INSIDERS' GUIDE® SERIES

INSIDERS' GUIDE® TO
SOUTH DAKOTA'S
BLACK HILLS AND BADLANDS

FOURTH EDITION

T. D. GRIFFITH AND DUSTIN D. FLOYD

INSIDERS' GUIDE®

GUILFORD, CONNECTICUT
AN IMPRINT OF THE GLOBE PEQUOT PRESS

The prices and rates in this guidebook were confirmed at press time. We recommend, however, that you call establishments before traveling to obtain current information.

INSIDERS' GUIDE®

Text design by LeAnna Weller Smith
Maps created by XNR Productions Inc. © Morris Book Publishing, LLC

ISSN: 1539-3542
ISBN-13: 978-0-7627-4192-2
ISBN-10: 0-7627-4192-9

Manufactured in the United States of America
Fourth Edition/First Printing

CONTENTS

CONTENTS

Directory of Maps

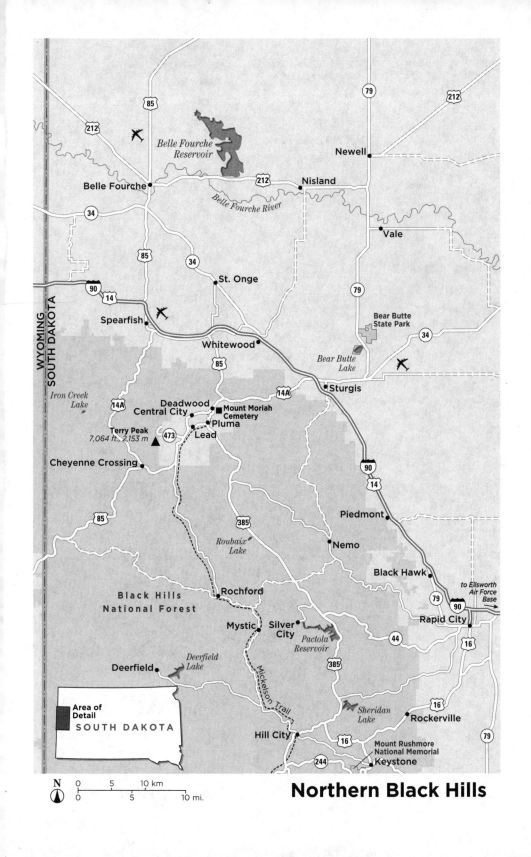

Northern Black Hills

N

| 0 | 5 | 10 km |

| 0 | 5 | 10 mi. |

Central Black Hills

Southern Black Hills

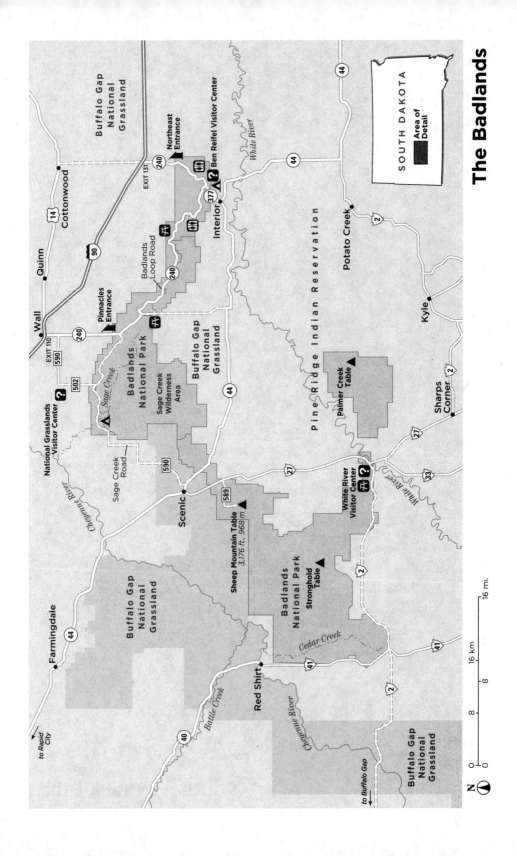

The Badlands

PREFACE

The Black Hills and Badlands form a region of contrasts. The Hills are an uplifted island of mountains in the middle of prairie flatland, and the Badlands resemble a sometimes spooky, prehistoric moonscape. Considered together, as they are in this book, they form a place that is welcoming, accessible, and quietly magnificent.

The Black Hills and Badlands are bounteous and beautiful, but sometimes tough and challenging, too. You'll find natural beauty of great power here: craggy mountains, mysterious geological formations, sudden weather changes, towering evergreens, grassy prairie, and vistas that will make your heart ache. This is still a homey kind of place where the good-hearted residents look you in the eye and say hello, and where visitors are welcomed with smiles, questions, and helpful hints.

In addition to the natural wonders and welcoming atmosphere, the contrasts, we believe, are what make life here so very interesting. You'll find ghost towns and modern towns, high-tech commerce and country life, and a taste of the combined Old West, Midwest, and New West. We have trendy restaurants and rustic bars, sophisticated art galleries and quaint attractions, and cowboys and businesspeople and artists. Recreation ranges from rough-and-tumble rodeos to skiing, skating, and mountain hiking. In some areas you can still view century-old wagon trail-ruts from modern highways. Life has changed quickly here in the relatively short history of settlement; yet, in other ways, it has hardly changed at all.

We've filled this book with places to visit, eat, and shop, fun activities for children, sights to see, trails to hike, history to discover, and much more. The table of contents will direct you to specific chapters, and the How to Use This Book chapter will help you use and enjoy some of the unique tidbits we've sprinkled throughout this book.

Whether you're an armchair traveler or tourist or new resident, we're glad for the opportunity to contribute to your enjoyment of our beloved Black Hills and Badlands. We think you'll love this place, too, and that you'll take pleasure in its delightful contrasts. We hope you'll feel at home here, just as we do.

Welcome. The Black Hills and Badlands await your exploration.

ACKNOWLEDGMENTS

As a fourth-edition book, credit for much of the research and writing goes to the authors of the first edition, Barbara Tomovick and Kimberly Metz. Assisting these writers were a host of individuals well-versed in the life and character of the Black Hills, including photographers and *Rapid City Journal* staffers, real estate agents, and many individuals who have worked in public service and the Black Hills visitor industry for many years.

Thanks also goes to the second-edition revisers, Bert and Jane Gildart, who provided some updated information and stunning new photographs.

Many of the first-edition sources were consulted for this fourth edition of the book, although a number of new faces deserve recognition. Among those are the staff of the Adams Museum and House, the employees of the Rapid City Parks and Recreation Department, the many helpful people at the chambers of commerce scattered throughout the Hills, the Deadwood Historic Preservation Commission, the Deadwood Gaming Association, the South Dakota Department of Tourism, Amanda Kille, Chad Blair, and Toni Lehman at TDG Communications, the Interpretation Centers of the many national and state parks in the Black Hills, the hundreds of small business owners across the region who answered their telephones and e-mail, and, of course, all the helpful—and sometimes anonymous—voices not mentioned here who provided us with the facts, figures, snapshots, and information you now hold in your hand. Last, but never least, editors Jennifer Quint, Elizabeth Taylor, and Glenn Novak also deserve recognition for their efforts to make this edition come together so smoothly.

HOW TO USE THIS BOOK

et's say you've just opened this book for the first time. The cover is glossy and smooth, the page corners sharp, the spine a bit stiff. So you've opened it somewhat gingerly, wondering where to begin.

The fact is, you'll get hooked on the Black Hills and Badlands no matter where you start your journey. Naturally, the table of contents will give you an idea of the sort of information you'll find here. The comprehensive index at the back will help you zero in on specific things you'd like to learn more about. But maybe you just want to chapter surf and get a feel for what this guide is all about. Go right ahead. The ride's on us.

To make it more fun, we've sprinkled interesting tips throughout the text, flagged with the ℹ symbol. And because we wanted to make our book unique among the Insiders' Guides, we borrowed from the South Dakota state slogan, "Great Faces, Great Places" (a reference to the faces of Mount Rushmore National Memorial), to bring you vignettes about some outstanding people and places you might not otherwise hear about. You'll find those stories under the headings Great Faces and Great Places. We've also included some Legends and Lore we thought you might enjoy and a dozen close-up features for an in-depth look at some of what makes this a special place.

Most of our chapters are arranged geographically, from north to south. Since locals customarily refer to various sections of the Black Hills as the Northern Hills, the Central Hills, and the Southern Hills, we've done that, too. The boundaries aren't necessarily hard and fast, so for our purposes we've divided the area up as follows:

The Northern Hills include Belle Fourche in Butte County, all of Lawrence County (primarily Deadwood, Lead, and Spearfish), and Sturgis and Bear Butte State Park in Meade County.

Piedmont and Black Hawk, in southwestern Meade County, come under Central Hills listings because those communities tend to be closely tied to Rapid City (in Pennington County) and are even listed under Rapid City in the phone book. Hill City, Keystone, Mount Rushmore National Memorial, and Harney Peak, all of which are in Pennington County, also come under the Central Hills umbrella.

The Southern Hills in this book encompass Custer and Fall River Counties, which include the towns of Custer and Hot Springs, respectively, plus Custer State Park, Wind Cave National Park, Crazy Horse Memorial, and Jewel Cave National Monument.

Some might argue with our geography, and we would agree there's a certain amount of latitude in defining these locations. Nevertheless, we think our divisions will help you plan and navigate through the Black Hills and perhaps come to a better understanding of the area. You'll get better acquainted in the Area Overview chapter, which describes each region in detail.

In our chapters on Attractions, Kidstuff, Gaming and Casinos, and Annual Events and Festivals, you'll learn about fun and fascinating things to see and do. In Campgrounds and Accommodations you'll find out where to rough it and where to relax in comfort. The Restaurants chapter will point you toward the best places to eat, whether you want a plain bagel, a homemade pizza with the works, or an elegant multicourse dinner. You'll get a closer look at the Black Hills lifestyle in the Education, Child Care, Relocation, Retirement, Health Care, Arts, and Wor-

If you're using a mobile phone, you should know that only two providers service the region: Alltel Wireless and Verizon Wireless. If you use a different company, you'll probably be roaming.

ship and Spirituality chapters. And in our chapters on History, Recreation, Parks and Mountains, The Badlands and Nearby, and Day Trips and Weekend Getaways, you'll find out why we and so many others choose to make this area our home.

We've done our best to be thorough in every chapter, but chances are you're still going to have to make some phone calls while you're here. Luckily, South Dakota is "small" enough to have just one area code, 605. Although there are no rules for which calls are long distance and which aren't, many calls between the Central Hills and Northern Hills are now considered local, but all calls to and from the less populated Southern Hills are long distance.

Some attractions include sales tax in their admission prices, and some add tax at the time of purchase. You'll need to inquire. Tax rates vary depending on where you are and what you're buying. Take note that state law requires groceries to be taxed, so don't be surprised if a checker adds on a few cents to your bushel of corn or fresh bison steaks.

We've included general credit card information in chapters that have to do with accommodations and dining, but when shopping or visiting attractions you should ask whether plastic is accepted.

You'll notice that we do a lot of cross-referencing among chapters, and that's because we want to make sure you don't miss anything.

You'll find, too, that the terms *Native American, American Indian,* and *Indian* are used throughout the book. The three are interchangeable, though most locals will use the latter two when referring to North America's aboriginal peoples. We also use both *Sioux* and *Lakota* in writing about the tribes of western South Dakota, because although all Lakota people are Sioux, not all Sioux are Lakota. We explain the distinction in a Great Faces section in the History chapter.

We hope you'll have as much fun reading about and exploring the Black Hills and Badlands as we did in putting this book together. But if you think we've left something out or made a mistake, let us know. You can write to us at Insiders' Guides, P.O. Box 480, Guilford, CT 06437. Or contact us on the Internet at www.GlobePequot.com. Of course, you can tell us what you like, too.

Soon, we hope, the volume you hold in your hands will look a bit dog-eared, its pages filled with underlines and notes, and its spine creased from constant use, like well-earned laugh lines.

AREA OVERVIEW

The Black Hills are ancient, some of the oldest mountains in North America. Although they don't claim the same attention as younger, taller mountain ranges, they're recognized for their quiet splendor.

But mountains they are; they could as easily have been christened the Black Mountains as the Black Hills. The Lakota Sioux named them Paha Sapa—*paha* meaning any "height," whether mountains or hills, and *sapa* meaning "black." It seems likely that early translators settled on Black Hills for this, the only mountain range in Dakota Territory, to avoid confusion with North Carolina's Black Mountains, a range of the rolling Blue Ridge.

But why black when the Hills are covered with thick stands of evergreens? Quite simply because from a distance these pine-covered slopes loom like a backlit silhouette against the vastness of the Great Plains. The Black Hills have been called an oasis in a sea of grass, a description you're likely to appreciate after a long drive across the boundless prairie to reach us.

We are no longer surprised to meet people who don't know where the Black Hills are or who think all of South Dakota is flat. Yet the Hills claim a substantial number of distinctions. For starters, this area is home to one of the largest concentrations of national parks, memorials, and monuments in the world. It's also a region rich with history, a land once trod by the likes of Crazy Horse, Sitting Bull, Lt. Col. George Armstrong Custer, Buffalo Bill Cody, Wild Bill Hickok, and Calamity Jane (see the History chapter), among others. In fact, the latter two are still here; they are permanent residents of Deadwood's Mount Moriah Cemetery.

The Hills are home to the nation's first national forest (discussed in the History chapter) and to one of our country's most prominent and defining symbols, Mount Rushmore National Memorial (see Attractions). Yet even among those who easily recognize Mount Rushmore, many don't know that the famous mountain carving is in the Black Hills, in South Dakota.

Nevertheless, some four million people from around the world find their way here each year, making tourism one of our top industries, along with agriculture and mining. Visits to Mount Rushmore, Custer State Park (see the Parks and Mountains chapter), and Deadwood (see Gaming and Casinos and Attractions) are likely to capture your imagination. A climb to the top of Harney Peak or a trek in the Black Hills National Forest (see Recreation) could very well make you want to stay forever. But to understand the nuances of life here takes more time.

For in some ways Black Hills residents have a bit of an identity crisis. We cherish and brag about our area's natural beauty and fascinating sights while tolerating a profusion of billboards that mar the view and a fair number of embarrassingly tacky roadside attractions. The vast majority of us are solidly politically conservative, yet we cry out for new industry and complain when our young people leave.

We proudly call ourselves South Dakotan, but we cite deep philosophical differences with our neighbors east of the Missouri River, which divides the state in half. In fact, "East River" is practically a curse in the Black Hills (as much as "West River" is a dirty word in Sioux Falls or Vermillion). East River, with its thicker population, rolling farmland, quaint villages, and conservative mind-set, is decidedly midwestern. West River, on the other hand, with its rough-and-tumble gold-rush past, ranches, arid plains, granite peaks, and even deeper conservative thinking, is clearly western. We Black Hills residents feel more akin to our neighbors in Wyoming, Montana, and Colorado, who

You'll find copies of two free visitor publications, South Dakota Vacation Guide *and* Exploring the Black Hills and Badlands, *at many area attractions, motels, and chambers of commerce. You can request copies from the Black Hills, Badlands, and Lakes Association, 1851 Discovery Circle, Rapid City, 57701; (605) 355-3600. The office is located off I-90, exit 61.*

share our mountain time zone, than we do to our East River brethren, who all happen to be on central time. Indeed, we commute to Cheyenne, Billings, and Denver more often than we travel to Sioux Falls, Minneapolis, or Omaha, which are about as far. The two sides of South Dakota are two different worlds. Of course, that's not taking into account the Badlands (see the Badlands and Nearby chapter), which seem to belong on another planet altogether.

Some locals like to call the Black Hills "God's country," but like any earthly paradise, this one has its imperfections. For instance, most of us work hard for dishearteningly low wages, and although some argue that our cost of living is lower than in many other places, few families here can survive on a single paycheck (more about that in the Child Care chapter). For too many would-be homeowners, "affordable housing" is an oxymoron, and for all of us property taxes are high. Limited career options and low pay drive many of our best and brightest young people to other states. So when locals say they live here for the quality of life the area offers, they're talking less about material objectives and more about intangibles such as neighborliness, clean air, elbow room, and a sense of safety.

Add the fact that only a portion of the Black Hills is privately owned. The rest is public land and, for the most part, unspoiled. The Black Hills National Forest takes up 1.2 million acres, or about 2,000 square miles—that's about one-third of our total area. National and state parks, monuments, and recreation areas make still more of the land surface off-limits to expansive development. All of this makes the Hills an extraordinarily unfettered playground.

The Hills are remarkable in other ways as well. There is a strong Native American presence, particularly in Rapid City, that manifests itself in our public art, museums, interior design, local products, and even architecture (see the Arts chapter). The same holds true for our Scandinavian pioneer heritage. Jokes about Norwegian bachelor farmers abound, as do surnames that end in *son* or *sen, ahl* or *al*.

Place names are revealing, too, often summoning images of land formations and wildlife. Many towns were named for their natural features, straightforward descriptions consisting of the plainest word combinations: Belle Fourche (French for "beautiful fork"), Spearfish, Deadwood, Rapid City, Hill City, Hot Springs.

Roads meander as if they had minds of their own, seeking out the irregular more than the smooth spots. It's not uncommon to see riders sweeping across the foothills on horseback. And only in the harshest winter weather do we fail to pass roadside bicyclists or joggers on even our most mundane jaunt into town.

Nestled within the Hills are a couple of dozen small towns, each with a personality all its own. Rapid City, with a population of more than 60,000, is the largest city by far. Yet even in Rapid City it's practically impossible to go anywhere without pausing to talk to someone you know. To our way of thinking, that's one of the best reasons to live here.

The information below is meant to serve as an introduction, a verbal handshake from people all over the Black Hills. Not every community is included, though, so we urge you to check a map, explore on your own, and get acquainted with us face to face. And be sure to check other chapters in this book such as Relocation, Education, Health Care, and the Arts for additional information about our Black Hills hometowns.

NORTHERN HILLS

Northern Hills residents enjoy small-town life enhanced by the presence of a four-year liberal-arts college (see the Education chapter) centrally located in Spearfish. To the north is Belle Fourche, to the east is Sturgis, and to the south are the twin cities of Deadwood and Lead. Each of these communities is unique in character and contributes something in the way of goods, services, and employment to the area as a whole.

Belle Fourche

As the northern gateway to the Black Hills, Belle Fourche, the Butte County seat, is a prairie town with close ties to the Northern Hills community. Near the fork of the Belle Fourche and Redwater Rivers, it's home to about 4,500 people, small enough that one longtime resident described it this way: "Even if you dial the wrong number, you still know who you're talking to." With its railroad tracks and rodeo grounds, it's not hard to imagine Belle Fourche when it was a dusty cow town. Although tamer now than in its heyday as a cattle and sheep shipping center (see History), the downtown business district retains a strong ranching flavor with stores that cater to folks who work on the land.

The town was built on cattle, but sugar beets and sheep also were big industries in the early days. Though not as lucrative as they once were, they remain economic pillars of Belle Fourche; the wool warehouse, livestock exchange, and grain elevator are community landmarks. Today, bentonite mining is the big industry, although the school system and hospital are major employers, too.

The city's real crown jewel is its community center, built in 1992. There are racquetball courts, basketball courts, a walking track, exercise room, and indoor pool with a waterslide. Residents from all over Butte County—numbering upward of 9,000 and growing—come here to relax and work out.

Deadwood and Lead

The Lawrence County towns of Deadwood and Lead (with about 1,300 and 3,000 people, respectively) are so closely associated with each other that it seems appropriate to couple them here. Through the years their list of cooperative efforts has included anything from a school district to a street sweeper. The mountainous twin cities were at the heart of the Black Hills gold rush and quickly prospered after San Francisco–based Homestake Mining Company acquired the area's richest gold deposit in Lead in 1877 (see History).

Until it closed in 2002, Homestake Gold Mine remained the economic pillar of the Northern Hills for more than 120 years, which made it the nation's longest-running underground gold mine. Both communities knew the yellow metal would run out eventually, so the closure was no surprise. In fact, the towns had begun to prepare years earlier, hoping to lessen the impact of losing more than 1,000 jobs.

In the 1980s, Deadwood was dying. Most miners and supporting businesses had established themselves in Lead, and Deadwood's elegant brick storefronts and Victorian mansions, holdovers from its Wild West heyday, were left to crumble. Citizens saw an unlikely savior in the form of gaming, and in 1989 Deadwood became the third venue in the nation after Nevada and Atlantic City, New Jersey, to legalize gambling (see the Gaming and Casinos chapter). Today, Deadwood's streets are once again paved with brick, its mansions

---

You have a chance to see Deadwood before you arrive by visiting Digital Deadwood, found on the Internet at www.digitaldeadwood.com. This free site enables you to create a character and navigate around an accurately re-created version of Main Street, where you can visit real businesses, chat with other users, play games, and perform historical research.

---

restored, and its Main Street bustling with travelers seeking their fortunes. The gaming industry has helped to market the Black Hills as a world-class destination and is Deadwood's current economic cornerstone. In fact, there are more jobs in Deadwood than there are residents.

Lead, on the other hand, was harder hit by the mine's closure. While casinos have revived Deadwood, no single industry has come in to save Lead—at least not yet. Plans are in the works to build a science and engineering laboratory deep underground in the old mine, funded by the National Science Foundation. At the bottom, shielded by 8,000 feet of limestone and granite, scientists could conduct subatomic experiments with minimum interference from cosmic radiation. Though the lab's future is still caught in red tape, South Dakota's senators are lobbying hard on its behalf. The hope is that the lab would provide jobs for several dozen people and attract similar high-tech industries to the area that

might employ hundreds or perhaps thousands more.

In the meantime, Lead is capitalizing on its proximity to downhill skiing and some of the best cross-country skiing and snowmobiling in the world. Lead's small-town atmosphere and location near the mouth of stunningly beautiful Spearfish Canyon attract more and more visitors each year (see the Recreation chapter).

Spearfish

Black Hills State University and an accessible location off Interstate 90 have provided Spearfish with some priceless advantages. The town has grown quickly in recent years, boosted to a population of nearly 9,000 (with another 3,500 in the surrounding 3-mile area) in part by retirees who succumb to its charms: a progressive outlook, tidy appearance (notice the pretty porches on houses along Main Street), convenient shopping, assorted medical facilities, and handy recreational opportunities. The Donald E. Young Sports and Fitness Center on the BHSU campus is open to community members, and an 18-hole golf course and outdoor swimming pool (see the Recreation chapter) are situated at the mouth of Spearfish Canyon. The unspoiled canyon, which beckons with stunning views of cliffs and streams, offers excellent trout fishing in Spearfish Creek (see the Recreation chapter for information about licenses and regulations).

The creek runs through town, not far from an attractive city hall–library and a paved 2-mile-long bike path. With a couple of large department stores, strip malls (see the Shopping chapter), and a vital downtown, Spearfish is the subregional shopping center for the Northern Hills.

Ranching, the timber industry, retail stores, health care, light manufacturing, and the school district are top employers, along with the university. Pope & Talbot Sawmill has operated here for close to two decades; a Premier BankCard call center is in one of three industrial parks on the east edge of town. Many people see Spearfish for the first time when they attend a summer performance of the Black Hills Passion Play, a premier visitor draw you can read about in the Attractions chapter. But for those familiar with the town, Spearfish has long been a favorite place to conduct meetings, and that has meant plenty of business for the town's convention center.

Sturgis

Although best known as the home of the annual Sturgis Rally & Races motorcycle gathering (see Annual Events and Festivals), Sturgis is much more. The Meade County seat of about 6,500 residents is a retail and service center for those who live on outlying farms and ranches. Located roughly a half hour's drive from both Spearfish and Rapid City, it's also home to professional couples who go their separate ways to work each day. Sturgis citizens are proud historians as well, and they love reenacting the 1870s at Fort Meade during the annual Calvary Days celebration.

We don't know of any town that gets more use out of its community center, either. Everything, it seems, takes place at the center, from recreation and meetings to concerts and school plays. Fort Meade Veterans Administration Medical Center (in the Health Care chapter) is the town's top employer, with the school district, the local hospital, and Black Hills Special Services Cooperative also providing jobs. Majestic Bear Butte (turn to Parks and Mountains for details) rises from the prairie northeast of town, a landmark for recreation and Native American spiritual rites.

Many Black Hills towns post signs at their city limits proclaiming "GOLD Community." In this context, GOLD stands for Guide to Opportunities for Local Development, a resource every bit as precious as the yellow metal. The program is administered by the governor's Office of Economic Development.

CENTRAL HILLS
Hill City

After the national magazine *Men's Journal* declared Hill City one of the country's 25 "truly cool" places, the little village that accurately calls itself the Heart of the Hills seemed poised for a population boom—and soaring property values. But a scarcity of available houses and building sites made the town's "cool" phase short-lived, no doubt to the relief of many of the 800 or so people already living here (and worried about their property taxes).

Part of the town's charm is its ready access to hiking and snowmobile trails and some of the Hills' most popular bodies of water: Sheridan and Deerfield Lakes and Pactola Reservoir. Sylvan Rocks Climbing School & Guide Service, an accredited climbing school, is located here, convenient to some of the area's foremost climbing spots (see Recreation).

As seasonal shops along Main Street attest, a certain number of residents rely on tourism for their livelihood, and Black Hills Central Railroad/The 1880 Train (see the Attractions chapter) has long been the main tourist draw. Some residents find year-round work at the Rushmore Forest Products sawmill, the Black Hills Institute of Geological Research, the school district, and the forest service; others commute to jobs in Rapid City. The Railroad Avenue truck bypass and the inviting Old World Plaza boutique mall on Main Street show that Hill City is on the move; further proof

Saga of Sue

In some ways the saga of Sue is a classic, the tale of a simple country girl transformed into a superstar worth millions of dollars. Thrust unwillingly into the spotlight, she quickly became world famous. Men fought over her, and one even went to prison. Today Sue is in Chicago, a skeleton of her former self—just as she has been for millions of years. Sue, you see, is a nearly complete set of *Tyrannosaurus rex* bones and for now, anyway, the largest, most complete *T. rex* ever found.

Sue the dinosaur fossil was named for Sue Hendrickson, a field-worker for the Black Hills Institute of Geological Research in Hill City. After Hendrickson found the giant skeleton on land belonging to rancher Maurice Williams in 1990, the institute paid Williams $5,000, and workers removed Sue's remains for restoration. But before long there were allegations that institute president Pete

Larson, his brother, Neal, and their partner, Bob Farrar, had been stealing fossils from public land. An investigation started.

In 1992 the FBI confiscated Sue along with other fossils and records from the institute, and a federal indictment charged the Larsons and Farrar, among others, with 153 crimes. None of the charges had to do with Sue, but the institute couldn't get her back. The courts said Williams couldn't sell the fossil without government permission because his land, which is on the Cheyenne River Indian Reservation northeast of the Black Hills, was held in trust. So the government kept custody of Sue, and Williams kept the institute's money, saying it was payment for disturbing his land. A federal jury ultimately rejected most of the charges in the federal case against the fossil hunters, but Pete Larson spent 18 months in federal prison for transporting

---

comes from the infusion of excellent art galleries showcasing regional talent.

Keystone

Mount Rushmore is the raison d'être for Keystone, a town that at first glance looks like a T-shirt mecca but bears closer scrutiny. True, you could probably fill several pickup trucks with logo-emblazoned shirts, fudge, and jewelry made of Black Hills Gold (see the close-up in the Shopping chapter) from the 40-plus summer

tourist shops that line Winter Street— known as the Strip.

But there are major attractions here, too (as you'll see in the Attractions chapter), such as Borglum Historical Center (Rushmore-Borglum Story), Big Thunder Gold Mine, and Beautiful Rushmore Cave. And although fewer than 250 people live in Keystone year-round, a keen interest in local history—gold and tin oxide were among the minerals mined here decades ago—has spawned the impressive West River History Conference, held each September at the Keystone Community Center.

undeclared traveler's checks through customs.

Meanwhile, Williams asked the government to sell Sue for him, and in October 1997 the 65-million-year-old fossil went on the auction block at Sotheby's in New York. In less than nine minutes she was sold to the highest bidder for $8.3 million. Williams became a multimillionaire, and the Field Museum of Natural History in Chicago became Sue's new owner. However, Walt Disney World Resort and McDonald's had put up most of the money to buy Sue. So, although the fossil will be properly curated and exhibited at the museum, a full-size cast of Sue eventually will be on display at DinoLand USA. McDonald's-sponsored DinoLand is part of Disney's Animal Kingdom, a feature of Walt Disney World in Florida.

After the auction, the Black Hills Institute kept the rights to the regis-

tered trademark name "Sue," and "Dakota" was chosen as the winning entry in a contest to rename the fossil. The institute later relented so Sue could keep her name, but paleontologist Bob Bakker (who is not affiliated with the institute) already had figuratively pinned a new tag on the world's most famous *T. rex*. Because of her star power, Bakker called Sue "the Marlene Dietrich of dinosaurs."

Rapid City

Rapid City, with more than 60,000 residents, is the largest community in the Black Hills—and all of western South Dakota for that matter. Not surprisingly, then, this gateway to the Hills off I-90 is also the medical, educational, cultural, air-transportation, and shopping hub for the entire region. But even in the face of ongoing expansion, Rapid City remains a low-key place with friendly shopkeepers and minimal traffic hassles. Its 22 parks (one of which surrounds Canyon Lake) and the

paved 13.5-mile bike path that runs beside Rapid Creek are some of its most attractive features. The bike path is symbolic of the city's ability to survive tragedy: After a 1972 flash flood killed 238 people and injured more than 3,000 others, the city established a parklike floodway along the creek so no one could build there and live in harm's way again. Even today, Rapid City and its longtime residents continue to define themselves in terms of "before the flood" and "after the flood."

While Rapid Creek divides the city into north and south, the forested ridge

The nonprofit InterTribal Bison Cooperative in Rapid City, www.intertribal bison.com, provides financial and technical assistance and other services to Indian tribes that want to restore bison to tribal lands, primarily for cultural and spiritual purposes.

known as Skyline Drive splits it the other way. To the east lie the oldest development, the downtown core, and Central High School; the west side, with its newer housing, golf courses, expansive Sioux Park, and Stevens High School, is almost a community unto itself. In fact, to get across town, you either have to loop several miles north and take I-90, or you have to pass through the Gap, a narrow canyon carved by Rapid Creek that barely has room for two six-lane roads. These streets are among the busiest in South Dakota, and congestion there inspired a bypass over the ridge several miles southwest of the city.

The Rapid City economy depends heavily on Ellsworth Air Force Base to the northeast of the city (read about the base in the History chapter). Ellsworth employs some 3,000 military personnel and another 500 or so civilians, injecting about $140 million a year into the local economy in wages alone. Other major employers include several Black Hills Gold manufacturers, Merillat Industries (makers of particleboard), Rapid City Regional Hospital, the school district, Green Tree Financial Servicing, Sanmina–SCI (an electronic-components manufacturer), the federal government, and the State of South Dakota, to name just a few.

Phone book listings for Rapid City and Keystone alone include some 70 businesses that start with Rushmore, and another 10 that include Mount Rushmore in their names.

When not working, Rapid citizens enjoy recreational opportunities at a massive indoor aquatic center and ice rink (see the Recreation chapter), cultural events and entertainment at Rushmore Plaza Civic Center (listed in Annual Events and Festivals), and artistic expression at the Dahl Fine Arts Center (see the Arts chapter). Other advantages include the Journey Museum (see Attractions), South Dakota School of Mines and Technology (see Education), Rapid City Regional Airport (see Getting Here, Getting Around), and easy access to I-90.

SOUTHERN HILLS

Like the Northern Hills, the Southern Hills are characterized by small towns, but the pace might be even a step slower.

Custer

Custer is home to fewer than 2,000 people despite the extraordinary landmarks that lie right outside its borders. Incomparable Custer State Park (see the Parks and Mountains chapter)—at approximately 71,000 acres one the nation's largest state parks—is just minutes east of town; inspirational Crazy Horse Memorial (see Attractions) is to the north. Although summer brings a flood of visitors to both, as well as to Flintstones Bedrock City and other attractions (see Kidstuff), Custer lacks the spit and shine and amenities of, say, Cody, Wyoming, a sophisticated tourist town that has made the most of its location near Yellowstone National Park.

Indeed, when the visitors vanish in the fall, Custer emerges as what it really is: a tightly knit community whose citizens are united by their love of high school basketball and who faithfully attend games whether they have a relative on the team or not (read about the team's accolades in the Education chapter). Social life revolves largely around school and youth activities, banquets, and church events.

The Custer Youth Corrections Center, a state-run boot camp for juvenile offenders, is south of town; headquarters for the Black Hills National Forest is on the north end. Both are major employers, as are the school district, Custer Regional Hospital, Crazy Horse Memorial, and the park. Ranching, lumbering, and mining (primarily feldspar, mica, and quartz) also add to the town's economy.

Hot Springs

When desirable attributes were being handed out, Hot Springs must have been near the front of the line. For starters, the southernmost town brags that it has the best climate in the Hills, and we wouldn't argue to the contrary. Pick a day, any day, and it's likely to be warmer and drier here than anywhere else nearby. Other marvels of this city include the thermal waters that made it a health resort for buttoned-up Victorians with or without physical complaints. They probably walked right over the top of what is now the Mammoth Site of Hot Springs, the serendipitously discovered spot where ancient elephant-like mammals succumbed to the forces of nature and were preserved for all time (see Attractions). Visitors and residents alike must have delighted in the area's lovely pink sandstone that positively begged to be turned into eye-catching buildings in the town and, in fact, was (see the close-up in the Attractions chapter).

Southern Hills Municipal Golf Course, historic Evans Plunge warm-water swimming pool, and nearby Angostura State Recreation Area are other bright gems in the crown of this prom queen called Hot Springs. So it makes sense that the Miss South Dakota pageant takes place here the third weekend of June each year. Likewise, it seems fitting that the health-care industry is a key employer for Hot Springs' 4,000-plus citizens, along with the school district. Hot Springs Veterans Administration Medical Center and the State Veterans Home are here.

A sense of well-being is furthered by well-placed city parks and the Freedom Trail hiking and biking path beside the Fall River, which runs through town. If you can tear yourself away, you'll find unspoiled, uncrowded recreational spots in just about any direction, including Wind Cave National Park to the north (see the Parks and Mountains chapter) and Cascade Falls to the southwest, on the way to the Black Hills Wild Horse Sanctuary (see Attractions).

GETTING HERE, GETTING AROUND

S et in the middle of the country, the Black Hills are landlocked, a bit remote, and far from any huge metropolitan area. Still, getting here is easy enough and not too inconvenient, and their relative remoteness allows the not-yet-spoiled Hills to remain their charming selves. Most of us who live here wouldn't want it any other way.

Once you get here, however, you have quite a variety of options for getting around. There are bus, van, airplane, helicopter, and balloon tours, as well as some great bike paths and rentals. Of course, there are taxis and rental cars, too. Still, your best bet is to drive and see the Hills at your own pace. Although the Black Hills encompass 6,000 square miles, it's easy to get around quickly via Interstate 90 and some well-maintained U.S. and state highways. But because the fastest way isn't usually the most interesting way, we've included lesser-known scenic roads, too. These more lightly traveled routes meander through some of the most pleasant scenery in the Hills. Although it may take you twice as long to get where you're going via these routes, you'll have twice as much fun getting there. And fun is why you're here, isn't it?

If you're from a metropolitan area, you'll be pleased to note that South Dakota drivers are laid-back and patient with slow-traveling visitors. Angry honks are rare, but passing is not. Black Hills residents, who have grown up navigating the narrow canyons, like to speed. Law enforcement officials are usually tolerant of some speeding, but don't expect much leniency at night, when animals are more likely to bound across highways, or for drunk driving.

Though the Black Hills don't have the parking difficulties you'll find in big cities, parking is trickier here than in other, similar-size places. The increased traffic brought by visitors is one factor, but so is the simple issue of space. When you build towns in narrow mountain gulches, you barely have room for businesses and homes, let alone parking lots. Hill City and Keystone are challenging only during the day in summer, though Deadwood can be troublesome on evenings and weekends year-round, especially during special events.

In Rapid City the only parking problems you'll find are downtown and at Rushmore Mall, though things improve after the summer tourist rush subsides. Traffic, however, can be quite slow all year during "rush hour"—which is nothing like its big-city counterpart. All the same, cars frequently back up in the Gap, the narrow corridor between east and west Rapid City. Things can be further complicated by trains, which tend to lumber through the Gap shortly after 5:00 P.M.

Overall, transportation problems are few here, making the Black Hills a beautiful and exciting place to travel any time of the year.

GETTING HERE

By Air

If you fly in on a commercial flight, you'll land at Rapid City Regional Airport. If you're flying your own plane, you have more choices.

NORTHERN HILLS

Black Hills Airport—Clyde Ice Field
300 Aviation Place, Spearfish
(605) 642-4112, (800) 843-8010

Planes both small and large land here. The airport can even handle large corporate craft; in fact, Kevin Costner's big private jet occasionally sets down here. There are three grass strips, two of which are 4,000 feet long, one 5,600-foot asphalt strip, two overnight hangars, and four county hangars. The airport also has an instrument approach. Fuel, maintenance, and repair services are available (though no food service), and you can even camp on the grounds. Rental cars are available. The airport is 3 miles east of Spearfish on U.S. Highway 14A. It is managed by Eagle Aviation, which also offers Eagle's View Air Tours (see listing under Eagle Aviation) and provides aircraft rental, flight instruction, and Cessna service and parts.

Sturgis Municipal Airport
13345 Alkali Road, Sturgis
(605) 347-3356
www.sturgiscityofriders.com/airport.php

This small, city-owned airport is 5 miles east of Sturgis on Highway 34, then another mile down Alkali Road (turn right off the highway onto Alkali). The airport has 4,600 feet of asphaltic concrete runway; fuel, hangars, and maintenance service are available. You can't buy food or rent a car here, but for a lift into town you can call Courtesy Taxi, (605) 347-4253. C&B Aviation manages the airport, which can accommodate small planes and jets, turboprops, and twin-engine craft.

CENTRAL HILLS

Rapid City Regional Airport
4550 Terminal Road, Rapid City
(605) 394-4195
www.rcgov.org/Airport/pages

This city-managed regional airport is a user-friendly and family-oriented facility. Inside the 90,000-square-foot terminal, which is cozy and pleasant, you'll find thoughtful services. The airport is one of only two in the country originally built with nurseries. The unattended nursery room—furnished with sink, chairs, and diapers—gives moms and dads a chance to let a child nap, change a baby's diaper, or find a moment of peace and quiet for themselves. Each elevator, escalator, and restroom has information in braille, and there is one TDD phone in the terminal. The public-address system broadcasts outside the terminal entrance, so you won't miss important information if you leave the terminal.

The airport, 10 miles from downtown Rapid City off Highway 44, has several runways for commercial and general aviation use. Jets the size of 747s and 757s can land here, but larger jets and international flights are not accommodated.

Car rental agencies with desks at the terminal include: Avis, (605) 393-0740, (800) 331-1212; Budget, (605) 393-0488, (800) 676-0488; Hertz, (605) 393-0160, (800) 654-3131; National, (605) 393-2664, (800) 227-7368; and Thrifty, (605) 393-0663, (800) 847-4389. Listings of additional car rental agencies are in the Getting Around by Rental Car section of this chapter.

Airport Express Shuttle, (605) 399-9999 or (800) 357-9998, serves the airport. Other shuttle and taxi services are available, but you must call them to schedule service. All are listed later in this chapter in the Getting Around by Taxi, Shuttle, and Limo section.

If you fly your own plane into Rapid City Regional Airport, two fixed-base operators can service your plane while you tour the Hills. JetStream, 3900 Air-

---

Temperature differences in the Northern, Central, and Southern Hills can be as much as 10 to 15 degrees. You may leave Rapid City, for example, on a warm afternoon only to find it much cooler in Deadwood or windier in Hot Springs. Pack the proper clothing for your drive.

---

port Road, Rapid City, (605) 393-0000, (888) 830-2800, has both tie-downs and hangars and offers full service for your airplane. It's open 24 hours, and the staff can help with almost anything you might need during your stay, including catering and lodging arrangements. They even provide a tourist information center. Westjet Air Center, 4160 Fire Station Road, Rapid City, (605) 393-2500, (800) 888-4270, provides full maintenance services and aircraft sales. Both fixed-base operators offer charter flights, though not air tours of the Hills.

SOUTHERN HILLS

Custer State Park Airport
Custer State Park, Custer
(605) 255-4515
You can fly your small plane into Custer State Park, land on the paved runway, park, and tie down your plane (no hangars are available). No car rentals or pickup services are available, however, and whoever picks you up must purchase a state park entrance license. The airstrip is in the east-central portion of the park, off Wildlife Loop Road.

Hot Springs Municipal Airport
Highway 79 South, Hot Springs
(605) 745-3555
The city of Hot Springs manages this airport, which has one asphalt runway (4,500 feet) and one turf runway (4,000 feet). It can handle aircraft such as business planes or small jets. The airport has no maintenance service, but it does have hangars, tie-downs, fuel, car rentals, a lunch counter, and a customer lounge area. The airport is 7 miles from Hot Springs.

By Bus

The Black Hills are apparently considered so remote that Greyhound buses don't directly serve the area. Fortunately, if you favor traveling by bus, you can make connections from Greyhound routes to two regional bus services, which operate out of Milo Barber Transportation Center in Rapid City and share a local telephone number and ticketing staff. The small transportation center terminal has a pleasant waiting area and vending machines but no food service.

Jefferson Lines
Milo Barber Transportation Center
333 Sixth Street, Rapid City
(605) 348-3300 and (612) 332-8745
(charters and tours),
(800) 451-5333 (schedules)
www.jeffersonlines.com
Jefferson offers bus service to points east of Rapid City. The staff can schedule your entire trip, even the portions you'll travel by Greyhound. Rapid City is the only Black Hills town at which Jefferson buses make stops. The company also offers charters and sightseeing tours for groups.

Powder River Coach USA
Milo Barber Transportation Center
333 Sixth Street, Rapid City
(605) 348-3300, (800) 442-3682

1700 East U.S. Highway 14, Rapid City
(307) 682-0960
Powder River has service to points west of Rapid City. You can schedule your complete route, even the Greyhound connections, through the Powder River office. In addition to stops in Rapid City, buses make scheduled stops in Sturgis and Spearfish. Powder River also provides charters and sightseeing tours to groups.

By Car

Denver is about 400 miles from the Black Hills; Kansas City, Missouri, is nearly 700 miles away; the Twin Cities of Minneapolis and St. Paul are about 600 miles distant; and Omaha, Nebraska, is some 500 miles away.

The major (and easiest) route to the Hills is I-90, which skirts the northern and northeastern boundaries of the Black Hills. I-90 has convenient exits to Rapid City,

Sturgis, and Spearfish. Alternatively, if you're crossing the northern Midwest on Interstate 94, you can exit at Belfield, North Dakota (near Dickinson), onto U.S. Highway 85, which goes south to Belle Fourche. Interstate 80 runs through the midsection of the Midwest, where you can catch U.S. Highway 26 at Ogallala, Nebraska, then U.S. Highway 385 at Northport, Nebraska, and head north to Hot Springs, South Dakota, at the southern edge of the Black Hills.

Check out the rules of the road in the Getting Around by Car section that follows, so you'll be aware of South Dakota's traffic regulations as soon as you cross the state line.

GETTING AROUND

By Air

If you're a fan of flying, try an air tour or a balloon or helicopter ride. For those who fly a private plane into the Hills, there are several places mentioned in the Getting Here by Air section to park your aircraft, have it serviced, and leave it safely while you go off to sightsee. Two balloon companies in the Hills can take you for a very special ride. Dakota Balloon in Rapid City, (605) 393-8808, and Black Hills Balloons in Custer, (605) 673-2520, are listed in the Recreation chapter under Ballooning. A helicopter ride is another thrilling way to see the Black Hills. Black Hills Aerial Adventures in Custer, (605) 673-2163, is listed in the Attractions chapter under Tours and Byways.

And if you're really fearless and want to see the Hills from the air—without an aircraft—read about Black Hills Air Sports and its skydiving opportunities in the Recreation chapter.

NORTHERN HILLS

Eagle Aviation
300 Aviation Place, Spearfish
(605) 642-4112, (800) 843-8010
www.eagleaviationinc.com

The Black Hills Visitor Information Center (at Elk Vale Road and exit 61 off I-90, east of Rapid City) has displays, picnic and pet exercise areas, information hosts, video theater, gift shop, and the office of the Black Hills, Badlands, and Lakes Association. The telephone number is (605) 355-3600.

Eagle Aviation, which is based at and also manages Black Hills Airport—Clyde Ice Field, offers Eagle's View Air Tours for two to five people in a Cessna high-wing aircraft (the wings are above the windows for unobstructed views). Fly over gold country (Lead, Deadwood, Spearfish Canyon, and the Homestake mines) or Devils Tower, Mount Rushmore, and Crazy Horse Memorial on 20- to 120-minute tours. Upon request, pilots can fly you over some nearby Wyoming and Montana attractions. Eagle Aviation also has a charter service.

By Bicycle

Bicycling is a great way to see the Hills up close, at a more leisurely pace. If you didn't bring your own equipment, you'll find bike rental information in the Bike Tours and Rentals section of the Recreation chapter.

Rapid City has a wonderful bike path that meanders 13.5 miles through the city, following sparkling Rapid Creek and bisecting the city's extensive park system. This foresighted city's policy is that all new streets will incorporate bike paths in their construction. The town of Sturgis has a Centennial Bike Path that runs from Brown High School, east of town, to Highway 34 on the south side of town. Spearfish has a bike path that runs in sections (some are concrete paved, others are sections of streets) from the northwest side of town to the south side. Even the streets of most small towns that lack

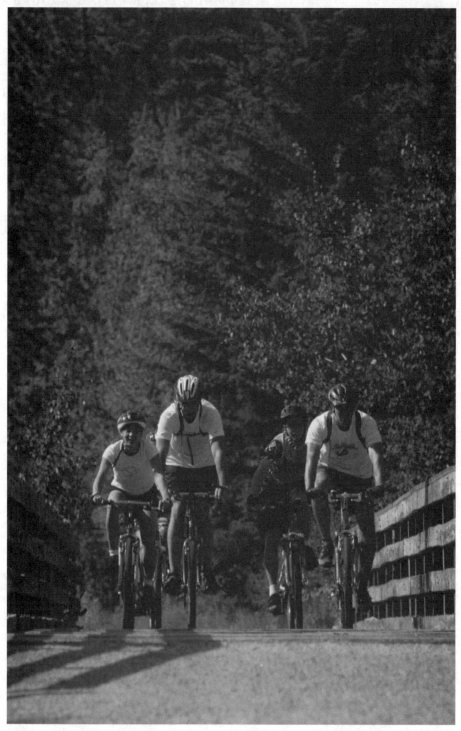

Mountain bikers, hikers, climbers, and other outdoor enthusiasts are attracted to the million-acre emerald oasis of the Black Hills. SOUTH DAKOTA TOURISM official bike paths are usually lightly traveled, which makes biking them a treat.

The best-known bike paths in the Black Hills, however, are recreational gems: the George S. Mickelson Trail and the Centennial Trail (both multiuse and open to bicyclists, hikers, horseback riders, and cross-country skiers). You'll find more about both in the Recreation chapter.

By Bus and Van Tour

Many companies will customize your tour; just tell them what you'd like to see and they'll take you there. We recommend you write or call for a brochure to determine if the tour fits your plans, then call to schedule before you arrive. Some companies adjust their operating hours for winter weather.

NORTHERN HILLS

Alkali Ike Tours
Deadwood
(605) 578-3147
www.alkaliiketours.com
These are history-packed, narrated, one-hour tours of Deadwood and Mount Moriah Cemetery. Look for the ticket booth in front of Old Style Saloon No. 10 at 657 Main Street. Tours begin at that location five times per day. Alkali Ike Tours' 46-passenger buses operate from May through October 1, weather permitting.

Boot Hill Tours
Deadwood
(605) 578-3758
www.boothilltours.com
This tour company provides one-hour narrated tours of Deadwood and Mount Moriah Cemetery in a 40-passenger bus. Tours start at the Bodega, 662 Main Street, five times each day.

Dakota Bus Service
631 South 32nd Street, Spearfish
(605) 642-2353
This service offers shuttles to Deadwood as well as charters and customized sightseeing tours to destinations in the Black Hills and throughout the country. It accommodates only groups.

Original Deadwood Tour
Deadwood
(605) 578-2091
www.originaldeadwoodtour.com
Since 1974, the Original Deadwood Tour has provided factual, entertaining, and humorous one-hour narrated tours of Deadwood and Mount Moriah Cemetery conducted in 40-passenger buses. The ticket booth is located in front of the Midnight Star at 677 Main Street, where the tours begin.

Western Transportation, Inc.
Sturgis
(605) 347-5066
Take a sightseeing tour around the Hills or a chartered trip across the country. Customized and escorted tours are offered in 47-passenger coaches. Step-on guide service is available, too, which means a Western Transportation guide will accompany and narrate any tour. If you wish to write for tour information, send a request to P.O. Box 700, Sturgis, SD 57785.

CENTRAL HILLS

Affordable Adventures
Rapid City
(605) 342-7691
A very flexible tour company, Affordable

In 2003 the South Dakota Department of Transportation and the South Dakota Highway Patrol joined several other states in launching a 511 information system. Anyone in the state can dial 511 toll free to receive complete weather and road construction reports that are updated regularly.

South Dakota's Low Profile

In 1987, Frank and Deborah Popper of Rutgers University in New Jersey proposed turning parts of the Great Plains (which include South Dakota) into a Buffalo Commons—a game preserve of sorts. They predicted that climatic and economic hardship, and even the landscape, would drive away what remained of the already sparse human population. Two years later an article in *Newsweek* magazine included our fair state in what it called "America's Outback," a region on the brink of decay.

At the same time, publisher Rand McNally omitted South Dakota, North Dakota, and parts of other apparently insignificant states from portions of its *Photographic World Atlas* for lack of

space. Insulting? Not really. The truth is, we kind of like it when others think we live in a throwaway state. As Custer State Park once noted in a promotional piece, "Out Here" a traffic jam is when the bison herd crosses the highway in the park.

Adventures offers jaunts all over western South Dakota and serves domestic and international clients. The owner is a "receptive operator," which means she can customize your tour to your needs and specifications. Vehicles are 7- and 11-passenger vans, but larger vehicles are available, too. The tours are informative, are conducted by knowledgeable guides, and accommodate parties from two up to 100 people. To write for information use P.O. Box 546, Rapid City, 57709.

Gray Line of the Black Hills
Rapid City
(605) 342-4461, (800) 456-4461
www.blackhillsgrayline.com
Gray Line is a worldwide company, and this locally owned franchise has 50 years of experience. It offers four- to eight-hour narrated sightseeing tours around the Hills and customized package tours that include accommodations and attractions.

Gray Line also has a nationwide charter service. Many campgrounds, motels, and hotels can arrange a Gray Line tour for you, so inquire where you're lodging.

Stagecoach West
Rapid City
(605) 343-3113, (888) 343-3113
www.rushmoretours.com
Groups of 10 or more can take both standard and customized narrated tours with Stagecoach West. The company also offers nationwide charters. If you'd like to write, send queries to P.O. Box 264, Rapid City, 57709.

SOUTHERN HILLS

L & J Golden Circle Tours
Custer
(605) 673-4349, (877) 811-4349
www.goldencircletours.com
Golden Circle's owners say their 14-

passenger vans travel roads that large buses can't. They add that their drivers are experienced and knowledgeable and that their tours (including available narrated tours) are flexible. For more information write to P.O. Box 454, Custer, 57730.

Plenty Star Ranches
U.S. Highway 385, Pringle
(605) 673–3012
www.plentystarranch.com
You'll find more information about Plenty Star Ranches in the Horse Camps section of the Campgrounds chapter. The wildlife tours around Custer State Park are especially popular because drivers follow little-used county roads as well as the more heavily traveled Wildlife Loop. The owners conduct tours in cars, small buses, or large coaches, depending on the size of the group. They provide step-on guide service and can direct you on a self-guided tour, if you prefer.

By Car

The Black Hills provide a majestic back-drop to any car ride, from multiday tours to grocery-store runs. Roads are wide and traffic laws are few, but there are some things you should know before making major forays into the Hills.

First, motorcyclists love it here. Thousands of visitors and locals alike ride their steel horses through South Dakota every summer. If you're used to watching for automobiles, you might find motorcycles easy to overlook—so keep an eye out. Only bikers under the age of 18 are required to wear a helmet. The only other equipment motorcyclists are required to have is eye protection (or a windshield) and rearview mirrors.

Second, remember that there is an abundance of wildlife here. It's common to see deer, antelope, porcupine, and even the occasional coyote standing on the shoulder, especially at dawn or dusk. It's just as common for them to dart out in

It's a good idea to fill your gas tank before touring the Black Hills, especially if you're using back roads and scenic routes. Gas stations are sometimes few and far between, and you'll be driving for miles, possibly quite far from the nearest town. You don't want worries about running out of gas to spoil your enjoyment of the scenery.

front of passing vehicles, so be vigilant and keep a finger on the horn.

The narrow, winding quality of Black Hills roads makes traveling fun, but only if you keep your eyes on the pavement. Let the passengers do the oohing and aahing, or you might end up approaching a tight corner too quickly. Most major bends have suggested speeds posted before the turn—many signs recommend speeds appropriate for RVs, but some suggested speeds may seem tight even for compacts. If in doubt, slow down.

South Dakotans hate it when anyone tries to dictate their behavior. All the same, the state's seat-belt laws are getting more aggressive. Any adult in the front seats must wear a belt, but you cannot be ticketed for not wearing a seat belt unless you have been pulled over for another offense. On the other hand, anyone under the age of 18 may be cited for not wearing a safety belt even if you weren't pulled over for something else.

Drinking and driving is not taken lightly in South Dakota. A person is legally intoxicated with a blood-alcohol content of .08 or more. Highway patrol officers

In 2003 South Dakota joined many other states by passing a "move over law" which requires motorists on a four-lane highway to use the left lane if a law enforcement vehicle is pulled off on the right shoulder and is flashing amber lights.

CLOSE-UP

Nellie Zabel Willhite, Pioneer Aviatrix

In the early days of aviation it took a courageous person to fly those "orange crates"—rickety biplanes that would never pass the aircraft safety standards of today. That's why the pilots were called daredevils, for only truly daring people risked life and limb to soar through the air, betting skill and wild courage against the high odds they'd never make it safely back to the ground.

In the 1920s, in the midst of excitement over aviation's arrival in the area—which brought wing walkers, barnstormers, stunt fliers, and ride-for-a-dollar pilots—came Nellie Zabel Willhite. She was skilled and adventurous, brave and strikingly pretty, with determined eyes and a bright smile . , . and she was deaf.

Nellie was born in a log cabin in Box Elder in 1892. Her father, Charley "Pard" Zabel, was also a pioneer. He left Wisconsin for the Black Hills when he was 17 and took up freighting: driving oxen teams loaded with merchandise over the Fort Pierre–Deadwood route. Nellie's uncle was the famous Russ Madison, known as Mr. Rodeo for his role in founding many rodeo events as well as the organization that would later become today's Professional Rodeo Cowboys Association.

When Nellie was two, a bout with measles robbed her of her hearing. When she was eight, her mother died. She was unable to communicate, so her grieving father took her to the State School for the Deaf, where she was taken in by a kindly doctor and his wife, who taught her lipreading and other skills. She later studied drawing at Yankton College and music at the Boston Conservatory.

But it was another talent that changed Nellie's life in a most dramatic way. In late 1927 she learned to fly, just five days before her 35th birthday. She

carry digital breath-analyzer devices. If you're suspected of driving under the influence, you'll be asked to take the test. If you are arrested for DWI and refuse, your driver's license will be confiscated at the time of arrest. And if the officer smells alcohol on your breath, you can be taken directly to jail.

The speed limit on South Dakota interstate highways is 75 mph, except through cities, where it is reduced to 65 mph. Most state and U.S. highways have a speed limit of 55 through the Black Hills.

Right turns on red are permitted in South Dakota unless otherwise posted.

If you're traveling on school days, you may meet school buses on the roads. When the yellow lights of a bus flash, prepare to stop. When the red lights flash, all drivers (in all directions) must stop at least 15 feet from the bus and remain stopped until the lights no longer flash. When the bus's yellow hazard lights flash (for example, at a railroad crossing), motorists must stop and then proceed with caution. Bus drivers are authorized to turn in the license numbers of offenders.

was the 13th student at the Dakota Airlines Flying School in Sioux Falls. She soloed on Friday, January 13, 1928, after 13 hours of instruction, then landed smack-dab in a mud puddle. Thereafter, 13 was her lucky number.

The first licensed woman pilot in South Dakota, and probably the first woman in the state to pilot an airplane, Nellie told her father of her dreams to fly. He promptly bought an old Eaglerock biplane, which she christened with the number 13 and the nickname "Pard" in Charley's honor. He returned the compliment by joyfully telling her she had "the instincts of a wild goose" when she found her way, using road maps and with Charley aboard, to Wisconsin.

Nellie and winged Pard barnstormed the country, racing, stunt flying, and giving rides to awed onlookers. Once they were swept up into a tornado and went from 2,000 to 8,000 feet in a matter of seconds. Keeping her head, Nellie pushed Pard into a downward 3,000-foot-spiral and restarted the stalled engine, escaping with only badly shaken nerves. Her most memorable experience, however, was the time "at the top of a loop-the-loop maneuver two or three mice fell out from somewhere in the floor of my plane—and I hoped there wouldn't be any more of them."

Nellie belonged to the "99s," the prestigious club of women pilots of which Amelia Earhart was the first president. She was a friend and student of Clyde Ice, another early South Dakota Aviation pioneer, for whom the field at Black Hills Airport in Spearfish is named.

Nellie Willhite passed away at the age of 99 in 1991. Before she died, however, she was inducted into the South Dakota Hall of Fame and the state's Aviation Hall of Fame in recognition of her achievements as both a pioneer aviatrix and a woman whose handicap never got in her way.

THE FASTER ROUTES

Northern Hills

If you need to get where you're going in a hurry, I-90 is the route to travel. It follows the boundaries of the north and northeastern Black Hills and, thus, is the ideal route to Sturgis (exits 30 or 32) and Spearfish (exits 10, 12, or 14). From those towns you can pick up routes to take you farther north to Belle Fourche or south to the towns of Lead, Deadwood, Nemo, Rapid City, and others.

Central Hills

From I-90, use exits 55 through 61 to reach Rapid City. If you're heading to the Central Hills, U.S. Highway 16 South has four lanes from Rapid City to Keystone. U.S. Highway 16A to Mount Rushmore, which branches off U.S. 16 near Keystone, is also a four-lane highway. From that area, U.S. 16 South becomes a two-lane road.

Southern Hills

The fastest route to the Southern Hills is Highway 79, which runs from Rapid City,

In Rapid City, Main Street runs one-way west and St. Joseph Street (locally known as "St. Joe") runs one-way east. West Boulevard and East Boulevard mark the west and east borders of downtown, and numbered streets from First to Ninth run north and south between them. Mount Rushmore Road (U.S. 16) is sometimes called Eighth Street or Rushmore Road by longtime residents.

past Hermosa, to the Hot Springs area. Highway 79 rolls through prairie hills and Buffalo Gap (where legend says the buffalo entered the Black Hills). It intersects U.S. 385, which will take you 3 miles west into Hot Springs. There you can journey farther south on Highway 71 to Angostura State Recreation Area or use U.S. Highway 18 to go farther west or east.

THE SCENIC ROUTES

Ah, the scenery! That's what you came here to see, and there's no better way to view it than on scenic routes. We can truthfully say there are no unscenic highways in the Black Hills, but we've listed our favorites below. Take a leisurely drive through some of the most picturesque landscape west of the Mississippi, with plenty of opportunities to pull over, park, and look around.

If you favor quiet, little-traveled routes known only to locals, we have plenty to offer. The Black Hills National Forest is positively laced with county and forest service roads—most graveled and rather narrow—where you'll see sights only locals usually see. If you have a good sense of direction and an adventurous spirit, you'll love exploring these roads. Get a detailed road map and plenty of gasoline first, and be prepared for emergencies or car trouble, because you may not meet another car, and you'll be far from help should you need it.

Northern Hills

The 19-mile Spearfish Canyon State Scenic Byway, U.S. 14A, is one of the best drives around. It runs between Spearfish and Cheyenne Crossing, and you'll meander along the paved road, following pretty Spearfish Creek past towering limestone cliffs and evergreen and aspen forests. There are some great places to hike just off the highway, including Roughlock Falls and Spearfish Peak, and there's information about biking, climbing, and cross-country skiing in Spearfish Canyon in the Recreation chapter. You'll find more information on the Spearfish Canyon State Scenic Byway in the Attractions chapter.

U.S. 14A also runs east and west between Deadwood and Sturgis, through beautiful Boulder Canyon. Traveling west, you'll reach a wide valley that is being developed with houses and businesses, then the road enters the canyon again and twists, turns, and climbs. The last mile or so is a steep grade that drops down into the town of Deadwood.

Central Hills

A great Central Hills drive is along Highway 44 (Jackson Boulevard west from Rapid City), then U.S. 385 North. Highway 44 is known as the Rimrock Highway. It passes Cleghorn Springs State Fish Hatchery, Thunderhead Underground Falls, and other attractions (there's information about these in the Attractions chapter). It runs along Rapid Creek through spectacular canyons, where rimrock cliffs tower above you, and the little town of Johnson Siding. Rimrock Highway dead-ends into U.S. 385, the Black Hills Parkway, from which you can head north to Deadwood and Lead, taking side trips on county roads to the little towns of Rochford, Silver City, or Mystic. You can also follow the road south to Hill City, Custer, and Hot Springs. The Black Hills Parkway bisects the Hills, north to south, from Deadwood/Lead to Hot Springs.

Nemo Road (Pennington/Lawrence County Road 234) begins at West Chicago Street in Rapid City and winds through lovely woods to the quaint town of Nemo. The road ends at U.S. 385 south of Deadwood and Lead.

Pennington County Road 323, the Old Hill City Road, will take you from Keystone to Hill City through some pleasing scenery. The narrow road follows Battle Creek and crosses and recrosses (several times) the tracks used by The 1880 Train (see Attractions). Watch out for the train in the summer. You'll see some gorgeous rock formations along this winding route, too.

One of our favorite drives is Forest Service Road 17 from Hill City to Deerfield Lake. The road occasionally runs parallel to the George S. Mickelson Trail, which is detailed in the Recreation chapter. This area has interesting and surprising examples of rolling prairie in the middle of the pine-covered Black Hills. From Deerfield, F.S. 17 (this section is unpaved) turns north and intersects with Forest Service Road 231, which leads to the whimsical mountain town of Rochford, founded in 1878.

Highway 40 travels from the subtle prairie plains of the Hermosa area to the wooded foothills around the little town of Hayward, then into the higher hills of Keystone. As you drive toward Hayward, look to your left (the south side of the road) to see Mount Rushmore in the distance.

Southern Hills

You simply must not miss the exquisite Peter Norbeck National Scenic Byway, 70 miles of road that loops through the Black Hills National Forest, Norbeck Wildlife Preserve, and Custer State Park. The byway includes the Needles Highway (Highway 87/89), Horse Thief Lake Road (Highway 244), and Iron Mountain Road (U.S. 16A). You'll see historic sites, wild animals, nifty switchbacks, pigtail bridges, lakes, and towering granite spires as you pass through tiny tunnels. Because we consider the byway a major attraction, you'll find complete information in the Attractions chapter, but note that sections of Iron Mountain Road and the Needles Highway close during the winter.

Most interstate information centers (plus one at Mount Rushmore and one at Custer State Park) have interactive kiosks. Touch the screen to find information on attractions, accommodations, and routes. Some centers stock travel tapes. For $20, you can listen and learn about the sights as you drive across the state. When you return the tape you receive $15 back.

Custer State Park's Wildlife Loop is another drive you mustn't miss. Its 18 miles of paved road literally loop through the beautiful park. You will probably see bison, deer, hawks, pronghorn antelope, prairie dogs, and the park's begging burros. If you're really lucky, you'll also spot Rocky Mountain goats, bighorn sheep, elk, and coyotes. There's more about Custer State Park and its wonderful roads in the Parks and Mountains chapter. We also recommend Highway 36 from Hermosa to Custer State Park, a delightful road that winds through pretty farm and ranch country. The landscape becomes increasingly beautiful as you approach the park. Near the park entrance, Highway 36 becomes U.S. 16A.

By Public Transportation

Unfortunately, the Hills lack public transportation systems, except for the two below.

NORTHERN HILLS

Deadwood Trolley
Deadwood Visitors Bureau
3 Siever Street, Deadwood
(605) 578-1876, (605) 578-2600 (City Hall)
Not many communities with fewer than 2,000 residents can afford a public transportation system, let alone one this complete. Trolleys run from one end of town to the other seven days a week,

stopping at all the major hotels, casinos, and attractions. In the summer trolleys operate 24 hours a day and hit each stop as often as every 10 minutes, although the coming of winter sees a trolley at each stop every hour, and only until midnight or 2:00 A.M. Fares are simple—one ride costs 50 cents—and though the system was designed primarily for tourists, locals love its convenience. Alas, the trolleys themselves are rubber wheeled, but steel-wheeled trolleys have been suggested by historic preservation consultants on multiple occasions. Still, the vehicles are very attractive, marked with bright green and gold paint, with wooden benches and open-air seating in summer.

CENTRAL HILLS

RapidRide/Dial-A-Ride
333 Sixth Street, Rapid City
(605) 394-6631
These small buses operate Monday through Friday, 6:25 A.M. to 6:00 P.M. Fares are $1.00 for adults and students and 50 cents for seniors 60 and older and disabled individuals. Those with transfers from another route and children younger than age five (with adults) ride for free. The RapidRide office is in the Milo Barber Transportation Center. Its four designated routes cover schools, the hospital, the mall, the library, and popular shopping areas rather than visitor attractions, so it's more a service for residents than for tourists. If you want to try it, however, get a schedule at the transportation center so you'll know where the buses stop.

By Rental Car

We list the nationally recognized companies plus some local businesses. Some automobile dealerships also rent vehicles (look under Auto Renting in the Yellow Pages). Many rental car companies have SUVs, trucks, and vans, too; inquire if you need something bigger and more rugged than a passenger car.

In the Black Hills are Avis, (605) 393-0740, (800) 331-1212; Budget, (605) 393-0488, (800) 676-0488; Dollar, (605) 342-7071, (800) 800-4000; Enterprise, (605) 399-9939, (800) 325-8007; Hertz, (605) 393-0160, (800) 654-3131; National Car Rental, (605) 393-2664, (800) 227-7368; and Thrifty Car Rental, (605) 393-0663, (800) 847-4389. Budget also has a second location at 1947 Deadwood Avenue in Rapid City, (605) 341-9040.

Local rental car companies include Rent-A-Wreck and Rent-Rite car rentals in Rapid City. Rent-A-Wreck, located at 1318 Fifth Street, (605) 348-3050, (800) 733-WREK, provides pickup and return service. Rent-Rite car rentals, 926 Main Street, (605) 348-0611, (800) 722-0207, offers its customers pickup and delivery service, as do some of the national companies.

By Taxi, Shuttle, and Limo

Many of these services also offer customized sightseeing tours; call ahead if you're interested.

NORTHERN HILLS

Courtesy Taxi
Sturgis
(605) 347-4253
Courtesy Taxi serves the Sturgis Municipal Airport and the Northern Hills.

CENTRAL HILLS

Airport Express Shuttle
Rapid City
(605) 399-9999, (800) 357-9998
You'll find drivers waiting at Rapid City Regional Airport during scheduled flight arrivals, or you can call them for a pickup. They'll take you where you want to go, whether that's from the airport to downtown Rapid City, to your hotel, to Deadwood, or on a tour.

Premier Limousine & Sightseeing Tours
Rapid City
(605) 381–0971
Rent an eight-person luxury stretch limo for any occasion, including tours through the Black Hills and to Deadwood, or ride to the airport in style. Premier has 20-passenger minibuses for larger groups.

Rapid Taxi
Rapid City
(605) 348–8080
This taxi service will take you around town or out of town.

By Train

Black Hills Central Railroad/The 1880 Train
222 Railroad Avenue, Hill City
(605) 574–2222
www.1880train.com
You can take an old-fashioned train ride from Keystone to Hill City and back again on this delightful train. There's information in the Attractions chapter on these 20-mile round-trip train rides, which are a terrific way to see the Black Hills the way the old-timers used to.

Specialty Transportation

Wheelchair Service of the Black Hills
(605) 341–2577
This company specializes in nonemergency transportation for people in wheelchairs. Although its drivers usually transport people on errands and to appointments, the service also offers sightseeing tours around the Hills. Its vans with lifts have a capacity of three wheelchairs. Operating hours are 6:00 A.M. to 6:00 P.M. Monday through Friday. Call ahead to arrange a customized tour.

HISTORY 🏛

In geologic terms, Black Hills history dates back millions of years. Because that part of our past is covered in the Natural World chapter, this chapter focuses on what is known about humans' presence here. (For a history of the Badlands, please see the Badlands and Nearby chapter.) It's an abbreviated account, however, because so much took place in a very short time. Scores of books have been written on the subject, and you'll find many of them in libraries, bookstores, and gift shops.

South Dakota attained statehood on November 2, 1889, more than a decade after pioneer settlement of the Hills had begun in earnest in 1875–76. From that time forward the story has been one of boom and bust, fire and flood, hunger and plenty—but always one of diligent efforts toward the building of strong, enduring communities.

Black Hills history, however, isn't just about the spread of European civilization on the western frontier. For the Native inhabitants, white encroachment on the Black Hills region was an invasion of a bountiful and cherished domain, and the struggle for its control was long and bloody. Although American Indians and non-Indians later learned to coexist, bridging the ideological and cultural chasm between the two groups is still a work in progress.

Tensions flared anew in 1973 when members of the American Indian Move-

ment (AIM) rioted and set the Custer County Courthouse on fire to protest the killing of an Indian by a white man. The conflict grabbed national headlines when AIM members occupied Wounded Knee village on the Pine Ridge Indian Reservation, staging a symbolic 71-day standoff to protest the treatment of American Indians in general. Wounded Knee II, as it came to be called, is considered a turning point in modern American Indian life, but it took almost another two decades before Indians and non-Indians in South Dakota reached out their hands in friendship. Accepting a challenge by then *Indian Country Today* newspaper publisher Tim Giago, the late Gov. George S. Mickelson declared a Year of Reconciliation in 1990, the 100th anniversary of the infamous Wounded Knee Massacre. It was the first step of a long journey.

WHO WAS HERE FIRST?

Archaeological evidence indicates the presence of prehistoric hunters called Paleo-Indians in the area as early as 11,000 years ago. Believed to have originated in Asia and crossed the Bering Land Bridge to the New World, these nomads and their successors left a record over the course of several millennia. Their ancient petroglyphs have been found carved, painted, and pecked into the rock at various places in the southern Black Hills; you'll get to examine some of them if you tour the Black Hills Wild Horse Sanctuary near Hot Springs (see Attractions). More recently, roughly between 200 and 500 years ago, aboriginal peoples left evidence of hunting activity at the Vore Buffalo Jump west of nearby Beulah, Wyoming (see Day Trips and Weekend Getaways).

That American Indians were here when the first Euro-Americans arrived is

---

i *Some early-day denizens of the Black Hills had colorful nicknames. Cold Deck Johnny, Swill Barrel Jimmy, Three Sixes Joe, Slippery Sam, Bummer Dan, Mineral Jack, Bedrock Tom, and Madame Mustachio are monikers that arouse conjecture about their owners.*

---

undisputed, but there is disagreement about much else. According to a Sioux creation story, the Lakota (Western, or Teton, Sioux) tribes have always lived here. They entered the world through Wind Cave, lured from their subterranean home by a trickster who falsely promised them wealth. However, anthropologists say the Lakota didn't arrive in the Dakotas until the 18th century. In fact, their homeland was farther east in Minnesota and Wisconsin—perhaps even as far east as Virginia. But other tribes, outfitted with guns and pressured by white settlers, drove them to the plains. Before the Lakota were free to settle the region, however, they had to drive out the preexisting Crow and Arikara tribes.

Whatever the date of their arrival, events since the last quarter of the 19th century are clearly documented. The United States' last great gold rush forever changed the Black Hills and ended a way of life for a proud, powerful people who found themselves confined on desolate reservations and reduced to poverty and government dependence.

We might never know the name of the first person who set foot in the Black Hills, but we do know that a white man traveled through during the late summer of 1823— it was none other than fearless, pious Jedediah Smith, on his way west. But while Smith's presence is little more than a footnote in history, the unfinished chapter on the ultimate battle for control of the Black Hills begins with the name of bold, brash Lt. Col. George Armstrong Custer. For it was Custer who led an 1874 expedition authorized by the war department to gather information and also, perhaps above all, confirm rumors of gold in the streams and soil of Paha Sapa.

TREATIES AND LAND CLAIMS

As the westward push brought competition for land, the U.S. government devised treaties that set aside territory for exclu-

The Homestake Gold Mine caused the city of Lead to be rearranged several times. Before mined-out tunnels were properly backfilled, streets and buildings had to be moved as the ground above the mine gradually sank. In the 1990s the mine rerouted U.S. Highway 85, the city's Main Street, and moved buildings to allow expansion of the surface mine.

sive use by Indian tribes in exchange for promises that westering pioneers and settlers would not be harmed. The Fort Laramie Treaty of 1868 was one such agreement; it ceded western Dakota Territory (which includes the Black Hills) and parts of neighboring states to the Sioux— oblivious to claims that might legitimately have been made by other tribes.

Enter Custer and a series of events that changed minds in the nation's capital. First, the Custer expedition—which was itself illegal by the terms of the Fort Laramie Treaty—confirmed and greatly exaggerated the presence of gold in the Black Hills. That left the government powerless, and soon unwilling, to turn aside the wave of prospectors that quickly followed. In addition, the gold rush of 1876 coincided not only with the nation's centennial but with Custer's death at the hands of Indian tribes in the Battle of the Little Bighorn. We can assume that federal officials and the nation as a whole did not look kindly on Indians after that. Congress, determined to annex the Black Hills, demanded in 1877 that they be sold, and opened the area for settlement in spite of Sioux resistance. Refusing to accept the terms, the tribes filed suit in 1923, claiming that the Black Hills had been seized unlawfully.

More than half a century later, in 1979, the U.S. Court of Claims agreed, awarding the tribes compensation and damages in excess of $100 million, a decision upheld by the U.S. Supreme Court the next year. However, the Sioux have refused to take the money, which has approximately tripled in interest-bearing accounts in the Sioux Nation's name. Now there are demands for the return of the land itself in accordance with the Fort Laramie Treaty.

U.S. Sen. Bill Bradley of New Jersey tried to settle the controversy in 1985 with a bill that would have given the Sioux all federal land in western South Dakota except Mount Rushmore National Memorial, along with natural-resource and jurisdictional rights as well as the settlement money. The Bradley bill never made it to the Senate floor, however, and a second attempt failed as well.

There is a great deal of opposition to the concept of conveying the Black Hills to Native American ownership, for several reasons. To many in the wider society, this concept appears as a threat to the social and economic order that has taken hold over the last century. In addition, there are those who argue that the Fort Laramie Treaty was broken by both sides and is no longer valid or even relevant; that whites acted no differently from Lakotas in displacing prior occupants of the land.

There is also disagreement over the role of the Black Hills in American Indian life. Plains-dwelling Indian tribes are not known to have lived within the boundaries of the Hills but did enter the area at times for various purposes and do consider them sacred.

If consensus about who can rightfully claim the Black Hills is ever reached, it's not likely to happen anytime soon.

BLACK HILLS OR BUST

Once word of the Custer expedition's discovery of gold in French Creek was out, adventurers began organizing illegal for-

---

The State of South Dakota has committed $35 million in funds to use the former Homestake Gold Mine as an underground science laboratory.

---

ays to the Black Hills. The first group to evade the military units assigned to keep fortune hunters out was the Gordon Party, which departed from Sioux City, Iowa, in late 1874. Among the party were Annie Tallent, the first white woman known to enter the Black Hills, and her nine-year-old son, Robert. Arriving at French Creek on Christmas Eve, the invaders set about building a sturdy log stockade. Their presence was soon detected, however, and the next April they were escorted out of the Hills by blue-coated soldiers. Today you can visit a re-creation of the Gordon Stockade in Custer State Park (see the Parks and Mountains chapter).

The escapade made headlines, and soon prospectors were entering the Hills in a brazen fashion. By 1876 a full-blown gold rush was under way. Although early efforts to find treasure focused on the French Creek and Custer areas in the Southern Hills, news of a gold strike in Deadwood Gulch quickly shifted the action north—so quickly, in fact, that the population of Custer City dropped from an estimated 6,000 or more to just 14 in a mere two weeks.

The first workings were placer (rhymes with Vassar) deposits that could be washed out of the gravel where gold had been dropped by slow-moving streams. As the easy diggings played out, miners began looking for rich hard-rock lodes on which to patent claims. The most famous of these was the Homestake, discovered in 1876 by brothers Fred and Moses Manuel and sold to George Hearst in 1877. By that time, the Hills were teeming with tens of thousands of prospectors, many of whom eventually returned home with empty pockets. Others successfully developed mining properties, harvesting gold, silver, or other minerals; in time, many of the deposits were mined out, and once-thriving communities decayed into ghost towns.

The Homestake Gold Mine in Lead had a different fate, continuing to produce gold decade after decade and making mining the cornerstone of the

The Custer Expedition of 1874

When George Armstrong Custer led an expedition into the Black Hills in the summer of 1874, he handed himself his own death certificate. The illegally conceived Custer expedition led to the gold rush of 1876, which triggered the U.S. government to forcibly take the sacred Black Hills from Sioux control. This land seizure contributed greatly to the Indian Wars of the late 1870s and 1880s. One of the ensuing battles, fought near the Little Bighorn River, would take Custer's life.

Word of the gold found during Custer's trip might have been the catalyst that released wave after wave of white fortune-seekers, but the flood had been building for years. In fact, Secretary of the Interior Columbus Delano wrote a letter as early as 1872 bluntly spelling out the government's plan:

> I am inclined to think that the occupation of this region of the country is not necessary to the happiness and prosperity of the Indians, and as it is supposed to be rich in minerals and lumber it is deemed important to have it freed as early as possible from Indian occupancy.
>
> I shall, therefore, not oppose any policy which looks first to a careful examination of the subject. . . . If such an examination leads to the conclusion that country is not necessary or useful to Indians, I should then deem it advisable . . . to extinguish the claim of the Indians and open the territory to the occupation of the whites.

Although Delano was supposed to protect Plains Indian territorial rights, his words clearly contradicted the Fort Laramie Treaty of 1868, which prevented whites from ever setting foot in the "country" he mentioned. Nevertheless, two years after Delano's letter, Custer was off to conduct a "scientific survey" of the protected Great Sioux Indian Reservation.

Custer, his troops, and a small contingent of scientists arrived at the Belle Fourche River before entering the Black Hills on its western side. For two months the Seventh Cavalry scaled the mountainsides of the Lakota's Paha Sapa, collecting samples and writing reports about the valleys, the forests, and, eventually, the gold. These reports were regularly sent west to Fort Laramie, where they were telegraphed to army posts farther east.

Even if the official military reports hadn't leaked out, the journalists Custer took with him would have informed the country immediately on their return. In a matter of months prospectors were preparing to invade the forbidden Black Hills. The military was officially dispatched to escort any intruding pioneers off the protected Sioux lands, but it gave up in 1875, permitting thousands of gold seekers to descend upon the Black Hills. The Sioux, outraged over the broken Laramie Treaty, did their best to launch an organized rebellion. They scored their greatest victory in 1876 at the Battle of the Little Bighorn, where Custer and most of the men who were with him on the Black Hills expedition were killed.

But the resistance was doomed before it began. The Sioux, along with their Cheyenne and Arapaho allies, were ultimately defeated and forced onto the much smaller reservations we see on maps today. Their once-protected territory, land that covered parts of present-day Wyoming, Nebraska, and both Dakotas, was divided and sold to ranchers and prospectors.

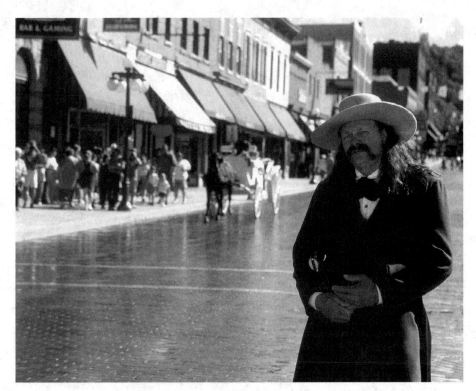

Wild West reenactors mingle with guests in Deadwood and stage daily shootouts on historic Main Street. SOUTH DAKOTA TOURISM

Northern Hills economy for generations. Mining and related business opportunities provided secure jobs and cash flow for the area, attracting immigrants of many nationalities who often formed their own ethnic neighborhoods in the new country. Some of these can still be seen in Lead today.

The roster of early-day citizenry also included many characters whose names and exploits are legendary. James Butler "Wild Bill" Hickok, dubbed the Prince of Pistoleers, was an early arrival in Deadwood. So was Martha Jane Cannary (or Canary) Burke—Calamity Jane. Wild Bill, already famous as a lawman and a dead shot, made a grand exit when he was murdered during a card game by drifter Jack McCall. Salty-tongued Calamity, who often wore buckskins and carried six-

guns, was reputed to be a down-and-out, not altogether honest, but kindly drunk who nursed the sick during a smallpox epidemic before succumbing to alcoholism in 1903. The origin of her nickname is uncertain, but many accounts attribute it to a venereal calamity that befell the gentlemen with whom she consorted. She and Wild Bill ("the only man I ever loved," she claimed after his death in 1876, although the then-recently wed Hickok doesn't seem to have returned the compliment) are buried along with other Deadwood notables in Mount Moriah Cemetery in Deadwood (see the Attractions chapter). Elfin 4-foot 3-inch prospector Potato Creek Johnny, martyrized Preacher Smith, and quick-witted Sheriff Seth Bullock also found their final resting place there, and a considerable

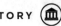

tourist industry quickly took hold around all their legends. You can learn more about them at the Adams Museum in Deadwood, which you'll find listed in the Attractions chapter.

Tourism has become a top industry in the Black Hills, but it was mining that sustained the area during the Great Depression, when the federal government promised to pay top dollar for all the gold that was produced. Many who had lost their livelihoods found work as miners, and the value of Homestake stock soared. The company continued to prosper and pay good wages, and a new gold rush began after the price of gold reached $800 an ounce in the early 1980s. New heap-leach technology and the development of giant earthmoving machines led to the resurrection of mines that had closed decades before, and in the mid-1980s modern-day surface mining was introduced to the Black Hills. State permits were granted for operations that would dig deep pits totaling hundreds of acres and use cyanide solution to treat huge piles of crushed ore—as well as provide good jobs and substantial tax revenues.

Those developments produced a passionate, bitter conflict between environmentalists and mining supporters that ruptured the community and ruined friendships. In early 2004, local politicians reached an agreement with Barrick Gold Corporation, owner of the now-defunct Homestake Mine. The state government agreed to indemnify Barrick of various environmental liabilities in exchange for a free-and-clear donation of the mine for use as a National Underground Laboratory. As a result, the legislature has been allocating funds to construct a temporary lab at the mine's 4,850-foot level, which officials hope to open in 2007. Although the National Science Foundation has yet to select a site for a permanent lab, community leaders are doing everything in their power to attract high-technology firms to the region in anticipation of scientific research at Homestake.

The original name of the town of Deadwood was "Dead Wood Gulch." The hills around the mining camp had suffered a forest fire years before the first prospectors arrived, and dead trees were everywhere. It wasn't long before enterprising entrepreneurs were selling firewood and the town had become known simply as "Deadwood."

LAW AND ORDER

A shooting a night was the rule when a tent city sprang up in Deadwood Gulch in 1876. In no time at all there were 75 saloons in the town, and the local newspaper deplored the presence of claim jumpers and dance-hall girls. "The summer air is filled with profanity and curses," an editorial protested. Was Deadwood much different from any other western mining camp? Likely not. Things began to settle down, though, when court was called to order on May 10, 1877. (One account says it was the first court session held in the Hills; another has the first session taking place about the same time in now-defunct Sheridan.)

Meanwhile, a Canadian hardware dealer who had come to Deadwood by way of Montana had become the first officially appointed sheriff in the Black Hills. An imposing figure, mustachioed Seth Bullock gained a reputation as the lawman who never killed anyone. He went on to success in many ventures, including a stint as the first Black Hills forest supervisor. He also became a close friend of Theodore Roosevelt, who was his frequent guest. A Belle Fourche rancher, he's even credited with introducing alfalfa to South Dakota.

Law officers in Belle Fourche probably could have used Bullock's help when handsome Harry Longabaugh—the Sundance Kid—and a group of outlaws tried to hold up the Butte County Bank there on June 28, 1897. The bungled job netted a trifling $97, but most of the bandits were quick enough to get as far as Red Lodge, Montana, before they were cap-

In 2005 South Dakota ranked fourth in the nation in total ethanol production. This could be an important asset as vehicle manufacturers increase production of vehicles that can run primarily on ethanol.

tured. They later escaped from the Deadwood jail and were never prosecuted for their crime.

History books recount many hairraising stories of drunken judges and astonishing jury verdicts in the region's early days. But on some occasions irate citizens took the law into their own hands, as when masked vigilantes broke into a temporary jail in Rapid City and hanged three alleged horse thieves the night of June 21, 1877. Many people believed one of the executed men, 19-year-old Jas. (presumably James) "Kid" Hall, was innocent. The incident caused a rift among the citizenry and earned Rapid City the unflattering nickname Strangle Town. A dead tree on Hangman's Hill on Skyline Drive in Rapid City may or may not be the actual tree used in the lynching, but, rooted in cement, it serves today as a grizzly reminder of do-it-yourself frontier justice.

Nowadays, judgment is handed down in hushed courtrooms according to uniform, codified laws that take up many volumes on law library shelves. But even after the law became more organized and orderly, a wild streak persisted in the Black Hills for many years. Brothels like Pam's Purple Door continued to operate in Deadwood until an FBI raid closed them down in 1980. The bust made national news, and Deadwood once more made headlines as a sinful city.

RANCHING

While others were busy with the pursuit of shiny yellow metal, would-be cattle barons had their sights set on green gold.

To them, the waving grass on the fringes of the Black Hills looked like a giant pasture for fattening livestock. Soon cattle herds that plodded up the dusty trails from Texas were grazing on vast spreads where, not long before, huge bison herds had roamed. White hunters, eager for buffalo robes, had decimated the native animals and by so doing, driven a stake into the heart of Plains Indian life.

The first herd of cattle turned loose on the range was driven away by the Sioux, but in 1875 a Coloradan named Joe Reynolds brought Hereford stock to the Central Hills and established the area's oldest ranch. Historic Reynolds Stage Stop is still a working ranch.

Once settlers arrived for good in the Black Hills and it became clear that there weren't enough gold mines to go around, some turned their attention north to the wide-open grasslands of what is now Butte County. Ranching flourished there, and so did the city of Belle Fourche in its southwest corner. By the end of the 19th century, Belle Fourche had become the cattle-shipping capital of the world, with herds lined up for miles waiting to be loaded into railroad cars bound for eastern markets.

Early on, however, in the 1880s, an enterprising Minnesota judge noticed that the short-grass prairie would also be ideal for raising sheep. H. J. Grant brought the first sheep to western Dakota Territory from Texas in the 1880s, much to the indignation of the cattle ranchers. They listed all kinds of ways sheep would ruin their grazing land and contaminate their water. They were wrong, it turned out, and when they discovered that wool could be at least as profitable as beef, some either switched altogether or added sheep to their operations. Today, a wool warehouse in Belle Fourche still buys wool from ranchers in a wide area and sells it to mills all over the country.

Ranching is important to the modern Belle Fourche economy, and its heritage is celebrated each year during the Black Hills Roundup. You can read about this

The Sioux

Tepees. Buffalo hunts. Beadwork. Feather headdresses. The movie *Dances with Wolves.* This is how the Sioux are most often portrayed. Is it an accurate picture? Yes and no.

The term "Sioux" refers to a group of American Indian tribes originally united by a common language, Siouan. The name is a French-English corruption of the Ojibwa (Chippewa) *nadow-is-iw,* a derisive term meaning "adders," or "snakelike." But many don't realize that the people known today as the Sioux are made up of three divisions that have distinct dialects and cultural attributes. The primary divisions are Dakota (Santee, or Eastern), Nakota (Yankton, or Middle), and Lakota (Teton, or Western), and each of these has further subdivisions.

Dakota and Nakota tribes, who settled in woodland and river areas respectively, often lived in bark dwellings or earth lodges and grew crops. The largest and most powerful division, the Lakota, was made up of nomadic, tepee-dwelling, horse-mounted bands that dominated the Great Plains when white settlers arrived. The Lakota came to represent the quintessential Plains Indians.

Lakota subdivisions, known as the "Seven Tents," are Oglala (Red Cloud was a famous chief), Hunkpapa (Sitting Bull's people), Minneconjou (Big Foot's followers), Sicangu (also called Brule), Sans Arcs, Sihasapa (Blackfeet, distinct

from the Algonquian Blackfeet), and Oohenanpa (Two Kettle). The Pine Ridge Indian Reservation east of the Black Hills is home to many members of the Oglala Lakota tribe.

Skilled buffalo hunters, the Lakota also became well known for their bold geometric quillwork and beadwork. Today, many examples of traditional Lakota artwork, both old and new, can be seen in Black Hills museums and stores (see the Attractions, Arts, and Shopping chapters).

By the way, the book *Dances with Wolves* is about a Comanche tribe. The multiple-award-winning movie is about a Lakota tribe because, according to author Michael Blake, it was hard to find anyone who spoke fluent Comanche. (Native Americans in the film speak Lakota with English subtitles.) And anyway, the movie was filmed in South Dakota, including several locations in the Black Hills.

three-day festival in the Annual Events chapter.

Between 1898 and 1910 the granddaddy of local ranching celebrations took place in Rapid City. Cowboys from all over the region as well as dignitaries from Chicago and other faraway places looked forward to April each year so they could attend the three-day meeting of the South Dakota Stock Growers Association.

Stockmen's Days was their time to buy supplies and have fun as they raced their horses down Main Street, played games, danced, and generally made a racket.

The celebration died out, some say because the ladies of Rapid City found it too boisterous, but the Stock Growers Association is still headquartered in the foothills town staked out by energetic Denver hotelier John Brennan. Brennan, who quickly gave up a hard miner's life in favor of civic development, envisioned a new Denver when he chose a town site near the banks of Rapid Creek. Rapid City began life as a hay camp where freight crews could revive themselves and their animals before pushing on to the mining camps deep within the Hills. The town quickly became the area's commercial center, a role it continues to play today while retaining a good deal of its cowboy flavor.

TIMBER AND THE FOREST

Once prospectors arrived in the Hills, primitive lumbering operations couldn't produce board feet fast enough to meet the demand for mine shorings, buildings, and fuel. It didn't take long for steam-powered sawmills to get up and running just about everywhere, but by the mid-1880s, railroad construction increased the need for timber still further. Much of the

area was clear-cut as a result. The situation was exacerbated by a rash of major forest fires in 1893, moving President Grover Cleveland to establish the 1.2-million-acre Black Hills Forest Reserve in 1897. The next year the nation's first commercial timber sale on federal forested land was authorized here, with Homestake Mining Company as buyer. In 1907 the reserve was renamed the Black Hills National Forest, having come under the jurisdiction of the USDA Forest Service two years earlier.

During the Depression, the forest provided jobs for Civilian Conservation Corps laborers who worked at improving timber stands, preventing and fighting forest fires, and numerous other tasks. Historical markers along many roads remind us of the CCC's contributions during those tough times. Its legacy remains intact at the Black Hills Playhouse, a once-abandoned CCC camp in Custer State Park where theatrical performances are staged each summer (see the Arts chapter).

The Black Hills National Forest has been a leader in the concept of multiple use, a practice that became law with the 1960 Multiple Use–Sustained Yield Act. This law ensures that national forests are managed for a variety of public uses, from logging to wildlife habitat and recreation, while maintaining productivity of land and harvestable resources. Logging and the manufacture of wood products remain important industries in the Black Hills today, employing more than 1,800 people in logging and milling alone. In addition, timber sales provide 97 percent of income from the forest (25 percent of those receipts go to counties with national forest acreage). But in recent years timber sales have come under a barrage of challenges by environmentalists who think too many trees are being cut and too many roads are being built for logging.

Babe the Blue Ox and the Beginning of the Black Hills

Geologists will argue, but we think this whimsical tale of mythological giant lumberjack Paul Bunyan and his beloved blue ox, Babe, offers a perfectly good explanation for the creation of the Black Hills.

One morning, so the story goes, Babe spied a batch of pancakes baking for the logging crew's breakfast. The sight made her so hungry that she gobbled up all 400 flapjacks, but even that wasn't enough to quiet her rumbling stomach. So with one bite, Babe devoured the scorching hot griddle and then gulped down the cookstove, flames and all. Suffering from the worst case of indigestion ever known, Babe galloped off with a mighty bellow, tearing up the prairie in her distress. When Paul finally found her, poor Babe was flat on her back, feet sticking straight up in the air, dead as a post. Grieving, Paul started to

dig a grave but changed his mind and instead covered his pet with a layer of dirt and rocks. Babe's burial mound became the Black Hills, and if you don't believe it, we have proof: The Belle Fourche River and South Fork of the Cheyenne River still flow all the way to the Missouri with the tears Paul shed while performing this sad task.

THE RAILROAD

Because the Black Hills were part of the Great Sioux Reservation and off-limits to the railroads, iron horses bypassed the area during the height of the 19th-century rail boom. In the first decades of white settlement, people came on horseback, in ox-drawn wagons and, later, in stagecoaches.

Nevertheless, narrow-gauge rail lines were used within the Hills to carry fuel and materials to the mines. Homestake Mining Company built the first such railroad in 1881. The first outside train arrived in Rapid City during the 1886 Fourth of July celebration after the Fremont, Elkhorn & Missouri Valley Railroad

built a branch from Chadron, Nebraska, to the Black Hills. The Elkhorn soon laid track to the Northern Hills, reaching Whitewood in 1887, Belle Fourche in 1889, and Deadwood in 1890. Other lines such as the Chicago, Milwaukee & St. Paul Railway Co., the Grand Island Railroad, and the Chicago, Burlington & Quincy Railroad brought supplies and tourists to the area. You can still ride part of the old CB&Q route on the Black Hills Central Railroad (The 1880 Train) in Hill City (see Attractions).

Because it was a destination resort, Hot Springs had two rail lines that delivered visitors eager to soak in its mineral baths, starting in 1892. Ironically, though,

Pactola Reservoir and Sheridan Lake bear the names of gold-rush towns that were flooded when the lakes were built.

western South Dakota didn't connect via rail to the eastern part of the state until the next century, and one historian has speculated that the continued isolation may help to account for ongoing differences between "East River" and "West River" South Dakota (see the Area Overview chapter).

Competition for invaluable rail service was stiff and often underhanded. In the push for the first train, Rapid City got the upper hand when citizens executed a legal maneuver that skirted a ban on financial aid to railroads while raising money for a depot and other improvements. To the north, Seth Bullock cut a deal granting the Elkhorn a right-of-way across his acreage in exchange for a station that would give rise to the town of Belle Fourche, even as residents of nearby Minnesela were negotiating for a depot in their town. (Belle Fourche later "stole" the county seat away from the now-abandoned town of Minnesela, too.) It just goes to show how vital rail service was for economic and social progress.

Railroads declined in importance as interstate highways and airlines provided efficient alternatives. Many miles of track were abandoned, and now, through a rails-to-trails project, a 114-mile section that belonged to the Burlington Northern Railroad has new life as a recreational trail. You can read about the George S. Mickelson Trail in the Recreation chapter.

Creosote, a substance used as a wood preservative, is commonly found in the railroad timbers that crisscross South Dakota and can cause neurological disturbance if inhaled in strong concentration.

The Burlington Northern Santa Fe Railway still has a crew change point in Edgemont, and the Dakota, Minnesota & Eastern Railroad chugs along the eastern slope of the Hills. In fact, the Sioux Falls–based DM&E is in the midst of a $2 billion project, the country's largest railroad expansion since the Civil War. The proposal, which includes building and upgrading 1,000 miles of track to Wyoming's coalfields, has been under legal attack since 1998. But federal agencies continue to rule in the company's favor, making the project's future more certain.

EDUCATION AND REFINEMENT

The first business to get a foothold in any rough-and-tumble mining camp was generally a saloon, and a newspaper often followed on its heels. Once respectable women and children arrived, settlers lost little time in starting schools, churches, and other cultural institutions.

At first many of these activities took place in crude shared or rented quarters, but within a few years pupils were attending classes in schools built just for them. The area's first teacher arrived long before that, though: Annie Tallent, the first white woman in the Hills, was a teacher. After she and the rest of the Gordon Party were expelled from their stockade in 1875, she returned to the Black Hills and, after being deserted by her husband, taught school and later became a school superintendent. She also wrote a book, *The Black Hills, or Last Hunting Grounds of the Dakotahs.* Her typically 19th-century views on Native Americans later branded Annie Tallent a bigot in some people's minds, and a Rapid City elementary school named for her was rechristened South Park Elementary School.

A prevailing philosophy in Tallent's day was that Native Americans' best interests would be served through acculturation. With that in mind, the federal government chose Rapid City as the site for an Indian school much like the one at Carlisle, Pennsylvania, where students were forced to cast off their Native dress, language, and religion and try to become Christian farmers and ranchers. Rapid City Indian School opened in 1887 and operated for several decades.

Perhaps some of the teachers at the Indian school were trained at Spearfish Normal School, which opened in 1883. And perhaps some of their students went on to study at Dakota School of Mines, where classes were offered for the first time in 1885. Both schools have grown and undergone name changes over the last century-plus, and you can read about Black Hills State University and South Dakota School of Mines and Technology in the Education chapter.

Many early settlers must have gone to school and learned to read before arriving here, because newspapers were in demand from the beginning. Not surprisingly, the first paper was published in Deadwood, where the action was. Deadwood was first, that is, if you don't count the single issue published in Custer by W. A. Laughlin and A. W. Merrick before they packed up their press and headed north. Before long their *Black Hills Pioneer*, founded in 1876, had lots of competition, and at one point Deadwood had three dailies and three weeklies.

In 1878 pioneer newspaperman Joseph Gossage arrived from Nebraska to start the *Black Hills Weekly Journal* in Rapid City. But Gossage's industrious, intelligent wife, Alice, gets much of the credit for the newspaper's success and longevity as well as for breaking ground for early women reporters. Together, and with help from the talented reporter Richard B. Hughes, the Gossages built the paper into an outstanding daily publication. Today the *Rapid City Journal,* as it's now called, is the largest newspaper in all of western South Dakota.

News on the spiritual front showed notorious Deadwood to be a leader, a reassuring achievement given the town's early reputation as a wicked place. Con-gregationalists founded the area's first religious institution there in 1876, although they didn't get a church building until almost a year later—and then they shared it with two other Protestant sects. Catholic worship came first to Deadwood in 1877 as did Baptist church services in 1881.

The Black Hills got its first martyr when Henry Weston Smith was found shot outside Deadwood in 1876. Though Indians were blamed for the murder of the staunchly Methodist Preacher Smith, the crime was never solved. Some historians believe he was killed by prospectors and gamblers who didn't take kindly to his fiery sermons. Today, however, most Black Hills residents consider themselves devoutly religious; you can read more about that in the Worship and Spirituality chapter.

For entertainment, settlers joined fraternal organizations such as the Masons and Oddfellows, and many immigrant groups had their own ethnic societies. Theater troupes were often among the first to arrive in a new settlement, and as cities gained a foothold, elaborate theaters were built. The Matthews Opera House in Spearfish was the most ornate theater in South Dakota when it opened in 1906; it was quickly upstaged by the Homestake Opera House in Lead, constructed eight years later. Though both eventually decayed (the Matthews from neglect, the Homestake from fire damage), the Spearfish theater has been restored and hosts regular performances, while Lead's opera house continues to undergo massive restoration.

By 1881 Rapid City had its first public building, Library Hall, and the townspeople used it for all kinds of civic and social activities. As the city became the area's population center, it also became the cultural center, and today western South Dakota's largest city, with a population of more than 60,000, hosts most of our major cultural events. (Turn to the Arts chapter for an in-depth look at the local cultural scene.)

Not surprisingly, the Black Hills today are home to many talented artisans who appreciate living in such an aesthetically

The Lawrence County Courthouse

The fight to save the Lawrence County Courthouse in Deadwood didn't provoke gunplay, but it had all the intrigue of a full-blown range war.

The Beaux Arts–style courthouse, with a cupola on top and hand-painted murals on the walls inside, opened for business in 1908. Three years later President William Howard Taft came for a visit, and the courthouse was decorated in his honor.

As time went by, county offices grew cramped, and in the 1970s a new public safety center was added on. But a decade later the original part of the courthouse was declared structurally unsafe, and everybody had to move out. That's when the fighting started.

At first, the Lawrence County Board of Commissioners couldn't decide whether to fix the building or demolish it. So a citizens group, Save the Courthouse, held a rally on the front steps and got up a petition to have county voters decide. Then the commissioners voted to tear the building down, but the public vote went the other way. That meant the commissioners had to figure out how to renovate the building and accommodate ongoing expansion in county government at the same time, and also how to pay for the mandated work. The discussion lasted more than three years. In the meantime there were efforts to stop the county

from issuing bonds to pay for the project, a proposal to move the county seat to Spearfish, a dispute over land for a new courthouse annex, and an attempt to block the annex project altogether. In addition, a leader of Save the Courthouse was convicted of arson for setting fire to her own restored Victorian home in an attempt to collect insurance money.

Fortunately, though, the courthouse was repaired, and while the job was in progress, workers uncovered all kinds of beautiful artwork that for decades had been hidden under false ceilings and behind wall panels. Restoration experts cleaned and touched up murals and refurbished original stenciling with paint and gold leaf. When the building reopened in 1991, the citizens of Lawrence County reaffirmed what they'd known all along—they had saved a national treasure.

pleasing environment. Two of the most conspicuously inspired pieces wrought by local artists, however, can't be seen in any gallery. Mount Rushmore National Memorial near Keystone and Crazy Horse Memorial near Custer are monumental works whose very existence makes their creators themselves seem larger than life. You can read about both of them in the Attractions chapter.

THE MILITARY

From the arrival of the first warrior society to the present, the Black Hills have had a military presence. It wasn't until 1878, however, that Fort Meade, east of Sturgis, became the first official military post in the area. By then, there was little fighting left to do on the frontier, and the soldiers' role was largely one of peacekeeping and community service. What remained of the Seventh Cavalry after Custer's defeat built Fort Meade, and many of the regiment's major players were in service there. Among them was Maj. Marcus Reno, the senior surviving officer of the Little Bighorn. Reno's troubled career ended in an 1880 court-martial at Fort Meade after he was accused, unjustly it is now believed, of window peeping at the home of his commander, Col. Samuel Sturgis. Another renowned Little Bighorn survivor, the horse Comanche, lived out his life as a pampered mascot at Fort Meade (see the Retirement chapter for a write-up on Comanche).

Relations between the fort and the nearby town of Sturgis were not always amicable. Racial tensions arose when a black soldier from the 25th Infantry, Cpl. Ross Hallon, was hanged by vigilantes for allegedly killing a Sturgis doctor in 1885. And in 1924 citizens were shaken when two soldiers fired machine guns on a burning cross erected by the Ku Klux Klan. The Klan was so well organized in the Black Hills at that time that newspapers reported on the activities of its hooded members, which included giving money to churches and marching in parades.

Overall, though, Fort Meade was a community asset where civilian girls attended dances and military operations continued for 66 years, far longer than the average army fort. During World War I, South Dakota National Guard troops trained there, and during the Depression the facility was headquarters for all South Dakota CCC camps. In 1942 the Fourth Cavalry's horses were retired and exchanged for motorcycles and light tanks.

The USS South Dakota *was the most decorated battleship of World War II.*

The next year, Fort Meade became a training ground for glider troops, and then, in 1944, it ceased to be a military post and in 1945 became a prisoner-of-war camp for German soldiers. Today Fort Meade is the site of a Veterans Administration primary-care facility (see the Health Care chapter) and houses a fine museum.

The same year Fort Meade soldiers turned their horses out to pasture, the army gained a new foothold in the isolated southwestern corner of South Dakota. Work began in 1942 on the Black Hills Ordnance Depot (later called the Black Hills Army Depot), a long-term storage facility for weapons and supplies, and soon a whole new community had sprung up near the tiny hamlet of Provo. The new town called itself Igloo, after the igloo-shaped concrete bunkers used for storing ordnance at the site. The depot brought a degree of prosperity to the area, where the agriculture-based economy had suffered tremendous losses during the Dust Bowl years. The depot closed in 1967, and much of the land reverted to livestock grazing. Igloo is now deserted, a veritable ghost town.

About the same time that work first started on the depot, the army also established an air base near Rapid City as a place to train B-17 bomber crews. Unlike the depot, Rapid City Army Air Base shut down for about six months after World War II, but it soon reopened under the auspices of the U.S. Air Force. It became a permanent installation in 1948 and after a series of name changes was dedicated to the memory of Brig. Gen. Richard E. Ellsworth in 1953. Ellsworth, commander of the 28th Strategic Reconnaissance Wing, and a crew of 23 died in a plane crash while returning from a routine mission in Europe.

A study of Ellsworth Air Force Base prompts contemplation about some of

In 1879 Deadwood became the first city in South Dakota to get telephones. The next year, it was the first to get its own telephone exchange.

the critical developments in modern-day world events. For example, during the Cold War increasingly sophisticated weapons, from surface-to-air missiles to intercontinental ballistic missiles (ICBMs) were assigned to the base. Nuclear warheads were stored in 150 heavily guarded underground silos under base command. A new age dawned, however, with the toppling of the Berlin Wall and the Strategic Arms Reduction Treaties between the United States and Russia. Ellsworth began deactivating its missile silos in 1991 and finished destroying them in 1996. A silo and launch capsule east of Wall has been preserved as a Minuteman Missile National Historic Site. Tours are by reservation only and give the general public a very real glimpse into the heart of the nation's military during the Cold War.

As recently as 1992 Ellsworth was dubbed the Showplace of Strategic Air Command, home to four wings plus two squadrons with separate missions of their own. It's a smaller operation now, due to general military cuts, but the base remains a key heavy-bomber facility. The 28th Bomb wing, which started at Ellsworth and fought in World War II, is still based there, in charge of a fleet of B-1B bombers and still adapting to the nation's military needs. Today it stands ready for conven-

In 2006 Ellsworth Air Force Base outside Rapid City was selected as the new location for a consolidated financial services center, as well as a 24-hour call center for use by all air force personnel. This, just months after the Base Realignment and Closure Commission voted to remove Ellsworth from its list of bases slated for shutdown.

tional rather than nuclear warfare.

Ellsworth is the largest, but not the only, military presence in the Black Hills today. The South Dakota Army National Guard established itself in Rapid City and other Black Hills towns almost two decades before Ellsworth was built, in fact. Camp Rapid, the army guard's state headquarters, was established in the mid-1920s.

The South Dakota National Guard itself formed in 1862 to protect settlers while regular troops were busy with the Civil War. Under the command of the state governor, today's guard fulfills a threefold mission that includes providing reserve forces for federal service, helping local agencies during emergencies, and being active in community service. Local units, which are based in Belle Fourche, Spearfish, Sturgis, and Custer, as well as Rapid City, have helped quell forest fires, served in overseas conflicts, completed construction projects, and performed numerous other vital tasks. Along with Ellsworth, the guard provides government jobs and purchasing power that have a significant impact on the local economy.

TOURISM

Modern Black Hills tourism began at the end of the 19th century in the Southern Hills, where thermal springs along Fall River, long revered by indigenous Indian tribes for their healing powers, were a trendy sell to Victorian visitors from metropolitan areas. Clever marketing, along with a railroad connection and a few modern resorts, captured the interest of travelers from all over the country who came to soak their aching joints in the warm waters.

It wasn't long before the rest of the Black Hills caught on. The Sylvan Lake Hotel, built right on the shore of Custer State Park's crown jewel in 1895, was an upscale regional hot spot until it burned to the ground 40 years later. Deadwood, ever on the cutting edge of technology, saw its first automobile in 1891; highways and roadside motels were quick to follow.

However, President Calvin Coolidge—"Silent Cal"—gets much of the credit for bringing widespread tourism to the Black Hills in the 20th century. The reticent Vermonter decided to make Custer State Park his summer home in 1927, and while he was here he took time out from trout fishing and running the country to dedicate Mount Rushmore (see the Attractions chapter). Newsreels of the day gave untold numbers of Americans—many of whom apparently didn't know where or even what the Black Hills were—their first glimpse of the area's pine-covered mountains and dramatic rock outcroppings.

And so it was that tourism in the Black Hills expanded northward. Today, most visitors to the area come to see Rushmore, America's Shrine of Democracy, or the revived streets of Deadwood. Of course,

The city of Deadwood is a National Historic Landmark.

while they're here they take time to view wildlife, explore caves, hike hillsides, snowmobile down narrow canyons, ride motorcycles around forested bluffs, and visit the dozens of other attractions in the region, among other things.

Tourism is critical to the economy of the Black Hills, bringing in over four million people—and many times that in dollars—to the region every year. Residents proudly point out that over half of the state's visitor dollars are spent in the Black Hills, proving that the area is secure in its position as the regional capital of commerce, culture, and art.

THE NATURAL WORLD

For many visitors, the natural world of the Black Hills is the awe-inspiring main attraction, their main reason for coming. And this delightful aspect of the Black Hills makes so many other activities and attractions possible. For example, camping and recreational opportunities abound here. We also have some great art, as well as geology- and paleontology-based museums and sites. Many accommodations boast gorgeous locations; some restaurants serve Black Hills trout. All of these are inspired and sustained by our natural world.

We talk a lot about nature and its many facets throughout this book—it's integral to our way of life—and we'll make a point here of directing you to the Recreation chapter, which provides thorough information on outdoor activities. In this chapter, however, we'll tell you a bit about our natural history: the Hills' elements and how they came to be; the animals, birds, fish, and flora you can expect to see; the insects you'll likely swat; and the weather you will alternately bask in and curse (sometimes all in the same day).

GEOLOGY

The Black Hills are a unique geologic formation. They rise out of the Great Plains like an oasis and are unlike the landscape of the rest of South Dakota. Do know, however, that Hills is a misnomer; they're definitely mountains, smaller than the Rocky Mountains but higher than the Appalachians. From a distance, they look black—the effect of dense pine and spruce cover.

The Hills' Precambrian formations have been estimated at 1.7 billion to 2.5 billion years old. During the Cambrian period the area was covered by ancient seas, and changes during the Mississippian period left the lower deposits of limestone, sandstone, and shale some 300 million years ago. Younger rocks cover and surround these deposits, including a purple limestone at least 230 million years old. Higher layers are composed of more sandstone, limestone, and shale, including Pierre shale and Niobrara chalk, remnants from the bottom of a Cretaceous sea.

The Black Hills were uplifted during the Paleocene epoch, some 63 million years ago, by the same geologic forces that created the Rocky Mountains. Although the mind envisions this as a noisy, cataclysmic, cinematic event, it actually happened very slowly, and over the span of eons the Hills changed many times.

Over the slow millions of years, the area was arid, then subtropical, and then nearly buried in volcanic ash. New rivers and streams carved their own paths, and rain and wind carried away surface particles. Toward the end of the Eocene era, the climate became arid once again, turning South Dakota into a windy desert. Hundreds of feet of clay and sand nearly covered the Hills and buried the Badlands. Nature sculpted the eerie Badlands formations through erosion by wind and water, then supplemented them with sediments washing and blowing eastward from the Black Hills.

During those days the Black Hills formation became elliptical, and today the area is approximately 50 miles wide and 120 miles long. Much of it is now the Black Hills National Forest. But the land hasn't changed much since Lt. Col. Richard Irving Dodge viewed it. Dodge accompanied the Jenney-Newton expedition here in

Bear Butte: A Lakota Legend

In Lakota mythology, Maka is the Earth spirit, second only to Inyan, who created her. Inyan's spirit is Wakan Tanka (The Great Mystery) and Maka's is Makaakan (Earth Goddess). Their home is the Black Hills, The Heart of Everything That Is.

Long, long ago, Maka became deeply disappointed by the behavior of her children, whose many nations had grown away from her and who had begun to fight among themselves. She called to them, but most ignored her, so she shook herself, causing earthquakes, floods, and volcanoes, breaking the surface of the Hills, and changing life for all the inhabitants.

The four-legged creatures held a meeting to discuss this disaster, and Buffalo declared that the two-legs should be destroyed, since they had caused all the trouble. Magpie heard this discussion and flew back to the winged creatures, who held a meeting of their own. Owl made the point that Bear was a two-legged creature and the symbol of wisdom, which must be spared at all costs. The winged creatures declared that the two-legs must, therefore, be saved. A great race was proposed; the winners would decide the fate of the two-legs.

Four times, over many days, the creatures ran and flew clockwise around the sacred Black Hills. The Magpie didn't stop except to sleep for a bit at night; many times he passed exhausted animals who were forced to rest. The pounding feet, hooves, and paws left a red trail of blood on the racetrack, and the earth shook with the running. With Buffalo nearing the finish line at Bear Butte, clever Magpie hitched a ride on his back, then flew ahead at the last moment to win the race and save the two-legs.

During the contest, a strange swelling had risen from beside Bear Butte, which you can still see there today. They opened it and found Inyan's sacred staff there. In commemoration of Bear, whose wisdom was spared that day, Maka named Bear Butte his home. She left the trail of blood, the Red Racetrack, in place to mark the sacrifice of her children and to remind all the creatures—the four-legs, the two-legs, the winged, and the growing things—to always live in peace as equals and to remember that we are all relatives.

1875; it was the second government-sanctioned visit to the mysterious and then-unknown territory. He wrote:

"There can scarcely be a country where the scenery is more varied. From the top of some lofty peak the explorer gazes in wonder at the infinite variety at his feet. Grand mountains, frowning crags, gloomy abysses, dense forests, and intricate jungles alternate with lovely parks,

Rose quartz is the South Dakota state mineral. You can find large and small specimens and gifts made from the pink mineral in local rock and gift shops.

smooth lawns [grasslands], and gentle slopes. Each portion of the Hills has its own especial peculiarities of scenery. One struggles through dense, apparently interminable thickets, over masses of broken rocks, up and down steep ravines, to emerge at the most unexpected moment upon a smooth, well-kept flower-covered lawn, as varied and beautiful in form . . . as was ever conceived by the most enthusiastic landscape gardener. One finds himself continually saying, 'What perfect taste.'" More than a century later, visitors and residents still agree with his assessment.

The geologic island that is the Hills is made up of four distinct subregions. The Great Hogbacks form the outer ring. These sandstone ridges were turned upward when the dome of the Hills broke through the surface of the earth and pushed skyward. They got their name because their sharp ridges look like the backs of razorback hogs. The best-known break in the Hogbacks is at Buffalo Gap, where Highway 79 cuts through it.

Just inside the Hogbacks is the Red Valley, or Red Racetrack, a lower, narrow feature composed of the red sandstone of the Spearfish Red Beds. It drops down sharply from the Hogbacks and is from a quarter mile to 2 miles in width. The Lakota knew this valley, and their mythology includes a wonderful legend about its formation, which you'll find in this chapter's Legends and Lore.

A limestone plateau lies inside the Red Valley, circling the core of the Hills. The western portion of this plateau is wider and higher than the eastern, in places reaching some 7,000 feet above sea level and rivaling only Harney Peak—the Hills' tallest mountain—in height. Within this plateau lies our famous network of caves and caverns, although no one knows for sure if they are actually connected to each other. The soft limestone was deeply carved by water and time, resulting in modern-day Wind Cave National Park, Jewel Cave National Monument, and many privately owned and operated caverns (the latter are listed in the Attractions chapter).

The fourth region, the inner core of the Black Hills, is crystalline. This is where the oldest rocks and the tallest mountains can be found. Eighteen peaks higher than 7,000 feet are here, including Harney Peak at 7,242 feet above sea level and Terry Peak at 7,064 feet. Harney, by the way, is North America's highest point east of the Rockies.

The crystalline core was formed from volcanic magma about 1.7 billion years ago, and it's estimated that the crystallization occurred some 8 miles deep in the earth. This core was later transformed during the geologic uplift into quartzite, granite, schist, and mica. The soft schist and mica eroded away, leaving the tougher granite to form craggy mountain peaks (some geologists believe that if Harney Peak had never eroded, it would be 15,000 feet above sea level). This area also contains deposits of gold, silver, and other minerals as well as the less financially valuable but more accessible granite Needles, which are the result of erosion.

The bones and fossils of prehistoric creatures have been discovered in the Black Hills and Badlands regions. The most famous is Sue, the *Tyrannosaurus rex* who has her own Great Faces feature in the Area Overview chapter. Another is a genus of dinosaur discovered by paleontologist O. C. Marsh of Yale University on Piedmont Butte. In 1889 Marsh spotted a bone fragment displayed at the Piedmont Post Office, visited the site where it was found, and named his new find barosaurus. Mammoth Site of Hot Springs is an ancient sinkhole; you can visit its mammoth graveyard (see the Attractions chapter). The remains of a "big pig," an archeotherium or wild boar, were found in the Badlands, which has its own abundance of fossils and finds. If you're fascinated by paleontology, you'll thoroughly enjoy a visit to the Museum of Geology at South Dakota School of Mines and Technology in Rapid City (see Attractions) and to the Black Hills Institute of Geological Research in Hill City.

Rock hunters will enjoy searching for clear and white quartz and, less often found, rose and smoky quartz, as well as feldspar, apatite, mica, columbite, agate, jasper, tourmaline, petrified wood, and beryl. Near the town of Keystone, you may find pieces of schist containing tiny but lovely rough garnets. Just make sure you're on land where collecting is allowed before you dig or take anything away with you.

If you'd like to further explore the geology of this area and see the natural roadside (and off-road) attractions most visitors whiz right past, we recommend John Paul Gries's fine book, *Roadside Geology of South Dakota*. You'll find other books in local bookstores on dinosaurs, fossils, rockhounding, and natural history. Our Badlands and Nearby chapter talks about the geologically wondrous Badlands and the natural treasures you will discover there.

WILDLIFE

Here in the Hills, perhaps more often than in many other states, you're likely to come across animals you've never seen in the wild and those you've always wanted to see. Perhaps it's because they are abundant here, or perhaps it's because the wilderness areas that are their homes are so close to our towns and cities.

If you want to meet some of these animals up close and personal, where they can't run too far away, try Bear Country U.S.A., Black Hills Wild Horse Sanctuary, or Reptile Gardens, all detailed in the Attractions chapter. It's more difficult, but also more rewarding, to get out into the Hills and find these animals on your own, on their turf, and under more natural conditions.

In 2005 the South Dakota Game, Fish & Parks Department opened mountain lion hunting season in the Black Hills, as well as other portions of South Dakota, for the first time.

Remember to keep your distance (the animal's reaction will tell you if you're too close), and never feed a wild animal. Use extra caution during rut (mating season) and when viewing mother animals with their young. Keep your camera and plenty of film handy. We recommend a telephoto lens so you don't have to get close. If you come upon a wild animal while hiking, it's usually best to stop immediately and back away slowly, making some noise and avoiding direct eye contact. Like you, most animals prefer to avoid a confrontation and will do so unless they feel threatened. Please also watch out for wildlife while you're driving; many species cross roads at all times of the day and night.

The early morning and evening feeding hours are the best times to see wildlife. Most species virtually disappear during broad daylight, preferring to rest and conserve energy before resuming their quest for food.

Nothing quite defines South Dakota like the buffalo, pounding across the plains and hills the way their ancestors did so long ago. Actually, the animals you see today are bison (North American bison, to be exact), but most everyone calls them buffalo. We discuss these immense creatures in the Parks and Mountains chapter, where we extol the beauty of Custer State Park, home of a fine and easily viewable herd. Small groups also live at Bear Butte State Park and Wind Cave National Park (also detailed in that chapter) and in the Badlands. When driving through these areas, you may come upon shaggy bison standing in the road. It's best to just enjoy the awesome view and wait until they move—you wouldn't want your car gored by a perturbed buffalo. You're on their turf, after all. We'll say this several times in

The Black Hills are home to large herds of elk, bison, deer, pronghorn, Rocky Mountain goats, and bighorn sheep. SOUTH DAKOTA TOURISM

this book: Bison are wild and unpredictable. If harassed, the 2,000-pound beasts can pursue you at speeds in excess of 30 mph.

Custer State Park and Wind Cave National Park are probably the best places to see elk, although they are more shy than bison. Elk were reintroduced here from Yellowstone National Park in the early 1900s, after being exterminated by over-hunting. You may need to hike off the road a ways, at sunset or sunrise, to see a herd moving down into a valley to feed. If they see you first, which they likely will, they will move away. Carry binoculars to get a better view. You haven't lived until you've

heard an elk bugle. During the fall rut, males call females with a strange hooting, echoing sound that really can't be described, but it will give you goose bumps.

You may see shaggy white mountain goats standing precariously on the rocks above you at Mount Rushmore National Memorial and in the Needles area. Their ancestors came to Custer State Park from Canada as a wildlife display, but the wily creatures escaped and made their way to the Northern and Central Hills, where their progeny live happily today. They consider these high, rocky areas safe and cozy.

The Audubon bighorn sheep native to

Prairie Dog

If you stop in certain grass-clipped prairie areas of Wind Cave, Custer State Park, or the Badlands and hear a barking sound, chances are you've stopped at the home of the prairie dog, one of the most social of all mammals. Once entire "cities" stretched hundreds of miles across the prairies of the West. Because prairie dogs cut all plants growing within 100 feet of their burrows, and because their "towns" required such expansive areas, these communities eventually had to give way to agriculture.

As social animals, prairie dogs communicate with one another using body language and often calls. You might see them grooming one another, for they are fastidious. Wait long enough and you might also see them standing erect and whistling or "throwing" themselves backward. Gestures such as these have evolved as survival techniques, serving as warnings that their homes are about to be invaded by a hawk, coyote, snake, or ferret, and that it may be time to seek refuge in their burrow.

Life for the prairie dog centers around the burrows. Invariably, each member in the community has a guardroom located about 3 to 6 feet below the entrance. Though the room itself may be little more than a shelf, nevertheless it is adequate as a sanctuary from predators. From the guardroom a tunnel turns horizontally and leads to a bathroom and a separate bedroom. To prevent flooding during times of heavy rainfall, generally these two chambers are elevated above the level of the guardroom.

For increased surveillance, prairie dogs reduce grass heights around the burrows to about 6 inches, which in turn serves to attract other species of animals. Bison are attracted to the barren grounds to wallow in the dust on hot summer days. The short grass and burrows attract one of the most interesting species of owls, the diminutive burrowing owl, which you might well see should you stake yourself out for an early morning watch. All in all, biologists say prairie dog communities attract more than 26 different species of animals, including the endangered black-footed ferret, which preys on the prairie dog.

Because the "dogs" serve as such wildlife magnets, we are fortunate the Black Hills provides a safe haven for these remarkable creatures.

the Black Hills unfortunately became extinct in the 1920s. Rocky Mountain bighorn sheep were introduced years later to the Badlands, the area around the Stratosphere Bowl near Rockerville, and Custer State Park. They have done well, despite an early die-off caused by disease.

Unfortunately (although ranchers and farmers wouldn't agree), grizzly bears and wolves were eliminated from this area by the early 1900s, although rare sightings of black bears, wolves, and wolf-dog cross-breeds are still reported. There were even sightings of two moose in the Black Hills in 2003. Where do these transients come from? Either Wyoming's Bighorn Mountains, 150 miles to the west, or Minnesota's woodlands, 500 miles east.

Black-Footed Ferret Reintroduction Project

The rarest mammal in North America is making a comeback in South Dakota. Endangered black-footed ferrets, once common in the Black Hills and Badlands, are being reintroduced here through a project of the National Park Service and the USDA Forest Service.

Ferrets live in prairie dog towns, because their required diet, prairie dogs, lives there, too. Decades ago, poisoning and shooting were common means of exterminating prairie dogs to prevent their burrowing on ranch land. With their decimation came a decline in their predators, the ferrets, until the only known group of black-footed ferrets in the world survived in Mellette County, South Dakota.

Captive breeding of black-footed ferrets was attempted unsuccessfully, and eventually they disappeared. The species was considered extinct in the late 1970s. Then one day in 1981 near Meeteetse, Wyoming, a rancher's dog brought him a black-footed ferret, and the human race had a second chance to save the species. The total population of the Meeteetse group was estimated at 129. The group was monitored for four years, until an outbreak of deadly canine distemper struck in 1985 and 1986; officials then captured 24 animals, of which 18 survived to become the core of the reintroduction program.

Black-footed ferrets have been successfully bred and released into Badlands National Park and Buffalo Gap National Grassland since 1994. More litters of wild kits are born each year, including 64 litters in 2003. The forest service estimates that five to nine wild black-footed ferrets lived in the Badlands National Park in 2003, and at least 200 more lived in the Conata Basin outside the park in Buffalo Gap National Grassland. Park officials don't plan on releasing any more captive-born animals in the area, although officials are considering taking some of the wild-born ferrets from the Conata Basin and moving them to the prairie dog towns inside the park boundaries of the Badlands.

Ferret breeding season begins in March, and kits are born in May and early June. In July and August, mother ferrets

Though you'd never know it by observation, mountain lions and bobcats are more abundant. Both of the reclusive species have made a comeback in recent years, thanks to legal protection and plenty of prey. Even lynxes, which are rare and very shy, are growing in number. All the same, you'll be lucky if you find any tracks or scat to mark the presence of these nocturnal hunters.

If you're out in the Hills in the evening, far away from the lights and noise of civilization, count on hearing eerie howls and screeches echoing through the forested valleys. Though coyotes, the state animal, are as abundant in the pines as they are on the prairie, don't expect to spot these skittish, stealthy creatures. It takes a sharp eye to catch a glimpse of one slinking between some trees.

Delicately beautiful creatures you'll see plenty of are mule deer, white-tailed deer, take their offspring above ground to learn, explore, and play. Nighttime spotlight surveys by volunteers estimate the range and size of the population. Volunteers stay awake from 8:00 P.M. to 6:00 A.M. sidestepping prairie rattlers and watching for bison, and wield high-powered spotlights that reveal animals by their eye shine. A ferret's eyes glow emerald green due to a corneal film that reflects that color. (A rabbit's eyes shine red, an antelope's glow green-yellow, and a coyote's reflect green, but not that distinct ferret emerald.) Since ferrets are solitary, several dancing emerald-green eyes mean a mother and her kits—and success for the program.

Bill Perry, district ranger for Buffalo Gap National Grassland and the regional black-footed ferret coordinator for the forest service, says the reintroduction program is the most exciting he has participated in during his career. He has helped reintroduce big-game animals such as Rocky Mountain bighorn sheep and mountain goats, but he has a special fondness for the ferrets, which he calls "enchanting." "We're dealing with an ani-

mal threatened with extinction," he says. "If we can't make this program work, there's very little hope for the ferret."

On a visit to the Black Hills and Badlands, you'll see plenty of prairie dogs. You probably won't see a ferret, though, because they've adapted to nocturnal hunting to capture their diurnal prey. Sleeping prairie dogs are perfect targets for wily ferrets, and—despite their enchanting faces—a fight between the two is anything but cute. "Pound for pound," Perry says, "the only fighter more vicious than a ferret is a wolverine." This is especially impressive when you consider that prairie dogs are more than twice the size of ferrets.

Read the Badlands and Nearby chapter and read about Buffalo Gap National Grassland in the Parks and Mountains chapter; at the National Grasslands Visitor Center in Wall, you can watch a ferret from the captive-breeding program. And if you'd like to participate in a spotlight survey (volunteers are especially needed during July and August), call the National Park Service at (605) 279–2464 or the forest service at (605) 279–2125.

and pronghorn antelope. The deer, with their ghostly gray-brown coloring, are easy to miss, especially in low light. Antelope, with their bold splashes of white, are easier to spot. You'll often see both grazing on distant hillsides, even in the middle of the day, and you can see them close up at state and national parks, especially Custer State Park.

A begging burro population also populates Custer State Park (there's more

about them in the Parks and Mountains chapter). Not technically wild animals and introduced in the 1920s, they are nonetheless great fun to watch (from your car, because they can be aggressive). Park officials don't want you to feed them, which will annoy the burros very much, but your consolation is an almost-assured sighting of the shy little foals that hang back from the group and watch you with their big, dark eyes.

CLOSE-UP

Celebrating a Species of Pine

Essentially, because of a species of tree rare in the Black Hills, in 1977 Congress proclaimed the Cathedral Spires Trail a Registered National Natural Landmark. Limber pine—a five-needled pine tree—grows a ways in from the trail. To find this same species elsewhere, one must travel hundreds of miles north or go west to the Bighorn Mountains.

Core samplings indicate that the limber pines here are hundreds of years old. The question is: How did they ever establish themselves along this remote trail deep within the Black Hills of South Dakota? Glaciologists say that some 10,000 years ago, massive ice fields isolated these stands of *Pinus flexilus*. Botanists theorize that the trees' seeds could have been transported into the area in bird droppings. Whatever happened, limber pine now grows along this trail as an isolated group that remains peculiar to the Black Hills. By hiking the Cathedral Spires Trail, you'll have an opportunity to see stands of this beautiful species as well as a multitude of other aspects such as the area's geological features. Still, it's the trees for which Congress designated the trail, and it's the trees that will make you want to take the short hike of less than one hour.

Kids and grown-ups alike will love the prairie dog towns at Custer State Park, Wind Cave National Park, and Badlands National Park. These little critters chirp, whistle, and bark (but not like a dog does); dive underground and poke their heads up again; and sit up to nibble at food held in their paws. You'll swear they're performing and long to feed the cute little fellows, but don't do it. They're wild, and their cute little teeth are uncommonly sharp.

You may also see jackrabbits and cottontails, foxes, squirrels and chipmunks (great photo subjects), skunks, badgers, marmots, porcupines, raccoons, mink, and beavers (along with their beautifully engineered dams and the pointed stumps of the trees used to build them).

Birders will love the Black Hills. Because of their proximity to the Rocky Mountains, the Platte River, and the Missouri River, there is a good mix of western and eastern birds here. Expect wild turkey, pheasant, ruffed and sharp-tailed grouse, magpies, golden and bald eagles, turkey vultures, and many species of owls and hawks. There are plenty of smaller birds, including eastern and western meadowlarks, mountain bluebirds, mountain chickadees, dippers, and a type of dark-eyed junco that only inhabits the land in and around the Black Hills.

Amphibians and reptiles to watch for include prairie rattlesnakes, bull snakes, western painted turtles, snapping turtles, and various lizards and toads. If you're hiking or climbing, watch out for the

There are 18 peaks in the Black Hills that rise to an elevation of greater than 7,000 feet. It is possible to climb to the summit of each one.

prairie rattler, the only poisonous reptile in the Black Hills and very common. To avoid rattlers, a good rule is to never put your fingers or feet where you can't see what you're touching, especially behind logs and rocks. If you are bitten, get help immediately.

The streams in the Hills afford blue-ribbon fishing, and that includes Rapid Creek, which winds its way through Rapid City. We can't name many cities where people can fly fish downtown.

Trout are the big draw, including brown and brook trout, rainbows and splake, but you'll also find some walleye, perch, crappie, bluegill, and bass. The trout aren't native, but they have been raised and stocked here since the late 1800s. Anglers can visit the D.C. Booth Historic Fish Hatchery and the National Fish Culture Hall of Fame and Museum in Spearfish, or the Cleghorn Springs State Fish Hatchery west of Rapid City (all discussed in the Attractions chapter) to learn about the process of stocking sparkling streams with healthy, hearty, feisty trout.

FLORA

The Black Hills are home to a great variety of wildflowers, plants, trees, and native grasses. The Hills are, in fact, unique due to the combined effects of climate, geology, topography, relative isolation, and location where several botanical zones meet and overlap, creating interesting diversity not seen elsewhere.

Some of the trees and shrubs you'll see here include ponderosa pine, white spruce (recognizable by its drapery of lichen on the lower branches), ground juniper, quaking aspen (which turns a beautiful yellow in the fall against a backdrop of dark spruce), western red cedar, mountain mahogany, currant, buffalo berry, and sumac. Ponderosas grow above the 4,000-foot elevation mark, preferring rocky soil and drier growing conditions. Spruce prefers moist, northern exposures.

Noxious weeds can be spread when people pick wildflowers and take them home or to their campsite. Weed seeds can stick in the tread of automobile tires or boots, or lodge on a sleeping bag or tent. What can you do to contain the spread of weeds that choke out necessary plants and sometimes poison livestock? Drive and walk only on established roads and trails, don't pick unknown flowers, and feed your horse certified weed-free hay and feed.

At lower elevations you'll see burr oak, box elder, American elm, cottonwood, willow, and much more.

A small population of lodgepole pines grows on 150 acres in Lawrence County, some 150 miles from the nearest stands in Wyoming's Bighorn Mountains, where it commonly occurs. A tiny population of limber pines grows near Harney Peak; again, the nearest stands of this species are in the Bighorns. Botanists believe both have been growing in the Black Hills for more than 200 years, but no one knows for sure how they arrived and came to thrive here in relative isolation from their kin.

Just outside the Great Hogbacks that surround the Hills are grasslands, with mixed grasses and shrubs such as prairie June grass, buffalo grass, blue grama, little bluestem, and western wheatgrass, plus prickly pear cactus and yucca. Inside the Hills, however, you can see examples of high-elevation prairie. Gillette Prairie and Reynolds Prairie are west of Deerfield, in the Central Hills, and beautifully illustrate a striking transition from coniferous forest to grassland. Another high-elevation prairie is in Danby Park, west of Custer in the Southern Hills. Although their existence is a bit of a mystery, these small prairies are beautiful examples of nature's unaccountable whims and fancies.

There's an incredible variety of landscapes to view here—at all seasons of the year—but we hope you won't overlook the

Disasters in the Black Hills

Frontier life is traditionally connected with natural disasters, and nowhere is that more evident than in the historical records of early Black Hills mining towns. Paging through books and newspapers, you can't help but notice that tragedies, especially those weather related, seem to come one right after the other in the 1870s and 1880s, perhaps giving the impression that seasons were harsher back in the "old days."

And while our grandfathers' assertions that they walked uphill both ways to school in 10 feet of snow would support that impression, in fact the climate probably hasn't changed much in the past century. On the other hand, building methods have. The first waves of settlers and prospectors quickly erected humble shacks and hastily constructed mines, paying little attention to where or how they put structures up. Hundreds of wooden shacks constructed just inches apart, on cliffs and the bottoms of narrow gulches, all without building codes, were a temptation too great for fate to resist.

Since Deadwood was long the most populous gold town in the Black Hills, records on disasters here abound. With its founding the city faced trouble when a series of blizzards struck in 1876 and 1877. These were just a premonition of the blizzard that would come in March 1878, when a light rain turned to three days of snow that reached a height of 7 feet and produced drifts over 20 feet deep. The flimsy wooden roofs of Deadwood's early buildings snapped under the weight. Fortunately, the snow quickly melted.

understated but lovely changes on prairies and plains. Native grasses and plants put on subtle shows all the time: in fertile spring, high summer, winter, and chilly fall, when grasses as well as trees change color. Mountain sunsets are wonderful, but prairie sunsets are, too; we think you'll love watching pastel evening light flood over the prairie, sinking every hollow and draw into deep shadow.

Romantically named wildflowers and herbs found locally are prairie coneflower, Indian paintbrush, black-eyed Susan, wood lily, yarrow, wild bergamot, fleabane, yellow lady slipper, blue larkspur, Rocky Mountain iris, and aster. There are many more, but our favorite is that harbinger of spring, the pasqueflower, South Dakota's state flower (also called wild crocus or mayflower). This dainty, tuliplike, white-to-purple beauty pops up through the melting snow in late winter and early spring, determined to share news of the coming warm season.

Because the climate of the Hills varies so drastically from region to region, and because elevations range from high mountains to low valleys, with the varied moisture and light levels that accompany such differences, we can't tell you where to find all these examples of flora. Instead, we recommend a good field guide, which you can find at local bookstores. Put on some sturdy shoes, long

Unfortunately, it created a flood that was followed in April by more heavy rains that washed out bridges, roads, houses, stores, and mines. A second destructive flood came through in 1883, causing $250,000 worth of damage. Black Hills Historian Watson Parker notes that while the waters wiped out the city school and Methodist Church, the Gem Theater and most of the saloons were left virtually untouched.

Water was a terrible enemy, but so was fire. The great fire of 1879 was relatively small when it broke out in a downtown bakery, but the situation quickly turned tragic when flames spread to a nearby hardware store and ignited eight kegs of gunpowder. The resulting explosion spread burning timber across town, resulting in the eventual destruction of 300 buildings and $3 million worth of property. Deadwood had been wiped out twice by flood and once by fire in a five-year period. Afterward, property owners rebuilt their structures with brick and stone, giving them the ornate Victorian facades visitors to the town can still see today.

Although Black Hills residents have gotten more careful over the years, disasters still happen. In fact, one of the most destructive floods in the history of the United States occurred in 1972 in the Black Hills. One million metric tons of water doused the region, causing $165 million worth of damage, destroying or damaging more than 4,000 homes and killing 238 people, most of them in Rapid City. Forest fires continue to be a threat; the Westbury Trails blaze in 1988 drove hundreds from their homes in West Rapid City, while the Grizzly Gulch fire in 2002 forced the evacuation of Deadwood and half of Lead.

pants, a light heart, and a sense of adventure, and take an exploratory trip into the Black Hills.

INSECTS

Since there are more than two million acres of pine forests, grass prairies, and clear-flowing streams in the Black Hills, you're bound to run into a number of bugs. Fortunately, the Black Hills are dominated by a mostly dry, mountainous climate, which means that less desirable creepy crawlers (mosquitoes for instance) aren't nearly as numerous as they are farther east and north.

Abundant wildflowers draw colorful butterflies (including the famous orange and black monarch) each spring. Other pleasant insect species native to the Hills include lightning bugs and dragonflies. Of course, there are biting or stinging insects in the area, such as yellow jackets, spiders (including wolf spiders and black widows, which are poisonous but rarely lethal), ticks, and carpenter ants. Since spring typically doesn't arrive in the Black Hills until late April and the first frost usually comes in mid-September, insects are only around for a few short months.

WEATHER

This is a region of weather extremes. Our weather has something for everyone's taste, often at the same time. The Southern Hills are usually warmer and drier than the Central or Northern Hills, which receive more snow in the winter and thunderstorms, hail, and rain in the summer.

However, anywhere in the Hills, summer temperatures in the 90s are not unusual, and winter sometimes brings temperatures well below zero and wind-chill factors considerably lower than that. On the other hand, the Rapid City area is sometimes called the Banana Belt because of its relatively mild climate compared with other parts of the Hills. It's known for an average of 300 days of sunshine each year and snowfalls that often melt before the next ones arrive. January thaws usually occur throughout the Hills, bringing warmer temperatures and a few days of blessed relief from winter's cold—as well as lots of mud.

Many first-time visitors have heard all about nearly mythical South Dakota weather: raging blizzards, howling prairie winds, dust storms, intense heat. Generally speaking, however, the Black Hills don't experience those events regularly, although our weather is indeed variable due to our elevation and location near the center of North America.

Gardening isn't always easy here, with an average frost-free date of May 20, a short growing season, and the possibility of snow or a freeze every month in the Northern Hills. Damaging hailstorms can occur during any summer month. However—and this points up the differences in regions—Hot Springs has a growing season a full 35 days longer than Deadwood's.

Usually winters are relatively mild (compared to the rest of South Dakota), although blizzards come through occasionally. Spring is often wet and wild, with fluctuating temperatures and snow well into summer (again, depending on the region). Summer is typically warm and sunny, with chilly nights, thunderstorms, and frequent hail. Fall arrives in September with pleasant, warm days and cool nights, sometimes with temperatures dipping below freezing. Tornadoes don't occur often, but high winds are frequent (although they're nothing like the winds the plains withstand). Statistically, Rapid City is windier than Chicago, the Windy City.

If you're visiting in the summer, watch out for thunderstorms, lightning, and some pretty large hailstones. Our storms are spectacular, but hail hurts (it can even cause concussions), so take shelter under a covered area, preferably in a hard-topped vehicle or building.

ACCOMMODATIONS

Whether you're visiting the Black Hills for pleasure or business, your accommodations are an important component of a pleasant visit. In this chapter you'll find a selection of accommodations that includes hotels, cottages, vacation homes, cabins, ranches, and bed-and-breakfasts. Although the Hills have literally hundreds of lodging possibilities—including inexpensive chain or mom-and-pop motels and single rooms in private homes—we've selected only the most interesting, comfortable, and enjoyable.

You may assume the accommodations in this chapter do not allow indoor smoking or accept pets and are not wheelchair accessible. If these features are important to you, read the write-ups closely, because we'll indicate all exceptions. You may also assume that each accepts credit cards, requires an advance deposit, and expects advance notice of cancellation.

The Black Hills tourist season runs from Memorial Day weekend through Labor Day weekend. Some accommodations are open before and after those holidays, and some close as soon as the season ends. Many remain open all year, catering to fall travelers and winter recreation enthusiasts. We'll give you the approximate dates of operation, but these dates are not set in stone, as they sometimes change with the weather.

Many lodging operators raise their rates during tourist season and lower them in the off-season, and almost all of them raise their rates during the Sturgis Rally & Races (more about that in the Annual Events and Festivals chapter). During rally time, the first two weeks of August or so, the Hills are filled to the brim with visitors and available accommodations are scarce, even if the rates are higher than usual.

PRICE CODE

The following price ratings are based on the cost of one night's lodging for two people (double occupancy) at in-season rates. Some businesses lower their rates during the off-season; inquire when you call. There is often an extra charge (not included in this code) for each extra person or child.

$	Less than $50
$$	$51 to $75
$$$	$76 to $100
$$$$	More than $100

BED-AND-BREAKFAST INNS AND RANCHES

In most bed-and-breakfasts, you get the chance to talk with the owners, meet other guests, and be pampered. Some of the Hills' B&Bs are ranches, too, offering you a taste of the western experience.

Northern Hills

Aunt Sophia's Bed & Breakfast $$$–$$$$
15 Washington Street, Deadwood
(605) 578–3257, (800) 377–1516
www.sleepindeadwood.com
Spend a night or two in this 1903 Victorian home that's within walking distance of historic downtown Deadwood. The full and ample country breakfast served during the summer will sustain you for a morning's stroll through town or a rest on the front porch. A continental breakfast is served in the winter. Breakfast is served in the Oriental-theme dining room, and the house is furnished with original art and antiques.

The owners like to pamper their guests and will entertain requests for special foods or treats for special occasions (extra charge). Aunt Sophia's is open year-round. Make reservations in advance for your choice of one of the four suites or two single rooms. Children ages 10 and up are welcome, as are weddings, receptions, and reunions.

Black Hills Hideaway Bed-and-Breakfast $$$$
11744 Hideaway Road, Deadwood
(605) 578-3054, (877) 500-4433
www.enetis.net/~hideaway

It's a tribute to the tranquillity of this property that it was selected by the owners, two corporate dropouts from the East who, after vacationing in the Hills 10 years, "downsized" themselves and created their hideaway in the forest. Now it's your turn. You can downsize your hectic life here, at least for a while, and bask in the peaceful mountain air. Once the site of a 1904 mining claim, these 67 acres are bordered by the Black Hills National Forest.

The owners invite you to "come and be pampered" in one of their eight guest rooms. They offer turndown service with chocolates in your room and a full, hot country breakfast that features their trademark dishes: homemade blueberry coffee cake and egg skillets. Hot and cold hors d'oeuvres are served in the evening, and cookies and fruit are available during the day. A light sandwich menu is available upon request, and the commercial kitchen can accommodate small parties (both at extra charge).

You can hike and mountain bike on the premises; snowmobile, ski, and golf nearby; and drive to Deadwood and Lead for gaming and sightseeing. But you may want to stay right here, soak in the hot tub or whirlpool, and just listen to the silence. Inquire about bringing children.

Black Hills Hideaway is 7 miles south of Deadwood off U.S. Highway 385. Watch for the Tomahawk Country Club, then turn onto Forest Service Road 247 and follow the signs.

Lown House Bed & Breakfast $$$
745 Fifth Street, Spearfish
(605) 642-5663
(800) 529-0105 (reservations)

This is a charming, historic Victorian house built by a local merchant in 1893. Your breakfast will be served in the formal dining room.

The house has interesting architectural features, and each of the four rooms is named for a past owner. The third-floor suite has a cupola and whirlpool, and two rooms have fireplaces.

The owners like to accommodate their guests' special requests for flowers, balloons, wine, chocolates, shuttles to Deadwood, and customized packages.

Old Stone House Bed & Breakfast $$$-$$$$
1513 Jackson Street, Sturgis
(605) 347-3007, (888) 447-3007
www.oldstonehouse.com

If you like lounging on a big, high, shady veranda and whiling away the hours, knowing you're close enough to everything to drive there if you want, this is the place for you.

The house is historic, built in 1885 of local sandstone. It's been beautifully restored, and the three rooms are furnished with antiques and quilts. In the 1930s it was used as the county poor farm. Today's amenities, however, are modern and lovely.

A four-course, hearty, family-style breakfast is served on antique china with elegant linens, either on the veranda or in the kitchen. The owner requests that guests inquire before bringing children. Alcohol is not permitted.

Old Stone House is close to Fort Meade, Bear Butte State Park, and the local bike/hike trail as well as Deadwood and Lead.

Poker Alice House $$-$$$$
1802½ Junction Avenue, I-90, exit 32, Sturgis
(605) 347-2506

Notorious Poker Alice Tubbs's historic house (a former brothel) is next to the

National 9 Junction Inn motel. The little house is bigger than it looks but does not have separate apartments, so it is best rented to one party at a time. It has a full kitchen, two bedrooms downstairs, four upstairs, and another in the basement. The basement also has a kitchenette and bathroom with shower. The full kitchen and the Poker Room—with player piano—are on the first floor, which is the common area. The house has old-fashioned decor (you'll think Poker Alice might still live here) and it can be used for meetings or reunions. Pets and smoking are allowed (Alice, with her ever-present cigar, would approve). The house is rented monthly during the winter and nightly during the summer season.

Strawberry Hill Bed & Breakfast $$$$
21291 Strawberry Hill Lane, Deadwood
(605) 578-2149, (866) 578-2149
www.strawberrybnb.com

Strawberry Hill is infamous among locals for its steep slopes and deep snow in winter, which can make for difficult driving. Fortunately, two summers' worth of construction have straightened and widened U.S. 385, which goes right up and over this local landmark. This makes it much easier to get to the Strawberry Hill Bed & Breakfast, perched near the summit of the mountain. Located about a mile from the highway in a stand of ponderosas, the inn provides private and secluded accommodations within 3 miles of Deadwood's city limits.

Privacy is further enhanced by the type of accommodations here. Guests don't have rooms; they have small cottages connected to the main house by a series of decks. As with most bed-and-breakfasts, each guest room is decorated differently. One has yellow and white country–style furnishings, one is made up to look like a hunting lodge, another has lacy Victorian accents, and one is contemporary, decorated in the forest-and-mauve color scheme you find in many hotels. Each cottage has its own modern bathroom and parlor/game area, but for breakfast guests must use the decks to climb to the main house. Breakfast is typical western fare, including eggs, sausage, and coffee, although waffles with spiced pears add some nice culinary color.

Two sleeping cabins are located farther down the hill. Set off from the other buildings in the forest, they're more rustic. Neither has its own bathroom, but there is an outdoor shower house. These lodge-style accommodations are especially popular with hunters in autumn. In winter, snowmobilers practically take over the place, and with good reason: A groomed snowmobile trail runs right across the property. If that weren't enough, two ski slopes are located only a few miles away.

Central Hills

The Anchorage Bed
& Breakfast $$$-$$$$
24110 Leaky Valley Road, Keystone
(605) 574-4740, (800) 318-7018
www.anchoragebb.com

Jim Gogolin promised his wife, Lin, that in return for her sacrifices during his years as a naval officer and their travels around the world, she could choose their retirement home. Although she could have selected Majorca, the Philippines, or other lovely places, Lin chose the Black Hills and announced that she wanted to open a bed-and-breakfast inn. Thus the name the Anchorage and the navy-eclectic decor.

Some accommodations are in a separate, private building called the Chart House. It sleeps up to eight people and is rented to just one party at a time. The kitchen is fully equipped, even supplied with some staple items, and there's a hot tub on the deck where you can watch the stars and the deer that come out of the woods. It's a real home with a handmade quilt, books, and a game table, but it doesn't have a television or telephone.

Then there are four rooms in the main quarters, each with private bath, fireplace, and access to a hot tub.

The houses sit on the rim of a lovely valley with a view of Harney Peak. You may see bobcats and coyotes and hear the whistle of the Black Hills Central Railroad/The 1880 Train as it chugs past. The Centennial Trail is just over the hill. There are 20 acres to play on here; if you need more room, you can go next door to national forestland.

The most-used word in the guest book is "wonderful," but that is hardly adequate for Anchorage breakfasts. "Spectacular" may be more apt. The specialty breakfast is pumpkin waffles with hot apple butter, smoked turkey sausage, rhubarb cake, and a compote of mango and fresh blueberries. Other delights include pepper and sausage quiche, wild raspberry crepes, and huge pecan caramel rolls. You might get to try Jim's Baked Pancakes, filled with apples, nutmeg, pecans, and sour cream, served with ham and muffins. Breakfast is served in the main house.

Anemarie's Bed & Breakfast $$$-$$$$
10430 Big Piney Road, Rapid City
(605) 343-9234, (888) 343-9234
www.bbonline.com/sd/anemarie
This is a bed-and-breakfast inn locals like to use as a getaway. The owners describe it as having European styling with contemporary convenience. Each of the four suites has a hot tub, television, VCR, and small refrigerator. All the rooms look out on peaceful views, and one room is wheelchair accessible.

Breakfast is served in the rooms, and the menu varies daily. Coffee is available in the rooms. When you wake in the

morning, you may see deer, rabbits, squirrels, and chipmunks outside.

Anemarie's is centrally located near Rapid City, 30 miles from Deadwood, across the road from a fine restaurant and lounge, the Fireside Inn.

Audrie's Bed and Breakfast and das Abend Haus Cottages $$$$
23029 Thunderhead Falls Road
Rapid City
(605) 342-7788
www.audriesbb.com
This glorious old-world estate was the Black Hills' first bed-and-breakfast; it was founded in 1985 and is still owned and operated by the same family. Its handsome antique furniture, purchased when the family was in Europe, adorns each room.

The beautiful buildings on the property are the Cranbury House, the Old Powerhouse (built in 1910 for water-generated electricity), and the chalet-style das Abend Haus (German for "the Evening House") Cottages. Each has two suites. You can also stay in one of seven big, high-ceiling log cottages, each of which is delightfully decorated.

The rooms, suites, and cottages are elegant and luxurious. They're beautifully furnished in rich colors, fabrics, and woods. Each has a private bath and entrance, latticed deck or porch, hot tub, cable television and VCR, refrigerator, and microwave.

Breakfast is placed in each refrigerator so guests can heat and enjoy it in privacy. It includes bacon-and-egg quiche for two, homemade baked goods, fruit, cereal, and juice.

Audrie's is in a pretty, quiet, and secluded canyon 7 miles west of Rapid City. You can easily drive to any Central Hills attraction, or you can take a walk, explore the Black Hills National Forest around the property, fish for trout in Rapid Creek, which flows right through the estate (you'll need a license—see the Recreation chapter), or bicycle up the road. Fishing poles and bicycles are provided for guests.

Each year at holiday time, the Old-World Christkindlemart is held at Audrie's Bed and Breakfast. The Old Powerhouse building is transformed into a festive marketplace, with vendors in costume and live music, on the first Saturday and Sunday in December. Admission supports the Black Hills Food Bank and the Cancer Institute of Rapid City. For information call (605) 342-7788.

Dedicated to comfort and privacy, Audrie's does not allow children or pets, and guests are asked not to bring visitors. The hot tubs can't be used after 11:00 P.M. or before 7:00 A.M. so that everyone can enjoy the nighttime peace and silence.

Black Forest Inn
Bed & Breakfast Lodge $$$-$$$$
23191 U.S. Highway 385, Rapid City
(605) 574-2000, (800) 888-1607
www.blackforestinn.net

You'll love the spaciousness here (10,000 square feet and 10 rooms), especially the huge great room with its rock fireplace. A wonderful deck overlooks the lawn and surrounding forest and holds a hot tub that's waiting just for you. Or settle into the game room, where you can read, play pool or games, or watch television.

A homemade breakfast is served in courses on silver and crystal. Meeting rooms are available for retreats and workshops. This is an especially lovely place for reunions, weddings, and anniversary celebrations.

Black Forest Inn is centrally located: It's near Pactola Reservoir, Sheridan Lake, Mount Rushmore, and Rapid City, as well as within a 30-minute drive of every attraction in the Central Hills.

Country Manor Bed
& Breakfast $$$-$$$$
12670 Robins Roost Road, Hill City
(605) 574-2196, (888) 560-5508
www.countrymanorbb.com

These pleasant accommodations are in a separate building next to the main house: The four rooms and one family suite have private entrances.

Other amenities include television, air-conditioning, and a theme for each room that honors an aspect of our American heritage. The three-room suite, which accommodates eight people, has a Wild West motif and features a double Jacuzzi bath, minikitchen, microwave, and refrigerator.

The full breakfast is served on the dining porch in the main house, and the

Many of the businesses listed under this heading are members of the Bed & Breakfast Innkeepers of South Dakota (BBISD). Members must meet standards for hospitality, cleanliness, and safety and must pass an association inspection conducted by state-trained inspectors. For additional information, or to request a member directory, call (888) 500–INNS.

hospitable owner describes it as a classic "Sunday morning breakfast." Her specialties include bacon quiche and strawberry waffles.

Here you'll be close to lovely Spring Creek and only a few minutes from Hill City, in the heart of the Black Hills. No credit cards are accepted.

Coyote Blues Village Bed
& Breakfast $$-$$$$
P.O. Box 966, Hill City 57745
(605) 574-4477, (888) 253-4477
www.coyotebluesvillage.com

The Swiss owners have given their bed-and-breakfast inn a contemporary European flavor. "Experience a piece of Europe in the Black Hills," they like to say. You'll love the original art scattered throughout the house, the huge deck, and the views across open land and forest.

Breakfast includes home-baked breads such as brioche, chocolate croissants, or *Gugelhopf* (an Austrian yeast cake), and other culinary delights including fruit, French toast, eggs, and another specialty, Swiss muesli.

When they purchased the property, the owners were intrigued by the nocturnal howling of coyotes, which they decided was coyote singing; thus the Coyote Blues name. You'll still hear the coyotes nearly every night, but that's about all; the peace and quiet will astound you.

The owners offer six theme rooms (one a suite), three basic rooms, and a conference room. There's an exercise area, a tanning bed, and a piano (for those who want to exercise only their fingers). The guest sitting room has a large-screen TV and VCR.

Coyote Blues Village is 12 miles from Hill City and 22 miles from Rapid City, just south of Pactola Lake off U.S. 385.

Deerview Bed & Breakfast $$$-$$$$
12110 Deerfield Road, Hill City
(605) 574-4204, (888) 622-5274
www.deerviewbb.com

Deerview is a beautifully appointed and carefully designed bed-and-breakfast that reflects the owners' attention to detail. The pine-studded property is bordered by national forest, where you can hike, snowmobile, look for old gold mines, or fish at Deerfield Reservoir, just 9 miles away. It's only 5 miles to Hill City along scenic Deerfield Road.

The cottage is set in the pines, apart from the main house, and has two rooms. A separate space between the rooms houses the shared hot tub. A third room is in the main house but has its own entrance and a private hot tub outside. Each room has a microwave (with complimentary popcorn), small refrigerator, satellite television, and a coffeemaker.

The owners are proud of their full, delicious breakfast, which is served in your room.

Flying B Ranch Bed-and-Breakfast $$$$
6324 North Haines Avenue, Rapid City
(605) 342-5324
www.flyingb.com

Immerse yourself in western ranch living. This 3,500-acre cattle ranch has been in the family since the 1940s. Three horse thieves were captured on the land in 1877, and two have suites named for them. Another, McClintock's Suite, is named for the owner of the last Deadwood stage line and has a secret passageway for kids to explore.

The house is beautifully decorated in western themes. Each large and comfortable suite has its own hot tub on a private deck and a loft where children can sleep (well-behaved children are welcome).

Old Man Wright's Keeping Room is a grown-ups-only common room with an open-hearth fireplace and antique cookstove. You can sit on the deck and look out over Box Elder Creek, or get comfortable on the sofa and listen to the owner tell some delightful tall tales. His stories are always free—just don't believe everything you hear!

The owners live on the property and will arrive each morning to fix your breakfast, which is served buffet style. The fixings are authentic ranch-style food because, as the owner says, "Real cowboys don't eat quiche."

You can swim in the pool, sit in Uncle Bill's Cowboy Cabaña, hike on the property, fish in the creek, and listen to the nocturnal coyotes and morning meadowlarks. You'll hardly believe you're only five minutes from the Rushmore Mall in Rapid City (see the Shopping chapter).

If you like, you can participate in the ranch chores. The Flying B is a working ranch, and the owners stress, "We don't do things just for show." There's always real work to be done, and you're welcome to help out. Guests who bring their own horses can help move cattle on a 10-mile trail drive on Mother's Day. Kids love to bottle-feed the calves in the spring. But the owners confide that a favorite guest activity is the CPCPC, Cow Pie Chip Pitching Contest, held in dry years only. Participants can experiment with throwing techniques—which is better, a Frisbee-style toss or the good old heave?

Horse accommodations include hay and feed and use of the barn, corral, and pasture. The Flying B is open from Memorial Day to Labor Day.

In Rapid City, take Interstate 90, exit 58, and follow Haines Avenue north and out of town. The ranch is 3 miles from the exit.

High Country Guest Ranch $$$-$$$$
12172 Deerfield Road, Hill City
(605) 574-9003, (888) CABIN28
www.highcountryranch.com

This one's not a dude ranch or a working

A stunning sunset captures the attention of a lone rider on the South Dakota Prairie. SOUTH DAKOTA TOURISM

ranch, but a real guest ranch where you can spend a few nights, relax, ride horses, eat a ranch breakfast, and still do your sightseeing. You can help care for the horses, participate in cattle roundups at nearby ranches or clinics on farrier work, and design your own custom trail rides. Read about longer trail rides in the Recreation chapter.

Other offerings include a pool, bicycle and four-wheel rentals, and rock climbing with a guide.

It you're looking for a place to both ride and bask in some luxury, there are 17 cabins here, and they're not rustic. Some have vaulted ceilings, bay windows, hot tubs, and fireplaces. Even your horse can be comfortable; board your equine for an extra charge (feed and hay are not fur-

nished). Alcohol use is limited and rooms are nonsmoking.

A traditional western breakfast is served, with simple but hearty food. Guests say the pancakes are "the best in the world," and there are also eggs, sausage, juice, and a cold-cereal and toast bar. Breakfast is served in a giant covered wagon—a perfect beginning to your western vacation. Other meals can be reserved for groups (ask about picnic lunches or steaks cooked on pitchforks) for an extra charge.

This ranch is "off the beaten path but close to everything," say the owners. The George S. Mickelson Trail goes right through the property. The ranch is open all year. No credit cards are accepted.

Shari's Sweetgrass Inn Bed and Breakfast $$$-$$$$
9356 Neck Yoke Road, Rapid City
(605) 343-5351
www.sweetgrassinn.com

This eight-room inn off U.S. Highway 16 boasts a great location between Rapid City and Mount Rushmore, with convenient access to many major attractions in the Central Hills. A spacious common room, a large parking area, and private entrances to each room are additional attractions for road-weary travelers who may be getting tired of cramped cookie-cutter chain hotels.

The decor is heavily Victorian, with pastel paints, floral-print furniture, and lace doilies accenting the entire house. Half of the rooms, which are all named for flowers, have their own whirlpool tubs, but a hot tub on the back deck is open to all guests during the summer months. Rooms have their own TVs, VCRs, and coffee pots, and the common room has a fridge and microwave. The owner encourages visitors to be on the lookout for the wildlife that roams the inn grounds, from the family of rabbits that lives under the porch to wild turkeys that shuffle past in the early morning hours. There's even Tiger—an orange tabby who keeps the inn free of mice.

Willow Springs Cabins Bed & Breakfast $$$$
11515 Sheridan Lake Road, Rapid City
(605) 342-3665
www.willowspringscabins.com

Two beautiful cabins and some wonderful breakfasts define the secluded Willow Springs accommodations. The cabins are decorated with family heirlooms and are cozy, comfortable, and private. The Willows Cabin sleeps four and is open all year. The Frontier Cabin sits on a little hill, sleeps two, and is open from May through September. Each has a private bath, hot tub, television and VCR, stereo, microwave, coffeemaker, and small refrigerator.

It's an easy drive to Rapid City, Sheridan Lake, and Pactola Reservoir, but you might want to stay right here and bask in the peace and quiet of 140 acres and adjoining national forest. Walk down to Spring Creek, fish (license required) and swim on the property, ice-skate in the winter, and get to know the friendly resident cats and dog.

Breakfast is served in the dining room of the house or brought to your cabin. The owner calls it "a wholesome and hearty gourmet breakfast." The cabins are stocked with coffee, tea, and popcorn.

Southern Hills

Custer Mansion Bed & Breakfast $$-$$$$
35 Centennial Drive, Custer
(605) 673-3333, (877) 519-4948
www.custermansionbb.com

This gorgeous and fascinating historic home is a charmer. Of Gothic design from the Victorian era (it was built in 1891), it is a tribute to both the success of the rancher/civic leader who built it and the current owners, who lovingly restored it. Listed in the National Register of Historic Places, it has seven gables, two staircases, transoms, stained-glass windows, a butler's pantry, and two rooms and three suites, all quaintly decorated. The mansion is filled with antiques, heirlooms, and lovely old framed prints from the owners' collection.

Breakfast often includes homemade granola (guests say it's the best they've ever had) and rhubarb-strawberry sauce for your pancakes or waffles.

You'll rest well in the gorgeous four-poster king bed in the Evergreen Room. Or you might choose to relax in the gabled-wall Shenandoah Room, which has a Jacuzzi. The Evening Star family suite has two rooms connected by a tiny charming hallway, and the bathroom features an antique claw-foot tub. You may also choose the Rose of Sharon Room or the Morning Dew Room. Whichever room you choose, you'll enjoy discovering the delightful idiosyncrasies of this historic house. Alcohol use is limited.

The Toal House $$$$
801 Almond Street, Hot Springs
(605) 745-4633, (888) 881-4633
www.toalhousebnb.com

Perched on a hill overlooking the elegant sandstone buildings of Hot Springs, this house was built in 1891 as a venue for the Sioux City Club, a society of elite Black Hills businessmen. For more than 30 years the turreted structure was a place where gentlemen came to read, smoke, drink, and gamble. In the 1920s a Chicago businessman turned it into a guesthouse for friends who came to visit the area. Though the house has been restored and renovated several times since, many of the building's original features have been preserved for guests, including the two-story octagonal turret that perches on top of the house. Once a place for men to smoke cigars and play poker, the comfortable wood-accented chamber is now a favorite among guests for reading and enjoying the view of Hot Springs below.

There are seven rooms, each with a different style. The most charming are the Stained-Glass Room, decorated with original pieces of stained glass and a headboard made from an old opera seat, and the Western Room, with a private entrance into the bathroom, which used to be the home's second kitchen—look for the original Victorian kitchen cabinets, porcelain sink, and icebox. Two smaller rooms are up in the attic, off of the octagonal living room.

Intrepid guests have only a short walk down the hill before they're in the town of Hot Springs, where a paved trail follows the warm waters of Fall River as it flows through town. The innkeepers can drop you and your bikes off along the nearby Mickelson Trail, which runs the entire length of the Black Hills. On the other hand, if you feel like relaxing, you can arrange for a professional massage in your room. As long as you make prior arrangements with your

On the third Saturday in September, the Bed & Breakfast Innkeepers of South Dakota sponsor a Pumpkin Festival and Open House. You can tour a member inn or ranch and meet the owners. Pumpkin treats are served and entertainment or activities are offered at each inn. Not every BBISD member inn participates, so call (888) 500-INNS to request a list by mail.

hosts, you don't even have to leave for food. For an extra charge, you can have dinner served to you in the home's elegant dining room.

CABINS AND COTTAGES

Camping cabins, cottages, and housekeeping cabins offer privacy and scenic settings, with facilities ranging from rustic to luxurious.

Northern Hills

Cheyenne Crossing $$$
U.S. Highways 14A and 85, Cheyenne Crossing, Lead
(605) 584-3510, (800) 529-0105

Built near the site of one of the old Deadwood-Cheyenne stage stops and locally known for home cooking, Cheyenne Crossing offers a three-bedroom lodge and a creekside rental cabin by Spearfish Creek that sleeps four people and has a whirlpool and deck. Fish for trout right out the back door.

Wickiup Village $$-$$$$
U.S. Highway 85, Cheyenne Crossing Lead
(605) 584-3382
www.spearfishcreekcabins.com

The setting is the best amenity here. These 19 log housekeeping cabins are surrounded by Black Hills spruce and near lovely Spearfish Creek. They are heated by gas-log fireplaces and furnished with everything you'll need, except groceries. Each cabin has its own bathroom and shower. Three cabins remain open in the winter. Leashed pets are allowed. Here you'll be within just a few miles of Lead, Deadwood, and Spearfish.

Central Hills

Deerfield Lake Resort $$
11321 Gillette Prairie Road, Hill City
(605) 574-2636
www.deerfieldlakeresort.com
Deerfield Lake Resort has four heated cabins, each with one large room, two double beds and one roll-away bed, a kitchenette, and private bath. It's a year-round resort and there's always something to do here. Deerfield Reservoir is next door, with great fishing in both summer and winter, and Hill City is just 14 miles away. Winter, however, is the resort's busiest season, as the property is adjacent to popular snowmobile trails; you can even rent a snowmobile here. From November through March breakfast is available. You can camp at the resort, too, and that information is in the Campgrounds chapter.

Elk Creek Camping Resort
and Lodge $-$$$
Elk Creek Road, Piedmont
(605) 787-4884, (800) 846-2267
www.elkcreek.org
This 11-acre resort has four cabins and five ranch-style houses that enclose 17 "cottage rooms." Each motel-style cottage room shares only a wall with adjoining rooms and has a private bath, coffeepot, and refrigerator. Some rooms have kitchens, too. Cabins have one main room and a small bunk room that sleep up to eight people. The cabins have no plumbing (shower facilities are nearby), but they do have air-conditioning and refrigerators. An outdoor, shared hot tub is on the premises, as is a heated pool. Breakfast is available for purchase on summer weekends. Your pet is welcome, but an additional deposit is required. One cottage is wheelchair accessible. Elk Creek Resort is open year-round, and a campground is also on the property. To get there, take I-90 to exit 46.

Harney Camp Cabins $-$$$
24345 Highway 87, Hill City
(605) 574-2594
www.harneycamp.com
Seventeen housekeeping cabins share this quiet, secluded property in the tall pines. Each has a private bath and sleeps from two to eight people. Sunday Creek runs through the property, and you can select a cabin that is accessible by a little bridge across the creek. Fire pits, grills, and a playground are available, and pets are allowed (please inquire). There's a hot tub and sundeck by the creek, and you can hike on the forest service land that surrounds Harney Camp. The cabins are open from April through October. Call to make reservations; the address above is not a mailing address.

Holy Smoke Resort $$-$$$
U.S. Highway 16A, Keystone
(605) 666-4616, (866) 530-5696
www.blackhills.com/holysmoke
This great place is nestled off the highway in Buckeye Gulch, the site of old gold, silver, and copper mines. Stay in one of 13 cabins, including an 1893 mining-camp cabin, soak in the outdoor hot tub, and stable your horse in the stalls for $10 per day (bring your own feed). You can ride your horse (or rent one here) or hike on the fire roads that lace the 75-acre property. The cabins have one or two bedrooms. A duplex unit is perfect for two couples traveling together, or you can stay in the one guest room in the charming 1920 main lodge. The Holy Smoke is open from May 1 to September 30. Register at the nearby Holy Smoke Restaurant and Lounge (see the Restaurants chapter), just down the road.

Little Elk Canyon Cabin and Cottage $$$-$$$$
100 Dalton Lake Road, Nemo
(605) 578-2012
www.littleelkcabin.com

This beautiful 1930s cabin was built by the Civilian Conservation Corps and moved to its present site in Vanocker Canyon. It's just 3.5 miles from the little town of Nemo, close to Dalton Lake and great hiking in Little Elk Canyon, yet right off Lawrence County Road 26 for convenience. Set in a pleasant meadow and surrounded by tall pines, it feels quite secluded. You may see deer, elk, or eagles during your stay. The cabin was lovingly restored by its talented owners and is charming, modern, and comfortable with two woodstoves. It sleeps several people in the one bedroom, a loft with two twin beds, and a sofa bed in the living room. The owners have added to the property a lovely new cottage with two full bedrooms. Lounge under the open beam ceiling and skylights, or relax next to the fireplace. Privacy is guaranteed, as each guesthouse sits on its own five acres. Both the cabin and the cottage have a warmly glowing wood interior, furnished kitchen, full bathroom, microwave, telephone, satellite TV, VCR, baseboard heat, and a picnic table and grill outside. Bedding and towels are furnished. The friendly owners live just "over the hill and through the woods."

The Lodge at Palmer Gulch Resort $$$-$$$$
Highway 244, Hill City
(605) 574-2525, (800) 562-8503
www.palmergulchresort.com

Palmer Gulch Resort has a lovely 62-room lodge and 30 cabins. Some of the one- to three-bedroom cabins have kitchens of various sizes and some are sleeping cabins. All have private baths. Outdoor and indoor hot tubs and two outdoor pools are available for use. The cabins are open only from May 1 through October.

The lodge has both rooms and mini-suites, which have fireplaces (some mini-suites also have kitchenettes and balconies). It's a popular place for family reunions, as it has meeting facilities, a conference room, indoor sauna and hot tub, a reunion hall with kitchen, a picnic shelter outside, and a restaurant and lounge across the parking lot. Pets are allowed, and the lodge is wheelchair accessible (one room has a roll-in shower). The lodge is open from April 15 through October 15. Smoking is permitted in the cabins, but there are designated non-smoking rooms in the lodge.

The resort is 5 miles west of Mount Rushmore. See the Campgrounds chapter for information about the Mount Rushmore KOA, which is located at Palmer Gulch.

Mystery Mountain Resort $$$-$$$$
13752 South U.S. Highway 16 West, Rapid City
(605) 342-5368, (800) 658-CAMP
www.blackhillsresorts.com

You have your choice of 22 lodging facilities that offer seven different kinds of accommodations. There are camping cabins (one room, no bathroom, and lower rates than those designated by the above price code), guesthouses, and the big reunion cottage with three bedrooms, one-and-a-half baths, and kitchen with microwave and dishwasher. All remain open throughout the year, except for the camping cabins and one small cabin. Pets are allowed. You can enjoy the rest of Mystery Mountain while you're there, too: pool, hot tub, playground, camp store, and laundry. There's also a campground, which you can read about in the Campgrounds chapter.

Nemo Guest Ranch $$$-$$$$
Main Street, Nemo
(605) 578-2708
www.nemoguestranch.com

There are 14 cabins and houses at the Nemo Guest Ranch, with private baths and one to five bedrooms that sleep 4 to 13 people. Some have kitchens or kitchenettes. The Ox Yoke Motel, 2 miles southeast of the main ranch, has motel rooms with lower rates, plus two cabins that sleep four to six people. Pets on leashes are allowed, as is smoking. The motel is open from Mother's Day until October 1, and the cabins are open from mid-April until December 1. The ranch is rustic and designed for outdoor fun; there are no televisions or phones (except pay phones). Campground and horse accommodations are available (see the Campgrounds chapter). You can shop for supplies at the late-1800s general store, dine at the Brandin' Iron Cafe, or have a drink at the Ponderosa Bar, all nearby. The ranch is on Lawrence County Road 234, which is also called Nemo Road, and is 16 miles northwest of Rapid City and 30 minutes from Deadwood.

Pine Rest Cabins $$-$$$
P.O. Box 377, Hill City 57745
(605) 574-2416, (800) 333-5306
www.pinerestcabins.com

You can get your rest in rustic little cabins with their backdrop of pine forest, yet they're only 1 mile south of Hill City. There are seven one-bedroom cabins, one guest room, and four two-bedroom cabins to choose from. Some have kitchenettes with basic utensils, coffeepot, toaster, and outside grill and picnic table. Linens and towels are provided. Your pet is welcome in some rooms at an additional charge. There is cable television, a playground for the kids, and a hot tub. The George S. Mickelson Trail is across the highway. Call for reservations.

Robins Roost Cabins $$-$$$
12630 Robins Roost Road, Hill City
(605) 574-2252
www.robins-roost-cabins.com

Eight housekeeping cabins are on the property—these are fully furnished cabins with private baths and showers, fireplaces, two double beds, and furnished bedding and towels. Some of the cabins have been set aside for pet owners; please inquire. Robins Roost is in a pretty pine setting close to Hill City, just 12 miles from Mount Rushmore, and near tiny Mitchell Lake, which is reported to have great fishing.

Spokane Creek Resort $$-$$$$
U.S. Highway 16A, Keystone
(605) 666-4609
www.spokanecreekresort.com

This family-oriented resort is just a mile from Custer State Park and has some fine amenities, too, such as laundry facilities, trout fishing, a deli/general store, heated outdoor pool, miniature golf, fresh cinnamon rolls each morning, and a playground for kids. There are 17 cabins, two of which have no bathrooms or kitchens but do have electricity and use of the nearby shower. The 15 housekeeping cabins have private baths and from one to four rooms that sleep two to eight people. The resort is open from mid-May to mid-September. There's information about the resort's campground in the Campgrounds chapter.

Spring Creek Inn $$$-$$$$
23900 U.S. Highway 385, Hill City
(605) 574-2591, (800) 456-2755
www.springcreekinn.com

This pretty property is just off the highway and a short distance from Hill City. You can rent the cottage house or one of three chalets. The cottage house has three bedrooms, two bathrooms, kitchen, air-conditioning, and outside picnic tables. The chalets have three bedrooms, one or two bathrooms, living rooms, decks, kitchenettes, and air-conditioning. The facility is open year-round, and motel units are also available. Spring Creek runs through the property, which is surrounded on three sides by forest service land. Barbecue grills and a playground are available for use. Smoking is permitted, but you should inquire before bringing your pet along.

Whispering Pines Campground
& Lodging $
22700 Silver City Road, Rapid City
(605) 341-3667
www.blackhillscampresort.com

Four camping cabins are for rent here. These are simple one- and two-bedroom cabins without bathrooms (facilities are nearby). A campground is on the property, too, with a general store and snack bar where breakfast specials are served. Nightly cookouts and movies are offered to campers and cabin renters. Whispering Pines also has two luxury vacation homes, which you can read about in the Vacation Homes and Condominiums section of this chapter. The property is on the Centennial Trail (see Recreation) and close to Pactola Reservoir and Central Hills attractions.

Southern Hills

American Presidents Cabins
& Camp $$-$$$$
U.S. Highway 16A, Custer
(605) 673-3373
www.presidentsresort.com
A serene country setting makes American Presidents a popular place for family reunions. There are 45 cabins, all with private bathrooms, although a few are sleeping cabins. The more luxurious cabins sleep from 10 to 12 people, have several bedrooms, two bathrooms, and their own decks. Other cabins vary in size; ask which will best suit you. Guests can use the 60-foot-by-40-foot heated pool and hot tub, then hit the convenience store for snacks. There are some nonsmoking cabins, but most allow smoking, and pets are permitted. A few cabins are wheelchair accessible, as is the shower house on the grounds. American Presidents has a campground (see the Campgrounds chapter), and the facility is open from approximately April through November.

Blue Bell Lodge and Resort $$$$
Custer State Park
Highway 87, Custer
(605) 255-4531, (605) 255-4772
(800) 658-3530 (reservations)
www.custerresorts.com
The Blue Bell Lodge houses the Tatanka Dining Room, with family-style dinners, the Buffalo Wallow Lounge, and the White Buffalo meeting room. Around the lodge are log cabins, including sleeping cabins, a honeymoon cabin with one room and fire-

place, and housekeeping cabins that accommodate four, six, or eight people. The Commissioner's Cabin has four rooms, a full kitchen, and sleeps eight. Some cabins are open in winter.

Calamity Peak Lodge $-$$$$
U.S. Highway 16A, Custer
(605) 673-2357, (800) 591-5949
www.blackhills.com/calamitypeak
If you stay here, you'll be just 2 miles east of the town of Custer and look out on both French Creek and Calamity Peak, a craggy granite mountain across the highway. You have your choice of accommodations. A house that sleeps 10 is available. One cabin sleeps four people, the other sleeps six; both have a kitchen and private bath. Motel units are also available, including two that sleep six people and have fully furnished kitchens. Grills and picnic tables are outside. Calamity Peak Lodge is open only from May through September.

Custer Mountain Cabins
& Campground $-$$
U.S. Highway 16A, Custer
(605) 673-5440, (800) 239-5505
www.custermountain.com
The eight log housekeeping cabins here have two or three bedrooms, private baths, and decks. You can hike on the adjoining forest service land, and you'll be near both the city of Custer and Custer State Park. There's a campground on the property, too, and you'll find information about it in the Campgrounds chapter.

Need help finding accommodations in the Black Hills and Badlands? Call the Black Hills, Badlands, and Lakes Association, (605) 355-3600, or visit Black Hills Visitor Information Center, 1851 Discovery Circle (exit 61, I-90), Rapid City. You can also call or visit the Rapid City Convention and Visitors Bureau, (605) 343-1744, 444 Mount Rushmore Road.

Larive Lake Resort & Campground $-$$
1802 Evans Street, Hot Springs
(605) 745-3993
www.larivelake.com

This lakeside resort has 11 cabins—some are very simple (without kitchens) and others have one to two bedrooms, kitchens, and decks. All have air-conditioning, private bathrooms, and cable television. Larive Lake has plenty of amenities: fishing, swimming, and boating (nonmotorized) as well as a store, playground, and laundry. RV and tent sites are available, too. See the Campgrounds chapter.

Legion Lake Resort $$$-$$$$
Custer State Park, Custer
(605) 255-4521, (605) 255-4772
(800) 658-3530 (reservations)
www.custerresorts.com

Another pretty little spot in Custer State Park, Legion Lake has a store, a gift shop, and dining room, plus 25 cottages, some with kitchens.

South Dakota State Parks Camping Cabins $
Angostura Recreation Area, Hot Springs
(605) 745-6996, (800) 710-CAMP
www.state.sd.us/gfp/sdparks

Six one-room cabins are available at Cascade Campground at Angostura. These are the only cabins operated by the state parks in the Black Hills, although the park system operates others in recreation areas and parks elsewhere in the state. These simple cabins are available year-round, and guests use outside vault toilets (basically a more sophisticated pit toilet) and nearby shower facilities (shower buildings are closed in the winter). Each has electricity, beds, table, and benches. Food concessions at Angostura are open only in the summer. Reservations in advance are required, but the above toll-free number is not answered in the winter (call the local number instead). Out-of-staters pay an extra $5.00. Leashed pets are allowed.

State Game Lodge and Resort $$$-$$$$
Custer State Park, Custer
(605) 255-4541, (605) 255-4772
(800) 658-3530 (reservations)
www.custerresorts.com

The charming State Game Lodge and Resort offers cottages or motel units on its grounds. The motel rooms accommodate up to four people. Cottages range in size from one room with two double beds to the Creekside Cabin and Bunkhouse or the Gamekeeper's Cabin, both of which accommodate up to 16 people. Some of the cabins have kitchens or kitchenettes and fireplaces. If you'd prefer to stay in the lodge, you can read about it in the Resorts and Lodges section of this chapter.

Sylvan Lake Resort $$$-$$$$
Custer State Park, Custer
(605) 574-2561, (605) 255-4772
(800) 658-3530 (reservations)
www.custerresorts.com

Thirty-one one-room sleeping cabins on the lodge grounds have fireplaces and television, but no kitchens. Housekeeping cabins have televisions, and the Senator's Cabin accommodates up to 10 people. It has four rooms, full kitchen, fireplace, three beds, and two sofa beds. You can also stay in the lodge's guest rooms; see the Resorts and Lodges section.

HOTELS

Found in the heart of Black Hills towns, these hotels give you easy access to historic and cultural sites.

Northern Hills

Bullock Hotel $$$$
633 Main Street, Deadwood
(605) 578-1745, (800) 336-1876
www.heartofdeadwood.com

Deadwood legend Seth Bullock, the town's first sheriff and a friend of Teddy

Roosevelt, built this elegant and charming hotel in 1895. It soon became known as one of the finest hotels in the region. When Deadwood's renovation began, the Bullock was meticulously restored to its early grandeur. Today, you can bask in the fascinating history of the building while enjoying some very modern luxuries. The old ballroom is now a casino, and you can dine beside the ornate fireplace in Bully's Restaurant and Lounge (named in Teddy's honor). Seth's Cellar can accommodate your private party or banquet. Like many Deadwood hotels, the Bullock offers tour packages (food, lodging, and gaming) for groups. The hotel also operates the Branch House, 37 Sherman Street (about a block away), which offers mostly suites; rates are slightly higher than the Bullock's.

**First Gold Hotel and
Gaming**   **$$$–$$$$**
270 Main Street, Deadwood
(605) 578-9777, (800) 274-1876
www.firstgold.com
Although not a historic hotel, First Gold has a lot to offer, including two restaurants (one with a bar), 11 casinos, and two hotels. The main hotel has three suites with Jacuzzis; two of the suites have kitchens. An entire floor of the main hotel is set aside for smokers, while the other hotel is completely smoke-free. Pets are permitted in certain rooms (deposit required).

**Historic Franklin Hotel/
Motor Inn**   **$$$–$$$$**
700 Main Street, Deadwood
(605) 578-2241, (800) 688-1876
www.historicfranklinhotel.com
The Franklin has a rich and lively Deadwood-style history. Built in 1903, it was the site of the first South Dakota radio broadcast, and it is the traditional place to stay for visiting celebrities, from Babe Ruth and John Wayne to Kevin Costner and country music stars Big & Rich. It also was a famous gambling house, even though the practice was outlawed until 1989. In fact, rumor says that an illegal poker

game was being held in the hotel's basement in the moments leading up to legalization.

The Silverado casino across the street purchased the Franklin in late 2005 and closed it for remodeling. The completely renovated main floor reopened in July 2006. Among other things, the new owners restored the front entrance to its original appearance, revealing portions of the original tin ceiling that were covered up over the years, investing more than $100,000 on chandeliers, and constructing a new wing on the Franklin's western side.

Historic Town Hall Inn   **$$$**
215 West Main Street, Lead
(800) 336-1876
This Italianate building, renovated into a charming and unusual hotel, served as Lead's first city hall, police headquarters, municipal courtrooms, and Homestake Mining Company's payroll offices. The two-story inn was built in 1912 and is listed on the National Register of Historic Places. The rooms, named for their former purposes, have been beautifully decorated with floral themes and oak reproduction furniture, including lovely dressers and armoires. Stay in the Auditor's Office, the Vault Room, the Jury Room, or the Municipal Judge's Chambers. The 13-foot ceilings and 10-foot windows are still in place, as is the open stairway and its oak banister, but private bathrooms, phones, and televisions have been added for modern visitors. There are just 12 rooms in the inn, so you should call ahead. Refunds are not possible if you cancel during the Sturgis Rally & Races (the first two weeks or so of

Some accommodations will help you arrange bus and van tours. Tour companies are listed in the Getting Here, Getting Around chapter, but if you haven't had time to make a tour reservation, your accommodations operator may be able to help.

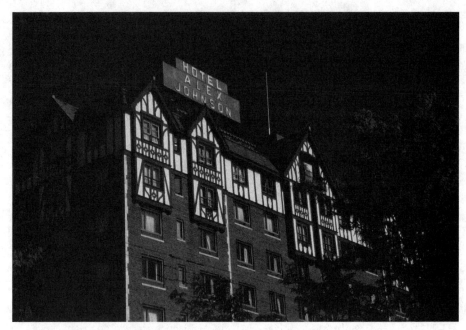

The historic Alex Johnson Hotel in Rapid City. SOUTH DAKOTA TOURISM

August). Reservations are made through the Bullock Hotel at the above number.

Mineral Palace Hotel **$$$–$$$$**
610 Main Street, Deadwood
(605) 578-2036, (800) 847-2522
www.mineralpalace.com

The Mineral Palace is a new hotel, at least compared to others in town that are housed in historic buildings. Each of its rooms and suites has a big bathroom, television, and clock radio. Some rooms are wheelchair accessible, and you can request a nonsmoking room. The Royal Suite has a Jacuzzi, wet bar, and fireplace. The multiroom casino and restaurant are on the first floor of the hotel. A new three-story expansion with additional hotel and casino space is due to open in mid-2006.

Central Hills

Alex Johnson Hotel **$$–$$$$**
523 Sixth Street, Rapid City
(605) 342-1210, (800) 888-ALEX
www.alexjohnson.com

The Alex was built in the 1920s by the businessman whose name it carries. The hotel is one of the treasures of Rapid City's historic downtown (Franklin Roosevelt once stayed there), and its lobby is beautifully furnished with Lakota art and artifacts. Here you'll be in the heart of town, yet within an hour or so of every attraction in the Black Hills. The 143 rooms are elegantly furnished, and two suites (the Presidential and the Bridal) have hot tubs. Some rooms are wheelchair accessible, and some are reserved for smokers. The Landmark Restaurant is on the first floor, as is Paddy O'Neill's Pub and Casino, and meeting and banquet facilities are available.

Radisson Hotel   **$$$-$$$$**
445 Mount Rushmore Road, Rapid City
(605) 348-8300, (800) 333-3333
www.radisson.com/rapidcitysd
We've included this chain hotel here
because it's in the heart of Rapid City and
has special accommodations for business
travelers. It is located on the corner of
busy Mount Rushmore Road and Main
Street. The rooms have coffeemakers,
microwaves, and dataports. Other ameni-
ties include free shuttle to and from Rapid
City Regional Airport; restaurant and
lounge; banquet facilities; indoor pool and
hot tub; exercise area; and business center
with fax, copier, and computer. There is
half a floor reserved for smokers, and four
rooms are wheelchair accessible. The
restaurant at the hotel went through
major changes in late 2003 and now
offers one of the classiest continental din-
ing experiences in the region. Read more
about it in the Restaurants chapter.

**Rushmore Plaza Holiday Inn
and Conference Center $$$-$$$$
Rushmore Plaza Civic Center
505 North Fifth Street, Rapid City
(605) 348-4000, (800) 315-2621
www.rushmoreplaza.com**
This eight-story chain hotel is adjacent to
the Rushmore Plaza Civic Center and
quite convenient for those attending con-
ventions, meetings, or events there. The
hotel's amenities include a lovely atrium,
indoor pool, sauna, whirlpool/hot tub,
exercise room, cable television and HBO,
the Tiffany Grille restaurant, and the Foun-
tain Court piano lounge. The Presidential
Suite has its own Jacuzzi. Some rooms
and floors are nonsmoking, and pets are
allowed (please ask, deposit required).
Rapid City also has two Holiday Inn
Express hotels (750 Cathedral Drive and
645 Disk Drive), which have no restaurant
or lounge but do offer free continental
breakfast.

RESORTS AND LODGES

Black Hills resorts offer lodging, restau-
rants, and other conveniences in a single
setting.

Northern Hills

**Deadwood Gulch Resort $$$
U.S. Highway 85 South, Deadwood
(605) 578-1294, (800) 695-1876
www.deadwoodgulch.com**
Deadwood Gulch is a complete resort, with
something for everyone, including 98 motel
rooms of various sizes and styles. The
resort is on the Mickelson Trail—the part
that can be accessed by snowmobiles. It
has a convention center, two casinos, a fitness room, a large indoor hot tub, and
restaurant.

**Spearfish Canyon Lodge at
Latchstring Village $$$-$$$$
U.S. Highway 14A, Spearfish
(605) 584-3435, (877) 975-6343
www.spfcanyon.com**
This 54-room resort in glorious Spearfish
Canyon offers lodging, conference facili-
ties, gift shop, restaurant, a lounge, and a
sports center. The accommodations vary
in size from guest rooms to suites, with
amenities like coffeemakers, fireplaces,
balconies, and microwaves. At adjacent
Latchstring Village you'll also find trails,
fishing, a botanical garden, and snowmo-
bile rentals. Although you'll be close to
Deadwood, Spearfish, and Northern Hills
attractions, the incredible scenery may
entice you to stay right here.

Southern Hills

**State Game Lodge and
Resort $$$-$$$$
Custer State Park, Custer
(605) 255-4541, (605) 255-4772
(800) 658-3530 (reservations)
www.custerresorts.com**
This beautiful structure was President

Coolidge's summer White House in 1927, and you'll enjoy it as much as he did. The charming lodge is listed on the National Register of Historic Places and is one of the treasures of Custer State Park. You can stay in one of the lodge's seven guest rooms, which come in a variety of styles and sizes and accommodate up to four people each. While you're there, dine in the Pheasant Dining Room or have a drink in the lounge. Meeting and banquet facilities are available, too. Cabins and motel rooms are also for rent; there's information in the Cabins and Cottages section of this chapter.

Sylvan Lake Resort   **$$$–$$$$**
Custer State Park, Custer
(605) 574-2561, (605) 255-4772
(800) 658-3530 (reservations)
www.custerresorts.com
This is a cozy lodge next to picturesque Sylvan Lake, close to the trails to Harney Peak, and on the way to both Mount Rushmore National Memorial and Crazy Horse Memorial. Sit by the pleasant fireplace in the lobby or have dinner in the Lakota Dining Room. The lodge has 35 rooms that vary in configuration and size and accommodate from one to six people. Read about the cabins on the grounds in the Cabins and Cottages section of this chapter.

VACATION HOMES AND CONDOMINIUMS

For longer visits to the Hills, consider renting a vacation home or condominium.

Northern Hills

Barefoot Resort   **$$$$**
21111 Barefoot Loop, H.C. 37, Lead
(605) 584-1577, (800) 424-0225
www.barefootresort.com
Located on the site of the historic Barefoot mining claim, and (at 6,400 feet) higher than any other lodge east of the Rockies, these 27 condos are across the

road from the Terry Peak Ski Lodge and 15 minutes from Deadwood. One- to four-bedroom units are available, and each has a private bath, kitchen, living and dining room, fireplace, and a great view from the balcony. A pool and hot tub are on the premises. Time-share programs are available, as is one four-bed cabin.

Mountain Stream Estates   **$$$$**
Rockford Road, Lead
(605) 229-1619, (605) 226-2904
www.mountainstreamestates.com
These two luxurious vacation homes are near Cheyenne Crossing, deep in the Hills and close to Deadwood, Spearfish, skiing, snowmobile trails, and hiking. A stream runs close by, and there's a trout pond near the houses. Each fully furnished house has five bedrooms, three baths, and kitchen with dishwasher and microwave. Both houses have a jet-spray tub and garage. No credit cards are accepted.

Terry Peak Condos   **$$$–$$$$**
H.C. 37, Lead
(605) 584-2723, (888) 584-2723
www.terrypeaklodge.com
These 18 condos are attached to the main lodge, which faces the Terry Peak Ski Area. Each has its own private entrance. Seven of the condos have two bedrooms and two baths; the remainder have one bedroom and bath. This is nice but simple lodging for people who are more interested in being outdoors—the condos have no phones, cable television service, or air-conditioning, but they do have fully equipped kitchens. Guests have access to an indoor pool, hot tub, and game room.

Central Hills

Edelweiss Mountain
Lodging   **$$$–$$$$**
U.S. Highway 385, Rapid City
(605) 574-2430
www.edelweiss-blackhills.com
More than 25 vacation homes are available through Edelweiss Mountain Lodging in

the summer, and 15 of those are available in the winter. The office is off the highway, between Sheridan Lake and Pactola Reservoir; the homes are all in the immediate area. Homes with one to four bedrooms and private baths are available. Some have hot tubs and pool tables, and all but one have fully furnished kitchens. Some of the homes are accessible to the disabled. All have great views of the surrounding pine-covered hills.

Whispering Pines Campground & Lodging $$$$
22700 Silver City Road, Rapid City
(605) 341-3667
www.blackhillscampresort.com

Two lovely vacation homes will give you the chance to relax in luxury. One is a four-bedroom, two-and-a-half-bath home, and it's open all year. The other has three bedrooms and two baths and, like the rest of the facilities here, is open only from May 1 through September. Both homes are fully furnished and include a kitchen, living room, dining room, deck

Tourist season in the Black Hills and Badlands begins Memorial Day weekend and ends Labor Day weekend. But spring, fall, and winter are great seasons in which to visit and enjoy the scenery and recreation (although many attractions are closed), as well as to take advantage of lighter traffic and smaller crowds.

with grill, two-car garage, woodstove with furnished firewood, and private driveway. Both smoking and pets are allowed, and the three-bedroom home is wheelchair accessible. Whispering Pines is in the midst of some great attractions, close to Hill City and Rapid City, 2 miles north of Pactola Reservoir, and right on the Centennial Trail (the Deer Creek trailhead is on the property; see the Recreation chapter). Camping cabins are also available; see the Cabins and Cottages section.

CAMPGROUNDS ⌂

Thousands of people come to the Black Hills each summer to camp among the pines, and both public and private campground operators are happy to oblige them. Whether you want to pack all your amenities on your back and hike to a primitive tent site, settle down with cable TV in your RV, or bring your horse with you, you'll find plenty of choices that meet your needs. We've listed a number of fine places we would recommend to our camping friends, but understand that these entries merely scratch the surface. There's an abundance of well-run camping spots from one end of the Hills to the other.

Many of the campgrounds in this chapter offer a wide range of creature comforts, but you'll find the owners have also done a commendable job of preserving the natural surroundings that beckon people to the Hills in the first place. And even those with the most campsites have a spacious feel—the great outdoors is all around you. Listen closely and you'll probably catch the strains of a coyote serenade at dusk. Of course, you're more apt to see wildlife if you hike deep into the forest, find a flat spot of ground, and pitch your tent. As long as you don't want a campfire and pack all of your supplies in and out, this is a pleasant (and free) option almost anywhere in the Black Hills National Forest.

Privately owned campgrounds often have swimming pools and other recreational opportunities on-site, and many are located near major attractions. But if you'd like to go touring and let someone else do the driving, be sure to ask whether any bus tours stop for passengers where you intend to stay. If you're looking for a public campground with fewer amenities, refer to the listings for state and national parks and recreation areas. You'll find 26 public campgrounds operated by the USDA Forest Service (see the Black Hills National Forest heading later in the chapter.) Lastly, we have a separate section for horse camps.

For information about camping in or near the Badlands, consult the Badlands chapter. If you're looking for a cabin to rent, the Accommodations chapter is your best source.

Unless we state otherwise, the campgrounds listed here have showers, flush toilets, and RV dump stations. Full RV hookups mean water, sewer, and electricity; partial means electricity and water or

State Park Camping Reservations

The state reservation center handles summer reservations for campsites, cabins, and picnic shelters in South Dakota state parks and recreation areas from early January until early September. (To make arrangements for the off-season, fall through mid-May, call the individual parks.) In general, your stay is limited to 14 days, and all fees, including a small processing fee for out-of-state residents, must be paid in advance. Call (800) 710–CAMP to make reservations up to 90 days in advance. For general park information, call (605) 773–3391; for information about a particular park, call the park.

Bison skull at Bear Butte. BERT GILDART

electricity only. Each listing includes a breakdown of RV and tent sites to help you gauge which campgrounds suit your camping style. And unless a listing states otherwise, assume your major credit card will be accepted and your pet is welcome on a leash.

You'll notice that many campgrounds give opening and closing dates "depending on the weather." Well, that's just the way we operate here, where winters can be long and blustery—or comparatively brief and mild. Be aware that campgrounds and other accommodations are apt to be packed in early August during the Sturgis Rally & Races (see Annual Events and Festivals). Although it's a good idea to make advance reservations any time you're coming to the Hills, it's especially wise to do so for stays during Rally week.

Whenever you arrive, and wherever you stay, don't be surprised if you find a family reunion or two in progress. Black Hills campgrounds are a popular choice for such activities, and when you think about it, what better way to spend time with those you love?

NORTHERN HILLS

Bear Butte State Park Campground
Highway 79, Sturgis
(605) 347-5240

If beautiful views and peaceful solitude are your top priorities, you'll appreciate the opportunity to stay here. On clear days you can see Bear Butte reflected in Bear Butte Lake, which is just a short walk from the campground. To the south, the Black Hills form an inviting silhouette on the horizon. You'll find 15 campsites for tents and RVs, but amenities are limited to a pit toilet and a hand pump for water; there are no showers, hookups, or dump stations. Also, because trees don't grow well here, shade is scarce. But there's a picnic shelter for you to use, and, of course, the lake for you to play in (see the Recreation chapter for boating information). East of the main camping area are four fairly well-shaded tent sites with a vault toilet and no water. Overflow camping is available during the Sturgis Rally & Races.

Credit cards and reservations are not accepted, but since the campground is not heavily used except during the Sturgis Rally in August, you should have no trouble finding a site on a first-come, first-served basis. There's a self-registration fee of $6.00 per camping unit (such as a tent or RV) but no park entrance fee to use the campground. If you drive into the eastern portion of the park to see the visitor center or use the hiking trails, you'll need a park entrance license. If you walk over (a hike in itself), you can get in for free.

The campground is open all year, although the water is shut off during the winter. To get there, go 3 miles east of Sturgis on Highway 34, turn left onto Highway 79, and go about 4 miles. Turn left again onto the dirt road where you see the campground sign and go another mile.

Chris' Campground
701 Christensen Drive, Spearfish
(605) 642–2239, (800) 350–2239
www.blackhills.com/chriscampground

Two-legged kids will delight in the opportunity to bottle-feed the four-legged variety at the petting farm here. Baby animals such as goats, lambs, and calves from local ranches spend the summer at this shady, grassy campground, which has been owned and operated by the Christensen family for nearly 50 years. Feedings are at 8:00 A.M. and 5:00 P.M., and guests are welcome to join in. The rest of the time, a heated pool, rec room, and playground are good places to pass the time.

There are 132 campsites: 45 basic ones for tents or trailers and the rest with full or partial RV hookups. Six camping cabins offer another option for summer nights.

Laundry facilities, paved interior roads, a convenience store, cable TV, volleyball, horseshoes, a basketball court, and lovely mountain views all make your stay that much more enjoyable. Weather permitting, you can visit between mid-April and mid-October. Limited camping is available all winter. Rates for four people range from $16 to $25.

Elkhorn Ridge RV Park
20189 U.S. Highway 85, Spearfish
(605) 722–1800, (877) 722–1800
www.elkhornridgervpark.com

Opened in the spring of 2006, this 75-acre resort is among the more luxurious campgrounds in the Black Hills. And with a location in the Centennial Valley near Interstate 90 and U.S. Highway 85 between Spearfish and Deadwood, there's hardly a lack of things to do nearby. Nevertheless, the campground developers saw fit to construct a heated outdoor swimming pool, hiking trails, a playground, and courts for horseshoes, basketball, and tennis. There are Internet and satellite television hookups available for RVs, full laundry facilities, and they've even staked out places to build a pavilion and outdoor amphitheater in the future.

Because the campground is fairly new, there isn't a great deal of greenery. A stand of mature trees sits on the northern edge, and new plants have been included in the landscaping, but it will be many years before this becomes a well-shaded place to pitch a tent or park your rig. In the meantime, large mounds of earth (topped by tasteful statues of elk and other wildlife) have been sculpted to separate the campground from the adjoining highways, which ensures relative privacy for the 186 full hookup sites, 30 tent sites, and 12 cabins.

The campground is located on the Frawley Ranch property, an estate once owned by a pioneer Deadwood lawyer. Indeed, the entire Centennial Valley was once a major source of food for the once-bustling city of Deadwood, which lies only a few miles above in the hills. Many of the original homestead structures have been preserved and make up one of the few National Historic Landmarks inside South Dakota's borders. Although the ranch buildings are normally closed to the public, they are opened on special occasions. If you're interested in a peek at this piece of frontier history, inquire at the front desk about the next time the ranch's unusual stone buildings—including a one-room schoolhouse and a traditional dugout—might be open for public viewing.

Glencoe Campresort
20555 Glencoe Drive, Sturgis
(605) 347-4712, (800) 272-4712
www.glencoecamp.com
A magnificent view of Bear Butte greets you as you turn off Highway 34 into Glencoe Campresort. Although serving groups of about 200 or more is the specialty here, the facility also welcomes families and solitary campers. The 1,000 RV sites with full hookups are close to the entrance, and then the dirt road winds around to more than 100 cottonwood-shaded, creekside acres for tent camping. Chemical toilets and water faucets are located throughout the grounds.

During the Sturgis Rally & Races each August, campers can buy meals that are prepared in an enclosed kitchen and served in a covered eating area with seating for 320. Geared mainly toward Rally business, the campground nonetheless is open between May 1 and October 1.

Weekly and monthly rates are available; otherwise, plan to pay $8.00 a night for a tent site, $15.00 to park your RV, and, in either case, $3.00 less if you don't use the showers. The campground is 3 miles east of town.

Mountain View Campground
625 Christensen Drive, Spearfish
(605) 642-2170, (800) 365-2170
www.mountainview-campground.com
Trees and grassy areas make this a homey little place to stay in your tent or RV, and the heated pool, game room, and small playground provide good fam-

ily recreation. There are 80 sites altogether, most with partial or full hookups. Laundry facilities and a convenience store provide more comforts. Some of the picnic tables have shelters to keep you out of the rain.

The campground is open from early May until mid-October, weather permitting. Rates for up to four people range from $16 to $30.

Spearfish City Campground
404 South Canyon Street, Spearfish
(605) 642-1340
city.spearfish.sd.us
Don't be fooled by the name; this quiet, shady campground is on the outskirts of town, alongside Spearfish Creek and D.C. Booth Historic Fish Hatchery and little more than a stone's throw from the mouth of incomparable Spearfish Canyon.

Thousands of people descended on the campground in 1989, when the National Horseshoe Pitchers Association held its annual tournament here, but the dust has long since settled. The campground offers about 100 basic sites; there are also 57 RV sites with full hookups and cable TV.

Depending on the weather, you can camp here from early May through mid-October. Prices start at $13 for one person at a basic site and $22 for up to four people using full hookups. Children ages five and younger stay for free. Campers who pay for six consecutive nights get a seventh night's stay for free.

Whistler's Gulch RV Park & Campground
235 Cliff Street, Deadwood
(605) 578-2092, (800) 704-7139
www.whistlergulch.com
Like just about everything in Deadwood, this campground a mile south of historic Main Street is situated on a hill. But the brief climb brings you to 126 immaculately groomed, level campsites and a fabulous view across the gulch. Twenty-six of the sites are reserved for tents, and the rest have full hookups for RVs. You won't find a dump station, but other comforts

include a sports court, a heated outdoor pool, arcade games, and a small store. The Deadwood Trolley stops here and for 50 cents takes you downtown to casinos and restaurants. The campground operates May 1 to October 1, weather permitting. Rates for two adults start at $20 for a tent site and $30 for an RV site. If the pool hasn't opened for the season yet, inquire about a discount.

CENTRAL HILLS

Mount Rushmore KOA at Palmer Gulch Resort
Highway 244, Hill City
(605) 574-2525, (800) 562-8503
www.palmergulch.com
If you're looking for a home away from home, this is it. Just about everything your family needs or wants is here, from recreational opportunities to nondenominational Sunday-morning worship services. That's because the resort, which started as a guest ranch in the mid-1930s, pays close attention to customer surveys. The state tourism department recognized its efforts with the George S. Mickelson Hospitality Award.

The list of services is impressive. Besides a grocery store, there's the Dakota Store that sells South Dakota–made products and squares cut from huge slabs of fudge. There's an outpost where you can buy tickets for 18-hole minigolf, the waterslide (an all-day pass gets the whole family into both), and trail rides; or you can watch a free movie every evening. Two outdoor pools, two hot tubs, two wading pools, two playgrounds, bicycle and paddleboat rentals, and a free trout pond (you

do need a fishing license) will probably occupy a good deal of your time. At night, free family activities are on tap, including hayrides and Native American dancing, and there's free transportation to evening lighting programs at nearby Mount Rushmore and Crazy Horse memorials.

If all the activity leaves you with hunger pangs, a restaurant serving three meals a day, a lounge with a full bar, an ice-cream parlor, and a sandwich shop come to the rescue. You can even rent a car and fill the gas tank here! And—need we say so?—there are laundry facilities and cable TV. All this is set against the Black Hills National Forest.

In case you find time to sleep, there are 150 tent sites, 185 partial hookups and 130 full hookups for RVs, 35 full deluxe sites, a group camping area, and 55 camping cabins. There's also an attractive new lodge and a number of furnished cabins (see the Accommodations chapter). The resort, 5 miles west of Mount Rushmore, is open from May 1 until October 1. Prices for campers range from $28 to $55 a night. Camping cabins start at $52. Tent spaces are $28.

Rafter J Bar Ranch Campground
U.S. Highway 16/385, Hill City
(605) 574-2527, (888) RAFTERJ
www.rafterj.com
Meadows, mountain views, and spacious campsites are among the first features you notice at this pristine campground. If you like outdoor recreation, you could spend your whole vacation right here, riding horseback, bicycling, and hiking, because the George S. Mickelson Trail borders the property. A swimming pool, rec room, playground, and hot tub are good places to spend the day, too. In the evening you can watch cable TV in your RV or join fellow campers for a free movie or other family entertainment.

The Ranch Store sells supplies, groceries, and gas for your car (your own or one you've rented at the campground), and there's a laundry for your convenience. There are some 220 campsites,

Campers. SOUTH DAKOTA TOURISM

more than half of which have full or partial RV hookups. Some of the tent sites have electricity, too. There are 23 heated camping cabins, 12 with kitchens and bath; the other 11 are sleeping cabins.

The campground, 3 miles south of Hill City, is open from May 1 to October 1. Nightly rates for two people range from $27 to $41 for a campsite. Cabins are $48 to $86 a night for two. There's no charge for children seven and younger, but horse and bicycle rentals cost extra.

Spokane Creek Resort
24631 Iron Mountain Road, Keystone
(605) 666-4609, (800) 261-9331
www.spokanecreekresort.com
You're just a mile north of Custer State Park and a short drive south of Mount Rushmore when you camp here. Plus, this campground in the Norbeck Wildlife Preserve is along what many consider to

be the most interesting road in the Black Hills—also known as Iron Mountain Road—with rock tunnels and curly "pigtail" bridges.

If that doesn't entice you, perhaps the thought of waking up to the scent of freshly baked cinnamon rolls will. You can buy them, along with breakfast sandwiches and coffee, in the general store each morning; later in the day you can munch on pizza made to order and sub sandwiches prepared on fresh bread. When not eating or exploring, you can swim in the outdoor heated pool or play a variety of sports, including nine-hole minigolf.

The campground has 31 sites for tents and 30 RV sites with full or partial hookups. Two of 17 cabins are for roughing it without plumbing, and the rest have bathrooms and kitchen facilities. (See the Accommodations chapter for more about the cabins.) A picnic pavilion with electricity and room for 100 can be reserved for family reunions and other events. The cost for two people ranges from $18 to $28, and cabins start at $39. The campground is open from May through September.

SOUTHERN HILLS

American Presidents Cabins & Camp
U.S. Highway 16A, Custer
(605) 673-3373
www.presidentsresort.com

Its location a mile east of Custer places this campground within minutes of many of the Black Hills' biggest attractions, including Custer State Park, Crazy Horse Memorial, Jewel Cave, and Mount Rushmore. The place has bragging rights to a heated shower house, a spa, and a heated outdoor pool advertised as the Hills' largest. There's also space for basketball, volleyball, horseshoes, minigolf, a playground, and an arcade. A convenience store and laundry simplify life on the road.

You'll find 36 sites with full or partial hookups and 30-plus shaded tent sites. There is no dump station, but the management will let you empty your RV holding tank at a vacant full-hookup site if you need to. Water spigots are plentiful, and picnic shelters are available for family reunions or other gatherings. See the Accommodations chapter for information about the 45 cabins and 15 motel units here.

The campground opens around mid-March if the weather permits, but water might not be available until the first of April. The place shuts down around mid-November, but you probably won't get a

shower here after October. Prices for two people range from $25 to $30. Inquire about off-season rates.

Angostura State Recreation Area
Off U.S. Highway 385, Hot Springs
(605) 745-6996, (800) 710-CAMP
www.sdgfp.info/Parks

Angostura Reservoir is the star attraction in this 1,125-acre park, and if you can't bear to leave after a day of water sports, you might as well plan to stay at one of 167 campsites spread among four campgrounds. Three of them—Cascade, Hat Creek, and Horsehead—are along the shore; the fourth, Cheyenne, is 150 yards distant. Cascade, close by the marina and with two camping cabins (see the Accommodations chapter) is the shadiest and most popular.

The Breakers Beach Club serves a beachside burgers-and-beer menu during the summer, and there's a convenience store with camping and boating supplies. The concessionaire also has six fully furnished, two-bedroom cabins for rent; call (605) 745-6665 for more information.

The campgrounds 10 miles southeast of Hot Springs are open all year, but the comfort stations close when it gets cold in October. You'll have to settle for vault toilets from then until spring, but you can still have electricity for a small fee. Peak-season rates, from mid-May through Labor Day, range from $10 to $13; camping cabins with heat and air-conditioning rent for $32 a night. The four furnished cabins are $175 a night. When you make your reservation, be sure to ask whether to reach your campground by the north or south entrance.

If road grime has you ready to trade your firstborn child for a shower, Beaver Lake Campground west of Custer has a far less drastic solution for you. For a small fee ($4.50), you can use the showers there and be on your way, your family still intact.

Beaver Lake Campground
U.S. Highway 16, Custer
(605) 673-2464, (800) 346-4383
www.beaverlakecampground.net

Once the kids find out about the 360-foot waterslide at this campground, you might have no other choice than to stay here. But think of the benefits to yourself, too. While the youngsters are happily sliding (and burning off a great deal of energy), you're taking your leisure under a pine tree or beside the heated pool. And the owners make the following promise: If their restrooms aren't the cleanest you've ever found, your stay is free.

There are approximately 96 campsites here, about 37 of which have full or partial hookups for RVs. A year-round full-service cabin is available also. Your family will have the use of a laundry, small convenience store, arcade, and playground. The campground, 3.5 miles west of Custer, is open from May to October. Peak-season (early June to late August) rates start at $18 for four people, with an additional charge for hookups and use of the waterslide. Inquire about off-season, monthly, and group rates. Children ages five and younger stay for free. Pets are welcome.

Cold Brook and Cottonwood Springs Recreation Areas
Hot Springs
(605) 745-5476

If you're looking for solitude and outdoor activities rather than modern amenities, these small recreation areas run by the U.S. Army Corps of Engineers are excellent choices. Somewhat remote, both are situated at reservoirs that are off-limits to noisy, high-speed watercraft.

Cold Brook, reputed to have the clearest, warmest water in the Black Hills, has a small beach for swimming; Cottonwood doesn't have a beach but offers fine fishing. Both have hiking opportunities, a wildlife area, and playgrounds.

Neither campground has hookups or showers, but Cottonwood Springs has flush toilets and running water.

Reservations are not accepted: It's first-come, first-served only. Cold Brook has 13 campsites and is open year-round; Cottonwood Springs has 18 sites that are open from mid-May to mid-September or longer if the weather permits. Both cost $5.00 a night, payable through self-registration.

Cold Brook is less than a mile northwest of Hot Springs; follow Evans Street and take the hard left that leads to the

project. Cottonwood Springs is west of town off U.S. Highway 18; follow the signs from either direction, then go 2 miles on gravel roads. Credit cards are not accepted.

Custer Mountain Cabins & Campground
U.S. Highway 16A, Custer
(605) 673-5440, (800) 239-5505
www.custermountain.com

If *quiet, spacious, shady,* and *close to wildlife* are the words you'd use to describe your ideal campsite, you'd do well to check out this place. You'll be nearly surrounded by USDA Forest Service land that invites you to follow wildlife trails on a hike. (There are no marked trails.)

Smack-dab between the city of Custer to the west and Custer State Park to the east—either one is just 1.5 miles away—the campground can accommodate more than 30 tents in a grassy meadow. For RVs there are 21 full-hookup sites plus several more with electricity only and cable TV. Two camping cabins are also available. See the Accommodations chapter to find out about the modern, year-round log cabins. Tents and RVs are welcome between mid-April and late October. Prices are $22 for a tent site and $25 to $29 to park your RV. Camping cabins are $55 a night.

Custer State Park
Custer
(605) 255-4515, (800) 710-CAMP
www.campsd.com
www.custerstatepark.info (information), custerstatepark@state.sd.us (reservations)

Campsites in Custer State Park are in great demand among out-of-staters, and, in fact, the state reservation center starts handling requests for Custer several weeks ahead of those for other parks. You'll find a variety of camping opportunities in the park, all with at least two things in common: showers but no hookups. Yet each of these campgrounds has its own personality.

Center Lake Campground (no flush toilets) is, naturally, near Center Lake and adjacent to the Black Hills Playhouse. Set

Bison in a Custer State Park campsite. BERT GILDART

amid dramatic granite outcroppings, Sylvan Lake's popular namesake campground has a higher elevation that ensures cooler summer temperatures. Blue Bell, the southernmost site, is handy to a stable offering trail rides and is a good place to watch for wildlife. All three of these campgrounds offer total shade.

Stockade Lake Campground is shaded on the west side and offers good access to Mount Rushmore and Crazy Horse Memorials. Centrally located Game Lodge Campground (the only one with a dump station) is ideal for large motor homes but also has well-shaded sites along Grace Coolidge Creek. Grace Coolidge Campground, also centrally located, is mostly shaded and close to the park's walk-in fishing area. Legion Lake Campground is in a valley setting across the road from a playground and a lake and lodge of the same name.

It's also close to the Badger Hole (see the Parks and Mountains chapter for a close-up on South Dakota poet laureate Badger Clark) and the Centennial Trail.

Sites at Center Lake, Grace Coolidge, and Stockade Lake South are first-come, first-served; Blue Bell, Game Lodge, Legion Lake, Stockade Lake North, and Sylvan Lake campgrounds are reservation only—but if you show up before noon, you might be able to reserve an unclaimed site on the spot. Game Lodge is open all year with limited facilities and reduced rates during the winter; the others are open from early May until late September, with variations due to weather and maintenance schedules. Except at Center Lake, where the fee is $13, nightly rates are $15 per camping unit (such as a tent or camping trailer) per site.

Group camping is available near two of the developed campgrounds as well. Game Lodge group area has showers and flush

Custer Campsites

GREAT PLACES

By the time Lt. Col. George Armstrong Custer and his Seventh Cavalry arrived in the Black Hills in 1874, rumors of gold had been trickling out of the area for years. Up to that point the U.S. government, determined to honor the Fort Laramie Treaty of 1868 (which ceded the Hills to the Sioux), had refused to provide military escorts for prospectors eager to invade the forbidden territory in search of riches. Inevitably, however, the war department at last authorized a Seventh Cavalry expedition to explore the Black Hills. It was to be a reconnaissance mission only, but Custer took miners along to look for gold. (At 23, the vain and daring Custer, who graduated last in his class at West Point, had become the Civil War's youngest general. But the "boy general" was dropped to captain after the war and later made a lieutenant colonel in the Seventh Cavalry, the rank he held on this mission. Nevertheless, you'll often see references to "General Custer" in the Hills.)

One of Custer's party, Horatio Ross, did indeed find specks of gold in French Creek on August 2, and by the end of the year a band of adventurers led by John Gordon had snuck in, intending to stay. Little more than a year later, the Black Hills gold rush of 1876 was in full swing. Today you can pull off the highway at Wheels West Campground, 3 miles east of Custer on U.S. 16A, and read a histori-

cal marker at the site of Custer's base camp. The expedition stayed here for five days, and its leader named the area Golden Valley. A half mile farther east, the Gordon Stockade has been re-created.

Another more obscure Custer campsite is 5 miles south of Bear Butte in Meade County. At the intersection of Highway 34 and County Road 12C, County Road 6L heads south. As it narrows you'll find a flagpole and a stone monument with a hand-lettered sign that reads: CAMPSITE, GENERAL CUSTER EXPEDITION, AUGUST 14-15, 1874. ENTIRE COMMAND OF SEVENTH US CAVALRY CONSISTING OF 1,200 MEN AND HORSES, 110 WAGONS AND EQUIPMENT. Custer, on the return trip and two weeks' ride from home, wrote a note to his wife, Elizabeth ("Libbie"), here, saying, "I have the proud satisfaction of knowing that our explorations have exceeded the most sanguine expectations."

toilets; Stockade Lake doesn't, but they're within walking distance. The rate is $3.00 per person per night, with a $60.00 per night minimum. Reservations are required.

Hikers might prefer the tranquillity of primitive campsites at French Creek Nat-

ural Area in the approximate center of the park. Hike in a mile from French Creek Horse Camp on the west end or 2 miles from the Wildlife Loop on the east end. At either end, occupancy is limited to 15 people, but both are open all year on a first-come, first-served basis. The fee is $2.00 per person. For more information call (605) 255-4464 or stop at the Peter Norbeck Visitor Center from May to October.

For information about French Creek Horse Camp, see the Horse Camps section of this chapter. Information on Custer State Park's cabins and lodges is in the Accommodations chapter. To find out what makes this park such a popular place, read the Parks and Mountains chapter.

Elk Mountain Campground
Wind Cave National Park
U.S. Highway 385, Hot Springs
(605) 745-4600
www.nps.gov/wica

Like the rest of the park, this serene campground is unspoiled and beautiful, with rolling, grassy hills and a wide prairie sky. A self-guided nature trail loops around the campground for about a mile.

On summer nights, free ranger-led programs start around sundown in the outdoor amphitheater that has bench seating and a projection booth for slide shows. Check the park's visitor center for the program schedule, because it varies as the days get shorter.

The 75 campsites have no hookups, and there's no dump station or showers.

The sole modern comforts—flush toilets and running water—are operational from mid-May until mid-September. The campground in the west central part of the park is open year-round. The rate is $12 per night during peak season, half that when the plumbing is shut off. Reservations are not accepted, and payment is by self-registration, but there's always a volunteer host on hand to welcome you and answer questions. During extremely dry conditions, a campfire prohibition will be posted. Credit cards are not accepted.

Flintstones Bedrock City Campground
U.S. Highway 16 West, Custer
(605) 673-4079
(605) 673-4664 (summer only)
www.flintstonesbedrockcity.com

You'll especially want to consider staying here if you have little ones who will appreciate the adjacent Flintstones amusement park (see the Kidstuff chapter for more about that). For one thing, your stay allows you unlimited entries to the park once you've paid admission.

In addition to 127 tent and RV sites—52 with full hookups—the 30-acre campground on the edge of town has laundry facilities, a game room, outdoor heated pool, nine holes of miniature golf, plus volleyball, basketball, and horseshoe courts. The campground is open mid-May to Labor Day. Prices range from $19.50 to $24.00 for two people. Six cabins are also available at $42.00 for two people.

Larive Lake Resort & Campground
1802 Evans Street, Hot Springs
(605) 745-3993
www.larivelake.com

Just as the name implies, you'll find a lovely little lake to play in when you stay here. Fishing and swimming are free to guests, and you can rent a paddleboat or canoe for a small charge; or you can bring your own nonmotorized watercraft.

The well-kept grounds with a view of nearby colorful, rocky cliffs offer 20 RV sites with full hookups and 20 or more tent sites, a laundry, game room, playground, cable TV, and camp store. See the Accommodations chapter for information about the eight cabins. The resort is open from May 15 to October 1. Rates range from $20 to $30; your seventh night in your tent or RV is free.

BLACK HILLS NATIONAL FOREST

National Forest Supervisor
R.R. 2, Box 200, Custer
(877) 444-6777 (reservations only)
www.reserveusa.com
The South Dakota portion of the Black Hills National Forest has 26 designated campgrounds, from lakeside to rugged. For specific information you need to call or write to the forest supervisor's office at the phone number or address above. Ask for the latest copy of the *Black Hills National Forest Recreation Guide.*

None of these campgrounds have utilities, but that's probably one reason you wanted to camp in the forest. In most cases, though, you do get the luxury of drinking water. Most have spacious RV sites with lots of trees and bushes for privacy. More than half of the campgrounds are open or partially open all year, but what services do exist are shut down during the winter, and you have to carry out your trash yourself. Be aware that snow can close the roads, blocking your way in or out.

About half operate on a first-come, first-served basis, but others have reservable sites. Your stay is limited to 14 days. In general, fees are charged between Memorial Day and Labor Day weekends only. Rates range from $8.00 to $17.00 a night, except at four remote campgrounds that are maintained with the help of donations, and at the Bear Gulch and Sheridan Lake group areas, where fees start at $40.00. Inquire about specifics. If your horse will be traveling with you, see the Horse Camps listings below. Also see the Hiking and Backpacking section of the Recreation chapter to learn about backcountry camping in the forest.

HORSE CAMPS

Horse camps cater to visitors who wish to explore the Black Hills with their equine friends.

Northern Hills

Nemo Guest Ranch
Main Street, Nemo
(605) 578-2708
www.nemoguestranch.com
The atmosphere at this well-kept ranch in Paradise Valley is nothing short of charming, with its western-style buildings and hitching-post trim. There are plenty of comforts, too, from the Ponderosa Bar and Brandin' Iron Cafe to the turn-of-the-20th-century Nemo Mercantile general store, which also houses a laundry. You can even gas up your truck right here. Take your pick of 14 modern cabins and houses with one to five bedrooms, which rent from $75 to $350 a night; a nearby motel (see the Accommodations chapter for complete information about those units); and 25 RV sites with full hookups or unlimited tent sites—but leave your horse in one of the corrals.

The ranch is open year-round. Nightly rates range from $20 to $30 for a campsite. Horses stay for $10 per night. The ranch is 21 miles from the junction of U.S. 385 and Nemo Road, southeast of Deadwood, or 16 miles northwest of Rapid City from the other end of Nemo Road, also called County Road 234.

Central Hills

Deerfield Lake Resort
11321 Gillette Prairie Road, Hill City
(605) 574-2636
www.deerfieldlakeresort.com
This year-round facility actually caters to many types of sporting, so depending on the season, you can bring your horse, fishing pole, hunting rifle, or even your snowmobile. Snowmobile and ATV rentals are available for use at the resort, too, and a

maintenance shop is right there. You'll find more than 66 miles of marked and mapped horse trails as well as more than 340 miles of groomed national forest snowmobile trails that depart from the resort. Deerfield Lake gleams quietly across the dirt road, offering top-notch trout fishing and no-wake boating for a small fee, payable at the lake.

For lights-out you can either reserve one of four two-bed, heated housekeeping cabins (see the Accommodations chapter) or, mid-May through September, pick a spot for your tent or RV—all 25 sites have electricity, and six have full hookups. There's no dump station, but there is a gas pump as well as a convenience store where you can purchase hunting and fishing licenses, five-day snowmobile permits, groceries, fishing tackle, and worms. From mid-October to March, a small cafe on the premises serves meals.

Camping fees are $16 to $18 per night; cabins start at $55. Horses board for $6.00 a day in corrals. You must be 18 or older to rent a snowmobile or a four-wheeler. Call for rates and reservations.

Southern Hills

Black Hills National Forest
(877) 444-6777
www.reserveusa.com
The national forest has two public horse camps with sheltered hitching areas, Willow Creek and Iron Creek. Of the two, Willow Creek is the more deluxe: It has drinking water. Neither has showers or utility hookups. Reservations are recommended at both during the summer. Iron Creek, east of Custer, has nine campsites; Willow Creek, on Highway 244 between Hill City and Mount Rushmore, has eight group sites.

Rates are $22 per night at Iron Creek; at Willow Creek, group rates apply.

French Creek Horse Camp
CSP No. 4, Custer State Park
(605) 255-4515, (800) 710-2267
www.campsd.com
No more driving 3 miles to Blue Bell Campground to take a shower when you stay here. A new era began in 1998 with the opening of a comfort station housing showers, flush toilets, and sinks with hot and cold running water from a newly drilled well. The familiar vault toilets were left in place, though, to save you a potentially lengthy hike in the middle of the night. There are no hookups or dump station.

The campground has 25 reservable sites and five that are available on a first-come, first-served basis. As popular as this place is, it's a good idea to reserve a site well in advance, especially for the summer months. The campground, 3 miles east of Blue Bell Lodge, is open all year. Unlimited corral space is available. The fee is $18 per night per camping unit.

Once here you can ride just about anywhere in Custer State Park except the Sylvan Lake watershed area and the walk-in fishing area that links Grace Coolidge and Center Lake Campgrounds. Both areas are posted. Four trails depart from the campground; see the Recreation chapter for more information.

Plenty Star Ranches
U.S. Highway 385, Pringle
(605) 673-3012
www.plentystarranch.com
Owners Jack and Isa Kirk have designed this restful camp for those whose primary purpose in going camping is to commune with nature. A Native American theme prevails here, and a pastoral tepee camp a short distance from the main area is kept free of cars and other modern trappings that would be out of context. Camping fees are $20 to $30 per night, while cabins start at $45.

You can stake out your own tent site (for $20 per night) behind the 19th-century ranch house, in a meadow bordered by graceful cottonwood and golden willow trees that grow on the banks of Cougar Creek. The ranch offers cabins, which can accommodate four to six persons each, plus 20 RV sites. The old ranch house can be rented for groups year-round; prices for that start at $100. A washer and dryer are in the heated shower house.

Box stalls and spacious pens are provided for your horse for $12 per day, and you'll find about 4,000 acres of public and private property on which to ride. The own-ers pride themselves on the horse-camper, hands-on vacations offered to kids. Call Jack or Isa for details. Bicycle riders love to stop at Plenty Star, as the Mickelson Trail runs right along the property. A public breakfast buffet is offered in the summer, beginning in May. The ranch is open from April through November but often has winter campers when the weather is mild. Reservations are taken year-round. Be sure to ask about group rates and packages. The ranch is approximately 9.5 miles south of Custer. Credit cards are not accepted.

RESTAURANTS

Here in cattle country prime rib reigns supreme, and you'll find any number of steak houses, restaurants, and cafes that cater to those who relish a hearty slab of beef. Indeed, some of the best steak and prime rib in the world is served right here. And while you won't find the diverse array of exotic cooking you might see in a more metropolitan area, the Black Hills has begun to branch out from the traditional steak house. New ethnic eateries are popping up all the time, and some restaurants now serve dishes for vegetarians (still a dirty word in some small ranching towns).

We've arranged the restaurants in this chapter in five categories—coffee and sandwich shops; American, eclectic, and ethnic cuisines; and sweet treats—with geographic subheadings under each. Some restaurants serve breakfast, lunch, and dinner, and some serve only one or two meals a day; the individual listings will tell you. The write-ups under Sweet Treats direct you to places you'll want to go for snacks and desserts. Most eateries are open seven days a week year-round, and we've noted those that aren't as well as those that extend their hours during the summer—that is, between Memorial Day weekend and Labor Day. If you plan to dine out on a holiday, it's a good idea to call ahead, because some restaurants close to give their owners and employees those special days off.

We've provided general price information with each listing, and unless you see the notation "no credit cards," assume you can pay for your meal with a major card. South Dakota prohibits smoking in any public building unless it possesses a liquor license. Most of the restaurant listings here include information on smoking policies, but if in doubt, follow this rule of thumb: If you can order a beer, you can smoke. Otherwise, you'll have to take it outside.

If you don't see any mention of alcohol in a write-up, none is served in that particular establishment. We've noted which places provide parking; at others you'll need to park curbside or in a public parking lot.

If you didn't believe that the Black Hills were in the West, here's your proof: There isn't a single restaurant here that requires a tie. Even at Jake's, a Kevin Costner–owned establishment on Deadwood's Main Street and arguably the classiest restaurant in the state, blue jeans and a cowboy hat are the standard. Of course, you may feel more comfortable at places like this in a sport coat or dress, but you'll be just as welcome in less-formal attire.

The listings below, while comprehensive, are not exhaustive. Your wanderings will take you near many fine eateries, including well-known chains not listed here because we assume you know them by reputation.

PRICE CODE

Prices are the average cost of dinner (or lunch, for coffee and sandwich shops) for two adults. Drinks, appetizers, dessert, and tip are not included.

$	Less than $12
$$	$12 to $25
$$$	$26 to $40
$$$$	More than $40

COFFEE AND SANDWICH SHOPS

Although these places specialize in breakfast and lunch, some serve dinner or stay open long enough for a late-afternoon or early-evening meal. Be sure to check the other categories for places that serve early in the day; you'll find a couple of

24-hour establishments listed under American Cuisine.

Northern Hills

Common Grounds $
111 East Hudson Street, Spearfish
1301 West Omaha, Rapid City
(605) 642-9066, (605) 721-1878

This gourmet coffee shop offers a full line of espresso drinks (including icy java slushes) and Italian sodas plus muffins, bagels, soups, salads, and wrap sandwiches for the vegetarian and carnivore alike. An eclectic mix of furniture and displays of student and local artwork make this a homey place to relax with a newspaper or good book while you munch and sip, and the rich aroma of bulk coffee you can buy to brew in your own kitchen just adds to the comfortable atmosphere. The cafe serves breakfast and has an all-day deli bar. Hours are 7:00 A.M. to 6:00 P.M. Monday through Friday, 7:00 A.M. to 7:00 P.M. Saturday, and Sunday 7:00 A.M. to 5:00 P.M. Smoking is not permitted. No credit cards are accepted at the Spearfish location only.

Central Hills

B&L Bagels $
512 Main Street, Rapid City
(605) 399-1777

There's nothing quite like a fresh bagel to start the day or provide a pick-me-up at lunch. Bagels are mixed from scratch, then boiled and baked on a stone hearth the old-fashioned way. You'll have around 15 kinds to choose from, and you can order your bagel plain or spread with any of 15 flavors of light (less fat) cream cheese or another topping such as hummus or honey peanut butter. Or order it stuffed with a sandwich filling such as turkey, pastrami, roast beef, veggies, or cream cheese and lox. Soups and fat-free pasta salad round out your meal, but if a snack is all you

need, try a frosted bagel knot or an energy bar. A full espresso bar offers java or tea or a refreshing Italian soda. During the summer, ice cream and smoothies made with fruit and yogurt are available. The shop is open daily for breakfast and lunch. Smoking is prohibited.

The Beanery "Deli & Bakery" $
201 Main Street, Rapid City
(605) 348-6775

The Beanery serves food fast but not fast food. Everything on the menu is made fresh daily, from breads and pies to soups and quiche. The service is cafeteria-style, but the dining area is homey, decked out in cheerful green-and-white check tablecloths, quaint wooden crates, retired milk cans, a comely antique cookstove, and a grand old wooden Hoosier cabinet that once did duty in a North Dakota farm kitchen. The Beanery serves lunch Monday through Saturday, featuring a daily special (often a pasta dish), a meat and a meatless quiche, soups, salads, and both cold and grilled sandwiches. Tuesday is fettucine Alfredo day and Thursday is lasagna day. Beverages include premium bottled sodas and fruit juices, and for dessert there's an assortment of pies, cheesecakes, and cookies. According to the owner, someone once bought one of the cafe's raspberry peach cream-cheese pies, entered it in a contest, and won. Blatant cheating? Certainly. But it speaks well for the Beanery, which is smoke-free and located in the basement of the Creamery Mall on the corner of Main and Second Streets. No credit cards are accepted.

Black Hills Bagels $
913 Mount Rushmore Road, Rapid City
(605) 399-1277

In addition to 37 kinds of bagels, 14 cream cheeses, and a variety of bagel sandwiches, you'll find tasty homemade salads here, including Oriental noodle, Italian, and fresh fruit. Or, if you're in the mood for a snack, a homemade cookie, muffin, or cinnamon bagel knot—the low-fat alternative to doughnuts—could be just the thing. A full espresso bar serves a wide variety of coffees plus Italian sodas and frappé freezes.

The shop is open from 6:00 A.M. to 6:00 P.M. Monday through Friday and 6:00 A.M. to 1:00 P.M. Saturday and Sunday. There is no smoking in the restaurant. Limited parking is available.

Coffee Garden $
303 Main Street, Hill City
(605) 574-9081

Greenery is in season all year, and so are the yummy treats in this delightfully decorated coffee shop. You might sample the hot chocolate, which can only be described as a liquid chocolate bar (it's made with steamed milk, not hot water). The shop also sells bread mixes, pretty teacups and infusers, dainty coffee spoons, locally roasted coffee beans, and biscotti in unusual flavors such as oatmeal cinnamon currant. There's a complete line of espresso beverages and Italian sodas, of course, as well as muffins, cookies, pastries, and bagels. Organic sandwiches and soup provide more substantial fare. The shop is open daily, but hours depend on the season. Smokers are welcome on the outdoor deck.

AMERICAN CUISINE

Listed here you'll find restaurants and cafes that specialize in familiar foods such as steak, hamburgers, chicken, fish, and seafood. Some of these places are plain, some are fancy, but each has a definitive place in its community.

You can buy bagels by the dozen at bagel shops, but be sure to store them properly: in a plastic bag overnight or chilled if you actually have any left for longer than that.

Northern Hills

Big Al's Buffalo Steakhouse $$
658 Main Street, Deadwood
(605) 578-1300

This buckaroo-theme restaurant practically shouts "beef" and moos. The eating establishment at the back of the gaming hall serves prime rib as its special daily from 3:00 to 11:00 P.M. It's open 24 hours, Friday and Saturday, and open until 11:00 P.M. every other day. That's a lot of delicious beef served from the brick barbecue pit. You say you'd rather have breakfast today? Try the bacon and sausage to go with the pancakes and omelets. Or how 'bout the steak, burgers, ribs, or chicken for lunch? And you want a beer or a glass of wine to go with that? Sure thing, partner.

Bob's Family Restaurant $$
1039 Main Street, Sturgis
(605) 720-2930

A barbecue pit and the world-class pork ribs it produces aren't the only special features of Bob's Family Restaurant. It's also home to one of the nation's largest collections of hot sauces, and hundreds of bottles make a striking display. They are enclosed in cabinets as part of a permanent collection. Breakfast is served all day, as well as lunch and dinner. The menu includes such hearty items as skillet breakfasts, hotcakes, omelets, pork chops, chicken-fried steak, grilled chicken, and homemade coconut cream and banana cream pies. On Sunday you can treat yourself to brunch. Bob's is one of the few businesses on Main Street that stays open during the Sturgis Rally & Races.

Regardless of where your booth or table is located, make it a point to view the 1880s photos of Sturgis hanging in the nicely furnished Heritage Room at the back. In the adjoining conference room is a large framed photo of local character Poker Alice, her trademark cigar clenched firmly in her mouth as she deals faro. The photo appeared in the December 3, 1927, edition of the *Saturday Evening Post,* and this print was made from the original negative, then hand tinted. The restaurant itself has been a fixture of the town for a good 50 years or more. New owners took over Bob's in 2003 and did some remodeling, but the atmosphere is the same.

Latchstring Inn Restaurant at Spearfish Canyon Resort $$$
U.S. Highway 14A, Spearfish Canyon
(605) 584-3333
www.spfcanyon.com

Pan-fried trout is the signature menu item at this beautiful log restaurant overlooking Spearfish Creek, and the management was generous enough to share the recipe with us. You'll find it, along with some fascinating background about this historic eatery, in the close-up in this chapter.

We make it a point to stop at the Latchstring for a cold drink on the deck after summer bike rides through Spearfish Canyon, but you don't have to work that hard to enjoy a pleasant, leisurely meal in the restaurant's fabulous surroundings. Here it's equally lovely indoors and out because the dining room is decorated with antiques from the original Latchstring Inn (see the close-up). Look around and you'll see a Stalwart bobsled, a shaggy buffalo hide, dainty dishes, a prim pump organ, and much more. Plaques that accompany many of the displays provide a mini-tour through local history. In the evening, the electric lights are dimmed to enhance the romantic glow of kerosene lamps and candles. Every window offers a dazzling view of the canyon, and a bird book will help you identify the little creatures that frequent the feeder out back.

For breakfast you can order trout, deep fried or pan fried (and with the head removed if you so request), along with eggs and hash browns or eggs and pancakes. Omelets and other items also are available. For lunch, burgers, sandwiches, and salads provide a hearty midday energy boost. Trout makes an encore appearance on the dinner menu, prepared amandine. Walleye, shrimp, rib eye, beef steaks, and chicken prepared in a variety

of ways are other choices. Beer and wine can accompany your meal, which you'll want to polish off properly with crème brûlée, tiramisu, or Chocolate Decadence. Don't worry about the calories, because after you eat you can hike to Spearfish Falls or Roughlock Falls. Both are nearby, so ask for directions. Reservations are recommended for dinner at the Latchstring all year except in the winter. Parking is provided.

Sanford's Grub & Pub $$
545 West Jackson Boulevard, Spearfish
306 Seventh Street, Rapid City
(605) 642-3204, (605) 721-1463, (800) 504-6840

You don't need to be a car buff to appreciate the automotive-repair-shop humor that went into naming the dishes served here (but it helps to know what was popular on TV a couple of decades ago). For instance, a Thermostat is a half-pound burger with jalapeño peppers and mozzarella cheese. Fonz-a-Relli is the name for an Italian-style marinated chicken breast topped with shaved ham and mozzarella. Then there's the Dip Stick, a sliced roast beef sandwich au jus on a sourdough roll. The number of choices on the menu is mind-boggling! In addition to burgers and sandwiches, you'll find appetizers (Tune Ups), homemade soups, Cajun food, pasta dishes, salads, steaks, shrimp, chicken, fajitas, meatless items, and rich desserts. And that's just the food—Sanford's has some 110-plus varieties of beer, most bottled but many on tap. You can also top off your tank with wine, wine-based cocktails, alcohol, and ice-cream drinks (they have a full bar). Sanford's has smoking and nonsmoking sections. Getting to the Spearfish location is a little confusing, though—turn where you see the Sanford's sign on Jackson Boulevard and look for the corrugated-metal building tucked away in the alley. You'll pass it on your left on your way to the parking lot, which is clearly marked. Rapid City's location is easy to find—just look for the big warehouse and sign on Omaha Street. Sanford's is open from 11:00

CLOSE-UP

Black Hills Trout

Imagine a weary 1876 prospector laying down his tools at the end of another fruitless day, eyeing the sparkling stream that refused to make him wealthy, and reckoning that if he couldn't have a gold pan full of riches he'd just as soon have a frying pan full of fat, fresh trout. Unlike today's vacationer though, that unhappy fortune seeker would have considered himself doubly unfortunate, because as recently as the Black Hills gold rush (see the History chapter), there were no trout in Black Hills streams. It wasn't until the 1880s that enterprising pioneers brought sloshing wagonloads of trout to this area, and, luckily for anglers ever since, the slippery swimmers took to the habitat like. . .well, like fish to water.

Anglers have come to the Black Hills in search of rainbows, browns, and brookies for more than a century now, and one of their favorite fishing spots has always been Spearfish Canyon. From the late 1800s until the 1930s, when a flood washed out the tracks, they would ride the Chicago, Burlington & Quincy Railroad to the canyon, fish all day, and take the train back to wherever they were staying. Or they might stay several days at Savoy, a bend in the canyon road between Spearfish and Cheyenne Crossing, where an inn has operated since the early 20th century. At first it was called Glendoris Lodge, but in 1919 it became the Latchstring Inn, a cluster of rustic cabins and a restaurant that started as a lumber company office in 1892 and was added onto. For decades, cooks at the inn happily fried up trout caught in nearby streams by proud, hungry anglers.

But by 1989 the beloved Latchstring had aged beyond repair, and the owner, Judy Woodworth, sold it to Homestake Mining Company. Homestake razed the old buildings and put up a beautiful log structure that houses the new Latchstring Inn Restaurant at Spearfish Canyon Resort. In the restaurant are many

A.M. to 10:00 P.M. every day, all year. See the Nightlife chapter for more.

The Stadium Sports Grill $$
818 Fifth Avenue, Belle Fourche
744 Main Street, Spearfish
(605) 723-9521, (605) 642-9521
www.stadiumsportsgrill.net
With menu items such as Huddle Up Sandwiches, what sports fan wouldn't want to eat here? The Stadium in Belle Fourche has lots of advantages for game buffs, too, as you'll see in the Nightlife chapter. But it's also won renown for its Rancher tenderloin tips, a specialty acquired from the once-famous (but now defunct) Rancher Bar and Lounge formerly in the nearby hamlet of St. Onge. The restaurant, once known as Prime Time, was dubbed one of the nation's top 10 places to eat and its tenderloin tips called one of the unique meals in the United States. However, you can also order 16-ounce steaks; steamed, grilled, or breaded fish and seafood; homemade soup; lemon-pepper chicken; salads and

antiques from the old Latchstring Inn, but another precious relic has been preserved as well: a simple recipe for pan-fried trout that dates back so far that no one, not even Woodworth, knows when it was first used in the Latchstring kitchen. Pan-fried trout is reported to be the most popular item on the menu even today, and the management graciously shared the recipe with us. The measurements are imprecise, but that only adds to its charm.

Latchstring Inn Pan-Fried Trout

Bread crumbs
Italian seasoning to taste
A dash of paprika
A pinch each of parsley and
 rosemary
A touch of thyme
A sprinkle of sage
Seasoning salt and black pepper
 to taste
Flour
Egg
Vegetable oil

Combine bread crumbs and seasonings. Filet the trout open. Dip in flour, then in beaten egg, then in seasoned crumbs. Pan fry in vegetable oil until the eyes turn white and pop out of the sockets. Serve at once and enjoy—but watch for bones!

(In case you're wondering whether the Latchstring Inn Restaurant serves trout caught from Spearfish Creek, which runs behind the restaurant, the answer is no. The entree on your plate came from a nearby trout farm.)

other tasty lunch and dinner items; plus Oreo fried ice cream to top it off. Hand-cut meats, generous portions, and a full bar are hallmarks of the Stadium Sports Grill, and you'll enjoy the pub's atmosphere (take note of the hand-built oak bar) minus cigarette fumes, thanks to a state-of-the-art smoke-extraction system that lets smokers and nonsmokers share space comfortably. A Sunday breakfast buffet is offered. There's plenty of seating, so you won't need reservations unless you're in a party of 15 or more. In any

case, it should be easy to find a space in the Belle Fourche parking lot.

The Stadium in Spearfish serves up just the kind of food you want to accompany your favorite game. Choose shrimp, raw veggies, onion rings, nachos, hot wings, burgers, sandwiches, salads, Indian tacos, steaks, chili, and more from the tabloid-size, newsprint menu, then read the sports pages while you wait for your lunch or dinner. The Stadium in Spearfish has a full-service bar as well as nonalcoholic beverages to go with your food.

Stampmill Restaurant & Saloon $$-$$$
305 West Main Street, Lead
(605) 584-1984

Back in gold-rush days, the local stamp mills kept up a steady pounding, pulverizing ore so the gold could be extracted. This restaurant in the heart of Black Hills gold-mining country pays tribute to the industry that created and has sustained the city of Lead for more than a century. Fittingly, then, the Stampmill occupies an 1897 sandstone structure that is one of the oldest buildings in town.

Beautifully renovated by a previous owner, it features a brick-and-wood interior with high ceilings and a gas fireplace to warm those snowy winter nights in the Northern Hills. Lunch items, named for some of the old stamp mills, are mainly burgers and sandwiches on homemade buns. For dinner, steaks cut from lean North Dakota beef plus shrimp and chicken dishes bear the names of former mining claims that became part of Homestake Mining Company's open cut. A full bar and dessert of the day, generally cheesecake or pie, add the finishing touches to your meal. Be sure to take a look at the old mining photos on the wall while you're waiting to be served.

Valley Café $
608 Main Street, Spearfish
(605) 642-2423

The Valley Café has been a Spearfish fixture since before 1921. The cafe's reputation rests largely on its hot beef sandwiches, chicken-fried steaks, and breakfasts. A breakfast buffet is served daily during the summer and on Saturday and Sunday the rest of the year. The regular menu ranges from old standbys such as omelets and waffles to liver with bacon, onions, and gravy. Desserts include pies (ask which ones are homemade) and old-fashioned ice-cream treats such as malts, sundaes, and banana splits. You can order a beer to go with your meal and choose to sit in either the smoking or nonsmoking section.

Central Hills

Art's Southern Style Smoke House Barbecue $$
1012 East North Street, Rapid City
(605) 348-5499

A mecca for barbecue devotees, Art's serves up a feast for the senses as well as tantalizing, down-home southern food. The rich scent of Artis and Marilyn Holmses' homemade barbecue sauce combined with their choice of music—all blues, all the time—will surely satisfy your hunger for atmosphere. ("Blues and barbecue, they kind of go together," Marilyn says. She ought to know—she and Artis are both from the Deep South.) There's a lunch buffet daily that features meats swimming in barbecue sauce, but you can order from the menu too—pulled pork (shredded pork shoulder that's smoked until it falls apart, then smothered with sauce); zesty, Cajun-style red beans and rice; collard greens seasoned with smoked ham hocks; sweet corn-bread muffins; barbecued ribs and chicken; and homemade peach cobbler. You can also order meats in bulk to feed a crowd and a beer or wine cooler to wash down all that tasty sauce. A dinner buffet is offered every night. After placing your order, take a look at the posters on the walls—they're stunning black-and-white portraits of blues greats including Billie Holiday and a youthful B. B. King at age 16. Art's serves lunch and dinner Monday through Saturday; closed Sunday. Smoking is not allowed.

Chute Roosters $$
101 Chute Rooster Drive, Hill City
(605) 574-2122

Occupying an old dairy barn, Chute Roosters has plenty of country charm and friendly service. Horseshoe sculpture, a rope twister, a tapestry sidesaddle, and other antiques along the same theme decorate the stone-and-board walls, making this a cross between casual and fancy. That means you'll fit in whether attired in blue jeans or your Sunday best. That even goes for Sunday brunch (summer only), which features a huge buffet in the main dining room. Breakfast and lunch are served in the summer. The nightly dinner offerings consist mostly of steaks, burgers, prime rib, pasta, seafood, and chicken, as well as a soup and salad bar. In the homey lounge you'll find a full bar serving cocktails, beer, and wine (see the Nightlife chapter). Smoking is permitted except in the Shebang Room, where a large mirrored back bar is the visual centerpiece. Chute Roosters, on the north end of Hill City, has plenty of parking. It is usually closed after Christmas until mid-February.

Elk Creek Steakhouse & Lounge $$-$$$
Interstate 90 and Elk Creek Road
Piedmont
(605) 787-6349
Western garb fits right in at this popular restaurant, and you'll see many customers enter the ranch-style building in their best hats and boots. Steaks and seafood are the main menu items, but the kitchen also cooks up such varied dishes as chicken Kiev and liver with onions and bacon. Steak sandwiches are a favorite here and are a bit less expensive than a full dinner. Don't overlook the buffalo rib eye and New York steaks, though, for a genuine taste of the Old West. The lounge has a full bar where you can order your beverage of choice. Elk Creek opens nightly for dinner, and reservations are recommended on weekends. The lounge opens at 1:00 P.M. on Sunday and will serve food. Take I-90 exit 46 and you'll be there.

Firehouse Brewing Company $$
610 Main Street, Rapid City
(605) 348-1915
South Dakota's first brewpub isn't just about beer, although the 15 varieties made here (only a few available at a time) provide many reasons to visit the Firehouse. (See Nightlife.) This is also an excellent place to stop if you're looking for a hearty, appetizing meal in memorable surroundings. As the name and

phone number suggest, the restaurant occupies Rapid City's historic 1915 fire station, which is listed in the National Register of Historic Places. Firefighting equipment of yore is suspended near the high ceiling, and garage doors are still in place in the front of the building. There's seating for diners downstairs near the rectangular bar, but nonsmokers will want to climb the stairs to the mezzanine, where the brewing vats are on display behind giant windows.

The menu changes with the season, but the food is always filling and plentiful. Popular dishes include the Reuben sandwich and Brewer's Burger. When you're in the mood for just a beer or cocktail and a snack, you'll find Fire Fightin' Nachos (jalapeños optional) among the tasty appetizers. Or you might find that Gorgonzola ale soup, made with the pub's Wilderness Wheat brew, hits the spot. Be sure to sample the freshly baked beer bread, too, and maybe order a loaf (with 24-hour notice) to take home. And yes, you can buy beer by the half gallon. The Firehouse is open for lunch and dinner Monday through Saturday. On Sunday, when it is open for dinner only, kids 12 and younger (one per family) eat for free.

The Fireside Inn Restaurant
and Lounge $$$
23021 Hisega Road, Hisega
(605) 342-3900
The inn takes its name from the 8-foot-square stone fireplace in the middle of the dining room, but it's not atmosphere alone that has made the Fireside a hit. The menu begins with a two-page wine list and progresses from there to some 50 or so dinner entrees. Prime rib is the house specialty, but beef, seafood, veal, pork, chicken, and pasta find their way into all manner of elegant dishes, such as Cajun rib eye, salmon en croute, chicken Wellington with tarragon cream sauce, crab-stuffed chicken, and stuffed pork tenderloin. Two salads are on the menu; so are two vegetarian pasta dishes, and the kitchen can prepare other meatless

entrees upon request. On Wednesday evening cuts of prime rib are offered for a reduced price. Quality is prized here, which is why all steaks are hand cut and why the sauté chef prepares sauces individually for each order. The full bar will fill your drink orders, and if you really must have dessert after all that good food, you'll find Chocolate Suicide and other cheesecakes at your disposal.

The Fireside serves dinner daily from 5:00 to 9:00 P.M. in the smoke-free dining room. The inn permits smoking in the lounge and provides parking for its clientele. Reservations are recommended for parties of six or more. The restaurant is 6 miles west of Rapid City on Highway 44.

The Gas Light $$$
13490 Main Street, Rockerville
(605) 343-9276

Rockerville was once a bustling gold camp. Thousands of miners settled in this section of ponderosa forest south of Rapid City, enough to warrant the construction of a flume to carry water from Spring Creek more than 20 miles away. Over time the gold ran out, the flume rotted, and nearly everyone left. The town tried to reorganize in the 1950s as a tourist attraction, hoping to catch visitors on their way to Mount Rushmore, but it seemed that Rockerville was destined to become a ghost town. It almost is, save for the Gas Light. Decorated in Old West memorabilia and antiques, this spacious restaurant is popular with groups and parties who like the meeting rooms in the back and with hungry travelers on their way to the Central Hills.

You could start with a cocktail, beer, or glass of wine at the bar, taking care to admire the century-old back bar from the former Harney Hotel in Rapid City. For an appetizer, you might try saloon-style nachos made with buffalo strips, then choose either a salad (chicken Waldorf for lunch, perhaps) or something more substantial. The lunch menu includes sandwiches and buffalo burgers, and dinner offers many choices in chicken, pasta,

seafood, and steaks. A special list of "old-world delights" such as Black Angus bourbon strip and chicken Oscar includes recommendations for the appropriate bottle of fine wine. The Gas Light is open daily for lunch and dinner as well as Sunday brunch between Memorial Day and Labor Day weekends. During the winter, dinner is served all week, but there is no lunch. The Gas Light is 12 miles south of Rapid City via U.S. Highway 16. Reservations are recommended, and parking is plentiful.

Holy Smoke Restaurant & Lounge $$
U.S. Highway 16A, Keystone
(605) 666-4616

The proprietors vow you won't find a deep-fat fryer or a can opener here, but we'll get to the food in just a minute. First we want to rave about the restaurant itself, which is an authentic log cabin with a southwestern flair. The dining room features an adobe fireplace, a knotty-pine floor, and a center post that was cut and peeled right on the property. Mexican furniture and a beehive-shape stucco-and-lath fireplace invite you to enjoy a cocktail in the comfortable lounge. And who could resist the opportunity to dine alfresco on the deck on a warm summer evening? Back in the kitchen, hand-cut steaks, barbecued ribs, and homemade jellies and desserts are the Holy Smoke's culinary hallmarks. Chicken dishes and Mexican specialties are available, too. Smoking is allowed everywhere but in the dining room, and reservations are accepted for parties of six or more. The restaurant serves breakfast, lunch, and dinner daily from May 1 through September 30. It is 1.25 miles north of Keystone.

Horse Creek Inn $$$-$$$$
23570 U.S. Highway 385, Rapid City
(605) 574-2908

If the topic were real estate, Horse Creek Inn would meet all three criteria: location, location, location. Not only is this quaint mid-20th-century cabin just a short drive from all the fun at Sheridan Lake, but it has a horse pasture out back where you're likely to see deer and coyotes. Formerly known as Old Wheel Inn, the pine-interior restaurant and lounge has retained its rustic ambience and simple furnishings, making it a delightful place to enjoy some fine food. Beef—top sirloin and filets—is the most popular item here, but chicken, seafood, pork chops, and a couple of vegetarian dishes (fettuccine primavera and Oriental stir-fry) are available as well. You'll see them all listed on the hand-drawn and -lettered menus that are framed and propped up on easels in the dining room. Steaks are hand cut and can be ordered with Cajun spices, and you can request a hamburger or appetizer to eat in the lounge, where there's a full-service bar.

During the summer you can take your drink or sandwich out to the deck, although you won't actually be served there. Nightly specials are offered, and the soups, salads, and desserts (such as mud pie and German chocolate cake) are made on the premises. The inn is open daily for lunch and dinner from May through September, for lunch Saturday and Sunday all year, and for dinner Monday through Sunday the rest of the year. Reservations are recommended on weekends. The restaurant is nonsmoking, but you can smoke in the lounge. The inn, with its own parking lot, is one-quarter-mile north of Sheridan Lake Road on U.S. 385, 18 miles west of Rapid City and 7 miles north of Hill City.

Powder House $$
U.S. Highway 16A, Keystone
(605) 666-4646
www.powderhouselodge.com
www.custerresorts.com
You'll do more than dine at this well-known eatery—you'll be transported back to the time when a real powder house stored explosives for local mines. Built at the site of the original (the area was called Crossville then), the Powder House dishes up old-time Black Hills atmosphere in a log cabin furnished with pine-board tables and a working fireplace. The menu

offers traditional western fare such as steaks and buffalo stew but appeals to other palates as well. You can get an assortment of chicken and fish entrees, fettuccine primavera topped with feta cheese, or even a veggie burger. Full bar service provides you with the cocktail, beer, or wine of your choice. For dessert, there's Bourbon Street bread pudding accompanied by a cup of freshly ground coffee. The Powder House, which is a mile north of town, is open for breakfast (trout and eggs, anyone?), lunch, and dinner, seven days a week from mid-May until September 30. Reservations are recommended for dinner during the summer. Smoking is not permitted in the dining room. Parking is provided.

Shooters Restaurant & Sports Bar $$
2424 West Main Street, Rapid City
(605) 348-3348
Warning: Parental permission is required for the hottest of Shooters' famous hot wings. The menu even says so. You're allowed to order spicy chicken wings mild, hot, or thermonuclear on your own, but you need a note from your mother to go all the way to extreme. Not to worry, though, because Shooters has plenty of other menu offerings, from appetizers, soups, and salads to wrap sandwiches, burgers, steaks, ribs, chicken, southwestern fare, pasta, and stir-fries. You can also choose from a large selection of beers, cocktails, premium wines, and single-malt scotches from the full bar. Desserts include homemade cheesecake and peanut butter pie. What's more, four satellites bring the wide world of sports to Shooters' TV sets. The clientele includes people of all ages, from 8 to 80, according

to the manager, and you can find a table for up to 12 or 15. Shooters accommodates both smokers and nonsmokers and provides ample parking.

The Windmill Restaurant $$
2803 Deadwood Avenue, Rapid City
(605) 342-9456

If you're a fan of truck-stop food, this is your kind of place. And it's open 24 hours a day, ready to get your order from the kitchen to the table in five minutes no matter what time hunger strikes. Breakfast is available around the clock, and the truckers' specials (various meat and egg combinations) come with a choice of toast, biscuits, or cake. You'll also find satisfying hot and cold sandwiches, burgers, fried foods, Indian tacos, John's homemade meat loaf, barbecued ribs, a soup and salad bar, and ice-cream treats on the menu. If you like, try the Friday and Saturday evening buffet or the Saturday and Sunday breakfast buffet. Beer and wine are available, and both smokers and nonsmokers will find a comfortable place to sit. As you can imagine, there's plenty of parking. Take I-90 exit 55 and you can't miss this place—just look for the big windmill.

Southern Hills

Blue Bell Lodge and Resort $$
Custer State Park
Highway 87, Custer
(605) 255-4531
www.custerresorts.com

The last guy to criticize the bartender here is still hanging in the resort's Buffalo Wallow Lounge. However, we feel safe saying you won't find much to criticize at Blue Bell, either in the saloon-style lounge (with a full bar) or the family-style Tatanka Dining Room. Tatanka means "buffalo" in Lakota, so expect to find plenty of menu items based on that wild game, from steak to meat loaf. In fact, the smell of buffalo leather emanating from the cushy lobby furnishings greets you the minute you

enter. You'll also find trout, walleye, and other entrees, but no matter what you order, everything comes to the table in big bowls so you can serve yourself, just like at home. You'll have to refrain from smoking.

The Blue Bell complex (see the Accommodations chapter for lodging information) on the west side of Custer State Park takes its name from the Bell Telephone symbol, honoring the phone company executive who built Blue Bell in the 1920s. This is also the departure point for Blue Bell's chuckwagon cookouts, which you can read about in the Attractions chapter. You can park for the restaurant right outside.

Pheasant Dining Room $$$
State Game Lodge
Custer State Park
U.S. Highway 16A, Custer
(605) 255-4541
www.custerresorts.com

Welcome to the dining room of American presidents. Both Calvin Coolidge and Dwight Eisenhower took meals in the State Game Lodge's Pheasant Dining Room during their presidencies. In fact, the table in the northwest corner is still referred to as the Eisenhower table, the one where Ike could sit and see all his guests. Just as you'd expect, game is the specialty here, so buffalo, venison, and the South Dakota state bird, pheasant, figure prominently on the menu. You might begin your meal with pheasant sauté or buffalo ribs, then progress to filet of venison sautéed with garlic and topped with mushrooms on wild rice. Or perhaps you'd be interested in marinated, sautéed ring-necked pheasant breast topped with plum brandy sauce. If fish is your game, you might prefer a flavorful walleye pike or rainbow trout. Lunch features a deli-style sandwich buffet, buffalo stew, elk burgers, and other items. Chocolate Thunder—fresh brownies layered with vanilla ice cream and hot fudge—is a fitting dessert tribute to the thundering herd of buffalo for which Custer State Park is famous.

The dining room is on the lodge's second level, but downstairs you'll find a lounge with a bar and a welcoming fireplace. Be sure to take note of the lodge's blueprints on the wall as you descend the stairs to the lower-level gift shop. Reservations are recommended for dinner in the smoke-free game lodge, which is open from Mother's Day until early October. Parking is available at the lodge in the northeastern quadrant of the park.

ECLECTIC CUISINE

The restaurants listed here serve dishes that cross many culinary borders. They often have a good selection of vegetarian offerings, and in fact, you'll see that we've even included a vegan eatery. But extraordinary meat dishes are on many of these menus, too.

Northern Hills

The Bay Leaf Café **$$**
126 West Hudson Street, Spearfish
(605) 642-5462
The menu describes the cafe's rosemary linguine this way: "Oh sigh. Oh heavy sigh." We suspect a few sighs of delight will have escaped your lips even before you see the menu, though, because the Bay Leaf itself is a collection of lovely architectural features. Right off you'll notice the beveled, stained-glass window in the front door and the ceramic tile floor. Regional artists' works hang on the walls.

Entrees run the gamut from trout amandine, elk, and buffalo rib eye to tempeh with sautéed vegetables and Cajun-style Bourbon Street pasta, plus ever-changing daily specials. Beer and wine are available, and after your meal an espresso drink, Italian soda, or herbal tea goes well with the rich, chocolaty homemade desserts. The food here is completely MSG free and largely preservative free as well. And in keeping with the emphasis on health, smoking is not permitted. The Bay

Leaf serves lunch and dinner daily during the summer, and because that's an especially busy time of year, it's a good idea to call ahead and ask whether reservations are needed. The cafe is closed on Sunday from early October until Memorial Day weekend.

Deadwood Thymes Café
& Bistro **$$$–$$$$**
87 Sherman Street
(605) 578-7566
www.deadwoodthymes.com
Set among a row of brick office buildings about 2 blocks from the busy tourist traffic on Deadwood's Main Street, the Deadwood Thymes is modest and unassuming. Unless you talk to the locals (who dine here regularly), you probably won't find it advertised anywhere, and a small wooden sign above the lonely brick facade is the only indicator of what lies inside. Even the interior—a remodeled funeral parlor—is relatively plain, accented only with some Old World–themed paintings and wrought-iron chairs and tables.

Despite the plain appearances, this is easily one of the best restaurants in Deadwood. Owner Mike Chaput and his talented culinary staff create a constantly changing array of European-inspired dishes for breakfast, lunch, and dinner. Brioche French toast, smoked salmon quiche, Thai burrito with peanut sauce, roast beef on rye with cream cheese horseradish and alfalfa sprouts, pecan encrusted shrimp and lobster cakes, breast of duck with orange sauce and forbidden rice, and pork prime rib with raspberry jalapeño salsa have all appeared on past menus. It is especially noteworthy that everything—from granola and doughnuts to salad dressings and the parsley gin sauce that accompanies the lamb chops—is homemade in the bistro's kitchen.

The Deadwood Thymes is open Tuesday through Saturday for breakfast and lunch, but dinner is available only on Thursday, Friday, and Saturday evenings. Brunch on Sunday gives you the option of sampling a full range of the bistro's signature dishes.

Jakes $$$$
677 Main Street, Deadwood
(605) 578-3656, (800) 999-6482
www.themidnightstar.com

You just can't help feeling glamorous when you dine at Jakes, located on the top floor of the Midnight Star casino. Although you're not likely to rub elbows with the glitterati here (but it's not impossible, either), just knowing this splendid restaurant was created by Hollywood celebrity Kevin Costner and his brother, Dan, lends panache to the evening. Jakes opens each night for dinner on the top floor of the 1879 Phoenix Building, Deadwood's first brick structure—and the only building in town that had a three-story privy out back (demolished in the 1940s). The Deadwood City Council held its first meeting in this space in 1881, but it's doubtful the early-day city leaders had as much fun as you will in this lofty chamber of cherry, mahogany, and double-lead crystal. (The original third floor was torn off several decades ago because of damage from a leaky roof, but the Costners' replacement is architecturally faithful.) With its tall windows and domed skylight, this is an exciting place to be during a summer thunderstorm, but you don't need a taste for thrills to appreciate the amenities. A propensity for stellar cuisine will do you just fine, because there's plenty of that at Jakes.

Begin with a tasty appetizer such as escargot, roasted portobello mushrooms, buffalo carpaccio, shredded pheasant quesadillas, or duck satay. After your salad, let the sorbet intermezzo, served on a lemon leaf, cleanse your palate for full enjoyment of an entree, such as sautéed walleye, honey-glazed shrimp, grilled pork tenderloins with cinnamon plum sauce, steak fillets, or Cajun seafood tortellini. These are just a few of the selections from the menu, which varies a bit every few months. What remains constant is the elegance of the food, including handmade desserts, such as macadamia white-chocolate cheesecake. The luxury of two fireplaces, a full bar, and live piano music Tuesday through Saturday are the final exquisite touches. Because this is a popular place, reservations are recommended. Jakes is open daily for dinner.

The Midnight Star has a sports bar, Diamond Lil's, which serves lighter fare, and you'll find it listed in the Nightlife chapter.

Seven Grill $$$
447 North Main Street, Spearfish
(605) 717-5701

The Seven Grill is actually two different eateries in one—a soup shack and a steak house. The soup is homemade, as is just about everything on the menu, including the salad dressing. Try starting your meal with creamy potato or southwest chicken artichoke soup, and top your salad with creamy dill or Italian vinaigrette dressing. The soup is served with warm, fresh-baked bread, usually made with wholesome grains or herbs and sun-dried tomatoes. The entrees are just as unique. The owner, Nic, describes the cuisine as distinctive to South Dakota—in other words, big, fresh, tasty meals. He uses steak and fish from the Black Hills and adds his own creativity to the dishes. Nic's signature rum-cured salmon is absolutely delicious. Of course, Seven Grill also serves prime steaks such as rib eye and tenderloin. It offers nightly specials, including the popular Friday night sushi.

The Seven Grill underwent remodeling in 2004 to expand the bar. It received a full liquor license, allowing it to add martinis and quality scotches to the usual beer and wine lineup. The Seven Grill is fast becoming a local favorite, especially among the younger college crowd in Spearfish. The interior is warm and inviting, with a wooden bar and tables and a large stone fireplace. The outside patio has a fire pit, and it is covered in cold weather for those who still wish to dine outside. Local artwork decorates the walls, and regional musicians are frequently invited to play and entertain the crowd. It's open year-round for lunch and dinner until 11:00 P.M., but the bar will most likely stay open until the crowd tapers.

Central Hills

Alpine Inn $$
225 Main Street, Hill City
(605) 574-2749

For dinner you have your choice of filet mignon or filet mignon—that is, you may order the six-ounce filet or the nine-ounce, depending on the size of your appetite. For such a small menu, this restaurant in the 1886 quarters of the former Harney Peak Hotel has a big reputation and a loyal clientele. Those who want more variety wait for dessert, when there are some 30 selections, including homemade apple cheese strudel and bread pudding. Or they come here for lunch, which features a good choice of sandwiches served with sides such as Swabian German potato salad. Hearty bratwurst and schnitzel are on the menu, but so is more delicate fare such as a turkey croissant Parisienne and a cheese board. Beer, wine, and lattes are among the beverages served. Reservations are not accepted, but if your party has eight or more people, call ahead and the staff will do its best to make space available for you. The inn is closed on Sunday. When it's nice out you can eat on the veranda for lunch (assuming there's a free table!), but if you eat indoors be sure to note the hotel's original wooden banister on the staircase and the sturdy old safe beneath the cash register. Credit cards are not accepted.

Enigma $$$$
445 Mount Rushmore Road, Rapid City
(605) 348-8300

Sitting in a quiet corner of Enigma, it would not be difficult to imagine yourself dining on the banks of the Seine or sipping cocktails off Broadway after a show. This small, unobtrusive restaurant is incredibly intimate, with a quiet atmosphere and contemporary cuisine found only in metropolises 10 or 20 times the size of Rapid City. Located off the lobby of the downtown Radisson Hotel, Enigma has fewer than 20 tables; most of them are booths with a distinctive cozy, private feel. All the same, the dining room maintains a warm and open ambience, due in part to the large pieces of continental artwork hanging on the walls and soft lighting from candle sconces. More striking light comes from the blue neon sign on the far end of the restaurant, proudly reminding patrons that Enigma has one of the only martini bars in the five-state region. This is the domain of restaurant manager Jamel Safir, an ethnic Moroccan who was trained in France and ran nightclubs in Germany for a number of years. He keeps a well-stocked bar complete with European and North African liqueurs; if you're feeling adventurous, ask for *bombas*.

The kitchen is run by Chef Janati, a childhood friend of Jamel classically trained in France; Chef Gunter, trained by the Master Chefs of Austria; and Chef Scott, a South Dakotan specializing in northern Italian cuisine. Items on the menu vary with some regularity but can range from a simple Greek salad and filet mignon to more elegant tortellini a la Provençale with beef, peppers, and garlic sauce and saltimbocca a la Romana, with prosciutto ham, pasta, vegetables, and a sage cream sauce. Traditional European desserts include crème brûlée and fruit tarts. The wine list is impressive, but don't be afraid to opt for the fine quality house red or white. Also on the menu is the Mystery Dinner, a four-course, two-hour affair that lets you hand over the creative fate of your meal to the chefs.

Rushmore Supper Club
& Lounge $$-$$$
253 Swanzey Street, Keystone
(605) 666-4501

This popular restaurant, formerly called the Historical Rushmore Grill & Bar, is a block and a half east of the Strip (Winter Street, the town's main drag) in Keystone,

---

If you see Rocky Mountain oysters on a restaurant menu and wonder what they are—well, ask your waitstaff. All we'll tell you is that they're not seafood.

---

but its reputation for authentic, made-from-scratch Mexican food draws hungry crowds in search of the cook's famous fajitas and other specialties served in heaping portions for lunch and dinner. Cajun blackened prime rib is on the menu, and so are half-pound buffalo and beef burgers, steaks, Cajun chicken sandwiches, and shrimp and taco salads, to name a few of the choices. A So-Sweet Burrito filled with apple and pineapple pie filling, deep fried and garnished with ice cream, three toppings, whipped cream, and a cherry is a special-request-only dessert that could pose as a meal in itself. The bar—note the ornate, century-old back bar from a long-ago Custer watering hole—serves highly regarded margaritas frozen, blended, or on the rocks, as well as beer, wine, and other cocktails. After many years of operation, the restaurant moved into larger quarters and added a sports bar in the basement. There's also a covered deck for outdoor dining. During the summer when it's busy, reservations are recommended for parties of seven or more.

Tiffany Grille $$$
505 North Fifth Street, Rapid City
(605) 348-4000
This elegant restaurant, lushly decorated with live greenery, is in the spacious atrium lobby of the Rushmore Plaza Holiday Inn. The serving day begins with traditional breakfasts accompanied by a cappuccino cart on weekdays; on Sunday the brunch buffet features a pastry bar and made-to-order omelets. At midday you can order a lunch of a turkey club on a spinach wrapper; a Reuben, chef, or Caesar chicken salad; vegetarian wrap; or something equally delicious. Dinnertime is when the kitchen pulls out all the stops, however. Tempting dishes include rib eye, fillets of beef, Key West chicken breast with a blend of Caribbean spices and pineapple salsa, almond walleye, pork medallions, herb-crusted orange roughy filet, or roasted-vegetable lasagna. While you're waiting for your order, you might ready your palate

with crab-stuffed mushrooms with Mornay sauce. All of the breads are tasty, as are the pies you'll see grouped with Chocolate Obsession Cake and other rich offerings on the dessert tray. Tiffany Grille has a full bar, both smoking and nonsmoking areas, and plenty of parking. Groups of 10 or more should make a reservation.

Southern Hills

Lakota Dining Room $$$-$$$$
Sylvan Lake
Custer State Park Resort, Highway 87
Custer
(605) 574-2561
www.custerresorts.com
The first hotel on Sylvan Lake was built in 1895, just six years after the lake itself. Unfortunately, a fire destroyed the popular Victorian-style inn in 1935, but its replacement opened just two years later. Today stone-columned Sylvan Lake Resort hosts Custer State Park's most elegant restaurant, the Lakota Dining Room. Dinner specials the night we stopped in included bacon-wrapped elk tenderloin, sautéed calamari with red chili pasta, and grilled orange roughy with creamed crab. Beef fajitas with guacamole, buffalo steak, grilled Black Hills trout, and South Dakota ring-necked pheasant also were on the menu. On this same late-summer evening diners were relaxing on the stone veranda that overlooks the quiet lake, chatting and sipping cocktails from the bar. The resort, which is in the northwestern corner of the park, serves breakfast, lunch, and dinner daily from mid-May until late September. Smoking is prohibited as it is in all state-owned buildings. Parking is provided.

ETHNIC CUISINE

Here, we've grouped Asian, German, Italian, and Mexican restaurants to help you satisfy your craving for food from a particular part of the world. Be sure to check the Eclectic Cuisine section above as well, because many of those places serve ethnic dishes.

Northern Hills

Chinatown Cafe $$
649 Main Street, Deadwood
(605) 578-7778
www.heartofdeadwood.com

Chinese immigrants played an important role in early-day Deadwood, and this restaurant honors their contribution to local history. Your order is prepared individually from fresh ingredients and seasoned to your taste while you sip tea or a beer or wine-based cocktail from the bar. Lunch and dinner feature many standard Chinese favorites, from egg rolls and wonton soup to chop suey, chow mein, fried rice, and sweet-and-sour chicken, shrimp, or pork. However, you'll find plenty of more complex dishes such as Szechuan beef, walnut shrimp, orange-flavored chicken, and two kinds of *war ba* served on sizzling platters. Daily luncheon specials offer a choice of sweet-and-sour pork or another dish. Although you'll probably be focused on your meal, take a moment to notice the graceful Chinese lanterns and unusual circular seating arrangement. Chinatown accommodates nonsmokers as much as possible, so be sure to state your preference. The restaurant is on the second floor of Miss Kitty's gaming hall.

Deadwood Social Club $$$
657 Main Street, Deadwood
(605) 578-1533, (605) 578-3346
www.saloon10.com/

Nestled atop the internationally famous Old Style Saloon No. 10, the Deadwood Social Club offers an astonishing wine selection and outstanding service in addition to excellent food. The kitchen specializes in northern Italian cuisine with selections that feature appetizing chicken, seafood, and meatless dishes, all made from scratch with fresh ingredients. While you peruse the menu, your server will bring you a basket of fragrantly irresistible herb focaccia and, if you wish, a beverage from the full bar. The Social Club has one of the most complete wine lists in South Dakota. The restaurant, with its high-backed wooden booths and charmingly eclectic ambience, has established a reputation for heavenly cheesecakes, which are made on the premises. You won't merely eat, you'll bask in your lunch or dinner experience. When winter is full-blown, the Social Club closes on Sunday. Reservations are recommended.

Guadalajara Mexican Restaurant $$
U.S. Highway 14, Spearfish
(605) 642-4765

The Rodriguez family, owners of all Guadalajara restaurants in South Dakota, has brought a little piece of Old Mexico with them to the small college town of Spearfish. Dagoberto (Dago for short) played soccer for several teams in Mexico before he and his wife, Claudia, made the move from (you guessed it) Guadalajara, Mexico, to the states. They run the restaurant in Spearfish with the help of several other family members, including their two children, who pitch in occasionally. But everyone is family at Guadalajara, and the staff goes out of its way to make you feel welcome. You'll catch Dago making the rounds, shaking hands, and he'll speak Spanish with you if you'd like him to.

Great service is not the only noteworthy feature here—the food is as authentically Mexican as the family who makes it. Everything is made from scratch, from the chips and salsa all the way to the fried ice cream and sopaipillas. You'll find all the traditional Mexican favorites, but the chimichangas are a local favorite. The sauces add flair to any dish; the Rodriguezes make their own red, green, and mole (pronounced *mow-lay*) sauces, but there is also the delicious red ranchero sauce and other concoctions they refer to as "special" sauces. Portions are large, food is served piping hot, and a full bar can provide you with all the best Mexican drinks (be sure to try the margarita). Lunch is always a good deal at Guadalajara, but there are dinner specials every night and a kid's meal for 99 cents on Sunday.

The experience doesn't end there—Guadalajara's decor reflects the old country. Everything is brightly colored, artwork and crafts all come from a small market town back home, and chairs and booths are brightly painted hand-carved wood made by one of Dago's friends in Old Mexico. The Rodriguezes have also brought traditions along with them, and if they find out it's your birthday, they'll plop a gigantic sombrero on your head, sing "Happy Birthday" in Spanish, and take a picture so you can remember the embarrassment! Guadalajara is open every day of the week. There is a smoking section by the bar.

Roma's $$$
701 Fifth Street, Spearfish
(605) 722-0715
www.romasristorante.com

This local favorite has set up shop in a building that once served the farming town of Spearfish as a dry-goods store. Although the farms vanished in time, this two-story castlelike structure, and most of the storage containers inside, remained. The owners of Roma's have taken full advantage of their historical digs, using some of the old flour bins for tables and tapping a wall of shelves to stand in as a massive wine rack. Enlarged historic photos of town grace each wall except for those in the very small upper seating area, where rotating art displays from regional artists serve as a backdrop. A 20-foot ceiling and an open kitchen make the dining area feel especially spacious and amplify conversation, making the place feel loud and alive even when there are only a few patrons inside. Although the large brick facade gives the building an imposing air, the bright blue trim around the windows and doors and decorative strings of white lights warmly usher diners inside.

The food is distinctively Italian and includes entrees such as steak Florentine, an herb-encrusted rib eye with greens, and smoked pheasant ravioli. A number of choices, including a spicy seafood dish called Angry Shrimp, give diners the option of three pastas to accompany their meal: linguini, ziti, and fuselli. Roma's also has a respectable wine list, which is of special interest on half-price wine night every Wednesday. The restaurant is open for lunch and dinner all week long. Reservations usually aren't necessary, but it might not be a bad idea. Visitors fill the dining room in summer, while faculty and students from nearby Black Hills State University keep the place packed when the snow starts to fly.

Central Hills

B.J.'s Grinder King $
902 Main Street, Rapid City
(605) 348-3166

First of all, grinders are just that—they're grinders, not subs. So expect olive oil rather than mustard or mayo on your sandwich (with an exception or two—ask when you order). And don't look for mozzarella, Swiss, or any other unbecoming cheeses, because only provolone belongs on a grinder. The bread, although not made on the premises, is preservative free, and the staff uses shredded cabbage instead of lettuce. The filling, however, is up to you, and you can choose from a variety of meats (turkey is the best seller), tuna, or eggplant. For the deep-dish pizzas, nearly everything is made in-house. The sauce, too, is homemade, and all meats are fresh and not saturated with preservatives. Crowning your pizza is a distinctive white cheddar cheese, or white cheddar with mozzarella on the vegetarian special.

B.J.'s closes on Sunday and from Christmas Eve until February 1 each year. Otherwise it's open for lunch and dinner, and parking is provided. Smoking is not permitted.

Botticelli Ristorante Italiano $$$
523 Main Street, Rapid City
(605) 348-0089

Why pay for plane tickets when you can take a virtual trip to northern Italy by simply walking through the door of this captivating restaurant? From the old-world decor and Italian background music to the authentic cuisine, you'll lose yourself in the ambience. Although good service makes it possible to eat a delicious lunch here (Monday through Saturday only) and still get back to the office on time, meals here are best if you can ignore the ticking of the clock. Most who venture into this tiny nonsmoking bistro for dinner tend to do just that, which makes a table difficult to find most evenings unless you've made reservations.

Before your meal arrives you're presented with a bowl of fresh bread just right for dipping into the herbed olive oil and balsamic vinegar on your table. If this isn't enough of an appetizer, there are several choices of antipasti, soups, and salads on the menu.

For lunch, entree selections include small pizzas with assorted meats, vegetables, herbs, and cheeses; sandwiches served on focaccia; pasta dishes including ravioli, fettuccine, and lasagna; chicken prepared in various ways; plus steak and fish. The dinner menu exchanges sandwiches for more chicken, veal, and seafood dishes. A fine wine or Italian beer adds a truly continental touch to your meal, which is further improved when polished off with a stout espresso beverage and extravagant tiramisu—lady fingers soaked in rum sauce, topped with mascarpone cream cheese, espresso syrup, and ground chocolate.

Curry Masala $
2050 West Main Street, Suite #7
(605) 716-7788
www.currymasalainc.com

One doesn't dine at Curry Masala for the ambience. Set in a nearly empty office suite on the west side of Rapid City, the restaurant's dining room is little more than a few wooden tables, a handful of folding chairs, and some secondhand booths that remain unattached to the wall—a section of which is formed from white canvas stretched across a wide doorway. Traditional and pop Indian music drifts pleasantly from a boom box in the open kitchen, from where the staff will serve you your food buffet-style on foam plates with plastic flatware.

In fact, the entire restaurant can be summed up in one word: cheap.

That said, the food here is spectacular. Owner Al Rodriguez keeps six curries on the menu at any one time, along with rice, naan bread, chai tea, and rotating selections of dessert items. Despite its somewhat hidden location and lack of publicity, the restaurant has gained a steady local following, thanks to the quality of the cuisine. The price point doesn't hurt, either—a lousy $5.95 will buy you more food than you could hope to eat in one sitting.

To keep up with the growing crowd who come here to dine, Rodriguez has begun to schedule small community events in his establishment, including Bengali language classes and an Indian cooking school. The restaurant is open every day but Sunday for lunch and dinner.

Great Wall Restaurant $$
315 East North Street, Rapid City
(605) 348-1183

You'll find several varieties of Oriental food here, such as Cantonese Triple Delicacy pan-fried noodles, Mandarin-style sesame beef, Szechuan beef Taiwanese Happy Family, and Shanghai-style minced lobster with pine nuts. Those are a few of the house specialties, and you'll find tried-and-true lunch and dinner favorites on the menu as well, such as egg drop soup, chow mein, broccoli beef, almond chicken, and sweet-and-sour shrimp. You can also get vegetarian meals here, and there's never any MSG added to your food during cooking. Subdued lighting and a saltwater fish tank create a somewhat mysterious mood in the dining area. Beer and wine are available. Reservations are recom-

Aunt Sally

Sarah Campbell called herself "the first white woman that ever saw the Black Hills." But anyone who knew jolly "Aunt Sally" must have chuckled upon hearing that. For Aunt Sally was African American, and we can assume she meant she was the first non–Native American woman in the Hills.

Aunt Sally arrived here with the gold-seeking expedition led by Lt. Col. George Custer in 1874, which you can read about in the History chapter. The only woman to go along on the trip, she had hired on as a cook for John Smith, a civilian trader who sold food, spirits, and other goods to the soldiers. After engineer Horatio Ross found sparkling flecks of gold in French Creek, a young newspaper reporter who had accompanied the excursion, William Curtis, interviewed the corpulent, well-liked cook for the *Chicago Inter-Ocean*. Curtis affectionately called her "a huge mountain of dusky flesh" and reported that she was more excited than anyone else about finding gold.

After all, Aunt Sally had left her comfortable home in Bismarck, North Dakota, and undertaken the journey for the sole purpose of seeing the Black Hills. Perhaps surprised to find that the Hills were in fact green rather than black, Aunt Sally apparently decided bright yellow was her favorite color and lost no time in filing a mining claim—illegally, we might add. The expedition was soon on its way again, but not before Aunt Sally had decided to return to the Black Hills at the first opportunity.

And return she did, although just when is not known. In time she filed a new claim at Elk Creek in Lawrence County and lived nearby, befriending her pioneer neighbors. They appreciated her cooking and midwifery skills, enjoyed her amusing anecdotes and tall tales, and took her pipe smoking in stride. At some point Aunt Sally reportedly adopted a 10-year-old white orphan boy, whom she had found crying in the street in Deadwood.

Aunt Sally lived to a ripe old age for her day. When she died on April 13, 1888, she was in her 70s. With fondness and respect, her friends laid her to rest on Vinegar Hill west of Galena, an old silver-mining district in Lawrence County. Flattering obituaries appeared in two local newspapers, acknowledging her stature in the community. Though gone, Aunt Sally was never to be forgotten, and today the simple wooden marker that first graced her grave is on view in the Adams Museum in Deadwood.

mended for five or more people. Parking is provided right outside the door.

Hunan $$
1720 Mount Rushmore Road, Rapid City
(605) 341-3888

A huge menu is just the beginning at this popular Chinese restaurant. The health conscious will be pleased to know that the food here is MSG free, and that special low-fat, sugar-free, and salt-free dishes are available. The regular menu includes everything from egg rolls and wonton soup to a Peking duck so elaborate it must be ordered 24 hours in advance. Although beef, pork, seafood, and vegetarian selections are offered in abundance, chicken—hot and spicy or sweet and sour—seems to be a favorite with guests. Beer and wine can accompany your meal, and cheesecake or lychee nuts (a Chinese fruit) can be your dessert. Take note of the magnificent photos in the entryway and behind the cash register, which are the work of owner Robert Wong, a native of China. We're sure you'll be impressed, not only by his skill as a photographer but also by the many ribbons, medals, and trophies he has won for his breathtaking images. His work has been featured in *National Geographic*. The prizes are on display in a cabinet in the restaurant. Smoking is prohibited at Hunan. Ample parking is provided. Hunan is open for lunch and dinner.

La Costa $$
603 Omaha Street, Rapid City
(605) 388-8780

This south-of-the-border-style restaurant has built its reputation on fajitas and fast service while preparing food the old-fashioned way, from scratch. That means tomatoes and peppers for your complimentary salsa are roasted each morning, and the tamales are encased in real cornhusks. You'll find all your Mexican favorites here, along with seafood, combination plates, and weekday lunch specials. Popular entrees from the menu include fajitas, *costenas* with char-broiled beef or chicken accompanied by sautéed shrimp and crab, and char-broiled *carne asada* steak. The sopaipillas topped with honey, cinnamon sugar, and whipped cream get rave reviews for dessert. You can order beer, including several Mexican varieties, and wine with your meal. La Costa is open for lunch and dinner seven days a week. And there's always a premeal bonus, because in addition to the obligatory homemade chips and salsa, your waitperson will bring refried beans to your table. Reservations are recommended for groups of more than 10. Ample parking is provided.

Piesano's Pacchia $-$$
3618 Canyon Lake Drive, Rapid City
(605) 341-6941
www.piesanospacchia.com

Don't be fooled by the amusing play on *paesano,* the Italian word for countryman. Piesano's takes *pacchia*—Italian for feast— very seriously. Everything is homemade, starting with the cinnamon rolls (with and without pecans) that come out of the oven in time for the 8:00 A.M. coffee crowd. Piesano's attracts a loyal clientele with scrumptious gourmet pizzas—sweet-and-sour cashew chicken is popular, but you can also order chicken Bar-B-Q, healthful vegetable, Happy Hawaiian, and more conventional varieties including primo, with the works. New combinations, such as bratwurst-and-sauerkraut and a breakfast pizza, appear from time to time. Pizzas are created on hand-tossed dough made fresh daily, and we're told that the owners are so fussy they follow the wheat crop to make sure they get top-quality flour. Pizzas come in four sizes, including an 8-inch noon special; other choices include sub sandwiches, salads (with hand-torn lettuce), and special meals such

Deadwood casinos sponsor clubs that entitle members to free meals once they accumulate enough points. Inquire at those that house your favorite restaurants.

as calzones on Tuesday, lasagna (with meat or meatless) on Wednesday, prime rib subs on Thursday, and Italian chicken-breast subs on Friday. And for dessert there's homemade chocolate-marble cheesecake. It was no surprise to learn that the *Black Hills Restaurant Guide* named Piesano's the best local pizza establishment several years in a row. You can have a bottled or draft beer with your meal, but not a smoke. Featuring homey red-check tablecloths, the decor is simple. So is parking—there's space right out front.

Saigon Restaurant $$
221 East North Street, Rapid City
(605) 348-8523

Vietnamese food must build brain cells, because the people who run this popular restaurant have phenomenal memories. It doesn't matter how long ago you ate here, they remember what you ordered and whether you prefer your glass of water without ice. They recall what Harrison Ford had on his plate when he ate here in 1995 and which vegetarian dish Lindsay Wagner had in 1997. Wagner, TV's bionic woman, could have been speaking for all of the Saigon's loyal clientele when she sent proprietress Mai Goodsell an autographed photo that says, "Mai, both you and your business are a joy!"

Mai, a native of Vietnam, and her daughter, Rebecca, are the most visible members of the staff, but we suspect the

kitchen harbors a team of wizards who whip up magical dishes for lunch and dinner. The menu contains many items you'd expect to find at an Asian restaurant, but you'll also find unusual dishes such as tofu lemongrass, a combination of noodles, bean sprouts, herbs, and tofu sprinkled with chopped peanuts and served with fish sauce; or chicken pad thai with shredded cabbage, carrots, cilantro, bamboo, rice noodles, and peanuts. The staff is amazingly flexible, so spicy items come in varying degrees of "heat," and you can request that the cook not use MSG in preparing your order.

When the restaurant moved into a spacious new building, the great food and welcoming atmosphere moved in, too. Longtime patrons will recognize the exquisite enamel and mother-of-pearl pieces from the former location amid the new decor, which features oval windows and interesting interior angles. Beer and wine are on the menu. There's handy parking in front. The Saigon closes on Sunday and in late January.

Southern Hills

The Bavarian Inn Restaurant
and Lounge $$$
U.S. Highway 16/385 North, Custer
(605) 673-4412
www.bavarianinnsd.com

This restaurant's name is your cue to its specialties, which are of the German persuasion. Rouladen, a stuffed, rolled top-round steak, is the most popular item on the menu, according to the staff. Many diners come here for the prime rib au jus, but the restaurant also has a solid reputation for its schnitzel, bratwurst dinner, sweet-and-sour cabbage, spaetzle and gravy, rib eye, and sirloin steak. Fish and seafood, vegetarian lasagna, bratwurst sandwiches, mesquite-flavored steaks, and a burger deluxe satisfy all kinds of appetites, and the bar serves cocktails, beer, and wine to complement the food. A

Although South Dakota isn't premier grape-growing habitat, two vineyards grow fruit and produce wine here. You can find products from Hill City-based Prairie Berry Winery (877-226-9453, www.prairieberry.com) at Black Hills restaurants and liquor stores. Wines from Valiant Vineyards (605-624-4500, www.buffalorunwinery.com), located in the east part of the state, are also common.

large selection of desserts includes German chocolate cake and, during the summer, homemade apple dumplings. The inn is open only for dinner through the winter, but from late May until Labor Day breakfasts are also served.

The inn offers a nice outdoor deck for candlelight dining (in warmer weather) and has a 200-seat banquet hall for receptions, weddings, and reunions. Another added attraction is the $2.99 menu for children under age six. Smokers and nonsmokers alike are welcome, parking is provided, and reservations are recommended.

SWEET TREATS

Like people everywhere, Black Hills locals develop regular cravings for ice cream and other desserts. Luckily, we have industrious purveyors who are more than happy to cater to our collective sweet tooth.

Central Hills

Armadillo's Ice Cream Shoppe $
202 Main Street, Rapid City
(605) 355-0507
The two families that run Armadillo's are masters of deliciously smooth ice cream. All of their ice cream is soft serve, and the decor adds to a 1950s feeling. The shop is located in an old gas station in downtown Rapid City, but the new look includes a black-and-white checked floor and red-top stools. But flashbacks are not what droves of people come here for; Armadillo's is known in the area for its inventive sundaes and fabulous sherbet. Family members and employees concoct both familiar and unfamiliar sundaes and tag them with their own name. Mike's Peach Cobbler has fresh peaches, caramel, and pecans; Rosie's Apple Pie has flame-roasted apples, caramel, and pecans; Tyler's Turtle simply has fudge with caramel and pecans. The creamy, smooth, low-fat sherbet is a local sensa-

Gotta have chocolate? Go directly to Mostly Chocolates, 1919 Mount Rushmore Road in Rapid City, (605) 341-2264. You'll find made-on-the-premises truffles and other sweets, plus a fine assortment of coffees, teas, and gift items. Be sure to stock up for Sunday, when the shop is closed.

tion, with flavors such as strawberry cheesecake, wild blackberry, raspberry, strawberry, and root beer. Armadillo's serves only one flavor of sherbet each day and alternates the flavors every couple of days, but you can ask for a schedule of flavors in the summer.

There is more to this little shop than ice cream. Armadillo's also serves malts, fresh market-deli sandwiches, steamburgers (they're like sloppy joes), and homemade soups. As at any quality ice-cream parlor, prices aren't the lowest, but the portions are unusually large. The shop is open March through October from about 11:00 A.M. to 10:00 P.M. Lines are long in the summer, but it is worth the wait. No smoking inside, of course, but there are tables and benches outside.

Fjord's Ice Cream Factory Inc. $
3606 Canyon Lake Drive, Rapid City
(605) 343-6912
Fjord's small and aging building on a quiet street in west Rapid City may not look very impressive, but this meager store is consistently designated as the best ice-cream factory in the Black Hills, whether by word of mouth or in regional magazines and newspapers. Locals know that it's the dozens of flavors of homemade ice cream inside that really count, and Fjord's has been faithfully turning them out for decades from this same location. Although simple varieties such as butter brickle, cookie dough, French vanilla, coffee, and mint chip are incredibly rich and creamy (there's a reason a water cooler stands watch in the corner), elaborate

One way to satisfy your sweet tooth in the Black Hills is to cover it in home-made saltwater taffy. Rushmore Mountain Taffy Shop (605-666-4430, www.rushmoremountaintaffy.com) in Keystone offers dozens of flavors, including huckleberry, buffalo berry, piña colada, and key lime.

concoctions like Black Hills gold (butterscotch ice cream, pecans, crushed Butterfingers, and cashews), Outback strawberry (strawberry-marbled kiwi ice cream), peanut butter M&M, sour cream raisin, banana split cream, and chocolate malt ball are Fjord's trademarks. The factory manufactures more than 100 flavors, although you can order only from about 40 at any given time, depending on what ingredients are in stock. Toppings also vary, but Fjord's is bound to have an interesting mix for its frozen marble slab. This trendy idea, borrowed from ice-cream parlors in more urban settings, allows the staff to pound your favorite toppings right into your selected flavor of ice cream, letting you further customize your frozen treat.

It's hard to see beyond the ice cream, but Fjord's also has homemade hot fudge, bread pudding, ice-cream pies, cakes, waffle cones, sugar-free ice cream, sorbet, sherbet, and frozen yogurt. There are only a few tables crammed into the small room adjacent to the counter and a sprinkling of benches outside, so you're welcome to take your treats home with you. It's even possible to buy a quart or half gallon of

your favorite flavor, but watch out—the stuff melts quickly. Lines form rapidly on summer evenings, so be prepared to wait or make it a point to arrive before the after-dinner rush. Fjord's closes for the winter. Dates vary from year to year, but don't count on getting any ice cream from December through February.

Southern Hills

Old Fashion Ice Cream Parlor $
19 Mount Rushmore Road, Custer
(605) 673-4070

Co-owner Arle Reetz says if they ever stop serving her homemade rhubarb pie in this cheery pink-and-purple shop, she and her partner-husband, Terry, will be run out of town. One bite of the flaky crust and not-too-tart, not-too-sweet filling tells you why. It's good a la mode too, but the ice cream is just background music. Proponents of the "life is uncertain, eat dessert first" philosophy, Arle and Terry also serve bumbleberry and other fruit pies, plus a different meringue pie every day, ice-cream concoctions, and frozen yogurt (including sugar free). Afterward, you can have a big cup of homemade soup with a sandwich. In contrast to the eye-popping exterior, the decor inside is simple. Free wireless Internet access is available. When it's nice out, the porch is a pleasant place to eat. The shop opens for lunch and stays open until late in the evening from early May until October 15. Smoking is not allowed, but ample parking is provided.

NIGHTLIFE �

The Black Hills are known for many things: unspoiled alpine vistas, herds of wild-roaming bison, epic mountain carvings, and woolly western legends. Nightlife, however, does not immediately spring to one's mind when the words "South Dakota" are uttered in conversation. In fact, the idea never occurs to many who visit here; there's even a good number of residents who never go for a night out on the town.

All the same, the Black Hills have a significant number of places that don't open until the sun sinks below the horizon. Rapid City's population base and Spearfish's college crowd make both communities regional nightlife capitals, though Deadwood's saloons, casinos, and frequent free concerts on Main Street make it the busiest nightlife headquarters in a 500-mile radius.

In fact the following listings feature a few bars and pubs that have been here since gold-rush days. You'll find coffeehouses where you can hear live music and sometimes poetry, sports bars with TVs galore, a couple of nightclubs, and comedy clubs for a truly lighthearted night out.

A state law requires businesses that serve wine or hard liquor to also serve food if they're open on Sunday, even if the fare is just hot dogs, snacks, microwave pizza, or sandwiches. The South Dakota Department of Revenue calls this Sunday privilege. We call it your guarantee that you can at least find a snack or a meal at a bar or pub on Sunday. Remember that the drinking age in South Dakota, as in the rest of the country, is 21. Expect to be carded anywhere, but especially in Deadwood. We can't guarantee that you'll be able to buy wine or liquor in a package store on Sunday or certain holidays, because those regulations vary from town to town. And our source at the revenue department tells us hard liquor can neither be sold nor served anywhere in South Dakota on Memorial Day or Christmas. Keep in mind that the South Dakota Highway Patrol doesn't take kindly to drunk drivers, and penalties can be aggressive. Checkpoints in Rapid City and outside Deadwood are common.

Speaking of legal matters, video lottery (see the Gaming and Casinos chapter) remains controversial, and lawmakers continue to scrutinize this form of state-sanctioned gambling. Unless or until a decision is made to abolish video lottery, you'll find machines in just about any establishment where you can buy a drink. Because they're so prevalent, we've noted those places that don't have them.

We've handled closing time the same way—unless otherwise noted, it's 2:00 A.M. You also can assume a business is open seven days a week unless we've mentioned that it's closed on certain days. Most bars and pubs offer discounted drinks during a late-afternoon or early evening weekday happy hour, so we've noted only the exceptions or those that serve food as an accompaniment. And because so few of our bars and pubs require a cover charge, we tell you those that do.

BARS, LOUNGES, AND PUBS

We wrote this section to direct you to what a friend calls local color. At the following establishments you'll experience our unique Black Hills culture and meet interesting residents. A few of these places may be a bit rough around the edges—they're not exactly Planet Hollywood. But all the bars listed here are great places to mingle with locals. If you're a fan of bars as cultural icons, you'll find the following a fascinating addition to your Black Hills adventure.

Northern Hills

B&B Lounge and Back Porch
703 North Main Street, Spearfish
(605) 642-8292, 642-2134
www.backporchbar.com

A popular nightspot for dancing and listening to rock 'n' roll music by local bands and DJs, the B&B boasts a clientele whose ages generally range from 21 to 50-something. It has a full bar and serves snacks and fried foods. When you get tired of dancing, you can play pool.

Knight's Cellar
604 Main Street, Spearfish
(605) 642-4292

The English owner describes this local favorite as a "pre-going-out stop," a place to relax, have a snack, hoist a brew, listen to music, and actually have a conversation. There is only one television in the upstairs loft for whatever customers want to watch, and the ubiquitous video lottery machines are absent.

Knight's stocks nuts of all kinds, cigars, specialty sodas, wine coolers, and 100-some microbrew and import beers that you can mix and match. Select your treats, then sit down and enjoy them to the accompaniment of local artists playing acoustic music every Friday and Saturday. The main event at Knight's Cellar, however, is open-mike night every Thursday from 8:00 to 11:00. A variety of area musicians stop by and play a few songs for the pub crawlers.

Back in the good ol' days, state law prohibited the buying or serving of spirits on election day. Sometime before 1971, lawmakers changed their minds. Perhaps they were hoping for a different outcome at the ballot box!

Smoking is not allowed in this establishment. It's closed on Sunday and is open from 4:00 P.M. to 2:00 A.M. Monday through Saturday.

Moonshine Gulch Saloon
Forest Service Road 231, Rochford
No telephone

The Moonshine Gulch is a local secret—a remote mountain bar with no telephone, a handful of electric lights, and genuine western character.

This is a real saloon—a bit wacky, pretty funky, and gloriously idiosyncratic. The rustic old building has a wooden front porch where you can lounge on a bench and view the tiny town of Rochford, pretending you've gone back in time to its decades-ago mining days. Inside there's simply too much to look at: wildlife trophies, hundreds of hats, antiques, junk everywhere, and stuff covering the walls in a visual extravaganza. Even the restrooms have quotable quotations on their walls. The food is great—homemade fries, burgers, and sandwiches—and you can have a brew with your meal. You won't find video lottery here, but you will find real locals enjoying real life, deep in the Black Hills. Moonshine Gulch is on the main road through Rochford, a town so small that—if you find it—you can't miss this saloon: It's the main attraction.

Nite Owl Tavern
1111 Main Street, Sturgis
(605) 347-9846

A basic, unpretentious bar, the Nite Owl caters to locals of all ages, who were having a good time the night we walked in. Some were playing pool or electronic darts, others were watching the seven television sets and chatting comfortably over their drinks. The establishment is in a long, narrow, high-ceilinged room in an older building, and you'll want to get a close look at the old, attractive bar with its interesting art deco features. Patrons can buy dart and pool supplies in addition to fried foods, snacks, and sandwiches. The Nite Owl, in the heart of Sturgis, is especially popular and crowded during the August Sturgis Rally & Races (which you can read about in the Annual Events and Festivals chapter).

Old Style Saloon No. 10
657 Main Street, Deadwood
(605) 578-3346, (800) 952-9398
www.saloon10.com

Local color is an understatement at the Saloon No. 10, a place tagged as the only museum in the world with a bar. A quick look around at the cluttered interior and you'll agree. The decor is much the same as it was in the early 1900s, with sawdust on the floor, western artifacts all around, and pictures of Deadwood's good, bad, and ugly surrounding you anywhere you sit. One face you're sure to see is that of Wild Bill Hickok, who in 1876 sat in the wrong chair at the Saloon No. 10 and played his last game of poker before getting shot from behind. You can watch this scene if you'd like—from Memorial Day through mid-September, the shooting of Wild Bill is reenacted daily at the bar.

Of course, there's plenty of gambling at the Old Style, and you're sure to have better luck than Wild Bill on that fateful day. The blackjack and poker tables have a room all to themselves, and there are also slot machines. With all that history under their belt, people at the Saloon No. 10 know how to entertain. Enjoy service by saloon girls in lacy period costumes or dance each weekend to a live band. If you get hungry, just step upstairs to the classy but casual Deadwood Social Club for some fine northern Italian dining and exceptional wine (read more about the Social Club in the Restaurants chapter). There's also the Charlie Utter Theatre, which hosts live shows (many related to Deadwood's history) throughout the year. Call the Saloon No. 10 and ask for theater show information.

Sanford's Grub & Pub
545 West Jackson Boulevard, Spearfish
306 Seventh Street, Rapid City
(605) 642-3204, (605) 721-1463

Sanford's decorative theme is "junkyard

chic." This charming place is full of antiques, old Coke machines, aging bicycles suspended from the ceiling, and memorabilia from nearby Black Hills State University. It opens at 11:00 A.M. for lunch and closes at 10:00 P.M., seven days a week in the summer. Call for winter hours.

You'll want to read more about Sanford's menu in the Restaurants chapter, but you'll find foods in jumbo portions, half-pound burgers, crawfish, barbecue, pasta, steaks, and seafood—and nightly dinner specials. Choose from among more than 99 beers and 20 taps. This pub offers hard liquor, beer, and wine. For recreation, after putting away all that food and drink, you can play pinball or pool, or watch one of the 25 televisions.

Central Hills

Brass Rail Lounge
624 St. Joseph Street, Rapid City
(605) 341-1768

This tiny bar might be in the middle of Rapid City's bustling downtown, but it's fairly quiet, very down to earth, and the sort of place where—if you showed up often enough—everyone would indeed know your name. It's so casual, in fact, that it may close before 2:00 A.M. if business is slow.

The jukebox has a good selection of tunes, and electronic dartboards stand along one wall. You won't find a pool table, live music, or meals (just hot dogs and snacks). Instead, you will find interesting Rapid City residents and friendly bartenders. The sign over the bar that reads SALOON NO. 8 refers to the fact that the Brass Rail holds the eighth liquor license issued in South Dakota after Prohibition, making it one of the oldest bars in Rapid City.

Cheers Lounge and Casino
Ramada Inn
1721 North Lacrosse Street, Rapid City
(605) 342-2273, (800) 2RAMADA

This hotel bar is popular with locals, businesspeople, hotel guests, and travelers. It's a relaxed place to hang out, whether you're staying at the hotel or elsewhere. Snack foods are always served at happy hour. Local bands occasionally play here, and there's room to dance, though not a lot. The bar has a pool table, electronic darts, and a dart league, and it serves wines as well as liquor and beer. In the winter Cheers may close earlier than 2:00 A.M.

Chute Roosters
103 Chute Rooster Drive, Hill City
(605) 574-2122

Wondering about the name? A chute rooster is a kind of backseat-driver rodeo cowboy, the kind who perches on the chute and tells the real cowboy how to do his job. We didn't meet any chute roosters here, but we're told cowboy poets sometimes provide entertainment in this charming lounge. Karaoke begins at 8:00 P.M. on Friday. A huge loft above the adjacent restaurant (read about that in the Restaurants chapter) has party facilities. Downstairs the cozy bar has a full array of cocktails and a menu with such items as burgers, rib eye, and chili. Dressed up or dressed down, everyone gets a warm welcome here.

Dublin Square at the Radisson Hotel
445 Mount Rushmore Road, Rapid City
(605) 348-8300

The two big-screen televisions here are almost always tuned to NFL and college games during football season, which draws a great weekend crowd. During weekdays, the 5:00 to 7:00 P.M. happy hour attracts a good show of downtown businesspeople. The later hours of Saturday and Sunday are the domain of karaoke devotees, while live bands provide entertainment Wednesday through Friday. The loud and boisterous patrons of the bar often mix with the quiet and dressy diners headed for the hotel's restaurant, Enigma, in the lobby, which separates the two very different venues. Read more about Enigma in the Restaurants chapter.

Firehouse Brewing Company
610 Main Street, Rapid City
(605) 348-1915

The Firehouse—which occupies the historic 1915 Rapid City firehouse building—has something for everyone. The restaurant welcomes families with its cuisine (see the Restaurants chapter). Both the rectangular bar and the second-floor mezzanine are comfortable places to relax and watch the crowd. In the summer the big, partially covered patio is a perfect place to eat and listen to the bands that play on its stage. It even has overhead radiant heaters for chilly nights.

The Firehouse brews its own terrific beer on the premises. Several recipes are rotated, and you'll find five to six on tap at any time, ranging from Wilderness Wheat (a light beer served with lemon) to Smokejumper Stout (a dark, coffeelike, and heavy-bodied brew).

Paddy O'Neill's Pub & Casino
523 Sixth Street, Rapid City
(605) 342-1210, (800) 888-2539

This classy pub is part of the Alex Johnson Hotel and is named for the hotel's first guest, who registered on July 1, 1928.

Carry A. Nation

The most famous and feared leader of the temperance movement, hatchet-wielding Carry Nation, twice visited the Black Hills. Born Carrie Amelia Moore, she married Rev. David Nation and legally changed her name to Carry A. Nation, to better express her iron-willed commitment to ending the use of alcohol as well as its kindred sins, smoking and gambling. Many saloons and gambling halls came under her attack, and she was not averse to using rocks, canes, iron rods, and anything else she could get her hands on to break bottles, destroy furniture, and physically punish the sinners.

Rapid City storyteller Carl Leedy, in his book *Golden Days in the Black Hills,* says that Carry visited Rapid City in 1905 but refrained from breaking any saloon windows. However, he tells that she jerked a pipe away from a smoker and angrily stomped on it, and during her speech to the crowd she addressed more smokers at the back of the auditorium. "You fellows down there by the door," she shouted, "if the Good Lord had intended you to smoke he would have turned your noses up the other way, for a smoke stack."

In 1910 Carry visited Sturgis. Apparently, passionate activism agreed with her. "Carrie [*sic*] is a pretty spry old lady for her age [she was 64] and moved around like a young girl at the age of 16," the *Sturgis Weekly Record* reported. Four brave male community leaders accompanied her to nearby Fort Meade for a visit, without telling her that two of them—between whom she was seated—were Sturgis saloon keepers. Later, the *Weekly Record* stated, "When informed, she took the joke good naturedly and said it made no difference, that the devil could not be routed until you got next to him."

Paddy's clientele includes businesspeople and hotel guests, but the live music by local bands—presented on Wednesday through Saturday nights—draws a younger, enthusiastic crowd. The pub is small and the music tends to be a bit loud, so don't count on intimate conversation or dancing on live-music nights.

Paddy's patrons can enjoy snacks and dinners (from the adjacent Landmark Restaurant's menu); yards and half yards of any tap beer; Guinness Stout on tap and one of the largest selections of imported beers in the area; and small-batch bourbons. You might want to become a member of the Pewter Mug Club—buy one, have a drink, and the staff will put your mug on display and your name on a brass plaque. When you come back for another visit, you can quaff from your very own mug.

You'll find the Alex Johnson Hotel in the Accommodations chapter.

Tana's Mangy Moose Saloon
24090 U.S. Highway 385 South, Hill City
(605) 574-4417

If the band's not very good, the bartender will entertain you. But since folks come here to dance on Friday and Saturday nights once or twice a month, we think it's safe to assume the music is up to par, be it country, rock, two-step, or something else. Live music begins at 9:00 P.M. In addition to a full bar, there's a selection of imported beers. You can get a bite to eat, choosing from a limited Mexican menu, burgers, an assortment of fried foods, and daily specials. The local clientele here is friendly—and loves to dance. The lounge is a mile south of Hill City.

Southern Hills

A.J.'s Ore Car Saloon
537 Mount Rushmore Road, Custer
(605) 673-3051

This small, slightly cramped bar seems like a good place to make friends, and apparently Australians think so, too. According to the owner/bartender, A.J.'s and Crazy Horse Memorial are the only two Custer listings in a U.S. travel guide published Down Under. (He got his hearsay information from an Aussie patron who made it a point to stop in one summer.)

This is a strictly casual place where 30-somethings sit and shoot the breeze while downing a few beers of the domestic variety. Happy hour, which occurs between 11:00 A.M. and noon on Sunday in addition to weekday evenings, could be a good time to study the shelves full of slow-pitch softball trophies garnered by teams the saloon has sponsored. Having done that, you're ready to turn to the pool table, listen to the stereo, or watch sports on TV. During the summer you can sip a brew or play horseshoes in the beer garden out back. If you're looking for a pool tournament or other games, check with the bartender for the schedule.

Frontier Bar
U.S. Highway 16 West, Custer
(605) 673-8870

The Frontier has a band every Friday at 9:00 P.M. in the summer, every other Friday in the winter, and the music varies from week to week. You might dance to rock, blues, or country, depending on the night. All told, the bar is pretty quiet, though. The Frontier offers appetizers from fried gizzards to mini-tacos, and a burgers and chicken-strips menu for those wanting a meal. In addition to happy hour on weeknights, it has happy hour on Saturday from 5:00 until 7:00 P.M. This is a spacious place with a big dance floor and an impressive mounted elk head on the wall.

The Gold Pan Saloon
508 Mount Rushmore Road, Custer
(605) 673-8850

The swinging doors and the sawdust on the floor say "Old West." The antlers, bovine skull, and cattle horns over the bar—not to mention the framed ammunition display—say "hunters' hangout." The saloon has a full bar and also offers pool tables. Happy hour is from 4:30 to 6:30 P.M. Monday through Saturday. Though some distance from Sturgis in the Northern Hills, the Gold Pan is a popular stop for visitors to the Sturgis Rally & Races in August (see the Annual Events and Festivals chapter).

COFFEEHOUSES

There's nothing like watching the world go by over the rim of a steaming cup of espresso, latte, or cappuccino. You don't necessarily have to wait until nighttime either. The coffeehouse listed here opens in the early morning.

Northern Hills

Common Grounds
111 East Hudson Street, Spearfish
1301 West Omaha, Rapid City
(605) 642-9066, (605) 721-1878

A classy, comfortable coffeehouse in a century-old building in Spearfish and a new building near downtown in Rapid City, Common Grounds entertains a mixed crowd of young people, Black Hills State college students and faculty at the Spearfish location, retired folks, and visitors. It serves great specialty coffees (including local Dark Canyon Coffee Company's blends) as well as bagels, muffins, sandwiches, soups, cookies and biscotti, and it offers a deli bar. A popular community gathering place, Common Grounds hosts poetry readings, live music performances, and open-mike nights. It's open 6:00 A.M. to 7:00 P.M. Monday through Saturday and 6:00 A.M. to 5:00 P.M. on Sunday.

NIGHTCLUBS

If there's a common element among the most popular nightlife venues in the Black Hills, it's music, whether it's boot-scootin' country or good old rock 'n' roll. If you want plenty of room for letting loose and busting a move, however, the following nightclubs are exactly what you're looking for. They all have dance floors, of course, and play music of almost any genre.

Central Hills

Phatty McGee's
321 Seventh Street, Rapid City
(605) 388-3232

If you go up to Phatty's above Hooky Jack's sports bar when it opens at 5:00 P.M., the place doesn't seem different from any other bar. There are places to sit and enjoy your drink, pool tables, foosball, video lottery, and some arcade games. Hang around until 9:00 P.M., though, and everything will change. That's when the DJ starts to play and the dance floor fills up with a crowd ranging in age from 21 to 55. Phatty's plays a wide range of dance music, including hip-hop, trance, and house. It has karaoke on Monday and Thursday. Occasionally the crowd pushes the 300-person limit, forcing Phatty's to resort to the "take a number" system, so show up early if you don't want to chance a line. To make dancing even more fun, the bar offers different drink specials every night, but ladies' night is every Wednesday. Phatty's also has employee appreciation night on Monday, when workers from other bars and restaurants get an exclusive special, and college night on Thursday when drinks are buy one, get one for a penny. When you're hungry, you can just go downstairs to Hooky's for some oven-cooked food (see Hooky's listing under the Sports Bars section).

Robbinsdale Lounge
803 East St. Patrick Street, Rapid City
(605) 342-7271

Robbinsdale Lounge promotes itself as Rapid City's music showcase. Live bands perform here Thursday, Friday, and Saturday nights. The music begins at 9:00 P.M., but the lounge's 300 seats start filling up much earlier as patrons settle in with a cocktail or a beer. Two pool tables also help pass the time until the band starts playing. On Wednesday and Friday the bar treats its patrons to free pizza or sub sandwiches during happy hour. Other nights, snacks are served. A more substantial meal of burgers, hot dogs, and the like is available from the cafe in the attached bowling alley, and you can order right at the bar. Customers get to show-

Nineteenth-Century Nightlife

On May 15, 1885, the *Black Hills Journal* reported on a meeting of Methodist ministers in Deadwood. Apparently the clergy members were concerned about nightlife in the region, and the discussion centered on which of two evils they considered to be the worse—the roller rink or the dance. Some claimed the rink at least took sinners away from the saloons, but the *Black Hills Journal* said Reverend Bartholomew insisted that "if he had a daughter old enough to go into society, he wouldn't want her associating in the rink with those who, but for the rink, would be in the saloon." Another preacher proclaimed, "The devil invented dancing when he was young. The roller rink was the product of his maturer skill, as a means of bringing the fallen elements into the midst of good society." If these reverend gentlemen came back to experience today's Black Hills nightlife, they wouldn't have to worry much about roller rinks, but we do wonder what they would think of video lottery.

case their own vocal cords when karaoke opens at 8:30 P.M. on Sunday, Tuesday, and Wednesday. The lounge opens at 10:00 A.M. Monday through Friday, 9:00 A.M. on Saturday, and 1:00 P.M. on Sunday.

Woody's (formerly the Boot)
826 Main Street, Rapid City
(605) 343-1931
Woody's is all about high-energy dancing, and the staff pulls out all the stops to get the crowd moving. The bar is young and so is its crowd—ages range from 22 to 40. It's open Tuesday through Saturday from 4:00 P.M. to 2:00 A.M., and you might want to get there early to avoid a line outside when the club reaches its 500-person limit. The sound system matches the energy level of the crowd, and a light show and fog amplify the whole experience. You'll hear mostly Top 40 rock and dance music. When the dancing wears you down, you can make your way through the crowd to the full bar, grab a drink, and enjoy everything else Woody's has to offer. There's a casino, pool tables, dartboards, mechanical golf, and Skee-Ball.

Woody's does offer some munchies, but if you want food head across the street to Murphy's Sports Bar.

SPORTS BARS

These places seem to be in competition over the number of televisions they can pack into their premises, and the benefit for you is that you can watch several favorite sporting events at once.

Northern Hills

Diamond Lil's Sports Bar
Midnight Star
677 Main Street, Deadwood
(605) 578-1555, (800) 999-6482

Televisions are all over the place here, broadcasting your favorite sports. If you get tired of watching, take a look instead at owner Kevin Costner's movie costumes and photographs on display. Barring that, you can always eat. Here you'll find sandwiches, appetizers, steaks, and other hot foods as well as video games and the popular National Trivia Network. Lil's is open every day from 11:00 A.M. to 10:00 P.M.

The Stadium Sports Grill (formerly Prime Time)
818 Fifth Avenue, Belle Fourche
744 Main Street, Spearfish
(605) 723-9521, (605) 642-9521

This establishment gets quite a variety of customers: families, locals, and tourists. The Stadium in Belle Fourche opens at 11:00 A.M. for lunch and stays open until 2:00 A.M., although it closes a bit earlier in the winter. It has no fewer than 16 televisions, a pool table, pinball machines, dartboards, and a state-of-the-art ventilation system that whisks away cigarette and cigar smoke. The Stadium is a great place to eat (the kitchen closes at 11:00 P.M.), offering burgers, sandwiches, seafood, and salads, but it is best known for the specialty of the house: Stadium Beef Tips, once enthusiastically extolled by none other than the *Chicago Tribune* and the *Houston Chronicle*.

Although the Stadium in Spearfish is a sports bar, it's also a family place and offers a full menu of good food served in large portions. After 5:00 P.M. it attracts a crowd of businesspeople; the college crowd arrives later. You can play pool, darts, video games, and the jukebox, or watch the 13 televisions, including one large-screen TV. The Stadium in Spearfish also provides interactive fun via the satellite broadcast National Trivia Network,

which is free and very popular with the bar's clientele.

There's more about both Stadiums in the Restaurants chapter.

Central Hills

Hooky Jack's
321 Seventh Street, Rapid City
(605) 388-3232

Things are as hoppin' at Hooky Jack's as the dynamite that led to its name. As the story goes, in 1882 local miner John Leary was warming a stick of dynamite by rolling it between his hands when it exploded. He survived, but he lost his hands and decided to replace them with hooks. After the incident, Leary changed jobs and became a night watchman, essentially Rapid City's first policeman. Locals started calling him Hooky Jack, and the bar is named in his honor.

You'll hear this story (in one of its various tellings) at Hooky Jack's, but the bar is otherwise strictly for sports, alcohol, and food. It has a full bar, plus about 30 televisions tuned to all sorts of sports. If you don't like to stare at the TV, check out all the sports memorabilia hanging around the place, or the shells of actual racing cars and the airplane suspended from the ceiling. However, the pride of the establishment is the open stone oven. In it the staff makes some appetizers, desserts, and their signature pizzas.

Hooky Jack's is open Monday through Friday from 5:00 P.M. to 2:00 A.M., Saturday from 11:00 A.M. to 2:00 A.M., and Sunday from 11:00 A.M. to midnight. The kitchen usually closes around 10:00 P.M., and this is when any underage customers must leave the building. The older crowd likes to swing upstairs to Phatty McGee's for some dancing (see Phatty's listing in the Nightclubs section).

Kelly's Sports Lounge
825 Jackson Boulevard, Rapid City
(605) 348-1213

Satellite sports are the main event here. TV

sets are everywhere, but you'll also find two pool tables, foosball, and electronic darts. The most popular game at Kelly's is Golden Tee, a multiplayer golf video game that's sprung up at many sports bars in the past few years. There's a full bar, and the kitchen cooks up burgers, steaks, prime rib (Wednesday only), wings, and chicken strips for a diverse crowd that ranges in age from 21 to 101.

Murphy's Sports Bar
510 Ninth Street, Rapid City
(605) 348-7270
Murphy's is a local favorite, and, as one employee claims, it really is "the place where everybody knows your name." Regular patrons and bartenders are incredibly friendly and hospitable, and the establishment rightfully claims some of the best service in town. One thing that makes Murphy's stand out is the food, which is tasty and comes in huge portions. The business crowd likes to stop by between 4:00 and 6:00 P.M. for happy hour, when appetizers are half price and deals are offered on drinks from a full bar. Murphy's is open 11:00 A.M. to 2:00 A.M. Monday through Saturday.

Of course, Murphy's has all the sports you could ever want. Find a TV from wherever you sit and watch everything from *Buck Hunter* and basketball to snowmobiling and golf. If you'd rather participate than be a spectator, there's always pool, darts, foosball, and ice ball (a newer version of Skee-Ball).

Shooters Restaurant & Sports Bar
2424 West Main Street, Rapid City
(605) 348-3348
Shooters has more of a restaurant atmosphere, but the regulars here really love football, and a sizable crowd consistently gathers to watch professional and college games on the TVs throughout the establishment. There are a few video lottery machines in a side room. Hours are earlier than standard bar time; it's open Monday through Thursday 11:00 A.M. to 11:00 P.M., Friday and Saturday 11:00 A.M. to midnight, and Sunday 11:00 A.M. to 9:00 P.M. The setting leans toward upscale, the attitude is mellow, and the crowd is laid back. Since it's a restaurant, everyone (from kids to seniors) is welcome, but the bar section is separate from where families sit to eat.

Shooters has a full bar and a menu that includes choice Black Angus steaks. The most famous item on the menu, however, is the outstanding hot wings. Shooters consistently wins local awards for them. Visitors are encouraged to challenge the cook to make the wings as hot as possible, but such challenges are often followed by several pitchers of ice water. Of course, the wings come in mild, medium, hot, and thermonuclear for those who want the standard range of hot wings. Read more about the food offered at Shooters in the Restaurants chapter.

Valley Sports Bar & Grill
1865 South Valley Drive, Rapid City
(605) 343-2528
Eleven televisions, pool tables, electronic golf and darts, and a separate room for video lottery players make this establishment a favorite of sports bar enthusiasts. Sit at the big, dark-wood bar and have a brew or munch one of the popular half-pound burgers. A full menu is served seven days a week, and on Wednesday you can order fresh prime rib. Live music is presented Friday and Saturday nights.

GAMING AND CASINOS

When Deadwood was young, saloons were the mainstay of the town. Thousands of prospectors—many unsuccessful and disheartened—needed entertainment to lift their spirits. Spirits, in fact, were the elixirs to which many of these miners turned. But the bar and its stock of liquor was only one part of the saloon. Upstairs, ladies of the evening held court, and at the back of the building, there were the card tables.

Professional gamblers quickly followed the merchants and bar owners, hoping to play the precious metals right out of the miners' hands. In fact, if one thing bound Deadwood's early residents together, it was lust for gold: Some mined it, some traded for it, and others shuffled for it. Practiced card players could indeed walk away from a table with a profit if they stayed sober, didn't challenge other professionals, and understood the odds. Of course, the inexperienced and less clever didn't fare so well, often losing everything to an unlucky turn of a card.

Men sometimes gambled away all their money in one poker game, leaving their families destitute and struggling. It's said that one fed-up wife cured her husband's gambling problem when she stalked into the saloon (it was unheard of that a proper lady would enter such a place), raked all the money on the table into her apron, and stalked back out, followed by her humiliated husband. The woman certainly remedied her husband's compulsive gambling, if only because no one would ever play cards with him again.

When the founding fathers in the Dakota Territory were trying hard to create a state in 1889, the open gambling going on in the wild town of Deadwood was a source of embarrassment to them. A prohibition against gambling was written into the constitution of the new state of South Dakota, but it continued, although most often in the back rooms of saloons. Even Prohibition barely crimped Deadwood's style.

Slot machines arrived in the late 1930s. The one-armed bandits, technically prohibited by law, were profitable and popular. In 1947, however, the state attorney general organized a surprise raid on the gambling establishments in Deadwood. All the gambling equipment was seized and, after the trials were over, hauled to the local dump and burned. That event ended open gambling in town for many years, although, true to tradition, it continued in a few back rooms. The other back rooms were used for prostitution, which wasn't shut down until 1980.

But running both industries underground and (mostly) out of business did little to improve the economy of the town. With the closure of public gambling came the slow demise of Deadwood; the raids on prostitution in 1980 only hastened it (longtime residents will tell you that hunting season has never been the same since the brothels closed). The once-proud Victorian buildings on Main Street crumbled; those that weren't abandoned were occupied by businesses that didn't make enough of a profit to maintain them. This and other factors led to the fires of the 1980s, blazes which took as victims the Ranger Bar and Brothel, the Homestake Opera House, the oldest part of Deadwood Elementary School, and the Syndicate Building. But the more the town decayed, the more proactive residents became, until they bravely forwarded a progressive idea in the late 1980s: Legalize gambling, then take a massive percentage of the profits to use for historic preservation and visitor advertising.

Of course, this meant altering the state constitution. Fortunately for Deadwood, the lure of restoration and the idea of increasing visitors to the state was enough for the conservative voters of South Dakota. On November 1, 1989, at high noon and marked by ceremonial gunshots, Deadwood officially became the third place in the nation to legalize gambling (after Nevada and Atlantic City). In the years since, Deadwood has been returned to the glory of its golden Victorian Age, thanks entirely to this now highly regulated and strictly monitored industry.

Some two million enthusiasts now gamble in Deadwood each year, and since 1989 they have wagered more than $6.8 billion (of that, $6.2 billion was won by gamblers). From this staggering amount, many millions have funded grants and low-interest loans to restore historic buildings and landmarks, both public and private. The scale of this restoration—both in terms of funds and number of buildings—makes Deadwood one of the largest historic preservation projects in the nation.

Gambling funds have been used to improve Deadwood's infrastructure and to repair and renovate the Adams Museum, Days of '76 rodeo grounds, the town's Carnegie Library, Mount Moriah Cemetery, and historic Main Street. Such renovations have in turn increased the wage scale and provided jobs in city and county government as well as in private businesses. In fact, there are far more jobs in Deadwood than there are residents. Though the precise figures vary from year to year, reports consistently show about 1,800 gaming-related jobs in the city. Population estimates, however, show that Deadwood has only 1,300 inhabitants.

Although modern Deadwood's gaming is somewhat controversial, and some citizens still believe the focus on gaming was an unfortunate choice, no one can argue with the positive changes in the town and the amazing improvements to both its appearance and economic outlook.

Today's Deadwood offers limited-stakes gaming, which means the maximum bet is $100 per blackjack hand, poker bet, or slot machine play.

About 90 gaming establishments—few business names include the word casino—offer live poker, blackjack, Let It Ride, three-card poker, and Rainbow 21 card games, progressive and other slot machines, and video lottery machines. Most have nickel, quarter, and dollar slot machines; you may even find some dime and penny machines. Many businesses also have special events such as slot tournaments and leagues, car giveaways, cash drawings, ladies' nights, and happy hours; some offer gaming clubs for frequent visitors. Many have restaurants, bars, adjacent motel or hotel accommodations, or offer travel packages with discounts and incentives. There are several special events in Deadwood each month, ranging from a Professional Rodeo Cowboys Association rodeo and an American Indian Christmas concert to a classic car show and two-day outdoor music festival with national recording artists. Many casinos and hotels anticipate these citywide events with their own parties or package deals; call the business and see the Annual Events and Festivals chapter for more information.

Deadwood gaming establishments line historic Main Street, but a few are on nearby Sherman Street, too. You'll find slot machines where you never expected to see them: the VFW, Decker's grocery store, even the Super 8 Motel. A walk down Main Street is nothing like a walk down the Strip in Las Vegas. Perhaps low stakes also means low-key, because you

CLOSE-UP

Deadwood Booms on the Small Screen

The rough-and-tumble ways of the Old West have been portrayed in Hollywood for decades. Legends such as John Wayne, decked out in leather chaps, leather vest, and cowboy hat while toting a shiny revolver, have been permanently embedded in our imaginations. Unfortunately, these westerns have been dolled up and typically aren't the best representation of how difficult and brash life in the Old West truly was.

In the spring of 2004, the HBO cable television network debuted a rough and realistic portrayal of a small mining encampment in western South Dakota that goes by the name of Deadwood. The show begins in the early years of the encampment when nearly 10,000 miners, mule skinners, and madams rushed to the gold-filled gulch in hopes of striking it rich. Whiskey was purchased with gold dust, disputes were settled with six-guns, and homes were constructed with canvas and businesses with wood. Life in those times, in that town, was difficult and, at times, deadly.

Of course, not all viewers are pleased with the show. Some are taken aback by the harsh nature of some of its content—which can include graphic nudity, violence, and foul language. Nonetheless, people in the small real-life Black Hills community of 1,800 have been eager to strengthen ties with the program and have welcomed its actors to town on several occasions.

Now, more than two years after the show's premier, its namesake is beginning to reap the rewards. According to community leaders, Deadwood hasn't seen this kind of boom since the gold rush that created it 130 years ago. Thanks largely to the success of the new drama, which has also been shown in a half-dozen foreign countries, thousands of visitors are now coming to Deadwood not only to enjoy the shopping, gambling, and scenic beauty of the Black Hills, but also to see where legends—now household names thanks largely to HBO—lived and died.

won't see building-size neon signs or chorus lines of dancing showgirls, and no football-field-size casinos or skyscraping hotels. We'd be surprised, in fact, if you heard a police car siren. As you stroll down the sidewalks that line the brick-paved streets and past the buildings restored to their former glory, you'll see gamblers hurrying from door to door, carrying their containers of coins. Some stop to browse in the shops, but most are looking for that slot machine with their name on it, the one that calls seductively, "You're a winner if you put just one more quarter in the slot."

Elsewhere in the Black Hills, South Dakota's state-operated video lottery—the machines that offer poker, keno, blackjack, and other electronic games—can be found in both casinos and other types of businesses in most Hills towns. Video lottery is highly controversial and has been the focus of repeal efforts in the state legislature, but the state has come to depend on the revenues from thousands of video lottery machines. Video lottery is purported to be one of the most addictive forms of gambling. A study published in the *South Dakota Medical Journal* reported that players who don't have problems with other types of gambling, and who don't display tendencies toward gambling addictions, tend to have problems with video lottery.

For this and other reasons, including government dependence on the revenue, some state legislators believe it was a mistake to institute video lottery, which was legalized in 1989. Replacing that revenue (which includes a 50 percent take on the machine's winnings, plus licensing fees and gaming taxes) will be difficult, however, especially since the most likely replacement would be a sales or income tax, an alternative that is unpopular with voters.

Video lottery also generates income for the business owners and communities offering it, and they are understandably less than enthusiastic about losing that source of revenue.

The future of South Dakota video lottery thus remains uncertain, but, at this writing, you can still play the machines, which you'll find in restaurants, bars, hotel and motel lounges, and convenience stores in addition to casinos and gaming establishments.

For fans of lottos—the kind played with paper tickets instead of electronic machines—the state offers several options. There's a Cash for Life game and a Wild Card game. One of the most popular is the South Dakota Powerball game; its large jackpots come from a pool of bets placed in several states. Several kinds of instant-win scratch tickets are available, too. You'll find them for sale at most convenience stores.

Gamers vie for a new luxury car at Deadwood's Silverado Casino. SOUTH DAKOTA TOURISM

The few bingo parlors in the Hills are run by private organizations; they are listed in the Yellow Pages under Bingo Games.

Although Black Hills gaming definitely isn't Las Vegas, fans of gaming will find a great variety of lotteries, games, machines, and events (albeit low stake and mild mannered) from which to choose. Gaming is part of both the tourism and local entertainment scenes in the Black Hills and generates income for many. However, if gaming becomes a problem, you'll find the Gamblers Anonymous hotline listed in a tip in this chapter.

DEADWOOD GAMING ESTABLISHMENTS

Deadwood still has an old-time, Old West flavor. It revels in its rich history and has mined its past to create a modern-day gold rush. Enter a casino and you'll hear the metallic clinking and clanking of coins pouring out of slot machines. Twinkling lights and neon illuminate the interiors of beautifully decorated businesses, music plays over the loudspeakers, the smell of good food is in the air, and both players and employees are relaxed and friendly. Many casinos boast handsome wood trim, elegant bars, and enticing light and color, and their pleasant ambience is enhanced by the lively electronic music of gaming devices. Although we can't list all the Deadwood casinos in this chapter, here are several you may want to visit.

Bullock Hotel
633 Main Street, Deadwood
(605) 578-1745, (800) 336-1876
www.heartofdeadwood.com
The historic Bullock has been beautifully redecorated to exceed its original elegance, and we've written about the charming features of the hotel in the Accommodations chapter. The first floor casino has huge windows, gorgeous chandeliers, and a wide staircase that, from the bottom, seems to go up forever. It's decorated with lovely wainscoting and wallpaper, and wicker and Victorian furniture. You can eat in Bully's Restaurant, have a drink in the bar, and play the many slot machines.

Cadillac Jack's Gaming Resort
360 Main Street, Deadwood
(605) 578-1500, (866) 332-3966
www.cadillacjackscasino.com
About a half mile north of Deadwood's core historic district sits Cadillac Jack's, which opened in 2002. The facade makes the complex appear to be a block of a half-dozen historic brick buildings like the ones you might find farther up on Main Street; the interior, however, is one large gaming floor with slot machines, blackjack, and live poker tables. Like many of the larger casinos, Cadillac Jack's offers regular drawings, contests, and giveaways. A favorite promotion includes the occasional stockpile of free Krispy Kreme doughnuts, which Cadillac Jack's has brought in from nearby Denver. The resort's distinguishing features include its convention facilities, which few other hotels or casinos in Deadwood can match, and a small, Denny's-like diner on the main floor, one of only two places in Deadwood where you can get food 24 hours a day in summer (the other is Big Al's Buffalo Steakhouse at the Stockade, which is open 24 hours all year; see the Restaurants chapter).

First Gold Hotel & Gaming
270 Main Street, Deadwood
(605) 578-9777, (800) 274-1876
www.firstgold.com

South Dakota's video lottery machines reward players with quietly printed paper tickets in lieu of cold, hard cash. Redeem the tickets at the establishment's counter, bar, or cash register, where the clerk or bartender will then hand over your winnings, in bills and coins.

First Gold is located out where it's quieter on Lower Main Street, on the northern edge of town. An ATV giveaway is often in progress inside this big building, and you can stay in the adjacent rooms and dine in the Horseshoe Restaurant on the premises. Up the hill several yards is the Terrace Hotel and Casino. Its commanding views of Deadwood Gulch and White Rocks (a mountain peak on the edge of town with bare granite spires on the summit) are among the best in town, but it's better known as being one of the only smoke-free venues in Deadwood.

Four Aces
531 Main Street, Deadwood
(605) 578-2323
fouracescasino.org
The Four Aces boasts lovely floral carpeting, cherry-stained woodwork, swanky chandeliers recessed into the high ceilings, and elegantly tall windows. It has a big, beautiful bar and its own restaurant. Here you can play blackjack, three-card poker, and many slot and video lottery machines.

Gold Dust Gaming and Entertainment Complex
688 Main Street, Deadwood
(605) 578-2100, (800) 456-0533
www.golddustgaming.com
The Gold Dust is a classy place. The floral-pattern carpet is an eye-catching bright red. The walls are rose and glass, and the trim is polished brass. Small, cozy lounges are scattered throughout the complex, or you can have your drink on the upstairs balcony. If you're hungry after cranking a slot machine or studying a hand of cards, have a bite in the buffet restaurant. You can

also wander over to the Gold Dust's Holiday Inn Express across the street, one of the newest structures in the core historic district. It was built in 1999 on top of a hole once occupied by the Syndicate Building, which was destroyed by fire in 1987—just after its 100th birthday. Officials say that had the December temperature been above zero, they would have lost the whole block. Ultimately the fire helped bring on legalized gambling, which in turn helped to fund the hotel's construction. Today, the only remnant of that tragic event is a large interpretive sign affixed to the yellow-brick facade near the hotel's front door.

Midnight Star
677 Main Street, Deadwood
(605) 578-1555, (800) 999-6482
www.themidnightstar.com
Actor and director Kevin Costner has said repeatedly that he has a fascination with the American West, especially the Dakotas and the Black Hills. It was that fascination which led him to star in and direct the Academy Award–winning movie *Dances with Wolves* in 1990, which was filmed primarily on the plains near Fort Pierre and in Spearfish Canyon west of Deadwood. That fascination also led him to restore Deadwood's Phoenix Building in 1991 and turn it into the Midnight Star, the tallest building on Main Street. Named for (and decorated to resemble) the saloon in Costner's 1985 *Silverado,* the establishment is lavishly adorned with etched glass, hardwood accents, plush carpet, a beautiful bar, a massive chandelier, and an imposing grand staircase with huge wooden banisters. There are dozens of slots on the main level and blackjack tables and a gift shop on the mezzanine. The second floor hosts Diamond Lil's Sports Bar (see the Nightlife chapter), while the third floor is home to Jakes, one of the best restaurants in the state (see the Restaurants chapter). Throughout the building you'll find costumes and props from some of Kevin's movies. A regular free shuttle service takes people up to Tatanka in summer (see the Attractions chapter).

Some 80 gaming halls attract the attention of Deadwood visitors. SOUTH DAKOTA TOURISM

Mineral Palace Hotel & Gaming
601 Main Street, Deadwood
(605) 578-2036, (800) 847-2522
www.mineralpalace.com
Hotel rooms make this gaming business a perfect place to spend some time; you'll find more about them in the Accommodations chapter. The Mineral Palace has multiple gaming rooms you can stroll through, with a gift shop, liquor store, both small and large bars, and a cafe.

Miss Kitty's Gaming Emporium
647 Main Street, Deadwood
(605) 578-1811
www.heartofdeadwood.com
Between 1876 and 1920 Deadwood was said to have had the largest population of ethnic Chinese in the United States outside San Francisco. Although Chinatown was incorporated into Deadwood after the fire of 1879, it remained separate from the rest of town for several decades, even operat-

ing its own legal system and fire department. The Chinese community eventually left the Black Hills, but Miss Kitty's Gaming Emporium stands as a tribute to that part of Deadwood's history. You can play slots, blackjack, and poker inside Miss Kitty's, which occupies a number of small 1880s-era buildings just south of the original Chinatown. However, the establishment is best known for its Chinese and Mexican restaurants, the only such ethnic eateries in town (see the listings for Chinatown Cafe and Consuela's Cantina in the Restaurants chapter). The festivities surrounding Deadwood's annual Chinese New Year Celebration, which takes place in late winter, are centered here.

Old Style Saloon No. 10
657 Main Street, Deadwood
(605) 578-3346, (800) 952-9398
www.saloon10.com
Arguably the most famous establishment

The Gamblers Anonymous (Gam-Anon) hotline at (888) 781-4357 can provide a referral to a local chapter or meeting.

in Deadwood, Saloon No. 10 is the watering hole where gunslinger James Butler "Wild Bill" Hickok met his end. Shot in the back by Jack McCall in 1876, Wild Bill was playing poker when he fell over dead. The cards he was dealt also fell—revealing a pair of aces and eights, forever known as the Deadman's Hand. You'll find pictures of Wild Bill—along with photos of other famous patrons, including Calamity Jane, Poker Alice, and Potato Creek Johnny—hanging on the walls here, though they're a bit hard to find amid the other artifacts that clutter the walls. Once you walk the sawdust floors and gaze at the photos, game trophies, and Wild Bill's death chair hanging above you, you'll understand why they call this the only museum in the world with a bar. In fact, the bar is so crowded that come Christmas the tree has to be hung from the ceiling. Things are a bit more open at the adjacent Utter Place, named for longtime Wild Bill companion Colorado Charlie Utter. You'll find some slots here, but mostly single-deck blackjack and, of course, poker. If you happen to get a Deadman's Hand while playing here, don't get nervous; get out your wallet, because you've just won $250.

Silverado Gaming Establishment & Restaurant
709 Main Street, Deadwood
(605) 578-3670, (800) 584-7005
www.silveradocasino.com

Two cars a month are always up for grabs by lucky winners at the Silverado, which is appropriate because it occupies a building that was formerly an automobile showroom. This is a big, wide-open space with beautiful decor, a restaurant, and plenty of gaming action, both at tables and at machines.

Tin Lizzie Gaming & Garden Cafe
555 Main Street, Deadwood
(605) 578-1715, (800) 643-4490
www.tinlizzie.com

Seniors are the primary patrons here, and the Tin Lizzie works hard to get them. Visitors over age 60 get price breaks on everything from food to gaming tokens, and there are regular special events in their honor that usually feature free food and giveaways. The building is relatively small compared to other Main Street venues, though the owners have managed to pack in plenty of classic car memorabilia. There's a cafe and snack bar, as well as a small stage for occasional live entertainment. One of the more popular musical groups in Deadwood usually plays here. A tribute to the Beatles, the Abbey Road Band has a strong following in town, even among the younger crowd, and are consistently noted for their striking similarity (in sound and appearance) to the Fab Four.

Wild West Casino and Entertainment Block
622 Main Street, Deadwood
(605) 578-1100
www.heartofdeadwood.com

You can tell when you reach for the six-guns that double as door handles that you've come to the Wild West. The carpet has a cowboy pattern, western art hangs on the walls, the ceiling is embossed tin, the casino floor has a slate fireplace, and the chandeliers are made of rawhide (really!). The building sits on the site of the old Saloon No. 10, the place where Wild Bill Hickok met his famous end at the hands of Jack McCall. There is an interpretive display in the basement that re-creates his murder and explains the historical events surrounding it. Also in the basement is an extensive model-railroad setup operated by the Black Hills Railway Society. The large model is incredibly detailed and fascinates as many adults as it does children. Upstairs is a coffee shop and homemade-candy store that proves to be a convenient stop for families marching up and down Main Street.

SHOPPING

For the folks who live in sparsely populated western South Dakota and northeastern Wyoming, the Black Hills probably look like shopping mecca. It's true that the stores and businesses do a good job of meeting the locals' material needs, and there's a lot of support for local commerce. At the same time, however, there's a limit to what a low-density area can support, and many locals head south to Denver or east to Minneapolis and the Mall of America when they can't get what they want here. So you won't find giant department stores with mind-boggling arrays of goods or streets lined with rows of specialty boutiques in the Hills. Unfortunately, you *will* find dozens of tacky gift stores peddling rubber tomahawks and plastic snow globes. But tucked between these tourist traps are small shops with an array of original and attractive items that you'd be hard-pressed to locate elsewhere—items that truly reflect the culture and history of the Black Hills.

You'll discover these regional qualities mostly in American Indian and western art; there are more details about galleries in the Arts chapter. There are other Black Hills products to watch for, such as Black Hills Gold jewelry, items made from honey (a major South Dakota export), and custom cowboy hats, boots, and saddles. Specialty stores often keep limited hours, however, so be sure to call ahead.

THE MALL

When Black Hills locals talk about "the mall," it's a safe bet that they're referring to Rapid City's Rushmore Mall (www.rushmoremall.com), the area's largest fully enclosed shopping center. Anchor stores at the mall include four national giants: Herberger's, Sears, JC Penney, and Target. There are lots of specialty stores, too, including casual-clothing stores that cater to a youthful clientele. Among them are the Buckle, Pac-Sun, Maurice's, and the Gap.

The Pro Image stocks sport jerseys, jackets, caps, and team banners. Athletics North, Foot Locker, Lady Foot Locker, and Kids Foot Locker carry athletic shoes and a few clothing items; Famous Footwear, Tradehome, Payless Shoe Source, and Payless Kids all specialize in fashionable shoes. Men will find suits and sweaters at Halberstadt's, and Victoria's Secret caters to women. Both genders can find good-looking casual wear at American Eagle Outfitters, and the entire family can find the latest sportswear at Eddie Bauer.

Western Outlet and RCC Western Store carry extensive inventories of boots, jeans, shirts, and dresses for all sizes. Top off your new outfit with a jacket, attaché case, or purse from Wilsons Leather. Gold, gems, watches, and other fine accessories can be found at Riddle's Jewelry, Kay Jewelers, and Zales Jewelers.

To maintain that healthy glow, visit General Nutrition Center for nutritional supplements and Bath and Body Works for skin care. Then reward the kids for their patience with a trip to Sam Goody's or Musicland for CDs, Suncoast Motion Picture Company for videos, or K-B Toys. With your children happy, you're free to browse for bestsellers, cookbooks, foreign dictionaries, and travel guides in Waldenbooks.

Now it's time for refreshments (this would be a good time to drop off that roll of film for one-hour processing at Ritz Camera, too) before heading for Someone's in the Kitchen, a gourmet cookware shop, and Scheels All Sports, which has clothing and equipment for just about any sport you can think of: fishing, camping, hunting, tennis, baseball, football, basketball, soccer, hockey, pool, darts, snow and waterskiing, snowshoeing, golf, kayaking, canoeing, mountain biking, in-line skating—have we left anything out? You'll also find athletic and good-looking casual shoes here.

Rushmore Mall is open seven days a week at 2200 North Maple Avenue in Rapid City. For more information call (605) 348-3378.

Separate from the mall but just across the parking lot is Toys R Us, at 400 East Disk Drive, (605) 399-9410. The name is self-explanatory: It's a wonderland of toys. You can get baby furniture and supplies, too.

You'll find additional shopping in the hearts of downtown centers and in small shopping areas on the outskirts of them. There are too many of the latter to list here, but we would like to mention Heritage Plaza on Colorado Boulevard off Interstate 90, exit 14, in Spearfish. This complex is anchored by Kmart and includes Corral West Ranchwear, Payless Shoe Source, Maurice's, Gallery 21, and Andrew's Hallmark. Keep reading to find out about some of the outstanding independently owned stores.

ANTIQUES

If you like to browse among old things, you'll have ample opportunity at any number of places that hang out an ANTIQUES shingle. Many offer a jumble of items in raw, just dug-out-of-the-barn condition, but other dealers are discriminating about their inventory and take pains to display their wares to best advantage.

Central Hills

Antiques & Art
21424 Clover Place, Piedmont
(605) 347-5016
www.antiquesandart.com
There's a reason many of the western and Plains Indian items in this bursting-at-the-seams shop look like museum pieces:

They once were. Owners James and Peg Aplan spurn reproduction and modern artifacts, often buying museum collections in their quest for authentic Old West treasures and collectible guns. They even sell rare and out-of-print books on western Americana. There's hardly room to turn around in here, but each time you do you discover something delightful: remarkable photographs, eye-catching beadwork, stunning military uniforms, star-shaped sheriff's badges, well-worn stirrups, creaky saddles, fierce-looking branding irons, sturdy stone tools, an extraordinary Crow woman's dress decorated with elk teeth, exquisite dolls, and much more. Look up and you're likely to be startled by a mounted bison head sporting three hats. The store is open daily, so you can return as often as you like. To get there, take I-90 to exit 40.

St. Joe Antiques & Gift Mall
615A St. Joseph Street, Rapid City
(605) 341-1073
This massive downtown Rapid City fixture displays items from an eclectic array of dealers. On the bottom floor you might run across vintage Star Wars toys or comic books, while a search through the upper floor might yield weathered ranching tools or an alligator-skin purse. Of course, there is plenty of antique furniture, and much of it can be seen displayed in front of the glass windows that surround the main entry. The stock of merchandise is substantial, but it's well organized and less cluttered than in many of the smaller antiques stores you'll find in less-populated towns. You can drop by the antiques mall, which is across the street from the imposing Alex Johnson Hotel, any day of the week except Sunday.

Talking Leaves
23849 U.S. Highway 385, Hill City
(605) 574-9090
This tidy little shop has just the right mix of old and old-timey items begging to go home with you. In fact, past and present blend so well it's sometimes hard to tell

which is which. Whether it's vintage dishes sweetly displayed in an antique cupboard or a collection of brand-new but unusual candles that catches your eye, it would be hard to leave empty-handed. It even smells good in here, and the owners keep the CD player stocked with soothing music by local artists. The shop, and a separate shed where you'll find more primitive antique furniture and other decorative items, is open daily May through December; call ahead January through April. You'll find Talking Leaves approximately 3 miles northeast of Hill City.

Southern Hills

Shaman Gallery
108 North Chicago Street, Hot Springs
(605) 745-6602
Owner Linda Heath and her husband, manager Adam Heath, are justifiably proud of the Shaman Gallery, located on one floor of a historic sandstone building next to the post office. The room has a 14-foot-high ceiling and stretches from 26 to 60 feet, boasting a huge inventory. One transplanted California artisan said the displays were better than anything he had ever seen in California. Here you can find Native American artifacts, works by well-known Native American painters, a large collection of western art, works by New York artists, illustration art from the 1940s and 1950s, and offerings by local artists and potters. In a small building out back, Adam does framing.

Shaman Gallery is open each day in the summer from 10:00 A.M. to 6:00 P.M. and on Thursday through Monday from 11:00 A.M. to 5:00 P.M. in the winter.

BOOKSTORES

If you love books, you know how much they enrich your life. When you visit our bookstores, be sure to look over the titles of local and regional interest, especially those by local authors.

Central Hills

Everybody's Bookstore
3321 West Main Street, Rapid City
(605) 341-3224
Bargain-hunting bookworms can have a field day in this used-book store, which has "previously read" books, mostly in paperback editions, in just about any category you can name: arts and crafts, how-to, religion, history, romance, biography, travel, and literature. You'll find French, German, Spanish, and Norwegian titles. If you're looking for an out-of-print title and it's not on the shelves, the staff will conduct a search (ask about fees). The only new items regularly in stock are books of regional, Native American, and western interest, plus maps, including topographic maps and globes. If you don't want to pay for your purchases, you might be able to trade for some of your old books. The store is closed on Sunday.

Prince & Pauper Village
902 Mount Rushmore Road, Rapid City
(605) 342-7964
www.princeandpauperbooks.com
This independently owned business is justly proud of its extensive collection of children's books, literary classics, and titles of local interest, including books by local authors. As the largest independent bookstore in town, it can be on the expensive side, especially when compared to the city's giant Borders store near the Rushmore Mall, and the shop charges for some search services.

But the emphasis on customer service is unmistakable. If you're looking for a special book, or one that's out of print, or if you want a list of available books on a given subject, just ask for help. In stock you'll find a wide range of titles, from a complete set of Hardy Boys mysteries to the latest best sellers. There are also sections on Native American fiction and Sioux history, racks of lovely greeting cards, and baby books. The shop, which hosts book signings for local and nationally known authors, is closed on Sunday except during December.

Black Hills Gold and Silver

A few specks of shining gold were all it took to touch off a wild stampede to the Black Hills in 1876 (see the History chapter). The rush didn't last long—such phenomena seldom do—but a style of world-famous jewelry that dates from those turbulent days ensures that they will not soon be forgotten. Accounts vary about the origin of the yellow, green, and pink jewelry that is the signature of Black Hills Gold. Legend says the original grape-and-leaf pattern appeared to a French jeweler in a starvation-induced vision at the height of the gold rush; another variation says that early prospectors found grapes where they discovered gold. Yet another version has the motif originating in the California goldfields of 1849 and making its way east through other gold camps. We do know that Deadwood merchant S. T. Butler was making jewelry from Black Hills Gold here in 1878, but whether he created the design, or perhaps borrowed it from the ancient Romans, is unclear.

What matters is that the design endures today, and that Black Hills Gold is still being made by hand right here. Variations on the original pattern are the most popular, but local manufacturers are coming up with new ones all the time. They still use the lost-wax method, in which each piece is cast in a plaster mold made around a wax model. The wax is melted out and replaced by molten gold. The colored accents—leaves, grape clusters, and whatever else—are spot welded on, then "wriggled" to give them a frosted look, and finally engraved for intricate details. The different colors are made by alloying gold with copper, silver, and other metals in varying proportions; some outfits still make their own alloys.

You can see artisans handcrafting 10-, 12-, and 14-karat Black Hills Gold jewelry at several places around Rapid City. Mount Rushmore Black Hills Gold, 2707 Mount Rushmore Road, (605) 343–7099, offers tours six times a day, Monday through Friday, during the summer and

The Storyteller
520 Sixth Street, Rapid City
(605) 348–7242
Comic books rule at this storehouse of fantasy. Look for entertaining books, games, and other items with a sci-fi or comic-related focus plus nonsport trading cards and collections of old and new comic-book series. The clientele is mostly between the ages of 14 and 25, but it also includes college professors and doctors. You can shop at the Storyteller every day except Sunday.

CHRISTMAS SHOP

This fun shop gets its own category. It's located in the Central Hills.

Mistletoe Ranch
23835 U.S. Highway 385, Hill City
(605) 574–4197
www.misletoeranch.com
Who said you can't have Christmas every day of the year? You can if you visit Mistletoe Ranch, where there are always

by request the rest of the year; call ahead to make arrangements. At Stamper Black Hills Gold Jewelry Manufacturing Inc., 4 miles south of Rapid City on U.S. Highway 16, (605) 342–0751, and at Landstrom Original Black Hills Gold Creations, 405 Canal Street, (605) 343–0157, (800) 843–0009, you can watch through windows and see a video.

But does the gold in Black Hills Gold actually come from the Black Hills? Until recently, we could say an assured "yes" because Homestake Gold Mine in Lead (see the History and Area Overview chapters) used to sell gold directly to local manufacturers. Now that Homestake is closed and gold mining in the Black Hills is but a remnant of a bygone era, the metals in Black Hills Gold jewelry are assuredly from sources outside South Dakota.

The same is true for Black Hills Silver, a brand created by Spearfish resident Jim Langer. Langer's Jewelry used to create its trademark leaf-and-acorn items from silver created as a by-product from Homestake gold extraction. Though the family-owned company gets metals from other sources now, its distinctive creations are still sold by many Black Hills merchants. You can also buy them directly by dropping in at the factory at 638 Main Street, Spearfish, (605) 642–2383, (800) 526–4377. There are modest mineral and gem displays, and you can make special arrangements to tour the production floor.

You'll find many brands of Black Hills Gold and Black Hills Silver rings, bracelets, brooches, pendants, earrings, watchbands, belt buckles, money clips, and other items offered for sale in jewelry and gift stores across the country and in Europe and Asia. The tricolor gold in particular has become such a classic that it has been imitated by other manufacturers who know a good thing when they see one. However, only jewelry made right here in the Black Hills can legally carry the name "Black Hills Gold." Be sure to check before making your purchase.

more than 30 artificial trees decorated in different themes plus high-quality gifts, ornaments, and collectibles galore. The selection changes all the time, but expect any variety of traditional Saint Nicholas dolls, chubby fleece Santas, dancing reindeer, and porcelain villages, as well as all kinds of ornaments. The red plaid carpet, Christmas music, and sweet scents here could turn the grumpiest Scrooge into a right jolly old elf anytime of the year—he'd probably even want to play the antique pump organ (it really works). Believe it or not, co-owner Joan Davis said she never gets tired of Christmas, not since she stopped hearing carols in her sleep. The store, 3 miles northeast of Hill City, is open daily, and refreshments are served during open-house events each Saturday and Sunday Thanksgiving through Christmas.

You can cut your own Christmas tree in the Black Hills National Forest by obtaining an $8.00 permit from any forest service office (see the Recreation chapter for a list of locations). You can cut up to five trees as long as you have a permit for each one. Choose from pine, spruce, or juniper.

CLOTHING

These shops feature custom western apparel and footwear.

Northern Hills

Trevino's Leathers
U.S. Highway 385, Deadwood
(605) 578-1271
www.trevinosleathers.com
Outside, it's a charming log cabin. Inside, it's black-leather heaven. Rhea (pronounced like Ray) Trevino has been stitching leather for a quarter century, and for most of that time he's had a steady clientele for his custom elk-hide chaps and vests. His rustic shop 6 miles south of Deadwood caters to motorcyclists with a yen for all kinds of leather garments, and the racks are hung with ready-made jackets, vests (both fringed and plain), belts, caps, and gloves. Wallets, handmade leather purses, and select jewelry items (yep, those rattles were once attached to real live snakes) round out the inventory. It's worth stopping here even if you're not in the market for some new leathers, because Trevino has some nice Native American artifacts displayed in glass cases. The shop is open seven days a week in summer and Monday through Saturday in winter. At Trevino's it's always leather weather.

Central Hills

Star of the West Hat Company
2255 North Haines Avenue, Rapid City
(605) 343-7345
Brad Montague makes custom hats with varying percentages of beaver fur and trimmings as plain or fancy as you like—and in just about any color, too. One time his stock included a dainty bone-colored bonnet shaped with a women's dress crease and adorned with a cascading ivory veil trimmed with ribbons and roses. He offers reconditioning services for hats that have been in service for a while. The average wait for a beautiful custom hat of your own is six to eight weeks. The shop is closed on Sunday.

Southern Hills

Stockman Boot and Saddlery Co.
106 South Chicago Street, Hot Springs
(605) 745-6771
www.stockmanboot.com
You won't give brand-name cowboy boots a second glance once you've seen this custom-made footwear. Imagine boots that fit perfectly not by coincidence but because they were made that way. Boot and saddle maker Jim Bultsma can create from virtually any type of leather available. Some of his past work has been made from the hides of kangaroo, bison, horse, elephant, bull, calf, shark, snake, lizard, and ostrich feet. The leathers can be dyed in any color, from slick black and bright yellow to metallic silver and gold. To get a pair of custom boots, which start at around $600, you'll have to make an appointment and see Jim personally. He'll take a footprint mark of both feet and several measurements, then he'll let you pick out the colors, cuts, and types of leather you'd like. The last step is waiting, and it's probably the most difficult of all. Expect Jim to take up to a year to get the boots done. You can stop by the Bultsma store any day of the week except Sunday.

NATIVE AMERICAN AND OTHER ETHNIC ITEMS

Long revered by various Native American tribes, the Black Hills became a richly diverse melting pot with the gold rush of 1876. To enjoy the artistic expression of some of those cultures, as well as others from around the world, visit the shops listed below and find wonderful handmade decorative items, clothing, and even foods.

Northern Hills

Shankar Arts
29 Deadwood Street, Deadwood
(605) 578-3808
Shankar Arts is owned by Phil Breland and his Moroccan-born wife, Georgette Ohayon. They've been traveling to the far side of the globe for more than two decades, bringing back exquisite silver and gemstone jewelry, woolen jackets, brass Buddhas, hand-knotted tribal carpets, crystals, antique ritual pieces, and other fascinating items. Their buying trips take them to North Africa, India, Thailand, Tibet, Indonesia, Nepal, and the Middle East, where they search out markets, fairs, and festivals for new folk crafts. Every piece reflects the culture from which it came, and Breland and Ohayon can tell you its story. You can buy unset gemstones here, order custom work, or have your gold and silver jewelry repaired.

Shankar Arts is open daily from early May through January, when it closes for three months while the owners travel the globe to replenish their inventory.

Central Hills

Global Market
617 Main Street, Rapid City
(605) 343-4051

617 Main Street, Spearfish
(605) 642-9014
It's said that if you can remember the

1960s, you weren't part of it. Well, Global Market will transport you back to those days of head shops and clothes from the India Imports of Rhode Island catalog. This is the place to find imported hand-batiked clothing, garments woven from flax and other natural fibers, incense, candles, silver-filigree jewelry, South American wool sweaters, bongo and conga drums (made in New Jersey), kilim rugs, carved masks, handmade soap, baskets, books, tapes, CDs, and more.

By the way, that's not a typo in the listing—the identical street numbers for the two stores were a cosmic coincidence. (We're convinced the owner has good karma.) Both are open daily.

House of Scandinavia
13774 U.S. Highway 16, Rapid City
(605) 348-3858
If you're of Scandinavian descent, you've probably been teased about lutefisk, the odoriferous Limburger of fish dishes. Well, here's a place where you can bask unabashedly in your ethnic heritage. For many decades this red-and-white chalet 9 miles south of Rapid City has stocked quintessential Northern European goods, from Norwegian sweaters (to die for) to *lefse* mix. Sweden, Norway, Denmark, Finland, Iceland, Holland, and Germany are represented here in such items as brightly painted Dalecarlian horses, needlepoint kits, delicate pewter jewelry, pretty table linens, glassware, china, funny troll dolls, kitchen utensils, food items, clogs, toys, glass Christmas ornaments, and blue delftware. The shop is open daily from May through October; in November and December, when co-owner Jean Watkins

---

Looking for a slinky little number covered in sequins or accented with spangles? See the scintillating selection of party dresses at Kathleen's, 622 Main Street in Spearfish, (605) 642-3843. This ladies' boutique also carries dressed-up casual clothes and fashionable sportswear.

(she's of Swedish parentage) serves hot cider and glogg and homemade *lefse,* it's open Friday through Sunday and by appointment. It's closed from the weekend before Christmas until May 1.

The Indians
141 Winter Street, Keystone
(605) 666-4864, (605) 341-7452, (866) 845-3426
www.theindianskeystone.com
Items on the shelves here represent the work of artisans from many tribes, and the store's Indian Arts and Crafts Association membership certificate (it's a charter member) is your guarantee of authentic Native American craftsmanship. There are works by local artists and crafters and an array of southwestern silver-and-turquoise jewelry, baskets, sand paintings, kachina dolls, and genuine Navajo rugs. Beadwork, quillwork, pottery, dance sticks, drums, moccasins, denim clothing, toys, and a great selection of books also keep you browsing. The store is open seven days a week year-round.

Prairie Edge Trading Co. & Galleries
606 Main Street, Rapid City
(605) 342-3086, (800) 541-2388
www.prairieedge.com
If you're captivated by Native American crafts and culture and you love fine handmade items, go straight to Prairie Edge. You'll know you're someplace special the instant you step into the spacious showrooms gleaming with polished-wood floors and fixtures. Set aside plenty of time for your visit, not only because there are three floors' worth of wonderful merchandise to look at, but also because the serene beauty of the displays makes you want to linger to examine each exquisite piece.

When you enter, locally made star quilts and colorful Pendleton blankets catch your eye, and cases of jewelry, beadwork, and intricate quillwork beckon. You might feel inspired to buy supplies for your own creations in the Sioux Trading Post portion of the store. The toy assortment offers games, marbles, puzzles, and many breeds of fuzzy stuffed animals. You're sure to be dazzled by the Italian Glass Bead Library, where jars upon jars hold beads in all kinds of colors and almost as many sizes—intriguingly, they're from a Venetian supplier that provided beads to 19th-century fur traders.

Most enchanting of all, perhaps, is the Plains Indian Gallery, where you'll see magnificent reproductions of traditional clothing and artifacts, including beaded cradle boards, fringed and beaded leather dresses, ceremonial garments embroidered with porcupine quills, decorative vessels, dolls, and more. From here, climb the wide staircase to browse among the fascinating books on Native American subjects, crafts, and the West, as well as a selection of tapes and CDs by Native American musicians. Finally, visit the third-floor art gallery to see works by acclaimed regional and national artists, sculptors, photographers, and craftspeople. If once is not enough, you can return seven days a week to see it all again at this 125-year-old building.

Sioux Pottery
1441 East St. Joseph Street, Rapid City
(605) 341-3657, (800) 657-4366
www.siouxpottery.com
This isn't just a place to buy beautiful, hand-decorated pottery in muted rainbow colors. You're also invited on a self-guided tour through the plant to ask questions and watch the craftspeople and artists at work. It's an interesting process. Clay slip, a liquid mixture of Black Hills red and Kentucky white clays and water, is poured into molds. After the edges harden, the excess slip is poured out, leaving a perfectly formed vase or other vessel. Once dry the pieces are unmolded, trimmed, sanded, painted, hand decorated, glazed, and fired. The artists use traditional geometric designs and their own imaginations in their etching and painting, which makes each piece unique. You can buy one piece or several, as well as other Native American-crafted items in the gift shop. Sioux Pottery is open daily June through August and weekdays the rest of the year.

Phoebe Apperson Hearst—and Family

Great wealth and personal popularity never went to Phoebe Apperson Hearst's head. Even as a much-courted Missouri belle, the lively brunette was known for her kindheartedness and generosity, traits she continued to cultivate after becoming the wife of George Hearst—she was 19 and he 41 when they married in 1862. George would later become a founder of Homestake Mining Company (see the History chapter) and a U.S. senator from California. The couple, who lived in San Francisco, occasionally visited the Black Hills city of Lead, where the Homestake Gold Mine was located.

Although the couple never made the rough-and-ready mining camp their home (George found the Black Hills a bit crude for his refined tastes), Phoebe's philanthropic efforts there earned her the admiration and affection of its citizens. In 1896 Phoebe gave Lead a public library for Christmas, and it bears her name to this day. She also came to the aid of the Lead Women's Club when financial problems threatened to shut down its free kindergarten. Her support for education spread far beyond Lead, however, as she helped found the PTA (originally the National Congress of Mothers) in 1897. That same year she became the first woman regent of the University of California, a post she held until her death in 1919.

In return for her many gifts to Lead, the citizenry and business community commissioned a Boston silversmith to create a large, ornately decorated and engraved loving cup in Phoebe's honor. No doubt the gesture pleased her, and perhaps the trophy did as well. Phoebe's love of fine things showed in her patronage of the arts and in the elegant clothes and jewels in which she posed for her portraits. The fact that she had Homestake stock issued in her own name (albeit misspelled "Phebe") hints that she was as astute in the acquisition of money as she was lavish in her dispensation of it.

Less well loved than his mother was George and Phoebe's only child, publishing tycoon and yellow journalist William Randolph Hearst, believed to be the model for Orson Welles's film *Citizen Kane.* William Randolph's ostentatious California home, Hearst Castle, is the setting for *Murder at San Simeon,* a book blending fact and fiction written by his granddaughter, Patty Hearst. The heiress made headlines of her own when she was kidnapped by the Symbionese Liberation Army in 1974 and transformed into the terrorist Tania. After her 1975 arrest and subsequent conviction for bank robbery, Patty married a prison guard, Bernard Shaw, and is reported to be living happily (and quietly) ever after.

NATURAL FOODS

If it tastes good it's bad for you, right? Wrong. Stock up on food from the stores listed here and you'll have everything you need for a yummy, nutritious feast. All of these stores are closed on Sunday.

Northern Hills

Good Earth Natural Foods
138 East Hudson Street, Spearfish
(605) 642-7639

The displays here are so attractive and welcoming you feel good even before you buy any of the healthful merchandise. Along with a good selection of grains are books, nutritional supplements, bulk herbs, grooming supplies, biodegradable cleaning products, frozen and canned foods, lots of bottled and canned beverages, and many other items.

Central Hills

Main Street Market
512 Main Street, Rapid City
(605) 341-9099
www.themainstreetmarket.com

The shelves in Main Street Market are well stocked with nutritional supplements, herbs, personal-care products, books, pasta, tea, soups, condiments, and lots of other tasty, tempting goods for wholesome meals and nutritious snacks. Add the personal service and attention on which the owners pride themselves, and you will come away with a warm feeling as well as a filled market basket.

Staple & Spice Market
601 Mount Rushmore Road, Rapid City
(605) 343-3900
www.stapleandspice.com

Since 1921 this tried-and-true market has been able to boast the largest selection of bulk herbs and spices in South Dakota. The current confines are bursting with nutritional supplements, homeopathic

remedies, personal-care products, teas, and staples for wholesome eating. Special items include free-range buffalo, chicken, turkey, and beef, whole-bean coffee, organic fruits and vegetables, and bulk honey. If the item you want isn't in stock, the staff will bend over backward to try to get it for you.

Southern Hills

Earth Goods Natural Foods
738 Jennings Avenue, Hot Springs
(605) 745-7715

Owner/herbologist Jackie Gericke offers nutritional supplements, herbs, and a generous variety of bulk dried fruits, nuts, flours, seeds, grains, and beans, plus frozen entrees and desserts, essential oils, juices, teas, and the usual items you'd expect to find in a natural-foods store. It's all offered in a comfortable, friendly atmosphere.

PHOTO SUPPLIES AND SERVICE

We've wondered how many professional photographers per square mile live in the Black Hills—we're betting it's quite a few. So it's rather baffling that we don't have a large camera store to serve them. If your photo needs are limited to basic cameras, print film, and quickie processing, you won't have any trouble finding what you're looking for. Fortunately we also have a few places that offer specialized services and higher-end equipment.

Northern Hills

Deadwood One Hour Photo
83 Charles Street, Deadwood
(605) 578-3015

Owner John Bing is exceptionally friendly and a fair businessman, two qualities that make his store a favorite among Northern Hills photo enthusiasts. His developing and printing charges might be more expensive than some area drugstores, but the quality of the prints that come out of his shop is unsurpassed—guaranteed. If a picture doesn't turn out right, you won't pay for it, period. He also does portraits for very competitive prices, sells a limited supply of new and used camera equipment, and does minor repair work. The studio and store are located in a historic house on the south side of town, next door to Northern Hills General Hospital.

Southern Hills

Camera Corner and Carroll Photo Studio
819 Mount Rushmore Road, Custer
(605) 673-4856
This shop, about 3 miles west of Custer State Park, offers one-hour 35mm color-print processing (ask about extra charges), black-and-white printing, enlargements, contact sheets, color copying, and basic camera repair. A limited selection of cameras, tripods, and other equipment is available as are Polaroid, slide, and 120 roll film. The shop also houses a studio specializing in family and group reunion portraits. It's open Monday through Saturday and by appointment on Sunday.

ROCK SHOPS

The subject of Black Hills rocks covers a wide spectrum that includes precious metals, gemstones, and fossils. To learn more about this mineral diversity, see the Natural World chapter.

Central Hills

Dakota Stone Co.
23863 Palmer Gulch Road, Hill City
(605) 574-2760
www.dakotastone.net
Stones for your fireplace, patio, rock garden, or rock veneer—they're all here, along

The Black Hills Farmers' Market sets up booths two to three times a week in Rapid City from early July through the end of October. To find out when and where to buy those farm-fresh fruits and veggies, contact the Rapid City Area Chamber of Commerce, 444 Mount Rushmore Road, (605) 343-1744.

with local alabaster for the sculptor in you. Not surprisingly, beautiful rose quartz, the South Dakota state mineral, is this store's biggest seller, and you'll find many lovely specimens from which to choose (the owners have their own quarry). Browse among the outdoor bins, where you'll see everything from milky selenite to jet-black obsidian, then do the same in the gift shop, where you'll find speckled leopard-skin rock, tumbled and polished stones, books, carvings, jewelry, and geodes—hollow rocks you can break open with a hammer to see the pretty crystals inside. The store, 3 miles north of Hill City on U.S. Highway 385, is open daily June through August but is closed on Sunday the rest of the year.

SADDLES 'N' STUFF

Around here folks rely on horses for the three R's: ranching, recreation, and rodeoing.

Northern Hills

Croft's Saddlery
U.S. Highway 385, Deadwood
(605) 578-3228
croftsaddlery.com
If you saw the Tom Selleck movie *Quigley Down Under,* you saw one of Jerry and Duffy Croft's saddles. Make that two—in movie work, matching pairs of everything are required for the actors and their stunt doubles. Croft's meticulously handcrafted saddles appeal to working cowboys as

well as to filmmakers, since the saddles combine an authentic antique look with modern comfort. The Crofts, a husband-and-wife team, pride themselves on using top-quality materials and not cutting corners. Then again, corners are a Croft signature—look for the classy spot braiding in them. The Crofts do most of their business by phone, taking measurements for both horse and rider that way. A custom saddle order takes six to eight months to fill, but other items such as chaps and bridles can be completed in two to three weeks. Croft's is open Monday through Friday.

J&S Saddle & Tack
2221 Junction Avenue, Sturgis
(605) 347-4667

It's hard to think of anything the equestrian needs that can't be found here. There's a room full of new and used saddles plus saddle blankets, bridles, and other tack for the horse to wear. For the rider, the shop has boots, chaps, decorative leather belts, and gift items such as pretty key rings. Of course, you don't have to own a horse to shop here; if you just like the western look, that's a good enough reason. The store is open every day but Sunday.

Central Hills

Bader Saddles
317 Main Street, Rapid City
(605) 342-5791

Everything you need to outfit your horse in style is here: saddles (new and used), saddle blankets, tack, and rodeo equipment such as bronc saddles and bareback riggings. But the truly discerning horse will want his or her own custom-made saddle, fashioned by the expert hands of store owner Boyce Bader. A custom order takes about a year and a half to fill, but both you and your horse know it'll be worth the wait. Boot and shoe repair is also available. Stop in any day but Sunday for more details.

Southern Hills

Stockman Boot and Saddlery Co.
106 South Chicago Street, Hot Springs
(605) 745-6771
www.stockmanboot.com

Jim Bultsma specializes in custom-made saddles but also does repairs and just about any other kind of leatherwork you might call for. His shop (see the listing under Clothing) stocks ready-made saddles and tack, too. Operations are in full swing Monday through Saturday.

SPORTING GOODS

If you've seen the Recreation chapter, you understand why we have so many sporting-goods stores.

Northern Hills

Terry Peak Ski & Sport
32 Fantail Gulch, Lead
(605) 584-3644, (866) 250-1606
www.rentmyskis.com
www.buymyskis.com

Terry Peak is a retail and rental store for winter sports. It's a great place to visit if you find yourself exploring the Black Hills in winter but unprepared for fun in the snow. Skis, snowboards, snowblades, boots, pants, goggles, and personal attention to your needs are all found at Terry Peak. The store is open daily between Labor Day and early spring and is closed the remainder of the year.

Central Hills

Dakota Angler & Outfitter
513 Seventh Street, Rapid City
(605) 341-2450
www.flyfishsd.com

When you think about it, an entire store devoted to fly fishing makes sense in the Black Hills. Just ask any local fly fisher (and

Cornish Pasties

First, some clarification. We're talking here about an ethnic food called a "pasty," which rhymes with "nasty" but is really very pleasant to eat. A pasty is a turnover filled with heavy foods like meat and potatoes. The resourceful wives of tin miners in Cornwall, England, concocted pasties long ago as a sustaining meal to tuck into their hardworking husbands' lunch pails.

According to Bonnie King, who has made more than one million pasties in her hometown of Lead, the first such hand-held pies had a barley crust and were filled with fish. Today's "traditional" pasty consists of a pastry crust with a steak, potato, and onion filling. When Cornish miners and their families immigrated to the Black Hills goldfields (see the History chapter), they brought their pasty recipes with them. That was fortunate for women like Bessie Richards, who lost her husband to silicosis and supported her 14 children by baking and selling pasties.

Local descendants of immigrant miners say they're not sure whether the Cornish folk imported their custom of leaving a bit of pasty crust at the mine to keep the tommyknockers from making mischief. Tommyknockers were dwarf creatures believed to live in the mines; their exis-tence explained knocking noises miners heard while digging.

You might never get to hear a tommyknocker, but you can experience the time-honored taste of a pasty during your trip to the Black Hills. Bonnie, who made and sold traditional pasties from her grocery store in Lead when the Homestake Mine was still open, now distributes her creations to FreshStart convenience stores across the Black Hills. For custom orders you can call her at (605) 722-3875. Bonnie, who learned to make pasties from a daughter of early-day immigrants, offers several varieties, including traditional, pizza (with a yeast crust), ham, sausage, and sausage 'n' sauerkraut.

there are plenty of women among them). Need a float boat? No problem. Looking for fly-tying supplies? There's a whole wall full. In addition to all the practical items like rods, reels, books, magazines, and maps, there are items to keep you in the spirit even when you can't be streamside: jewelry, watches, artwork, T-shirts, dishes, and even wild rice to serve alongside your catch. For information about Dakota Angler's guide service and lessons, see the listing in the Fishing section of the Recreation chapter. The store, which is an authorized Orvis dealer, is closed on Sunday all year and on Monday during January and February.

CLOSE-UP

Made in the Black Hills

You'll notice lots of South Dakota–made items on the shelves in stores and gift shops. Here are some that are made in the Black Hills: the Country Caterer jellies, bread mix, and more, Belle Fourche; Dakota Delights and Homespun Naturals vegetable soaps, Custer; Dakota Gold Mustard, Spearfish; Dark Canyon Coffee, Rapid City; Daystar Candles, Custer; eggspressions! hand-decorated goose and other eggshells, Rapid City; Heart of the Earth bath products, Fruitdale; Jewelry by Waldron, including the Circle of Nations and WaterSong lines and Earth-Charms ornaments, Rapid City; and Prairie Gold Coffee Co., Rapid City.

And then, of course, there is our very own Black Hills Gold.

Edge Sports
922 Main Street, Rapid City
(605) 716-9912

32 Baltimore Street, Lead
(605) 722-7547
www.grabanedge.com
Edge Sports, with locations in both Rapid City and Lead, provides thrill seekers with a variety of adventure sports equipment. Their friendly and helpful staff is well trained and will assist you in finding the most suitable equipment for skiing, snowboarding, skateboarding, and rock climbing. During the winter months, they also provide the newest in ski and snowboard rentals at their Lead location. The Rapid City shop is open seven days a week all year long, and the Lead shop is open primarily from November to March.

Granite Sports
301 Main Street, Hill City
(605) 574-2121
www.sylvanrocks.com
Granite Sports' mission statement includes a commitment to stocking the largest selection of climbing equipment in the area. But owner (and climber) Susan Scheirbeck also shows great taste in her assortment of camping gear, backpacks (both human and canine), hiking boots, brand-name outerwear, technical clothing, casual duds (for kids, too), and rugged sweaters. The shop is the Patagonia dealer for the area. The shop is open daily from May through October, and closed Thursday the rest of the year.

Peak Sports
1002 Jackson Boulevard, Rapid City
(605) 341-5445
This shop specializes in downhill skis, snowblades, snowboards, and everything you need to be attired for playing in the snow. Personal attention is yours when you need the proper fit in a boot or a custom insole, and certified personnel are on hand to keep your skis or board in topflight condition. The store does not carry rentals. Peak Sports is open daily between Labor Day and early spring and is closed the rest of the year.

The Runner's Shop
41 East Omaha, Rapid City
(605) 348-7866
www.sdrunnersshop.com
Lots of stores sell athletic shoes, but how

many have this kind of selection, or offer the kind of knowledgeable service you find here? At last count it carried 90 styles of running shoes in stock and at least that number in other types of footwear for hiking, walking, and other activities. The staff has more than 45 years of combined experience fitting runners—and they're runners themselves, which helps. The shop specializes in modifying shoes for optimal comfort and performance to avoid problems. If it's too late for that, they'll work with you on problem resolution. You can pamper more than your feet here, though, because the shop carries the latest high-tech running wear plus accessories and books, shoe-care products, and even free maps to help you find the best trails. You can also get information about competitive and fun runs. The store is closed on Sunday.

Two Wheeler Dealer Cycle and Fitness
100 East Boulevard North, Rapid City
(605) 343-0524

215A Jackson Boulevard, Spearfish
(605) 642-7545
www.twowheelerdealer.com

So you want to get in shape. Now all you have to do is decide whether to buy a bicycle, treadmill, elliptical trainer, glider, strider, weight machine, or some other type of fitness equipment to help you get the job done. The decision will be much easier after you visit with the folks here, who carry all of the above and more. In bikes alone they stock mountain, road, BMX, fitness, and cruiser models. You can rent bikes also. The clothing and accessories you need for your active lifestyle are here, too, along with a full-service repair and maintenance shop. You can drop in any day of the week in Rapid City; the Spearfish location is closed Sunday.

ATTRACTIONS

The Black Hills aren't nearly as massive as some of the mountain ranges you'll find farther west, but they aren't small either. Spreading across a swath of land 125 miles long and 65 miles wide, they take up well over two million acres in South Dakota and Wyoming. The natural wonders of this expansive region alone would provide enough activities to keep a visitor busy for weeks on end. However, the creativity and industriousness of the land's 160,000 residents continue to give travelers here more opportunities to relax and have fun.

Diversity of attractions is one of the Hills' greatest resources, yet the sheer number of things to do makes it hard to separate the activities that will capture your imagination from the ones that will make you yawn. In the following pages you'll find a selection of the best the Black Hills have to offer—but it is by no means exhaustive. If there's a specific attraction you're looking for but can't find in this book, your best bet is to ask a local. They're friendly, helpful, and willing to show off just how much they know about the area.

If you're looking for diversions geared primarily toward children, see the Kidstuff chapter. Day Trips and Weekend Getaways, Recreation, and the Badlands and Nearby are other relevant chapters to read. In these chapters, as in this one, you'll find a sampling of both major roadside attractions and out-of-the-way sights—the secluded settlements and hidden wonders known only to insiders.

Glorious Black Hills summers are the high point of the year, and most visitors come here in June, July, August, and September. Some attractions open a week or two before (or on) Memorial Day weekend and close for the winter on (or a couple of weeks after) Labor Day. Many shorten their hours and days of operation in the early and late part of the season, too. Other attractions are family owned and operated and may be a bit casual about their operating seasons (due in part to our rather unpredictable winters). Many attractions may plan to close in November, but if the snows begin in October, they'll close early. Some may open in early May, only to find that spring rains are keeping visitors away. They may close again until later in the month or shorten their hours. South Dakotans have learned to adjust to their weather, so it always pays to call ahead before driving to an attraction.

Not only can seasons affect times of operation, but they might also affect prices, as can age makeup and group size. Many establishments have a sliding scale of rates for seniors and children. Rates for large groups may be less than for small groups. Rates may also be less in the winter months if the establishment is even open. Again, because things can change so rapidly, call ahead.

Many places listed in this chapter have the additional benefit of being educational. You'll be entertained while you learn about geology, the history of the Wild West, the culture of old Dakota Territory, and the critters and folks who inhabit the present-day Black Hills. By the time you've worked your way through this chapter, you'll feel like a local.

PRICE CODE

The following price ratings refer to the cost of one adult ticket; however, many places offer discounts for children, students, and seniors.

$	Less than $5.00
$$	$5.00 to $10.00
$$$	$11.00 to $20.00
$$$$	More than $20.00

Calamity Jane

Calamity Jane, one of Deadwood's most famous citizens, passed away in 1903 in debt to the Goldberg Grocery for the sum of $7.00. Calamity is buried at Mount Moriah Cemetery. In recent years the grocery changed ownership and is now a casino, but the ledger book with Calamity's still-outstanding balance can be seen at the Adams Museum.

CAVES

Caves lace the limestone beneath the central Black Hills. Exploration is difficult, so no one knows for sure about their depth, whether they are connected, or what natural wonders the unexplored regions may conceal. You can, however, tour the previously explored nether regions of each cave listed below. Stalactites, stalagmites, popcorn and frost crystals, cave flowers, and flowstone are just some of the fascinating geological formations you'll see.

The caverns have easy and safe walking trails, although the nature of caves makes them inaccessible to wheelchairs. Cave temperatures are in the range of 45 to 50 degrees, and they can sometimes be damp—take a jacket and wear your walking shoes (preferably with sturdy rubber soles).

The following caves are privately owned and operated and many have gift and rock shops, snack bars, hiking trails, and picnic areas. Some are open only during the summer, approximately Memorial Day to Labor Day. In planning your trip to the caverns, remember that the last tours of the day often leave sometime before the official closing hour. It's a good idea to call ahead.

You'll find the Southern Hills' Jewel Cave and Wind Cave discussed in the Parks and Nature Areas section.

Northern Hills

Wonderland Cave Natural Park   **$$$**
Vanocker Canyon Road, Nemo
(605) 578-1728, (605) 343-5043
This cave is accessible from U.S. Highway 385 from Deadwood or via Interstate 90, exit 32. Hours are 8:00 A.M. to 4:00 P.M. seven days a week, from May 1 through November 1 (or until the first snowfall, sometimes as early as October).

Central Hills

Beautiful Rushmore Cave   **$$**
13622 Highway 40, Keystone
(605) 255-4467, (605) 255-4384
www.beautifulrushmorecave.com
During its season, this cave is open seven days a week. From May 1 through Memorial Day, hours are 9:00 A.M. to 5:00 P.M. After Memorial Day and through Labor Day, hours are 8:00 A.M. to 8:00 P.M. After

Labor Day until its closing on October 31, hours are 9:00 A.M. to 5:00 P.M.

Black Hills Caverns $$
2600 Cavern Road, Highway 44 West
Rapid City
(605) 343-0542, (800) 837-9358
www.blackhillscaverns.com
Guided tours start every 20 minutes in summer. Hours are 8:00 A.M. to 8:00 P.M. seven days a week, from mid-June through Labor Day. From May 1 to mid-June and from Labor Day until October 15, hours are 8:30 A.M. to 5:30 P.M., seven days a week. There's an additional fee for gold panning.

Crystal Cave Park $$
Highway 44 West, Rapid City
(605) 342-8008
Summer hours are 8:00 A.M. to 8:00 P.M. seven days a week. After Labor Day, hours are 9:00 A.M. to 5:00 P.M. on weekends only, but call ahead for fall and winter hours.

Sitting Bull Crystal Caverns $$
U.S. Highway 16 South, Rapid City
(605) 342-2777
www.sittingbullcrystalcave.com
This cave is open approximately May 1 through September, seven days a week 7:00 A.M. to 7:00 P.M. and on weekends only in October 8:00 A.M. to 5:00 P.M.

Stage Barn Crystal Cave $$
Interstate 90, exit 46, Piedmont
(605) 787-4505
This cave is open from Memorial Day through Labor Day; hours are 8:00 A.M. to 7:00 P.M. Open seven days a week, the cave is in beautiful, natural Stage Barn Canyon; all the flora and fauna native to South Dakota is found in this canyon. The excellent interpretive guides are prepared to lead you on the one-hour tour as you arrive; usually there is no waiting time.

HISTORIC SITES

Step back in time by visiting the places where history was made in the Black Hills.

Northern Hills

Buckskin Johnny Spaulding
Cabin Free
415 Fifth Avenue, Belle Fourche
No phone
If you admire the pioneers for their courage, independence, and toughness, you should see this reconstructed cabin to understand how strong they really were. It's difficult to imagine braving a South Dakota winter in this vulnerable home. Built in 1876, the original tiny cabin sheltered pioneer and adventurer Buckskin Johnny and his sister's family, the first white settlers in the area. The cabin is now a minimuseum and an eye-opening glimpse into the primitive lives of the early settlers.

Be sure to read the story on the plaque on the cabin's outside wall (or ask a volunteer) of how Johnny and his childhood sweetheart, Nettie, were separated in their youth. They were finally reunited after a 53-year separation and were married from 1927 until 1932, when Johnny died.

The cabin is open year-round from 8:00 A.M. to 5:00 P.M. Monday through Friday. Hours may expand to include the weekends during the summer, but visitors should stop by or call the Tri-State Memorial Museum in Belle Fourche (see the listing) to be sure. Donations are appreciated.

D.C. Booth Historic Fish
Hatchery Free
423 Hatchery Circle, Spearfish
(605) 642-7730
www.dcbooth.fws.gov
You don't have to be a fishing enthusiast to enjoy this attraction. If you are, though, you'll find the historic hatchery and museum a delight. Trout hatchlings were once raised here to stock streams across the West. You'll learn about the hatchery process and how it evolved as technology and knowledge improved. The fish car, an early 1900s railroad car that was equipped to transport fish all over the country on their way to new trout streams, is open for viewing.

If you're less than enthusiastic about fishing, you'll still enjoy strolling the grounds, feeding the ducks and fish, and touring the Booth home. The house was built in 1905 and is listed in the National Register of Historic Places. Furnished with period antiques and Booth family memorabilia, it is a delightful example of the attention to design and detail obvious in the gracious homes of that era. Be sure to visit the underwater viewing window near the entrance to the grounds, where the resident rainbow trout and brown trout swim by. It's a chance for a rare fish-eye view as well as a humorous glimpse from below of paddling duck feet.

The hatchery, museum, and home are open from mid-May through mid-September, seven days a week from 10:00 A.M. to 5:00 P.M. Donations are accepted. The hatchery and grounds are next door to the Spearfish City Park and are open from dawn until dusk.

Mount Moriah Cemetery (Boot Hill) $
Lincoln Street, Deadwood
(605) 722-0837

No dedicated Deadwood visitor leaves without paying respects to those who lie at Boot Hill. Calamity Jane's and Wild Bill Hickok's graves are the main attractions, though lesser-known—but no less interesting—folks are also buried here. Pick up a walking-tour guide at the ticket booth. It will furnish the human-interest stories lacking on traditionally succinct tombstones. Take note of the nearly empty Chinese section (most bodies were eventually returned to China), the Jewish section (where many stones are inscribed in Hebrew), and the three potter's fields.

Among the colorful characters buried here are madam Dora Dufran, who is buried with her parrot, Fred, and Blanche Colman, the first woman member of the South Dakota Bar, who was self-taught.

The entire cemetery completed a three-year, $3.1 million restoration in the summer of 2003, enhancing the peace and beauty of its location overlooking the gulch. The renovations didn't alter its mountainous terrain, however, so keep in mind that some parts can be quite steep to access. Be sure to check out the new interpretive center at the base of the cemetery, which houses a small gift shop and exhibits from the collection of the Adams Museum (see the listing under Museums). Check out the stained-glass window, massive leather-bound Bible, and other artifacts from Deadwood's First and Second Methodist Churches, which were destroyed in 1885 and 2002, respectively.

The cemetery is open all year, but the ticket booth is open from May to Labor Day from 7:00 A.M. to 8:00 P.M., then from 9:00 A.M. to 5:00 P.M. for the rest of September, and intermittently until winter sets in. Residents and those with relatives buried here are admitted at no charge.

Central Hills

Big Thunder Gold Mine $$
604 Blair Street, Keystone
(605) 666-4847, (800) 314-3917

Learn about the history of Black Hills gold mining, explore an 1800s underground mine, and try panning streamside for your own specks of gleaming treasure. Guided tours begin with a 10-minute film, and each hard-hatted visitor is rewarded with a sample of gold ore at the end of the 68-foot tunnel. If your best panning efforts fail to yield anything, you can purchase a small vial of pure, 24-carat gold leaf in the gift shop, which also carries souvenirs, books, rocks, and that great pretender, fool's gold.

The mine is open May through September. Hours are 8:00 A.M. to 8:00 P.M. from Memorial Day through Labor Day and 9:00 A.M. to 5:00 P.M. the rest of the season. For an additional small fee, you can go gold panning, too.

Prehistoric sinkhole at Mammoth Site of Hot Springs. SOUTH DAKOTA TOURISM

Southern Hills

1881 Custer County Courthouse
Museum & Book Store   Free
411 Mount Rushmore Road, Custer
(605) 673-2443

The exhibits here provide a good overview of early life in the Custer area. Old photographs play a prominent role in telling the story, but you'll also see George Armstrong Custer's dress epaulets and antelope rifle. Rocks and minerals, native bird and animal specimens, authentic costumes, Native American artifacts, and exhibits depicting mining, lumbering, farming, and community life round out the displays. Don't miss the chilling stone jail in the basement, the courtroom on the second floor, or the buildings out back—where Custer County's only legal hanging took place. Bookstore attendants are ready to answer your questions as you browse among the reading matter.

The museum, which is staffed by volunteers, is open from June 1 to August 31, 9:00 A.M. to 9:00 P.M. Monday through Saturday and 1:00 to 9:00 P.M. Sunday. Donations are appreciated.

Mammoth Site of Hot Springs $$
1800 U.S. Highway 18 Bypass, Hot Springs
(605) 745-6017
www.mammothsite.com

If you think an elephant is big, wait until you meet Sinbad the mammoth. The full-size replica of a Columbian mammoth skeleton greets you at the Mammoth Site, where scientists have unearthed the fossilized remains of ancient creatures that became trapped in a sinkhole and died. The find was discovered accidentally in 1974, when the ground was being excavated for housing construction. Since then, the site has provided research data about animals and the environment from thousands of years ago. It is the only in situ mammoth fossil display in the United States—that is, the only one in which the bones are left lying where they were found. This may be the only place you'll ever see mammoth hair on display, too.

You can take a guided tour or walk through the exhibits yourself with a guidebook from the ticket counter. (The text is available in English, French, German, Dutch, Italian, and Japanese.) In the gift shop, children will find a hands-on paleontological dig. The shop features a big selection of books for all ages, in addition to other items.

Mammoth Site is open daily; during the peak season, mid-May to late August, hours are 8:00 A.M. to 8:00 P.M., with the last tour at 7:00 P.M. Hours vary the rest of the year, so call ahead.

MUSEUMS

Tour restored historic homes or visit museums of mining, trains, and motorcycles. Dozens of museums offer ways to deepen your knowledge of the Black Hills and Western history.

Northern Hills

Adams House $
22 Van Buren Street, Deadwood
(605) 578-3724
www.adamsmuseumandhouse.org

William Emery (known as W. E.) Adams became a successful businessman in Deadwood during the late 19th and early 20th centuries (see the Adams Museum listing below). By 1925 he and his wife were living in the finest mansion in town and awaiting the arrival of their only daughter's first baby. But by a terrible twist of fate, W. E.'s wife, daughter, and grandchild all died within a 48-hour period, each from a different cause. The once-proud Deadwood patrician was left devastated at the loss of his entire family and wondered if he'd ever find happiness again.

The details of this story, and many

others relating to W. E. and the original builders of the home, Deadwood's influential Franklin family, are now a part of the regular tours through this historic house. Though there are many such historic homes scattered throughout the American West, this massive estate is different: It sat empty and unchanged for half a century. Age had taken its toll on paint and structural integrity, but all of its furnishings and decor were intact, from elegantly carved hardwood tables and hand-painted frescoes to porcelain bathroom fixtures and a jar of sugar cookies in the pantry. Using gaming proceeds earmarked for historic preservation, the city of Deadwood meticulously renovated the entire house, restoring its 1892 color scheme, original stained glass, and metal shingles. When it opened as a museum in July 2000, locals agreed that it was worth every penny of the $1.5 million bill.

You can tour the home Memorial Day through Labor Day from 9:00 A.M. to 6:00 P.M. Monday through Saturday and from noon to 4:00 P.M. on Sunday. From Labor Day through Memorial Day, you can catch a tour between 10:00 A.M. and 3:00 P.M. Monday through Saturday. Tours usually begin and end on the hour, but they are more frequent in summer.

Adams Museum   Free
54 Sherman Street, Deadwood
(605) 578-1714
www.adamsmuseumandhouse.org

W. E. Adams came to the Black Hills in 1877 as a miner and eventually became one of Deadwood's most influential and prosperous citizens. The city approached him in the 1920s about funding a museum. It was the perfect time. People were taking a keen interest in history, and many early Deadwood pioneers were still alive. Thus, the museum has many objects and collections that came straight from the collectors, their history and authenticity intact.

You can view displays on Wild Bill Hickok, Calamity Jane, Potato Creek Johnny, the Chinese workers and business owners who came here for the gold rush, the ladies of the night, the gamblers and miners, the first locomotive in the Black Hills, and much more.

A skilled staff and good funding have helped to turn the once cluttered and disorganized exhibits into modern, state-of-the-art displays. The lower and main levels of the museum were completely reorganized and redeveloped in 2001 and 2002, and upper-level work began in 2004. Only the much larger (and far more expensive) Journey Museum in Rapid City matches the professionalism, comprehensiveness, organization, and quality you'll find at the Adams Museum.

The Adams is open during the summer (May 1 through September 30) from 9:00 A.M. to 7:00 P.M. Monday through Saturday and noon to 5:00 P.M. on Sunday. Winter hours (October 1 through April 30) are 10:00 A.M. to 4:00 P.M. Monday through Saturday. The museum is closed on Thanksgiving Day, Christmas Day, and New Year's Day. Admission (by the stipulation of Mr. Adams himself) is free, but a small donation is suggested.

Black Hills Mining Museum $
323 West Main Street, Lead
(605) 584-1605
www.mining-museum.blackhills.com

This museum is a trip through the industry that created the city of Lead: mining. You'll find plenty of historic photographs and exhibits on mining culture and local history. The museum offers a video program, guided five-minute tours of a simulated underground mine, and gold-panning demonstrations. Plan to try your hand at panning your own gold, too.

All displays and tours are available from mid-May through August, seven days a week, from 9:00 A.M. to 5:00 P.M. Kids age six and younger get in free. Gold panning is $4.25. From September 1 through early May, the museum is open from 9:00 A.M. to 4:30 P.M. Monday through Friday for self-guided tours and video programs. During these months, admission is discounted. Groups should call ahead to book special tours.

CB&Q Engine House Free
Sherman Street Parking Lot, Deadwood
(605) 578-2082

Deadwood was already a well-established city of brick and stone buildings when the railroad finally came in 1891, but this vital transportation link helped to solidify Deadwood's position as a regional economic capital. The displays at this interpretive center detail the railroad's contribution to the Black Hills and explain its role in Deadwood. The building is the actual 1930 engine house where huge steam-driven Mallet locomotives were serviced and readied for their trips. The engine house is in the parking lot next to the old depot (now First Western Bank). It is not staffed and there is no phone.

It is open mid-May to mid-September, and hours are from 8:00 A.M. to 8:00 P.M. (they do vary). For information or to check on hours, call Deadwood's Department of Planning, Zoning, and Historic Preservation at the number above during business hours.

Days of '76 Historic Museum Free
17 Crescent Drive, Deadwood
(605) 578-2872

This museum will remind you of a rancher's attic or old barn, and with good reason: That's where many of the artifacts here came from. Less organized, more cluttered, and a bit rawer than the nearby Adams Museum (see the earlier listing), the Days of '76 Museum is literally filled with piles of Old West artifacts. There are letters, family photographs, saddles, Lakota ceremonial items, rifles, branding irons, and even some of the original bricks from Deadwood's early streets. The horse-drawn vehicle collection is extensive. You'll see real buggies, buckboards, carriages, covered wagons, three hearses, and the original Cheyenne–Deadwood Stage, which navigated wild western terrain for 11 years.

The museum is open approximately late April to early October, from approximately 9:00 A.M. to 5:00 P.M. You'll find it off U.S. Highway 85/14A on Crescent Drive next to the Days of '76 rodeo grounds. Donations are accepted.

High Plains Western Heritage Center $
Heritage Drive, Spearfish
(605) 642-WEST
www.westernheritagecenter.com

The center's impressive building sits alone atop a high hill, where it is whipped by wild plains winds and overlooks the green hills beyond. If you're lucky you might get to watch a High Plains thunderstorm blow in from far away—complete with roiling black clouds and jagged lightning. The setting is perfect for a museum dedicated to High Plains life, which is greatly affected by the landscape and the weather.

Inside the center you'll see many forms of western art and artifacts, including old buggies and wagons; saddles and spurs; a barbed-wire collection (old barbed wire is an art form itself); re-creations of shops from the past; wood carvings; original art and photographs; and plenty more. A 17-foot-high sculpture of legendary trail boss Tennessee Vaughn astride his rearing horse is especially impressive.

Outdoors, get a close-up look at grazing longhorn steers and buffalo, a one-room schoolhouse, a log cabin, and a sod dugout. Kids will love the petting farm in the summer months.

The museum is open year-round seven days a week, 9:00 A.M. to 5:00 P.M. To get there, take I-90 to exit 14 south and go to Heritage Drive, 1 mile south.

Old Fort Meade Museum and
Old Post Cemetery $
Highway 34, Fort Meade
(605) 347-9822

Constructed in 1878 by the remnants of Custer's Seventh Cavalry, Fort Meade was designed to keep the peace between native Lakota and Cheyenne tribes and the invading white settlers. Amazingly, there is still a military presence there. Today Fort Meade includes the Veterans Administration Medical Center and the Veterans Affairs complex.

The museum chronicles historic events and changes with displays chock-full of artifacts, clippings, photographs, and stories. Fort Meade was the home of Custer's Seventh Cavalry (after Little Bighorn and the death of Custer) and the Buffalo Soldiers of the 25th Infantry, Dakota Territory. It was also one of two South Dakota prison camps during World War II, housing soldiers from General Rommel's Africa Corps.

To get to the museum building, enter the grounds at the Fort Meade complex entrance and follow the blue signs. It is open daily from May 15 through September 15. From Memorial Day weekend through Labor Day weekend, hours are 8:00 A.M. to 6:00 P.M. Hours are 9:00 A.M. to 5:00 P.M. from May 15 until Memorial Day weekend and from Labor Day weekend until September 15.

The Old Post Cemetery is on a hill south of the museum, accessed by a gravel road. It's best to ask for directions at the museum before attempting to find it on your own. Soldiers, their relatives, and civilians were buried in the cemetery from 1878 until about 1948, when the Black Hills National Cemetery opened. In the tradition of the time; headstones have very little detail (some even lack dates), and the number of children buried there may shock you. It's open all year, 24 hours a day. There is no fee for admission to the cemetery.

Sturgis Motorcycle Museum
& Hall of Fame $
Junction and Main (the Old Post Office
across the street from the Armory)
Sturgis
(605) 347-2001
www.sturgismuseum.com

For many, Sturgis is synonymous with motorcycles. Though the first Sturgis Rally & Races was held in 1938, the event didn't gain national notoriety until the 1980s. Since then, the event has consistently attracted a crowd of around 500,000, nearly doubling the size of

South Dakota and turning Sturgis into the largest city in a five-state area (read more about the Rally in the Annual Events and Festivals chapter).

This museum is a popular destination for bikers during the weeklong Rally—so popular that the museum makes enough money during that single week to support regular year-round hours, despite only a trickle of visitors during the winter months. One of the biggest draws is the collection of vintage motorcycles, including Harleys, Indians, and Triumphs. There are also a few historic photos and interpretive displays and a gift shop. As is typical of many small-town museums, the interpretive information is bland and there is little interactivity. However, the museum is run and staffed by motorcycling enthusiasts, and their inside knowledge and passion help fill in the holes left by the museum displays. Staffers especially love to talk about members of the museum's Motorcycle Hall of Fame.

In general, those inducted into the Motorcycle Hall of Fame are drawn from those cyclists who support the Rally and have in some way made a substantial contribution to the sport of riding. Names in the list include entertainer Jay Leno and the late publisher Malcolm Forbes, as well as many politicians associated with motorcycling.

The museum is open 8:00 A.M. to 4:00 P.M. Monday through Friday during summer; winter hours are 9:00 A.M. to 3:00 P.M. Monday through Friday. It is open on weekends in both seasons, but the doors are unlocked an hour later.

Tri-State Memorial Museum   Free
415 Fifth Avenue, Belle Fourche
(605) 892-2676, (888) 345-5859

This small and traditional museum features artifacts from ranchers and businesses in both Dakotas and Montana, giving the institution its name. There are dozens of photos depicting life around early Belle Fourche, which was once the largest livestock shipping point in the West. There are also collections of dolls and clothing that belonged to early home-steaders. For a taste of the bizarre, examine some of the 4,000 old salt and pepper shakers on display.

The entire collection was reorganized in the spring of 2004 when the museum opened the doors of its new 5,000-square-foot building near the chamber of commerce. Though it is staffed by only a few part-time people and some passionate volunteers, the enthusiasm and knowledge of the museum's caretakers are more than enough to accommodate even the toughest questions from visitors.

The Tri-State Museum is open 8:00 A.M. to 5:00 P.M. Monday through Friday year-round. In summer it may be open on the weekends, but interested visitors should call ahead. Donations are appreciated.

Central Hills

Black Hills Institute of Geological Research   Free
217 Main Street, Hill City
(605) 574-3919 (tour information)
www.bhigr.com

What this small, unassuming museum lacks in size it more than makes up for in outstanding fossil exhibits. You'll be just as impressed by the displays of smaller creatures as you are by gargantuan Stan, the mounted *Tyrannosaurus rex* skeleton. There are rocks, minerals, meteorites, and fossilized plants, too. Some of the specimens are on loan, but others belong to the Black Hills Institute of Geological Research, which has a lab in the basement (closed to the public) and a reputation for quality work. Even the gift shop, Everything Prehistoric, is a wonder world of ancient life-forms, with drawers full of specimens for sale. You'll want to linger over the fossils, minerals, cast items, books, and toys.

From May through September the museum is open 8:30 A.M. to 6:30 P.M. Monday through Saturday and 10:00 A.M. to 5:00 P.M. Sunday; the rest of the time, hours are 10:00 A.M. to 5:00 P.M. Tuesday through Saturday. Donations are welcome.

Group tours are free by reservation. Guided tours of the paleontology lab are available by appointment for a fee.

Borglum Historical Center (Rushmore-Borglum Story) $$
342 Winter Street, Keystone
(605) 666-4448
www.rushmoreborglum.com
Get acquainted with Mount Rushmore sculptor Gutzon Borglum before visiting the mountain he carved. A self-guided, narrated tour provides background about the artist's personal and professional history as well as the significance of the masterpiece that immortalized him. Texts of the tour are available in English, French, Spanish, German, Japanese, and Mandarin Chinese. (See the Mount Rushmore listing in the Parks and Mountains chapter.)

The tour, begun in 1978, includes a 25-minute newsreel compiled from old photos, news clips, and broadcasts. The gallery displays more of Borglum's work. The large museum/gift shop features artwork, books, and videos; more sculpture is displayed outside.

Located in Keystone, 3 miles north of Mount Rushmore, the center is open daily May through the first week of October. The hours are 8:00 A.M. to 7:00 P.M. June through August. Call for hours in May, September, and October. Admission is discounted during Sturgis Rally & Races week each August.

The Journey Museum $$
222 New York Street, Rapid City
(605) 394-6923
www.journeymuseum.org
Housed in a spectacular building, this museum is a techno-wonder. Your own journey through it starts with a dramatic movie about the geologic and cultural history of the Black Hills. Then continue with a self-guided tour that's both educational and entertaining, thanks to hand-held sound sticks that allow you to walk, stop, and listen at your own pace. The sound sticks explain the exhibits in Lakota or English.

The Journey was designed as an interactive excursion through time, beginning with the earth-shattering birth of the Hills and moving through detailed accounts of the Native American way of life, the arrival of white explorers, the gold rush, pioneer days, paleontology and archaeology, ranching and farming, and much more.

Here's a secret: When you reach the tepee, sit on the bench in front of it, hold the sound stick to your ear, and wait for the moon to come up over the tepee. You'll be treated to a holographic visit with Nellie Two Bulls, Lakota elder. Other exhibits also "materialize" if you wait for them. The museum was designed to provide a contemplative experience; it's not to be hurried through—take your time and enjoy.

We recommend you make the Journey one of your early stops: It will enhance your understanding of the rich culture of the Black Hills. The gift shop, stocked with Native-made crafts, is above average. The Journey houses two galleries, the Sioux Indian Museum Gallery, and another displaying original South Dakota and midwestern artists.

The museum is open daily year-round. From Memorial Day to Labor Day, hours are 9:00 A.M. to 5:00 P.M. In winter it's open 10:00 A.M. to 5:00 P.M. Monday through Saturday and 1:00 to 5:00 P.M. on Sunday.

Motion Unlimited Museum and Antique Car Lot $
6180 Highway 79, Rapid City
(605) 348-7373
www.motionoldcars.com
You don't have to spend half your life under the hood of a car to appreciate the automobiles, motorcycles, and memorabilia on display here. Even the toys in glass cases look like they've been lovingly restored. The car collection spans several decades and changes over time, but you might find among the more unusual exhibits a 1926 Model T paddy wagon with bars on the rear windows, an airplane car, a 1925 Studebaker motor home, and a 1932 Ford dragster.

Historic Houses

The historic houses of Lead and Dead-wood appear to perch—some quite pre-cariously—on the rocky hillsides on which the towns are built. Some houses have been beautifully renovated and others allowed to decay. Most streets are quite narrow, some are one-ways or dead ends, and you don't want to attempt them in the winter.

Both Lead and Deadwood sprang up during the gold-rush days, although Lead was a camp built for the employees of the Homestake Gold Mine. Today the mine spreads out beneath much of the town, and Lead home owners own just the surface rights to their properties. The

Homestake Mine owns the rights to everything underneath—dirt, minerals, and maybe gold.

What you see is all the more impres-sive when you learn that owners Bill and Peggy Napoli have done much of the restoration work themselves. They have a parking lot full of "project" cars waiting for the right owner to purchase and fix up. How about an Edsel?

The museum, 2 miles south of Rapid City, is open 9:00 A.M. to 6:00 P.M. Monday through Friday and 9:00 A.M. to 4:00 P.M. Saturday, April through September. There's no charge to look around the car lot, which is mostly open all year. Call ahead for winter hours.

Museum of Geology   **Free**
501 East St. Joseph Street, Rapid City
(605) 394-2467
(800) 544-8162 ext. 2467 (weekdays)
www.sdsmt.edu
Even if you're not a scientist, it's easy to spend hours among the exhibits in this museum on the Tech campus of South Dakota School of Mines and Technology. The Badlands (see the chapter called the

Badlands and Nearby) and Black Hills provide a ready supply of fossils and min-erals, respectively, but you'll also see fas-cinating, colorful rocks from around the world on display here. There are mete-orites, models of famous diamonds, gold nuggets, and a case full of South Dakota minerals. Dinosaur skeletons (including a dino leg bone you can touch), polished agates, fossilized fish, and a slice of faulted sandstone (you can see where it buckled) are other eye-catching exhibits. And here's your chance for a close-up look at boxwork, popcorn, and frostwork, which are some of the mineral formations in Wind Cave National Park (see the Parks and Mountains chapter). There's a small selection of books and minerals for sale, too.

The museum is open year-round, with summer hours 8:00 A.M. to 6:00 P.M. Monday through Saturday and noon to 6:00 P.M. on Sunday. Winter hours are slightly shorter; call for information. Dona-tions are gratefully accepted.

The museum, where students and others do research, offers several two-week paleontology digs each summer, but you have to take your own tent and sleeping bag. Call or write for information about getting college credit, which costs more.

**South Dakota Air and
Space Museum**   **Free**
Ellsworth Air Force Base
Interstate 90, exit 67
(605) 385-5188

If you're a military or aviation history buff, or if you just love airplanes, you'll enjoy this museum. Outside displays include more than 27 planes and helicopters, including General Eisenhower's personal transport and a Mitchell B-25 bomber. Inside, explore the history of the base, tour a mock-up of a Minuteman launch control center, and see military memorabilia.

The South Dakota Aviation Hall of Fame is housed here, too, with tributes to pioneer aviators that are especially interesting. Read about Nellie Willhite, who—despite deafness—became South Dakota's first licensed female pilot (see the close-up in the Getting Here, Getting Around chapter); Clyde Ice, barnstormer, wing walker, and aerobat; and aviatrix Violet Cowden, who made her first parachute jump on her 74th birthday.

Hours are 8:30 A.M. to 6:00 P.M. from mid-May to mid-September and 8:30 A.M. to 4:30 P.M. the rest of the year. A narrated bus tour ($) is available from mid-May to mid-September, lasts about an hour, and includes a descent into a real Minuteman II missile silo. The museum is near the base's main gate; watch for signs and lots of parked planes.

Southern Hills

**Fall River County Historical
Museum**   **Free**
North Chicago Street, Hot Springs
(605) 745-5147

If taking a step back in time is one of your pleasures, this museum will delight you. The musty scent of yesterday greets you as you open the door and tread the well-worn wooden stairs of this three-story former schoolhouse. The 1893 sandstone structure, whose halls rang with the sound of youthful voices until 1961, houses extensive collections of everything imaginable, all smartly arranged in clusters and groupings. You'll find a room devoted to kitchen implements, for instance, and another filled with musical instruments and related items. There's a dentist's office well equipped enough to make you wince, and a Victorian parlor that makes you want to set a spell over tea and polite conversation.

The museum is open 9:00 A.M. to 5:00 P.M. Monday through Saturday from June 1 until September 30. The volunteer-run museum relies on donations.

National Museum of Woodcarving   **$$**
U.S. Highway 16 West, Custer
(605) 673-4404
www.blackhills.com/woodcarving

Ignore the old saw "Don't take any wooden nickels" when you get to the National Museum of Woodcarving: You're going to need three of them to take full advantage of the displays. The museum, 2 miles west of town, features the work of Dr. Harley Niblack, a Denver chiropractor who gave up his practice at age 42 to devote his time to wood carving and animation. His talent in that area made him one of Disneyland's earliest animators, and some of his work has been displayed by the Smithsonian Institution.

When you buy your ticket, you'll get enough wooden nickels to set three of the carvings in motion. But before entering the exhibit area, you'll want to watch videos in the Wooden Nickel Theater about the collection and about wood carving. The self-guided tour ends with a look at work by some of the nation's other top wood-carvers and a stop in the gallery where you can buy quality carvings. An adjacent gift shop sells snacks and souvenirs.

Rapid City's Place in Aviation History

Think pioneer aviation and you're likely to think of Kitty Hawk, North Carolina, where the Wright brothers made a short hop in the world's first airplane in 1903. But a spot near Rapid City in the Black Hills earned a place in aviation history in 1935, when two army officers, Orvil Anderson and Albert Stevens, set an altitude record in a helium balloon launched from the Stratosphere bowl. The balloon, *Explorer II,* ascended 72,395 feet, enabling its crew to collect new data on Earth's upper atmosphere. Today the gondola that carried the men and equipment is in the National Air and Space Museum in Washington, D.C.

The Stratobowl, as it has come to be called, is a flat, circular field sheltered by rocky cliffs. Its unique characteristics have attracted numerous other balloonists, including millionaire adventurer Steve Fossett, who launched an unsuccessful around-the-world flight from the bowl on January 8, 1996. The bowl itself is privately owned and not open to the public, but you can look down into it from the rim. (You'll have to hike in about three quarters of a mile.) In addition to the view, the rim has a plaque commemorating the 1935 launch, which was sponsored by the National Geographic Society and the U.S. Army Air Corps.

To get to the Stratobowl rim, look for the gate and cattle guard off U.S. 16 about 10 miles southwest of Rapid City. Pull in and park at the gate; if you find yourself at the Black Hills National Forest overlook, you've gone too far. The rim is on USDA Forest Service land, so all agency rules and laws apply.

The museum is open from May 1 until late October. Hours vary throughout the season, so call ahead.

MUSIC AND SHOWS

Historical plays, chuckwagon supper shows, and other musical events are held evenings in spring, summer, and fall.

Northern Hills

The Black Hills Passion Play   **$$$**
Interstate 90, exit 12, Spearfish
(605) 642-2646
(800) 457-0160 (reservations)
www.blackhills.com/bhpp
The passion play's history dates from 1242. Josef Meier brought this production to the United States from Germany in 1932, and it has been performed in Spearfish since 1938. The last days of Jesus Christ are reenacted by professional actors and more than 150

volunteer actors in a two-and-one-quarter-hour performance. The amphitheater seats 6,000 and has the largest outdoor stage in the nation. A covered section seats 1,000, but do be prepared for an evening spent outdoors: Bring a jacket and bug spray, just in case you need them.

The play is performed during June, July, and August only, on Sunday, Tuesday, and Thursday at 8:00 P.M. From exit 12 (Jackson Boulevard), follow the signs to St. Joe Street and the amphitheater.

Central Hills

Supper Music Shows $$$-$$$$

If you like beef with a little lively music on the side, you'll want to catch one of the area's nightly dinner shows. Starting times and prices vary for the attractions listed below. Cowboy boots and a Stetson are not required—but if you're not sure what to wear, ask.

For a cowboy-style chuckwagon supper of beef 'n' beans with all the trimmings, your choices include Circle B Ranch on U.S. 385, (605) 348-7358, north of Rapid City, where you'll find a western town, minigolf, trail rides, gold panning, and other activities.

Or perhaps you'd like to visit Fort Hays, (605) 394-9653, a movie set from *Dances with Wolves,* on U.S. 16 south of Rapid City, with continuous free showings of the four-hour version of the film. The owners offer a 99-cent cowboy breakfast from 6:30 to 11:00 A.M. and a chuckwagon supper beginning at 6:30 P.M. For about $54 you can join a daylong tour starting at 9:00 A.M. that takes you to Mount Rushmore, Custer State Park, and the Crazy Horse Memorial. Upon your return to Fort Hays, you'll be treated to supper and a show. Fort Hays is open daily from May 12 to October 1.

Flying T Cowboy Supper and Show, (605) 342-1905, also on U.S. 16 south of Rapid City, has provided western tradition since 1979 with a variety music and comedy show.

Southern Hills

Black Hills Playhouse
Highway 87, Custer State Park
(605) 255-4141, (605) 255-4551
www.blackhillsplayhouse.com

This rustic playhouse, fashioned from an abandoned 1934 Civilian Conservation Corps camp, has offered professional summer theater since 1946. Quality performances in a novel setting have made it a popular attraction for locals and tourists alike. For information about shows, see the Arts chapter.

Mountain Music Show $$
U.S. Highway 16, Custer
(605) 673-3135

The Pee Wee Dennis family's hillbilly style of entertainment dishes up two hours of country and bluegrass music and cornball humor in an indoor theater next to Flintstones Bedrock City. Sunday is country-gospel night. The show normally goes on each evening from Memorial Day weekend to Labor Day weekend, but the season may vary; call ahead to confirm. Curtain time is 8:00 P.M. Reservations are recommended. A free bus gets you there from any Custer motel or campground.

The Original Singing Cowboys $$$
Heritage Village
1 Village Avenue
Crazy Horse (Custer)
(605) 673-4761, (888) HAVEFUN
www.heritage-village.com

You might call this group the South Dakota version of the Sons of the Pioneers. And indeed, one of the members of this traditional western-style band, Jim Lovell, won the Old West Trail Foundation Award for the Preservation of Western Music in 1980, an honor also bestowed on the aforementioned Sons. Lovell and fellow Cowboys Buddy Meredith, Kenny Hamm, and Bill King sing enduring songs about enduring values, and their arrangements are so true, you just might get the urge to stretch out in a bedroll under the stars. That's especially so if you've had a

ATTRACTIONS

Belle Fourche claims the designation of Geographical Center of the United States. In 1959, after Alaska and Hawaii became states, the U.S. Coast and Geodetic Survey moved the center from Kansas to a point about 20 miles north of Belle Fourche. The actual site is on inaccessible land, but you can read the official plaque at the Center of the Nation Information Center, 415 Fifth Avenue, Belle Fourche.

filling meal from the buffet table on the main floor at Heritage Village before heading downstairs for the show in the Show Barn Theater.

Performances are at 8:00 P.M. Tuesday through Sunday from early May through Labor Day, and on weekends until mid-October. The buffet starts at 4:30 P.M. Group reservations are recommended.

PARKS AND NATURE AREAS

These sites are among the Hills' best-known and most beloved features. We also include some lesser-known gems, perfect for an afternoon of adventure and discovery.

Northern Hills

Black Hills National Cemetery and VFW Memorial Chapel   Free
Interstate 90, exit 34, Sturgis
(605) 347-3830
Row upon row of gleaming white head-stones framed against green grass and blue sky are an impressive sight. This is a place of tranquillity, where more than 14,000 veterans and their family members lie at rest. The cemetery opened in 1948; veterans from World War I and every war and conflict since are buried here.

If you're looking for the grave of a rel-ative, stop at the administration building

by the front gate, pick up a map, and use the locator book in the foyer to find the location. While you're in the foyer, note the human-interest stories jotted in the comments column in the guest book.

The cemetery is open all year and accessible 24 hours a day, although visi-tors are asked to restrict their visit to day-light hours. The administration building is open from 8:00 A.M. until 4:30 P.M. Monday through Friday, but the foyer is always unlocked.

The tiny Veterans of Foreign Wars Memorial Chapel is not part of the National Cemetery, but visitors use it as a place of contemplation before or after their visit. Take the cemetery road (which goes under the interstate) the short dis-tance to the grounds. The chapel is usu-ally unlocked, although it is closed in the winter and sometimes locked after occur-rences of vandalism.

Tatanka: Story of the Bison $$
U.S. Highway 85, Deadwood
(605) 584-5678
www.storyofthebison.com
When the 19th century dawned, an esti-mated 30 million bison roamed the plains of central North America. A century later their number had been reduced to fewer than 1,000. But the white hunters who slaughtered the continent's largest beast by the thousands weren't just wiping out an animal—they were wiping out the only way of life known by thousands of Native tribes.

This attraction serves as a memorial to the height of the buffalo culture in 1840. An interpretive center details the rise, fall, and recovery of bison; why the Lakota people were so dependent on these roaming herds; and how bison have found their place in modern culture. A re-creation of a tepee encampment nearby, staffed entirely by Lakota, serves as an interpretive center for everything from traditional weapons and courtship rituals to musical instruments and household tasks. A small cafe serves buffalo meat. The central component, however, is a mas-

Bronze sculptures at Tatanka: Story of the Bison outside Deadwood. SOUTH DAKOTA TOURISM

sive, heroic-scale bronze sculpture (the third largest in the world, according to the staff) depicting 14 bison being driven off a cliff by three mounted hunters. It's owned by Kevin Costner, who also owns the Midnight Star (see the Gaming and Casinos chapter) and shot some of his epic *Dances with Wolves* in nearby Spearfish Canyon.

The attraction, located on Deadwood Hill less than a mile above town off U.S. 85, is open from May to October, although it may be open in other months, depending on weather. Likewise, hours vary throughout the season, so it's best to call ahead. The one-time admission fee allows you to enter the attraction all season.

Central Hills

Berlin Wall Exhibit   **Free**
Memorial Park, Eighth Street Rapid City
Take a break from your busy activities and visit this quiet, thoughtful tribute to freedom. Take Mount Rushmore Road north from Omaha Street (there it becomes Eighth Street) and park in the Rushmore Plaza Civic Center parking lot. These are replicas of the Berlin Wall, but the wicked-looking steel tank traps in front of the wall sections are authentic. Read the story of the Berlin Wall—how it came about, its harsh history, and how it ended—on the displays.

Rapid City's sister city is Apolda, Germany, whose mayor attended the exhibit's opening in 1996. This exhibit is accessible 24 hours a day, year-round. After your visit continue your walk through Memorial Park and explore the fantastic Rapid City park system.

Chapel in the Hills (Stav Kirke Chapel)   **Free**
3788 Chapel Lane, Rapid City
(605) 342-8281
Known in English as Chapel in the Hills, and in Norwegian as Stav Kirke, the little

Colonel Carlton's Patriotic Legacy

In 1892 Fort Meade post commander Col. Caleb Carlton and his wife discussed their idea that the United States needed a national "air." Mrs. Carlton suggested the well-known "Star-Spangled Banner" written by Francis Scott Key. Colonel Carlton commanded the melody be played at the fort's retreats, parades, and concerts. He took the opportunity to explain this new custom to the governors of South Dakota and Pennsylvania, and interest spread. Soon Secretary of War Daniel Lamont ordered that the composition be played each evening at every U.S. Army post.

Colonel Carlton initiated the practice of standing and removing hats while the music played. The heart-stirring song and the respectful acts of patriotism accompanying its performances were so popular that in 1931 Congress declared "The Star-Spangled Banner" our national anthem.

wooden church in the pines is a 1969 replica of the 12th-century Borgund Church in Laerdal, Norway. The ornately carved, unique structure takes its name, which means stave church, from the 12 staves around which it is built. The staves represent the 12 apostles, the foundation of the Christian church. With its wooded backdrop and broad, well-kept lawn, the chapel and its grounds impart a sense of peace and well-being. It's no wonder couples from a wide area choose to be married here.

Visitors can sit on wooden benches in the chapel and listen to a continuous tape to learn more about the building's intricate features, including the dragon heads that adorn the roof. There's also a late-19th-century log cabin built by Norwegian immigrant Edward Nielsen that has been turned into a museum cozily furnished with Scandinavian antiques. The reception center/gift shop, housed in a grass-roofed *stabbur* (traditional pantry or granary building) imported from Norway, continues the Scandinavian motif with carvings,

handcrafts, and books. In addition to its spiritual and architectural significance, Chapel in the Hills reminds visitors of the northern Europeans who immigrated to South Dakota, imbuing the state with their steadfast, vivid heritage.

Chapel in the Hills is open from 7:00 A.M. until dusk daily, from May 1 through September 30. A half-hour nondenominational vespers service begins at 8:00 each evening from mid-June through late August. Weddings may be scheduled from mid-March until mid-November. Donations to support the nonprofit operation are appreciated. To get there, take Highway 44 to Chapel Lane in Rapid City and follow the signs to Stav Kirke.

Cleghorn Springs State Fish Hatchery   Free
Highway 44, Rapid City
(605) 394-2399 (summer only)
(605) 394-2391
No sense trying to worm your way out of it—even if you've never been caught by

the lure of fishing, you're likely to get hooked on the hatchery. Besides ponds full of trout for stocking South Dakota waters, there's an aquatic center where you can learn about watersheds, fish, and fishing. There are nature programs, too, and pellets are available if you want to feed the fish.

Hours are 9:00 A.M. to 4:30 P.M. daily from Memorial Day to the end of August, and you can call for information about free summer programs.

Cosmos Mystery Area $$
U.S. Highway 16, Rapid City
(605) 343–9802, (605) 343–7278
www.cosmosmysteryarea.com
If you want to stand up straight at Cosmos, just lean forward, especially if you're standing on the wall. To learn more about this baffling place, where the laws of physics are unenforceable, see the Kidstuff chapter.

Mount Rushmore National
Memorial Free
Highway 244, Keystone
(605) 574–2523
www.nps.gov/moru
One of South Dakota's most defining features and among the most recognizable of American icons, the massive granite faces of Mount Rushmore attract more than three million visitors from all over the globe each year. The busts of George Washington, Thomas Jefferson, Theodore Roosevelt, and Abraham Lincoln represent the events and philosophy of 150 years of American history and the lifelong dream of sculptor Gutzon Borglum.

A massive restoration project in 1998 revitalized the memorial, replacing many of the outdated structures with imposing granite and glass buildings, turning Rushmore into a world-class destination. Indeed, you're just as likely to see a family from Toulouse or Taipei as you

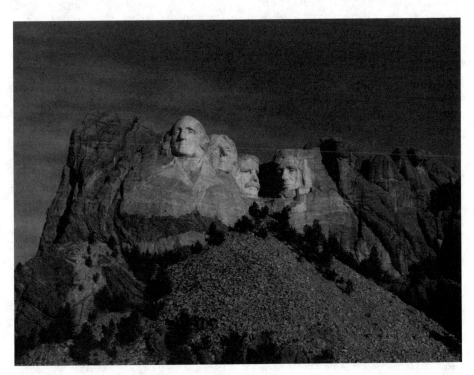

Mount Rushmore. SOUTH DAKOTA TOURISM

> **More than 90 percent of South Dakota's land was classified as farmland in the mid-1990s.**

are a couple from Cincinnati or San Francisco walking the Avenue of Flags. Of course, it's also likely that you'll see a Rocky Mountain goat lounging near the amphitheater or standing around the parking lot. These harmless creatures aren't native to the Hills, but they've been a part of the animal life that wanders the grounds at the memorial since they were introduced in 1924.

The massive Lincoln Borglum Museum, set into the earth beneath the Avenue of Flags and above the amphitheater, is a must-see for any visitor. Exhibits of original carving tools, the lives of all four presidents, and Mount Rushmore in popular culture (including a clip from the *Muppet Show*) are interactive and engaging—even for kids. A more detailed description of the mountain and services available is in the Parks and Mountains chapter.

Petrified Forest of the Black Hills $$
Interstate 90, exit 46, Piedmont
(605) 787–4560
www.elkcreek.org/forest

Start your self-guided tour of the Petrified Forest with the informative video made by the geologist owner, Jerry Teachout. The prehistoric formation of the Hills is explained clearly, and the video will enhance your knowledge and appreciation of the area. Next, visit the museum, where you'll see displays on geologic history and collections of rocks and minerals. Then head outside to walk the property and check out the petrified logs unearthed there. These once-wooden logs are so ancient that they predate the Hills themselves. In fact, they were already petrified when the slow geologic uplift that created the Black Hills exposed them, and that began 62 to 65 million years ago. Stop by the excellent

rock shop at the end of your tour. (See the listing in the Shopping chapter.)

The Petrified Forest is open from May 1 through October 15. Hours are 8:00 A.M. to 7:00 P.M. seven days a week and 9:00 A.M. to 5:00 P.M. after Labor Day.

Southern Hills

Blue Bell Lodge and Resort Hayride and Chuckwagon Cookout $$$$
Custer State Park, Highway 87 South
(605) 255–4531
www.custerresorts.com

An hour-long hayride with live, sing-along folk music winds through the park to Parker Canyon for a chuckwagon dinner and continued entertainment. The hay wagon is pulled by a vehicle, not by horses, but you get a complimentary cowboy hat and bandanna to take home plus your choice of steak or hamburger for supper. Plan to spend two-and-a-half to three hours relaxing and enjoying the park's splendid scenery.

The lodge recommends making your reservations by 2:00 P.M., but walk-ins are welcome until 5:00 P.M. if there's space left. Rides depart at 5:30 P.M., but guests are asked to arrive by 5:00 P.M. Group rates are available.

Crazy Horse Memorial $$
U.S. Highways 16 and 385, Custer
(605) 673–4681
www.crazyhorse.org

Seven years after work ceased on Mount Rushmore (see the listing above), a fifth granite face started to emerge from another Black Hills mountaintop. This still-unfinished carving-in-the-round of Lakota Sioux leader Crazy Horse will pay homage not to U.S. presidents but to the legacy of those who preceded them. The monument and the museum complex below it are dedicated to Native Americans of all tribes. Because no known portraits of Crazy Horse exist, sculptor Korczak Ziolkowski created one from oral reports of those who had known the chief, intending that

Evans Plunge

Although no longer a destination point for the weak and ailing, Hot Springs still draws tens of thousands of visitors each year with its famous Evans Plunge. The original 1890 Plunge Bath came into the hands of builder Fred Evans (see the "Hot Springs' Sandstone Buildings" close-up in this chapter) after the springs that feed it had traded hands several times—at one point, for a $35 horse. But legend says that long before white men claimed and bartered the renowned healing waters among themselves, Indian tribes fought each other for its exclusive use. The Sioux are said to have triumphed over the Cheyenne in a clash on Battle Mountain north of

present-day Hot Springs. When white settlers took over the land, they readily added their own stories of near-miraculous cures to those handed down by the Native people.

the monument stand as a symbol of the leader's spirit rather than an exact likeness.

The project was initiated by another Lakota chief, Henry Standing Bear, who wrote to the Connecticut artist after reading that Ziolkowski's marble bust of Polish pianist-composer-statesman Ignacy Paderewski had taken top honors at the 1939 New York World's Fair. Standing Bear's now-famous invitation read, in part, "My fellow chiefs and I would like the white man to know the red man has great heroes, too." The first blast at Crazy Horse removed 10 tons of rock on June 3, 1948. Hampered by South Dakota weather and dependent entirely on private funding (at Ziolkowski's insistence), it took 50 years to complete the sculpture's nine-story-tall face. When the last bit of rock is carved away at some unknown time in the future, the head alone will be big enough to hold all four faces on Mount Rushmore. Then, Crazy Horse, who was killed at Fort Robinson, Nebraska, in 1877, will sit astride

his horse for all time, his left hand pointing proudly toward home: the place where his people lived and lie buried.

Ziolkowski himself is buried near the mountain carving. Since his death in 1982, his wife, Ruth, and many of their 10 children have continued his work. Knowing from the start that he would not live long enough to complete the 563-foot-tall memorial—taller than the Washington Monument—the self-taught sculptor drew up a detailed master plan to guide his successors.

A visit to Crazy Horse begins on the Avenue of the Chiefs, which takes you to the visitor complex where there's a model of Crazy Horse's face carved from a native pine tree, a slide show, photos depicting the work on the mountain, and many examples of Ziolkowski's *Fighting Stallions* sculpture. Continue to the Native American Educational and Cultural Center to see beadwork and prehistoric tools and to watch a documentary video. In the Indian

---

 CLOSE-UP

Hot Springs' Sandstone Buildings

When late-19th-century white settlers discovered natural warm waters in the southern Black Hills, a health resort was the inevitable result. (See the History chapter for more information.) But enterprising developers of the day were quick to capitalize on a second treasure trove to promote Hot Springs as a premier destination. It seemed that local sandstone quarries held the perfect material to build an illustrious city, for the giant, rosy blocks that were cut and hauled to construction sites were not only enduring but also beautiful.

Present-day Hot Springs boasts 32 sandstone buildings from the late 1800s and early 1900s. They are what you notice when you arrive in town and what you remember after you've gone. Fred T. Evans, whose name resounds throughout Hot Springs today, must have had that in mind when he set about building the Minnekahta Block in 1891 and the Evans Hotel

a year later. Both structures are included on a walking tour of historic buildings; you can pick up a color brochure and go on your own or make an appointment for a guided tour by calling the Hot Springs Chamber of Commerce at (605) 745–4140 or (800) 325–6991.

Your tour will take you to the sprawling, tile-roofed 1907 Veterans Administration Medical Center and the world's smallest Union Depot, built in 1891; to the 1889 State Veterans Home, the first major stone building; and to the 1932 post office, the last local building to be built from local stone.

As you walk around town, look for details such as the carved face and purple accent blocks on the Petty building on Albany and Chicago Streets, and the multiple styles of tooling on City Hall. Before it got serious about preservation, the town lost some of its old beauties, and even now public opinion is divided

---

Museum of North America, tribes from every corner of the nation are reverently represented in collections of artifacts and costumes. The sculptor's studio-home showcases more of his work. In years to come, Ziolkowski's master plan calls for a new museum, a university and medical training center for Native Americans, and other additions.

The visitor complex, where you can also buy Indian-made and South Dakota products, is open all year, with summer hours from 7:00 A.M. to dark and off-season hours from 8:00 A.M. until dark. The Laughing Water Restaurant is open

from early May to late October. Children six and younger, Native Americans, active military personnel with I.D., and Girl Scouts and Boy Scouts in uniform get into the memorial free. There are reduced rates for motorcyclists, bicyclists, walkers, and groups—call for more information.

Evans Plunge $$
1145 North River Street, Hot Springs
(605) 745-5165
www.evansplunge.com
You'll find not only the world's largest natural warm-water indoor swimming pool but also a host of other recreational facilities

on whether to try to save others. The 1913 Carnegie Library building, for example, was condemned and vacated in 1995 because of cracking, and at least some preservationists are unhappy about plans to raze all but the facade and build anew.

Since 1976 the city-appointed Hot Springs Historic Preservation Commission has headed up efforts to save what remains of the town's grand architectural legacy. Things got under way in 1977 when the National Trust for Historic Preservation named Hot Springs one of three pilot sites nationwide for a Main Street USA restoration project funded with matching grants. The commission has since strengthened its own ability to obtain grants for additional projects by gaining certified local government status in 1994. It's also begun stockpiling sandstone blocks from fallen buildings to use in restoration work. In addition, the local Save Our Sandstone Foundation Inc. raises money and provides labor to acquire and restore buildings. The two

groups acted together to save the Evans Hotel after it was gutted by fire in 1979; it now houses 84 low-income apartments for the elderly.

The city's historic district is listed in the National Register of Historic Places, making tax credits and other advantages available for preservation work. But the high cost of restoration means that saving all the buildings, some of which are privately owned, would take many years and millions of dollars.

Nonetheless, although the trains that used to puff into town four times a day have vanished along with the red carpets and bands that greeted passengers, it's nice to think that if Fred Evans arrived today he'd be able to recognize the little city he so energetically endorsed. He'd find tourists relaxing at his old Plunge Bath (now Evans Plunge), and he'd surely note with satisfaction that sandstone from his quarry still graces the streets of Hot Springs.

for the entire family, including waterslides, a sauna, steam room, and fitness center. Evans Plunge is open all year; for more information, turn to the Recreation chapter.

Jewel Cave National Monument   **$$**
U.S. Highway 16, Custer
(605) 673-2288, (800) 967-2283
www.nps.gov/jeca
Among the first national monuments declared by President Theodore Roosevelt, Jewel Cave is rich in geological splendor. The sparkling calcite crystal that gives the cave its name is just one of its many features, however. The cave's greatest claim

to fame is probably its length. With more than 130 miles of explored passages (and perhaps another 4,900 miles to go, according to some studies), Jewel Cave is the second-longest cave in the world.

Above ground there are over 1,000 acres of ponderosa forest to explore. The diverse ecosystem is famous for its bats (nine species) and vibrant wildflowers. A fire started by an arsonist in 2000 ripped through 90 percent of the park, destroying many of the trees, but the fallen timber has helped fuel the growth of many small shrubs, wildflowers, and ground cover. Three trails lead through the park above ground.

> *Know the difference between a national monument and a national park? A monument can be set aside for preservation by a simple presidential declaration, but it takes an act of Congress to establish a national park.*

Several types of daily tours run through the cave itself, including a historic lantern tour and a four-hour wild caving tour. All start from the visitor center, which is open 8:00 A.M. to 4:30 P.M. all year, seven days a week. You'll also find interactive computer terminals and interpretive exhibits there. Extended information on Jewel Cave can be found in the Parks and Mountains chapter.

Wind Cave National Park $$-$$$
U.S. Highway 385, Hot Springs
(605) 745-4600
www.nps.gov/wica
One of about half a dozen caves in the world to harbor honeycomb-like boxwork formations, Wind Cave offers four informative guided tours ranging from an hour to 90 minutes. Reservations are recommended for special candlelight and spelunking tours. See the Parks and Mountains chapter for more information.

TOURS AND BYWAYS

See the Black Hills through a customized tour or by traveling one of the state's remarkable scenic byways.

Northern Hills

Homestake Gold Mine Surface
Tours and Visitor Center $
160 West Main Street, Lead
(605) 584-3110, (888) 701-0164
www.homestaketour.com
The Homestake Gold Mine was the oldest continuously operating underground gold

mine in the world until 2001. Financial considerations, however, forced closure, and today the former mine retains only its visitor center and gift shop, which features Black Hills Gold and a deck overlooking the massive open-cut mine. Hours of operation are flexible, but count on the facility to be open from 8:00 A.M. to 5:00 P.M. daily in summer. In winter, you can visit Monday through Saturday from 9:00 A.M. to 5:00 P.M. There's a charge for tours, but admission to the visitor center is free.

Spearfish Canyon State Scenic Byway
U.S. Highway 14A
www.spearfishcanyon.com
One of the glories of South Dakota is the amazing diversity of scenery: mountains, prairie, badlands, forest, high plains. But nothing quite compares to Spearfish Canyon. The canyon—six times older than Grand Canyon—is so spectacular, in fact, that it is a State Scenic Byway, a designation that acknowledges its famous beauty. U.S. 14A is a 19-mile winding paved road that ends at Cheyenne Crossing and U.S. 85 at its south end and at the Spearfish city limits at its north end.

The byway is often a bit crowded, especially in summer and also in fall, when the aspens burst into autumn color framed by deep green spruce and pine. The highway follows Spearfish Creek through towering limestone cliffs and thick forests and goes past Bridal Veil Falls, Roughlock Falls, and the mighty Spearfish Falls, restored after nearly a century of diversion by the now-defunct Homestake Mine. The shoulders of the highway are wide enough for bicycles (the grade is a comfortable 3 percent), and there are picnic areas and pullovers so you can safely stop and take photographs.

Allow enough time to hike into the woods or an adjoining canyon. The creek is known for its trout. You can find plenty of listings for nearby places to dine or spend the night in the Restaurants and Accommodations chapters. Be sure to allot enough time for a relaxed drive through

Wild Bill Hickok's Last Hand

When the legendary Wild Bill Hickok was shot in Deadwood by the infamous Jack McCall (the first and last time Bill ever sat at cards with his back to the door), he reportedly was holding black aces and eights, known ever after as the "dead man's hand." Deadwood's Adams Museum displays what are purported to be the actual cards.

the idyllic canyon. Your only concern should be the other drivers, who are gazing around in awe as much as you are.

Central Hills

Black Hills Central Railroad/ The 1880 Train $$$
222 Railroad Avenue, Hill City
(605) 574-2222
www.1880train.com
A favorite among visitors, this attraction features vintage railroad cars pulled by a steam locomotive that chugs along the original Chicago, Burlington & Quincy route that served Hill City and Keystone more than a century ago. Before or after your ride you can dine at the Highliner snack shop, where seating is available on the deck or in a railcar decorated with railroad memorabilia. In the gift shop you'll find train-related videos, books, and other items.

After Memorial Day and before Labor Day, the train pulls out from Hill City at 7:15 A.M., 9:45 A.M., 1:15 P.M., and 4:00 P.M. Monday through Friday. From Keystone the train pulls out at 8:30 A.M., 11:00 A.M., and 2:30 P.M. Before Memorial Day and after Labor Day, the schedule is limited.

Reservations are recommended because space for the two-hour rides is limited. A restricted timetable is in effect from mid-May to mid-June and after Labor Day until early October; call for information. You also need to call if you want to board at the Keystone junction or to find out about special evening rides during July and August.

Peter Norbeck National Scenic Byway
This 66-mile loop, named for the late nature-loving South Dakota governor and U.S. senator Peter Norbeck, takes in some of the most rugged scenery in the Black Hills. The byway will take you into the Norbeck Wildlife Preserve, the Black Hills National Forest, and Custer State Park when you travel the Needles Highway (Highway 87), Iron Mountain Road (U.S. 16A), Horse Thief Lake Road (Highway 244), and Sylvan Lake Road (Highway 89). Norbeck laid out portions of the route himself on foot and horseback.

Along the way you'll encounter switchbacks, looping "pigtail" bridges, narrow 1930s tunnels that open onto breathtaking views (look for Mount Rushmore and the Needles Eye, an aptly named granite spire) and Sylvan Lake, so be sure to have your camera ready. There are historic sites, too, such as the spot along U.S. 16A that served as a base camp for Lt. Col. George Custer's 1874 expedition to the Black Hills, when reports of gold set off a human stampede to the area.

The Needles Highway is in the Custer State Park fee area, so you'll need to buy a park entrance license if you go that way. You'll also need a license if you plan to tour or stop in the park. See our Parks and Mountains chapters for information about park features and license fees. Parts of Iron Mountain Road and the Needles Highway are closed during the winter.

Rushmore Aerial Tramway   **$$**
U.S. Highway 16A, Keystone
(605) 666-4478
www.rushmoretramway.com
Trams depart about every five minutes for a short ride to an observation deck where you can look out over a scenic valley to Mount Rushmore, about a mile and a half away. Trails lead to other overlooks, and you can pack a picnic and stay as long as you like before returning to the gift shop to browse for souvenirs.

The tramway runs 9:00 A.M. to 6:00 P.M. or later, weather permitting, from late May through mid- to late-September.

Southern Hills

Black Hills Aerial
Adventures   **$$$-$$$$**
U.S. Highway 385, Custer
(605) 673-2163
www.coptertours.com
The Black Hills are breathtaking any way you view them, but few are the individuals who get to look down upon their pine-covered slopes. Black Hills Aerial Adventures hopes to change that with some help from their Bell 47 helicopter. Resembling a giant one-eyed dragonfly, this helicopter with its giant glass cockpit provides passengers with incredible views of the Black Hills' more famous locations, including Crazy Horse Memorial, Mount Rushmore National Monument, and the

Needles. Tours range from a quick 8-minute ride to longer 30-minute excursions, although pilots are happy to create custom tours on request. Prices vary depending on the length of your tour but start at $20 per person and go all the way up to $189 per passenger. The well-marked helipad is located 1 mile north of Custer on U.S. 385.

WILDLIFE EXHIBITS

Learn about the Hills' animals—including bison, elk, fish, wild horses, reptiles, and more—at these sanctuaries and exhibits.

Central Hills

Bear Country U.S.A.   **$$$**
13820 South U.S. Highway 16, Rapid City
(605) 343-2290
www.bearcountryusa.com
It's not every day you have to brake for a big, burly bruin or a gaggle of geese, but at Bear Country you can count on it. Here it seems natural for the animals to roam about while the people are confined to their cars with the windows up. Besides bears you'll see elk, reindeer, mountain goats, bighorn sheep, wolves, bison, mountain lions, and other species as you drive through the 200-acre park on paved roads.

After your drive you'll be able to get out and walk through the Wildlife Center and Baby Land for a (relatively) close look at bear cubs and other small animals. The youngest visitors can take a few turns around the pony pen. (Pony rides are $1.00.) You'll find more critters, though not live ones, in the Bear's Den gift shop and gallery, where collectibles, clothing, and other items are for sale. There's also a snack bar and picnic area for hungry folks and brownbaggers.

Bear Country, 8 miles south of Rapid City, is open from early May to late November, weather permitting. During peak season, mid-June to mid-August,

The Cathedral Spires embrace the skyline in the southern Black Hills. SOUTH DAKOTA TOURISM

hours are 8:00 A.M. to 7:30 P.M. daily; the rest of the time it's roughly 8:00 A.M. to 5:00 P.M., but it would be wise to call ahead. Plan to spend at least an hour and a half once you get there.

Reptile Gardens $$
U.S. Highway 16, Rapid City
(605) 342–5873, (800) 335–0275
www.reptilegardens.com

Everyone from lizard lover to flower fancier will be enchanted by the displays and plantings at Reptile Gardens. This award-winning attraction—the pink building capped by the Sky Dome 6 miles south of Rapid City—claims the world's largest reptile collection as well as the largest variety of venomous species on exhibit anywhere.

But if creepy, crawly creatures make you cringe, you can soothe your nerves with an extravagant indoor orchid display or the more than 40,000 bedding plants in the outdoor gardens.

Reptile Gardens offers educational 20-minute shows featuring alligators, snakes, birds, and trained animals. The shows promote conservation and understanding of the important role animals play in our world. The U.S. Fish and Wildlife Service's Raptor Rehabilitation Center, based at Reptile Gardens but closed to the public, treats injured birds of prey in an effort to return them to the wild.

Millions have toured Reptile Gardens since it opened in 1937 after a local man, the late Earl Brockelsby, found that visitors enjoyed meeting the pet rattlesnake he kept under his hat. Along with your self-guided tour, you can have a light meal or snack in the Green Parrot Cafe and shop for jungle- and rainforest-related items, New Guinea tribal art, and other treasures in the gift shop.

The complex is open from April 1 to October 31. Hours are 8:00 A.M. to 7:00 P.M. from Memorial Day through Labor Day and 9:00 A.M. to 4:00 P.M. the rest of the season. During the summer, shows run throughout the day, with the last one starting at 7:00 P.M.

Trout Haven $–$$
U.S. Highway 385, Rapid City
(605) 341–4440

Here you can catch a trout (all fishing gear furnished), have it cleaned and fried up fresh, and you won't even get your hands dirty. It's a family place, and you can read all about it in the Kidstuff chapter.

Southern Hills

Black Hills Wild Horse Sanctuary $$$
Rocky Ford Road, Hot Springs
(605) 745–5955, (800) 252–6652
www.wildmustangs.com

The drive to Black Hills Wild Horse Sanctuary is worth every dusty mile (the last 5.5 are on gravel roads), for the preserve is a place of tranquillity and wild beauty. Two-hour bus tours through the 11,000-acre sanctuary stop for unforgettable views of the Cheyenne River, an intact set from the TV movie *Crazy Horse,* ancient petroglyphs, sacred caves, and, of course, free-roaming horses. Along the way you'll learn about the area's natural and human history, and whether you're a novice or an expert equestrian, you'll have plenty of opportunity to talk horses with your fellow passengers.

Author, rancher, and conservationist Dayton O. Hyde established the sanctuary in 1988 as a haven for unadoptable wild horses. The grounds support 350 mares and their foals; stud colts are sold to help support the nonprofit operation. Registered Cheyenne River paints also are for sale. If you're interested in helping out with work around the place, call for information about the volunteer program. You can also inquire about sponsorships.

Tours leave at 9:00 A.M., 10:00 A.M., 11:00 A.M., 1:00 P.M., and 3:00 P.M. April through October. Call for information about group rates or to make special arrangements for off-season tours. The sanctuary is 14 miles west of Hot Springs; to find it, follow Highway 71 south and turn right after the Cheyenne River Bridge.

KIDSTUFF

The Black Hills attract people from all walks of life, but two groups travel the highways and walk the streets here more than others: retired couples and young families. As a result, you'll find many attractions that cater especially to older crowds or children. In this chapter, we discuss an extensive list of places designed for the latter.

Though there are plenty of developed sights and fun parks for kids, the natural beauty and expansiveness of the Black Hills is a great asset for parents. Kids are free to roam (and hopefully tire themselves out) in the national parks, forests, and grasslands while remaining free from the dangers found in the wilder parts of Wyoming, Montana, or Colorado. There are no bears or wolves and few big cats, though poison ivy and snakes can be a nuisance. Check with park or forest service personnel if you have questions specific to an area, and read the Natural World chapter.

PRICE CODE

The following price code ratings refer to the cost of one child's ticket or admission fee.

$	Less than $5.00
$$	$5.00 to $10.00
$$$	$11.00 to $20.00
$$$$	More than $20.00

The Black Hills, Badlands, and Lakes Association (a nonprofit promotion group) publishes an annual list of Family Approved Attractions. While not all of the businesses on the list are specifically designed for children, they are appropriate for any age group. Many businesses have joined the listing system and display the pine tree logo with bright yellow and red lettering.

FUN PARKS

Get wet, get wild—there are plenty of fun parks in the Hills where youngsters (and their parents) can burn off energy and have good, clean fun.

Northern Hills

Gulches of Fun Family Fun Park $-$$$$
U.S. Highway 85 South, Deadwood
(605) 578-3386, (800) 961-3096
www.gulchesoffun.com
Ride the bumper boats and go-karts, play through the 18-hole miniature golf course, test your skill in the batting cages, play every arcade game, and fill up at the snack bar. For little kids, there are kiddie go-karts and rides. This place does birthday parties (with pizza), too.

Gulches of Fun is open from Memorial Day through Labor Day but may be open earlier and later in the season if weather permits.

Each activity at the park requires one or more tickets, which are $1.75 each. All-day wristbands are available for $18 and $30 and are more cost-effective. Gulches of Fun is on Deadwood's south side, on the way to Lead.

Central Hills

Black Hills Maze & Amusements $$
6400 South U.S. Highway 16, Rapid City
(605) 343-5439
www.blackhillsmaze.com
If you like puzzles you'll love this bilevel, ever-changing maze with more than a mile of mind-boggling paths. Time yourself to see how quickly you can find your way out of the fortresslike network of towers, bridges, stairs, and sharp corners.

There's also Bankshot Basketball and Water Wars with water balloons, a climbing wall, a zipline, and scooterlike Roller-Racers. Worn out yet? Take a break at the snack bar and pick up a South Dakota souvenir at the gift shop.

The maze, 3 miles south of Rapid City, is open 8:30 A.M. to 9:00 P.M. daily from Memorial Day through Labor Day, except on Flashlight Fridays, when it's open an hour later and the lights go out. During September and October it's open Friday through Sunday on a varying schedule, so call ahead for times.

South Dakota law prohibits fireworks of any kind, including firecrackers, in the Black Hills Forest Fire Protection District, except within the incorporated boundaries of municipalities. The district encompasses pretty much all of the Hills from Spearfish to Edgemont and Rapid City to the Wyoming border.

Flags and Wheels $-$$$
405 12th Street, Rapid City
(605) 341-2186
If you want to go fast, get excited, and let off some steam, this is the place. Also known as Flags of Fun, this 47,000-square-foot fun park is one of the largest indoor racing facilities in the region. There are small go-karts and an arcade area for younger children, but the primary attractions here are for the bigger "kids." Biz-Karts, high-speed competitive racers built in England, are available for anyone over 16 (although the average age of racers is probably twice that). The indoor urban paintball is open to anyone (kids and parents sign a waiver form), but it's usually the domain of kids in their 20s and 30s. There are also batting cages, a snack bar, and some small party rooms.

Flags and Wheels is open all year. Hours are 4:00 to 10:00 P.M. during the week and noon to 10:00 P.M. on weekends. Prices range from 75 cents for a few pitches in the batting cage to $17 for a round of paintball.

Gigglebees $
937 East North Street, Rapid City
(605) 399-1494
The name of this pizza arcade says it all. There's enough to do to keep you giggling for hours. Check out the kiddie rides, video games, Skee-Ball, pinball, and the play space. The restaurant—specializing in kid food—will help you keep up your energy for play. Gigglebees hosts birthday parties, too, with cakes, game tokens, even hats.

Gigglebees is open year-round; its hours are 11:00 A.M. to 10:00 P.M. Monday through Thursday, 11:00 A.M. to 11:00 P.M. Friday, and 10:30 A.M. to 11:00 P.M. on Saturday.

There is no admission fee, but all games and rides require one or more tokens that cost 25 cents each. Token specials are often available.

The Ranch Amusement Park $$-$$$$
6303 South U.S. Highway 16, Rapid City
(605) 342-3321, (877) 302-3321
This modest facility doesn't hold a candle to big-city amusement parks, but it does seem to have attractions for all ages. The go-karts are by far the favorite for both kids and adults. The slick track is fairly long (three-quarters of a mile) and well designed, and the slow pace of the go-karts will make it safe and fun for younger drivers. The bumper boats, inflatable jumping castle, and two 18-hole miniature golf courses with a Wild West theme are also popular with the younger crowd. The climbing wall and arcade cater to the older kids, but everyone seems to appreciate the small snack bar after a round of golf or few laps in a go-kart.

On the downside, the park is expensive when compared to many Black Hills attractions. Two laps on the go-kart track (which take a little over five minutes to complete) are $5.00. Repeated activities quickly add up, so wristbands, from $13 to

Laura Ingalls Wilder

Laura Ingalls Wilder gently drew the curtain on her *Little House* books in DeSmet, the "little town on the prairie" in eastern South Dakota. But several characters from her enduring tales of pioneer childhood went west and left their imprint on the Black Hills.

Laura's younger sister Carrie pursued a newspaper career that took her to Keystone in 1911. There she married a widower with two children, David Swanzey (who played a part in naming Mount Rushmore), and lived there until her death on June 2, 1946. Mary, the blind sister of the stories, died at Carrie's house on October 17, 1928; both sisters are buried with Ma and Pa in DeSmet.

Laura's Uncle Henry and Aunt Polly, from the Big Woods of Wisconsin, also came to the Black Hills and are buried with their daughter, Ruby, in Harney Cemetery east of Keystone.

Laura herself traveled to Keystone with her husband, Almanzo, to visit Carrie and see the sights.

But long before any of that, when Laura, Mary, and Carrie were still little girls on the banks of Plum Creek and before sister Grace was even born, their Uncle Tom Quiner, Ma's brother, ventured to the Hills in search of gold with the Gordon Party. (See the History chapter for more.) Years later, Uncle Tom visited Laura and her family in DeSmet and told them about his adventure; much later still, when Laura was in her 70s, she recalled Uncle Tom's story and wrote it down in *These Happy Golden Years*.

$30, are usually the way to go. The staffers here don't go out of their way to be friendly—a rarity in the Black Hills, where hospitality is the major industry.

The Ranch is open 10:00 A.M. to 10:00 P.M., from Memorial Day to mid-August. Hours vary from April to May and from mid-August to September, so it's best to call ahead. While you're on the phone, ask about the weather—thunderstorms shut down most attractions here. "Wacky Wednesday" is especially busy, since all visitors receive $5.00 off the price of a wristband. Call ahead for group rates and schedules.

Rushmore Waterslide Park　　**$$–$$$**
1715 U.S. Highway 16 Bypass (Catron Boulevard), Rapid City
(605) 348-8962
www.rushmorewaterslide.com
In the mood for some liquid refreshment? Make a splash at the waterslides, where you can take your pick of the superspeedy Bonzai or something slightly more sedate. In addition to the two steep slides, there are four 400-foot descents, an inner-tube river ride, a short ramp, and a kiddie slide. You'll also find volleyball, basketball, and horseshoe courts. If constant motion isn't your

mode of operation, you can soak in the 30-foot hot spa, take shelter in the shaded picnic area, mosey along the minigolf course, sneak over to the snack bar, or browse among the beach accessories in the gift shop.

The park, which is 3 miles south of Rapid City, is open early June to the end of August, 10:00 A.M. to 7:00 P.M., depending on the weather. Call ahead if it's questionable.

Coin-operated lockers and hot showers are available, as are swimsuit, life-preserver, and towel rentals. There's even a fenced area to keep your dog safe while you play.

Southern Hills

Evans Plunge $$
1145 North River Street, Hot Springs
(605) 745-5165
www.evansplunge.com
Take your pick of the waterslides before taking the plunge into a swimming pool heated with naturally warm water. For information about other things to do at Evans Plunge, see the Recreation chapter.

Flintstones Bedrock City $$
U.S. Highway 16 West, Custer
(605) 673-4079
www.flintstonesbedrockcity.com
Fred, Wilma, and the gang are ready to welcome kids of all ages to Bedrock City. Enter the Stone Age and see the faces of Mount Rockmore, ride the Flintmobile and the Iron Horse train, and zip down the Slideasaurus. Then get your strength back with a Brontoburger or Dino Dog at the Drive-In, and check out the licensed Flintstones items in the gift shop.

Bedrock City, at the west end of town, is open from mid-May through Labor Day. From early June to mid-August, hours are 9:00 A.M. to 8:00 P.M.; call for times the rest of the season.

For information about the park's campground, see the Campgrounds chapter.

HISTORIC SITES AND MUSEUMS

History comes alive at these sites and museums. Each has an emphasis or special feature that appeals to kids.

Northern Hills

Broken Boot Gold Mine $
U.S. Highway 14A, Deadwood
(605) 578-9997
So you think you might strike it rich here? It could happen, but, more likely you'll get rich quick in historical knowledge. The Broken Boot is a real gold mine, abandoned and closed for about 50 years, then reopened in 1954 for tours. When modern-day engineers explored the mine, they found a miner's boot that had been abandoned half a century before; hence the name.

Today you can follow a tour guide 840 feet back and deep into the hillside. You'll learn about the way early miners looked for gold and about the history of the Black Hills gold rush.

Mining is hard work, but this tour isn't, and you should have enough energy left over for gold panning. The Broken Boot will provide the pans and other supplies, show you how to look for gold in the panning troughs, and let you keep the shiny stuff if you find some.

The mine is at the intersection of Upper Main Street and U.S. Highway 14A, at the south end of Deadwood. It is open mid-May through mid-September, 9:00 A.M. to 5:00 P.M. seven days a week. Tours leave every 30 minutes during those hours. The mine is not wheelchair accessible. There's an additional charge ($) for gold panning.

Trial of Jack McCall $
715 Main Street, Deadwood
(605) 578-3583
Deadwood may have been only a few months old in the summer of 1876, but

the illegal gold camp already claimed 5,000 inhabitants—mostly prospectors, gamblers, and opportunists of dubious origin. Wild Bill Hickok, a legendary lawman and gunslinger, was one of them. It was no secret that he was in Deadwood to profit at the card table, which is what he was trying to do on August 2, 1876, when he walked into Saloon No. 10 on Main Street. After failing to convince fellow gambler Charlie Rich to give up his stool, Wild Bill reluctantly took the only open seat and joined the game. Forsaking years of cautious habit in a moment of greed, the gunman sat with his back to the door. The decision would prove fatal when drifter Jack McCall sidled through the door. Hickok, distracted by his losses to another player ("The old duffer, he broke me on the hand," he was muttering), didn't notice when McCall finally walked up to the table, gun drawn. "Damn you! Take that!" McCall shouted, discharging the death-dealing round into Hickok's head.

Hickok's murder happens four times a day, seven nights a week, in summer at the Old Style Saloon No. 10 (657 Main Street; more in the Nightlife chapter), subsequently followed by McCall's brief escape and capture farther up the street. The last performance at 7:00 P.M. is followed by McCall's trial in the Masonic Temple's theater at 715 Main Street.

Southern Hills

Four Mile Old West Town $
U.S. Highway 16, Custer
(605) 673-3905
www.fourmilesd.com
A talking outhouse with a sense of humor? That's just the beginning of your self-guided trek through the Old West at its most rustic. More than 50 wooden shacks house artifacts from days gone by, and there are plenty of witticisms sprinkled in with the history lesson—for

Kids younger than 21 are welcome in Deadwood gaming halls if they come with a parent or guardian. But according to state law, they are not allowed to touch or play the gaming machines or handle money used for gambling, and they must stay 3 feet behind any player.

instance, the proprietress of the seamstress shop is Mrs. Hattie Coates. But only the worthy may enter through the front door. A sign outside admonishes, TINHORNS, GAMBLERS AND LAYABOUTS, USE THE BACK DOOR. There is even a rebuilt stockade.

Stagecoaches used to stop here to water their horses at Four Mile Spring, and the town of Moss City was located here more than a century ago.

The owners offer lots of hands-on activities for the kids.

The present-day tourist complex 4 miles west of Custer has regular tours 8:00 A.M. to 5:00 P.M. Monday through Saturday and 9:30 A.M. to 7:00 P.M. on Sunday, May through September, and by appointment or chance during the winter.

Mammoth Site of Hot Springs $$
U.S. Highway 18 Bypass, Hot Springs
(605) 745-6017
www.mammothsite.com
How is an elephant's ear like an air conditioner? Find out at Mammoth Site, where you can touch an elephant's ear, see the giant (and sometimes tiny) bones of ancient animals that died here, and "dig" for fossils. To find out more, see the Attractions chapter.

PARKS AND NATURE AREAS

Playgrounds, open space, and fresh-air activities are found in these parks and nature areas.

The South Dakota Triceratops

The South Dakota state fossil is the triceratops, one of the last dinosaurs to live in North America. The word *triceratops* means "three-horned face." This 30-foot-long, 12-ton dino had a head more than 6 feet long, protected by those three fierce horns. His neck was topped by a bony plate and beaked snout. A heavy, pointed tail made him well armed against his predator, the much larger tyrannosaurus.

The South Dakota triceratops's skull was discovered in Harding County in 1927 and is on display at the Museum of Geol-

ogy, but his concrete likeness can be seen at Dinosaur Park. Both are in Rapid City.

Northern Hills

Spearfish City Park   **Free**
Canyon Street, Spearfish
The playground here isn't just another collection of swings and slides. Local kids worked with an architect to design it, and it was built by local volunteers, including kids, in 1996. You'll find an area with a sandbox and smaller equipment just for tots as well as swings, slides, monkey bars, a tire swing, and other fun equipment for older children. A wooden fence encloses the entire playground. When you're played out, soak your feet in Spearfish Creek, which runs along the west side of the park. City Park is on the south end of town.

Central Hills

Cosmos Mystery Area   **$$**
U.S. Highway 16, Rapid City
(605) 343-9802, (605) 343-7278
www.cosmosmysteryarea.com
You'll be confounded by the Cosmos,

where balls roll uphill, people get shorter, and the laws of physics are unenforceable. What's more, your guide on a half-hour tour will do everything possible to confuse you. Don't expect to get an explanation for the odd things that occur here; according to the staff, even scientists can't agree on what causes folks to feel off-balance at the Cosmos. It's been a tourist attraction since 1952, when two college boys discovered the area known as "the strangest location in the Black Hills."

The Cosmos is open 7:00 A.M. to dusk daily, June 1 to Labor Day; and from 9:00 A.M. to 5:00 P.M. Monday through Friday during April, May, September, and October.

Cosmos is 18 miles south of Rapid City; look for signs pointing to the turnoff.

Dinosaur Park   **Free**
Skyline Drive, Rapid City
(605) 343-8687
It's not every kid who gets to slide down the face of a dinosaur. That's because most towns don't have a special park full of the green monsters. The seven concrete giants aren't very detailed, and

they look a bit out of place (perhaps even tacky) atop a giant hill that overlooks the city, but it's their symbolism—not their appearance—that matters. Built in the depths of the Depression by the Works Progress Administration, the bright green dinos represent a determination to survive in tough times, even by very creative means. Among the first roadside dinosaurs ever constructed, they are listed on the National Register of Historic Places, and Rapid City park officials continue to tend them with pride. The giant brontosaurus (as the apatosaurus was known in 1936) is the only structure visible from both the east and west sides of town. He's usually lit up at night, and he marks the holiday season with a big red bow that hangs from his neck.

Dinosaur Park is open 6:00 A.M. to 10:00 P.M. year-round. A gift shop and snack bar are open 8:00 A.M. to 8:00 P.M. daily, June through August, and 9:00 A.M. to 5:00 P.M. in May, September, and October. It's closed from November through April.

From Quincy Street in Rapid City, follow the signs west to Dinosaur Park. It's seven-tenths of a narrow, twisting mile up Skyline Drive.

Mount Rushmore National Memorial   Free
Highway 244, Keystone
(605) 574-2523
www.nps.gov/moru

Youngsters ages 5 to 12 can do much more than tag along with Mom and Dad when the family visits Mount Rushmore. Kids who participate in the park's learn-and-earn Junior Ranger Program pick up a booklet at the information center and fill it out as they gather information about the monument by watching a video, taking a tour, or doing other activities. When they're done an hour or so later, a park ranger will sign their book, entitling them to a certificate. Those who wish to may also buy a patch for a small charge to sew on their hat or coat.

The American Lung Association of South Dakota offers the Children's Fun Pass that gives youngsters ages 6 to 12 free or reduced rates on admission, games, and food at more than 40 Black Hills area attractions (and others across South Dakota). The pass costs $15 but is valued at more than $250. Call (800) 873-5864 for more information.

The park's children's program offers age-appropriate talks on a variety of topics related to Mount Rushmore. Talks are offered once each afternoon and last about 30 minutes; call ahead for the schedule or check at the information center when you arrive.

Take U.S. 16 south from Rapid City or U.S. 16A south from Keystone and follow the signs to Highway 244 and Mount Rushmore. For more information about the memorial, see the Parks and Mountains chapter.

Storybook Island   Free
1301 Sheridan Lake Road, Rapid City
(605) 342-6357
www.storybookisland.org

Nursery rhymes are the theme at Storybook Island, where tykes and grown-ups enter the world of characters from some of the best-known children's stories. Cinderella and her pumpkin coach are here, along with Dorothy and Toto, the Crooked Man, and many others. The Storybook Island Theatre Troupe performs all season; call for the schedule.

The park is open 9:00 A.M. to 8:00 P.M. daily from Memorial Day weekend through Labor Day. It reopens on weekends from the day after Thanksgiving through Christmas, when miles and miles of lights deck the trees and displays, and special events are planned. Call for more details.

The Rapid City and Rushmore Rotary Clubs support Storybook Island. However, donations are always welcome.

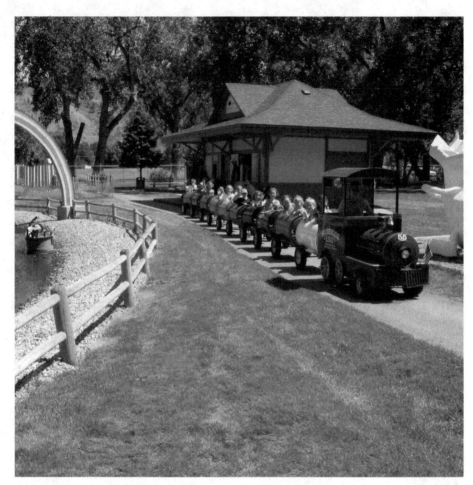

Storybook Island in Rapid City. T. D. GRIFFITH

WILDLIFE PARKS

Youngsters get a close-up view of alligators, bears, bison, elk, fish, lions, reindeer, reptiles, and more at these wildlife attractions.

Central Hills

Bear Country U.S.A. $$$
13820 South U.S. Highway 16, Rapid City
(605) 343–2290
www.bearcountryusa.com

Lions and reindeer and bears, oh my! Look who's looking at you, kid, as you drive through this wildlife park. Here, you're in a "cage" and the animals get to wander around. For more about Bear Country, turn to the Attractions chapter.

Reptile Gardens $$
U.S. Highway 16, Rapid City
(605) 342–5873
www.reptilegardens.com
Like rattlesnakes? How about tropical flowers? Either way, you'll find what you're looking for at Reptile Gardens. Plus, you'll get

to know more about alligators, birds, and other animals. See the Attractions chapter for a more complete description of one of the Black Hills' most popular stops.

Trout Haven $-$$
U.S. Highway 385, Rapid City
(605) 341-4440

This place is quite a catch. It's your chance to hook a trout, and you won't have to stand in the middle of a stream and get cold water in your waders to do it. It's also your chance to tell a big fish story.

Trout Haven furnishes poles and bait, encouragement and advice. When you've got that big one, they'll clean it and either fry it up in the restaurant or pack it in ice. If you and your family are traveling for a while, they'll even keep your filleted and frozen fish until you return.

Trout Haven is open from approximately Memorial Day to late September, but call ahead to be sure. Hours are 8:00 A.M. to 6:00 P.M. seven days a week during the summer.

Your big catch will cost you 50 cents an inch, or $4.95 for a meal that supplements your fish with french fries, Texas toast, and coleslaw. Breakfast is also served (and if you've never tried fresh trout for breakfast, you're in for a treat). Other items are available on the restaurant's menu if you don't like fish.

Trout Haven is 19 miles west of Rapid City, 20 minutes south of Deadwood on U.S 385. There are plenty of signs on the highway to guide you.

ANNUAL EVENTS AND FESTIVALS

Black Hills residents have always known how to have a good time. Since the land was settled, festivals and special events have been important here. Out on the range the ranchers learned to plan cowboy-style rodeos and fairs, while the more rowdy miners and mountain men deeper in the Hills threw wild parties and street dances. To this day you'll find a great series of events out on the plains, but the closer you get to the ancient mining towns of the Hills, the more spirited and more frequent the festivals become.

Deadwood, for example, has more special events than any other town in the region. There's always something cookin' there, and the town really knows how to throw a party—often rolling the shindigs, which usually include live music, dancing, and open containers, right out onto the streets.

Because some events change dates from year to year, only approximate dates are listed here. Call ahead or check the local papers or visitor guides for firm dates. The information here is not meant to be exhaustive—many events change,

new events are added, and those decreasing in popularity fall by the wayside.

You'll notice a minimum of events in January, February, March, and April. Blame it on South Dakota winters and wet springs, which make getting out and about a bit difficult and undesirable. If you're visiting during those months, you'll still find plenty to do, but don't expect the variety of festivals you'll find in the summer.

Our festivals and events are your chance to get in on some local celebrations and festivities. Have fun!

JANUARY

Central Hills

Black Hills Stock Show and Rodeo
Rushmore Plaza Civic Center
444 Mount Rushmore Road, Rapid City
(605) 394–4115
www.bhssf.com
Begun in 1958, the Black Hills Stock Show and Rodeo is the third largest stock show in the country. This annually anticipated event is a place for ranchers to show, buy, and sell cattle and horses, and a great community get-together.

If you've never been to a stock show, you'll find that they're highly educational and a great way to learn about the trials, tribulations, and rewards of the South Dakota ranching life. You may even learn to tell the difference between one breed of cow and another. There are plenty of other things to look at, too: art, clothing, gifts, and food.

The show is held in late January or early February and runs for about 10 days. Admission to the stock show is free, but tickets must be purchased for the rodeo and a few other events.

According to the **Guinness Book of World Records,** *on January 22, 1943, the temperature in Spearfish rose 49 degrees in just two minutes! A thermometer disc marked the 7:30 A.M. temperature at -4 degrees; at 7:32 A.M., a temperature of 45 degrees was recorded. This astounding change was the result of a chinook, and the sudden change from frigid to mild cracked windows around town.*

Lion dancers entertain the crowd during Deadwood's annual Chinese New Year celebration.
SOUTH DAKOTA TOURISM

FEBRUARY

Northern Hills

Chinese New Year Celebration
Miss Kitty's Casino
647 Main Street, Deadwood
(605) 578-7777, (605) 578-1811
www.deadwood.org
Since Chinese New Year is a lunar holiday, it's hard to pin down the exact date of this celebration, which takes place in early February.

Deadwood history has a fascinating chapter on the Chinese immigrants and businesspeople who joined in the glory days of the gold rush. The city celebrates that culture on Chinese New Year with lion dancers, a parade, firecrackers (which drive away evil spirits that threaten the coming year), and a display of photographs and artifacts from the Adams House and Adams Museum. Miss Kitty's also has a buffet for the event.

Hot Chocolate Days
Various locations in Spearfish
(605) 642-2626
Warm up winter at this community event, held during mid-February in charming downtown Spearfish. Most of the stores and businesses along Main and its adjoining streets display all kinds of artwork, so you can grab a warm, steamy cup of hot chocolate at one of the cafes or restaurants and stroll through the town to check out the show. Matthews Opera House (614½ Main Street) has its Winter Art Show at this time. There's also a children's carnival, a chili cook-off, shopping promotions, and an ice-skating evening (with lots of hot chocolate, of course).

Mardi Gras Celebration
Main Street, Deadwood
(605) 578-1876, (800) 999-1876
www.deadwood.org
It's the Mardi Gras of the West, with costumes, a night parade, a Cajun-food cook-off, and all the trappings (well, most of them) of New Orleans. But this one also has gaming and the charming amenities and atmosphere of Deadwood, South Dakota—something New Orleans can't claim.

Mardi Gras takes place in late February or early March, and it's an outrageous party you won't soon forget, done up Deadwood-style.

Central Hills

Black Hills Community Theatre Season
Dahl Fine Arts Center
713 Seventh Street, Rapid City
(605) 394-1786, (605) 394-6091
www.bhct.org
The community theater presents five quality performances—a good mix of drama, comedy, and music—throughout the year, with the first scheduled for February. Performances are professionally staged by dedicated local actors in the theater at the Dahl. Ticket prices vary and season tickets are available, so call ahead to check prices and reserve seats.

The Black Hills Community Theatre also conducts classes and workshops and presents plays for children. You can read all about it in the Arts chapter.

MARCH

Northern Hills

Black Hills Box Sled Championships
Deer Mountain Ski Area
U.S. Highway 85, Lead
(605) 584-3230
www.skideermountain.com
Yes, the sleds are literally boxes. Kids of all ages are welcome to build a cardboard

box sled using tape, glue, and imagination. Sharks, Vikings, and Model Ts have all plowed through the snow in the past. And, if their sleds actually stay together (there are quite a few wrecks at this race), competitors have a chance to win! There are all kinds of prizes, including best of show and best costume. The entry fee is $15. Deer Mountain has several other fun events and also serious competitions. Check its Web site for the latest dates.

Campfire Series
High Plains Western Heritage Center
Heritage Drive, Spearfish
(605) 642-9378
www.westernheritagecenter.com
If you want to hear and be part of a "real deal," catch one (or more) of the four-series Campfire shows held at the Western Heritage Center theater. One show per month is held in March, April, September, and October. The dates may be tentative, so call ahead to find out the schedule.

The idea behind this informal presentation around a fire is for area descendants, artists, writers, craftspeople, and storytellers to have the opportunity to relay their unique stories of the High Plains and to display their crafts.

Afterward, the audience is invited to ask questions and perhaps reminisce, as well as to view the articles from the show. The Chuckwagon Hour (finger food) begins at 6:00 P.M., and the show starts at 7:00 P.M. Admission is $5.00.

Ghost Towns of the Black Hills
High Plains Western Heritage Center
Heritage Drive, Spearfish
(605) 642-9378
www.westernheritagecenter.com
This program is a fun way to explore the history of the Black Hills through classes offered by a local history buff. The expert who runs this six-week course has a personal collection of photographs and information that was started by his father; the two men's research and findings are exclusive. The class is informal but the teacher is very knowledgeable. The class costs

$50 and space is limited to 75 people because of the field trip included (they don't want to lose anybody in the ghost towns). The group takes a day to visit several sites in the Hills and see history's mark on the world firsthand. The most popular sites in the area are closed-down mines, such as the ones in the Iron Hill District or the Galena area. The Western Heritage Center plans to make a video of the class and field trip to sell in the bookstore (it has the largest bookstore in Spearfish), so you could buy one for memorabilia or just as a gift. Read about the Western Heritage Center in the Attractions chapter.

St. Patrick's Day Celebration
Downtown Deadwood
(605) 578-1876, (800) 999-1876
www.deadwood.org
Show your colors (as long as they're green) at St. Paddy's parade and celebration in Deadwood. There are usually Irish bands, great food, green beer, a parade that tosses out money, and special events taking place in the casinos and restaurants on Main Street.

Central Hills

Country Fair Arts and Crafts Shows
Various locations in Rapid City
(605) 342-3694, (605) 343-8783
Six shows are held each year, beginning in late March (with others held in July, early October, mid- and late November, and December). Most are at the Rushmore Plaza Civic Center, but the mid-July show takes place outdoors in pretty Canyon Lake Park.

Crafters come from all over the country, and local and regional artisans participate. This is the largest indoor craft show in the area, and it's been a popular annual event for more than 20 years.

Sometimes there is informal musical entertainment, and homemade baked goods and candy are available from vendors. You'll find the newest craft and gift

trends here, as well as old favorites. Admission is free for the summer shows, $1.00 for benefit at the other shows, and vendors pay for their booth space.

APRIL

Easter Egg Hunts and Festivities
Various locations throughout the Hills
Many Black Hills towns celebrate Easter and the pending arrival of spring weather with Easter egg hunts and other activities. Most are small community celebrations and, thus, aren't planned as organized annual events, but we mention them here because they're fun, especially for children. Check local papers and visitor publications for current information.

Northern Hills

Historic Matthews Opera House
614½ Main Street, Spearfish
(605) 642-7973
www.moh-scah.com
The delightful community theater performances are presented in the restored opera house. You can read about them, and the beautiful venue, in the Arts chapter, or call the above number for information.

MAY

Black Hills Moonwalks
Various locations throughout the Hills
(605) 343-1567
Moonwalks take place one day each month, May through October (usually the Saturday nearest the full moon), and each is held at a different park or recreation area. They are sponsored by the Black Hills National Forest and the Black Hills Parks and Forests Association and conducted by people who can tell you a lot about each place.

The moonwalks take participants to a certain destination where an expert in a field related to the hike's location gives a 30-minute presentation. Past talks have

Elvis

Elvis Presley performed one of his final concerts at Rapid City's Rushmore Plaza Civic Center on June 21, 1977, less than two months before his death on August 16 at the age of 42. And, no, he hasn't been seen in Rapid City since.

focused on wildlife such as bats and coyotes, archaeology in the Deadwood area, the Battle Creek forest fire, and the history of the Williams Ranch near Pringle.

The moonwalks begin in the evening (between 7:00 and 9:00) and are usually 1- to 3-mile round-trips that last two to three hours. There is no charge, and you can call any of the forest service offices in the area to request current information. Bring your binoculars, something to drink, sturdy shoes, and layers of clothing (it can be chilly at night).

Check with the Mystic Ranger District office (at the number above, or visit 803 Soo San Drive, Rapid City) or see local newspaper listings for details and directions.

Spring Open House and Free Fishing Weekend
Various locations throughout the Hills
(605) 773-3391
www.state.sd.us/gfp
This is a very special event held at all 38 South Dakota state parks and recreation areas. It's a sort of visitor appreciation weekend, a way of inviting visitors back to the parks in the spring.

The open house is held the weekend before Memorial Day, and from Saturday morning through Sunday evening there is

no charge for park entrance, and fishing licenses are not required. Each park and recreation area offers entertainment, naturalist programs for kids, fishing tournaments, and presentations.

For more information call the South Dakota Parks and Recreation Department in Pierre at the above number.

JUNE
Northern Hills

Summer Institute of the Arts
Black Hills State University
1200 University Street, Spearfish
(605) 642-6241; (605) 642-6420
In June, Black Hills State University sponsors this competitive program that not only benefits the participants but the community as well. Students 17 and older from across the nation and around the world audition to study with international opera star Johanna Meier and other professors, and the students present at least two performances for the public. The educational program is called the Vocal Arts and Opera Theatre School, which is the main part of the Summer Institute of the Arts. The focus is on vocal, opera, and theater performance.

The programs' events (which also include classes and lectures) most often take place in BHSU's new recital hall, finished in 2003, that has been named in Meier's family's honor. Meier Hall is small (280 capacity), but the design is beautiful and created especially for music performances. The performances are open to the public, but you need to buy tickets. An opening performance by the students includes a reception; admission is $5.00 for adults, $2.50 for children under 15 and seniors. At the final performance, *A Night at the Opera,* students and teachers present a selection of opera scenes and arias; admission is $10.00 for adults, $5.00 for children and seniors, with a reception afterward. There is also a preperformance dinner and lecture for an additional $12.00, but you need to make reservations the day before.

Center of the Nation All Car Rally
Herrmann Park
Off Eighth Street, Belle Fourche
(605) 892-2676, (888) 345-JULY
www.bellefourche.org
Collectible cars and trucks from across the nation show up here to show off. Owners can participate in the show-and-shine competition, and the event runs in conjunction with the South Dakota State Chili Cook-off, which is open to the public for spicy sampling and bears a cash prize for the winner.

Most types of collectible cars and trucks are welcome, but call ahead to learn if there are restrictions.

There's a registration fee for vehicle owners, but spectators and those who just want to ooh and aah don't have to pay. The All Car Rally is held the second weekend of June on Friday, Saturday, and Sunday.

Sturgis Cavalry Days
Various locations in Sturgis and
at Fort Meade
(605) 347-2556
www.sturgis-sd.org
Honoring the history of the West, and Sturgis's part in it, this mid-June event takes place at different locations and offers some interesting western-style activities. Past ones have included an arts festival, horse and carriage rides, living-history and cavalry reenactments, a buffalo feed, a trial of Lt. Col. George Custer by real-life modern-day lawyers, a military ball, and a trader rendezvous.

Wild Bill Days
Downtown Deadwood
(605) 578-1876, (800) 999-1876
www.deadwood.org
Deadwood celebrates history in June by remembering one of its most famous permanent residents: James Butler "Wild Bill" Hickok. You'll see reenactments of Wild Bill's famous murder and the carousing of his friends Calamity Jane and Charlie Utter, and you'll also see these characters at the parade. If that's not enough excitement for you, the fast-draw and gun-spinning competitions are sure to get your heart racing. The activities are free and include two free concerts by national recording artists on Main Street (past performers have included Loverboy, Blackhawk, and Big & Rich).

Central Hills

Music in the Park
Memorial Park
Fifth and Omaha Streets, Rapid City
(605) 343-5176
Free outdoor concerts are presented each summer at the Memorial Park band shell, and indoor winter concerts are held at coffeehouses or the Dahl Fine Arts Center. Read about Music in the Park, listed under Backroom Productions, in the Arts chapter.

Family Cruiser Night
Various locations in Rapid City
(605) 394-4133
www.rcgov.org
On one hand, this is a chance for proud car owners to parade down Mount Rushmore Road, then display their shiny vehicles at the Rushmore Plaza Civic Center parking

lot or downtown. It's also a chance to participate in the long-standing pastime of cruising. But it's really an evening for families—an opportunity for parents to cruise with their kids and to spend time together. Spectators have great fun, too, watching the streams of beautifully restored, well-cared-for, and customized cars, from classic '57 Chevys and antique Model A's to snazzy low-riders with fuzzy dice dangling from their rearview mirrors. With good weather, Cruiser Night will get as many as 500 cars.

The event starts and ends at the civic center, next to Memorial Park, and is sponsored by the Rapid City Police Department. There's usually music downtown or at the band shell, plus public-safety displays and demonstrations that show what's new in law enforcement. Food and T-shirt sales benefit the DARE program.

Family Cruiser Night is held on a Friday evening in mid-June, but it is sometimes canceled because of rain, so call ahead.

West Boulevard Summer Festival
Wilson Park
Mount Rushmore Road, Rapid City
(605) 348-9439, (605) 343-1744

A very popular community arts-and-crafts festival, this one is held in pretty Wilson Park, just a block from historic West Boulevard, in mid-June.

You'll enjoy shopping for creative arts and crafts, listening to the musical performances, and sampling a variety of ethnic food. Then stroll over to West Boulevard and take a look at the beautiful historic houses.

Vendors pay a fee for their booth space, but browsers are admitted free.

Black Hills Bluegrass Festival
Mystery Mountain Resort
U.S. Highway 16, Rapid City
(605) 394-4101

It's a weekend of toe-tapping, feel-good bluegrass and acoustic music. For more than 20 years, the festival has taken place on the last full weekend in June, starting Friday night and ending Sunday morning with a gospel show.

The festival is a warm and homey event, with concerts by nationally known entertainers, workshops, informal jam sessions, food, and plenty of music. The organizers describe it as a big family reunion because so many people come back year after year.

Prices for a single show are $10; a ticket for all day Saturday is $20; a weekend ticket is $30. Discounts are available for advance purchases, and children under 12 are admitted free. The resort offers special camping rates for the bluegrass event. Call the resort at (605) 342-5368 or (800) 658-2267.

Southern Hills

Black Hills Playhouse
Custer State Park, Custer
(605) 255-4141, (605) 255-4551
www.blackhillsplayhouse.com

A visit to the playhouse is a perfect chance to tour beautiful Custer State Park and catch a great stage performance, too. The summer season runs from June through August each year. You'll need a South Dakota state park sticker to access the park. You'll find detailed information about the playhouse in the Arts chapter.

Crazy Horse Volksmarch
Crazy Horse Memorial
U.S. Highway 16/385, Custer
(605) 673-4681
www.crazyhorse.org

Just once each year, participants are allowed to walk right up to the huge carved face of Crazy Horse and view the work in progress close-up. (You can read about Crazy Horse Memorial in the Attractions chapter.)

In recent years, between 10,000 and 14,000 hardy folks have made this 6.2-mile trek.

The Crazy Horse Volksmarch, the largest *Volksmarch* in the country, is held on Saturday and Sunday during the first full weekend of June and costs just $2.00 per person.

Mattie Goff Newcombe

From the time she was a teenager, Mattie Goff Newcombe had a reputation. She was known as the fastest trick rider on the fastest horse in rodeo.

Even when she was a little girl, Mattie knew she was born to ride. When she sat astride a horse for the first time, she was just three years old. Luckily, growing up on her family's Meade County ranch gave her plenty of opportunity to break wild horses and become a skillful rider, and at 14 she entered her first rodeo. Back then, in 1921, not many women competed in rodeo, and Mattie helped pave the way for other talented riders of her sex.

Weighing only 100 pounds, Mattie was an agile woman who wore a wide-brim hat atop her smiling face and fancy boots on her tiny feet. She quickly earned fame for performing exciting stunts with names like "the slick saddle liberty stand," "spin the horn," "under the neck," "under the belly" and, most dangerous of all, "the suicide drag." She loved to square-dance on horseback in a quadrille made up of four couples. And no one could beat her at relay racing—she was that fast and that good at leaping from horse to horse without touching the ground.

Mattie was fearless. The only time she felt nervous was just before she performed for President Calvin Coolidge in 1927. But once she got on her horse, her jitters faded. She later reported, with some disappointment, that Silent Cal had talked to her and wasn't silent after all.

She never intended to retire, but Mattie married Maynard Newcombe in 1927 and discovered, as she often said, "You can't run a ranch and rodeo, too." So she came home to South Dakota and a life of hard work but no regrets. She stayed active, and 60 years after she entered her last rodeo she could still fit into her trick-riding costume.

In 1961 Mattie became a charter member of the National Cowboy Hall of Fame, and for more than 30 years after that she continued to accumulate honors. In 1989 she was inducted into the South Dakota Hall of Fame, and three years later Mattie was named South Dakota Rodeo Personality of the Past by the Casey Tibbs Foundation. Local sculptor T. R. (Tony) Chytka cast a small bronze statue of Mattie that's on display in First Western Bank in Sturgis, where she settled after her husband died. A life-size version will go in the Casey Tibbs South Dakota Rodeo Center in Fort Pierre, in central South Dakota. In 1994 Mattie became a Cowgirl Honoree in the National Cowgirl Museum and Hall of Fame.

To receive official credit for your *Volksmarch*, you must pay $2.00; to receive the "Volksmarch Crazy Horse" medal, you must pay $7.00.

JULY

Fourth of July celebrations
Various locations throughout the Hills

Most Black Hills towns and cities hold their own Fourth of July celebrations, patriotic community events that may include parades, picnics, barbecues, street dances, craft fairs, special events for children, and, of course, fireworks after dark. Check local papers and visitor publications for details.

Northern Hills

Black Hills Roundup
Roundup Grounds
Roundup Street, Belle Fourche
(605) 892-2643, (888) 345-JULY
www.bellefourche.org

The first roundup in 1918 was a Red Cross benefit. This long-standing and entertaining event still takes place over five days around the Fourth of July, and there's a lot to see and do. You can enjoy carnival rides, a free barbecue, roundup and horsemanship performances, a 10K run, a parade, and the Miss Rodeo South Dakota Pageant.

The roundup itself is a Professional Rodeo Cowboys Association (PRCA) event, with traditional rodeo competition and entertainment. Brothers Marvin and Mark Garrett, Belle Fourche's world-champion riders, usually attend and compete as well.

Casey Tibbs, from rural Fort Pierre, South Dakota, was the youngest cowboy to win the national saddle bronc riding championship (he has won six of them!), plus a bareback championship and two all-round cowboy championships. His record is still unequaled in the Professional Rodeo Cowboys Association.

Ticket prices for the rodeo range from $9.00 to $16.00 for adults, depending on seating selection, with discounts for children. Most other roundup events are free.

The Roundup Grounds are 1.5 blocks west off U.S. 85 (Fifth Street).

Family Creek Fair
D.C. Booth Historic Fish Hatchery
423 Hatchery Circle, Spearfish
(605) 642-7730
dcbooth.fws.gov

The fair is held on Father's Day on the lovely grounds of the hatchery. It's designed as a family event, a day when dads, moms, kids, and extended families can be together in a beautiful setting and have fun.

Besides children's activities, there's brunch in Mrs. Ruby Booth's garden at the historic house. Parents can watch the demonstrations on fishing and wildlife, and everyone will enjoy feeding the trout and ducks and touring the hatchery museum. It's all free, except for the brunch (advance reservations are required). Read more about the D.C. Booth Fish Hatchery in the Attractions chapter.

Festival in the Park
Spearfish City Park, Spearfish
(605) 642-7973

The Festival in the Park, held on a mid-July Saturday and Sunday, is a huge, popular event with more than 200 vendors. This juried art show is held in a lovely setting: Spearfish's city park on the banks of Spearfish Creek.

Arts and crafts of every variety, having passed the jury's discriminating eye, are presented in booths for the public's pleasure and purchase. In addition, there's a wonderful variety of food, jazz bands, dancing, music, and children's events and performances. These entertainments run all day long, so you can rest and snack, then walk around and look some more.

The vendors pay a fee to display their work, but the festival is free to everyone else, except for the first night, when there is a $5.00 charge.

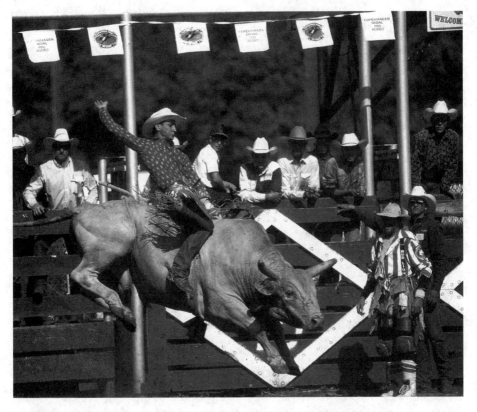

Deadwood's Days of '76 is one of American's oldest rodeos. SOUTH DAKOTA TOURISM

Black Hills Corvette Classic
Various locations in Spearfish
(605) 334-1625
www.blackhillscorvetteclassic.com
In 1971 the Sioux Falls Corvette Club (which consisted of seven couples and their cars) took a vacation together in the Black Hills. The event took on a life of its own, and hundreds of people and their Corvettes have been having fun together ever since.

In recent years, some 1,700 people and 900 cars from 38 states have attended. The Corvette Classic takes place on the third full weekend of July (Thursday through Sunday). On Thursday, the group caravans from Sioux Falls to Spearfish, and everyone is welcome to tag along (not just club members, and not just

Corvette owners). On the way home Sunday morning, everyone takes a detour to Mount Rushmore.

The main event is "Vette Street USA," when all those cars park on Main Street for a giant car show. Music, food, and merriment abound, plus competitions, touring and side trips, autocross, and drag races.

The registration fee is $120 per couple or $70 for one person, and participants can preregister by July 1. You can also register on-site at the Holiday Inn of the Northern Hills. The fee includes entrance to all the parties. If you just want to wander and browse through all that gleaming, curvy steel (no drooling on the cars!), there's no charge.

CLOSE-UP

The Sturgis Rally & Races

Every year in mid-August, tens of thousands of black-leather-clad folks ride their roaring steeds into Sturgis, South Dakota. They take over the town, park in every available parking space, fill the restaurants, crowd the sidewalks, and stay up half the night partying. The air is filled with the thundering sound of their steel horses, and normal conversation is downright impossible.

Why don't the good citizens of Sturgis do something about this intrusion, you ask? Don't they resent this yearly invasion of their peace and quiet, of their quaint little town? Heck, no! They invited these invaders, and they even gave the event a name: Sturgis Rally & Races.

It all started in 1938 when J. C. "Pappy" Hoel (who owned the local motorcycle shop) and his friends organized a race. Nineteen people showed up, and it was so much fun that they formed the Jackpine Gypsies Motorcycle Club and started an annual tour of the Hills. Events and activities were added each year; attendance grew, and the whole thing snowballed.

Now, most of the businesses on Main Street and neighboring blocks clear out and make way for hundreds of vendors, including custom-bike builders such as West Coast Choppers (owner Jessie James, a devout biker, usually rides his chopper all the way up from California). Bikers still race and tour the Hills, but there are also Motorcycle Hall of Fame inductions (Jay Leno and Peter Fonda are members), rock 'n' roll concerts, fighting competitions. . . . One thing for sure, you'll never be bored at the Rally.

The Rally has really picked up since the 1980s. An estimated 30,000 people attended in 1981; the 50th Rally in 1990 saw a whopping 400,000 attendees. And the 60th, a landmark event commemorated in the year 2000, played host to 600,000 people! (The mathematical discrepancy in the dates is due to the two years during World War II when the Rally was canceled.)

Nearly everyone attending the Rally takes the opportunity to show off in some way. You'll see incredibly creative custom bikes and paint jobs, wild headgear, bikers with parrots, bikers with snakes, bikers with dogs in sidecars, Christian bikers and unregenerate ones, tattoos that cover more square inches of skin than clothing, piercing on every conceivable body part, and rude (but funny) T-shirts.

Although "biker" might sound a bit scary—conjuring up visions of burly, mean, criminal types—most bikers aren't like that at all. Few rally-goers are hardcore bikers anymore; very rarely will you

Days of '76
Various locations in Deadwood
(605) 578-1876, (800) 999-1876
www.deadwood.org
This is rightfully billed as "the best rodeo in the hills—no bull." To prove it, the rodeo holds six consecutive awards from the Professional Rodeo Cowboy Association (PRCA) for the best rodeo in its class. This action-packed event runs for five days and includes the rodeo, three nights of street dances, and two historic parades on Main Street in downtown Deadwood.

see someone who might belong to an infamous biker gang. The vast majority are middle-aged professionals (doctors and lawyers especially) from the East and West Coast who don black leather and grow their beards out or abandon the makeup bag for a week. For them, the Rally is time to let loose in a way that isn't ordinarily possible.

But while the adults reign, you'll notice a fair share of kids at the event, too. It's not uncommon to see a toddler on a bike in a leather jacket or kids as young as six geared up with helmet and pads, ready to race on bikes just their size. Many locals and visitors like to make the Rally a family event. Others stay clear of the event altogether, citing stories of licentiousness and rowdy behavior. True enough, some venues can get a bit shady and family unfriendly during the week, but they're clearly identifiable (and carry age restrictions to boot). And admittedly, no matter where you are it's not uncommon to hear a little rough talk or see some bare skin.

Regardless of how rough, scraggly, or naked bikers may look, they all have an interesting story to tell, and most are pretty sociable if you can get up the nerve to talk to them. If you need an ice-breaker, just ask about their bikes; whether they built them themselves or just bought them yesterday—all bikers take pride in their steel beast. It will probably be a Harley-Davidson, which is the official bike of the Rally. Other brands,

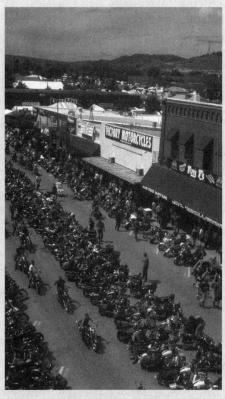

Motorcycles line Main Street during the Sturgis Motorcycle Rally. SOUTH DAKOTA TOURISM

such as Kawasaki and Honda, are minorities and may even get a few laughs. Unless, of course, the owner sports a studded leather jacket and outweighs everyone by 100 pounds.

The traditional parade is 3 miles long and mostly horse powered. The PRCA rodeo events attract enthusiastic crowds, and sometimes the Budweiser Clydesdales show up. President Coolidge attended the Days of '76 in 1927. It's a real (and real entertaining) tradition around Deadwood.

National Impala Association's International Convention
Various locations in Spearfish
(605) 642–5864
www.nationalimpala.com
You don't have to be an Impala owner to appreciate those roomy old beauties; in

If you want to tie the knot while attending the Sturgis Rally & Races (which many couples do each year), there are rules. Both persons must be present, older than 18, and carry identification. The license is $40, and neither waiting period nor blood test is required. You can get the license at the Meade County Register of Deeds in the courthouse at 1425 Sherman Street, Sturgis.

fact, any full-size Chevrolet made from 1958 to 1969 is welcome.

Anyone who wants to participate can join the National Impala Association for $35 and then register for the convention (there are extra charges for meals and some events). But there's no charge for just being in Spearfish during the convention and watching all those shiny cars cruise down Main Street and around the Hills.

Going on each year since 1980, the convention is held over six days in late July and is headquartered at the Holiday Inn of the Northern Black Hills, though many of the events take place at other locations. There are two show-and-shine competitions, tours of the Hills, a car-part swap meet, breakfasts, a 1950s and 1960s dance, a picnic, an evening excursion to Deadwood, and an awards banquet.

Central Hills

Black Hills Heritage Festival
Memorial Park
Off Mount Rushmore Road
Rapid City
(605) 209-4339
www.bhheritagefest.com
It's among the largest festivals in western South Dakota, in existence for more than 20 years. The Heritage Festival celebrates the arts (literary, visual, performing, and all the rest), as well as the Black Hills' ethnic and cultural heritage.

Held in Rapid City's Memorial Park, the festival takes place over the Fourth of July weekend (Thursday through Sunday), and admission is free. National and regional touring artists perform, and there are fireworks, arts-and-crafts displays and demonstrations, an international food bazaar, a children's area and carnival, strolling performers, and concerts.

Independence Day Celebration
Mount Rushmore National Memorial
Highway 244, Keystone
(605) 574-2523, (605) 574-3171
www.nps.gov/moru
Largely considered one of the top-10 fireworks displays in the nation, the Independence Day Celebration at Mount Rushmore is one of the more extravagant annual festivals held in the Black Hills. Besides the incredible pyrotechnics show, produced by internationally famous Zambelli Fireworks, there are live bands from local organizations and all branches of the military; flybys of F-16 fighters, Black Hawk helicopters, and B-1 bombers by Air National Guard and U.S. Air Force personnel; and daylong entertainment from comedians, professional presidential impersonators, and others.

The main event, of course, is the explosive fireworks display directly above the four presidential heads. Crowds of people pack into the memorial, cars line the highway all the way to Keystone, and groups watch from mountainsides throughout the Black Hills, many listening to local radio stations that broadcast patriotic music during the show. If you want one of the coveted places in the memorial's amphitheater, plan to arrive no later than mid-morning on the day of the display. On the other hand, if you can't handle the crowds, which number into the tens of thousands, the show is televised by local stations, South Dakota Public Broadcasting, and by some national news networks.

Gem and Mineral Show
Rushmore Plaza Civic Center
444 Mount Rushmore Road, Rapid City
(605) 394-4115

This is a great show for rock hounds, gem and mineral fans, and folks shopping for interesting gifts and treasures. Vendors come from all over the country to sell, buy, swap, and exhibit their collections. You can find jewelry, rough rock, fossils, and specimens here and enjoy demonstrations, educational programs, and the silent auction.

It's sponsored by the Western Dakota Gem and Mineral Society and held on the third weekend in July.

Black Hills Jazz and Blues Festival
Memorial Park, Civic Center Grounds, Off Mount Rushmore Road, Rapid City
(605) 787-6619
This is a very special event for jazz and blues lovers. Each year on the last Saturday in July, five nationally and regionally known performers make Memorial Park come alive with the sound of their music. It starts at noon and lasts until 10:30 P.M., and it's a great family day spent in a beautiful setting, with music all around.

Food is available; bring lawn chairs and blankets for seating. Wristbands, which cost $10, enable you to come and go as you like, skipping one performance and reentering the grounds for another. Discounts are available for children, too (please inquire).

AUGUST
Northern Hills

Hawg Draw and Buffalo Feed
High Plains Western Heritage Center
Heritage Drive, Spearfish
(605) 642-9378
www.westernheritagecenter.com
The only hogs you'll see at this event are the motorcycles, as the Hawg Draw is scheduled at the same time as the Sturgis Rally & Races (read more about the Rally in this chapter). Bikers and everyone else are welcome at this entertaining display of artistic talent; admission is $7.50, but that also includes a chuckwagon buffalo meal served cowboy style—outdoors. The event

starts at noon or earlier so visitors can talk to the participating artists before they start drawing.

At 1:00 P.M., the "quick draw" begins. The artists go to work—drawing, sculpting, painting, using whatever medium they choose—for just one hour. The public gets to watch as the works progress. At 2:00 P.M., work stops and the auction begins. This is your chance to purchase a freshly created work of art and meet the artist, too.

Don't forget to tour the High Plains Western Heritage Center while you're there. Read about it in the Attractions chapter.

Ruby's Garden Party
D.C. Booth Historic Fish Hatchery
423 Hatchery Circle, Spearfish
(605) 642-7730
dcbooth.fws.gov
The elegantly beautiful D.C. Booth home and gardens on the fish hatchery grounds are the setting for Ruby's Garden Party. Mrs. Ruby Booth, a charming hostess, loved to entertain; this party is named in her honor and is patterned after her gracious style and evokes the charm of the early 1900s.

This lovely, dressy affair is held in mid-August in the garden behind the home and includes a champagne dinner with musical accompaniment. Advance registration is required. Proceeds from the party help the D.C. Booth Society maintain the historic home and grounds.

Sturgis Rally & Races
Sturgis and other locations
around the Hills
(605) 347-9190
www.sturgismotorcyclerally.com
The Sturgis Rally & Races, the Black Hills' biggest party, began in 1938. The little town of Sturgis, South Dakota (normal population about 7,000), swells to a temporary population of about 500,000 to 650,000 each year during the event. How this happens is a sort of motorcycling miracle. (For more about the history and idiosyncrasies of the Rally, see the close-up in this chapter.)

Need accommodations for your trip to the Sturgis Rally in August? Check the Campgrounds and Accommodations chapters. Or call Sturgis Rally & Events, Inc., at (605) 347-9190 or the Sturgis Area Chamber of Commerce at (605) 347-2556 and request accommodations information.

The Rally officially runs from Monday through Sunday in mid-August, but bikers begin to descend on the Hills weeks early, and some stay just as long after the Rally ends. For about two weeks each summer, the Black Hills vibrate constantly to the thunderous music only hundreds of thousands of motorcycles can make. After you're here for a couple of days, you can even sleep right through it.

So many events of vast and amazing variety are held during Rally week that it's impossible to describe them all. Official events include motorcycle auctions and displays, demonstration rides, concerts, parties, motorcycle jumps and hill climbs, races and ride-ins, guided tours of the Hills, exhibits, and poker runs. Four blocks of Main Street are closed to all vehicles except bikes, and you haven't seen anything until you've viewed thousands of shiny motorcycles parked perpendicular to the curbs, and in a double row down the middle, stretching as far as the eye can see.

Almost every downtown storefront is occupied by someone selling nearly every type of food you can imagine, or T-shirts, leather clothing, bandannas, cigars, motorcycle parts and accessories, and souvenirs.

Other Black Hills towns throw their own parties for bikers, and Rapid City's Rushmore Plaza Civic Center hosts the free Harley-Davidson show, with vendors, seminars, competitions, and demonstrations, plus a major concert (past performers have included ZZ Top, Willie Nelson, Lynyrd Skynyrd, and Def Leppard). You must purchase tickets to the concert. Deadwood is sometimes as crowded as Sturgis, since most casinos have weeklong activities

planned for the biker crowd. Expect rowdy concerts, custom-bike giveaways, and celebrity appearances by people such as G. Gordon Liddy and Playboy centerfolds.

Call the number or browse the Web site listed in the heading for information and schedules, to register, and for help in finding accommodations (which you should book months, maybe even a year, in advance). You aren't required to officially register (and there's no charge for doing so), but you can stop at Rally Headquarters in the Armory building on Main Street to enter your name in the guest book and put a pin in the U.S. or world maps to mark where you're from.

Black Hills Steam and Gas Threshing Bee
Hereford Road, Sturgis
(605) 347-2556
www.sturgis.sd.us

Elders remember the farming equipment you'll see at this show: early steam- and gas-powered machinery that (in those days) made work easier. At least it was easier than doing it by hand and with horses.

The Threshing Bee marks its 36th year in 2004. That's an indication of how popular it is, and how the old equipment still strikes a chord in the heart. More than 200 pieces of antique equipment are exhibited.

The Threshing Bee will transport you back to a simpler, but more strenuous, time. It may even be a chance for elders to share their stories and heritage with those who are younger. You'll see antique tractors, threshing machines, sawmills, steam engines, miniature engines, blacksmithing, a one-room schoolhouse, and more. There are plenty of demonstrations, threshing, and hay binding in the field next door, tractor races, and a daily parade. Music is provided by the Grimm Reapers (would anyone else be more appropriate?).

The bee takes place on Friday, Saturday, and Sunday of the third weekend in August, on the grounds owned by the Western Dakota Antique Club, a half mile east of the Sturgis Airport, off Highway

Classic cars and cool music are trademarks of Kool Deadwood Nites. TDG COMMUNICATIONS

34. Admission is $5.00 per day for anyone 13 and older.

Kool Deadwood Nites
Various locations in Deadwood
(605) 578-1876, (800) 999-1876
www.deadwood.org

It's the finest kind of retro concert 'cause you get to pretend you're back in the '50s and '60s again. It's held on Friday, Saturday, and Sunday in late August.

You can dance at the sock hop or attend the parade and show and shines. Classic cars are displayed, and prizes are awarded for beauty.

The "prom," complete with authentic music, is on Saturday night, and everyone is encouraged to dress up in style. (You can rent a tux in town.) In the past, music has been provided by the Turtles, Dion, and Chubby Checker.

Central Hills

Ellsworth Air Force Base Open House
Interstate 90, exits 63 and 67, Ellsworth
(605) 385-4414
www.ellsworth.af.mil

"There's always a plane in the air during

this exciting open house," say the organizers, and if you like planes, you'll get your fill of them here. You can watch aerial demonstrations, fly-bys, and parachute jumps and see both vintage and modern combat aircraft. The Golden Knights army parachute team has appeared, and attendees have been treated to aerobatic stunts and air rescue demonstrations.

Central States Fair & Rodeo
Central States Fairgrounds, Rapid City
(605) 355-3861
www.centralstatesfair.com
This is a traditional fair with those familiar events that make country fairs so much fun. You can browse 4-H and agricultural exhibits, sit in on classes and demonstrations on cooking and crafts, walk through the livestock barns, pet an exotic critter at the petting zoo, ride the carnival rides, catch a horse show or parade, and stuff yourself with cotton candy and caramel apples. Or sit back in the grandstand and be entertained by famous musical talent (past performers include the Nitty Gritty Dirt Band and Creedence Clearwater Revival). If you'd rather sit on the edge of your seat, try the Professional Rodeo Cowboys Association rodeo instead.

So many things go on at this eight-day fair that you'll have trouble finding time to enjoy them all, so check local newspapers and sort out each day's events. The Central States Fair takes place in mid- to late August.

 Autumn is a great time to visit the Hills. The weather is usually fine, traffic is lighter, leaves are turning gold, and most attractions are open. For a brochure on the "Autumn Expedition," annual events and festivals from mid-September to early October, call the Black Hills Visitor Information Center in Rapid City at (605) 355-3700 or stop by (exit 61 off I-90).

SEPTEMBER
Northern Hills

Black Hills Airport Fly-In
Black Hills Airport, Spearfish
(605) 642-4112, (605) 642-0277
Pilots and aviation buffs alike love this annual event, which takes place on a Saturday in September.

Seventy-some planes have been displayed, including vintage war birds as well as experimental planes, ultralights, and helicopters. Pilots can fly their planes in, and spectators can take rides and enjoy the displays. Demonstrations and food are offered, too. You can watch the South Dakota Aviation Hall of Fame induction ceremony, a very special event.

The fly-in is free to everyone, pilots and spectators alike.

Deadwood Jam
Downtown Deadwood
(605) 578-1102, (800) 999-1876
www.deadwoodjam.com
The "Jam" has become one of the largest musical festivals in the Black Hills, and if you're a music fan you won't want to miss it. It's held in mid-September each year, outdoors. Ticket prices are $18 in advance and $20 at the gate. Food and alcohol are available by vendors.

George Clinton and the Parliament Funkadelics, Collective Soul, Spin Doctors, Inner Circle, and Tonic have performed in the past.

Harvest Fest
Various locations in Spearfish
(605) 642-5421
www.spearfish.sd.us/dba
Two blocks of Main Street are blocked off for the annual Harvest Fest. Enjoy crafts, kids' entertainment, apple-pie-baking contests, music, displays, puppet shows, a quilt show, and more, all free.

A new addition to this event is the Fiddle Fest, the only sanctioned fiddling contest in South Dakota. Everyone is welcome to compete in this toe-tappin' hoedown—

the first performance in 2003 drew musicians from the entire midwest region. Impressive talent vies for a sponsored ride to the national competition. There is an entry fee to compete, but the public can watch for free.

Central Hills

Annual Dakota Polka Festival
Canyon Lake Viking Hall
2900 Canyon Lake Drive, Rapid City
(605) 787-5584
Admit it: You've always wanted to polka. This is your chance. This festival takes place on a September weekend, and all kinds of dance steps are performed, not just polka. Live bands provide the music, and the Friday and Saturday night dancing goes on until 11:00 P.M.

If you don't polka, you can observe, or ask one of the friendly enthusiasts to teach you on the 5,400-square-foot floor.

Homemade food and RV parking are available at the center. A two-day pass is $15.00 per person, a Friday-night pass is $6.00 per person, and a Saturday-night pass is $10.00 per person. Smoking and alcohol are not permitted.

Southern Hills

Crazy Horse Night Blast
Crazy Horse Memorial, Custer
(605) 673-4681
www.crazyhorsememorial.org
This ceremonial blast on the mountain takes place each year in early June and on September 6. (You can learn about the Crazy Horse Memorial in the Attractions chapter.) The latter date commemorates both Crazy Horse's untimely death in 1877 and the late sculptor Korczak Ziolkowski's birthday.

The blast takes place after dark for spectacular effect, and it's free with your entrance fee. An open house, during which you can tour the visitor complex and exhibits, is held on Labor Day weekend.

Badger Clark Hometown Cowboy
Poetry Gathering
The Mueller Center
801 South Sixth Street, Hot Springs
(605) 745-3446
www.hotsprings-sd.com
Locally and regionally famous cowboy poets tell their tales and play their music in this late September event. It's designed to pay tribute to both Badger Clark, South Dakota's "Poet Lariat," and the art of cowboy poetry. In addition to the performances, there are symposiums, displays of western gear, jam sessions, open sessions where amateur poets can give tale telling a try, and more cowboy boots in the audience than you can shake a stick at.

OCTOBER
Northern Hills

Oktoberfest
Downtown Deadwood
(605) 578-1876, (800) 999-1876
www.deadwood.org
This is a German celebration, presented Deadwood-style. It takes place over several days in early October.

You can enjoy German and other music, clog dancing, a microbrew expo, a German cook-off and food tasting, accordion music, a lederhosen contest, and a home-brewers beer contest. German folk band the Sauerkrauts usually provides the music.

It all takes place on Deadwood's Main Street, though most downtown casinos, restaurants, and hotels also have something special to offer. The entertainment and events are free.

Deadweird
Downtown Deadwood
(605) 578-1876, (800) 999-1876
www.deadwood.org
Don't miss out on this spooky event, because it happens only once each year—on Halloween night. It's a citywide bash, with trick-or-treating for the kids and a costume contest (for big kids older than

21) that rewards winners with cash.

Since Deadwood is haunted by such illustrious ghosts as Calamity Jane, Seth Bullock, and Wild Bill Hickok, this event is perfectly appropriate. It's doubly appropriate because Deadwood also is haunted by some very odd—and very alive—people who seem to descend into the town from their mountain homes only for Halloween. Despite the colorful crowds, Deadwood (and Deadweird) is safe and family friendly.

Central Hills

Black Hills Chamber Music Society
First Congregational Church
1200 Clark Street, Rapid City
(605) 718-5666
www.rapidcityweb.com
The society's five-performance series begins in October (and runs through April) and always boasts outstanding performances. We've included more information in the Arts chapter.

Mount Rushmore International Marathon
Various locations, Rapid City
(605) 348-7866, (605) 721-1251
www.mtrushmoremarathon.com
The annual marathon takes place on a Sunday in early October. The route winds through the scenic Black Hills and ends in Rapid City, and for the entry fee ($40) you can compete and enjoy the scenery at the same time.

A marathon relay is run in conjunction with the marathon itself (cost is $70 per group), and a pasta buffet at Mount Rushmore is on the schedule, too.

Rapid City Concert Association
Rushmore Plaza Civic Center Theater
444 Mount Rushmore Road, Rapid City
(605) 394-4101
www.rapidcitycvb.com
The annual six-concert series begins in October (and ends in April) and presents fun and exciting musical performances. You can read more about them in our chapter on the Arts.

Black Hills Pow Wow and Art Expo
Rushmore Plaza Civic Center
444 Mount Rushmore Road, Rapid City
(605) 343-5718
www.rapidcitycvb.com
Powwows are spectacular events and a rich opportunity to learn about Native American culture and tradition. To participants, pow-wows are a spiritual experience, a celebration of culture, a chance to dance together and to renew old friendships and make new ones. The steady drumbeats accompanying the dancers represent the heartbeat of the people, a powerful emotional experience.

The Black Hills Pow Wow and Art Expo take place in mid-October and last for three days. Call for exact dates.

Traditional and contemporary art is on display and for sale, and in past years there have been storytellers, flute players, dance and drumming performances, educational activities for children, and a Native American fashion show. Pre-powwow programs are held at the Journey Museum (see the Attractions chapter) several days prior to the event. There is a charge for daily sessions and three-day passes.

Be sure to watch the Grand Entry, an event that is repeated on all three days of the powwow. Observers, who are expected to respectfully stand during the entry, are treated to a stunning visual and auditory display of finery, drums, dancing, and passionate musical voices. The participants enter the arena in a line, singing and dancing as they go, accompanied by drumbeats and preceded by the sacred eagle staff and tribal and U.S. flags. Hundreds of dancers fill the arena in a sacred circle, winding round and round, until the floor is a whirl of movement, color, and sound. It's a spectacular sight, especially from the civic center's seats high above the arena.

Ski for Light Ski Swap
Rushmore Plaza Civic Center
444 Mount Rushmore Road, Rapid City
(605) 394-4115, (605) 381-1172
www.rapidcitycvb.com
The Black Hills Regional Ski for Light organization holds its annual fund-raiser in

Fall Color Heralds Bison Roundup

In the Black Hills, fall is a time when managers at Custer State Park reduce bison numbers to be compatible with the land's carrying capacity. The time is right, for the blood of the bison has cooled following the intensity of their summer ardor. Now, as the Black Hills begin to turn gold, bison plod along like patriarchs of old, at least that is until the roundup begins. Then, their blood is anything but cool.

Game Lodge campground is conveniently located for the roundup, which the park holds the first Monday after the last weekend in September as one of their fall interpretive programs. Set against the plains that thread throughout the hills and the ponderosa pine, the roundup has a splendid fall backdrop. The herd thunders over hills, finally charging through the coulees and ravines, urged on by riders. Once the bison are in motion, the direction is easy to sustain, for as managers say, "A moving herd is easier to contain than a stationary one."

After the herd is contained in a huge holding area, biologists begin the process of reduction. Bison are herded into various chutes according to age and sex. Culled animals are then auctioned off to the highest bidders. After the roundup, the much-reduced herd of about 950 is returned to roam the park, where it joins those that eluded the riders. The two-day event is one of the most dramatic in the Black Hills, and it's made even more spectacular as it coincides with a time when the Black Hills turn gold.

Bison charge during fall roundup at Custer State Park. BERT GILDART late October or early November. It's an equipment consignment swap, where 20 percent of the sale price goes to the non-profit organization to fund programs that help the visually impaired ski, camp, canoe, and enjoy the outdoors.

This is your chance to pick up some great used equipment at a fair price and help support the Ski for Light programs, too. There is no entrance fee to shop at the swap.

For information on outdoor and recreational programs for the visually impaired (including a January ski event at Deer Mountain, near Lead, which draws participants from all over the country), call Ski for Light at the second number above.

Southern Hills

Annual Buffalo Roundup and Arts Festival
Custer State Park, Custer
(605) 255-4515
www.custerstatepark.info
Organizers have called this event "Feel the Thunder." You can't quite understand why until you've seen, heard, and felt 1,500 buffalo running across the plains, herded by cowboys, cowgirls, and park rangers (riding pickups and horses) into corrals. It's really something to experience.

The roundup is held on a Monday in late September or early October in the corral area south of the State Game Lodge on Wildlife Loop Road. You can watch the critters being branded and vaccinated (but you need to arrive between 6:30 and 7:30 A.M. and stay until the "all clear" signal is given). The buffalo not returned to the park for the winter are sold at auction in November.

Plenty of less dramatic (but equally interesting) events take place during roundup weekend, on the Saturday and Sunday before the roundup itself. The arts festival is staged near the State Game Lodge, and you'll find great collectibles and gifts in the booths.

There's also terrific entertainment: Native American dancers, cowboy poets,

cloggers, fast-draw competitions, and western music. You can enter the Buffalo Wallow Chili Cook-off, or just sample the entries, and enjoy a pancake feed and chuckwagon cookout, too. It's all free, except for the food.

For convenience, you can stay at the Custer State Park campgrounds (see the Campgrounds chapter) or resorts (see the Accommodations chapter).

Native American Day Observances
Crazy Horse Memorial
U.S. Highway 16/385, Custer
(605) 673-4681
www.crazyhorsememorial.org
A special program and events are held each October at Crazy Horse Memorial to commemorate the struggles, triumphs, heritage, and legacies of Native Americans.

You can enjoy lectures and demonstrations, drumming, singing, dancing, and storytelling. Tour the Indian Museum of North America and the Native American Cultural Center; both are housed on the grounds.

A special day blast is planned on the mountain (see more about the sculpture in the Attractions chapter), and there's a buffalo stew feed at noon. It's all free with your admission to the memorial.

NOVEMBER

In November, holiday home tours, craft shows, "festival of lights" parades, and Christmas tree decorating festivals are popular. Check a local newspaper for details.

Central Hills

Black Hills Symphony Orchestra
Rushmore Plaza Civic Center Theater
444 Mount Rushmore Road, Rapid City
(605) 348-HORN (season tickets)
(605) 394-4111 (individual performance tickets)
Six fine concerts are presented by our very own symphony orchestra each season. Read about these great events in the Arts chapter.

Southern Hills

Buffalo Auction
Custer State Park, Custer
(605) 255-4515, (605) 255-4814
www.custerstatepark.info

Read about the Annual Buffalo Roundup and Arts Festival that takes place in Custer State Park in October's listing (Southern Hills) or in the Parks and Mountains chapter. The surplus animals culled from the herd along with the park's surplus burros are sold at this mid-November auction, which helps support the park's operations.

It's an interesting event to watch, even if you're not inclined to take a buffalo or burro home.

DECEMBER
Northern Hills

Adams Family Christmas
Adams Museum and Adams House
54 Sherman Street, Deadwood
(605) 578-3724
www.adamsmuseumandhouse.org

The Adams Museum and Adams House always celebrate Christmas in Victorian style, and one of their favorite events each December is *An Adams Family Christmas Carol,* an original play written for the organization that is based not on the Dickens classic but on Deadwood's historic Adams family during the 1920s. Performances usually take place at the house, not the museum (read about these two sites in the Attractions chapter).

Enjoy Christmas readings, a masquerade, dramatic musical presentations, and special exhibits (the events change from year to year).

Christmas Stroll
Downtown Spearfish
(605) 642-5421
www.spearfish.sd.us

This lovely community event takes place on a weekend afternoon in early December, on Spearfish's charming Main Street. With a little luck, you can bask in the sunshine of a Black Hills winter day, or at least listen to music and carolers, shop for crafts, enjoy the food, and take a horse-drawn wagon ride. The fun is free, although there is a charge for food. This old-fashioned Christmas is a fun event for all ages. Adults can enjoy chestnuts roasted on an open fire, and children can have their pictures taken with Santa, the Mystery Snowman, or the Snow Queen.

Festival in the Snow
Holiday Inn Convention Center
Interstate 90, exit 14, Spearfish
(605) 642-7973, (605) 642-4683

This large arts-and-crafts show, held the first full weekend of December, has a little bit of everything, including the Christmas spirit. Santa Claus makes an early appearance at this event: on Saturday afternoon, right next to a festive train display. The show is not just for kids, though; everyone can browse the show to shop for clothing and food or just look at all kinds of arts and crafts, especially things in traditional country style. Vendors are juried to take part in the show and pay a fee for their space, so you can bet the work will be good. Admission is $1.00, but entertainment is free once you're in.

Festival of Trees
Spearfish Park Pavilion
Fifth Street, Spearfish
(605) 642-7778

Beautifully decorated Christmas trees are on display for about four days in early December; you can view them without charge, but a donation of a can of food is appreciated.

The festival is sponsored by the businesswomen's community service organization, Zonta. At the end of the display period, the trees are auctioned at a gala event, and proceeds go to charity. You can take home a decorated tree and help out those less fortunate at the same time.

Hatchery Holidays
D.C. Booth Historic Fish Hatchery
423 Hatchery Circle, Spearfish
(605) 642-7730
dcbooth.fws.gov
The hatchery grounds and D.C. Booth historic home are lovely places and the perfect backdrop for a Christmas event.

The house is decorated in the finery of a long-ago Victorian Christmas, and the many trees on the grounds are draped in finery of their own. You can take a tour of the house and museum and enjoy the special displays and events. It's all free and a charming way to spend a holiday Sunday in early December.

New Year's Eve Celebration
Main Street, Deadwood
(605) 578-1876
www.deadwood.org
Deadwood has been a party town since the first rowdy prospectors descended upon the gulch in 1876. Though the gold is now gone, residents still throw some wild celebrations here, and with the possible exception of Mardi Gras, New Year's Eve is Deadwood's wildest shindig. People come from all over the Dakotas, Nebraska,

Wyoming, Montana, and beyond to usher in the new year in Deadwood. The casinos have parties and special giveaways, the saloons bring in bands that play all night long, and the hotels fill up fast. If you'd like to join in the festivities, be sure to reserve a room well in advance.

Southern Hills

Christmas in the Hills
Various locations in Hot Springs
(605) 745-5642
The folks in Hot Springs—who work hard to present this event—are rightfully proud of this old-fashioned festival, which goes back more than two decades. Traditions include a children's procession and living nativity, an arts-and-crafts fair, music, art shows, community dinners and chili suppers, a tour of local homes, and appearances by Mrs. Santa Claus. There is also a parade of lights, a tree lighting ceremony, and open house at downtown businesses. It takes place during the first weekend of December and attracts visitors from surrounding states as well as residents and folks coming home for Christmas.

THE ARTS

Many people don't associate the American West with fine art. True, there are no world-class ballet companies based here, nor are there any internationally famous art museums. But art imitates life—and there is plenty of life in the Black Hills. The landscape, with its physical and spiritual wonder, has triggered the imagination of countless artists. Anyone who spends time in the Hills will quickly see that art runs strong here, especially on the local front. Photographers, composers, poets, painters, singers, writers, and sculptors of all backgrounds and ages practice their craft and form the broad base of the area's cultural community.

You'll find art on display and for sale at many events (see the Annual Events and Festivals chapter). Especially worthy of note are the Black Hills Pow Wow and Art Expo, the Black Hills Heritage Festival, even the Black Hills Stock Show and Rodeo, all in Rapid City, and the Festival in the Park and High Plains Western Heritage Center's Hawg Draw & Buffalo Feed in Spearfish.

The rich traditions of this area also have an influence. Western themes and traditional Native American art predominate, although some visual artists choose other themes or abstract forms, and a growing number of Native American artists are exploring contemporary paths. Literary arts run from cowboy poetry and stories of western life to work that transcends the sense of place that defines the Black Hills.

As the Black Hills cultural community is strong, so are the organizations that support and fund them. Rapid City's Allied Arts Fund Drive, (605) 394-4106, is responsible for sponsoring many of the performances, concerts, exhibits, and readings that happen in the Rapid City area; several occur at the Dahl Fine Arts Center, which is owned by the city and administered by the independent Rapid City Arts Council, (605) 394-4101. The organizations continue to consolidate and work more closely with one another, which is important, since much cooperation will be needed to raise the funds for expanding the tiny Dahl, Rapid City's only community art venue. The current plan calls for a $6.5 million renovation and expansion, which will be paid for only partly by city taxes and open before 2007 (see the Galleries and Exhibit Spaces section of this chapter for more information).

The state government and nearly every town in the Hills support the arts. The South Dakota Arts Council, (605) 773-3131, is part of the state's Department of Education and Cultural Affairs. It funds residencies and grants to help local artists share their work with schoolchildren, who experience poetry, Lakota dance and flute music, stories, photography, mural painting, rodeo clowns, puppets, classical guitar, and more through the program.

The Sturgis Area Arts Council sponsors theater performances, Art for Lunch Bunch discussions, book signings, a juried art show, and the Community Sculpture Garden. The Spearfish Center for the Arts and Humanities, (605) 642-7973, helped restore the town's Historic Matthews Opera House, now a performing arts center, and sponsors art shows and an annual foreign-film series.

The Historic Deadwood-Lead Arts Council, (605) 584-1461, sponsors exhibitions in the under-renovation Historic Homestake Opera House, which will one day also be a performance space. South Dakotans for the Arts, (605) 578-1783, based in Lead, is an arts advocacy, service, and education organization that sponsors the U.S. West Artists in Rural Schools program, the five-state Art Beyond Boundaries Conference, and much more.

Hill City prides itself on a growing reputation as an art community. The Hill City Area Arts Council, (605) 574–2890, supports exhibits and demonstrations, including June's Heart of the Hills Art Show. The Hot Springs Area Arts Council, (605) 745–4225, manages the Main Street Arts and Crafts Festival (more than 20 years old) and children's programs and scholarships. Southern Hills Arts and Humanities, (605) 745–6473, promotes all types of arts activities, including a summer music series.

We encourage you to learn about the arts in the Black Hills in this chapter—then watch, listen, participate, and enjoy.

DANCE

One venue specializes in dance, including performances, workshops, and master classes.

Central Hills

Black Hills Dance Theatre
4939 Spring Tree Court, Rapid City
(605) 342–1564
www.bhdancetheatre.org
This dance theater is managed by an all-volunteer board, a sure sign of community commitment. It sponsors two professional dance performances each year, one in the spring and another in the fall, with master classes and school activities coinciding. In recent years, the Kothi modern dance group has performed, as has Kim Robards's modern dance company from Denver, the Joffrey Ballet from New York, and Spectrum, a jazz company from Seattle.

The theater performs the *Nutcracker* ballet biennially, bringing in a professional performer to complement local talent, and also offers weeklong summer dance workshops for both children and adults.

Ticket prices vary for each performance but range between $7.00 and $20.00.

FILM AND CINEMA

Choose from classic and foreign films or contemporary blockbusters that may one day become cinema classics.

Northern Hills

The Black Hills State University Film Series
1200 University Street, Spearfish
(605) 642–6249, (605) 642–6062
Visitors tired of special effects and simplistic plots will appreciate this program, which presents an eclectic mix of films for the benefit of the university community and the general public. These independent and foreign pictures, selected by the Black Hills State University Honors Program, are shown once a month in the fall and spring. Films shown in the past have included *The Pianist, Confessions of a Dangerous Mind,* and *Real Women Have Curves.* Showings are free and popular among members of the community, though the somewhat cramped room in Jonas Academic Hall is filled mostly with college students. Call the numbers above for upcoming shows.

The Foreign Film Festival
Northern Hills Cinema
1830 North Main Street, Spearfish
(605) 642–7973
The Spearfish Center for the Arts and Humanities sponsors this tribute to films from other nations. Four are shown on alternate weekends in September and October, and each is run twice, on Sunday afternoon and Monday evening. Season passes are available for $20.00, or tickets are $4.25 each. Those planning the event choose a variety of film subjects but often include one in English and three in other languages, with English subtitles.

Northern Hills Cinema 4
1830 North Main Street, Spearfish
(605) 642-4212
The six theaters in this cinema show first-run movies, and tickets are $7.75 for adults and $5.25 for children ages 3 to 11 and seniors age 65 or older. Matinee tickets are $5.00. The Northern Hills Cinema hosts a foreign film festival sponsored by the Spearfish Center for the Arts and Humanities.

Central Hills

Elks Theatre
512 Sixth Street, Rapid City
(605) 341-4149, (605) 343-7888
(reserved seating)
www.elkstheatre.com
If you missed that blockbuster the first time it came to town, you're likely to get a second chance at the Elks. You might wait a few weeks, but think of the savings: Seats are just $3.00. When you consider that this historic theater boasts the biggest screen in South Dakota—a whopping 48 feet wide by 22 feet tall—it's even more of a bargain. And an eight-channel digital sound system means you won't miss any all-important movie dialogue no matter which of the 605 comfortable seats you choose, even if it's in the balcony.

The more intimate Screening Room features a 10-by-20-foot screen and seating for 100. The Screening Room is on the third floor, above the balcony, in what was once the Elks Club's elegant ballroom.

The theater building dates back to the early 1900s, when the Elks hosted live vaudeville shows and, later, motion pictures. In fact, this is one of the oldest movie theaters in the nation. So think of it as carrying on tradition when you catch any of the daily or nightly shows. You'll find some services here that are reminiscent of the days when businesses catered to the public as a matter of course. Thurs-day is BYOB night—bring your own bag and get three free scoops of popcorn. And you can request reserved seating for any show by calling up to a week in advance.

The Elks also shows classic movies and local independent films from time to time; there's even an after-school movie program for kids. Call for more information.

Friends of the Devereaux Library
Film Series
Elks Theatre
512 Sixth Street, Rapid City
(605) 394-1262
The Friends of the Devereaux Library, at South Dakota School of Mines and Technology, sponsor this annual film series, a fund-raiser for the library.

Ten classic films are presented, one each Sunday evening from mid-January through mid-March. Previous showings have included *Rear Window, Meet Me in St. Louis,* and *North by Northwest.* The cozy, historic theater has a great old-fashioned balcony and a huge screen. You can purchase season tickets for about $30.

Rushmore 7
350 East Disk Drive, Rapid City
(605) 341-7021, (605) 341-6960
The seven theaters in this modern cinema boast chairs that rival those in your living room. Comfortably seated, you can see first-run movies, with matinees (before 6:00 P.M.) costing $5.50 for both children and adults. After 6:00 P.M., tickets for children younger than 12 and seniors 55 and older are $4.50; others pay $7.75.

Southern Hills

Hot Springs Theatre
241 North River Street, Hot Springs
(605) 745-4169
This circa-1912 theater features first-run movies now instead of the vaudeville acts of old. Showtime is at 7:00 P.M. Friday,

Saturday, and Sunday as well as 2:00 P.M. Sunday; the theater is closed on other days. Ticket prices are $6.00 for adults, $4.00 for children ages 2 through 11 and seniors 60 and older.

GALLERIES AND EXHIBIT SPACES

We've included galleries that carry original art (for display, for sale, or both), although many also offer prints, custom framing, art supplies, and gifts. All are great places to see what's being created in artists' studios around South Dakota or to purchase a work of art. Some galleries close for the winter or shorten their operating hours, so call ahead.

Northern Hills

The Photographer's Gallery
Black Hills State University
1200 University Street, Spearfish
(605) 642-6769; (605) 642-6062
Interest in photography is growing in the Black Hills, and BHSU has responded by dedicating a small display area to photographers. Exhibits are shown in the newly remodeled basement of Jonas Academic Hall in a long hallway next to the darkroom and studio, and you can check out the display anytime the building is open. Students often show their new work toward the end of each semester, and established local photographers, such as Ray Tysdal, are invited to fill the hall at other times. Known in the area for his abstract black-and-white pictures of Black Hills animals (especially buffalo), Tysdal displays his traditional work alongside sepiatone prints of African wildlife. Other local artists to grace the gallery's first year of exhibits included multimedia artist Bob Miller, who displayed interesting Polaroid prints, and photojournalist and nature photographer Dick Kettlewell.

Ruddell Gallery of Art
Black Hills State University
1200 University Street, Spearfish
(605) 642-6852, (605) 642-6104
A small gallery tucked away on the second level of the student union, the Ruddell is a pleasant space with some fine exhibitions.

A wide variety of work circulates through this gallery, including artistry by young and old alike. Students have two shows each year, one for photography and one for other visual arts, and alumni also have an annual display. In addition, the Ruddell makes room for four or five other artists each year, with work in many media. In recent years the gallery has hosted the South Dakota Health Care Association's Dakota Master Works exhibit, a touring show of work by artists age 60 and up. Toward the beginning of the schools' second semester, the Ruddell puts on an educational program show that deals with social issues through art. The displays often coincide with speakers. Past shows have included topics such as threats to democracy (which displayed war art from 1960 to 1975) and abused women and children. Displays usually last about a month, and the gallery is open year-round during regular campus hours.

Termesphere Gallery
Christensen Drive, Spearfish
(605) 642-4805
www.termesphere.com
Dick Termes has become internationally known for his six-point perspective spherical paintings, known as Termespheres. When you step across the threshold of his geodesic-dome gallery, you enter a magical room filled with so many colorful spheres and mobiles twirling from the ceiling that you'll be browsing in awe for an hour. If you're lucky, Termes himself may explain his complicated techniques for making these unique works of art.

One-of-a-kind originals, reproductions, and limited editions are on display and for sale.

In addition to spheres, you'll see cubes, tetrahedrons, polyhedrons, icosahedrons, and dodecahedrons. Each gives you the sense of standing in the center of the environment that is the subject of each piece, yet—at the same time—you are viewing it from the outside.

Call ahead for directions. The gallery is on Christensen Drive, in the countryside south of Spearfish.

Central Hills

Apex Gallery
South Dakota School of Mines and Technology
501 East St. Joseph Street, Rapid City
(605) 394-1254, (605) 394-2481

The fact that "Tech" encourages art studies (there's not yet a formal art program) impresses us; that outside-the-lines thinking shows in the quality of exhibitions at this gallery. There's more about Tech in the Education chapter.

As part of the School of Mines, the Apex welcomes exhibits not only by contemporary artists but also by scientists, many of whom are nationally and internationally recognized. The gallery often aims for educational enrichment in its exhibits and has included work that relies on interactivity. For example, installation artist Sandy Skoglund worked with art history students in 2001 to create a surreal environment. Exhibits are usually shown for six to eight weeks and often are launched with an opening reception.

Even though you'll have to park in the main lot and walk a bit to reach the gallery in the Classroom Building, it's well worth a visit.

Black Hills Glass Blowers
901 Old Hill City Road, Keystone
(605) 666-4542

This is the working studio of glass artists Gail Damin and Pete Hopkins. You can watch them create their glass art but, they stress, only when they're working, which is not all the time. It's best to call ahead if you want to see a glass artist in action, or in the winter months to make sure the studio is open. Gail and Pete do both lamp (or flame) working and offhand (or traditional) glassblowing. They make figurines, such as unicorns and dragons, and colorful art glass, including vases and bowls.

You'll find South Dakota Public Radio at 89.3 FM in Rapid City; 88.1 FM in Belle Fourche and Hot Springs; 99.1 FM in Spearfish; and 91.9 FM in Lead.

Dahl Fine Arts Center
713 Seventh Street, Rapid City
(605) 394-4101
ww.thedahl.org

Plan to spend some time at the Dahl. The Ruth Brennan Gallery has six to eight exhibitions every year, each with an opening reception. Themes vary widely, from Mexican folk art and impressionistic oils to photography and Black Hills landscapes. The gallery focuses on education—and this includes regional, national, and international work, and traveling exhibits.

The center has a 170-seat theater and offices and serves as the hub for several arts organizations in Rapid City. It's open 10:00 A.M. to 5:00 P.M. Tuesday through Saturday and 1:00 to 5:00 P.M. Sunday.

Adjoining the Ruth Brennan Gallery is the Central Gallery, which focuses on community work and involvement. Artwork, often from local schools or organizations, is displayed in three- to six-week-long shows. Art classes are offered for both children and adults, and the subject matter varies. Local artists regularly give talks and presentations.

The *Cyclorama* mural by Bernard Thomas is in a room adjacent to the Central Gallery. It is a representation of 200 years of American history from an economic perspective (it was commissioned by the Dahl's founder, a banker). Ask a staff member to turn on the taped narrative and lighting system to accompany your look at the mural.

The Northern Plains Watercolor Society sponsors a juried exhibition of watercolors each fall. The show includes the work of its members and is open to watercolorists from other states. The exhibition is usually held in November at Prairie Edge Art Gallery, Sixth and Main Streets, Rapid City. For information go to www.prairieedge.com.

Dakota Art Gallery
632½ St. Joseph Street, Rapid City
(605) 394–4108

This lively gallery in downtown Rapid City is operated by the Dakota Artists Guild. Each month the gallery features either a solo or group display by regional artists. Work on continuing display includes jewelry, paintings, pottery, and glasswork. The guild offers classes for adults and children in drawing, painting, pottery, and other art forms, plus some odd-but-fun classes for the kids, such as 3-D and sidewalk art, paper-bag puppets, and papier-mâché. And for even more of a learning experience, the guild offers workshops with visiting artists. Another unique program put on by the gallery is the occasional lunch and art series, where an artist is invited to speak or give a demonstration while participants kick back with a packed lunch or food available at the gallery. Call for information on upcoming events.

Jon Crane Watercolors
336 Main Street, Hill City
(605) 574–4440
www.joncranewatercolors.com

"Art That Takes You Home," this gallery's motto, perfectly describes the work of nationally known watercolorist Jon Crane. His subjects are often the rural landscapes of isolated farms and aging homesteads, lovely forests and trout streams, and heartwarming scenes that remind the viewer of home. Even the titles are nostalgic: *Home for Hot Chocolate, A Great Day to Be a Kid, Heartland Legacy,* and *Almost*

Christmas are among the many works you'll see here.

The pleasantly decorated gallery carries original work, framed and unframed open-edition miniature prints, and limited-edition prints and note cards. Custom framing is offered.

The Perfect Hanging Gallery
520 Kansas City Street, Rapid City
(605) 348–7761

The Perfect Hanging is a display space for prints by South Dakotan and internationally known artists. The gallery has Jon Crane watercolors and paintings by Terry Redlin and Gene Stocks. It also carries artist giftware, including music boxes, pins, sculptures, and mugs. If the Perfect Hanging doesn't have what you want in stock, the staff can order any print available and dress it up with custom matting and framing. They specialize in conservation and museum-quality mounting and framing.

Prairie Edge Trading Company & Galleries
606 Main Street, Rapid City
(605) 342–3086
www.prairieedge.com

Prairie Edge is a local landmark. It's a great place to shop (more about that in the Shopping chapter), and the restored building's stunning architecture alone is worth a visit. The second-floor fine art gallery is a gem in the Prairie Edge crown. Here, basking in the light from the huge old windows, you may see the amazing photographs of Robert Wong of Rapid City and the contemporary Native American work of Don Montileaux, or the work of local artists Paul Goble, Loy Allen, Jim Whartman, and James Van Nuys. Changing exhibits feature the art of many artists, but the astounding cast-paper art of Allen and Patty Eckman is on permanent exhibit, so be sure to have a look.

Rimrock Art & Frame Company
1108 Jackson Boulevard, Rapid City
(605) 342–7263, (888) 849–8485

The oldest frame shop in Rapid City, Rimrock Art & Frame is also an artists' gallery that displays original work and prints of regional artists, including the oils of Jan Wiedmeier, the original lithographs of Russell Chatham, and the fantasy art of John Backlund. Jon Crane's prints (both current and secondary-market editions) are here, as is the work of Kay Williams and Ron Holyfield, longtime summer artists-in-residence at Custer State Park.

The owners, Mike and Debbie McLane, are fine artists themselves: Mike, a certified professional framer, produces great watercolors, and Debbie is a talented photographer.

Sioux Indian Museum Gallery
The Journey Museum
222 New York Street, Rapid City
(605) 394-2381
www.journeymuseum.org

This small gallery is devoted to Native American art. It is inside the Journey Museum, near the gift shop, and your Journey ticket will admit you at no additional charge. The gallery has shown delightful and colorful contemporary Sioux quilts from the Journey's permanent collection; the paintings and three-dimensional art of Jim Yellowhawk of Rapid City; the beading, pottery, and batik of Linda Szabo of Mission; the acrylics and oils of Del Iron Cloud, also of Rapid City; and the sculptures of Tom Red Bear of Hot Springs.

Stanford Adelstein Gallery
The Journey Museum
222 New York Street, Rapid City
(605) 394-6923
www.journeymuseum.org

We've written about the Journey Museum in the Attractions chapter, but the adjacent Changing Exhibition Gallery is separate from the museum and has its own exhibitions. In fact, visitors can tour the gallery without paying the museum's fee. Each exhibit is launched with a reception, often held in the evening.

Exhibitions are accompanied by educational programs for children and gallery talks by experts. One of the more popular programs is the Storyteller's Series every Sunday from 2:00 to 3:00 P.M. (cost is $3.00). This event complements the display in the gallery at that time and may be geared toward children and adults. For one session, the mayor of Rapid City read stories to children while they sat with treats and drinks. The shows usually change monthly and range widely in topic. For example, they once held a World War II exhibit in which Black Hills residents contributed personal artifacts, such as a Japanese parachute and a German flag. A theme show during August is held in conjunction with the Sturgis Rally & Races.

Warriors Work Studio and
Ben West Gallery
310 Main Street, Hill City
(605) 574-4954
www.leatherframegallery.com

The smell of leather greets you as you open the door to this gallery. Artist Randy Berger creates deerskin-wrapped frames, each individually designed, hand cut, and handcrafted according to his IDT ("I Don't Tell") method. Each is an original work of art, although some are limited editions of two to seven.

The studio carries the work of several artists, including Jim Yellowhawk, Ryan Burr, Frank Howell, Peggy Detmer, Kirby Sattler, Ben Wright, Joe Geshick, and Mike Larsen. You'll find pencil and pen-and-ink drawings, original lithographs, serigraphs, giclée prints, and much more. A recent addition to the Warriors Work Studio is the Ben West Gallery, which shows contemporary work. The displays, always different and unique, have included wood turnings and tables by Craig Richardson, watercolors by Sarah Rogers; black-and-white animal and landscape photography by Ray Tysdal, and stone sculptures by Cheston Turnbul.

As for Berger's frames themselves, they sometimes have a symbolic message or tell a story related to the picture inside. He knows most of the artists and creates his frames as an extension of the spirit of their work. Some frames are inlaid with colorful beads or other decorative or symbolic items. Each takes from two days to more than a week to complete. One of Berger's favorite tools for detailed leatherwork is his pocket knife's bottle opener, a humble apparatus that helps create his exquisitely beautiful art.

Southern Hills

Cabin Fever
444 Mount Rushmore Road, Custer
(605) 673-2525

This downtown Custer gallery is a pleasant space that displays art all the way up to the high ceiling. You'll see Brenda Bruckner's pencil drawings of horses and the ranching life, silver handcrafted jewelry, photographs and pottery, as well as gifts and prints. Take note of the antler carvings by Custer resident Tony Ramer, a nationally known artist whose work graces the White House. Also represented are works by Tim Cox and Merle Locke, both local artists. Cabin Fever carries tack, blouses, and leather and suede jackets, among other offerings.

LITERARY ARTS

If you're a fan of reading, you'll be happy to know that a fair number of book signings, readings, and discussions take place here. In Rapid City, signings often are held at Prairie Edge Trading Company and Galleries, Borders, and Prince & Pauper Village (discussed in the Shopping chapter). In smaller towns, you might find events at bookstores (most of which have sections dedicated to local authors), art galleries, libraries (see the Relocation

chapter), or community centers. Check the local newspapers for announcements; book signings are great opportunities to meet local authors.

Black Hills Writers Group
(605) 341-3224

Founded in 1956 by local author Laura Bower Van Nuys, this group meets at the Rapid City Public Library, 610 Quincy Street, on the fourth Tuesday of each month (except December). Members plan events, read their work, critique, and conduct impromptu writing assignments. The group sponsors the Black Hills Writers Conference in the fall of odd-numbered years, and the Laura Bower Van Nuys Writing Contest in even-numbered years.

The contest, which receives entries from writers all over the United States and from other countries, is named for the author of *The Family Band,* a history of Van Nuys's family that was made into the Disney movie *The One and Only Genuine, Original Family Band.* The contest accepts fiction and nonfiction entries, has an April 15 deadline, and is judged by professional writers. Call (605) 341-3224 to request guidelines.

MUSIC

Concerts, both indoors and out, are offered year-round and enrich life in the Black Hills.

Northern Hills

Black Hills Area Music Teachers
(605) 642-6241; (605) 722-8033

The Music Teachers' Association is a professional group that works to make music education prevalent in the Hills. This private organization consists of teachers from the entire Black Hills area. Concerts are free and presented year-round. The association sponsors several student recitals and competitions throughout the Hills, and teachers join students for an

The Rapid City Journal *publishes an Arts Calendar each Sunday in its Life & Style section. It's a one-stop source to learn about upcoming events you won't want to miss.*

Ambrose Bierce

Ambrose Bierce was never happy. And after trying his hand at gold mining in the Black Hills, he was more miserable than ever.

Born in 1842 into a large, pious family, Bierce was a gloomy, withdrawn child. As a young man he distinguished himself during the Civil War but questioned the Union cause for which he fought. Later he became a renowned journalist but was contemptuous of the press. Even his wife, Mollie, and their three children didn't please him.

Settling in San Francisco after the war, "Bitter Bierce" became famous for his scathing "Town Crier" and "Prattle" newspaper columns. But at age 38, perhaps suffering from a midlife crisis (or trying to run away from himself), and hoping to quit journalism for good, Bierce resigned from his job and left home to become general agent for the Black Hills Placer Mining Company in Rockerville, in Dakota Territory. One of his assignments was to complete a 17-mile wooden flume to carry water from Spring Creek to Rockerville. That was in 1880, and today you can hike along the Flume Trail and see remnants of his work (see the Recreation chapter for more information). To protect the company's assets, Bierce hired a famous gunslinger named Boone May and listed him on the payroll as "Boone May, Murderer."

The mine proved unsuccessful, though, and Bierce returned to San Francisco within a few months, broke, depressed, and jobless. He soon was offered editorship of the *Wasp,* a satirical journal, and revived his "Prattle" column. Readers noticed he was more bitter than ever, hurling savage verbal attacks at seemingly every person and institution in sight. He later became chief editorial columnist for the *San Francisco Examiner* under William Randolph Hearst, and then Washington correspondent for Hearst newspapers. He wrote for *Cosmopolitan* and put together a collection of his works.

Bierce never "mined" his experiences in the Black Hills for his writing, and biographers speculate that he simply couldn't bear to admit failure, even though it wasn't his fault. His most enduring work is a short story, *An Occurrence at Owl Creek Bridge,* that influenced many later writers, including Stephen Crane and Ernest Hemingway.

In 1913, when he was 71 years old, Ambrose Bierce disappeared. Many people think he went to Mexico and died in Pancho Villa's revolution. But some think he took his own life in Grand Canyon. In any case, he got his last, bitter wish—that no one would ever find his bones.

annual performance in May at the Rush-more Mall in Rapid City. Performances are often held at Black Hills State University in Spearfish at the new Meier Recital Hall.

Central Hills

Backroom Productions
(605) 341–5940, (605) 348–6295
www.backroomevents.com

These guys have something going on every month, and then some. The main event is Music in the Park, a series of 8 to 10 free concerts at Memorial Park in Rapid City during the summer. Concerts may include jazz, country, rock, big band, bluegrass, or Native American music and dance. Additionally, Backroom annually hosts the Guitar Masters, an all-acoustic concert in March at the Journey Museum in Rapid City, and the Black Hills Sun Writers Workshop in June at Nemo Guest Ranch. The workshop invites participants to spend a weekend learning music, usually for guitar and keyboards, and holds concerts at the end. Sign up for the workshop or find out more information about each event online.

Black Hills Chamber Music Society
(605) 718–5666, (605) 342–8480

The society's series runs from October to May, and most performances are held at the First Congregational Church, 1200 Clark Street, Rapid City. The Dakota String Quartet has performed, as well as the

The Black Hills Symphony League supports the symphony orchestra, the Black Hills Chamber Music Society, the Music in the Schools program, and the Young Artists' competition. It also awards music lesson scholarships to children. This organization sponsors a Homes for the Holidays fund-raiser each year in early November; tickets can be purchased at the Dahl Fine Arts Center, (605) 394–4101.

Black Hills Chamber Orchestra, Nebraska Brass, the Rawlins Piano Trio, and the Dakota Woodwind Quintet. The Chamber Music Society has outreach programs for children and seniors, including performances in schools, local nursing homes, and rehabilitation centers.

Ticket prices range from $30 to $35 for season tickets and $10 to $15 for individual performances.

Black Hills Symphony Orchestra
(605) 348–HORN (season tickets)
(605) 394–4111 (individual performances)

Rapid City may be a small city, but it has a symphony with big-city quality. The orchestra was founded in 1932, and current conductor Jack Knowles has been with the group since 1972. Six concerts are scheduled each season, and all take place at the Rushmore Plaza Civic Center.

Ticket prices for adults range from $11 to $22 for individual performances; season tickets are available.

Cathedral Concerts
520 Cathedral Drive, Rapid City
(605) 342–0507
www.cathedralolph.org

The Cathedral of Our Lady of Perpetual Help boasts the largest pipe organ in a five-state region, a 62-rank Casavant. The Fifth and Broadway Dessert Theater, featuring Broadway tunes, is presented each June in the cathedral. And each December the South Dakota School of Mines and Technology choir presents two free concerts.

Dakota Choral Union
(605) 394–4111 (tickets)

The Dakota Choral Union is composed of more than 100 vocalists from the South Dakota School of Mines and Technology and the Black Hills community. It includes several choral ensembles and is the official chorus provider to the Black Hills Symphony Orchestra. Performances are held at varying locations around the Black Hills, including the Rushmore Plaza Civic Center.

Ticket prices for adults are $12 for

individual concerts and $35 for season tickets. Four to five concerts are presented each season.

Rapid City Children's Chorus
(605) 341-5304, (605) 394-2564

Children in grades three through eight audition to join the Children's Chorus, which has been performing since 1986. Most concerts feature classical choral music, but some include ethnic, jazz, and gospel. The chorus presents concerts the first Sunday of each May and December at Dakota Middle School, 615 Columbus Street, and travels around the country to perform as well. Tickets are $5.00 for adults and $12.00 for families.

Rapid City Concert Association Series
(605) 721-3914

The volunteer Rapid City Concert Association plans and schedules five concerts each year, presenting national touring artists who perform at the Rushmore Plaza Civic Center. Past performances have featured pianist Valentina Lisitsa, Czech Boys Choir Boni Pueri, and the brass group Side Street Strutters. The series runs from September through May. Ticket prices are $25 for students, $50 for adults, and $110 for families.

Southern Hills

Hot Springs Area Concert Association
801 South Sixth Street, Hot Springs
(605) 745-3886, (605) 745-4140

Four concerts are presented each season, and admission is by membership only (that is, only season tickets are sold). Ticket prices are $10 for students, $25 for adults, and $60 for families. Tickets include reciprocity to concerts in Newcastle, Wyoming, Belle Fourche, and Rapid City.

Concerts are family oriented music that can be instrumental or vocal. One of the association's goals is to pull in entertainment that appeals to all age groups in the area.

PUBLIC ART

You may want to make some side trips to see our noteworthy public art. In addition, two fine works of art grace the lobby of the Radisson Hotel at 445 Mount Rushmore Road, Rapid City. Both are mosaics; one a landscape of the Black Hills and the other a depiction of Mount Rushmore. These are not public art (they're owned by the hotel), but they are worth a visit.

Northern Hills

Bust of Wild Bill Hickok, Korczak Ziolkowski, Custer. Granite sculpture. Sherman Street Park, Deadwood.

Generation, Jim Maher, Belle Fourche. Bronze sculpture. D.C. Booth Historic Fish Hatchery, 423 Hatchery Circle, Spearfish.

Gold, Tony Chytka, Spearfish. Entrance to Days of '76 rodeo grounds, Crescent Drive, Deadwood.

Kinship, Dale Lamphere, Sturgis. Bronze sculpture. Community Sculpture Garden, 1401 Lazelle Street, Sturgis.

Lasting Legacy, Tony Chytka, Spearfish. Bronze sculpture. Centennial Park, U.S. Highway 85 and National Street, Belle Fourche.

Peace Memorial, Dale Lamphere, Sturgis. Bronze and granite sculpture. Visitor center, 415 Fifth Avenue, Belle Fourche.

Tickets—both season and individual performance—to many events can be purchased through the Rushmore Plaza Civic Center's box office. The toll-free number is (800) GOT-MINE, and the local number is (605) 394-4111.

Visitors will discover a bronze bust of Wild Bill Hickok on his grave at Mount Moriah Cemetery. SOUTH DAKOTA TOURISM

Spherefish, Dick Termes, Spearfish. Termesphere. Spearfish City Hall, 625 Fifth Street, Spearfish.

Wild Bill Hickok, James Borglum and Monique Ziolkowski, Custer. Bronze sculpture. Four Aces Casino, 531 Main Street, Deadwood.

Central Hills

Bluestem Woman, Dale Lamphere, Sturgis. Metal and found objects sculpture. Rapid City Public Library, 610 Quincy Street, Rapid City.

Cyclorama, Bernard Preston Thomas, Florida. Oil on canvas. Dahl Fine Arts Center, 713 Seventh Street, Rapid City.

Endless Horizon, Dick Termes, Spearfish. Termesphere. Rushmore Plaza Civic Center, 444 Mount Rushmore Road, Rapid City.

He Is, They Are, Glenna Goodacre, New Mexico. Bronze sculpture. Prairie Edge Trading Company and Galleries, 606 Main Street, Rapid City.

Iron Eagle, Vic Runnels, Aberdeen. Metal and wood sculpture. Central High School, 433 Mount Rushmore Road, Rapid City.

Legacy, Dale Lamphere, Sturgis. Bronze and concrete sculpture. Memorial Park, Omaha and Sixth Streets, Rapid City.

Mitakuye Oyasin (All My Relatives), Richard UnderBaggage, Rapid City, and Dale Lamphere, Sturgis. Bronze sculpture. Southwest corner of Sixth and Main Streets, Rapid City.

Monolith, Fiorenzo Berardozzi, Rapid City. Western Dakota Technical Institute, 800 Mickelson Drive, Rapid City.

Pinocchio, John Eng, Hill City. Wood sculpture. Rapid City Public Library, 610 Quincy Street, Rapid City.

Rapid Trout, Martin Wanserski, Vermillion. Concrete sculpture. Founders Park, Omaha Street near 12th Street, Rapid City.

St. Thomas More Mural, Fr. Peter Wilke and Julia Poage, Rapid City. Porcelain tile mural. St. Thomas More High School, 300 Fairmont Boulevard, Rapid City.

Spirit of Healing, Dale Lamphere, Sturgis. Bronze sculpture. Rapid City Regional Hospital, 353 Fairmont Boulevard, Rapid City.

The Ingalls Family, Harvey Hultquist, Minneapolis. Wood carving. Rapid City Public Library, 610 Quincy Street, Rapid City.

Toth, Andrew Leicester, Minneapolis. Timber, concrete, and steel sculpture on a hill above South Dakota School of Mines and Technology, 501 East St. Joseph Street, Rapid City.

Untitled, student artists under the direction of artist Vic Runnels. Painted mural. At the railroad overpass, East Boulevard near New York Street, Rapid City.

Vigilance, Peggy Detmer, Rapid City. Bronze sculpture. Memorial Park, Rapid City.

Learn what's going on in the world of South Dakota fine arts by listening to the Arts Advocate on South Dakota Public Radio. The Weekly Arts Calendar is broadcast Monday at 5:25 P.M. (mountain time). Hear the Daily Arts Calendar Tuesday through Friday at 6:50 A.M. and 7:50 A.M. Arts Advocate Report is broadcast Tuesday through Friday at 7:30 A.M. and 5:25 P.M.

THEATER
Northern Hills

The Black Hills Passion Play
Interstate 90, exit 12, Spearfish
(605) 642-2646
(800) 457-0160 (reservations)
Read about the Passion Play in the Attractions chapter. It is performed during June, July, and August in a 6,000-seat outdoor amphitheater. Ticket prices range from $16 to $20.

The Charley Utter Theatre
657 Main Street, Deadwood
(605) 578-3346, (800) 952-9398
www.saloon10.com
This small stage is part of the Deadwood Social Club, the restaurant above the Old Style Saloon No. 10 right in the middle of downtown Deadwood. (Read more about the Social Club in the Restaurants chapter and the Saloon No. 10 in the Nightlife chapter.) The theater, named for one of Wild Bill Hickok's best friends, stages old-fashioned melodramas or historical reenactments of Deadwood's famous history, such as Wild Bill's death (they also reenact this event downstairs in the saloon daily during the summer), or Calamity Jane's Wild West show. Every December the theater hosts a comedic *Christmas Follies* performance, plus it occasionally offers musicals and dinner shows. The Charlie Utter folks step out of historical bounds for holidays and special events, however; for one of the town's annual Deadweird cele-

brations, they showed the *Rocky Horror Picture Show* and encouraged participants to dress in character. Call for showtimes.

Historic Matthews Opera House
614 Main Street, Spearfish
(605) 642-7973
www.moh-scah.com
A working performing arts center, the renovated opera house (where operas are not performed) was built in that wonderful turn-of-the-20th-century western style that walks the line between ornate and practical. Year-round community theater productions, events, and exhibits are held here; it is also the home of the Spearfish Center for the Arts and Humanities.

Community theater performances run during March, May, August, October, and December for three weekends each month. Past plays have included *M.A.S.H.,* the musical *Annie,* and *Cowgirls.* Ticket prices are $12.50 for adults and $6.50 for children. You can sometimes purchase tickets at the door, but it's best to call ahead and reserve them.

Year-round Monday through Friday, you can tour the opera house. When plays are scheduled, you can visit until the plays begin at 7:30 P.M. Call ahead to ask about visiting during the remainder of the year. Staff members are available to answer questions during your visit, and there is no admission charge.

Central Hills

Black Hills Community Theatre
713 Seventh Street, Rapid City
(605) 394-1787, (605) 394-1786 (box office)
www.bhct.org
This community theater was established in 1968. Its five-performance series runs from September to May; each play runs three weeks, with both a Sunday matinee and evening presentations. Professionally staged performances are presented by dedicated local actors, and most take

place in the Dahl Fine Arts Center's theater, but larger productions and musicals may be held at the Rushmore Plaza Civic Center. Past performances included *Guys and Dolls, Great Expectations, Little Shop of Horrors, Dial M for Murder,* and a January dinner theater fund-raiser.

Season ticket prices range from $40 to $65. Tickets for single performances go on sale at the Dahl's box office a few days before each performance begins.

Black Hills Community Theatre presents plays for both children and adults and offers theater workshops and classes. A children's troupe gives at least two performances each year.

Southern Hills

Black Hills Playhouse
Custer State Park, Custer
(605) 394-7797, (605) 255-4141, seasonal (tickets)
www.blackhillsplayhouse.com
The playhouse is inside Custer State Park, which provides a beautiful setting for this professional theater. Summer season begins in June and continues through August. Each play runs two to three weeks and has matinee and evening performances. Past performances have included *I Hate Hamlet, Brigadoon, Crimes of the Heart, Steel Magnolias,* and *Cat on a Hot Tin Roof.*

Ticket prices range from $13 to $20. Discounts are available for groups of 20 or more. Reservations should be made at least 48 hours in advances.

You must purchase a park entrance license, since you'll be accessing the park to reach the playhouse (for license fees, see the Custer State Park listing in the Parks and Mountains chapter). Take advantage of the opportunity: Come early, and visit the park before having dinner and enjoying the play.

VENUES

You'll find several venues mentioned in this chapter: the Dahl Fine Arts Center's intimate theater, the Historic Matthews Opera House's restored stage, the band shell at Rapid City's Memorial Park, and various churches, schools, and community centers where the acoustics and size lend themselves to performances. But the largest and most versatile venue in the Black Hills is the Rushmore Plaza Civic Center, listed below.

Central Hills

Rushmore Plaza Civic Center
444 Mount Rushmore Road, Rapid City
(605) 394-4115, (800) GOT-MINE (tickets)
www.gotmine.com
The civic center is the major venue in the Black Hills. It has hosted ice shows, the Black Hills Stock Show and Rodeo on the last weekend in January, monster truck rallies, ballet and Broadway performances, theater troupes, concerts, powwows, art and antiques shows, and conventions. Its grand-opening concert in 1976 was one of Elvis's final performances.

The center boasts 150,000 square feet of exhibit space, a 10,000-seat arena, the 1,779-seat Fine Arts Theater, two large halls (La Croix and Rushmore), 27 meeting rooms, and 3,000 free parking spaces. It's set on nine acres adjacent to Rapid City's Memorial Park and is fewer than 100 steps away from the Rushmore Plaza Holiday Inn.

Among the many events here is the Broadway Play series, which recently included touring productions of *Cats, My Cousin's Wedding, The Music Man,* and *Saturday Night Fever.* Ticket prices for performances range from $25 to $60; season tickets are available.

PARKS AND MOUNTAINS

When it comes to finding places to play outdoors, the Black Hills can't be beat—and the numbers prove it. The region claims the highest concentration of national parks, memorials, and monuments in the country: Mount Rushmore National Memorial, Jewel Cave National Monument, Wind Cave National Park, Devils Tower National Monument (just a few miles across the Wyoming border), Badlands National Park, and opening sometime in 2005, the Minuteman Missile National Historic Site. Add to that four state parks and recreation areas (Bear Butte State Park, Custer State Park, Angostura Recreation Area, and the Mickelson Trail), and you'll start to see the essence of the region. Don't forget that the 1.2-million-acre Black Hills National Forest sprawls over the whole area, with Buffalo Gap National Grasslands almost touching its southern and eastern borders and the Thunder Basin National Grasslands only a few miles to the west in Wyoming.

Most of these places are also listed in the Attractions or Recreation chapters, but four of the most striking mountain parks in the Black Hills are detailed below.

If you'd like to support educational programs and research in Black Hills forests and parks, join the Black Hills Parks and Forests Association, which publishes books and educational materials and funds research and intern programs. Membership includes a semiannual newsletter and a discount on books, maps, and posters at their sales outlets (Custer State Park, Wind Cave, and Jewel Cave) and most national park bookstores. Call (605) 745-7020.

Even though many of these areas are located near each other (for instance, Wind Cave and Custer share borders), each has its own distinctive features. Indeed, some places in these parks will seem like worlds unto themselves.

NORTHERN HILLS

Bear Butte State Park
Off Highway 79, north of Sturgis
(605) 347-5240
www.state.sd.us/gfp

As you drive into the area around Sturgis, you'll see Bear Butte rising blue-gray in the distance. Isolated from the rest of the Black Hills by a mile or more, the mountain looks out of place, rising up from an otherwise unbroken stretch of prairie. That makes its distinctive silhouette (that of a bear sleeping on the plains) easy to spot from a distance. In fact, the peak has been guiding people to the Black Hills for millennia.

This is Mato Paha, Lakota for "bear mountain." The Cheyenne call it Noavosse ("good mountain"). For centuries it has been a place of worship, a powerful site from which to contact the holy, and a Native American landmark. Cheyenne legend tells that the prophet Sweet Medicine received four sacred arrows here and four commandments for his people to live by.

It appears that Bear Butte has always been sacred. Artifacts 10,000 years old and an ancient ceremonial site have been unearthed here. Today Native Americans still climb the mountain to pray and fast, leaving medicine bundles, tobacco offerings, and ribbons as physical manifestations of their prayers. Please respect this holy site and don't disturb the privacy of worshipers or the offerings, including

Peter Norbeck

The name of Peter Norbeck is one you encounter often as you travel around the Black Hills and Badlands. That's because Norbeck—art lover, conservationist, South Dakota governor, and U.S. senator—did so much for the area. Therefore it seems only fitting that an overlook, a wildlife preserve, a visitor center, and a scenic byway, all in or close to Custer State Park, as well as a pass through Badlands National Park, are among the places named in his honor.

Norbeck loved the outdoors and played a major role in the establishment of both parks. His efforts to set aside a game preserve and map out a scenic route through rugged, virgin Black Hills terrain also bore fruit. And he answered the call when South Dakota's state historian, Doane Robinson, sought his help in promoting and funding the carving of Mount Rushmore National Memorial.

His influence extended well beyond the borders of his home state, however, when he left his mark on the creation of Wyoming's Grand Teton National Park and passage of the federal Migratory Bird Conservation Act.

Born to Norwegian immigrant parents on a Clay County homestead in southeastern South Dakota on August 27, 1870, Norbeck learned early the value of hard work. Unwilling to become a farmer himself, however, he accumulated a modest fortune with a well-drilling business and Wyoming oil interests. His prominence in the private domain helped propel him to positions of leadership in public life.

Nicknamed "the benevolent buffalo," the 225-pound Norbeck inspired confidence and loyalty in his supporters with his honesty and can-do enthusiasm. Yet he had a stormy relationship with Mount Rushmore sculptor Gutzon Borglum, whom Norbeck deemed a poor businessman.

The two were still at odds when Norbeck, suffering from cancer, died at his home in Redfield on December 20, 1936. Fifteen years later, a decade after Borglum's own passing, they made a sort of posthumous peace when the sculptor's bronze bust of his most ardent backer, Norbeck, was placed in the state capitol building in Pierre.

rocks placed in the forks of branches, which are the traditional markers of someone's visit.

The mountain will offer you incredible views, both out over the plains and toward the Black Hills. Take all the scenic photographs you like, but do not photograph the ceremonial items, offerings, or worshipers. The signs at the trailhead ask that you walk quietly and reverently and speak in low tones. Use the same respect you would feel when touring a cathedral where the worship service is in progress, for that is what Bear Butte is.

The first white men to see the mountain, and the Black Hills, were probably the Verendrye brothers, François and Louis-Joseph, French explorers who climbed Bear Butte in 1743. They called it Montagne des Gens des Cheveaux, the "Mountain of the Horse People," because the inhabitants there (unlike some tribes of that era) had horses.

In 1855 Dr. Ferdinand Hayden, a geologist, climbed Bear Butte and discovered, 600 feet up, a previously unknown flower, *Anemone patens,* the pasqueflower. You may find it sprouting up through melting snow. It later was designated South Dakota's state flower. For more on this flower, see the Natural World chapter.

The Teton Sioux held a great council at Bear Butte in the summer of 1857. Men from Custer's 1874 expedition climbed it while the troops camped nearby, resting for the last leg of their trip back to Fort Lincoln. In 1880 Rev. George Pelton traveled through the area on his way to Deadwood and reported in his journal that it took "nearly three hours" to get around the mountain with horse and wagon.

A pioneer's landmark because it could be seen at such great distances, Bear Butte eventually overlooked three gold-rush roads, a stage line, and Fort Meade, the military post of the Seventh Cavalry.

Bear Butte State Park was created in 1961, and the mountain was named a Registered Natural Landmark in 1965. It was entered into the National Register of Historic Places in 1973, under the National Preservation Act, because of its spiritual significance to Native Americans and its importance as a landmark to early pioneers.

Geologically speaking, the mountain (which is not really a butte) is a laccolith, a dome of molten lava that expanded and bulged upward through the overlying surface rock, which slowly eroded away. Basically, it's a volcano that didn't erupt. From a distance Bear Butte looks almost touchable and soft. Rising more than 4,400 feet

above sea level, more than 1,200 feet above the surrounding plains, it is mostly bare rock, but some trees and vegetation are scattered on its sides.

History books cite eyewitness accounts of fires on Bear Butte in the 1800s and claim that it was once more heavily forested than in recent decades. Until recently ponderosa pine was the predominant species at the higher elevations, and elm, cottonwood, hawthorn, juniper, chokecherry, and native grasses dominated the middle and lower regions.

In August 1996 an out-of-control ceremonial fire burned much of Bear Butte in a spectacular blaze that lasted two days. Between 80 and 90 percent of the ponderosa pines died, and it will be decades before they reestablish themselves. Ceremonial fires are permitted for Native American ceremonies only (inquire at the visitor center). Campfires are not allowed.

Today Bear Butte's environment is making a comeback. For nearly a year the National Hiking Trail that climbs the summit was closed for repairs and to protect the mountain from erosion caused by the lack of vegetation and tree canopy. The summit trail reopened with new wooden steps and erosion edging, the lumber for which was airlifted to the top by National Guard helicopters. The trail is rocky but is only moderately difficult. The north end of the Centennial Trail starts at the summit of Bear Butte. Read more about the Centennial Trail in the Recreation chapter.

The state park is open year-round. At the visitor center (open 9:00 A.M. to 5:00 P.M., seven days a week, from May to early September only), you can learn about the geologic and cultural history of Bear Butte and the park. The center contains a museum and presents educational videos. The entrance fee is $5.00 per car per day. There is no charge for children 11 and younger. A Custer State Park entrance license or annual state park pass will admit you without charge.

Bear Butte State Park is a low-key entertain-yourself park. Organized activities are few, but summer programs for groups can be arranged with the staff naturalist, who will give presentations on history and natural history and conduct hiking tours. Special programs need to be arranged in advance.

No concessions are available in the park, but the town of Sturgis is just 5 miles away.

You can also watch the park's buffalo herd, fish (by state permit—see the Recreation chapter), swim in the lake, camp in the campground (see the Campgrounds chapter), and hike. Try photographing the mountain at different times of day, when it changes color and texture in the light of sunrise and sunset, thunderstorm and snow.

You can sit at its base and stare at it, mesmerized by its powerful beauty. Or you can climb it and look out over the plains and hills (which you can see stretching into Nebraska or North Dakota), imagining Custer and his men marching by, or the

Verendrye brothers climbing up beside you, or Sitting Bull waiting patiently for the mountain to speak.

CENTRAL HILLS

Mount Rushmore National Memorial
Highway 244, Keystone
(605) 574-2523
www.nps.gov/moru
Egypt has the pyramids, England has Stonehenge. But ancient artisans were not the last to create world-class stone monuments, for a modern-day example is found in the Black Hills at Mount Rushmore. One of the nation's most recognizable landmarks, the towering busts of four U.S. presidents—George Washington, Thomas Jefferson, Abraham Lincoln, and Theodore Roosevelt—stand in tribute to the American ideals of freedom and progress. But the carving by American sculptor Gutzon

Mount Rushmore. SOUTH DAKOTA TOURISM

Borglum can't help inspiring awe as an impressive feat of engineering and an extraordinary work of art as well.

Flamboyant, patriotic, and hugely talented, Borglum, the son of Danish immigrants, believed a great nation deserved public art as big as all outdoors. So when he was invited to Georgia in the 1920s to create a Confederate soldiers' memorial, he envisioned giant likenesses of Dixie leaders carved onto the granite face of Stone Mountain. With the work under way, a bitter quarrel with his sponsors led to Borglum's dismissal—and an invitation to start over in South Dakota.

Borglum was 60 years old in 1927 when he started work on Mount Rushmore, hiring nearly 400 workers to drill, blast, and chisel rock off the mountainside. They were almost done when the sculptor died on March 6, 1941, leaving his son, Lincoln, to oversee the job's completion. Ever since then there have been suggestions (some serious, most not) to add more faces. However, Gutzon Borglum was very clear in expressing his vision of just four presidential sculptures. Washington was chosen for his leadership in the Revolutionary War and as the first president, roles that signify the independence and establishment of the Republic. Jefferson was selected not so much for the Declaration of Independence but for the acquisition of the Louisiana Territory in 1803, effectively doubling the size of the country. As such, Jefferson represents western expansion. Lincoln symbolizes the permanent union of the nation and equality for all its citizens. And Roosevelt, who had been dead for only eight years when Borglum started work on the mountain, was chosen by the sculptor because he completed the Panama Canal, allowing the United States to exert its influence worldwide. The National Park Service is dedicated to preserving Borglum's choices and preserving the monument as it stands. Besides, there's no more rock suitable for carving.

Newsweek columnist George F. Will called Mount Rushmore "an agreeable example of American excess," and indeed, more than three million people from around the world visit the Shrine of Democracy each year. Before viewing the 60-foot-tall faces, you'll want to stop in the information center to learn about the memorial and the 1,240-acre park's other features and free activities. For starters, you can see original tools, models, and other relics in the Sculptor's Studio, and the wheelchair-accessible Presidential Trail will take you to the talus slope along the base of the mountain. The park service offers guided walks and talks daily throughout the summer, and those in the 5- to 12-year-old crowd have their own activities that make learning about Mount Rushmore fun. Parents can help their youngsters earn a certificate through the Junior Ranger Program or have them take part in a 30-minute ranger-led program. (Turn to the Kidstuff chapter for more details.)

In 1998 a new interpretive center/museum complex opened with 5,000 square feet of exhibit space and two theaters for viewing an informational video. It's just one of numerous recent improvements that include the pergola, or grand entryway, the information center and restroom complex, the amphitheater, a new Avenue of Flags, a spacious gift shop, and a food-service facility with two snack bars and a cafeteria.

Most of these additions are the product of a nearly $24 million fund-raising campaign by the Mount Rushmore National Memorial Society, an organization Borglum himself formed in 1930. Contributions poured in from dozens of South Dakota communities, all 50 states, and about 20 foreign countries. Private donors have included descendants of New York attorney Charles Rushmore, who was visiting the Hills on behalf of mining interests when the mountain was named for him, partly in jest, in 1885.

The campaign also made possible the completion of the Hall of Records. One of Borglum's greatest fears was that future civilizations would have no idea why these

Photographing Mount Rushmore

Visitors like to photograph Mount Rushmore through the tunnels on Iron Mountain Road, and that requires tricking your camera. The darkness of the stone is a high contrast to the light on the tunnel's other end. Your camera's meter will read the darker stone, overexpose the shot, and, when your photos are developed, the great faces will be washed out. The trick is to ignore your camera's meter reading. "Stop down," or close down, the lens aperture to let in less light. You'll need to use F8, F11, F16, and maybe F22,

and you should also match (or approximate) the shutter speed to the film speed. Another method to photograph Mount Rushmore from the nearby tunnels is to move to the mouth of the tunnel, point the camera directly at the faces and set your exposure by the meter reading you get. Then move back and photograph, ignoring the metering changes your camera wants you to make. Don't forget, too, that Mount Rushmore's southeastern exposure makes morning the best time to take pictures of the faces.

America's shrine to democracy. SOUTH DAKOTA TOURISM

four faces graced a mountain in the middle of the continent. It was always his intent to construct a cavernous hall on top of the sculpture, hidden behind the heads, into which would be placed copies of the Constitution and its Bill of Rights, documents

explaining the carving of the mountain, and busts of famous Americans. However, dwindling funds and the onset of World War II forced him to abandon the project. The hall remained unfinished until the 1998 renovations, when officials finally decided

Badger Clark, Poet Laureate

South Dakota once had a Poet Lariat.

In reality, Badger Clark was named the first poet laureate in 1939, but many people—including the poet—preferred the humorous cowboy title of honor, a tribute to his western heritage, a larger-than-life designation for a colorful, larger-than-life man.

Charles Badger Clark was born in Iowa in 1883. His family moved to the Dakota Territory when he was three months old. Just months shy of being born a Dakotan, he nevertheless is considered a native son and our own beloved poet.

When Clark was 15, his mother died. Several years later, his frontier-minister father married a strong woman with an interest in writing, a woman Clark loved and admired enough to call Mother Anna. She would push him along the paths of poetry, prodding him to write, to submit his work to publications, and to publish books.

As a boy, Clark spent vacations at his uncle's Wyoming ranch and developed a taste for the wide-open, romantic West

and cowboy life. In 1903, having given up on college and not knowing what he wanted for his future, he accompanied a party hoping to colonize Cuba. The expedition was a failure, but Clark stayed on, seeking adventure. After Cuba he came home, joined a Badlands surveying party, tried (and failed at) business, and got a taste of the writing life at the Lead newspaper.

Then near-tragedy struck: Clark was diagnosed with tuberculosis. On his doctor's advice, he moved to Arizona and found an ideal job on a Tombstone ranch, tending cattle and enjoying time to write and think. The dry air and rest sent his tuberculosis into remission. And when he mailed his stepmother a poem and she sent it on to a magazine that published it, a surprised new poet was born. Later he wrote one of his most famous poems, "The Cowboy's Prayer," in which he captured the souls of the men of the West:

Oh Lord, I've never lived where
churches grow.
I love creation better as it stood

to complete Borglum's dream. Today, a vault chiseled into the Hall of Records' floor contains porcelain tablets etched with the documents Borglum requested, encased in titanium and sealed with a half-ton block of solid granite. Though not completed on the scale Borglum had envisioned, the Hall of Records serves its original purpose: to protect and preserve the

ideals of the nation led by the men carved into the giant granite mountainside.

Of course, preserving the sculpture is important, too. Thus, restoration and maintenance efforts are a major priority here. Every fall hairline cracks in the faces are painstakingly sealed by hand with silicone caulk, ensuring that generations will have an opportunity to see the sculptor's dream.

That day You finished it so long
   ago . . .
I know that others find You in the
   light
That's sifted down through tinted
   window panes,
And yet I seem to feel You near
   tonight
In this dim, quiet starlight on the
   plains.

Clark, a bachelor, spent years in Hot Springs, then moved to a cabin he built in Custer State Park. Although a friendly, popular man, he craved the solitude and independence only a rustic cabin in the woods could provide. In the 30 years he lived there, he wrote and read, answered fan mail, fed pancakes to the deer, received intrigued visitors, and gave poetry readings.

His two cabins still stand. The first he lived in while building the larger home, which is just as he left it in September 1957 when he went to his nephew's Rapid City home three weeks before dying of lung cancer. His fans still visit Badger Hole, the property and the cabins. There you can delight in his fine library—the comfortable spot where he wrote late into the night—and his kitchen, still stocked with staples and utensils.

As any legendary character does, Clark always wore a trademark outfit: high riding boots and breeches and an officer's coat and hat. His boots still stand in his bedroom, and his jackets hang on their pegs, seemingly awaiting their owner's return.

You can walk the Badger Clark Historic Trail, which winds up the hill behind the cabin and down again. Carry a brochure (available at the cabin) with some of his many poems, and stop at the markers and read a verse that commemorates that spot.

When you reach this one, pay closer attention. It's called "I Must Come Back":

No, when the waning heartbeat
   fails
I ask no heaven but leave to wend,
Unseen but seeing, my old trails,
With deathless years to compre-
   hend . . .

Badger Clark is buried in Hot Springs, but his spirit lingers in Custer State Park.

One of the best ways to share Borglum's vision is to attend the lighting ceremony that begins with a talk and a film at 9:00 in the amphitheater each summer evening. Lights illuminate the faces at 9:30 P.M. (Everything begins an hour earlier between Labor Day and mid-September.) Weather-related cancellations are rare, but call ahead if in doubt. Even during the off-season, the faces are bathed in light for an hour or two each evening, beginning shortly after dusk. It's a tradition that at least some local people take seriously—a temporary federal government shutdown in 1996 left Mount Rushmore in the dark, so Keystone rancher Art Oakes dug into his own pocket and took up a collection to pay the light bill.

"Buffalo Are Dangerous. Do Not Approach."

You'll see this and similar signs in Custer State Park and Wind Cave National Park. But the animals we call "buffalo" are not buffalo. That species includes African cape buffalo and water buffalo, which are not native to North America. The big, shaggy creatures of the West are North American bison, but most people just call them buffalo. Their Lakota name is *tatanka*.

These big creatures may look docile, but they are not livestock, nor are they domesticated. Bison are wild, can run at 35 mph or faster and turn on a dime, and are equipped with sharp horns, which they use to make their point when they feel threatened. People have been gored and attacked when they got too close or harassed bison. Cows with calves are especially prickly tempered.

Males (standing 5 to 6 feet high at the shoulder and weighing 2,000 pounds) keep to themselves or live in bachelor groups, while cows and calves stay in a herd. The rut (breeding season) begins in July and lasts through September. Bulls fight for females, and you may hear their roars or witness fierce battles. The bison are temperamental at this important season, so don't leave your car to get a better look. Don't approach the buffalo!

Mount Rushmore is open 24 hours a day all year except Christmas Day. The information center is open from 8:00 A.M. to 10:00 P.M. during the summer and from 8:00 A.M. to 5:00 P.M. for the winter. The season for special activities is May 15 to September 30.

You can park for free if you don't mind climbing 60 or more steps from the parking lot. Otherwise, parking in the new trilevel ramp just outside the grand entryway costs $8.00 per passenger vehicle for as many visits as you care to make in a single calendar year. (Buses pay $25.00 every time they enter.) The parking fees were established to pay off an $18 million loan to the Mount Rushmore Society for the parking ramp and related roadways. So although admission to the actual park grounds is free, your Golden Eagle, Golden Age, or Golden Access pass won't be honored at the parking ramp.

SOUTHERN HILLS

Custer State Park
Highway 87 South or North, Highway 36 West, or U.S. Highway 16/16A East
(605) 255-4464 (Peter Norbeck Visitor Center)
(605) 255-4515 (general information)
(800) 658-3530
www.state.sd.us/gfp

One word defines all of Custer State Park: *big*. With 71,000 acres of ponderosa forest, towering granite peaks (including North America's tallest mountain east of the Rockies, the 7,242-foot Harney Peak), and grassy prairie, Custer is one of the largest state parks in the country. And then there are the bison, the largest land mammals on the continent. Custer State Park has about 1,500 of the animals in one of the largest free-roaming herds of bison in the world. It's fitting that these great one-ton reflections of nature's might reside here, for only a group of such powerful animals would suit such a powerful mountain landscape.

Custer State Park was the idea of Peter Norbeck, a popular U.S. senator and the governor of South Dakota from 1916 to 1920. Originally from eastern South Dakota, Norbeck visited the Black Hills in 1905 and conceived the idea of establishing a wild game park in Custer County. Legislation was passed in 1913.

A practical man, Norbeck planned that timber production and resource management would help keep the park self-sustaining. Today camping fees, revenue from buffalo sales, entrance fees, concession revenue, and timber sales generate the multiple-use funds that maintain the park and its facilities. Custer State Park is self-funded on a day-to-day operational basis, although major deferred maintenance projects are sometimes funded by tax dollars.

If you'd like to stay in the park, you have your choice of four resorts: the State Game Lodge (where President Calvin Coolidge stayed during his 1927 summer vacation), Legion Lake Resort, Blue Bell Lodge, and Sylvan Lake Resort. Both Legion Lake and Sylvan Lake resorts rent boats, kayaks, and hydrobikes, and you can reserve a mountain bike at Legion Lake. Each resort in the park has dining facilities and a store or gift shop where you can purchase food or a souvenir. Read about these resorts in the Accommodations chapter.

There are also seven modern campgrounds, two primitive and two group

campsites, and the French Creek horse camp, which has corral space. You can read about these facilities in the Campgrounds chapter.

At Custer State Park you can cross-country ski, fish, hike, and climb the rocks. Scale Mount Coolidge to its 6,023-foot peak and get a look at the Badlands 90 miles away. Or travel back in history at the re-created Gordon Stockade, where, in the summer, you can watch daily activities as they were carried out in 1874 by gold-seeking pioneers. Both Mount Coolidge and the Gordon Stockade are on the west side of the park. We recommend you pick up maps and brochures at the visitor centers or the park entrances, which will make everything easy to find.

When you're ready for a break from your own activities, there's plenty of daily organized entertainment in the park (summers only, though). You can enjoy educational programs, slides and films, guided nature and historic walks, informal lectures, and fishing demonstrations. Some great programs for kids are offered, too, including a Junior Naturalist Program that teaches children about nature. Call the Norbeck Visitor Center for more information about these programs.

At Blue Bell stables you can sign up for trail rides or overnight pack trips (see the Recreation chapter) or go on the Old-Fashioned Hay Ride and Chuck Wagon Cookout (with cowboy fixin's). If motorized transportation is more your speed, try the Buffalo Safari Jeep Tour and Chuck Wagon

Some state parks use prescribed burns to mimic the work of wild prairie fires: The destruction of vegetation and subsequent rejuvenation of the land help restore the natural balance between grasslands and pine forests. While traveling through a park, you may come across fire personnel monitoring the blazes, smoke, and wind direction. No need to worry, and it's fine to watch and learn.

Coolidge General Store

The Coolidge General Store at Custer State Park has a most amazing ceiling. It was built to resemble the hull of a ship (turned upside down, above you), and it's beautifully constructed of native ponderosa pine. It is said to have 11,000 angle cuts (the cuts made in the boards to make them all fit perfectly together). Virtually every board meets the adjoining board or beam at an angle, in a stunning display of fancy craftsmanship. If you try to count all those angles, however, you'll get a crick in your neck for your efforts. The ceiling was crafted in 1927 by shipbuilders from Minnesota, who built the general store and other buildings to

accommodate President Coolidge and his entourage during their summer vacation at Custer State Park.

Cookout Adventure, which start at the State Game Lodge. These activities are daily summer happenings. Each attraction and resort area is well marked with highway signs and easy to find on park maps. Some activities require advance reservations; call the general information number to inquire about hours and fees.

The State Game Lodge has a rotating artist-in-residence program for wildlife and western artists. In the gallery off the lobby, you can watch artists create, browse through their displayed work, and take home an original work of art.

Theater lovers will want to take in a summer theater performance at the Black Hills Playhouse (see the Arts chapter). Poetry buffs will enjoy a pilgrimage to Badger Hole, the carefully preserved cabin that was the home of Badger Clark, South Dakota's first poet laureate. It's open in the summer from 10:00 A.M. to 5:00 P.M. Monday through Friday and from 1:00 to 4:00 P.M. Saturday and Sunday. Admission

is free with your park entrance license.

You can take a scenic drive along the Needles Highway (14 miles), which wanders through the Needles formations, granite spires that point to the sky. The Needles Highway is closed in the winter (approximately November 1 to April 1, depending on the weather).

Or try Iron Mountain Road, which winds between the intersection of U.S. Highway 16A and Highway 36 and Mount Rushmore. Along that route you'll see the marvelous pigtail bridges, artistically engineered creations designed by Governor Norbeck that switchback up steep hills. The 70-mile Peter Norbeck National Scenic Byway is another great drive; there's more information about it in the Attractions chapter.

A drive on the Wildlife Loop is a must. Its 18 miles go directly through the areas most often frequented by the park's wildlife. Try it in the early mornings and evenings when you're likely to spot white-

Bighorn sheep in Custer State Park. SOUTH DAKOTA TOURISM

tailed and mule deer, pronghorn antelope, mountain goats, bighorn sheep, wild turkeys, and prairie dogs. You're less likely to see the elk and coyotes, but you might get lucky. You'll see many birds, including—quite possibly—hawks and golden eagles as well as small mammals such as squirrels, chipmunks, and skunks. You might even see a snake or two.

These roads were designed as scenic drives. Take your time, enjoy the scenery, and don't travel too fast. As Governor Norbeck himself said about the scenic byway, "You're not supposed to drive here at 60 miles an hour. To do the scenery half justice, people should drive 20 or under. To do it full justice, they should get out and walk."

While driving on the Wildlife Loop and Iron Mountain Road, you'll eventually be slowed by a wily burro (or two, or several). Do be careful and watch out for them. Attempted escape is not recommended,

sometimes not even possible. These guys will simply stand in front of your vehicle and solicit handouts. Or they'll poke their big heads in your window and stay there a while, keeping you effectively trapped. The burros are not indigenous; they are the descendants of those brought to the park in 1927 to take visitors to Harney Peak. The park management discourages feeding the critters. Roll up your windows and enjoy watching them until they become bored and let you pass.

The 1,500-head bison herd is the park's main attraction. You may find the animals standing in the road, too, or grazing alongside. In the spring the little red calves are born. They are shy, and their mothers are protective, but (from your car) you can get some good pictures. In October the herd is rounded up, corralled, vaccinated, and sorted during the Buffalo Roundup (more about this in the Annual

Narrow Tunnels

Three scenic roads within Custer State Park have tunnels that are great fun to drive through unless you're steering a big RV, camping trailer, or bus! Few of the tunnels have a bypass, so your overlarge vehicle will have to turn around, which may not be an easy task. These roads, and their pulloffs, are narrow. Plan ahead! Iron Mountain Road (U.S. 16A North) has three tunnels, each 12 feet 6 inches high and 13 feet 6 inches wide. The tunnel near Sylvan Lake on the Needles Highway (Highway 87/89) is 10 feet 8 inches high and 10 feet wide. There are two other tunnels on the Needles Highway (Highway 87 North). One is 11 feet 5 inches high and only 8 feet 7 inches wide, and the other is 12 feet high and just 9 feet wide.

Events chapter). Of these, about 950 are returned to the park to winter (that's the amount the range can support), and the rest are auctioned in November. The sale provides income for the park and helps control the herd population.

Custer State Park is open year-round, and you must purchase an entrance license to enjoy it. An annual license is $20.00 and a second license for another of your vehicles is $10.00. You can also purchase a daily license for $3.00 per person (six and older) or $5.00 per vehicle. Your entrance license allows you to enter any state park or state recreation area during the term of the license.

Custer State Park has a way of enchanting visitors. The animals, the landscape, and the history will all work their way into your heart.

Jewel Cave National Monument
U.S. Highway 16, Custer
(605) 673-2288, (800) 967-2283
www.nps.gov/jeca

The narrow, winding road to Jewel Cave primes travelers for a voyage into the mysterious depths of the earth. Rich in history and natural wonders, if not in actual gems, this cave 13 miles west of Custer was discovered by prospectors Frank and Albert Michaud and Charles Bush in 1900. Mistaking a sparkling layer of calcium carbonate (also called calcite crystal) for diamonds, the men staked a mining claim but failed either to extract anything of value or to mine tourists by turning the cave into an attraction. Yet Jewel Cave's vast chambers hold a treasury of stalactites, stalagmites, and other marvels, and in 1908 President Theodore Roosevelt declared it a national monument.

Continued exploration has established Jewel as the second-longest cave in the world, with more than 130 miles of mapped passages (outdone only by Kentucky's 346.20-mile Mammoth Cave, the world's longest). However, some cavers and scientists have forwarded the theory that Jewel Cave is connected to nearby Wind Cave (the fourth longest in the world; see the Wind Cave National Park listing in this chapter). If true, that would make the cave system the longest on the planet. Of course, that's assuming that there are very few passages left to explore. Air-volume studies show the opposite. In fact, regardless of whether the two caves are linked, research suggests that less than 10 percent of the cave system has been explored, and park rangers guess that there may be a total of 5,000 miles of passages.

But there's more to the monument than the cave itself. Above ground there are 1,274 acres of ponderosa forest and prairie grassland that are host to an array of native creatures. There are deer, coyotes, 9 species of bat, 120 species of birds, and a plethora of wildflowers that bloom in a colorful show of glory each spring. Three trails (two accessible from the visitor center, one beginning on the park's western boundary off U.S. 16) cut through the terrain and offer visitors an up-close look at the flora, fauna, and geology of the south-central Black Hills.

Of course, there are plenty of options for hiking the cave, too. Half-mile guided tours that depart from the visitor center last 80 minutes and incorporate 723 stairs—the equivalent of 40 flights, but it's mostly downhill. Sturdy, rubber-soled shoes and a light jacket are de rigueur.

Tours leave every 15 to 30 minutes beginning at 8:30 A.M. Tickets are sold on a first-come, first-served basis, so your best bet is to arrive during the morning. Historic lantern tours begin daily on a varied schedule, mid-June to mid-August, at the cave's natural entrance in Hell Canyon, a mile west of the visitor center. Prices are the same as for the regular tours, but children younger than six are not permitted on these tours, which last one hour and 45 minutes and cover a half mile. Call ahead for the tour schedule. The last tour is at 6:00 P.M.

Reservations are required for the two-thirds-mile, four-hour spelunking tours ($$$$) in the cave's undeveloped areas, where groups of five begin their adventure at 12:30 P.M. daily from mid-June to mid-August. Hard hats and headlamps are complimentary, but you're required to bring ankle-height, lace-up, lug-sole boots, gloves, and soft knee pads. Be prepared to crawl through a concrete-block tunnel to qualify for this tour, which is off-limits to anyone age 16 or younger. Those age 16 or 17 must have their parent's or guardian's written consent.

It's OK to take your camera but not your tripod on any of the tours. Touching any part of the cave's interior is prohibited, since skin oils and general wear and tear will damage the fragile formations.

Never feed a wild animal, even those that seem tame. The animal may suddenly bite, kick, scratch, or attack you. Moreover, park officials will be forced to kill wild animals that have sickened after eating human food. Animals that are hand-fed also lose their natural fear and are at greater risk of being struck by a vehicle or abused.

Anyone who's been recently hospitalized or who has respiratory or circulatory problems is advised to consult a park ranger before embarking on any cave tour. Jewel Cave is open all year except Thanksgiving, Christmas, and New Year's Day. The visitor center is open 8:00 A.M. to 4:30 P.M. year-round. Hours occasionally change, especially in summer months; call for information.

Wind Cave National Park
Highway 87 South or U.S. Highway 385 East or North, Hot Springs
(605) 745–4600 (visitor center)
www.nps.gov/wica
This park has as much to offer below ground as above. Adjacent to Custer State Park (directly south), it is a wildlife park as well, set on 28,000 acres. It has similar rolling prairie hills and pine-forest vistas, and it also boasts pronghorns, a bison herd, prairie dogs, deer, elk, coyotes, and more.

But this park has one feature Custer State Park lacks: Wind Cave, one of the most complex caves in the world. Its explored maze today totals about 121 miles, all within 1 square mile of land area. But there's more down there; scientists estimate that only 5 percent of the cave has been explored. An early adventurer, Alvin McDonald, wrote in 1891, "Have given up the idea of finding the end of Wind Cave." Fortunately, explorers who came after McDonald didn't give up, and the cave is still being explored and mapped.

Wind Cave became the nation's seventh national park in 1903. It was also the first cave to become a national park and is

Wind Cave Lint

No one would accuse Wind Cave of being dirty, but it does have a lint problem. Every visitor impacts the cave in the same way: by leaving behind microscopic skin cells, some hair, some clothing fibers. . . . It all adds up to lint! And with 100,000 visitors each year, lint is a big problem.

How do you clean a cave? Wind Cave National Park organizes lint cleaning camps, where volunteers carefully brush and vacuum sections of the cave and its trails, then remove bag after bag of lint. Wind Cave National Park management strives for a balance between public

enjoyment of the cave and protecting it from the impact of all those intrigued visitors.

the world's fourth-longest cave. More than 100,000 people tour the cave each year.

Wind Cave's natural opening is a (barely) adult-size hole in the ground. It was discovered in 1881 by two hunters, one of whom was Tom Bingham. When Bingham bent down for a look, the wind escaping from the hole blew his hat off his head. He excitedly went to tell his friends and brought them back to the opening. When he leaned down to show them, the wind sucked his hat inside.

Today we know that Wind Cave is a breathing cave; that is, the wind escaping or entering the cave is controlled by the atmospheric pressure outside. When the pressure rises, air is drawn inside the cave; when the atmospheric pressure lowers, the air blows out. You can stand outside the natural entrance today and experience the same phenomenon.

Wind Cave has beautiful and delicate subterranean formations such as flowstone, frostwork, popcorn, and helictites, but it is best known for a rare formation called boxwork. The cave has more box-

work than any other in the world. Millions of years ago, when the area was covered by ocean, limestone formations were created below the waters. Later the ocean receded, and over millions of years other waters seeped in and out, the limestone slowly dissolved, and passageways began to form. About 62 million to 65 million years ago, the slow geologic uplift that formed the Black Hills also caused the limestone to shift and crack, and more passages were opened.

Acid-laden water filled the cracks in the underground limestone. As the limestone dissolved in the slowly seeping water, hardened calcite boxwork formations were left behind. They are delicate and fragile, thin honeycombs clinging to the walls and ceilings of the cave.

Although early explorers and owners used the cave for commercial tours and blasted caverns and paved walkways, today it is carefully protected. Its vital signs (humidity, temperature, and water quality) are constantly monitored to spot environmental problems early.

This living, breathing cave is constantly changing, but the temperature inside is always around 53 degrees. Wear a jacket and sturdy, rubber-sole walking shoes, and remember that some of the ceilings are low and some paths are wet. It's fine to take flash photographs and video shots, but tripods are prohibited. It's also forbidden to touch the cave walls, disturb the formations in any way, or smoke, eat, chew gum, or leave litter behind. There are no restrooms underground either, so plan ahead.

Wind Cave and the visitor center are open year-round (the center does close on Thanksgiving, Christmas, and New Year's Day), but tour hours vary by season. You can take your choice of different walking tours, which during the summer season leave every 20 minutes or so. Each is led by a well-informed park ranger. The tours are popular, and in the summer you may have to wait. Try the morning tours, which aren't as crowded.

Children younger than six can participate free of charge in the first three tours listed. Golden Age discounts apply for each tour (you must show your Golden Age Passport).

The Natural Entrance Tour lasts 75 minutes. You will navigate 300 stairs, most of which go down, and exit the cave by elevator. Prices range from $4.50 for children 6 to 16 to $9.00 for adults 17 and older.

The Garden of Eden Tour lasts one hour and is the least strenuous (you will navigate only 150 stairs and enter and leave by elevator). Prices are $3.50 to $7.00. It is the only tour offered in winter.

The Fairgrounds Tour lasts 90 minutes and navigates 450 stairs. You'll enter and exit by elevator. Prices are $4.50 to $9.00.

The Candlelight Tour is conducted entirely by candlelight in an unlighted part of the cave. It's the longest tour: It lasts

The Black Hills are home to some of the longest caves in the world. SOUTH DAKOTA TOURISM

two hours and covers a mile of strenuous trails. You must make reservations (sometimes a month in advance), and children must be eight or older to participate. Prices are $4.50 to $9.00.

The Caving Tour is for the most adventurous types. It's a three- to four-hour tour with a beginning course in spelunking on trails the other tours don't cover. You'll be crawling quite a lot, so wear old clothes, long pants and sleeves, sturdy shoes, and gloves. The park will provide the hard hats and lights. Only those 16 and older may participate, and reservations are required. The cost is $23.

You can make reservations for tours by contacting Wind Cave National Park at (605) 745–4600.

There are also summer-only activities held outside the cave. Discovery programs are held three times each day (ask at the visitor center), a two-hour prairie hike takes place once a day, and evening campfire programs are presented at Elk Mountain Campground. You can stay at the campground or in the back-country (inquire at the visitor center for free permits), hike cross-country or on the trails, and bicycle on the roads (off-road biking is not allowed). You can also ride horseback.

Whether your preference is for the above-ground or below-ground sights and scenery, you'll thoroughly enjoy Wind Cave National Park, a South Dakota natural treasure.

THE BADLANDS AND NEARBY

Your first glimpse of Badlands National Park might well prompt comparison to a giant, mythological beast or bring to mind a bleak lunar surface. With its stony face and jutting spine, parched soil, and eroded, barren peaks, the Badlands give many visitors the impression of a place long ago forsaken.

Yet this eerie world is very much alive. Get acquainted with it, and you might find yourself warming to those thirsty slopes and windy plains that, like patient teachers, show us how to look beyond the surface. All they ask is that we take time to notice and marvel at their splendor. The more time you spend in the Badlands, the more familiar and precious its features become.

Badlands National Park is a place for meandering and making frequent stops, whether you are traveling by car or on foot. The scene changes minute by minute. The time of day and weather patterns constantly alter the way the Badlands appear. A winter sunset casts over the snow-covered peaks and white, frozen canyons a cloak of orange and gold, while a summer sunrise over the sandy buttes paints the landscape in shades of pink and red. One minute you'll think you're on the moon, and the next you'll imagine that you're on Mars. Perhaps that's why the Badlands have been the set for a few science-fiction movies, including the 1997 flick *Starship Troopers*.

There is much to observe and experience here, and we urge you to do both with care and deliberation. Hike along a dry wash and listen as curled leaves of parched mud crackle beneath your boots. On the compacted hardpan, look back and notice how you leave almost no trace at all. Watch closely as a long-tailed magpie takes flight, white wing patches flashing like outspread, gloved fingers against coal-black wings. Feel the wind brush your face like ghosts bearing ancient dreams.

A long thread of life weaves through the Badlands, both in its rich fossil beds and in stories handed down. Take time to learn and think about the living things, human and otherwise, that have found this to be a good land.

HISTORY

The Lakota Sioux called it Mako Sica, "land that is bad." Eighteenth-century French fur traders who traveled the area spoke of *les mauvaises terres à traverser,* "the bad lands to cross."

Not until the mid-19th century did scientists become convinced that this eerie place, with its rugged cliffs, baked soil, and ferocious weather, was in fact a storehouse brimming with information about the ancient past.

By studying the striated rock formations of the Badlands, researchers have learned that the area was covered by a warm inland sea millions of years ago. Then, as the Black Hills laboriously rose skyward, the sea drained away, and the seabed oxidized. Eons passed, and layers of silt, sand, clay, and volcanic ash were deposited. Today these mineralized layers are seen as varicolored bands sweeping across the craggy landscape.

Through millennia the land underwent many transformations, from dense forest to vast plain to grassland. The climate changed as well, from subtropical to cool and dry. Four-legged creatures roamed and grazed where invertebrates had lived submerged in the sea, and over time the four-leggeds' bones joined those of the sea-dwellers, settling into the earth to turn to stone. The Badlands are now an extensive source of fossils; local rocks from the Oligocene epoch, roughly 25 million to 35 million years ago, contain some of the world's best-known specimens. A fairly recent discovery, known as the Big Pig Dig, yielded the remains of an archeotherium, or ancient wild boar, and other animals from the Eocene period some 55 million years ago. Scientists digging at the site find more fossils each year, mostly of rhinoceros and boar ancestors. Paleontologists plan to dig each summer until there are no more bones to find, which probably won't be for years. If you'd like to visit the site, contact one of the park's visitor centers (phone numbers appear later in this chapter). Otherwise, you can see some of the Big Pig Dig bones at the Museum of Geology on the campus of South Dakota School of Mines and Technology in Rapid City (see the Attractions chapter).

Eventually, water and wind gouged out cliffs and canyons in the soft sediment, and the climate ripened into extremes of hot and cold. More than 10,000 years ago—recently, in geologic terms—humans appeared in the Badlands, hunting mammoths. (You can see bones and hair from these ancient creatures at Mammoth Site of Hot Springs, which is listed in the Attractions chapter.) Indian tribes followed—first the Arikara and later the Lakota Sioux—then white trappers, traders, fossil collectors, ranchers, and homesteaders.

In the 1920s, South Dakotan U.S. Sen. Peter Norbeck and Ben Millard, an early Badlands homesteader and founder of the Cedar Pass Lodge (see the listing below, under Accommodations), joined forces to create a national park in the Badlands, an effort actually begun by the South Dakota Legislature in 1909. President Franklin Roosevelt issued a proclamation establishing Badlands National Monument in 1939, three years after Norbeck's death. In 1976 the monument expanded to include the Stronghold (South) and Palmer Creek units, both on Pine Ridge Indian Reservation land that had been used as a gunnery range during World War II. In 1978 the monument achieved national park status through an act of Congress; today Badlands National Park contains 244,000 acres.

CLIMATE

Badlands weather is a lot like the landscape: often harsh and subject to rapid change. Most of the park's million-plus annual visitors arrive during the summer, when the thermometer can easily register three digits. But just as easily, blazing sunshine can give way to a downpour that turns hiking trails and back roads into a gummy mess. Lightning, high winds, hailstorms, flash floods, and tornadoes are other warm-weather hazards for which it is wise to be prepared. The climate is semi-arid (annual rainfall is about 15.5 inches). Add to this the prairie winds, and dehydration becomes a very real concern in hot weather, especially if you're hiking or otherwise working up a sweat. Carry plenty of drinking water with you, because opportunities to wet your whistle are few—essentially at facilities in the Cedar Pass area and at the White River Visitor Center (open only during the summer). Sunscreen and suitable clothing are essential.

During the winter, ice storms and blizzards can strike with little warning. Bitter cold and howling winds are to be expected, but so are mild, sunny days and picturesque snowfalls.

That said, spring, when baby animals are born and the land greens up, and fall, when the weather is generally more moderate, are lovely times to visit the Badlands.

 Badlands rock formations make a perfect reflective surface for sunlight. It's a good idea to wear sunscreen and a pair of sunglasses while touring the park, even during the winter.

Eroded bluffs in the Badlands. SOUTH DAKOTA TOURISM

THE NATURAL WORLD

The towering, 60-mile-long Badlands Wall dominates the Badlands moonscape with a series of eroded ridges and valleys running from the northeast to the southwest. Other, smaller rock formations have inspired comparisons to everything from castles and ancient ruins to oversized ribs and toadstools.

So it might surprise you to know that wide-open, mixed-grass prairies, not barren rocks, make up most of the Badlands. Some 170,000 acres nourish more than 50 species of grass (about 70 percent are native) and numerous varieties of wildflowers that flourish from early spring until the first hard freeze. Yellow plains prickly pear, pale green yucca, golden prairie coneflower, and white snow-on-the-mountain are just a few of the varieties of flowers to be seen. Theodore Van

Bruggen's *Wildflowers, Grasses & Other Plants of the Northern Plains and Black Hills* is a color-coded guide to local plants that you might find useful; also, a brochure titled *Badlands Nature Guide* is handy for identifying fauna as well as flora. Both publications can be purchased at the park.

A program of prescribed burns has been instituted in recent years to promote a balanced ecosystem in much the same way as wildfires of the past did, by recycling nutrients into the soil and promoting the natural succession of plant species.

Trees and shrubs are scarce in the Badlands, growing for the most part near creek drainages. Most notable are the aromatic Rocky Mountain junipers that give Cedar Pass its name. You can get a close look at these trees and enjoy their cooling shade on the Cliff Shelf Trail (see the listing below under Recreation). Cliff Shelf is

Of all the hazards you might encounter in Badlands National Park, lightning looms largest. During a storm, stay off ridges and away from lone trees to avoid being struck.

a slump, a place where surface runoff collects as it drains underground, thus providing sufficient water to nourish a sizable stand of trees.

Other forms of life find sustenance in Badlands National Park, which is a key player in efforts to save the black-footed ferret from extinction. These black-masked members of the weasel family prey on prairie dogs and live in their holes, and ferrets bred in captivity have been reintroduced to the wild here. You're not likely to see ferrets in the park, though, because the nocturnal little burrowers spend almost all their time underground. In the event of a sighting, however, please watch from a respectful distance—binoculars or a telephoto camera lens will give you a close-up look—so as not to disturb these endangered creatures. (For more on these creatures, see the close-up in the Natural World chapter.) Prairie dogs, on the other hand, are commonly seen—try Roberts Prairie Dog Town on Sage Creek Rim Road in the western portion of the park.

Audubon bighorn sheep were native to the Black Hills and Badlands, but unregulated hunting pushed the entire species to extinction sometime in the 1920s. Four decades later some closely related Rocky Mountain bighorn sheep were introduced to the park to take their place. Around the same time bison—barely saved from extinction—were reintroduced to the Badlands.

Wolves, elk, and bears no longer roam here. (Whether bears actually inhabited the Badlands is in dispute.) You might see antelope, deer, rabbits, coyotes, foxes, badgers, grouse, and many other animals as you explore the park, but remember that they are wild and potentially danger-

ous. Keep your distance no matter how placid they seem—the rule of thumb is, if an animal responds to your presence, you're too close. Be on the lookout for poisonous prairie rattlesnakes, especially around prairie dog holes, rocky areas, grass, and brush.

And remember, the only things you're allowed to take home from the park are your memories. Removing or harming the plants, animals, minerals, fossils, and other features is a federal offense, and it spoils the park for others. If you come upon fossils, notify a park ranger so the specimens can be handled professionally.

GETTING HERE, GETTING AROUND

There are several entrances to Badlands National Park. Most travelers arrive in the North Unit via Interstate 90; if you're approaching from the east, take exit 131 and follow Highway 240 (Badlands Loop Road) for about 3 miles to the park's Northeast Entrance and another 5 miles to Ben Reifel Visitor Center (see the write-up under Attractions later in this chapter). From the west, take exit 110 at Wall and head straight south on Highway 240 for 8 miles to the Pinnacles Entrance. Badlands Loop Road links these two entrances.

Once you've arrived, you can pick up a free official map and ask for information and directions at the visitor center. Roads and attractions in the North Unit are well marked with signs to help you find your way. One caution, though: Unpaved roads can be slippery from winter ice or summer rain, so use extra care under those conditions.

From the north or south, Bureau of Indian Affairs (BIA) Road 27 takes you to the White River Visitor Center in the southeast corner of the Stronghold (South) Unit, which is on the Pine Ridge Indian Reservation. The Stronghold and nearby Palmer Creek Units, although part of the park, are isolated, undeveloped, and not well suited to tourism. Grazing and subsistence hunting (with a permit) are allowed here, and there is only one official road, unpaved at that; Sheep Mountain Road (off County Road 589) narrows and turns from gravel to dirt, winding around until it dead-ends after 7 miles at a sheer drop on top of Sheep Mountain Table. There's the added complexity of private land that can't be crossed without permission—check on local access at visitor centers before you try to enter. And there's always the possibility of stumbling upon unexploded ordnance (UXO) from the gunnery-range days; information about what to do in that event is available at visitor centers.

For a less complicated backcountry experience, consider Badlands (Sage Creek) Wilderness Area in the North Unit. (See the Recreation section in this chapter for more information.)

North of the park, Wall Municipal Airport, at an altitude of 2,810 feet, has a hard-surface runway rated up to 12,500 pounds for single- and twin-engine planes. Services here are minimal; fuel is available on an emergency basis only, and there are no car rentals or taxis. However, motels, restaurants, and tourist attractions, including world-famous Wall Drug (see the close-up in this chapter) are within easy walking distance (9 blocks or fewer). For airport information, call (605) 279-2666.

Badlands National Park is open all year, and a $20.00 annual pass allows you unlimited visits. Seven-day passes cost $10.00 per noncommercial vehicle ($5.00 for Oglala Sioux tribal members). Single-person entry (on motorcycle, bicycle, or foot) is $5.00. Admission is free on National Parks Day, August 25.

ATTRACTIONS

Strictly speaking, the Badlands are one big attraction all in themselves. But we've listed the primary tourist draws, which are located along Badlands Loop Road in the North Unit of the park and within a few miles of its northern boundary.

Badlands National Park

Badlands Loop Road
Highway 240, Badlands National Park
www.nps.gov/badl
Badlands Loop Road is the most heavily traveled road in the park, doubtless because it takes you to the most popular hiking trails and overlooks. Points of interest along the road are well marked, and all are worth stopping for. The wheelchair-accessible Fossil Exhibit Trail, for instance, is a short, circular boardwalk along which you'll find "fossils under glass"—replicas of fossils found in the area and displayed in boxes with domed, heavy plastic lids. The Journey to Wounded Knee Overlook tells a poignant tale of a doomed people and a dying leader trapped between two worlds. (You'll find more information about the 1890 Wounded Knee Massacre in the Day Trips and Weekend Getaways chapter.) At the Seabed Jungle Overlook you'll see low, ancient hills that oxidized and turned yellow after the inland sea receded. There are other sights that you won't want to miss, so plan to take your time.

Ben Reifel Visitor Center
Highway 240, Interior
(605) 433-5361
www.nps.gov/badl
A stop at this visitor center 5 miles from the park's Northeast Entrance will make your journey through the Badlands more meaningful. By studying the geologic displays, you'll be able to recognize a variety of natural features throughout the park

---

If you encounter a rattlesnake, stop and back away slowly or allow the snake to retreat. Don't make sudden moves. Once the coast is clear, proceed on your way. If you get bitten, contact a park ranger at (605) 433-5361 or seek medical attention. The closest facility with antivenin is Rapid City Regional Hospital; call (605) 341-8222 for the emergency department.

Although Badlands National Park is in South Dakota, other badlands are found in other states, including North Dakota, Wyoming, and Montana. The South Dakota badlands are sometimes referred to as the Big Badlands or the White River Badlands to distinguish them from the others.

and understand how they came to be formed. Cultural displays will help you appreciate the area's human history. In the "You Can Touch" room, you'll get acquainted with the park's flora and fauna. A table there with fossil riddles and puzzles grabs the attention of kids, and so does a cow backbone you can try to assemble. Every half hour during tourist season and by request during the winter, you can view an 18-minute video on the natural and cultural history of the area; it's shown in audio and closed-caption versions simultaneously. Afterward, you might want to browse the gift shop. Services at the center include information, restrooms, water, a public pay phone, and brochures in German and French.

The center is named for the late Oglala Lakota leader Benjamin Reifel, known to his tribe as Wiyaka Wanjila, or Lone Feather. Reifel was superintendent of the Pine Ridge Indian Reservation, a U.S. congressman, and the U.S. commissioner of Indian affairs.

The center is open year-round; summer hours are 7:00 A.M. to 8:00 P.M. daily, with reduced hours at other times.

Naturalist Programs
(605) 433-5361

Free educational programs are available each day during the summer, including evening talks that begin at dusk at the Cedar Pass Campground amphitheater. Times and topics (such as Badlands natural or human history, fossils, geology, and animals) are posted on park bulletin boards at Ben Reifel Visitor Center, Cedar Pass Lodge, and park campgrounds. Addi-

tional programs offered recently were the twice-daily Evolving Prairie Talk and Fossil Talk; check bulletin boards for information. The park newsletter, *The Prairie Preamble* (you'll get a copy when you pay your entrance fee), lists regularly scheduled programs; you can ask at the visitor center about additional, special programs.

White River Visitor Center
Junction of BIA Roads 27 and 2
Badlands National Park
(605) 455-2878
www.nps.gov/badl

The center, cooperatively managed by the Pine Ridge Indian Reservation and the National Park Service (and on reservation land), features displays on Lakota Sioux history and culture. There's also a video you won't want to miss, *The Great Plains Experience,* which originally aired on public TV. The items for sale in the bookstore are also available at Ben Reifel Visitor Center, so you get two chances to make up your mind about what to add to your home library. Information, maps, restrooms, and water are available, too. The center is open from late May through August, from 10:00 A.M. to 4:00 P.M. daily.

Nearby

Buffalo Gap National Grassland
South of Wall and southeast of Hot Springs
(605) 279-2125

Don't be deceived. If you think you know about grass—that it's boring stuff—think again. Natural prairie grasslands aren't your suburban backyard. Home to prairie dogs, fox, prairie chicken, pheasant, bison, and coyotes, grasslands are vibrant places rich with life.

Modern living is often about speed and special effects, high color and haste. The grasslands, though indifferent to your presence, force you to slow down and look carefully. Their mysteries are not revealed to those in a hurry.

Be sure to stop at the National Grass-

Stronghold Table

In a last, desperate attempt to make their world right again, Lakota Sioux ghost dancers gathered at Stronghold Table, a remote mesa in what is now the Stronghold (South) Unit of Badlands National Park, to hold ceremonies in late 1890. The ghost dance belonged to a religion preached by Paiute prophet Wovoka, who promised that the Messiah would restore the old ways. Purifying themselves and eschewing violence, adherents danced in a circle, appealing to their deceased relatives and praying for a miracle to drive out the white invaders and bring back the buffalo.

Whites, viewing the ghost dance as a threat to their own safety and objectives, and hearing reports that ghost dancers wore special shirts to protect them from bullets, were suspicious and tried to repress the ceremonies. Efforts to prevent ghost dancing led to the death of Chief Sitting Bull, who was killed December 15, 1890, by Native American police sent to keep him from joining the ghost dancers on Stronghold Table. Two weeks later, on December 29, the Wounded Knee Massacre took place when the Seventh Cavalry intercepted Chief Big Foot's band, believed to be en route to Stronghold Table but in fact bound for Pine Ridge to meet with Chief Red Cloud in a quest for peace. You can read more about Wounded Knee in the Day Trips and Weekend Getaways chapter.

lands Visitor Center on Main Street in Wall (there's no admission charge). Outside, there's a black-footed ferret in his pen. He's endangered, and a project is under way to reintroduce his species to Buffalo Gap and Badlands National Park (see the close-up in the Natural World chapter).

When the Great Plains, in the heart of the United States, were first explored in the 1800s, the early explorers called it "the Great American Desert." They considered it a wasteland. But as the United States grew and civilization in the East pushed westward, there was a clamor for more room. All that vast emptiness in the middle of the country was available, so the government passed the Homestead Act of 1862. The cry of "Free land!" soon went up, and adventurous folks were on the move westward to the Great Plains.

The migration continued until the early 1920s. Until then, prairie farmers and ranchers had been relatively successful. There was enough rain, and the market for wheat and cattle was strong. Unfortunately, no one at that time understood that the Great Plains are much more fragile than they appear. By the mid-1920s the plains had been overgrazed and overcultivated and were ripe for the disaster that soon struck. The combination of the Depression, drought, and high winds of the 1930s added to the land's burden. It is estimated that during those dust-bowl years, 2.5 mil-

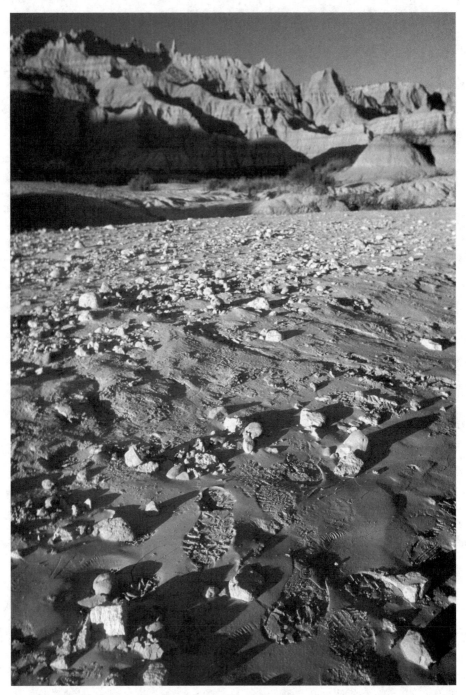

With numerous trails, hiking is a popular pastime in Badlands National Park. SOUTH DAKOTA
TOURISM

lion homesteaders gave up in despair and abandoned their ranches and farms.

· In 1934 the federal government's Resettlement Administration began to purchase both never-owned and abandoned acreage, eventually amassing more than 10 million acres and relocating thousands of failed homesteaders. In 1937 the Soil Conservation Service began to "rehabilitate" the wind-eroded land. Using Civilian Conservation Corps and Works Progress Administration labor, shelter belts and stock ponds were created and new grass was seeded.

In 1954 the management of the grasslands was transferred to the USDA Forest Service, and in 1960 nearly four million acres were designated national grasslands. The 20 national grasslands throughout the United States serve as multiple-use public land. Ranchers graze their livestock there, by permit, and have built stock tanks on the land at their own expense; the stock tanks water both livestock and wildlife. Hunting and fishing are also allowed (state laws apply).

Buffalo Gap National Grassland covers more than 591,000 acres of prairie and badlands, and there is no admission charge to enjoy it. On a detailed map (which you're encouraged to pick up at the National Grasslands Visitor Center), you'll see it is not a "solid" mass of land; its blocks of acreage are mixed with private and state-owned property. The eastern half of the grassland, for example, is near Badlands National Park, and the western half is south of the Black Hills. Buffalo Gap is one of three South Dakota national grasslands; the others are Fort Pierre and Grand River, which you can read about in the Day Trips and Weekend Getaways chapter.

It's important to get information and a map at the visitor center before entering the grassland. Camping here is primitive, with no designated campgrounds or concessions. There are no established hiking trails and only one bike trail, but you can trek cross-country or follow a road or animal path.

Grassland regulations are different from those for a national forest: You can pick wildflowers and hunt for rocks, and it's illegal to remove or disturb only the vertebrate fossils. You can dig for agate southwest of Kadoka and east of the old town of Conata, too; the exact sites are on the map.

If you drive in (four-wheel drive or high-clearance vehicles are recommended), stay on the roads and close all gates behind you. Don't disturb the cattle. Don't cross private land without prior permission, and do be aware that it's hard to identify that land without a map.

You'll need to pack everything in with you and pack it back out. Take plenty of water, and watch your campfire; this is semiarid, windy country. The folks at the visitor center ask that you use common sense about fires, and they'll tell you if fire danger is high while you are there.

The grasslands are home to many wildlife species. You might see pronghorn antelope, deer, meadowlarks, sharp-tailed grouse, hawks and eagles, badgers and weasels, fox, and prairie dogs. Watch out for prairie rattlers, too. For advice on handling wildlife encounters, see the Natural World chapter.

Remember that you're miles from anywhere and possibly from anybody. If your vehicle becomes stuck in wet clay after a rain or you get into trouble, help is a long way off. Use common sense and lots of caution.

The best approach to the grasslands is to drive into one of the vast Buffalo Gap areas and park your car. Get out and look around. This is your exercise in subtlety. Take close looks at everything. This country will not shout at you or perform for your benefit; it's up to you to pay attention. If you're used to smaller, closer landscapes, all that treeless vastness may unnerve you at first.

You're not likely to see other people or vehicles, an exhilarating experience in itself. The wind may be ferocious, the sky an extraordinarily blue bowl above you, but the silence is the best of all. Listen—

The best time to take pictures in the Badlands is when the sun is low in the sky and the softer light enhances the color in the rock formations. The harsher light of midday makes them appear almost white.

---

you won't hear a freeway, siren, or radio, only the sound the wind makes as it rushes past. The grass ripples like the ocean, prairie surf without roar or spray but comparable in majesty and beauty.

Prairie Homestead
Highway 240, Philip
(605) 433-5400
www.prairiehomestead.com

You'll experience something rare at this original 1909 sod dugout: an authentic sense of life on a prairie homestead, with all of its hardships and rewards. It's not hard to imagine the covered wagon coming to a stop at this spot, to picture Ed and Alice Brown and their son, Charles, newly arrived from Nebraska, scanning the landscape and saying, "Yes, here. This is home."

The family dug a hole into a low hillside, plowed bricks from the hard soil, and built themselves a sod house with a kitchen and a bedroom. Later, they dug a root cellar, built a chicken coop and barn, and moved a wooden claim shack into place beside the "soddie"—then they had a proper parlor where they could relax and entertain their neighbors.

Ed Brown died in 1920, but Alice stayed on the homestead with Charles until 1934, when she moved to California. The sod house was last occupied by bachelor George Carr until 1949, and then, abandoned, it started to decay. But in 1962 Keith Crew (who never lived more than 2 miles from the site) and his wife, Dorothy, started restoration work on the place. Today you can tour the grounds and authentically furnished buildings (still owned by the Crew family) at your own pace while prairie dogs scamper and scold, chickens roam and peck in the sweet-

smelling grass, and the calls of songbirds drift on the air like voices from the past. Take it all in, and you'll understand why the Browns and thousands like them were willing to sacrifice creature comforts to build a life on the Great Plains.

Prairie Homestead was entered into the National Register of Historic Places in 1974, and numerous prestigious publications carried articles about it—many of them are posted on the wall outside the gift shop. The shop has an excellent assortment of books about prairie life, featuring collections of Laura Ingalls Wilder, Willa Cather, and Mari Sandoz.

The homestead, which is 2 miles south of I-90, exit 131, is open for tours during daylight hours between mid-April and mid-October. Admission prices are $4.00 for adults, and $3.25 for seniors 62 and older and youths ages 11 to 17. Children 10 and younger get in free.

Wild West Historical Wax Museum
601 Main Street, Wall
(605) 279-2915

From Sitting Bull and the Sundance Kid to John Wayne and the James Gang, the displays here tell the ripsnortin' version of western history. You'll meet famous outlaws such as Billy the Kid as well as some whose names might be less familiar, like Clay Allison. But there are "good guys" in this hall of fame, too, including "Little Sure Shot" Annie Oakley, courageous Sacagawea, and a trusty Pony Express rider. Signs and taped narratives give lots of details about each of the 50 wax figures (although historians might take issue with a couple of pieces of information). You can see displays of barbed wire, antique cavalry swords, silver dollars, old photos, and more. There's a gift shop with jewelry, souvenirs, books, and CDs.

The museum is open from early May until mid-October or later. Summer hours are 8:00 A.M. to 8:00 P.M. Admission (which also gets you a coupon for post-tour free popcorn) is $4.50 for adults ages 16 to 61, $4.00 for seniors 62 and older, $2.50 for youths 6 to 15, and free for kids 5 and younger. Inquire about discounts for groups of 10 or more.

KIDSTUFF

Badlands National Park

Junior Ranger Program
Badlands National Park
(605) 433–5361
www.nps.gov/badl
Summer programs for kids ages 5 to 8 and 9 to 12 allow youngsters to learn about the fascinating Badlands in entertaining ways.

By purchasing a Junior Ranger booklet at Ben Reifel Visitor Center, kids are on their way to adventure. Once they complete the book, which usually takes a couple of hours, and have it signed by a park ranger, they receive a free certificate and badge. Booklets cost $1.50.

Ask at the visitor center about other summer kids' programs. Discovery hikes, games, and other activities are offered on certain days.

Nearby

Wall Drug
510 Main Street, Wall
(605) 279–2175
www.walldrug.com
You're not afraid of a little dinosaur, are you? Well, how about a big one? For a roarin' good time, visit the (mechanical) *T. rex* in the Back Yard at Wall Drug—he speaks his mind about every 15 minutes. Less intimidating are the 6-foot rabbit, Singing Sam the Gorilla Man, and a hitch of singing reindeer. A tepee from the movie *Dances with Wolves* and a video arcade offer hands-on fun. The Back Yard closes for the winter, but there's lots more stuff inside. Read all about Wall Drug, where admission is free, in the close-up in this chapter.

ACCOMMODATIONS

With all the fascinating things to see and do in and around Badlands National Park, you may need a place to stay for a night or two, or even longer. Several good motels are listed below. Major credit cards are accepted.

PRICE CODE

Prices are for double occupancy during the peak season—generally, June, July, and August. Inquire about off-season rates and senior discounts.

$	Less than $50
$$	$51 to $75
$$$	More than $75

Badlands National Park

Cedar Pass Lodge   **$–$$$**
Cedar Street, Interior
(in Badlands National Park)
(605) 433–5460
www.cedarpasslodge.com
An unobstructed view of the open prairie, rocky spires, and deep canyons of the Badlands is the primary feature of these 24 cabins in the eastern end of the park. Aside from two primitive campgrounds operated by the National Park Service, these modest lodgings are the only accommodations within park boundaries. The lodge operators—a private company that manages marinas, inns, and resorts in national parks across the country—assume that you'll spend most of your time exploring the park, not holed up in your room. Subsequently, the cabins are furnished with little more than the bare essentials: twin beds, air-conditioning, a sink, and a bathtub. Of course, amenities matter little when you realize that there's nowhere else in the world where you can wake up to the deep pink and purple hues of a Badlands sunrise, accompanied by the sounds of a western meadowlark or mountain bluebird. Also on-site at the

lodge are a small restaurant (see the listing later in this chapter), pay phones, a gift shop, and a cottage with a full kitchen that sleeps up to 10 guests. Pets are allowed, but there is a $5.00 fee. The entire lodge, including the restaurant, closes down in mid-October and doesn't open again until early May; the exact dates depend on weather. The complex is located 5 miles from the park's Northeast Entrance off Highway 240.

Nearby

Ann's Motel $$
114 Fourth Avenue, Wall
(605) 279-2501

Twelve clean, cozy units and more than the usual amenities make this a home-away-from-home kind of place. Whether you choose two double beds or one queen, you get a small refrigerator, microwave, coffeepot, phone, and remote cable TV in your room. Add a tub-shower combo and you've got all the basics and then some. Pets are allowed, but you can't leave them alone in your room.

Badlands Budget Host Motel $
Highway 377, Interior
(605) 433-5335, (800) 388-4643
(800) BUD-HOST

The 21 units here are simply appointed but adequate and reasonably roomy, and you can choose either two double beds or two queen-size. If a hot soak is on your list of must-dos, ask for a room with a tub-shower combination; some have a shower only. You won't have a phone in your room, but you will have a coffeepot, and there is a pay phone you can use. There's also a laundry at your disposal and a restaurant that serves simple, all-you-can-eat breakfasts and suppers. The motel shares the grounds with Badlands Interior Campground, which is listed in the Campground section of this chapter.

Open from May 1 to September 31, the motel is near the Interior Entrance to Bad-

lands National Park, on the southeast end of the park and the north end of Interior.

Best Western Plains Motel $$-$$$
712 Glenn Street, Wall
(605) 279-2145, (800) 528-1234

You'll get the royal treatment at this sparkling-clean place, where the beds come in either king- or queen-size. Best of all, you can choose family accommodations with two beds in a separate room for the kids. All 74 rooms have a tub-shower combination, coffeepot, phone, and TV with movie channel. There's a heated outdoor swimming pool and a game room. The lobby has free coffee and a gift shop with clothing and western gifts. Pets are allowed, and plenty of nonsmoking rooms are available.

Super 8 Motel $$
711 Glenn Street, Wall
(605) 279-2688, (800) 800-8000

This attractive, 29-room motel has a couple of outstanding features: a wheelchair-accessible room and extra-long double beds. (You can get a queen-size bed if you prefer.) Nonsmokers will appreciate the availability of smoke-free rooms. Other comforts include free local calls, cable TV with Showtime, tub-shower combinations, and free coffee in the lobby during the morning and evening. Babies have the use of a free crib and are welcome, but pets are not.

CAMPGROUNDS

Badlands National Park has two campgrounds with minimal amenities, plus backcountry camping opportunities for the strong of heart and back (see the Recreation section later in the chapter). Regardless of your camping preferences, it's important to keep in mind that campfires are not allowed anywhere in the park. If you plan to cook, bring along a camp stove or, if you're staying in a campground, a small charcoal grill. The same arid conditions that make fire such a hazard also make drinking water essential, and unless you stay at Cedar Pass Campground, which has potable water, make sure you take a good supply with you.

Group camping is available in Cedar Pass Campground for $2.50 per person, with a minimum fee of $25.00 per night. Groups must have a designated leader and make advance reservations by writing to Group Camping, Badlands National Park, P.O. Box 6, Interior, 57750, faxing (605) 433-5404, or calling (605) 433-5235 or (605) 433-5361. Otherwise, campsites are available on a first-come, first-served basis; for information call (605) 433-5361.

Private campgrounds are available outside the park, and you'll find two shady ones listed here. Both are just a short distance away.

Badlands National Park

Cedar Pass Campground
Highway 377, Interior
(605) 433-5361

About 100 sites are available for tents and RVs. You won't find hookups here, but the restrooms have flush toilets and electricity. When winter comes, however, the restrooms (and the RV dump station) are closed, but if you're a diehard camper, you'll gladly make do with pit toilets. Running water is available year-round from a spigot near the group loop area (which is the only section of the campground open during the winter). On hot days you'll welcome the relative shade of the covered picnic tables.

Stays are limited to 14 days and cost $10.00 per night during the summer, $8.00 during the off-season, which usually runs from sometime in October (depending on the weather) until May.

The campground is a short distance south of Ben Reifel Visitor Center and is well marked.

Sage Creek Primitive Campground
Sage Creek Rim Road
(605) 433-5361

There's no charge for your stay of up to 14 days here. Presently, there are unlimited sites to pitch a tent or park an RV, but the only comforts are picnic tables and two pit toilets. Be sure to bring your own water. The campground, which is 10 miles west of the park's Pinnacles Entrance, offers a semiwilderness experience without the hazards of more remote places, plus it's a good starting point for treks into Badlands Wilderness Area, listed later.

There are two areas with tie-offs for horse camping. Ask at the visitor centers for information and a brochure explaining horse regulations.

Nearby

Badlands Interior Campground
Highway 377, Interior
(605) 433-5335, (800) 388-4643

This modest little campground is surrounded by great views of the Badlands in all directions, and a generous sprinkling of trees and grass provides a nice contrast to the stark moonscape. Some 60 sites for tents and RVs, a swimming pool, playground, laundry, restrooms with showers, small convenience store, an arcade, and a restaurant serving basic breakfasts and suppers for a small charge take care of your basic needs when you're not out roaming. Full and partial hookups and a dump station are available. There are also two air-conditioned camping cabins and a 21-unit motel, which is described in the Accommodations listed earlier. If you're interested in an extended stay, the friendly owners let out a handful of mobile-home units. Be sure to inquire well before the summer season, however, because they get reserved quickly.

The basic camping rate for two people is $11.50, with an additional charge for hookups. Cabins are $29.95 with air-conditioning. The campground is open from May 1 until September 31 and is on the north end of Interior, a short drive from the park's Interior entrance.

CLOSE-UP

Wall Drug

The signs are everywhere. Paris. Vietnam. The North Pole. And of course you'll see the signs for miles along I-90 long before you get to the town of Wall in western South Dakota: ALL ROADS LEAD TO WALL DRUG. SHOOTIN' GALLERY, WALL DRUG. WALL DRUG OR BUST. And the most famous sign of all, the one that got things started: FREE ICE WATER.

It was a sweltering summer day in 1936 when Dorothy Hustead told her husband, Ted, that hot and thirsty travelers on the nearby highway would stop at their store, a pharmacy and soda fountain, if they knew they could get a free drink of ice water there. To spread the word, Dorothy said, they should post a series of signs along the road. Tourists have been flocking to Wall Drug ever since, and the business now takes up an entire city block, forming the heart of Wall (population about 900)—and still giving away ice water 361 days a year. (It's closed on Thanksgiving, Christmas, New Year's Day, and Easter.)

Wall Drug (officially, Wall Drug Store, Inc.) is still a Hustead family business, too. Now it's in the capable hands of Ted and Dorothy's grandsons, Teddy and Rick—the third generation. But what's the big attraction?

If Wall Drug had been founded 10 years ago rather than deep into the dirty 1930s, it would be nothing more than a big roadside tourist trap. However, its Depression-era roots, combined with some hokey western enthusiasm, give the store (which can just as easily be called an attraction) an almost irresistible appeal. Where else in the world can shelves of blue jeans and racks of leather chaps sit side by side with boxes full of tacky plastic snakes and rubber tomahawks?

But if shopping for turquoise jewelry and snow globes isn't your thing, not to worry. There's the Travelers Chapel (with antique stained glass), a poorly mechanized Cowboy Orchestra, and concrete dinosaurs to keep you entertained. Or, if you're in the minority of visitors who are really there for medicine, you can talk to a pharmacist and obtain any number of prescription or over-the-counter products.

Although visitors almost never tire of poking around to discover the latest cheap souvenir, they rarely leave without a visit to the Western Art Gallery Cafe. Its wooden walls are crowded with original western paintings, antique cowboy gear, and the brands of many area ranchers. The cafe serves any number of home-

Badlands/White River KOA
Highway 44, Interior
(605) 433-5337, (800) 562-3897
With more than 700 shade trees, this is a cooling, restful place to come home to after a day spent exploring under a searing Bad-

lands sun. Situated on the south bank of the White River, the campground has 56 grassy tent sites (six with water and electricity), 81 RV sites (38 with full hookups, 43 with water and electricity), and 8 camping cabins. A swimming pool, playground, nine-

A jackalope greets visitors at the Wall Drug Store. SOUTH DAKOTA TOURISM

style dishes, from simple buffalo burgers and BLTs to steak dinners and homemade apple pie. Traditionalists will appreciate the authentic soda fountain and the stainless-steel tub and ladle in the corner, where visitors still serve themselves free cups of ice water.

The best part of the cafe, however, is the doughnuts. Locals swear by them. The dining room is filled with area ranchers and businessmen in the early morning hours, and almost all of them start their day with a cup of five-cent coffee and a couple of these cholesterol-laden pastries, which come plain, maple iced, or chocolate iced. Feel free to take a dozen back home with you, but know this: They taste much better if you heat them up a little bit first.

Wall is 50 miles east of Rapid City along I-90 and 8 miles north of the Pinnacles Entrance to Badlands National Park on Highway 240 (the Badlands Loop Road). But approach from any direction, and we guarantee you won't have any trouble finding Wall Drug—all signs point that way. Once there, be sure to stop by the drug counter or the checkout stand in the souvenir department and ask for, you guessed it, a free WALL DRUG sign.

hole minigolf course, and game room provide recreation, but you might find yourself perfectly content to simply lap up the peace and quiet at this "oasis in the Badlands," as it calls itself. Showers, laundry facilities, and a dump station are provided, and a convenience store sells groceries, supplies, and souvenirs. A modestly priced pancake breakfast is available.

The campground is open from April 15 to October 15. Rates for two adults start at $18 per night for a tent site and $23 for

Visitors gaze at the 244,000-acre moonscape of Badlands National Park. SOUTH DAKOTA TOURISM

an RV site; hookups are extra. A night in a cabin costs $34. Campers ages five and younger stay for free.

The campground is 4 miles southeast of Interior.

RECREATION

Many who visit Badlands National Park are "windshield" tourists, folks who like to view the scenery from the comfort of their vehicles but who never get out and explore. Such visitors are missing out on the best part, as the enticing recreational opportunities in the listings below demonstrate.

This section deals only with the park because, Wall Drug notwithstanding (see the close-up in this chapter), that's the main attraction in this part of the country. Here we give information on hiking, back-

packing, and horseback riding. If you bring your bicycles, you'll be required to stay on the paved and unpaved roads; bikes are not allowed in the park's backcountry or on hiking trails. Climbing in the park is limited to scrambling, since the soft, crumbly rock that makes up Badlands cliffs won't support standard climbing gear.

The following advice applies to any remote area, but especially to the Badlands. First, take a compass and topographic map (available for around $10 at park visitor centers) whenever you venture away from the roads. Weather changes very quickly here in any season; in fact, temperatures have been known to jump or drop 40 degrees or more in a single day, windchill notwithstanding. Be prepared with equipment and clothing. Beware of any trails after a good rain, as the soft, clay-ridden earth is prone to become a sticky mud called gumbo, which is infamous for trapping both car tires and hiking boots. Most important, take your own water, and lots of it—at least a gallon per person per day. Most of the creek beds here are dry, but even when they flow the water in them is too chalky to filter. And, as always, if you pack it in, pack it out.

Hiking and Backpacking

BADLANDS NATIONAL PARK HIKING TRAILS

A number of mostly short, mostly easy trails are accessible from Badlands Loop Road in the park's North Unit— this well-traveled route and the wheelchair-accessible Fossil Exhibit Trail are covered in the Attractions section of this chapter.

Other popular trails include the half-mile Cliff Shelf Nature Trail, which meanders along a dirt track interspersed with wooden stairs and takes you through a cool, fragrant bower of Rocky Mountain junipers. At the end of the 600-yard-long Door Trail, it's not too hard to block out traffic noise and imagine the vast, bleak silence that greeted early denizens and explorers in the Badlands. Both of these trails, which are north of the Ben Reifel Visitor Center, have self-guiding brochures available.

To the west of the visitor center is Saddle Pass Trail. A mere two-tenths of a mile long, it's still a demanding climb from the base of the Badlands Wall, and you'll want to be in good condition before you attempt it. Make sure you carry your water bottle and camera in a pack, because the trail is covered with a layer of loose, crumbly soil and you'll need to use your hands when the scrambling gets tough, especially on the way down. But your effort will be rewarded by a terrific view at the top. You might want to keep going by picking up the Castle Trail (you

Pets must be on a leash or otherwise under physical control of their owners at all times in Badlands National Park. Pets are not allowed at all in the Badlands (Sage Creek) Wilderness Area.

can go east or west) or the Medicine Root Loop, which heads east for 2 miles and leads you back to the Castle Trail. The Castle Trail links the Badlands Loop Road (from the Door Trail parking lot) and the Fossil Exhibit Trail and can be done as a 5-mile, end-to-end excursion through badlands and prairie or taken in sections. Free maps available in the park will help you decide.

BADLANDS (SAGE CREEK) WILDERNESS AREA

If you've ever longed to experience the prairie the way its early inhabitants did, here is a place to realize that dream. Few visitors venture into this panoramic paradise, making it an ideal place to escape civilization—a plus when you're seeking solitude, a potential hazard if you run into trouble. At 64,144 acres, this is the nation's largest prairie wilderness, a home on the range to bison, pronghorn antelope, eagles, and other wild creatures. Although mixed-grass prairie dominates, you'll also find barren badlands formations to explore.

Vehicles are not allowed here, and the only trails are those of the bison. (You can leave your car at Sage Creek Primitive Campground.) You don't need a permit to hike or camp in this territory, but park officials recommend checking in with a ranger at Ben Reifel Visitor Center and signing a backcountry register before you head into the trackless wilds. Registers can be found at Conata Picnic Area off Badlands Loop Road, Rodeo Point Overlook off Sage Creek Rim Road (ask for directions), and Sage Creek Campground. Camping is prohibited within a half mile of any road or trail, and your campsite must not be visible from a road. Also, be sure to stay clear of bison trails when making camp, since the giant creatures are not likely to make a detour—after all, they were here first.

And make this your mantra: "No open fires." They are absolutely forbidden in Badlands National Park.

Horseback Riding

Horses are allowed throughout the park except on marked trails and roads or in developed areas. Horses usually don't like Badlands water any better than do humans (for whom it's not safe), so it's wise to pack at least five gallons of drinking water for your horse each day, along with your own gallon. You can park your horse trailer at an overlook or parking area if you just want to ride around the Badlands for the day; if you're staying overnight, you'll find Sage Creek Primitive Campground equipped for horse camping. See the Campgrounds section above as well as the Horse Camps section of the Campgrounds chapter for information about camping with your equine. Also check under Trail Rides and Pack Trips in the Recreation chapter to find out about commercial expeditions into the Badlands. Backcountry camping and grazing are allowed (remember, no campfires), but check with park rangers for the latest regulations. They can also tell you where to buy certified weed-free hay, the only kind allowed in the park.

RESTAURANTS

It would be hard to visit the Badlands and not work up an appetite. There are plenty of places serving good food throughout the area. Unless otherwise noted, major credit cards are accepted.

PRICE CODE

Prices are for two dinners not including appetizers, drinks, dessert, tax, or tip.

$	Less than $15
$$	$15 to $30

Badlands National Park

Cedar Pass Restaurant   **$$**
1 Cedar Street, Interior (in Badlands National Park)
(605) 433-5460
The first things you're likely to notice when you enter the dining room are the huge windows along two walls. Since you seat yourself, you can pick the booth or table with the view you want. The house specialty is Indian tacos (made with meat for dinner or scrambled eggs for breakfast), but trout and grilled halibut sound equally irresistible after a day of vigorous exploring. Sandwiches, buffalo burgers, steaks, chops, and ribs also are among the choices. You can have bottled beer or a glass of wine with your meal, but not a smoke.

The restaurant serves breakfast, lunch, and dinner daily from around April 1 until October 31. It's on Highway 240, 5 miles from the park's Northeast Entrance.

Nearby

Cactus Cafe and Lounge   **$$**
519 Main Street, Wall
(605) 279-2561
Steaks and Mexican entrees such as Butch's Barnbuster—a large burrito smothered in green-chili gravy—are the specialties at this cafe, which has been run by three generations of the Beach family for more than 40 years. (It's been in existence much longer than that, though.) Other choices include daily specials and a soup, salad, and fruit bar (although it's not available during the winter). There's ordi-

nary fare such as chicken strips, sandwiches, fish, and pasta, but you'll also find veggie burgers and, among the appetizers, breaded gizzards. Carrot cake and homemade pies appear on the dessert list.

The decor is simple but dressed up a bit with brick arches and hanging planters. In the lounge, which has a full bar (plus a pool table and other diversions), there's a mural depicting scenes of early prairie life, including the building of the railroads. The cafe serves breakfast, lunch, and dinner daily all year.

Elkton House Restaurant $-$$
203 South Boulevard, Wall
(605) 279-2152

Low-fat and low-calorie items distinguish this eatery. You'll have to ask for them, but nonfat sour cream, zero-cholesterol margarine, low-fat salad dressing, and steamed seafood and chicken are available. The rest of the menu is a mix of typical chicken sandwiches and grilled fish along with more distinctive dishes including buffalo burgers. The restaurant ages all of its own beef for steaks. There's a soup and salad bar, too. Bottled beer is available.

Elkton House serves breakfast, lunch, and dinner daily, year-round.

Wall Drug $
510 Main Street, Wall
(605) 279-2175
www.walldrug.com

This legendary attraction—known for free ice water and nickel coffee—has cafeteria service and a cafe with seating for more than 500. The fare is simple—burger baskets, soup and sandwiches, and the like—but wine is available. Breakfast, lunch, and dinner are served daily all year; during the summer a sub shop and restaurant serving low-fat food are open in the Back Yard. Although the food services here do a brisk business, there's far more to Wall Drug than you can imagine. See the close-up in this chapter to learn more.

RECREATION

The Black Hills are relatively isolated in the center of North America, separated from the nearest major population centers (Sioux Falls, Billings, and Denver) by several hundred miles. While that means that there's very little urban culture here, there are also very few urban problems—overcrowding, traffic jams, pollution, and high crime rates are unheard of. Unfortunately, good paychecks are also rare. The average salary in South Dakota is among the lowest in the nation, and Black Hills residents take bigger hits to their pay stubs than their counterparts east of the Missouri. So why do people continue to make the Black Hills their home?

Because people who choose to live and work here are content to take some of their pay in trees. They consider the 1.2-million-acre national forest in their backyard, and all the recreational opportunities that come with it, as part of their salary—a fringe benefit, perhaps. Locals spend their weekends hunting out new trails and mountain streams, getting acquainted with hidden forest service roads, and fishing or cross-country skiing in that beautiful, isolated spot passed on by a friend or family member. They never get bored, since there's always something new: National parks annex more land, new hiking trails are developed, new attractions open and others rebuild, and once-developed property is reclaimed, reforested, and returned to the Black Hills.

Hiking, biking, horseback riding, skiing, and snowmobiling on the hundreds of miles of trails that belong to the Hills are probably the area's most popular activities. You'll find some of them listed in this book, but the list is by no means exhaustive. For more information and detailed maps, check with forest and park service officials at any ranger station or visitor center, and look for any number of specialized books at local book and gift stores.

If staying on dry land isn't your idea of a good time, turn to the Boating and Fishing sections in this chapter for a preview of recreational waters. There are more than a dozen lakes, all of them man-made, and more than 300 miles of streams at your disposal. You'll find information about licensing regulations in the appropriate sections.

With additional sections on ballooning, climbing, golf, horseback riding (including commercial trail rides), hunting, jeep tours, skiing, swimming, and even skydiving, you might conclude (correctly) that this chapter is heavily weighted toward outdoor activities. However, notice the sections on bowling, roller-skating, and organized sports and other indoor recreation possibilities. And be sure to check the Spectator Sports chapter to find out where to see others competing in the games you love to watch.

We've provided information about where and how to get rental equipment for many of the activities listed here. Some rentals have to be reserved ahead of time. Even when it's not necessary, though, it's a good idea to call in advance so you have a better chance of getting what you need. Refer to the Shopping chapter if you've arrived minus some vital piece of gear or clothing.

Many activities on public land have their own set of regulations; before heading out, reference the appropriate recreation or park section in this book, or contact the park or ranger station that applies to your plans. However, there are a few all-inclusive guidelines to keep in mind before engaging in any outdoor pastime in the Black Hills.

Fires are allowed only in grates in designated campgrounds; if the year has been really dry, there may be a ban on even those fires (check with the forest service for information). Violations aren't taken lightly, especially after the rash of western wildfires in the late 1990s and early 2000s, which included major blazes that threatened Lead, Deadwood, Jewel Cave National Park, and the Black Elk Wilderness Area.

Watch for wildlife wherever you are, and keep your distance. Be especially watchful for bison. They are unpredictable animals, particularly during the rut, or mating season, and the only difference between being hit by a one-ton pickup going 35 mph and a bison is that the truck doesn't have two horns.

The weather in the Black Hills and Badlands is wildly unpredictable. Snow can fall in any month, although summer afternoons are more likely to yield thunderstorms that can produce high winds, lightning, flash floods, and softball-size hailstones. Snowfall in the northern hills averages 150 inches a year. Temperatures can vary by 40 degrees or more on a single day, due partly to an elevation range of 3,200 feet to 7,200 feet. Wear layers, and be prepared.

The rules in the Black Elk Wilderness Area are especially strict. No motorized equipment or transportation, and anything packed in must be taken out. It's a good idea to follow the latter rule no matter where you are. If we all practice zero-impact principles, the beauty of the Black Hills will endure for generations to come.

BALLOONING

What could be prettier than sunrise over the Black Hills? And what finer way to experience it than at a leisurely pace in a hot-air balloon? Most people choose this activity during the summer, but in winter you have the advantage of beating the windchill factor as you travel at the same speed as the breeze. Whatever time of year you go ballooning, dress in layers so you can make adjustments. And plan to be up before dawn—balloons fly mostly during the calm of early morning.

Central Hills

Dakota Balloon
3758 Jolly Lane, Rapid City
(605) 393-8808

A balloon ride is just the thing to sweep you off your feet for a special occasion. David Hendrickson, a licensed commercial balloon pilot, instructor, and designated FAA examiner, specializes in what he calls "personal rides" for anniversaries, birthdays, marriage proposals, and other significant events. You might kiss the treetops, dip low in the wicker basket for a "splash and dash" into a pond, or rise to 10,000 feet on your hour-long flight over Rapid City and the foothills. Depending on the wind direction, you might head for the Hills or soar over the prairie or Ellsworth Air Force Base. Upon landing you'll toast each other with champagne and receive a certificate as a memento.

Rides are available during early mornings and evenings year-round, weather permitting, or you can arrange a "night flight," a glorious predawn excursion that lifts off in the dark and is guided back to Earth with the first rays of the sun. The price is $175 per person; call for night-flight prices. All rides include transportation back to the launch site. Weather conditions and other factors dictate the number of passengers, with a maximum of four.

Southern Hills

Black Hills Balloons
U.S. Highway 16 West, Custer
(605) 673-2520, (800) 568-5320
www.rapidnet.com/~balloons

Gain a new perspective as you leave Earth and drift at altitudes of 7,500 feet (2,100 feet above the ground) or more, for an hour or longer. Seen from aloft, pine-clad peaks, bison herds, elk, deer, Mount Rushmore, or Crazy Horse Memorial will leave an indelible impression. Any way the wind blows, your hot-air balloon ride will be an unforgettable experience—and since no two flights are identical, the owners guarantee that yours will be unique. When you touch down you'll follow tradition and mark the occasion with champagne, croissants, muffins, and cheeses. Plan on three hours to accommodate launch preparations, flight time, and the return van ride. Flights with experienced, licensed balloon pilots are available daily (weather permitting) between early May and the end of September and during the rest of the year by special arrangement. Five balloons with leather and wicker gondolas are available to carry 2 to 12 passengers, but reservations are needed for all flights.

The fare is $165 per child and $210 per adult. Black Hills Balloons is just outside the Custer city limits across from Pizza Hut.

BOATING

For a region with no natural lakes, we have an astonishing number of places to launch boats. Most popular are motorized pleasure boats and personal watercraft, but you'll also see sailboats, catamarans, fishing boats, paddleboats, canoes, kayaks, and rowboats.

Power boaters, water-skiers, sailers, and riders of personal watercraft are drawn to our largest lakes, all of which are accessible from U.S. Highway 385: Pactola Reservoir west of Rapid City, Sheridan Lake southwest of Rapid City, and Angostura Reservoir southeast of Hot Springs. All three have marinas where you can rent boats and buy supplies (see below).

Many smaller lakes are set aside for no-wake boating (less than 5 mph) to heighten the enjoyment of trollers, canoeists, and others seeking a slower-paced, more contemplative experience. Among them is popular Deerfield Lake, which is off Forest Service Road 17 northwest of Hill City.

Motors are allowed on Bear Butte Lake, near Sturgis off Highway 79, but they have to be less than 25 horsepower. Electric motors are allowed at Cold Brook

and Cottonwood Springs Reservoirs west of Hot Springs, but they're prohibited on the lakes in Custer State Park.

This list is not exhaustive; for more information call the forest supervisor's office at (605) 673-2251 or the state Game, Fish & Parks Department at (605) 394-2391. The department's annual *South Dakota Fishing Handbook* also contains information about boating regulations.

The Cheyenne River offers limited canoeing, although the water level is often too low during the summer and fall. There are no designated access points, but the lower end of Angostura Reservoir is a convenient launch site. Angostura itself is popular among sailboarders and sail boaters. The large surface area, consistently powerful winds, and two marinas make the lake one of the only appropriate venues for these sports in the state.

Any boat more than 12 feet long and all motorboats must be registered either in South Dakota or your home state. If you dock here, you need a South Dakota license, which is available from any county treasurer's office or the licensing office of the state Division of Motor Vehicles, 118 West Capitol Avenue, Pierre, SD 57501. Boats can be licensed for one to three years, and license fees range from $11 to $81.

Life jackets are mandatory, as are proper lights between sunset and sunrise. The following locations rent boats to the public.

Central Hills

Pactola Pines Marina
23060 Custer Gulch Road, Rapid City
(605) 343-4283

Pontoon boats can be rented for two hours or a full day. Rates depend on the size of the boat and day of the week; generally they range from $75 to $250. Fishing boats with six-horsepower motors are also available for rent, either hourly or daily; the rates range from $30 to $70.

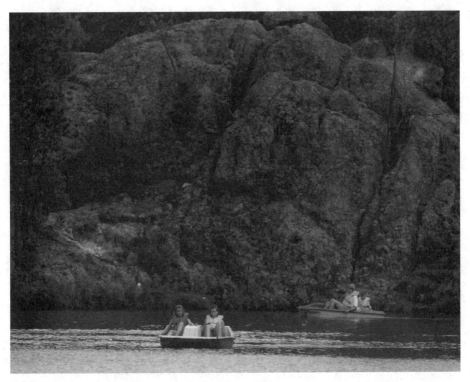

Boating on Sylvan Lake in Custer State Park. SOUTH DAKOTA TOURISM

Life jackets and instruction are included. A snack bar at the marina serves chicken, ice cream, and beverages.

The marina rents its 200-plus boat slips mostly by the season, but overnights can sometimes be accommodated with advance notice. Prices vary, so call for information.

The marina is on Pactola Reservoir's south shore. To get there, turn right off U.S. 385 at the Black Hills National Forest Visitor Center.

Sheridan Lake Marina
16451 Sheridan Lake Road, Rapid City
(605) 574-2169
www.sheridanlakemarina.com
Boats and recreational equipment can be rented here. Canoes that accommodate three to four people rent for $8.00 for the first hour, $5.00 an hour thereafter. Fourteen-foot, four-passenger aluminum fishing boats with outboard motors cost $25.00 for two hours, with reduced rates for additional time. Pontoons that can hold 8 to 10 people start at $70.00 for two hours. All rentals include fuel, life jackets, and other mandatory safety equipment. Call for age limits to rent various boats. The marina offers ice fishing in the winter.

About 4 of the approximately 70 boat slips are available for short-term rental at $10.00 a night; other prices vary, so call. The marina store with boat and equipment rentals is at the North Recreation Area, which is accessible from Sheridan Lake Road or U.S. 385. The marina is closed in March and October.

When it was built in 1927, the Custer Community Building at 644 Crook Street in Custer was reported to be the largest all-log building in the United States. Paid for with money raised by the Custer Women's Civic Club, it was dedicated by first lady Grace Coolidge. Now known as the Grace Coolidge Memorial Log Building, it is owned by the city and occupied by the Custer YMCA.

Southern Hills

Common Cents Marina
Angostura Reservoir
Off U.S. Highway 385, Hot Springs
(605) 745-6665
A 16-foot fishing boat and pontoons in two sizes can be rented here. Boat rental costs $100 per day. An 18-foot pontoon rents for $150 per day, while a 20-footer goes for $200. Life jackets and safety equipment are included, but you pay for your own gas. The minimum age for all rentals is 21.

Boat slips are available by the day, week, month, or season. Daily rates are $10; call for other rates. The marina is at the north end of the reservoir.

Custer State Park
Custer
(605) 255-4772, (800) 658-3530
www.state.sd.us/gfp
Paddleboats, rowboats, and one-person kayaks can be rented at Sylvan Lake and Legion Lake Resorts. Aquacycles and hydrobikes are also for rent. Call for prices.

BOWLING

Bowling is a serious sport for many Black Hills residents. Most of the bowling opportunities are in the Northern and Central Hills, and we've listed some.

Northern Hills

Bedrock Lanes
145 Glendale Drive, Lead
(605) 584-9013
There's a strong emphasis on youth league bowling here, but the 12 lanes of tenpins are open to everyone. Hours are noon to about 9:00 or 10:00 P.M. all week in winter and 6:00 to around 9:30 P.M. Monday through Friday in summer, and reservations usually are not needed. An arcade room, a pro shop selling equipment, a snack bar, a bar serving beer and wine coolers, and party facilities add to the amenities. You can bowl for $3.75 per game and rent shoes for $1.25. Lessons from a certified coach are available.

Buffalo Bill's Bowling
910 First Street, Sturgis
(605) 347-2741
Buffalo Bill's, formerly Key City Lanes, is a popular venue for Northern Hills league bowlers. Since league traffic can be heavy or light depending on the day of the week, it's a good idea to call ahead and ask how many of the 12 lanes are open at a given time. Friday nights will always be open, however, for Rockin' Bowl, a teen-oriented event that begins around 9:00 P.M. and lasts until midnight.

There is a full bar that serves snacks and a video game room. The lanes open around noon and close whenever demand tapers off, usually around 10:00 P.M. Games are $2.75 for adults and $1.75 for children under 15. Likewise, shoe rentals will cost grown-ups $1.25 a pair, while those 14 and younger pay half that much. Rockin' Bowl costs $8.00 for the three-hour event.

Lucky Strike Lanes
1740 Ryan Road, Spearfish
(605) 642-7367
League play is heavy at this six-lane bowling alley, especially in winter, so call ahead to check for available space. Your best bets for open bowling are Sunday from

noon to 6:00 P.M. and Saturday from noon to 10:00 P.M. Friday from 7:00 to 11:00 P.M. is Club Bowling, popular among the younger crowd for its neon lights and loud music. There are midweek student specials from Tuesday through Thursday from 9:00 P.M. until closing—call for details.

Hours vary, but generally Lucky Strike is open from noon to 10:00 P.M. daily. Rates vary, too, but during the times of heaviest play (after 6:00 P.M. and on weekends) games cost $2.50 and shoes cost 75 cents. Senior and student rates are available.

Central Hills

Meadowood Lanes
3809 Sturgis Road, Rapid City
(605) 343-5985
Meadowood is the Black Hills' busiest bowling venue. Its 36 lanes are packed all hours of the day, nearly every day of the year. In fact, the bowling alley used to be open 365 days a year, although it now may close for Christmas and Thanksgiving, depending on demand. Every other day of the year Meadowood is open from 9:00 A.M. to midnight. Leagues play from 5:00 to 9:00 P.M. almost every day of the week, and you can forget about open bowling anytime on Wednesday, Saturday morning and evening, and Sunday evening. The lanes are taken over late Friday and Saturday (sometime between 10:00 P.M. and 2:00 A.M.) by teenagers for Cosmic Bowling, an event marked by flashing neon and loud music. The event costs $12.00 per person and covers shoe rental and as many games as you can play. A regular game will run $3.10 per person, and shoes cost $2.00.

Facilities here include a lounge with a full bar, a full-service restaurant, pool tables, video games, and video lottery machines. For the serious bowler, the pro shop sells the accessories you need for your game, and there's an expert on hand to answer questions and make sure you get the right equipment.

Southern Hills

Winners Circle Lanes and Games
733 Jensen Drive (U.S. Highway 385 North), Hot Springs
(605) 745-5414
This medium-size facility claims some of the newest bowling equipment of any alley in the Black Hills. However, its primary distinguishing feature is that all 12 lanes are nonsmoking (smoking is only allowed at the full bar in the lounge, which is separated from the open public areas). A modest pro shop keeps bowling enthusiasts content, but the majority of patrons come to appreciate the full restaurant (which serves dishes like sirloin and prime rib), video game arcade, video lottery casino, and banquet room. Few visitors find their way here, so the staff can be a bit wary of strangers at first. Once they get to know you, however, they can be very hospitable.

Fees vary depending on events, ages, season, and times of day, but a game of open bowling will run $2.75 per person, and shoe rentals are $1.00. League action can be heavy in fall and winter, so call ahead to be sure there's a lane available. The facility opens at 9:00 A.M. It closes at midnight on Friday and Saturday and 10:00 P.M. every other night. Cosmic Bowling, complete with thumping music and neon, runs from 10:00 P.M. to midnight on Friday and from 8:00 to 10:00 P.M. on Saturday. The $10 admission covers all the bowling you can do in two hours.

CLIMBING AREAS

You'll find world-class rock climbing among our granite peaks and limestone outcroppings, and listed below are the areas most highly recommended by local climbers. There are specific guidebooks for some areas; a few of the titles are listed below.

Be aware that helicopter tours operate in the Hills during the summer (see the Attractions chapter), and climbers say the

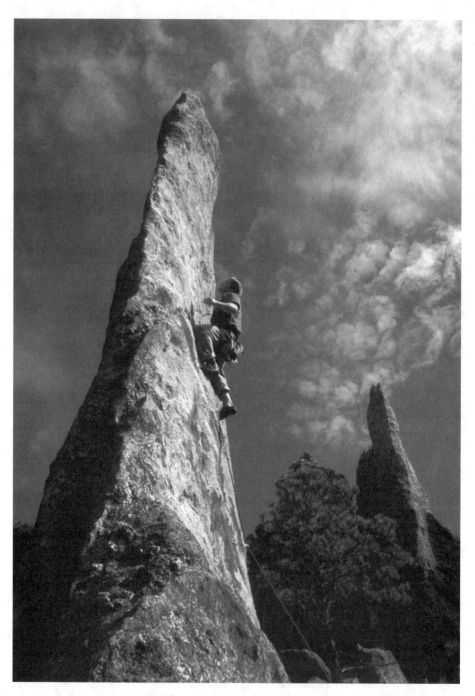

The Needles, fingerlike granite spires that rise from the forest floor, are a favorite destination for rock climbers. SOUTH DAKOTA TOURISM noise sometimes interferes with their communication. This is particularly true in the Cathedral Spires area of the Needles.

A growing number of rock climbers looking to expand their abilities are turning to ice climbing these days. Opportunities are limited here, but Spearfish Canyon (Bridal Veil Falls in particular) in the Northern Hills offers short, grade 1 climbs that are close to the road. The back side of Harney Peak, in the Black Elk Wilderness Area, develops 130-foot floes, but the area is hard to reach and you have to snowshoe in when the snow is deep. Also, there are no comprehensive guidebooks to tell you where to ice climb, so the best way to get information is to contact local climbing shops.

Northern Hills

Spearfish Canyon
U.S. Highway 14A, Spearfish
Spearfish Canyon's limestone palisades are becoming increasingly popular with climbers. These routes are primarily bolted sport climbs, requiring little in the way of your own hardware. No maps or guidebooks are available for this area, so you'll have to contact a climbing shop for information.

Central Hills

Falling Rock
Highway 44, Rapid City
Another bolted sport climbing area on a limestone ridge, Falling Rock is 3.1 miles west of Rapid City. Turn left (if you're coming from town) off Highway 44 onto Falling Rock Road, a dirt road where you'll find two parking areas a short distance apart, both on your left. Trails leading from the first parking area will take you to the top of the limestone cliff, and those leading from the second one go to the cliff base. Contact local climbing shops for information about routes.

Mount Rushmore Climbing Area
Highway 244, Keystone
The area northwest of the four famous faces has become increasingly popular among climbers. The routes along the granite here tend to be bolted. You can learn more about them in the *Mount Rushmore National Memorial Climber's Guide* by Vernon Phinney, which is widely available. You can park along the highway in any of several pull-offs between Horse Thief Lake (on Highway 244) and the monument. Recommended classic routes include Waves (5.6), Stardancer (5.8), Baba Cool (5.9), and Mr. Critical (5.11).

Southern Hills

The Needles
Highway 87, Custer State Park
Climbers popularized the granite spires along the Needles Highway (Highway 87) in the 1940s and 1950s, and this well-known area still offers traditional climbing as well as bolted routes. On many of them you'll have to pack various forms of hardware and place your own protection. The Needles area is recommended for more experienced climbers. Newer routes are not included in Paul Piana's comprehensive *Touch the Sky*, which was published in 1983; other titles include *Recommended Climbing Routes in the Needles of Custer State Park*, by John Page; *Black Hills Needles, Selected Free Climbs*, by Dingus McGee, and *Classic Rock Climbs No. 7 Devils Tower/Black Hills*, by John Harlin.

This area is within the boundaries of Custer State Park, and you'll need a park entrance license if you drive in. Parking is available along the highway from Sylvan Lake to the spires. Classic routes include Riddle (5.7), Tricouni Nail (5.8), and Nantucket Sleighride (5.10).

Wyoming

Devils Tower National Monument
U.S. Highway 24, Devils Tower
(307) 467-5283, (800) 354-6316
You'll find a wealth of information about Devils Tower in our Day Trips and Weekend Getaways chapter, but we include it here because it's one of North America's premier crack-climbing areas. *Devils Tower Monument National Climbing Book,* by Guilmette, Carrier, and Gardiner, lists more than 200 routes. Among the most popular are Durrance (5.7), Soler (5.7), Walt Bailey Memorial (5.9), and Matador (5.11). Climbers are asked to refrain from climbing here in June out of respect for Native American religious observances. However, many guide services ignore the voluntary ban.

CLIMBING LESSONS, EQUIPMENT, AND GUIDE SERVICES

If you need books, maps, gear, or information, don't hesitate to stop in at our local climbing shops, which are listed here. We also tell you where you can find lessons and guide services.

Central Hills

Granite Sports
301 Main Street, Hill City
(605) 574-2121
www.sylvanrocks.com
The helpful staff here is made up of experienced climbers. The shop is an excellent source for climbing gear and clothing, maps, guidebooks, and local climbing information. For lessons, guide service, and rentals, you can simply step around the corner to the climbing school.

Sylvan Rocks Climbing School & Guide Service
81 Elm Street, Hill City
(605) 574-2425
www.sylvanrocks.com

Started in 1989 by Black Hills native Susan Scheirbeck, Sylvan Rocks offers courses from entry level through advanced. The school is accredited by the American Mountain Guides Association, which has reviewed and approved its safety programs and operation procedures. Classes are available daily from May through October, weather permitting; you can sign up for a couple of hours or one to three days of instruction, and courses can include a climb to the summit of Devils Tower (see the listing above). Rates vary and include all the gear you need to learn the ropes. Reservations are strongly recommended.

Guide service, including guiding at the Tower, is available for climbers with solid technical skills who want to make optimal use of their climbing time. Climbing shoes can be rented.

CROSS-COUNTRY SKIING

The Black Hills' moderate altitudes and temperatures, combined with plenty of dry, powdery snow, provide just the right conditions for a satisfying, invigorating workout in a beautiful alpine setting. If you're feeling brave, you can strike out on your own and break trail in the Black Hills National Forest. The trails listed below are in the Northern Hills, where the snow is deepest and most dependable.

Northern Hills

Big Hill
Spearfish Ranger District
2014 Main Street, Spearfish
(605) 642-4622
(800) 445-3474 (conditions)
Beginners and experts alike will find something to match their skills on 16 miles of mostly groomed trails that wind through groves of aspen, pine, and spruce 8 miles south of Spearfish. The area is on forest service land but is maintained for skiing through an agreement with the

Northern Hills Cross-Country Ski Club, which pays for the grooming. The donation box at the trailhead is for that purpose. The popular Loop A1 is recommended for beginners; other trails are more challenging. The demanding Loops C and D cover a lot of ground and appeal mostly to accomplished skiers. C has the best overlooks, with views of dazzling Spearfish Canyon; a casual tour with time out for stops can easily take three hours. Maps are available at forest service ranger stations and at the trailhead.

To get to Big Hill, take Jackson Boulevard in Spearfish west, turn north onto Jonas Boulevard, and then turn west onto Oliver Street. Pass Pope & Talbot sawmill, turn south onto Forest Service Road 134, and go about 8 miles to the trailhead.

Deer Mountain Ski Area
U.S. Highway 85, Lead
(605) 584-3230
(888) 265-2197 (conditions)
www.skideermountain.com
About 10 miles (15 kilometers) of gently sloping, groomed trails wind through the woods, beginning near the base of the downhill slopes. You can ski from 9:00 A.M. until dark. You can also rent skis, poles, and boots at the ski lodge. Deer Mountain is open from approximately late November until about the end of March. It's closed Monday and Tuesday except during the Christmas season.

Eagle Cliff
Spearfish Ranger District
2014 Main Street, Spearfish
(605) 642-4622
(800) 445-3474 (conditions)
Approximately 23 miles of marked, ungroomed trails southwest of Cheyenne Crossing offer some of the finest skiing in the Hills. (Cheyenne Crossing is at the junction of U.S. Highways 85 and 14A on the south end of Spearfish Canyon.) The closest trail, Dead Ox, is about 4 miles from the crossing, with the nearest official trailhead (Bratwurst) and parking area another 3 miles down the road. Most of

It's against the law to damage, destroy, disturb, or remove any natural feature of the Black Hills National Forest. That means you can't take prehistoric artifacts home, collect wildflowers for commercial use without a permit, and so on. A good rule of thumb is, "Leave what you find."

these trails are easy to moderately difficult, but steep canyons and twisting turns test your mettle. If you're lucky enough to have two cars, you can park each in a different lot and enjoy a nice long trek without having to retrace a single glide of your skis. But the trails interconnect so that you can make a loop and wind up back at your starting point.

Sunny Meadow and Bratwurst are good trails for beginners and those with single vehicles. Eagle Cliff is a fairly easy trail, as well; Roller Coaster, Deep Snow, and Wipeout are more demanding. Dead Ox, the most popular trail in the system, gets twisty and steep, and Lily Park can be downright scary.

The forest service has made Eagle Cliff an official ski area, making it easier to maintain the trails and keep roadside parking areas plowed. Maps are available at forest service ranger stations, the Cheyenne Crossing Store, and the Bratwurst trailhead.

CROSS-COUNTRY SKI RENTALS
Northern Hills

Ski Cross Country
701 North Third Street, Spearfish
(605) 722-3851
All sorts of cross-country skiing equipment and clothing is for sale or rent here. Rental times and rates are flexible depending on your needs—call ahead for more information, or work out a deal with the operators when you arrive in town.

CYCLING

Many communities have recreational paths that are ideal for riding a bicycle, whether for fun or transportation. They're easy to spot, because they're almost always in use by cyclists, joggers, and walkers. If you're a mountain biker with a yen for the backcountry, keep reading: We've listed some local favorites. Don't bypass our back roads and cross-country ski trails (see the Cross-country Skiing section), which offer excellent riding, too.

Centennial Trail (No. 89)

Created in celebration of South Dakota's 100th birthday in 1989, the Centennial Trail stretches 111 miles down the length of the Black Hills, from Bear Butte State Park to Wind Cave National Park. Bikes are forbidden only on the sections in the Black Elk Wilderness and Wind Cave (see the Parks and Mountains chapter.) Alternate routes are available around the Black Elk Wilderness that add just a few miles to your trip—a trail map will help you choose your path.

Centennial Trail ends (or begins) in Wind Cave park, so avoiding the 6-mile stretch there is simply a matter of ending or beginning your trek at the park boundary. Along the trail you'll see lakes, streams, grasslands, dramatic rock outcroppings, and wildlife. There are more than two dozen well-marked trailheads and access points, some with night parking for extended trips. For complete information, consult the *Centennial Trail User's Guide,* which is widely available wherever you find brochures in the area.

Its length and accessibility make the Centennial Trail ideal for any style of trip—it's really just a matter of deciding where you want to start and where you want to end up. One section we recommend is the 10-mile stretch between Pactola Reservoir and Sheridan Lake. Start at the Rapid Creek trailhead at Pactola. From Highway 44 west of Rapid City go 2.1 miles south on U.S. 385, turn left onto gravel Pactola Basin Road, then go one-half mile to a four-way intersection, turn left, and park at the trailhead. Drop a second vehicle at Dakota Point trailhead by taking U.S. 385; go east 1.6 miles on Sheridan Lake Road southwest of Rapid City, turn right onto gravel Dakota Point Road (Forest Service Road 434), and go another 0.3 mile to the trailhead, which will be on your left. You can do this route in reverse if you want to.

Custer State Park
Custer
(605) 255-4515
www.custerstatepark.info

The park has trails that range from moderately difficult to difficult. The shortest goes through the 3-mile Grace Coolidge Walk-in Fishing Area, which runs between Center Lake and Grace Coolidge Campground, with a trailhead at either end. Three other trailheads—Iron Creek, Badger Hole, and French Creek—provide access to the 22 miles of Centennial Trail that thread through the park. The most difficult section, from Badger Hole to French Creek, is also the shortest at 4.2 miles. Less strenuous are the 7.3 miles between Iron Creek and Badger Hole, and the 10.3 miles from French Creek to the Wind Cave National Park border. Big Tree Robbers Roost Draw Trail makes a 10.5-mile loop that begins and ends at French Creek trailhead. Maps are available at Custer State Park visitor centers, but you can also ride on any trail or logging road in the park that isn't posted as closed.

See listings under Cycling—Tours and Rentals for information about where to find bicycles.

Deerfield Lake Loop Trail (No. 40L)

This easy 10-mile trail circles Deerfield Lake, which is not only scenic but gives you the added advantage of a place to take a cooling dip after, or during, your ride. Three campgrounds are a short distance from the trail—Dutchman, Whitetail, and Custer Trails—where you can refill your water bottle en route during the summer. Access points with free parking

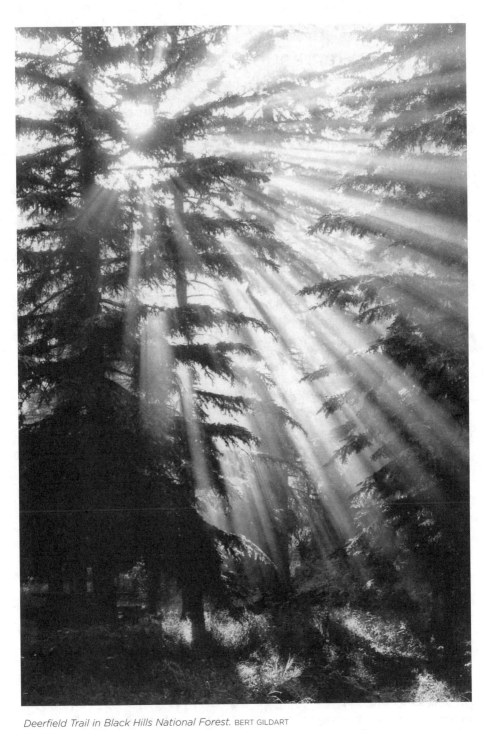

Deerfield Trail in Black Hills National Forest. BERT GILDART

Recreation Resources

RECREATION CENTERS

Here is a list of places to call for information about organized sports and other recreational opportunities in Black Hills communities. Also listed are public recreation centers with swimming pools, fitness equipment, and other facilities you can use for a daily fee. In some cases, the recreation center is also the place to call for information.

Northern Hills

Belle Fourche Area Community Center
1111 National Street, Belle Fourche
(605) 892-2467

Deadwood Recreation Center
105 Sherman Street, Deadwood
(605) 578-3729

Northern Hills YMCA
845 Miners Avenue, Lead
(605) 584-1113

Spearfish Parks, Recreation and Forestry
(Public Works Department)
625 Fifth Street, Spearfish
(605) 642-1333

Sturgis Community Center
1401 Lazelle Street, Sturgis
(605) 347-6513

Young Sports & Fitness Center
1200 University Street, Spearfish
(605) 642-6098

Central Hills

Hill City City Hall
324 Main Street, Hill City
(605) 574-2300

Hill City Youth Center
111 McGregor Street, Hill City
(605) 574-2010

Rapid City Recreation Department
235 Waterloo Street, Rapid City
(605) 394-4168

are Gold Run and Hilltop trailheads on the south side of the lake off F.S. 17 (also called Deerfield Road, which runs northwest from Hill City), and North Shore trailhead on the northwest side (follow F.S. 17 to Forest Service Road 461 and turn south). You can access the trail from Custer Trails Campground, too, but during the summer you'll pay a user or camping fee to leave your car there. The trail offers varied scenery from pine forest on the south side of the lake to an open meadow, known as Reynolds Prairie, on the north.

George S. Mickelson Trail (No. 104)
www.mickelsontrail.com
Named for the South Dakota governor who championed it and then met an untimely death in a 1993 plane crash, the Mickelson Trail is an abandoned railroad bed that has undergone a rails-to-trails transformation through the joint efforts of government agencies and local volunteers. Completed in 1998, the 10-foot-wide trail offers 114 miles of scenic beauty and gentle grades for nonmotorized recreation between Deadwood and Edgemont. Restored tunnels, trestles, and the ruins of section houses along the Rochford-to-Mystic stretch speak to its railroading past.

The Mickelson Trail is easily the most popular trail in the Black Hills, and with good reason. First off, it's accessible: There are 14 trailheads, each with parking and trail-pass vending machines, and all but one (White Elephant, between Custer and

Rapid City YMCA
815 Kansas City Street, Rapid City
(605) 342-8538

Southern Hills
Custer City Pool
Crook and Third Streets, Custer
(605) 673-3935 (summer)

Custer YMCA
644 Crook Street, Custer
(605) 673-3154 (school year)

Hot Springs City Hall
303 North River Street, Hot Springs
(605) 745-3135

FOREST SERVICE RANGER STATIONS

Here is a list of USDA Forest Service Ranger Stations where you can get information about the Black Hills National Forest. For general information, contact the

Forest Supervisor's Headquarters at R.R. 2, Box 200, Custer, SD 57730, or call (605) 673-2251.

Northern Hills
Spearfish/Nemo Ranger District
2014 North Main Street, Spearfish
(605) 642-4622
U.S. Highway 14A, Deadwood
(605) 578-2744

Central Hills
Pactola/Harney Ranger District
803 Soo San Drive, Rapid City
(605) 343-1567
23939 U.S. Highway 385, Hill City
(605) 574-2534

Southern Hills
Custer/Elk Mountain Ranger Districts
330 Mount Rushmore Road, Custer
(605) 673-4853

Pringle) have tables and vault toilets. Several trailheads are within the towns of Deadwood, Lead, Rochford, Hill City, Custer, Pringle, and Edgemont, giving riders and hikers access to food, water, lodging, entertainment, and bike equipment rentals. The trail is relatively easy. Since it was built on top of old railroad tracks, the grade is never steeper than 2 percent. And then there's the crown jewel of the trail: the landscape. The natural wonder of the land along the trail is spectacular, giving riders unparalleled views of bizarre granite rock formations, waterfalls, alpine meadows, wild berry patches, and vistas that stretch for miles. There's plenty of historical wonder, too. Telegraph poles, roundhouses, railroad signs, tunnels, rock bridges, stagecoach

stops, ghost towns, abandoned lumber mills, and ancient gold camps, some dating from the 1870s, are all easily visible from the trail. While some sites are off-limits on private land, other places can be explored on public property. Interpretive signs along the trail explain the sites' history.

This trail relies on small user fees to help with its upkeep. Those 12 and older are required to buy a daily ($2.00) or annual ($10.00) trail pass. Fees are payable at self-registration boxes and some businesses along the trail. No fee is required within city limits. Check out the Web site for great information and registration for the annual fall trail ride.

CYCLING—TOURS AND RENTALS

These Black Hills bike shops rent equipment and can direct you to nearby trails for memorable rides. Some offer guided tours.

Northern Hills

Deadwood Bicycles
180 Sherman Street, Deadwood
(605) 578-1345
www.deadwoodbicycles.com
Housed in Deadwood's 1890 Burlington engine house, Deadwood Bicycles couldn't be any closer to the Mickelson Trail; in fact, the trail runs right up to the front door. This modest shop sells bicycles and equipment, rents several types of bikes, and performs repair work. Next door is a trail visitor center that interprets Black Hills railroad history and tells the story of the Mickelson Trail's creation.

Latchstring Village All Season Sports Center
U.S. Highway 14A, Spearfish Canyon
(605) 584-2207, (800) 439-8544
www.spfcanyon.com
Mountain bikes and helmets can be rented here for a half or full day. Trails depart from the premises of Spearfish Canyon Resort.

Central Hills

Two Wheeler Dealer Cycle & Fitness
100 East Boulevard North, Rapid City
(605) 343-0524
www.twowheelerdealer.com
Here you can rent mountain bikes, kiddie carts, tandems, and car racks. Helmets are included with bike rentals; call for daily or extended rates.

Southern Hills

Custer State Park, Custer
(605) 255-4515
www.custerstatepark.info
You can rent mountain bikes for use in the park at Legion Lake Lodge, (605) 255-4521, during the summer. Rentals range from $8.00 to $35.00, and prices include a helmet. Reservations are recommended.

Trailside Bikes
35 Sixth Street, Custer
(605) 673-5526, (888) 673-2453
www.trailsidebikes.com
Suspension mountain bikes rent for $25 a day and solid-frame bikes for $22; half-day rentals are $22 and $18, respectively. All prices include a helmet and bike lock. Trailside Bikes also offers customized backcountry tours with optional support-and-gear wagon, food, camping gear, pickup, and delivery. A new feature is weeklong tours with the Mickelson Trail as the backbone for daily side trips. Tour prices vary. The shop is open from mid-May to mid-October. Bike sales and service are available.

FISHING

Around here, angling is a year-round activity. There are enough lakes and streams to satisfy all enthusiasts, whether they prefer to fish while standing on shore, sitting in a boat, crouched over a hole in the ice, tucked into a float tube, or slogging up to their wader tops in midstream.

Although trout aren't native to this area (having arrived by wagon in the 1880s), they're the main attraction for Black Hills anglers, along with walleye and largemouth bass. Most of our trout—brookies, browns, rainbows, and a brook-lake cross called splake found in Deerfield Lake—are spawned in our fish hatcheries. Nevertheless, some native reproduction is taking place, particularly among brook trout.

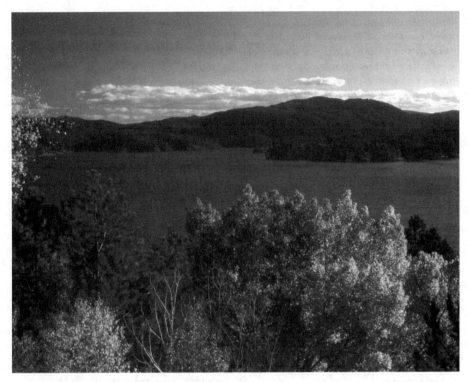

Pactola Reservoir provides ample opportunities for water recreation. SOUTH DAKOTA TOURISM

Walleye fishers tend to gravitate toward the warm waters of Angostura Reservoir near Hot Springs. Sheridan Lake southwest of Rapid City is a good place to cast for perch and northern pike. Colorful rainbow trout bite in Custer State Park's Sylvan Lake and in Spearfish Creek up north. And you'll find bass swimming in Pactola Reservoir west of Rapid City.

These are just a few of our excellent fishing holes. For a complete rundown, pick up a free copy of the Game, Fish & Parks Department's *South Dakota Guide to Public Fishing Waters,* which is available through license agents.

Speaking of licenses, you'll need one unless you're fishing at an attraction or campground where it's not required—you'll find those places listed in their respective chapters in this book. Licenses are available at sporting goods stores, convenience stores, and other businesses as well as at some county treasurers' offices. And don't forget about entrance fees at state parks and user fees at some lakes.

Daily and possession limits for trout have gotten stricter since a survey of local anglers showed they want to catch bigger fish. (Raising bigger fish in hatcheries means raising fewer of them.) Thus, the daily trout limit is five, with just one of those being 14 inches or longer. You're allowed to have no more than 10 trout in your possession—and that includes the ones back home in your freezer or packed in ice at your campsite—at any one time.

Limits are higher for other species, and you'll find all that information, along with regulations for organic bait, catch-and-release areas, and so forth, in the yearly *South Dakota Fishing Handbook* issued by Game, Fish & Parks. Make sure you get the current copy, which comes out around the first of the year.

Wheelchair-accessible fishing is available at Pactola Reservoir and at Strawberry Lake, which is off U.S. 385 south of Deadwood.

FISHING GUIDE SERVICES

Lessons and guided trips treat anglers to some of the best fly fishing in the region.

Northern Hills

Custom Caster
21207 Thunder Lane, Lead
(605) 584-2217
members.mato.com/bhangler
This one-man operation is locally known for custom rods, although the shop carries professionally manufactured rods, reels, flies, and tying accessories. Owner Dale Peters, a 40-year fishing veteran, performs repair work, and he conducts half-day or full-day guided fishing trips.

Central Hills

Dakota Angler & Outfitter
516 Seventh Street, Rapid City
(605) 341-2450, (888) 319-3474
www.flyfishsd.com
Everything here is geared toward fly fishing. The shop offers guided half- and full-day trips as well as fishing and fly-tying lessons. Trips cost from $165 to $275 and include transportation and lunch or a

snack. Reservations are required. The cost for lessons varies, so call for information. The shop sells equipment, clothing, gifts, and even artwork. You can rent a fly rod, reel, and waders.

GOLF

The beautiful landscape of the Black Hills has inspired countless outdoor enthusiasts, and golfers are no exception. Despite the brevity of summer, most Black Hills communities have their own small course, and Rapid City claims seven. And it's not unusual to see a few brave souls teeing off in December or January if warm chinooks have melted the snow and ice from the fairway.

All the courses below have pro shops, motorized and pull carts, club rentals, and grass greens. Most have policies about spikes and attire (which is usually pretty casual), so ask when you reserve your tee time. This list isn't exhaustive, but local parks departments (find their information in the gray box at the end of the chapter) can help you locate other courses.

Northern Hills

Spearfish Canyon Country Club
Intersection of U.S. Highways 14 and 14A
Spearfish
(605) 642-7156
www.spearfishcanyoncountryclub.com
The only 18-hole golf course in the northern Black Hills has a lot to recommend it, not the least of which is the historical integrity of its original nine holes (the front nine). You can play them today the same way golfers did in pre-heavy-equipment 1922, when the natural lay of the land dictated the design of greens and fairways. The views are beautiful, and at the eighth hole (par 3), which is situated on a ridge looking into the mouth of Spearfish Canyon, you're required to aim the ball through a narrow lane of tall pine trees.

Tee times are requested for the par 71, semiprivate course. You'll find bent-grass greens and a wide variety of elevation changes, plus an outdoor driving range, a Professional Golf Association (PGA) pro and teaching pro on staff, a full-service bar and restaurant, and a swimming pool.

In fall and winter, a round of 9 holes will run $15 and a round of 18 will cost $25. In spring and summer, fees jump to $20 and $36, respectively. A golf cart will cost $8.00 for a round of nine and $14.00 for the whole course per rider, irrespective of season. Rates will be higher on weekends and holidays, but there are twilight discounts for golfers who tee off after 4:00 P.M.

Tomahawk Country Club
U.S. Highway 385 South, Deadwood
(605) 578-9979, (605) 578-2080
You'll play on a true mountain course here, where five tee boxes are elevated to compensate for the rolling terrain. Two creeks run through the picturesque nine-hole course, making your game more challenging in spite of wide fairways. There are two par 5 holes for men and one for women, with a total par 36 for the 3,300-yard course. A practice range, full bar, and grill take care of your needs off the course. Open play means there's no need to reserve a tee time, but you do have to abide by the rules governing ladies' day, which begins at 2:00 P.M. on Wednesday, and men's day, which starts at 2:00 P.M. on Thursday.

The course opens as early as possible in the spring but for sure by May 1. It closes October 31. Hours are 7:00 A.M. until dark. Greens fees are $16 for 9 holes and $25 for 18. Carts are $12 for 9 holes, $21 for 18.

Tomahawk is 8 miles south of Deadwood.

Central Hills

Hart Ranch Golf Course
23759 Arena Drive, Rapid City
(605) 341-5703
www.hartranch.com

Bring your A game, not your B game, advises resident PGA pro Craig Hatch. This challenging 18-hole course is for veteran golfers who can play around Spring Creek where it winds through the 6,285-yard, par 72 course. Lessons and a complete practice facility are available, and there's a snack shop. Alcohol is not served and is not allowed on this well-manicured course.

The course is open daily from sometime in March through November, depending on the weather. Starting time varies with the season, but tee times can be requested before 5:00 A.M. in summer. At all times, the course closes at dark. Greens fees vary by season, but the peak summer rates are $36 for 18 holes and $22 for 9 holes. Cart rentals are $25 per person and $16 per person, respectively.

To reach Hart Ranch Golf Course from Rapid City, take U.S. 16 south for 8 miles, turn left onto Neck Yoke Road across from Reptile Gardens, and left again at Spring Creek Road, then go 1.5 miles to the entrance.

Meadowbrook Municipal Golf Course
3625 Jackson Boulevard, Rapid City
(605) 394-4191 (advance reservations)
(605) 394-4192 (same-day reservations)
This city-operated, scenic course rates high with golfers who like a challenging game. It also rates high on *GolfWeek* magazine's list of the top-50 public courses in the country.

Open daylight to dark whenever the weather permits, the 6,520-yard, par 72 course has 18 holes with bent-grass greens. A driving range, PGA pro, and lessons are at your disposal, and beer and snacks are available.

Greens fees are determined by age, residency, season, and day of the week. Moreover, the entire rate system changes almost yearly, usually increasing across the board by about 5 percent. Count on paying $15 to $18 for a round of 9 holes in summer, $27 to $30 for 18, and about $15 or $25 for cart rental on 9 or 18 holes, respectively. In winter, it'll only cost you about $20 for a round of as many holes as you can play, cart rental included.

A Tribute to Last the Ages

There is a little-known park just two and a half miles from Deadwood, hidden atop a forested hill, up a dusty gravel road. The park was constructed in 1919, but the story behind it begins with an unlikely meeting between a Harvard-educated New York politician and a Canadian-born lawman and rancher.

In 1844, while riding the range on his Belle Fourche ranch, U.S. Marshal and former Deadwood sheriff Seth Bullock came across three men. One of these three frontiersmen was current deputy sheriff and future U.S. president Theodore Roosevelt, who along with another deputy was transferring a prisoner he had just captured. Despite their differences in background, Roosevelt and Bullock hit it off immediately. Over the next 30 years, the two men formed a friendship that has truly lasted through the ages.

Following Roosevelt's death in January 1919, Bullock was deeply saddened and immediately enlisted the help of the Black Hills pioneers to erect a monument to the former president on what is now known as Mount Roosevelt. Dedicated on July 4, 1919, it was the first monument in the nation dedicated to the trust-busting conservationist president. The stone tower sits just above Deadwood, with views that stretch miles across the plains into Roosevelt's ranch country in North Dakota.

Bullock died a few months afer the dedication, secure in the knowledge that he had paid proper tribute to his longtime friend. In accordance with his wishes, Bullock was buried high above Deadwood near White Rocks, where those visiting his isolated grave site could cast their gaze across the gold-filled gulch toward Mount Roosevelt.

Today, Mount Roosevelt is maintained by the Black Hills National Forest. The park can be difficult to find, but visitor information centers in Deadwood will provide directions. There is a designated parking lot below the tower, with a well-marked, half-mile trail leading to the summit. A brisk hike can get you to the tower in about 10 minutes, although those with smaller children or who have trouble walking will need to take periodic rests. Several markers with information about the views along the way make for convenient stopping places.

Although visitors could once ascend stone stairs to the top of the tower, it has since been closed due to public safety concerns. While the tower's reopening remains uncertain, one thing is clear—the monument that was built to honor a friendship has stood the test of time and remains an enduring reminder of two frontiersmen who helped tame the West.

Southern Hills

Rocky Knolls Golf Course
U.S. Highway 16 West, Custer
(605) 673-4481
www.rockyknolls.com

Curious deer and marmots might be
watching while you tee off at this tree-
lined, nine-hole course, which borders
West Dam and French Creek. Following
the contour of the land, the 3,001-yard,
par 36 course features rock outcroppings,
bent-grass greens, and outstanding views
of the Black Hills. Off the course, you'll
find a grill, a full bar, and a putting green.
Tee times are by reservation.

Greens fees in summer are $15.00 for
a round of 9 and $25.00 for 18. There is a
$3.00 reduction in price from September
through May. Golf cart rentals are steady
at $10.00 for each round of 9 holes. You
can tee off almost anytime during daylight
hours, provided the fairways aren't too
snowy.

Southern Hills Municipal Golf Course
West U.S. Highway 18, Hot Springs
(605) 745-6400

These seemingly modest city-owned links
are actually part of one of the most-praised
golf courses in the country. Consistently
recognized in golf journals for its stunning
beauty and design, the course was hon-
ored at the start of the millennium by *Golf
Digest* magazine for being the best 9-hole
public course in North America. It will
never get that honor again: Sometime in
2004 or 2005 the course will open an
additional 9 holes, making it eligible for an
18-hole award.

The fairways here wind among abundant ponderosa pine trees, and most tee
boxes are set on cliffs where you're required
to shoot over canyons to the bent-grass
greens. Most golfers play 18 holes, making
the 5,700-yard course par 70. Riding is recommended because of the steepness, but
walkers are welcome. Lessons and a driving
range are available, and snacks and beer are
served. Reservations are recommended but
not required for tee times.

The well-groomed course is open from
early March to October 31, weather permitting; summer hours are 7:00 A.M. to
7:00 P.M. Greens fees are $15 for 9 holes,
$25 for 18 holes. Cart rentals are $10 for 9
holes, $20 for 18.

The golf course is about one-half mile
west of town.

HIKING AND BACKPACKING

Trails in the Black Hills National Forest
range from easy (see the George S.
Mickelson Trail listing under Cycling) to
steep (Crow Peak and Harney Peak,
below). That means everyone from small
children to veteran trekkers can ramble at
his or her own pace. There are scores of
scenic hiking opportunities not covered in
this chapter; you'll find at least some of
them in your wanderings, including those
in state and national parks.

Regardless of the length of your hike,
make sure you take a good supply of
drinking water, because in all likelihood
you won't find any on the trail. And if you
need water bottles or other equipment,
see the listings of sporting goods stores in
the Shopping chapter.

Of special interest are four wheelchair-
accessible trails. In the Northern Hills the
mile-long Roughlock Trail begins in the
parking lot at Spearfish Canyon Lodge
(see the Accommodations chapter) and
goes to Roughlock Falls; take U.S. 14A
through the canyon to the resort and turn
onto Forest Service Road 222. In the Central Hills are Veterans Point Trail (No. 56—
see the close-up in this chapter), at the
north end of Pactola Dam at Pactola
Reservoir, the trail at Norbeck Overlook on
U.S. 16A south of Keystone, and the Presidential Trail at Mount Rushmore.

Centennial Trail (No. 89)

All 111 miles of the Centennial Trail are open
to hiking, and if you've brought your tent
along, you can set it up either in a designated campground or in the wilderness. If
you want to camp in Wind Cave National

Park's backcountry zone in the northwest section of the park, you need a free permit that's available at the park's visitor center or at either end of the Wind Cave portion of the trail. You must stay 100 feet from the trail or any water source and out of sight of the road while camping. If you camp in Custer State Park, you must stay in one of the campgrounds. (See the Campgrounds chapter for information about reserving campsites in the park.)

Many of the trailheads have long-term parking space, but if you plan to leave your car overnight or longer in Fort Meade National Recreation Area, Bear Butte State Park, or Wind Cave National Park, be sure to notify a ranger.

Northern Hills

Crow Peak Trails (No. 64)

This hike is rated difficult, but you'll be glad you made the effort once you reach the summit of this historic landmark. Crow Peak takes its name from the Sioux Paha Karitukateyapi, "the hill where the Crows were killed" in a long-ago battle. After gaining 1,600 feet of elevation (to 5,800 feet) in a little more than 3 miles, you'll have a 360-degree view of South Dakota (including Bear Butte, which you can read about in the Parks and Mountains chapter) as well as parts of Montana and Wyoming. To reach the trailhead, which is southwest of Spearfish, take Utah Boulevard west out of town to Higgins Gulch Road (Forest Service Road 214), turn south, and go 4 miles.

Devil's Bathtub Trail

This is a popular hike in summer, but most of the people who ascend this rocky canyon are locals. Either visitors don't know about it, they can't find it, or they'd

Dogs are welcome on national forest hiking trails, but they must be on a leash or under voice control at all times.

rather not get their feet wet. And wet they will get, unless you are a deft acrobat and attempt hiking the creek bed during a very dry August or September, when the Devil's Bathtub is least impressive. Of course, most hikers appreciate the clear, icy waters when they make the climb in the heat of summer. The Bathtub itself, a massive boulder eroded into a smooth pool about 25 feet in diameter, used to hold water 4 or 5 feet deep. However, erosion and concerned forest officials have filled in much of the pool with small pebbles. It's still a good place for wading, and many visitors slide down the smooth rock waterfalls when the creek runs fast. To reach the Bathtub, you'll hike about 45 minutes up a narrow, heavily wooded canyon. When the trail disappears, you must walk in the creek. To find the trailhead, travel north on U.S. 14A through Spearfish Canyon. A few miles north of Savoy, turn right onto Cleopatra Place, which is marked by a blue street sign. Almost immediately you'll find yourself in a small parking area at the confluence of Spearfish and Squaw Creeks. The trail to Devil's Bathtub leads up the smaller creek branch.

Central Hills

Flume Trail (No. 50)

This National Recreation Trail is reserved for hikers and with good reason: Along it are fragile historic artifacts and tunnels from 1880s gold mines that relied on the Rockerville Flume to carry water from Spring Creek to their operations. Read the trailside signs to learn more about that, and see the History chapter for information about the Black Hills gold rush.

Trailheads are located at the east end of Sheridan Lake, which is off U.S. 385 southwest of Rapid City; at Coon Hollow, off County Road 233 about one-fourth mile west of the intersection with U.S. 16 in Rockerville (which is south of Rapid City); and at points in between. A trail map will help you locate them.

The Harney Range looms large in the Black Hills. SOUTH DAKOTA TOURISM

The Upper Spring Creek trailhead is closest to the two tunnels; it's about a mile west of the Spring Creek picnic area on Sheridan Lake Road southwest of Rapid City. You can leave the 11-mile-long trail for the 3-mile Spring Creek Loop at the north end or to ascend the trail to 5,331-foot Boulder Hill, whose summit provides awesome views of the Black Hills, Badlands, and prairies. The 1.5-mile stretch along the southeast shore of Sheridan Lake from the Calumet trailhead is flat and doable for young children. You'll have to pay the $2.00 daily fee to park at Sheridan Lake Southside Campground where the trailhead is. Turn east off U.S. 385 at the lake onto Calumet Road and follow the signs for the campground.

Harney Peak (multiple trails)

To the Lakota of the Black Hills, Harney Peak was a mystical mountain. Black Elk, a prominent medicine man among the Oglala people, considered Harney Peak the center of the world. For him it was a place for vision quests and spiritual rejuvenation. In addition to the mountain's spiritual embodiments, Harney Peak is a significant mountain because it is North America's highest peak east of the Rocky Mountains.

Harney Peak was named after Gen. William S. Harney, the commanding officer of Lt. G. K. Warren, who mapped the peak during a military expedition to the Black Hills in 1857. Valentine McGillycuddy also climbed the peak in the 19th century, completing the ascent in 1875 at the age

National Forest Trails

To build or to maintain—that is the question foresters face each year when presented with their limited trail budgets.

The Black Hills National Forest trail system consists of some 360 miles of track for hiking, horseback riding, bicycling, and cross-country skiing. The heavy use those trails receive shows how important they are. But in recent years, tighter purse strings in Washington, D.C., have meant tough choices about whether to build new trails to keep up with demand or maintain existing trails. Frequently, the choice is painfully obvious.

"When things start to deteriorate, they accelerate. You've got water coming down a trail and you've got to take care of it," said Rusty Wilder, a civil engineer at the forest supervisor's office in Custer.

The USDA Forest Service gets some very welcome help from volunteers who clear downed trees, clean drainage structures, work on trail surface maintenance, repair and replace trail markers and signs, and perform heavy tasks such as bridge repair. There's an Adopt-a-Trail program that allows a volunteer group or individual to assume official responsibility for maintenance of a trail, or portion of a trail, under specific guidelines.

First, of course, trails have to be planned for and built, and both processes are more complex than you might expect.

The first step is to identify a need and the type of users looking for new trails. Foresters survey potential sites—often old roads—by walking the area and examining aerial photos and topographic maps to ensure that a new trail will meet specifications for grade and varied terrain. Then a decision is made about whether to do the work themselves or hire a contractor.

Wolfgang Schmidt of Nemo is one contractor who has worked for the forest

of 26. McGillycuddy mapped the peak and photographed it. Later he served as an agent on the Pine Ridge Reservation and as the first president of the South Dakota School of Mines. When he died in 1940, his remains were cremated and placed at the base of a fire tower that had been constructed on Harney Peak. A bronze plaque is cemented in the base of the stairway to the tower containing an inscription that reads, in part, WASICU WAKAN. In Lakota, the words mean "holy white man."

The stone fire tower was constructed in 1938 and 1939 by the Civilian Conservation Corps (CCC). The CCC also constructed stone steps leading to the tower, steps that hikers still ascend today. The peak's importance for detecting fires had long been recognized. From 1911, the tower had made the life of a fire lookout here a little less extreme. In 1967, more modern techniques of spotting fires took over, and today the tower stands in mute testimony to the lonely life spotters led on the peak.

You'll find moderate or challenging hikes to the top of the Hills' tallest peak, depending on where you start. The easier—and more popular—hikes begin at Sylvan Lake in Custer State Park; the round-trip is about 7 miles. On the north side, Willow Creek/Harney Peak Trail (No.

service. In one instance, Schmidt said, he used a shovel and hand tools to build a trail in an area where heavy equipment couldn't be used.

"For me, to build one just by hand was quite a challenge," said Schmidt. "I like the hard work and being outside in nature. It's been a wonderful experience."

Loren Poppert, a recreation forester in the Custer/Elk Mountain Ranger District, also finds satisfaction in the hard labor of trail building. He helped cut trees, move rocks, dig out trail tread on a side slope, and build retaining walls for the Hell Canyon Trail. Especially gratifying, he said, is the positive feedback, "hearing the comments about how nice of a trail it is and the number of people who love to hike it."

Doing things the old-fashioned way extends to hauling materials on pack mules into the Black Elk Wilderness, where federal regulations prohibit the use of mechanized equipment of any kind.

Most years, local officials import a 10-mule pack string from Colorado for the beast-of-burden duties.

Most trail work is not so romantic, however. Without the help of present-day dirt-moving equipment, many of the trails we enjoy would not be so readily accessible.

But the human spirit can be just as powerful as any big machine. Thanks to a cooperative effort between the forest service and the Rapid City chapter of Disabled American Veterans (DAV), a paved trail at the north end of Pactola Reservoir allows people with disabilities to enjoy the outdoors in new ways. The DAV raised money to help with initial construction of the Veterans Point Trail, where anglers can fish from wooden piers.

So the next time you set booted foot, waxed ski, or nubby tire on a Black Hills recreational trail, we're certain you'll appreciate the hard work that's gone into making it available for you to enjoy.

9 North) ascends from just outside Willow Creek Horse Camp (off Highway 244, 3 miles east of U.S. 16) and is considerably more strenuous, somewhat longer (about 11 miles round-trip) and less populous. Either way, your reward for reaching the 7,242-foot summit is a spectacular, 60-mile view from the stone lookout tower, now listed in the National Register of Historic Places.

From the tower, hikers have distant panoramic views of South Dakota, Nebraska, Wyoming, and Montana, as well as close-up vantage points of the granite formations and cliffs of the Black Elk Wilderness Area. One caveat: Sylvan

Lake/Harney Peak Trail (No. 9 South), gets extremely heavy use during the summer, and the forest service is asking hikers to use alternate routes to the summit whenever possible. The most likely choices for hikers are No. 9 North and Cathedral Spires Trail (No. 4), which departs from Sylvan Lake and heads east, then picks up No. 9 South near the summit.

Southern Hills

Hell Canyon Trail (No. 32)
This 5.5-mile loop starts out steep, but after a half mile the going is easy along

One of the best ways to identify private property in the backcountry is to look for signs: those that say PRIVATE PROPERTY or the orange-and-black national forest markers posted at boundary corners. Visual signs, such as vehicles, outbuildings, and other indications of civilization also provide clues. If in doubt, contact any forest service office and ask.

fairly level grades. The trail winds along the base of the limestone plateau for about 2 miles, and the last 2 miles take you along the canyon floor, which is especially pretty in the fall when hardwood trees in riparian areas show their colors. Note the ruins of a Civilian Conservation Corps camp along the bottom of the trail. The trailhead is about 1 mile west of the entrance to Jewel Cave National Monument and 11 miles west of Custer on U.S. 16.

HORSEBACK RIDING

Horses are practically synonymous with the West, and they continue to occupy an important place in the local culture and economy. The trails listed below are a tip of the hat to our equine tradition. See the Campgrounds chapter for more horseback-riding opportunities. And, of course, you're free to ride almost anywhere in the Black Hills National Forest. Just be sure to avoid private land or get permission before you cross it.

Centennial Trail (No. 89)
See the Cycling and the Hiking and Backpacking sections earlier in this chapter for basic information about this trail. Note that horses are not allowed on the Wind Cave National Park section (although a free horse-riding permit from the park's visitor center allows you to ride alongside the trail or anywhere else in the park). Horses aren't allowed in the eastern por-

tion of Bear Butte State Park, where the Centennial Trail begins (or ends, if you're coming from the south).

Central Hills

Norbeck Wildlife Preserve and Black Elk Wilderness Area
The forest service's two horse camps, Willow Creek on Highway 244 between Hill City and Mount Rushmore and Iron Creek off U.S. 16A east of Custer, are the starting points for a dozen pathways in the 50-mile Harney Range Trail System in this protected area. All of these forested trails provide lots of opportunities to see wildlife, but we call your attention to other interesting features. The rugged Grizzly Bear Creek Trail (No. 7) will take you to beaver ponds and old-growth vegetation; Lost Cabin Trail, one of three National Recreation Trails in the national forest, passes near two old mining sites. This area has the highest concentration of trails in the Hills; any comprehensive trail map can help you sort them out. You can contact the forest service for information about the trails and about riding as well as horse camping in the backcountry.

Southern Hills

Custer State Park
Custer
(605) 255-4515
www.custerstatepark.info
A favorite riding place with abundant wildlife, the park gives almost free rein to equestrians. Horses aren't allowed in the Sylvan Lake watershed area or the walk-in fishing area that links Grace Coolidge and Center Lake Campgrounds (both areas are posted), but otherwise you're free to ride to your heart's content through this fabulous park. If you want to follow marked trails, you have options for both

Outfitters provide opportunities for visitors to live the cowboy life on the range. SOUTH DAKOTA TOURISM

long and short rides. The park's Trail No. 6, Blue Bell Lodge & Store (distinct from Trail No. 6 in the national forest system), takes 45 minutes from French Creek Horse Camp (listed in the Campgrounds chapter) to the lodge. Park Trail No. 1, French Creek, is a seven-hour loop that departs from the horse camp and joins up with the Centennial Trail on the return trip. Maps and detailed information about these and other trails are available at the park or by calling (605) 255-4464 or (605) 255-4515.

HORSEBACK TRAIL RIDES AND PACK TRIPS

Summer trail rides are plentiful, and a number of roadside corrals offer one- to two-hour rides. Those we've listed are a bit more off the beaten path or offer unusual opportunities. Some require reservations.

Central Hills

Gunsel Horse Adventures
P.O. Box 1575, Rapid City 57709
(605) 343-7608
www.gunselhorseadventures.com
Take a real Old West-style pack trip of 4

The South Dakota Professional Guides and Outfitters Association issues a free publication, Directory of Hunting, Fishing and Horseback Services, that you can obtain by calling (605) 945-2928.

to 10 days (or longer), camping along the way. No modern amenities are found along the trail, just plenty of fabulous scenery and folksy song and poetry entertainment at night. Trip choices include riding the length of the Centennial Trail, Fort Meade, the Badlands, or a ride to Deadwood's historic Main Street. Trips are available from mid-April through September or October, weather permitting.

Bob Lantis, proprietor of Gunsel, is one of the oldest (since 1968) outfitters in Yellowstone National Park. He is also the trail boss at the annual fall bison roundup at Custer State Park. For hearty souls, Bob offers a bison roundup trip, a cattle roundup, and a spring turkey hunt. Call, write, or use the Web site for more information, including prices.

High Country Guest Ranch
12172 Deerfield Road, Hill City
(605) 574-9003
www.highcountryranch.com
Ride for one to three hours, sheltered in seclusion in the Black Hills National Forest. Even the shortest ride treats you to a view of Harney Peak, and the longest takes you to an abandoned gold mine. If you feel like riding longer, call and ask about a custom trip.

Riders must be at least six years old to go on the trail, but little people can take a pony ride around the ranch as long as their parents accompany them on foot. You can ride from mid-May to mid-

If you know about poaching or other wildlife law violations, you can make an anonymous report by calling the South Dakota Turn In Poachers (TIPs) hotline at (800) 592-5522.

September here. Rates depend on the length of your ride and the season; call for more information. To get here, look for the little covered wagon 4 miles west of town. The guest ranch has 17 cabins for rent.

Southern Hills

Blue Bell Stables
Custer State Park
Highway 87 South, Custer
(605) 255-4571
There are many fine ways to view the natural wonders of Custer State Park, but sitting astride a horse has to be one of the best. On a one- or two-hour guided trail ride departing from the stables at Blue Bell Lodge and Resort, you can expect to come upon wildlife and learn about the park itself from your guide. The rides are extremely popular, and reservations are recommended; they're required for half-day and full-day pack trips. Children must ride alone and be four or older.

Rides are available daily from 8:00 A.M. until 4:30 P.M., mid-May until mid-September. Fees start at $21 for adults and $18 for children 11 and younger; ask about the special rate for groups of 10 or more. Other rides range from $33 to $150 per person.

HUNTING

South Dakota boasts some of the best hunting in the nation, due in no small part to the species diversity found in the Black Hills. Among the animals with hunting seasons are pheasant, grouse, partridge, deer, turkey, duck, geese, antelope, and coyote. It's even legal to hunt bison, elk, mountain goats, and bighorn sheep, although these exceptionally rare opportunities are usually open only to residents and, even for them, often once in a lifetime.

Licenses for big game are issued through a state-run lottery system. Applications are available at many hardware,

Black Elk

Most people think of John G. Neihardt's classic book when they hear the name of Black Elk. First published in 1932 and still in print, *Black Elk Speaks: Being the Life Story of a Holy Man of the Oglala Sioux* recounted Black Elk's visions so powerfully and affected readers so profoundly that it has been credited with planting the seed not only for the 1960s cultural revolution but for the ongoing revival of Native American cultural and spiritual life.

Born in 1863, Black Elk participated in the ghost dance movement and rescued an infant from the carnage at Wounded Knee (see the Day Trips and Weekend Getaways chapter for information about the Wounded Knee Massacre). He also toured with Buffalo Bill's Wild West show. In later life, he converted to Catholicism but also used the Red Road/Black Road (good actions/evil actions) approach in

his tribal ministry. In the wrenching conclusion to *Black Elk Speaks,* he climbed Harney Peak with Neihardt and cried, "O make my people live!" Now, thousands of people each year visit Harney Peak in the protected Black Elk Wilderness Area, and Black Elk's people are finding renewed strength and identity in the old ways.

---

sporting goods, and convenience stores; county treasurers' offices; and the state Game, Fish & Parks Department's Wildlife Division regional office, 3305 West South Street, Rapid City, (605) 394-2391. Or contact the department's main office at 523 East Capitol Avenue, Pierre, (605) 773-3485.

The seasons and prices for deer, turkey, and waterfowl are long and varied. For details, visit www.state.sd.us/gfp, or call one of the phone numbers above.

The list of licenses, prices, and other details for hunting grouse, rabbits, and other animals is also long and complex, so inquire for the information you need. Nonresidents are not allowed to trap predators and furbearers at all in South Dakota and are not allowed to take mink,

beavers, bobcats, and certain other species by any other means either; those privileges are reserved for state residents.

With a mishmash of public and private land, you need to know where you are and who owns what before you begin hunting. Make sure you have permission before you enter private property. Atlases and maps are available from Game, Fish & Parks and from the USDA Forest Service, R.R. 2, Box 200, Custer, 57730, (605) 673-2251. Game, Fish & Parks also issues an annual hunting handbook with all the latest regulations, including restrictions in state parks—be sure to get the current copy (which comes out around Labor Day) when you buy your license or pick up your application. Knowing the rules is your responsibility.

And one more thing: Uncased .22 caliber rimfire firearms are prohibited at all times in state parks and recreation areas and on the George S. Mickelson Trail. Further, firearms and bows may not be discharged on or across the Mickelson Trail right-of-way.

Custer State Park sponsors its own buffalo hunt from November through January. A trophy bull license is the most sought for, but the rarest: Fewer than 10 are issued each year. Since 2003 the park has made available three or four dozen cow and nontrophy licenses. None of the licenses are cheap or quick to obtain, as fees run from $1,000 to $4,000 and hunters may wait for two years before their name is drawn. The upsides are that nonresidents are welcome to apply, and the fee pays for a guide to accompany you on your hunting trip for up to three days. For an application or more information, call the park at (605) 255-4515.

JEEP TOURS

These are Custer State Park's enormously popular rides.

Southern Hills

Buffalo Safari Jeep Rides
Custer State Park
Wildlife Loop Road, Custer
(605) 255-4541
www.custerresorts.com
Feel the wind in your hair as you head out in an open-air jeep in search of wildlife

A Buffalo Jeep safari in Custer State Park takes visitors into the herd. SOUTH DAKOTA TOURISM

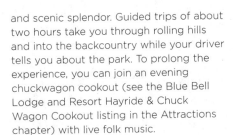
and scenic splendor. Guided trips of about two hours take you through rolling hills and into the backcountry while your driver tells you about the park. To prolong the experience, you can join an evening chuckwagon cookout (see the Blue Bell Lodge and Resort Hayride & Chuck Wagon Cookout listing in the Attractions chapter) with live folk music.

Rides are available from 8:00 A.M. to 6:00 P.M. daily, from Mother's Day until the weekend before the roundup in late September. Prices range from $20 to $25 per person, with a minimum of $100 per jeep. Group rates for 10 or more are available. Reservations are recommended.

The cookout ride departs at 4:30 P.M. and returns by 8:30 P.M. The price is $50 for those older than 12 and $40 for children. Reservations are required by 2:00 P.M.

ORGANIZED SPORTS AND OTHER RECREATION

Black Hills communities do a good job of providing organized sports for youths and adults, often thanks to the work of volunteers. Activities may include team sports such as baseball, softball, basketball, soccer, and volleyball. If you enjoy individual sports such as racquetball, swimming, tennis, running, and walking, you're likely to find free and low-cost indoor and outdoor facilities wherever you are. To help you get involved and find what you need, we've compiled the addresses and phone numbers of information and recreation centers for most of our communities; you'll find them in the gray box earlier in this chapter. More esoteric pursuits such as martial arts, yoga, and aerobics are available at certain public and private facilities, and you can inquire about them as well.

SKATING

All forms of skating are popular in the Black Hills, but ice-skating is especially

Forest service ranger district offices are open Monday through Friday year-round and are excellent places to get maps, brochures, information, and directions. They also sell Christmas tree- and firewood-cutting permits. Check outdoor racks for maps and brochures if the doors are locked.

big. In addition to the indoor rink listed below, Rapid City has four outdoor skating areas, at Wilson Park, Sioux Park, College Park, and near the fish hatchery on the west side of town. Outdoor rinks can also be found in Belle Fourche (Weyler Park) and Spearfish (the City of Spearfish Campground). There is a skateboarding park in Rapid City (at 221 New York Street), a snow-skate park at Deer Mountain Ski Area near Lead (see the Skiing and Snowboarding section in this chapter), and an old-fashioned roller-skating rink in Rapid City (listed below). If you plan on roller-skating or skateboarding in city limits, be sure to check at the city hall or police station for local ordinances.

Central Hills

Rapid Skate
2302 East St. Andrew Street, Rapid City (605) 342-8944
A popular place for roller-skating parties, Rapid Skate has a special party room and a snack bar in addition to a skating rink. Summer hours vary, so call for information. Winter hours also vary, but Rapid Skate is usually open Wednesday, Friday, Saturday, and Sunday. Hours on other days change weekly. Rates include skates; speed skates and in-line skates are extra. Lessons, including artistic dance skating, are available. Call for rates and times.

Roosevelt Park Indoor Ice Arena
235 Waterloo Street, Rapid City (605) 394-6161

This indoor complex receives heavy use by hockey leagues in winter, but there are plenty of opportunities for public skating, too—just call ahead. Times are set aside for public hockey and curling. If you're interested in either sport, call the arena for more information. If public skating isn't available, you can always come in to watch the leagues play or the figure skaters practice. Getting out on the ice will cost $3.75 for adults and $2.75 for children 18 and under. Skate rentals are available for $2.75.

SKIING AND SNOWBOARDING

The Black Hills aren't capped by sheer granite peaks in the same way that the Rockies are, but the beautifully forested landscape and gentle intimacy of the Hills make them a great place for downhill skiing.

Northern Hills

Deer Mountain Ski Area
1000 Mountain Road, Lead
(605) 584-3230, (605) 717-0422,
(888) 636-0626
www.skideermountain.com
Natural snow, night skiing, and groomed cross-country trails (which we've covered in the Cross-country Skiing section of this chapter) are hallmarks of Deer Mountain. At an elevation of approximately 6,800 feet, with a 750-foot vertical drop, Deer Mountain offers downhill slopes for all skill levels—Meadow and Snow Bowl for beginners, Racers' Cliff or the Chute for hotdoggers. A 3,000-foot triple chairlift and two other lifts serve the trails, which get plenty of use between 4:00 and 9:00 P.M. Friday and Saturday, when the area is lighted for night skiing. Snowboarders have their own territory in the regulation-size half-pipe and a terrain park with tabletops and jumps. Even tubers have a trail all to themselves.

When it's time to come in from the cold, patrons head for the cafeteria and full-service bar in the lodge. Lessons, equipment rentals, and a ski shop round out the amenities.

Lift ticket prices range from $8.00 to $29.00. Call for information about season passes and group rates. A half day of tubing costs $10.00, with tube rental included.

Ski rentals are $15.00 (day) and $10.00 (night) for adults, and $13.00 and $9.00 respectively, for kids. Snowboards are $20.00 day or night. Poles and boots are included.

Deer Mountain is closed on Monday and Tuesday except from about mid-December to early January, when the lifts run seven days a week. Hours are 9:00 A.M. to 4:00 P.M. Wednesday, Thursday, and Sunday, and 9:00 A.M. to 9:00 P.M. Friday and Saturday.

To get there, go 3 miles west of Lead on U.S. 85/14A and watch for the well-marked turnoff to the ski area.

Terry Peak Ski Area
Nevada Gulch, Lead
(605) 584-2165
(800) 456-0524 (conditions)
www.terrypeak.com
Our largest and tallest ski area (7,076 feet, with 1,052 feet of vertical drop), Terry Peak also sets itself apart with its high-tech, computerized snowmaking machinery. Five chairlifts, including a high-speed detachable quad chair, serve more than 20 miles of slopes for all skill levels. Stewart Slope and River Run offer beginners a gentle start, while Ben Hur and Holy Terror give advanced skiers a run for their money.

Snowboarders will find a terrain park on the Snowstorm trail. Stewart Lodge has a cafeteria, lounge, ski shop, and rentals. Nevada Gulch Base Lodge has a cafeteria, ski shop, and the adjacent Dark Horse Saloon. Lessons are available through the certified ski school.

All-area day passes cost $35 for adults ages 13 to 69 and $28 for juniors 6 to 12. Passes are free for children 5 and younger and seniors 70 and older. Reduced rates are available for limited access and for

The northern Black Hills offer two downhill skiing areas, hundreds of miles of cross-country trails, and heavy snowfalls. SOUTH DAKOTA TOURISM half days. Call for information about that and season passes as well as group rates.

Complete ski sets (skis, boots, and poles) rent for $20 for adults and $15 for juniors. Snowboards with boots are $22, and snowblades are $17.

Traditionally, Terry Peak opens the day after Thanksgiving, assuming there's enough snow, and operates on weekends until mid-December, when it's open seven days a week. Hours are 9:00 A.M. to 4:00 P.M.

To reach the ski area, turn off U.S. 85/14A at the Terry Peak billboard west of Lead.

SKI AND SNOWBOARD RENTALS

Additional rental information can be found in the Skiing and Snowboarding section.

Northern and Central Hills

Terry Peak Ski & Sport
32 Fantail Gulch, Lead
(605) 584-3644
www.rentmyskis.com
Owned by local ski fanatics, this shop lets you rent complete ski and snowboard packages or just the pieces of equipment you need. Full snowboard rentals are $24, while all of your skiing equipment will run $22. Special rates apply for children and holidays. The store is right before the turnoff to Terry Peak Ski Area, a quarter mile west of Lead on U.S. 85/14A.

SKYDIVING

Skydiving just might be the closest you'll ever come to sprouting wings. The sensation is more like floating in midair than falling, and even first-time jumpers almost universally report a feeling of accomplishment and exhilaration when they return to Earth.

Northern Hills

Black Hills Air Sports
Belle Fourche Airport, Belle Fourche
(605) 342-2180
www.blackhillsairsports.com
The certified instructors and jump masters at Black Hills Air Sports will teach you all you need to know for a tandem jump, in which you jump with your instructor, hitched to a parachute built for two, or a static-line jump, in which a 15-foot line attached to the plane opens your chute automatically. They also offer skydiving for experienced jumpers who want to free-fall and deploy their own chutes. A licensed pilot will take you and your instructor—and a cameraman, if you've ordered a video and/or still photos—10,000 feet up for a tandem or 3,500 feet for a static-line jump.

Skydiving is available on three weekends each month, year-round when the weather permits. Prices range from $235 for first-time jumpers needing instruction; for others, it's $195. Video and photos are extra. Reservations are required. When you call, be prepared to state your weight—there's a 210-pound limit.

SNOWMOBILING

The Black Hills are consistently ranked by enthusiasts as one of the best places on the continent to snowmobile. More than 350 miles of groomed trails, regular snowfalls, and more than two million acres of creek-carved canyons and ponderosa-covered hillsides make the Hills a favorite destination for sledders from all over North America.

Restrictions are few; just be sure you avoid logging areas, plowed roads, private land, cross-country ski trails, and wildlife winter ranges. Ski trails and winter range are defined on the South Dakota *Snowmobile Trails Map,* which is available at no charge at trailside businesses and other locations around the Hills, by calling the state tourism department at (800)

The Black Hills consistently rank among the top snowmobile destinations in the United States. SOUTH DAKOTA TOURISM

732–5682, or logging on to www.travelsd .com. Call (800) 445–3474 for current conditions.

Snowmobiles must be licensed (a valid out-of-state license is acceptable); if your machine isn't, you can purchase a five-day license for $10 at trailside businesses and other locations. A state license costs $20 for two years and is available at county treasurers' offices.

You can legally snowmobile in the national forest whenever there's enough snow, but the agreements on which the trail map is based (and which make it valid) are in effect only between December 1 and March 31. Trail grooming doesn't begin until December 15. If you snowmobile before then, be sure you sled on land that isn't off-limits, and watch for hunting parties.

The Northern Hills and the Deerfield area in the Central Hills tend to get more snow and colder temperatures than elsewhere, and those are two places we recommend; the O'Neill Pass area along U.S. 85 near the Wyoming border is especially consistent in the quality of its snow. The trail system, however, rambles through the western portion of the Hills from Spearfish practically to Custer, a stretch of almost 80 miles. And when the Needles Highway in Custer State Park is snow covered, it becomes a paradise of switchbacks, tunnels, and spectacular scenery for snowmobilers.

Parking is provided along the state trail system, and the map will show you where the lots are. Some trailside businesses also have space for your road vehicle, but it doesn't hurt to ask permission before you take to the trails.

SNOWMOBILE RENTALS

Here we've listed rental outlets that are close to popular trails and areas that get heavy snow. But you'll find rentals at other places, too, and several are listed on the snowmobile trail map mentioned previously.

Northern Hills

Latchstring Village All Season Sports Center
U.S. Highway 14A, Spearfish Canyon
(605) 584-2207, (800) 439-8544
www.spfcanyon.com
Single-seat sleds are $130 for a full-day rental on weekends and $100 on a weekday. Half-day rentals are half price. Double-seater sleds and other equipment are extra. Excellent package deals are available for guests of Spearfish Canyon Lodge, where the sports center is located. Call early for reservations—the machines are popular.

Recreational Springs Lodge
U.S. Highway 85 South, Lead
(605) 578-2774, (877) 584-1228
www.recsprings.com
Located just a few miles southwest of Lead, "Rec Springs" rents a variety of performance snowmobiles. Rates depend on the make and model of the sled, but they range from $65 to $95 for a half day and from $100 to $140 for a full day. There are modest accommodations here, as well as a restaurant, repair shop, and some clothing rentals. Before December the lodge is the domain of hunters.

Trailshead Lodge
U.S. Highway 85 South, Lead
(605) 584-3464
www.lead.sd.us/trailshead
Single sleds rent for $99 a day Monday through Thursday and $120 Friday through Sunday. Doubles are $120 and $145, respectively. Half-day rates start at $87. Prices include a helmet and the first tank of gas and oil. A full set of outerwear rents for $15, with varied prices for individual pieces. The lodge is 21 miles southwest of Lead.

SWIMMING

Here we've listed some of the most popular indoor swimming venues in the Black Hills. But don't forget about our lakes and reservoirs, some of which are mentioned in the Boating and Fishing sections.

Northern Hills

Deadwood Recreation Center
105 Sherman Street, Deadwood
(605) 578-3729
Built in 1912 by the Deadwood Business Club as the city auditorium, this beautiful brick facility fell into disuse and decayed with the rest of Deadwood over the years. However, historic preservation money from gambling proceeds has helped renovate and restore the structure. Today the building holds a massive indoor pool, changing rooms, exercise equipment, and basketball courts (indoor and outdoor). Few towns with populations of less than 1,500 sport such a facility, and Deadwood residents know it; the building gets used frequently all year, especially in the afternoons after school. There is a daily use fee of $2.75 for adults, but prices are reduced for families, seniors, children, and high school students. Hours vary, but the cen-

ter is usually open 5:00 A.M. to 9:00 P.M. weekdays, 1:00 to 9:00 P.M. Saturday, and 1:00 P.M. to 5:00 P.M. Sunday.

Central Hills

Roosevelt Park Indoor Aquatic Center
235 Waterloo Street, Rapid City
(605) 394-4168

Rapid City's antiquated public swimming pools went through a massive rebuilding project in the late 1990s and early 2000s, and the Roosevelt Aquatic Center is the pool system's crown jewel. The massive indoor structure, which opened in 2004 next door to the Roosevelt Indoor Ice Arena (see the Skating section), has a shallow play pool, a mock river for tubing, a giant waterslide, spray toys, a 25-yard racing pool with diving boards, a hot tub, and a "vortex area," a small pool that resembles a toilet flushing. The center hours vary depending upon programming, but it is generally open year-round, 6:00 A.M. to 10:00 P.M. Monday through Friday, 8:00 A.M. to 10:00 P.M. Saturday, and noon to 8:00 P.M. Sunday.

There are two other modern outdoor swimming areas, at Sioux Park, 1000 Sheridan Lake Road, (605) 394-1894, and at Parkview Pool, 4221 Parkview Drive, (605) 394-1892. The Horace Mann Pool, 818 Anamosa Street, (605) 394-1891, has yet to be renovated. Admission at all pools is $4.50 for adults, $3.50 for children under 18, and $3.00 for seniors over 60.

The outdoor pools are heated, have full-time lifeguards, and offer lockers and showers. They generally open Memorial Day weekend and close, one by one, between mid-August and Labor Day. Hours are 1:00 to 8:00 P.M.

Southern Hills

Evans Plunge
1145 North River Street, Hot Springs
(605) 745-5165
www.evansplunge.com

The warm mineral waters that made Hot Springs a turn-of-the-20th-century health resort still feed the swimming pools at Evans Plunge. Inside, a long, twisting waterslide and a short, zippy one will dump you into the 87-degree water in the 200-by-50-foot pool, touted as the "world's largest natural warm-water indoor swimming pool." Outside, you can speed slide into a smaller pool when the summer sun warms the water even more. Added attractions include giant tubes for paddling or floating, Tarzan rings for the strong of bicep, water basketball and volleyball, a 3-foot kiddie pool with tyke-size slide, spas, a steam room and sauna, weight and exercise rooms, a snack bar, and a gift shop.

Evans Plunge is open from 5:30 A.M. to 10:00 P.M. during the summer and from 5:30 A.M. to 8:00 P.M. in the spring, fall, and winter. Daily rates are $9.00 for ages 13 and older, $7.00 for children 3 through 12, and free for those 2 and younger. Use of the spa and fitness center costs $2.50 extra, or $7.50 if you don't swim. Inquire about group discounts and membership rates. Forgot your suit and towel? You can rent those here, along with life jackets and lockers. For your safety, lifeguards are on duty; children younger than 13 are not allowed in the weight room and exercise area.

SPECTATOR SPORTS

Physical activity is common in the Black Hills, and with good reason. The pine-covered bluffs and creek-carved canyons of this region are an incredibly beautiful backdrop for any number of recreational pursuits. Because of this, local residents usually prefer being in the thick of the action to being anchored on the sidelines.

There are a handful of venues for spectator sports, but not many. It isn't for a lack of trying, either; Rapid City has hosted several semiprofessional teams since the last decades of the 20th century, but few have lasted. The city had a fantastic semiprofessional basketball team in the 1980s, but attendance numbers dwindled, and the franchise packed up and left. A replacement team failed to keep local attention. Officials decided residents needed a change of pace, so they established an indoor football league in 2000. Though the team's permanence (and name) continues to be debated, the Rapid City Flying Aces maintain a respectable local following.

College and high school sports attract a more passionate group of fans than any regional pro franchise. Rapid City's two American Legion teams—Post 22 and Post 320—are especially popular, and each maintains high national rankings. Other Black Hills communities sponsor teams. Since the local American Legion officials change regularly, the best way to obtain information is to check the local newspapers. You can find out more on school-sponsored sports in the Education chapter.

Most Black Hills residents share a common trait: We spend time on sports—participating, watching, or both.

There are three universities in the Black Hills: Black Hills State in Spearfish, South Dakota School of Mines and Technology in Rapid City, and National American University in Rapid City. Each has a smattering of sports teams, and you'll find some information on the teams below. However, since each school is relatively small, sports teams are formed and disbanded depending on student and local interest. A phone call or a quick look on the sports page is your best bet for updated information.

BASKETBALL

Black Hills State University
1200 University Station, Spearfish
(605) 642-6882
www.bhsu.edu/athletics
The BHSU men's and women's basketball season runs from November until March. Yellow Jackets home games are at the Donald E. Young Sports and Fitness Center on campus. Tickets are sold on-site; prices are $6.00 for adults and $3.00 for students of all ages.

South Dakota School of Mines and Technology
501 East St. Joseph Street, Rapid City
(605) 394-2601
www.sdsmt.edu/athletics
The men's and women's basketball season begins in early November and continues until mid-March. Home games are in Goodell Gymnasium (called the New Gym) on the Tech campus. Women's games generally begin at 5:30 P.M. and men's at 7:30 P.M. Tickets are available at the gym; prices are $5.00 for adults, $2.00 for youths 10 to 18, and free for those 9 and younger. The Lady Hardrockers have appeared in the Division II national championships eight times since

1994, and they reached the final four twice. The men's team has also done well, competing multiple times in the national championships since 1997.

CROSS-COUNTRY

Black Hills State University
1200 University Station, Spearfish
(605) 642-6882
www.bhsu.edu/athletics
Men's and women's cross-country running events take place from September to November at Spearfish Canyon Country Club, (605) 642-7156, at the intersection of U.S. Highways 14 and 14A. Admission is free. Both men's and women's teams maintain high national rankings. In 2002, the women's team finished third overall in the country.

South Dakota School of Mines and Technology
501 East St. Joseph Street, Rapid City
(605) 394-2601
www.sdsmt.edu/athletics
Men's and women's cross-country events generally take place on Saturday during the fall. Each year a meet featuring regional teams is held in conjunction with the school's homecoming events. The meet is open to the public at no charge, but since the location varies you'll need to call for information.

FOOTBALL

Black Hills State University
1200 University Station, Spearfish
(605) 642-6882
www.bhsu.edu/athletics
Football season for the BHSU Yellow Jackets runs from early September until the first week of November. Home games are played at 1:30 P.M. on Saturday at Lyle Hare Field on the university campus. Ticket prices are $6.00 for adults and $3.00 for students of all ages. Tickets are sold at the stadium at game time.

Rapid City hosts a boys' high school basketball tournament each year in March, alternating between Class A and Class AA.

Rapid City Flying Aces
632½ St. Joseph Street, Rapid City
(605) 716-2237
www.flyingacesfootball.com
This semiprofessional football team is a part of the NIFL—the National Indoor Football League. Approximately seven home games are played between March and June, usually featuring teams from the other cities in the Pacific West division: Billings, Montana; Kennewick, Washington; Bozeman, Montana; Casper, Wyoming; Lincoln, Nebraska; Katy, Texas; Beaumont, Texas; Fayetteville, Arkansas; and Monroe, Louisiana. Games are typically held on Saturday at 7:00 P.M. Tickets can be purchased at the Red Dogs office or at the Rushmore Plaza Civic Center box office (call 800-GOT-MINE) and are $8.00 for general admission, $15.00 for reserved seating, and $25.00 for seats in the first four rows.

South Dakota School of Mines and Technology
501 East St. Joseph Street, Rapid City
(605) 394-2601
www.sdsmt.edu/athletics
The Hardrockers' season begins around the first part of September and goes until early November. Home games are usually at 1:00 P.M. on Saturday at O'Harra Field on the Tech campus. Tickets are available at the stadium, and prices are $5.00 for adults, $2.00 for ages 10 to 18, and free for anyone 9 or younger.

RODEO

Organized rodeo teams used to exist at the institutions of higher learning in the Black Hills, but as the region has become more metropolitan and the universities attract more out-of-state students, interest in the sport has waned. There are still informal rodeo groups at the colleges, but there are no regular events open to the general public. Your best bet for ridin' and ropin' action is going to be one of the many annual rodeo events that happen in the Black Hills. The Days of '76 in Deadwood, Black Hills Roundup in Belle Fourche, and Black Hills Stock Show and Rodeo in Rapid City are among the most popular and attract some of the biggest names in the Professional Rodeo Cowboys Association. More information on these competitions can be found in the Annual Events and Festivals chapter.

TRACK AND FIELD

Black Hills State University
1200 University Station, Spearfish
(605) 642-6882
www.bhsu.edu/athletics
The men's and women's indoor season is in January and February, with Yellow Jackets events at the Donald E. Young Sports and Fitness Center on the BHSU campus. Outdoor events take place from late March through May at Lyle Hare Field on the campus. There is no cost to attend.

South Dakota School of Mines and Technology
501 East St. Joseph Street, Rapid City
(605) 394-2601
www.sdsmt.edu/athletics
Men and women hold indoor track competition during January and February. Outdoor

events for the Hardrockers are generally on Saturday from late March through late April at O'Harra Field on the Tech campus, with one regional meet each year open to the public at no charge, usually at 10:00 A.M. on the first Saturday of April.

VOLLEYBALL

Black Hills State University
1200 University Station, Spearfish
(605) 642-6882
www.bhsu.edu/athletics
South Dakota–Iowa Conference champions in 1997, the women's Yellow Jacket team plays from August through November, with home games in the Donald E. Young Sports and Fitness Center on campus. Admission is free.

National American University
321 Kansas City Street, Rapid City
(605) 394-4825
Women's competition takes place between August and November, with home games played at the university gym. Most Mavericks games are in the evening. Admission is free.

South Dakota School of Mines and Technology
501 East St. Joseph Street, Rapid City
(605) 394-2601
www.sdsmt.edu/athletics
Women's volleyball competition takes place from early September through mid-November. The Lady Hardrockers' home games are in Goodell Gymnasium (the New Gym) on the school campus, but you'll need to call for the schedule. Tickets are sold at the door and cost $5.00 for adults and $2.00 for ages 10 to 18. Admission is free for those age 9 and younger.

DAY TRIPS AND
WEEKEND GETAWAYS

The Black Hills have often been described as an island of emerald forests in a sea of prairie. It's also true that the Hills are an island of people in a sea of relatively unpopulated land. There are about 200,000 hardy souls in the Black Hills, but the hundreds of miles of short-grass prairie that surrounds them are decidedly less peopled. The nearest towns with more than a few thousand people are Casper, Wyoming, and Billings, Montana, nearly 300 miles away to the west. If you travel 350 miles east you'll find Sioux Falls; 400 miles south and you'll come across Denver. In between is a stretch of vast and empty country, dotted only with cattle and bison ranches, a few tough cowboys, and a handful of small and dying towns.

Without a doubt, the Black Hills are gorgeous. Yet the wide tracts of prairie and clear skies beyond its foothills have a timeless beauty all their own. Inhabited by the descendants of resilient American pioneers, this land represents the nation's last great frontier. But the population grows older every day, and many towns and ranches are hanging on by a thread. In 2003, South Dakota Governor Mike Rounds suggested that unless circumstances change, the state could have fewer than 20 populated towns by 2025. Our neighbors Montana, Wyoming, Nebraska, and North Dakota might share the same fate.

The very emptiness of the land is what brought pioneers in the first place, and it's what continues to attract visitors today. There are few places in the country where the sky is wider, the air fresher, or the stars brighter. In this chapter you'll find destinations and attractions listed in most of the states mentioned above. For some attractions, the nearest town is several miles distant and claims only a couple hundred residents. Others are located in the middle of larger towns. Cafes and restaurants show up almost anywhere, but your best bet for accommodations is going to be the larger cities. As you watch your gas gauge, keep in mind that distances between service stations are usually several dozen miles or greater. However, none of the places listed below will require driving more than four hours from the Black Hills.

NORTH OF THE BLACK HILLS

Northwestern South Dakota

The **Sioux Ranger District** of Custer National Forest, (605) 797-4432, maintains Camp Crook and two National Natural Landmarks: Capital Rock (west of Buffalo, just across the Montana border) and Castles in Harding County (east of Buffalo, on Highway 20). These are mixed-use and mixed-landscape areas, with buttes, grasslands, and pine forests, where you can hike, hunt, watch wildlife, and camp (limited facilities only) at no charge, year-round. It's best to get a map because the district's land units are not always contiguous or easy to find. To get there, take U.S. Highway 85 north from Belle Fourche for about 70 miles until you reach the junction with Highway 20. Follow

A Bogus Banner

North Dakota and South Dakota were admitted to the Union at the same time, as the 39th and 40th states. When President Benjamin Harrison signed the statehood act on November 2, 1889, he intentionally shuffled the papers so neither state could claim admittance before the other. The Fort Meade Museum, near Sturgis, South Dakota, displays an old flag with 39 stars, but it's a bogus banner, for the United States never had only 39 states, having gone directly from 38 to 40, thanks to North and South Dakota.

Highway 20 east to the Castles, and west to Camp Crook. You'll cross into Montana to get to Capital Rock, but it's only a few miles across the border.

Grand River National Grassland, (605) 374-3592, is on 197,000 acres on the North Dakota and South Dakota border. It's a primitive place without developed facilities (except fishing ponds) and, like most grasslands, is broken up into blocks of federal, state, and private land. Call ahead for a map. It's open year-round, and there are no entrance fees. The Shadehill Reservoir Recreation Area is within the grassland, near the town of Shadehill. To get to the grasslands, take Highway 79 north from Sturgis. At Newell, turn onto U.S. Highway 212 and follow it northeast to the outskirts of Faith. There, turn north onto Highway 73, which will take you into the grasslands and past Shadehill Reservoir. The trip is about 190 miles one-way.

For more information on northwestern South Dakota, call the South Dakota Office of Tourism at (605) 773-3301 or (800) SDAKOTA, or, better yet, log on to South Dakota's Web site, www.travelsd.com.

North Dakota

The 19th-largest state, North Dakota is a huge expanse of prairie, farm, and ranch land that is quietly and understatedly beautiful. The state is rich in history and historical sites. Teddy Roosevelt, Sitting Bull, Custer, Lewis and Clark, and Sacagawea all left their mark there. Roosevelt said, "My experience when I lived and worked in North Dakota with my fellow ranchmen, on what was then the frontier, was the most important educational asset of my life." Outsiders often snicker when they hear the words "North Dakota," but that just makes it obvious they've never been there. The state is still relatively undiscovered, and that fact alone makes it a special place.

U.S. 85 from Belle Fourche is the fastest way to reach North Dakota from the Black Hills. Follow it until you reach Interstate 94, which you can take west to get to **Theodore Roosevelt National Park,** one of the best reasons to visit North Dakota. The only national park named for a person, it encompasses North Dakota's

Badlands, where Roosevelt rode and hunted in 1883. Teddy called the area "the romance of my life" and went on to work to preserve such beautiful places as national parks and monuments. The South Unit, (701) 623–4466 (on mountain time), is near Medora, and I–94 cuts through it. The North Unit, (701) 842–2333 (70 miles away and on central time), is near Watford City, off U.S. 85. The Little Missouri River flows through both, and the North Unit is more rugged and heavily forested. Views at both are glorious, and you can mountain bike, hike, ride horses, camp, or take a scenic drive and watch buffalo, wild horses, deer, and prairie dogs.

The **Little Missouri National Grassland,** (701) 225–5151, has one million acres that surround Theodore Roosevelt National Park. It's open year-round, and there are no entrance fees. It's primitive, although there are some established camping sites and hiking trails. It's a great (and great big) place to view wildlife, birds, and butterflies, or to fish and hunt and just get away from it all. Call ahead for a map.

Historic **Medora,** (800) 633–6721, (701) 623–4444, near the south entrance to the South Unit of Theodore Roosevelt National Park, is a 3-block-long restored Old West town owned almost entirely by the Theodore Roosevelt Medora Foundation. To get there, take I–94 to exit 27 (westbound) or exit 24 (eastbound). Walk on the boardwalks along gaslighted streets, visit the museums and galleries, and have a meal of beef or buffalo. Tour the 28-room Chateau de Mores, the historic 1880s home once owned by the Marquis de Mores, a local rancher, and his wife, Medora. Other attractions include the Doll House (antique dolls and toys), the Rough Rider Time Machine (a free multimedia presentation), and the Museum of the Badlands. Medora attractions operate from about Memorial Day through Labor Day.

The **Medora Musical** (call phone numbers for Medora above) is performed outdoors in the 2,750-seat Burning Hills Amphitheater on a bluff outside town (there's no official address, but there are plenty of signs). It has a nifty reversible outdoor escalator. The rollicking musical is a boot-stomping salute to Teddy Roosevelt and the American spirit. It is held nightly at 8:30 from early June through early September; ticket prices are $17.50 for adults, $10.00 for students (grades 1 through 12), and free for preschoolers and those younger. We recommend that you order tickets in advance. The trip from the Black Hills to Medora and the nearby Theodore Roosevelt National Park and Little Missouri National Grassland is about 200 miles one-way.

From Medora you can take I–94 35 miles east to Dickinson and the **Dakota Dinosaur Museum,** (701) 225–DINO, 200 Museum Drive, exit 61 off I–94. Here you can look at more than 12,000 fossils, rocks, minerals, shells, and re-created dinosaurs. The museum has educational activities for kids, including a once-daily Dino Dig (Memorial Day through Labor Day, kindergarten through sixth grade students only). The museum is closed September to May; however, groups of 20 or more can make advance arrangements to visit during that time. From May 1 until Memorial Day, hours are 9:00 A.M. to 4:00 P.M. Monday through Saturday, and 11:00 A.M. to 4:00 P.M. Sunday. From Memorial Day through Labor Day, hours are 9:00 A.M. to 6:00 P.M. seven days a week. Admission prices are $6.00 for adults, $3.00 for children under 13, and $5.00 for the Dino Dig. While you're there, visit the other museums on the grounds. The

Old West Trail Explorer, *a self-described "on-the-road tourist magazine," highlights the states of South and North Dakota, Wyoming, Nebraska, and Montana. It's published every spring and can be found at visitor centers, hotels and motels, attractions, and chambers of commerce. The issues are free. Or call (888) 700–8855 for a copy by mail.*

Joachim Regional Museum (local artifacts and displays) is open year-round. The Pioneer Machinery Museum and Prairie Outpost Park operate from Memorial Day through Labor Day.

Request a visitor packet from the North Dakota Tourism Office by calling (800) 453-5663, or log on to the Web site at www.ndtourism.com.

NORTHWEST OF THE BLACK HILLS

Montana

The landscape of the fourth-largest state is striking and gorgeous, and it makes a great backdrop for the places you'll visit there. Best of all, Montana—despite its size—has fewer than a million residents, which means you can find lots of elbow room. In fact, population in some parts of eastern Montana is measured in square miles per person, and in many counties the cattle outnumber the human inhabitants.

Cross into Montana from Belle Fourche on U.S. 212. The first town you'll come to is Alzada, in ranching country. Enjoy the empty scenery until you come to Broadus, about 100 miles from Belle Fourche, where you can visit the free **Powder River Historical Museum,** www.mcdd.net/museum, on the town square, and see the old county jail, a chuck wagon, artifacts, antique cars, and a collection of 200,000 seashells. The **Powder River Wagon Train and Cattle Drive** is an annual midsummer event in Broadus, and you can participate on horseback or by wagon. Call (406) 436-2388 or (800) 492-8835 to sign up.

Continue on U.S. 212 for 50 miles and you'll come to Ashland and Lame Deer, on the Northern Cheyenne Reservation. Custer's last camp before his troops began the Battle of the Little Bighorn was in the area. The free **Cheyenne Indian Museum** is in Ashland, (406) 784-2746, on the St. Labre Indian School campus.

There's no street address—Ashland is a small town—but you can't miss it. It's open year-round. The **Ashland Pow Wow** is held each year on Labor Day weekend, and the **Northern Cheyenne Pow Wow** is on the Fourth of July weekend. For information about the powwows, call the tribal offices at (406) 477-6284.

Fifty miles west of Lame Deer you'll reach the junction with Interstate 90, where the **Little Bighorn Battlefield National Monument,** (406) 638-2623, is located. For more than a century the only monuments here were to the battle's losers (in fact, up until 1991 it was called the Custer Battlefield), but in 2003 an elaborate memorial was finally erected to honor the Sioux, Cheyenne, Crow, and other Native American warriors who lost their lives here. You'll also find an interactive interpretive center and a national cemetery.

If you're feeling adventurous, you can follow I-90 60 miles west to Billings, Montana's largest city. In the middle of a metropolitan area claiming more than 120,000 people, you can enjoy fine restaurants, museums, and parks, including the **Yellowstone Art Museum,** (406) 256-6804, and **ZooMontana,** (406) 652-8100. This would be a long day trip, however, since Billings is 270 miles from Belle Fourche (you can make the same trip via I-90, but it will take you through Wyoming and add about 60 miles to the journey). Fortunately, Billings also has a number of good hotels.

You can get to Miles City by traveling northeast on I-94 150 miles from Billings, or by taking Highway 59 north for 80 miles from Broadus. Miles City is home of the annual **Jaycee Bucking Horse Sale,** (406) 232-2890, held downtown on the third weekend in May. You can watch as the horses run down Main Street, and there's a parade, good western home cooking at the steak fry and pancake breakfast, and more fun events. The annual **Western Art Roundup,** (406) 232-2890, is held in conjunction with the Bucking Horse Sale. At nearby **Pirogue Island State Park,** (406) 232-0900, Kinsey Highway, you can hunt for agates.

Don't miss the free **Custer County Art Center,** (406) 232-0635, Water Plant Road, which features work by local and regional artists. The **Range Riders Museum,** (406) 232-6146, just west of town and across the Tongue River on Highway 10, displays the town's original Main Street, a heritage center, and exhibits devoted to local history. There is an admission charge; call ahead for hours.

From Miles City head northeast to Terry, also on the Yellowstone River. The **Prairie County Museum,** (406) 635-4040, is located in the town's 1906 bank building and displays a collection of historical arti-facts related to the community. It also has a 19th-century caboose, a steam-heated brick outhouse, a reconstructed home-steader cabin, and a collection of photo-graphs taken by British pioneer women who arrived in the area in the late 1800s. It's open Memorial Day through Labor Day every day except Tuesday.

Seventy-five miles farther northeast is Glendive, home of the free **Frontier Gate-way Museum,** (406) 365-8168, Belle Prairie Road, a collection of Plains Indian, ranch, and farm artifacts that's open only in the summer. You'll also want to visit **Makoshika State Park,** (406) 365-6256, Snyder Avenue, where erosion has created some spectacular rock formations on 8,800 acres that also contain fossils, including those of the amazing tricer-atops, whose skull is on display in the visi-tor center (open year-round). A Montana state park license is required to enter the park; the license is $5.00 daily per car or $30.00 annually and admits you to any state park in Montana. A complement to the strange natural wonders of Makoshika, Montana's largest state park, is Buzzard Days, an annual spring celebration dedi-cated to the return of the turkey vultures to the park. Call for the exact date; it varies each year. You can take a bird-watching tour, participate in the 10K run, and enjoy breakfasts and barbecues. The park's entrance fee is waived during the celebration.

The anatosaurus, or duck-billed dinosaur, is the Montana state fossil, and the mighty ponderosa pine is the state tree.

Thirty miles to the east of Glendive on I-94 (and 35 miles west of Medora; see the previous section on North Dakota) is the town of **Wibaux,** named for cattleman Pierre Wibaux, who owned the Roubaix Mine and the 777 Ranch in South Dakota's Black Hills. The town is also the home of St. Peter's Catholic Church, downtown, built in 1885, which has an unusual lava-rock facade and beautiful stained glass. You can't tour the church, and there's no telephone, but you can take a look at the outside of the structure. At the free **Pierre Wibaux Museum Complex,** (406) 795-9969, Orgain Street, you'll learn about eastern Montana through the exhibits and by touring Wibaux's 1892 home and offices as well as the other historic build-ings in the complex, which is open only in the summer. The Wibaux County Fair is held in late August.

Drive 70 miles south and you'll come to **Medicine Rocks State Park,** (406) 232-0900, off Highway 7, 10 miles north of Ekalaka, where it is said Native Ameri-can hunting parties found magical spirits. The sandstone rocks there do indeed have strange and mystical forms. Ekalaka has an almost-complete anatosaurus (duck-billed dino) skeleton that awaits you in the downtown **Carter County Museum,** (406) 775-6686. It has been consistently rated one of the best county museums in the nation, despite being located in a town that, according to the 2000 census, claimed only 410 hardy souls. Another famous community landmark is the **Old Stand Saloon,** (406) 775-6661, Main Street, which is immortalized in town leg-end. The story claims that buffalo hunter Claude Carter was on his way to build a saloon on the railroad tracks in Montana Territory during the late 1880s when his

Wyoming and Montana are on mountain standard time, but the line between the central standard and mountain standard time zones runs through North Dakota, South Dakota, and Nebraska—and the dividing line takes a wild westward swing in northern North Dakota. Time zone lines are marked on most maps and on telephone directory maps, too.

wagon got stuck (or his horses refused to budge, depending on whom you ask) near the border with Dakota Territory. Carter stood up on his wagon full of logs, scanned the surrounding country, and spat, "Hell, anywhere in Montana is a good place for a saloon." Not only did the saloon thrive in its remote location, but it grew its own small town.

A bit farther south are the Chalk Buttes and Custer National Forest, but Highway 7 is unpaved after it leaves Ekalaka, so you may want to turn back to town and choose another route to your desired destination.

For a Montana travel packet, call Travel Montana's Custer Country offices at (406) 665-1671 or (800) 346-1876, ext. 6. You can also call Travel Montana's Helena office at (406) 444-2654 or (800) VISIT MT, or log on to the Travel Montana Web site at www.visitmt.com.

SOUTH OF THE BLACK HILLS

Nebraska

Nebraska, like North Dakota, is an "undiscovered" state, often believed to be just an uninteresting, flat expanse of rangeland. Although parts of the state are indeed flat and plain, western Nebraska—known as the Panhandle—may surprise you. This is a varied landscape of rocky geological wonders, grasslands, rolling hills, and the fabled, mysterious sandhills.

The western counties of Box Butte, Sioux, and Dawes hold a wealth of sightseeing adventures, especially for the traveler interested in history and natural wonders.

U.S. Highway 385 from Hot Springs will take you 55 miles to the town of Chadron, Nebraska. The **Chadron State College** Administration Building's second floor, (308) 432-5276, Main Street, has local author Mari Sandoz memorabilia and archives as well as a Sandhills library.

Chadron State Park, (308) 432-5167, 8 miles south of Chadron off U.S. 385, is set in the spectacular Pine Ridge cliffs and buttes of the Nebraska National Forest. You can camp, hike, swim, cross-county ski, and trail ride, and planned activities such as cookouts and demonstrations are offered in the summer. Cabins are available from mid-April through mid-November. A Nebraska state park entrance license is $2.50 daily per car or $14.00 for the season. The northern section of the park closes in the winter.

The fascinating **Museum of the Fur Trade,** (308) 432-3843, east of Chadron on U.S. Highway 20, will give you insight into how the trade helped develop western Nebraska. It is open only from Memorial Day through Labor Day, 8:00 A.M. to 5:00 P.M. Fur Trade Days are held in Chadron on the second weekend of July each year.

Twenty-five miles southwest of Chadron is Nebraska's largest state park. The 22,000-acre **Fort Robinson State Historical Park,** (308) 665-2900, U.S. 20 near Crawford, is both the site of the 1874 fort where Crazy Horse was murdered and a recreation area. It's open year-round for hiking, cross-country skiing, and mountain biking. The **Fort Robinson Museum,** (308) 665-2919, and the **Trailside Museum,** (308) 665-2929, are also on the grounds and are open Memorial Day through Labor Day. Cabins and the lodge are open mid-April through mid-November. You must purchase a state park entrance license to enjoy this or any other Nebraska state park. The annual **Western Art Show** is held at the fort over the Fourth of July weekend.

This is also the region of the Nebraska Badlands, with some spooky natural scenery. Visit strange **Toadstool Geologic Park,** (308) 432-0300, Toadstool Road, off Highway 2/71, a National Geologic Site that has hiking trails and picnic facilities. It's located 20 miles northwest of Crawford.

Drive 25 miles west of Crawford to get to Harrison, then take Highway 29 south for about 20 miles to reach the **Agate Fossil Beds National Monument,** (308) 668-2318. Here you'll see fossil beds 19 million years old and paleontology exhibits in the visitor center. The free center is open year-round, 8:30 A.M. to 5:30 P.M. daily.

For more sightseeing, return to Chadron. Then, as you journey south on U.S. 385, you will cross the Niobrara River, ranked among the top-10 canoeing rivers in the country. Then turn east (60 miles south of Chadron at Alliance) on Highway 2, and you will come to the **Sandhills,** once called the Great American Desert. Wildlife refuges and tiny lakes are scattered over this area; to learn more about them, call the Nebraska Game and Parks Commission at (402) 471-0641.

Check out the town of **Alliance,** the Coal Capital of Nebraska and a railroad town since the late 1800s. The town's Central Park encompasses the Sunken Gardens, Sallows Conservatory and Arboretum, and the Central Park Fountain, a WPA project listed on the National Register of Historic Places. The free **Knight Museum,** (308) 762-2384, 908 Yellowstone Avenue, has cavalry and Native American artifacts and is open May 1 through Labor Day weekend.

Somewhat less elegant, but equally fascinating, is Alliance's **Carhenge,** (308) 762-4954 or (308) 762-1520, 2.5 miles north of Alliance on U.S. 385, which replicates England's Stonehenge using old cars instead of stone. The satiric display was created in 1987 using Stone Age construction methods: lots of people pushing and pulling, and probably muttering and groaning. Although the state

Department of Roads insisted it was a junkyard and tried to have it removed, it is still maintained by the Friends of Carhenge, which accepts donations for its upkeep (admission is free). Sculptures on the grounds are also made of car parts. Some 80,000 people visit this pseudomystical shrine to used transportation each year.

Forty miles south of Alliance, near Bridgeport, are **Courthouse Rock, Jailhouse Rock,** and **Chimney Rock National Historic Site,** (308) 586-2581, impressive geologic formations that were milestones for pioneers traveling the Oregon and Mormon Trails. **Scotts Bluff National Monument,** near Gering, (308) 436-4340, is another great landmark, with a fine visitor center. To the pioneers, these formations were signs that they had made it through the vast prairie and were about to embark on the difficult trails through the mountains. History buffs will want to tour the **North Platte Valley Museum** in Gering, (308) 436-5411, where Nebraska pioneer history is lovingly preserved.

The Nebraska Division of Tourism can give you more information about the state on their Web site at www.visitnebraska.org.

Nebraska, the Cornhusker State, became a state in 1887. Arbor Day originated in Nebraska, the 16th-largest state.

SOUTHEAST OF THE BLACK HILLS

South Central South Dakota

South and east of the Black Hills lies the 11,000-square-mile **Pine Ridge Indian Reservation,** the second largest reservation in the country. Follow U.S. Highway 18 from Hot Springs east across the reservation. Pine Ridge is home to the Oglala

The Massacre at Wounded Knee

The Wounded Knee Massacre site, on a windswept hill sloping down to a valley and ravines, is a powerful place that marks a shameful incident. Here, in 1890, 14 years after their comrades and commander Lt. Col. George Custer were wiped out at Little Bighorn, and still nursing a grudge, the Seventh Cavalry opened fire on men, women, children, and elderly Lakota of Chief Big Foot's band, including the chief himself, who was dying of pneumonia.

Although the massacre started when an accidental rifle shot panicked the soldiers, eyewitness accounts say the cavalry then methodically hunted down the fleeing people. Bodies—including those of mothers with babies and small children—were found as far as 3 miles away, and many had been shot at close range. Although the military immediately began an investigation, charges against officers were soon dropped, and several soldiers received the Congressional Medal of Honor for their part in the massacre.

It is estimated that 100 to 300 Lakota died that day, or later, from their wounds. Many were found by their kin, taken to camps to die, and buried elsewhere. Of the cavalrymen, 25 died then and 39 were wounded, some of whom died later. Eyewitnesses' and researchers' accounts conflict. Some believe the Lakota were unarmed; others believe that despite being disarmed, a few warriors had hidden guns. Some historians think that many soldiers were killed by their comrades' panicky cross fire. Whatever the historical truth, that night, four days after Christmas, a number of survivors were taken to the nearby Episcopal mission where, it is said, a festive holiday banner still hung. Ironically, it read: "Peace on earth, good will to men."

On the night of the massacre, a blizzard hit, with raging winds and minus-40-degree temperatures. By the time the storm passed and a burial detail arrived, three days had gone by. A 60-foot-long trench was dug at the top of the hill, and frozen Lakota bodies were laid in it, after first being stripped of clothing and possessions, which were sold as artifacts. This grave is now fenced and marked by a monument at the Wounded Knee Cemetery, which is still in use.

Near the mass grave is the burial site of Lost Bird, who, just four months old, miraculously survived frigid temperatures for three days before being discovered beneath her mother's body. Her tragic story is told in *Lost Bird of Wounded Knee* by Renee Sansom Flood. Lost Bird died in 1920 at age 29 in California. In 1991 her remains were returned to Wounded Knee and reburied with her own people.

Lakota people, many species of wildlife, and some beautiful, expansive landscape. The Oglala tribe is one of the seven that make up the Great Lakota (Sioux) Nation. Famous leaders Crazy Horse, Red Cloud, and American Horse were Oglala Lakota.

For a taste of Lakota culture, time your visit with the **Oglala Nation Powwow,** (605) 867-5821, which is held each August. You can take scenic drives across the reservation, too, watching for spectacular geological formations with romantic names such as Yellow Bear Canyon, Slim Buttes, and Wolf Table. Some bus and van tour companies offer sightseeing tours of the reservation; these are listed in the Getting Here, Getting Around chapter. For information about Pine Ridge scenic drives, events, and tourism, call the Oglala Sioux Tribe's Office of Tourism at (605) 867-5301.

If you'd like to try your money-winning luck, your first stop as you enter the reservation could be the **Prairie Wind Casino,** (605) 867-6300, (800) 705-WIND, off U.S. 18, near the town of Oglala about 50 miles east of Hot Springs. The casino is open 24 hours a day.

Just west of Pine Ridge (about 15 miles south of Oglala) is the **Red Cloud Indian School,** (605) 867-1105, off U.S. 18, founded in 1887 when Chief Red Cloud asked the Jesuits to teach his people. The **Holy Rosary Church,** completed in 1898, was the first brick church west of the Missouri River.

In the original building on the Red Cloud campus (built in 1888), you can tour the **Heritage Center,** (605) 867-5491. The center houses a rich Native American art collection, with paintings, traditional artifacts, sculptures, beadwork and quillwork, and a gift shop. The **Red Cloud Indian Art Show** is sponsored annually by the school, from the first Sunday in June through the third Sunday in August. It is the largest juried show of its kind for Native American art in the country and is attended by collectors from all over the world. Other pieces remain on permanent display at the Heritage Center.

Ask at the administrative offices (adjacent to the Heritage Center) for a tour of the cemetery atop the hill, where the grave of the venerable Red Cloud is located. The great chief, who died in 1910, possessed admirable foresight about the education of the children of his people. Many others are buried in the historic cemetery, both Native American and white, including nuns and priests who served at the school.

Next you'll come to the town of **Pine Ridge,** headquarters of Oglala tribal government. And at the intersection of Bureau of Indian Affairs (BIA) Route 27 and U.S. 18, where a sign points to the town of **Wounded Knee,** you'll see a cemetery and church on the hill. Look for a cement block and iron arch at the entrance—it is not otherwise marked. This is the site of the 1890 Wounded Knee Massacre. You can look around without charge, but please don't disturb the offerings you see on the graves. The cemetery is open year-round all day long; if you need information, call the Oglala Tribe's Office of Tourism at (605) 867-5301. A large sign across the highway tells the story; note where the word "Battle" has been corrected to read "Massacre."

EAST OF THE BLACK HILLS

West Central South Dakota

As you head east on Interstate 90, you'll pass some interesting and quaint farming towns. The Badlands and Wall area east of the Black Hills are in their own chapter in this book (see the Badlands and Nearby).

Stop at Murdo, 135 miles east of Rapid City, where the line that separates the mountain standard time and central standard time zones is just to the west of the town limits—don't forget to reset your watch! Murdo is the home of the **Pioneer Auto Show and Antique Town,**

Just beyond the Black Hills lie prairie flatlands, the Pine Ridge Indian Reservation, the state capital, the broad Missouri River, and numerous pioneer-turned-tourist towns. Neighboring states beckon with attractions, too.

(605) 669-2691, I-90, exit 192, with the country's largest private collection of vehicles. Elvis Presley's motorcycle is there, as are 250 other classics. There are also collections of minerals, antique tractors, old china and crystal, antique clothing, organs and music boxes, and antique toys. The exhibits are housed in 39 buildings on 10 acres that also include a restored town. You can lunch at the food court and shop for gifts and antiques, too. The Pioneer Auto Show is open year-round. Call ahead for current hours and admission charges.

To take a side trip to South Dakota's capital, Pierre (pronounced "Peer"), turn off I-90 at exit 212; Pierre is about 35 miles farther north on U.S. Highway 83, and you'll pass through the Fort Pierre National Grassland on your way. The elegant **State Capitol,** (605) 773-3765, in the Capitol Complex between Fourth Street and Capitol Avenue, is worth a visit. Built in 1910 with a South Dakota granite foundation and solid copper dome, the building has been restored to its early-1900s glory. Free tours are conducted from 8:00 A.M. to 5:00 P.M. Monday through Friday, and must be scheduled in advance at the visitor information center in the capitol.

While you're at the complex, visit Capitol Lake, which hundreds of migrating Canada geese use as a stopover in the fall. You'll also want to see the memorial dedicated to the victims of a 1993 Iowa plane crash that took the life of popular South Dakota governor George S. Mickelson. The centerpiece is a replica of the *Fighting Stallions,* a piece designed by Crazy Horse Memorial sculptor Korczak Ziolkowski in 1935.

Pierre celebrates its visiting Canada geese with the annual **Goosefest** in late September. Festivities have included a wine tasting, arts-and-crafts displays, concerts, and the Honker 5K and 10K runs. Call the Pierre Area Chamber of Commerce, (605) 224-7361 or (800) 962-2034, for information about the annual event.

The **Museum of the South Dakota State Historical Society** and the **Cultural Heritage Center,** (605) 775-3458, are also on the Capitol Complex grounds, north of the capitol building. You'll find exhibits on cultural, pioneer, and Native American history, the State Archives (which the public can use for genealogical research), an observation gallery with views of the capitol grounds and Pierre, and a gift shop that carries South Dakota–made products. Admission for those 19 and older is $3.00; those 18 and younger are admitted free. Hours are 9:00 A.M. to 4:30 P.M. Monday through Friday, and 1:00 to 4:30 P.M. Saturday and Sunday (it's closed for Thanksgiving, Christmas, and New Year's Day).

Kids will enjoy the **South Dakota Discovery Center and Aquarium,** (605) 224-8295, 805 West Sioux, Pierre. It has more than 60 hands-on activities, planetarium shows, and several aquariums with fish from the local aquatic environment (no dolphins or performing sea lions). After Labor Day until Memorial Day, it's open 1:00 to 5:00 P.M. Sunday through Friday, and 10:00 A.M. to 5:00 P.M. Saturday. From Memorial Day through Labor Day, it's open from 10:00 A.M. to 5:00 P.M. Monday through Saturday, and 1:00 to 5:00 P.M. Sunday. Admission is $4.00 for those 13 and older, $2.00 for children 3 to 12, and free for kids younger than 3.

At Fort Pierre (across the river from the capital) visit the 60,000-acre **Triple U Buffalo Ranch,** (605) 567-3624, 2631 Tatanka Road. You can take a motorized tour of the ranch and see the herd of about 4,000 bison and the site where part of the movie *Dances with Wolves* was filmed. The cost is $21.00 for one to four adults or $5.00 each for five or more adults. For children 6 to 12, the cost is $3.00, and those younger than 6 take the tour without charge. Reservations in advance are required.

The 231-mile-long **Lake Oahe** reservoir, created from the great Missouri River, stretches from Pierre to Bismarck, North Dakota, and is the fourth largest man-made reservoir in the country. One of the state's greatest recreational treasures, Lake Oahe has more than 2,200 miles of shoreline (nearly twice that of California) and 900 square miles of water. It's a great place to fish for walleye, salmon, bass, and trout or to sail, ski, and windsurf. The Pierre Area Chamber of Commerce, (605) 224-7361 or (800) 962-2034, has more information.

Lake Sharp is another great fishing and recreation waterway, south of Lake Oahe, off Highway 47 on the way to Chamberlain. If you're there in the summer, you can also visit nearby Lower Brule and Crow Creek Indian Reservations and watch the annual powwows. Or try your luck at the tribes' casinos; the Crow Creek tribe operates the **Lode Star,** (605) 245-6000, and the Lower Brule tribe operates the **Golden Buffalo,** (605) 473-5577. For information about visiting the reservations, call the Crow Creek Sioux Tribal Office at (605) 245-2221 or the Lower Brule Sioux Tribe Office at (605) 473-5399.

Back on I-90, continue to Chamberlain (about 2 miles from exit 263), home of the **Akta Lakota Museum and Cultural Center,** (605) 734-3452 or (800) 798-3452 (there's no address, but you'll see it as you drive through Chamberlain). On the grounds of St. Joseph's Indian School, the museum has been amassing a rich collection of Lakota art and artifacts since the school was founded in 1927. Admission is free, but donations are appreciated. Both a gift shop and a gallery of original art are part of the museum. From May 1 through September 30, hours are 8:00 A.M. to 6:00 P.M. Monday through Saturday and 9:00 A.M. to 5:00 P.M. Sunday. From October 1 through April 30, hours are 8:00 A.M. to 5:00 P.M. Monday through Friday only.

WEST OF THE BLACK HILLS

Wyoming

Our neighbor to the west is Wyoming. A very small portion of the Black Hills creeps into Wyoming, but the terrain quickly flattens out until you reach the Bighorn Mountains, the start of the Rockies, more than 150 miles to the west. In reality, northeastern Wyoming and western South Dakota are very much alike—not just in geography, but in economy and the attitudes of their residents. It's not unusual for people to live in Wyoming and work in Spearfish or Deadwood, or for Rapid City businesses to serve clients in Gillette and Sheridan.

For your day trip, try the tiny town of Aladdin first. Take Highway 34 west for about 20 miles from Belle Fourche (Highway 34 becomes Highway 24 in Wyoming). Just east of town, you'll come to the free Aladdin Historic Interpretive Park, site of the coal mine that sustained the town. Only about 15 people live in Aladdin now, and its main attraction is the big old **Aladdin General Store** and post office, (307) 896-2226, right off the highway. It was built in 1896 and still operates both as a supplier to area ranchers and as a tourist draw. The funky store has groceries, gifts, and crafts, and there's a great antiques shop and boutique in the deteriorating, but charming, upstairs. The store is open every day, although hours are shortened a bit in the winter. The Hard Buck Cafe next door is a fun place to eat for adventurous visitors who aren't afraid of a casual cleaning philosophy. Ask about the homemade pies.

Wyoming is affectionately called "The Cowboy State." Ranching is one of the state's most important industries, and the cowboys who make ranching possible are among the state's most beloved assets. A cowboy's likeness is even on Wyoming's license plates.

CLOSE-UP

Devils Tower National Monument

There is no word for "devil" in the Lakota language. How, then, did Devils Tower get its name?

The massive landmark was christened by Col. Richard Dodge in 1875. Dodge and his army troops accompanied the Jenney-Newton expedition, a scientific team ostensibly studying the Black Hills region (although they were also looking for gold). The expedition was in violation of the Fort Laramie Treaty of 1868, which had ceded the Hills to the plains tribes.

Dodge wrote that when he asked Native American scouts about the Black Hills, they responded with what he called "studied silence." Perhaps they hoped the intruders would give up in disappointment and go away. If so, it didn't work. The scouts did say that the enormous tower's name was "bad god's tower," and again, this may have been an attempt to frighten the explorers, whose curiosity was then only more intensely piqued. Dodge decided the proper translation of

the tower's name was "Devils Tower."

For centuries, Native people have had great respect for the mystical tower. It was the site of the ancient Sun Dance and is still a place of great power that plays a consecrated part in seasonal rites. The Lakota call it *mato tipi la paha,* "the hill of the bear's lodge." Other tribes revere the tower, too, and have their own names for it.

Several tribes share a legend about its origin: It is said that seven little girls, playing outside their camp, were chased by a huge bear. Frightened, they jumped atop a rock and prayed for help. Hearing their pleas, the rock began to rise, higher and higher above the bear. The angry bear clawed at the rock as it rose, straining to reach its prey until the rock was so high that it had to give up. The little girls were pushed upward into the sky, where they became a group of seven stars, *wicincala sakowin,* the constellation Pleiades. The bear's claw marks are still there on the

Then journey on to **Hulett,** (307) 467–5430, where Devils Tower National Monument will appear on the horizon as you approach. You'll be passing through the Bear Lodge district of the Black Hills National Forest and the Bear Lodge Mountains. Hulett is a western logging town with interesting buildings and shops, and the town hosts a rodeo on the second weekend in June.

Nine miles south of Hulett on Highway 24 looms **Devils Tower,** (307) 467–5283, which entered into pop culture via the Steven Spielberg film *Close Encounters of*

the Third Kind. The formation has another reason for fame, however: It was the first national monument, having received that designation from President Theodore Roosevelt in 1906. The product of ancient volcanic activity, the spectacular tower is 865 feet high, 1,000 feet in diameter at the base, and 1,267 feet above the Belle Fourche River valley below. The 1.3-mile Tower Trail meanders around the base and past huge granite columns that have fallen from the tower. The 3-mile Red Beds Trail circles the tower and explores the nearby forest and river valley.

tower's sides, a legendary reminder, perhaps, of nature's power to aid respectful believers.

Those less interested in mystical nature and ancient legend offer a scientific explanation: Some 60 million years ago, molten volcanic magma forced its way upward through rock layers but did not break the surface, instead cooling and hardening below. This cooling process caused the volcanic rock to fracture into the huge columns on the tower's sides. Over millions of succeeding years, the softer rock above and around the core eroded away, and the tower rose higher as the rock around it disappeared. The sides of Devils Tower are nearly vertical, all the way to the slightly sloped top, which is about the size of a football field and covered in grasses, sagebrush, and cactus. Small animals—chipmunks, wood rats, snakes—live on the top, having apparently climbed there.

Since 1893 people have climbed the tower, too. That year, two entrepreneurs were first (it's not known if Native Americans climbed the tower), and many thousands followed. In recent decades climbers began to interfere with Native American religious observances still held at the age-old place of worship, creating controversy. In 1995 the National Park Service proposed a plan to curtail climbing during June's traditional summer solstice observances. The 1995 NPS voluntary closure plan was evaluated in 1999, found to be the best solution, and instituted as part of the monument's final management plan. Since the policy went into effect, the number of June climbs each year has held steady at about 250. (By comparison, there are nearly 5,000 climbs at Devils Tower each year, almost entirely between April and October.) Park officials estimate that 8 out of 10 climbers comply with the ban and refrain from ascending the mountain in June.

Devils Tower National Monument offers many opportunities, recreational and spiritual, for Americans both native and newcomer. The tower itself, however, is above it all. It is simply there, a place of power and wonder, reverence and beauty.

Devils Tower National Monument is open year-round, 24 hours a day. You can stay at the campground there from April through October. The visitor center is open daily 8:00 A.M. to 8:00 P.M. May through October only, and it has a museum and natural history exhibits. Daily programs and demonstrations on geology, wildlife, history, climbing, and more are conducted by staff in the summer. The park entrance fee is $8.00 per vehicle. You can find refreshments at the **Devils Tower Trading Post,** (307) 467–5295, at the entrance to the monument. For more on Devils Tower, see the close-up in this chapter.

Drive 30 miles down U.S. Highway 14 to Sundance (where the Sundance Kid got his name) and visit the free **Crook County Museum and Art Gallery,** (307) 283–3666, in the courthouse basement at 309 Cleveland. Kids love the exhibits about the Kid, who was tried for horse stealing in town. The museum has the original court records, even the "Wanted" posters, plus western artifacts and an exhibit devoted to the nearby Vore Buffalo Jump. Each month a local artist exhibits work at the

Black Hills' Time Zones

Until the 1880s, the United States had no time zones. Each town simply operated on its own "local time," which for farmers was nature's time, clocked by the sun's movement. As railroads became the most popular means of travel and transportation, "railroad time" was instituted to make timetables simpler. But eventually there were 100 different railroad times, and it became quite confusing. Travelers found themselves arriving at a station before they'd left the previous station—according to the timetable, that is.

In 1883 the railroads in the United States and Canada established four time zones to alleviate the problem. On November 18, the newly coordinated times were telegraphed to cities all over the country, and everyone—even farmers—adjusted his or her schedule to the newfangled way. It is said that a Mr. Sears, agent at the Minneapolis and St. Louis railroad station in Minnesota, made a tidy sum selling pocket watches to people who had never needed them before. And it wasn't long before he moved to Chicago and started a new business called Sears, Roebuck and Company.

The time zone system was so successful that Congress made it official in 1918. The dividing line between the central and mountain standard time zones runs through the Great Plains, but the railroads chose its exact route. Thus, the line meanders and jogs, apparently for the convenience of the railroads and their scheduled stops. You'll find some towns, even the mighty Missouri River, divided by the line and neighbors on central time living next door to folks on mountain time.

museum, too. It's open year-round, Monday through Friday, 8:00 A.M. to 8:00 P.M. in the summer and 8:00 A.M. to 5:00 P.M. in the winter.

A visit to the **Vore Buffalo Jump** is a must. Exit I-90 at Beulah and drive 2.5 miles west on the frontage road. Pull off the road at the sign, walk down the trail, and read the interpretive display there. Over a period of 300 years (beginning in the 1500s), Native American hunters drove 20,000 stampeding bison into a natural sinkhole to their deaths. There the animals were butchered (nearly every part was used) and their bones were left in the hole to slowly compress and be filled in with earth. The Vore site is one of the largest and best-preserved sites of its kind in the world.

The layers of bones (along with tools that were left behind) are some 20 feet deep and can be counted and studied, much like tree rings, to learn about ancient weather and ecological conditions.

In the summer you can look over the shoulders of University of Wyoming archaeologists and students as they work. For information about excavation schedules, call (307) 766-5136, (307) 766-2208, or (307) 283-1192. The Vore Buffalo Jump Foundation and the university are raising funds to construct a visitor center, so donations are appreciated.

For more exploring, backtrack 50 miles west on I-90 to Moorcroft, where the Old Texas Trail crosses the Belle Fourche River, and Pine Haven. Nearby **Keyhole State Park and Reservoir,** (307) 756-3596, 353 McKean Road, has mountain biking, camping in primitive sites and the backcountry, boating and swimming, fishing, and cross-country skiing.

Thirty miles west of Moorcroft is the very wealthy town of Gillette, Energy Capital of the Nation, and the **Rockpile Museum,** (307) 682-5723, U.S. 14/16, open all year. Gillette, founded in 1891 and originally a ranching town, is now the largest coal-producing city in the country. In fact, if Gillette and surrounding Campbell County were its own country, it would be the third-largest coal-producing nation in the world. Not bad for a town of fewer than 20,000 people. You can take a tour of one of the 16 mines in the area (summers only). Reserve your place by calling (307) 686-0040.

About 100 miles northwest of Gillette on I-90, a few miles from the Montana border, is the town of **Sheridan**. Only slightly smaller than Gillette, Sheridan sits on the edge of the Bighorn Mountains, a small range of the Rockies that are much taller, younger, and less developed than the Black Hills. You'll find a few modest ski slopes and snowmobile lodges outside town, and some good restaurants and museums, including the Trail End Historic Site, (307) 674-4589, and the Sheridan Inn, (307) 674-5440. The trip is about 200 miles from Spearfish via I-90, so if you plan on seeing much, you might want to consider making this an overnight trip.

Backtrack east on I-90 to Moorcroft and head south on U.S. 16 to see the towns of Upton and Newcastle. Newcastle (about 50 miles south of Moorcroft, or 40 miles west of Custer) is the home of the free **Anna Miller Museum,** (307) 746-4188, Delaware Washington Park, off U.S. 16, which has local artifacts, fossils, dinosaur bones, dolls, an original stone cavalry barn, treasures from nearby Cambria ghost town, a re-created country store, and old pioneer buildings. The museum is open year-round, Monday through Friday 9:00 A.M. to 5:00 P.M. Saturday hours (9:00 A.M. to noon) are added in the summer, but the museum is always closed on Sunday. The annual Sagebrush Festival is held in late June in Newcastle; it features cowboy poetry, arts and crafts, and parades.

The Wyoming Division of Tourism, (307) 777-7777 or (800) 225-5996, can provide more information and send you a visitor packet. Or, log on to the tourism Web site at www.wyomingtourism.org.

RELOCATION

The Black Hills have been luring people with their enchanting beauty and enduring mystery for centuries. Native tribes and European settlers alike have fought drought, flood, fire, famine, and each other for the right to make this timeless place their home. Fortunately, people who wish to live here today don't have to contend with such adversity.

All the same, finding a place to live in the Black Hills isn't without its challenges. One of the first challenges is deciding on your preference for housing, as there is property for any type of person. It isn't hard to rent a downtown loft in a multistory historic building, but it's also relatively easy to find a spot on a mountain slope, miles from the nearest town. And then there are the places in between: small houses bounded by acres of public forest, but only five minutes from the nearest traffic light.

If you're from Europe or the American coasts, prices for land and homes here will seem cheap. For instance, an average-size house on a small, forested lot might be appraised at four or five times its South Dakota value if it were located in California. On the other hand, Canadians, Australians, and visitors from the rural American Great Plains might find costs to be typical or slightly expensive. According to the last census, the average home in America was worth a little over $111,000. The median home value in the Black Hills will hover around $80,000, which means most buyers will get themselves a very good deal.

Wherever you're from, if you stick around the Hills long enough, you'll see real estate prices rise, thanks mostly to low mortgage rates and an influx of seasonal residents. Like western Wyoming and Montana, the Black Hills are slowly becoming a haven for wealthy out-of-state residents who fall in love with the pristine scenery but are unable to leave their urban jobs and families. Their solutions can be seen in the giant summer homes peeking out of the forest on mountaintops and along canyon rims.

But the Black Hills are still being discovered, and property remains both affordable and readily available. You'll find a few suggestions on the following pages, but by no means is the list exhaustive. Be sure to check the newspaper classifieds, real estate publications, and word of mouth. A real estate agent can be especially helpful if you're not familiar with the area; there are several listed at the end of this chapter.

For those of you relocating to the Black Hills from out of state, this chapter will also direct you to motor vehicle and licensing offices, chambers of commerce, and public libraries—all good resources for newcomers. The Black Hills cover a wide area (about the size of Delaware), so information about hospitals, schools, retirement homes, and other services of interest to potential immigrants were vast enough to include in separate chapters. If you're serious about relocating, be sure to look at the chapters on Education, Health Care, Child Care, Retirement, Media, and Worship and Spirituality for more details on the facilities and services available in Black Hills communities.

REAL ESTATE IN THE NORTHERN HILLS

People who want the hospitality and safety of small-town life but don't wish to be isolated from urban comforts find that the northern Black Hills provide a number of pleasing variations on that theme. The towns of Belle Fourche, Spearfish, Lead, Deadwood, and Sturgis all have their own personalities, yet all are reasonably close to the population hub of Rapid City. Some working folks choose to live in the Northern Hills and commute an hour or more to their Rapid City jobs.

Belle Fourche

A growth spurt in Belle Fourche has slowed, but the town continues to attract home owners looking for the last of the wide-open spaces, as one real estate agent so aptly put it. Many of those moving to the Belle Fourche area have pulled up stakes from metropolitan regions; others work in the surrounding towns but choose to own a home here, where prices tend to be lower.

Belle Fourche responded to growth with the in-town Ridgefield subdivision, where homes on the approximately 21 lots are wood frame. A bit farther out and established are the Sonoma Estates and Grandview subdivisions. Jewell Estates and rugged Redwater Ranchettes accommodate both wood-frame and mobile homes. At SRK Ranchettes east of town, lots of anywhere from 10 to 30 acres with water, electricity, and phone service—and in some cases, views of the Black Hills—are available for building a new home. Historic homes and fixer-uppers can be found closer to downtown. Home prices range from $25,000 to around $157,000 in Belle Fourche, with the average at $55,000. Rentals, primarily multifamily houses, are plentiful, which means that average rent is low—right around $315.

Spearfish

In Spearfish, growth and prices continue to rise, as is evidenced by robust construction and brisk property sales. A high percentage of homes in this picturesque college town (see the Black Hills State University write-up in the Education chapter) were built in the 1980s and 1990s, and many were custom-built for their owners. Accordingly, prices are similar to those in nearby Rapid City, which is about six times the size: The average value of a home in Spearfish today is $85,000, but you can easily find something for $200,000 or more. Nice homes have made developments such as the Jorgensen, Evans, and Mountain Plains subdivisions popular. Mountain Plains, above Spearfish City Park, features large lots with wood-exterior houses that are among the most expensive in town— around $170,000 to $300,000—even though city services aren't provided. Properties in the newer Sandstone Hills subdivision on the southern slope of Lookout Mountain do have city services, and houses being built here run $350,000 to $400,000. Mountain Shadows Estates is the newest, most modern mobile-home park, with about 300 well-groomed lots designed primarily for larger homes.

The university guarantees there will always be an abundance of mid-priced rentals in Spearfish, and in fact, a number of townhouses and apartment complexes have been built for just that purpose. Average rent runs from $350 to $400, slightly higher than the state average.

Lead and Deadwood

At the turn of the 20th century, Deadwood and Lead were populated by thousands of miners. Even after the surface deposits ran out and Homestake became the dominant mining company, the corporation continued to employ more than 1,200 workers, many of whom lived and played in the Twin Cities. Population numbers took a hit when Homestake closed in early 2002. Within a decade both communities lost a third of their population. However, the figures are misleading. With the introduction of gambling to Deadwood's Main Street in 1989, many once-crumbling storefronts were converted into casinos, eliminating the apartment space above and driving up rental costs. Developments outside city limits are thriving; the high-income homes in Shirttail Gulch and

The Wild West town of Deadwood attracts two million visitors a year. SOUTH DAKOTA TOURISM

Meadow Crest near Deadwood are valued from $400,000 to $750,000, while houses in the Hearst development on a mountain above Lead run from $200,000 to $400,000. Of course, there are plenty of isolated private lots outside the towns as well, and many summer homes and cabins are springing up on them. Less-expensive housing can be found among the historic residences within city limits, though some of the Victorian-era homes—which sell from $35,000 to $225,000—require substantial restoration work. Both towns have plans to create more affordable apartments and town houses; as it is now, the average rent payment is $350.

Sturgis

Situated along Interstate 90 between Spearfish and Rapid City, Sturgis is both smaller and slower-paced than either. That helps keep prices down, making it possible to find a nice home at a reasonable cost in a convenient location—as escapees from more crowded parts of the West are discovering. Many who choose Sturgis want to live in the country or on the outskirts of town, but new subdivisions called Pine Acres, Hurley, and Vernon Heights Estates are filling up quickly. The average price of a house in Sturgis is $70,000, and rent averages $300. Three new apartment buildings help make up the rental market in Sturgis, where few houses are rented, except during the Rally, when any real estate commands prime rates—even by Manhattan standards.

REAL ESTATE IN THE CENTRAL HILLS

With the entire Black Hills to choose from, people pick Rapid City for its economic and cultural advantages. Nevertheless, folks relocating here want to feel as if they live in the country; trees and privacy are top on the list of what they say they want in a home. As construction heads south, new housing developments offer just that type of setting, whether in town or miles away.

Rapid City

Early in Rapid City's history, west became the fashionable place to expand the growing municipality. It wasn't long before the hills got in the way, however, and the city started pushing north and east. But the flat, wind-swept land wasn't very attractive, and as property values dropped, these sections of town turned to commerce, which thrives there today. That left the southern district of the city as its only solid residential development option, and develop it has. South Rapid City, both to the east and west of Skyline Drive's divisive ridge, is one of the fastest-growing regions in the Black Hills. Terracita Hills, just south of the city's burgeoning medical district, is filled with homes that range from $250,000 to $400,000. On Rapid City's eastern edge, the unincorporated area known as Rapid Valley continues to see expanded residential development, with more than 9,000 people now living there. Several miles to the southwest, along U.S. Highway 16 outside the city limits, are housing developments such as Copper Oaks, Enchanted Hills, and Hart Ranch. The area around Neck Yoke Road

off U.S. 16 near Rockerville is noted for its secluded homes.

The Sheridan Lake Road area southwest of town is also the site of new, upscale housing developments such as Wildwood, Countryside (where all the streets are named for bird species), and Countryside South. Homes in Countryside South, which run in the $200,000 to $300,000 range, realize an exceptionally high appreciation rate. Chateaux Ridge and Autumn Hills subdivisions are along Sheridan Lake Road inside the city limits. Lots average $25,000 to $35,000.

Nemo Road (County Road 234) and Rimrock Highway (Highway 44), which link Rapid City and U.S. Highway 385 to the northwest and west, respectively, are the sites of smaller developments as well as gated Cinnamon Ridge on Rimrock Highway. This scenic road follows the route of the old Crouch Line, a rail line with so many twists and turns that it made what amounted to a dozen complete circles on every trip between Rapid City and Mystic, crossing more than 100 bridges each way.

Closer to downtown, New Robbinsdale in the southeastern part of the city is attracting home owners who like the newer housing and Parkview swimming pool there. Existing homes are in the $125,000 to $150,000 range (with the exception of those in the Rapid City Defense Housing subdivision for Ellsworth Air Force Base personnel, which are less). Several new apartment complexes and retirement communities have been built in New Robbinsdale in recent years. In Old

---

New in town? If you've moved to the Rapid City area in the last few months, New Neighbors Welcome Service will send a representative to greet you and supply you with literature, maps, and merchandise certificates to help you get acquainted with your new community. Call (605) 341-5737.

Before buying country property be sure to inquire about the availability of water. Ask adjacent landowners and check with a local well driller to find out whether you'd be able to drill a productive well on your piece of paradise and how deep it would have to be.

Robbinsdale, folks on a budget can find quaint post–World War II houses and fixer-uppers in the $60,000 range or even as low as $45,000.

West Rapid City experienced most of its growth from World War II through the 1970s, but several homes and buildings are new, and most have been well cared for and renovated. Because of west Rapid City's location in the upper foothills, forested land, and beautiful parks, land values here are generally high. Stevens High School occupies an expansive site in west Rapid. Prestigious developments in Pinedale Heights, Chapel Valley, and the older section of Carriage Hills have been established for some time and are filled up, but new multimillion-dollar mansions are taking hold in the uppermost reaches of Carriage Hills. Lots there carry price tags in excess of $80,000.

In the historic district around West Boulevard, buyers can find older but well-maintained, higher-end homes from about $150,000 for older and smaller homes on up to $500,000 for larger historic mansions and villas. The boulevard, one of downtown Rapid City's loveliest features, is popular with fitness-conscious residents who can be seen jogging or power walking down the tree-lined median just about any time of the day.

The northwestern and northeastern parts of town are well developed, and the area beyond is flat, windy, and less desirable for development. North Rapid includes some subsidized-housing neighborhoods and is becoming increasingly commercial. New businesses in this part of town include national giants Best Buy, Borders, Lowe's, Chili's, Applebee's, Pier

One Imports, Shopko, OfficeMax, and Super Wal-Mart. Rushmore Mall is out that way, and I-90 runs through the area.

Rapid Valley to the east offers attractive, affordable homes that are closest to Rapid City Regional Airport. Rapid Valley boasts a Blue Ribbon elementary school, which you can read about in the Education chapter.

The average value of a home (the price at which it would sell) in Rapid City is $85,000, while the average asking price for a house in the market was $130,000. Houses have been appreciating at the rate of 3 percent or more per year, a figure attributed at least in part to easy access to the interior of the Black Hills and to Mount Rushmore National Memorial.

Apartments and rental houses are plentiful in Rapid City, but so are people who want to occupy them. Rentals come in all types, so whether you're looking for a place over a store downtown, a furnished room, an apartment in someone's house, a duplex or multifamily house, a luxury space in an apartment, a townhouse complex beside a golf course, or a furnished or unfurnished house, you're sure to find listings. But expect lots of competition, too. The property management division of a real estate agency can sometimes be your best bet if you are in the market for something new and upscale. Average rent in Rapid City is $440.

North of Rapid City, homes and businesses are going up in the Black Hawk area, where property taxes are lower and building codes and zoning laws are less restrictive. Home owners not concerned with conformity in their neighborhoods or a certain proximity to commercial development may find their heart's desire here.

A few miles north of Black Hawk is the new Summerset development. This area is growing at the fastest rate in South Dakota; the developer hopes that by 2010 there will be more than 3,000 residents here. People are attracted to Summerset because of its proximity to I-90, seclusion in the pines away from Rapid City, growing commercial services, and comparatively low costs. Many of the houses here are middle-income homes, with the average price tag hovering around $200,000. Both Black Hawk and Summerset are in Meade County, although they serve primarily as bedroom communities for Rapid City and Pennington County.

Hill City

At one point in the mid-1990s, disillusioned exiles from populous places discovered tiny Hill City and dubbed it a cool place to live. But the influx of newcomers to this town of fewer than 1,000 people was short-lived, largely because 85 percent of the land around Hill City is controlled by the USDA Forest Service. That leaves little room for private development, although Hill City could be an up-and-coming bedroom community for Rapid City, a place where families can find small-town atmosphere and lower housing costs. It will take time, however, because growth here is slow, and development takes place on demand rather than on speculation. Older and smaller homes in town will run from $60,000 to $125,000, but a fair number of larger houses outside the community carry price tags from $200,000 to $400,000. The average home value is $83,000.

Top of the Hills subdivision in the city limits is helping to fill a need for subsidized housing for those on a modest income; an adjacent development offers buildable lots with utilities and maintained roads in the $18,000 range for middle-income home buyers. Matkins Addition No. 4, alongside Major Lake and also inside the city, offers improved lots as part of a four-acre parcel to be developed in phases. Few existing homes are for sale, and even fixer-uppers are scarce. Desirable out-of-town lots can run around $5,000 to $10,000 an acre along with potentially high costs for improvements because of rocky soil. That's something for prospective buyers to inquire about.

REAL ESTATE IN THE SOUTHERN HILLS

About 90 percent of Custer County is public land. But Custer State Park, Wind Cave National Park, Jewel Cave National Monument, and the Black Hills National Forest also make this area a special place where people want to buy a plot of land, build a nice house, and settle in to enjoy the wilderness. Trouble is, those places are pricey (by Black Hills standards, anyway), starting at around $150,000, and buildable land is becoming scarce. Finding water can be a tricky business, too, especially to the south and west. So although Custer was the state's fastest growing county during the late 1980s, the pace has slowed since then.

Custer

New subdivisions are appearing in Custer, such as Weaver subdivision, which accepts double-wide mobile homes on a foundation as well as frame houses. Lots in Boot Hill Ranch Estates, ranging in size from a half acre to two-and-a-half acres, run between $25,000 and $40,000. The subdivision, located a couple of miles east of town near Custer State Park, is heavily regulated by covenants.

A typical newer home runs anywhere from $125,000 to $200,000, and a fixer-upper in town runs around $50,000. Rentals, which average $230, are scarce in Custer, which makes it hard for college kids who work in the parks, restaurants, and gift shops to find summer lodging.

Hot Springs

The demand for farms and ranches is high around Hot Springs, especially from out-of-staters who want thousands of pristine acres on which to roam in privacy. Then again, many who are looking in this area want a lot in a subdivision so they can build a house. The 12-acre Hot Brook

Overlook 5 miles north of town, Water's Edge on Angostura Reservoir, and Battle Mountain Ranch on U.S. 385 next to Wind Cave National Park are among subdivisions where lots of several acres may be found. Cedar Hills is a development west of town with lots from 6 to 11 acres; prices hover at $50,000. Houses in town run from $60,000 to $100,000, depending on age and condition. There are plenty of ranches and homes on secluded lots outside town as well, and they can range in price from $175,000 to $775,000.

REAL ESTATE PUBLICATIONS

The following publications are available for free from real estate agencies and, in some cases, selected newspapers, information centers, and businesses.

The monthly *Home Journal* comes out in a Saturday edition of the *Rapid City Journal* around the middle of the month. The *Home Journal* contains listings for the entire Black Hills—turn it one way and you can leaf through the *Rapid City* pages; flip it over and turn it upside down to get listings for the rest of the Hills.

In Rapid City, look for *Rapid City Homefinder*, which is also available by mail for a subscription fee; write to *Rapid City Homefinder*, P.O. Box 9217, Rapid City, 57709, or call (605) 343-7684.

REAL ESTATE AGENCIES

You'll recognize some agencies as big-name franchises with solid reputations in real estate sales. But don't overlook

Need a plumber? A builder? A siding expert? The Black Hills Home Builders Association can provide you with a list of members for just about any home-building task. Stop in at 3121 West Chicago Street, Rapid City, or call (605) 348-7850.

smaller, independent agencies. Many of them are operated by agents who have been in the local real estate business for a long time and know the area intimately. You'll find additional agencies listed in the Yellow Pages, or you can contact local boards of Realtors, listed in the gray box in this section.

Hills-wide

Century 21
607 State Street, Belle Fourche
(605) 892-2021

50 Cliff Street, Deadwood
(605) 578-1417

123 East Jackson Boulevard, Spearfish
(605) 642-4607

942 14th Street, Sturgis
(605) 347-4567

503 Mount Rushmore Road, Custer
(605) 673-2433

646 Jennings Avenue, Hot Springs
(605) 745-5141
www.century21.com
One of the world's largest residential real estate franchises has six independent offices in the Black Hills. In addition to national name recognition, the franchise offers buyers and sellers a large coverage area. Although the offices operate separately, they do make referrals to each other whether for a house, commercial property, or country acreage. For rental information call individual offices.

The Real Estate Center
376 Main Street, Deadwood
(605) 578-3030

140 West Jackson Boulevard, Spearfish
(605) 642-2525

1921 Lazelle Street, Sturgis
(605) 347-9300, (800) 510-9301

8 West Mount Rushmore Road, Custer
(605) 673-2629

Boards of Realtors

Local boards of Realtors primarily serve the agencies in their territory, but they can also provide home buyers with a list of member firms and handle ethical complaints against real estate agents. Some also offer mediation service for a fee when buyers and sellers get into a dispute, or provide statistical data about property sales. Here's a list of our local boards:

- Northwestern South Dakota Board of Realtors, Inc., 121 West Hudson Street, Spearfish, (605) 642-0200

- Black Hills Board of Realtors, 1836 West Kansas City Street, Rapid City, (605) 341-2580

- Southern Black Hills Board of Realtors has no permanent headquarters because officers rotate, so you need to get in touch with a member agency for contact information. When this book was written, all of the Hill City, Custer, and Hot Springs agencies listed here were members, with the exception of Matkins Realty in Hill City.

310 Cleveland Street, Suite 1, Sundance (307) 283-2896

1401 Fifth Avenue, Belle Fourche (605) 723-7653
www.realestatecenters.com
These six independent offices are part of a limited partnership that started as a single office in Spearfish in 1992. Other agents liked founder Rich Harr's concept and, one by one, asked to be part of it. The partnership specializes in helping people relocate to the Black Hills, and all offices work together, making referrals between them. Combined, they cover the entire area, including the Wyoming Black Hills, through regional multiple listing services.

Northern Hills

Johnson Joy Real Estate
1230 North Avenue, Suite 5, Spearfish (605) 642-5723
www.johnsonjoy.com
This agency has been dealing in homes, ranches, land, and recreational properties in Spearfish and western Wyoming since

the mid-1960s. Its agents can help you learn about this beautiful area and will send you a packet of information if you're thinking of relocating here.

Johnson Real Estate
722 14th Street, Sturgis
(605) 347-0141, (888) 297-1334
johnsonrealestate.net
An all-purpose, independent agency, Johnson Real Estate has been handling residential and commercial listings in the northern Black Hills, Piedmont, and Black Hawk since 1995. The agents here handle numerous referrals from other agencies as well as their own walk-in clients.

The Keene Team RE/MAX Gold
134 Sherman Street, Deadwood
(605) 717-1544
www.keene-team.com
This small real estate agency is run by area natives and avid skiers John and Terri Keene. They list properties throughout the Northern Hills, including homes and businesses in Spearfish, Deadwood, Lead, and the surrounding canyons. If you're looking to build your own home on a wooded lot, they can help you with places in the

Meadow Crest subdivision. They work closely with an interior-design firm in Spearfish to help clients decorate their new home. The Keenes are also able to help with financing, as their son works for Wells Fargo Home Mortgage in Rapid City.

Real Estate 2000
506 ½ State Street, Belle Fourche
(605) 892-2000
The agents here handle a diverse mix of properties, from rural land, farms, and ranches to traditional residential listings. The company has covered northwest South Dakota and northeast Wyoming since the early 1990s.

Central Hills

Central Hills Real Estate, Inc.
441 Main Street, Hill City
(605) 574-6000, (800) 682-9149
www.blackhills.com/centralhillsrealestate
The residents-turned-real-estate agents here handle commercial and residential listings primarily in Hill City, Custer, and Rapid City. The company also sells real estate at auction.

Coldwell Banker Lewis-Kirkeby Hall Real Estate, Inc.
2700 West Main Street, Rapid City
(605) 343-2700, (888) 343-2700
www.coldwellbankerrapid.com
One of the nation's largest franchises, Coldwell Banker has been established in Rapid City since 1963. Approximately 40 agents handle residential, commercial, business, land, farm, and ranch sales in

Rapid City and the Black Hills. A separate property management department can help in your search for any type of rental, and relocation kits are available for prospective newcomers.

Hallmark Realtors Inc.
821 ½ Columbus Street, Rapid City
(605) 343-4545, (800) 343-8301
These agents sell business, commercial, and residential properties of all kinds in Rapid City and the surrounding Black Hills. The independent agency, which has been in operation since 1985, also provides information packets to clients who are interested in relocating to the area.

Heartland GMAC Real Estate
2210 Jackson Boulevard, Rapid City
(605) 343-1600
This local office of a well-known franchise has been specializing in residential listings since 1990. About 20 agents focus primarily on Rapid City but sometimes handle sales in other communities as well. They can also help you find a rental house. Their relocation packet has information about the Black Hills and Rapid City areas and includes a mover's guide to help you get organized, plus details about specific homes if you have something special in mind.

Matkins Realty
114 Main Street, Hill City
(605) 574-2628
www.matkinsrealty.com
This agency deals in all types of real estate in Hill City and the surrounding area, including Keystone and Custer. The office, which opened in 1983, can help you locate a rental house or apartment, too. Relocation information is available.

Prudential Kahler Realtors
2020 West Omaha Street, Rapid City
(605) 343-7500, (800) 658-5550
www.kahlerinc.com
After 35 years as an independent company, Kahler joined the Prudential franchise. The 30 or so agents here specialize

in residential and commercial sales throughout the Black Hills area. The property management division handles all types of rentals, from houses and apartments to offices, warehouses, and strip malls. The relocation division sends information packets upon request.

Raben Real Estate
302 Main Street, Rapid City
(605) 342-7272, (800) 888-1619
(relocation information)
www.rapidcityrealestate.com

Relocation is a major part of Raben Real Estate's business. Folks with serious inquiries receive a two-hour video tour of the Black Hills, from the backcountry to attractions and shopping; a book on many aspects of life here; several smaller publications; and even customized information for those with specific requests. About 25 agents handle primarily residential listings in this company, which opened in 1972. They can also provide you with a list of available apartments.

RE/MAX Realtors
1240 Jackson Boulevard, Rapid City
(605) 341-4300, (800) 456-0860
www.remax.com

The Real Estate Maximum concept that originated in Denver in the mid-1970s has made RE/MAX an internationally successful franchise. Under the formula, each agent is an independent producer committed to providing top-quality service, and the 30 or so agents in the Rapid City office are no exception. The office deals in residential and commercial properties in Rapid City and within a 50- to 60-mile radius. Relocation packets are available upon request.

Rossum & Neal, Realtors
2400 West Main Street, Rapid City
(605) 342-9112, (800) 888-1430
www.rossumneal.com

The motto at this independent agency is, "Our reputation is your guarantee." About 20 agents sell homes, commercial properties, and land in Rapid City and the imme-

diate area. Rossum & Neal can make the relocation process easier, by providing an information packet with a free video about the Black Hills or by helping you find an agency in your future hometown. Local rentals of all kinds are handled here as well.

Southern Hills

Black Hills Land Co.
428 Mount Rushmore Road, Custer
(605) 673-3167

Broker/owner Patrick D. Krantz has more than a decade of experience in selling land, which is his specialty. He started his own company, where he's the sole agent, in 1996 to handle sales of farms, ranches, recreational properties, and acreages for building a custom home (occasionally, he'll list one with a house already on it). Krantz's coverage area in western South Dakota and eastern Wyoming includes the entire Black Hills.

Wyatt's Real Estate
309 North River Street, Hot Springs
(605) 745-3140

Wyatt's has been selling real estate for nearly three decades. You'll find specialists in ranches and appraisals among the agents at this independent company, which also deals in residential, commercial, and undeveloped properties within about a 20-mile radius of Hot Springs. Requests for relocation information are handled individually.

MOTOR VEHICLE INFORMATION

If you're moving to the Black Hills, you'll need to register and license your vehicle in South Dakota. You can do this by heading to the treasurer's office of your local county courthouse (or the appropriate extension office). If you need a South Dakota driver's license or ID card, however, you'll need to go to an approved exam location—typically a fire station or community center. The exam locations are active only one day a week (or less often) in all Black Hills communities except for Rapid City, where you can take a driver's test Tuesday through Friday. Most of these locations don't have their own phone numbers, so for more information contact the South Dakota Department of Public Safety, Office of Driver Licensing, (605) 773-6883.

Northern Hills

Belle Fourche Driver's License Exam Station (Thursday only)
City Hall Council Room
508 Sixth Street, Belle Fourche

Butte County Courthouse, Treasurer's Office
839 Fifth Street, Belle Fourche
(605) 892-4456

Deadwood Driver's License Exam Station (Tuesday only)
Deadwood Fire Station
737 Main Street, Deadwood

Lawrence County Courthouse, Treasurer's Office
80 Sherman Street, Deadwood
1230 North Avenue, Suite 4, Spearfish
(605) 578-1862
www.lawrence.sd.us

Meade County Courthouse, Treasurer's Office
1425 Sherman Street, Sturgis
(605) 347-5871

Spearfish Driver's License Exam Station (Wednesday only)
Spearfish Fire Hall
622 Canyon Street, Spearfish

Sturgis Driver's License Exam Station (Friday only)
Sturgis Community Center
1401 Lazelle Street, Sturgis

Central Hills

Pennington County Courthouse Treasurer's Office
315 Saint Joseph Street, Rapid City
(605) 394-2161
www.co.pennington.sd.us

Rapid City Driver's License Exam Station (Tuesday through Friday)
South Dakota Highway Patrol Station
1301 East Catron Boulevard, Rapid City

Wall Driver's License Exam Station (call for days)
Wall Community Center
501 Main Street, Wall
(605) 394-2162

Southern Hills

Custer County Courthouse, Treasurer's Office
420 Mount Rushmore Road, Custer
(605) 673-8172

Custer Driver's License Exam Station (first three Wednesdays of the month)
Custer City Hall
622 Crook Street, Custer

Fall River County Courthouse, Treasurer's Office
906 North River Street, Hot Springs
(605) 745-5145

Hot Springs Driver's License Exam Station (Friday only)
Hot Springs High School Administration Building
1609 University Avenue, Hot Springs

CHAMBERS OF COMMERCE AND VISITOR INFORMATION

Each of the major communities in the Black Hills has its own chamber of commerce and visitor bureau staffed with helpful people and stocked with guides and printed material about the area. These business associations are more than happy to provide you with information about local stores and services, but they'll also give you an idea of a community's character and personality.

Northern Hills

Belle Fourche Chamber of Commerce
415 Fifth Avenue, Belle Fourche
(605) 892-2676, (888) 345-5859
www.bellefourche.org

Deadwood Area Chamber of Commerce & Visitor Bureau
767 Main Street, Deadwood
(605) 578-1876, (800) 999-1876
www.deadwood.org

Lead Area Chamber of Commerce
309 West Main Street, Suite A, Lead
(605) 584-1100
www.leadmethere.org

Spearfish Area Chamber of Commerce & Visitor Bureau
106 West Kansas Street, Spearfish
(605) 642-2626, (800) 626-8013
www.spearfish.sd.us/Chamber

Sturgis Area Chamber of Commerce
2040 Junction Avenue, Sturgis
(605) 347-2556
www.sturgis-sd.org

Central Hills

Hill City Chamber of Commerce
324 Main Street, Hill City
(605) 574-2368, (800) 888-1798
www.hillcitysd.com

Keystone Chamber of Commerce
110 Swanzey Street, Keystone
(605) 666-4896, (800) 456-3345
www.keystonechamber.com

Rapid City Area Chamber of Commerce
444 Mount Rushmore Road North
Rapid City
(605) 343-1744
www.rapidcitychamber.com

Wall-Badlands Area Chamber of Commerce
503 Main Street, Wall
(605) 279-2665, (888) 852-9255
www.wall-badlands.com

Southern Hills

Custer Area Chamber of Commerce & Visitors Bureau
615 Washington Street, Custer
(605) 673-2244, (800) 992-9818
www.custersd.com
Hot Springs Area Chamber of Commerce
801 South Sixth Street, Hot Springs
(605) 745-4140, (800) 325-6991
www.hotsprings-sd.com

LIBRARIES

Most Black Hills communities—even the very small ones—have libraries, thanks largely to Andrew Carnegie's philanthropic generosity at the turn of the 20th century. Aside from offering general reading material, local libraries are usually depositories for community historical archives and public Internet access points. You should be able to find several books devoted to the flora, fauna, and people of the Black Hills.

Northern Hills

Belle Fourche Public Library
905 Fifth Avenue, Belle Fourche
(605) 892-4407

Deadwood Public Library
435 Williams Street, Deadwood
(605) 578-2821
dwdlib.sdln.net

Grace Ballock Memorial Library
625 Fifth Street, Spearfish
(605) 642-1330

Phoebe Apperson Hearst Library
315 West Main Street, Lead
(605) 584-2013
leadlib.sdln.net
Sturgis Public Library
1040 Second Street, Sturgis
(605) 347-2624

Central Hills

Hill City Public Library
324 Main Street, Hill City
(605) 574-4529

Keystone Public Library
1101 Modill Street, Keystone
(605) 666-4499

Rapid City Public Library
610 Quincy Street, Rapid City
(605) 394-4171
rcplib.sdln.net

Wall Community Library
407 Main Street, Wall
(605) 279-2929

Southern Hills

Custer County Library
447 Crook Street, Custer
(605) 673-8178
www.custerlibrary.com

Hot Springs Public Library
1543 Baltimore Street, Hot Springs
(605) 745-3151

EDUCATION

Admittedly, South Dakotans aren't usually the first ones to champion a cause in the name of progress. People in the Black Hills tend to be conservative and resistant to change, embracing it only after much deliberation. All the same, South Dakotans can't be thought of as being backward, especially when it comes to education. That's because we're serious about educating our young people and preparing them to make their way in life. We provide school-to-work opportunities so students can experience the career world firsthand while earning credit toward graduation. For gifted students, we have academic enrichment programs to let them stretch their abilities to the fullest. And although we know there's always room for improvement, we see our efforts paying off in test scores that are slightly to significantly higher than the national average, particularly in math, science, and social studies. Approximately 75 percent of our high school students stay in school and graduate (our dropout rate is less than 2.5 percent a year); of those, more than 47 percent go on to a four-year college, and 20 percent attend other postsecondary institutions. Another 5 percent enter the military.

We face some difficult issues, nonetheless. One shortcoming is in teacher pay: South Dakota has been 50th or 51st in the nation (counting the District of Columbia) for more years than we care to recall. Another point of contention is the way we fund our public schools. Roughly half of school funding comes from property taxes, a system that has produced several citizen-initiated ballot measures aimed at shifting more, or all, of the burden elsewhere. So far, however, the state legislature has failed to come up with a satisfactory school-funding alternative, in part because the thought of a state income tax is anathema to most

South Dakotans. Currently, the state's funding formula provides half of school funds, paying districts approximately $4,200 per student.

Still, we've moved ahead on other issues. With the advent of open enrollment in 1998, parents and students entered an arena of brand-new choices and challenges. Under open enrollment, most students can attend any public school in the state without paying tuition, subject to limitations aimed at maintaining reasonable attendance levels. The idea is to help students find schools best suited to their needs.

Not everyone in South Dakota is concerned with open enrollment, of course. In a recent school year, 2,724 students were receiving alternative instruction, with 1,938 of them in home schools taught mostly by dedicated mothers. Alternatively schooled students must achieve proficiency in English and take math and reading/language arts as well as nationally standardized achievement tests, the same as their peers in public school. But it's up to individual districts to decide what course work they'll accept for credit toward graduation for students who want a diploma from an accredited public high school. For more information about alternative schooling, call your local school district.

Districts throughout the Hills contract with Black Hills Special Services Cooperative for special- and alternative-education services, various forms of therapy, and a full range of other benefits for special-needs students. In addition, the co-op's Technology and Innovations in Education (TIE) office is involved in a sophisticated technology project in schools across South Dakota. The co-op has been a national leader in rural education services since the 1970s.

Learning doesn't end at adulthood. Older learners find intellectual stimulation in community education programs. In most cases the local school district is the place to call for information about that as well as about General Educational Development (GED) preparation and testing; in Rapid City, however, contact the Career Learning Center, 730 East Watertown Street, (605) 394-5120.

Below you'll find thumbnail sketches of many school districts, private schools, and colleges. We couldn't squeeze all of their accolades into this chapter, but administrators and teachers at each one would be happy to fill in the blanks. Naturally, the best way to get acquainted with a school is to pay a call, or several, and observe it for yourself. The profiles here serve as an introduction.

PUBLIC SCHOOLS

Northern Hills

Belle Fourche School District
1113 National Street, Belle Fourche
(605) 892-3355

According to superintendent Bill O'Dea, Belle Fourche has the only school district in the country with a four-day alternative calendar. Regular classes are held four days per week, and the fifth is called an intercession day. Academically gifted students work on special projects, while those struggling with certain subjects can get help catching up. Attendance on this day is voluntary, but the schools are usually full, a sign of both parent and student support for the program. More than 1,400 students attend school in the Belle Fourche district, where the focus is on a child-centered curriculum that strives to meet each student's individual needs, especially in math and science. Spanish is offered in elementary school, and there's an eclectic approach to English that incorporates both whole language and phonics.

Advanced-placement classes allow high school students to earn college credit early. Vocational studies are another strength, as the district has articulation agreements with Western Dakota Techni-

cal Institute (WDTI). Students studying the building trades here can transfer their credits to WDTI without cost if they enroll there after graduation. Class projects have included building homes for people in the community from start to finish. Computer-aided drafting is a popular class.

District residents are serious about educating their youth, as evidenced by several community/school partnerships, such as the Community Council for Education and the School Improvement Council, which looks at curriculum changes before they go to the school board. Both are made up of professional educators and community members.

Belle Fourche teachers have won five national Presidential Science and Math Awards; honors among students include state football and girls' basketball championships; and the district has produced a Rhodes scholar.

The district has one elementary school spread out among several buildings, a new middle school, and one high school. High school students who don't do well in a traditional classroom setting may be referred to Education Connection, an alternative school in Spearfish. Read more about it in the Spearfish School District listing later in this chapter.

Lead-Deadwood School District
320 South Main Street, Lead
(605) 717-3890
www.lead-deadwood.k12.sd.us

This district in the heart of Black Hills gold-mining country is still proud of the fact that Lead High School won a prestigious National Bellamy Award for overall excellence and teaching of Americanism in 1970. But the school hasn't rested on its laurels in subsequent decades. In recent years LHS physics and chemistry students have excelled in regional competition with their peers, and the school band represented South Dakota at the 150th anniversary of the laying of the Washington Monument cornerstone in Washington, D.C., in 1998. Student athletes have brought recognition to Lead-Deadwood by winning state championships for the girls' cross-country team in 1997 and 1996, when they won a combined championship with the boys' team, which went on to become the 1998 Class A champ. The Debate and Speech team won the 2004 District Award, which means the entire team competed at the National Forensics League's national tournament. Although the team has sent individuals to the tournament every year since 1998, 2004 was the first year the entire team garnered a place there.

The district's approximately 1,000 students are divided among one elementary school, one middle school, and the high school in Lead.

Meade School District
1230 Douglas Street, Sturgis
(605) 347–2523, (877) 522–6251
meade.k12.sd.us
At 3,200 square miles, this is the state's largest school district geographically. Primarily encompassing Sturgis, Piedmont, Black Hawk, and rural Meade County (South Dakota's largest county), it also includes Whitewood, in Lawrence County. The Meade district is further distinguished by its eight rural schools, most of which are reached via miles and miles of gravel roads—the most remote one in the town of Opal is some 90 miles from school administrative offices in Sturgis. One principal oversees and visits them all. Students who attend these one- and two-room schools on the prairie benefit from a close-knit, family-style atmosphere and lots of individual attention from teachers, but those advantages can also make adjusting to a larger school difficult. The rural schools carry students through eighth grade in the same curriculum as their peers in town; after that it's on to high school in Sturgis or somewhere closer to home. Some rural families move into town during the week so their high schoolers can get to school more easily, or students might board with town families for the school year.

In addition to the rural schools, the Meade elementary system includes five attendance centers in Sturgis that are divided into various grade levels, one building each in Piedmont and Stagebarn plus one school in Whitewood. Some children in Black Hawk attend the Piedmont-Stagebarn schools, but others go to Black Hawk Elementary School, which is in the Rapid City Area School District. All Meade students, except those in the rural schools, are assigned to Williams Middle School in Sturgis. From there they go to Sturgis Brown High School. Black Hawk children attend middle and high school in either Sturgis or Rapid City.

Sturgis Brown High School is noted for its excellent wrestling and girls' basketball teams. The wrestling team is especially distinguished, having won both the state's dual and individual championship titles in 2001, and garnering the most dual wins in South Dakota in 2002. The school's vocational programs are noteworthy. In 2001, the Association for Career and Technical Education gave teacher Coleen Keffeler its national teacher of the year award for her efforts in Brown's Schools-to-Careers program.

The *USA Today* Community Solutions for Education Award and other honors have also gone to the district. An applied-academics curriculum helps Meade students find practical applications for their classroom studies, and a law-related education program helps them stay out of trouble—or see the error of their ways if they stray. An alternative academy associated with Brown High School serves students with a variety of needs, from work-related scheduling problems to struggles in the classroom.

Despite its large coverage area, the Meade district has a modest enrollment of about 3,000 students.

Spearfish School District
525 East Illinois Street, Spearfish
(605) 717–1201
spearfish.k12.sd.us
As the home of Black Hills State University (see later listing), Spearfish is able to offer its public school students dual enrollment, a popular option that enables

high school juniors and seniors to take certain classes at the university level and earn college credit.

Spearfish has dedicated a good share of its resources to making sure its students acquire current technology skills. In addition to its academic advantages, Spearfish is justly proud of its athletic teams—the high school football team won the state AA championship in 1997 and 2003, the boys' basketball team won the state title in 2002, and Spearfish boys won state and conference championships in track in 1999. Spearfish is also proud of its music programs: Some 200 students participate in band alone.

Recent enrollment was around 2,000. Currently, kindergarten through grade five are distributed among three elementary schools. The single middle school and one high school are in adjoining buildings. The Education Connection academy is available for students who need an alternative to a traditional classroom but still want to earn a diploma from Spearfish High School. At Education Connection, students who have been referred by their school district tackle a full, accredited curriculum through independent study, block courses that focus on one subject area, and self-paced computer course work. Students who are at risk of dropping out or are behind on credits find help through a combination of group work and individual tutoring, and they must also complete a careers course and be involved in job-related activities.

Central Hills

Douglas School District
400 Patriot Drive, Box Elder
(605) 923-0000
www.dsdk12.net
Named for the family that founded it in 1891, the Douglas School District started as a one-room school and expanded to meet the needs of military families who arrived when Rapid City Army Air Base— now Ellsworth Air Force Base—was built in

1942. Today, Douglas educates about 2,400 students a year from Ellsworth, the town of Box Elder, the surrounding rural area, and part of Rapid Valley.

There are three elementary schools, each containing just two grades. Students attend Douglas Middle School for grades six through eight, then move on to Douglas High School, which in 1971 became first in the state to have an ROTC program. The air force discontinued its rating system for ROTC programs in 2000, but the Douglas High School program consistently garnered Honor Unit or Meritorious Unit awards before then, and it continues to be very popular among students.

The school has an outstanding family and consumer sciences classroom with a progressive home economics and life-skills curriculum that's a hit with both male and female students. In the building and trades classes, students are building houses that are for sale to the public. In one program sponsored by Cisco, students split up into teams to learn about computer networking, then compete to design a campus or office building with the most efficient network. The School-to-Work program has been implemented at all levels, from kindergarten through 12th grade, to help students "learn a living." (On-the-job training doesn't begin until the later grades.) Educators, parents, and other community members work together to improve education through the Douglas Community Partnership Council and the Curriculum Coordinating Committee.

Hill City School District
421 Main Street, Hill City
(605) 574-3030
hillcity.k12.sd.us
Though Hill City has only 800 residents, the town is vibrant and thriving. Without a doubt, its prosperity is directly tied to the millions of visitors who pass through here each summer on their way to or from nearby Mount Rushmore. However, the community's push to become the regional art-gallery capital certainly helps. Several

major Black Hills artists have set up shop here, adding vitality to the commercial district along Main Street that bustles even after the tourists are long gone.

The constant ring of cash registers means more taxes for the Hill City School District. Even so, it took many years of careful saving and planning to construct a new $5.5 million high school in 2001 without any bonds or loans. This is remarkable not only because of the town's small size but also because the district managed to add 9,000 square feet and a new hardwood gym floor (also without debt) to the middle school just two years earlier. But officials have long recognized that nice buildings aren't very useful without proper equipment, and it was this attitude that led the tiny district to become the second in the state to connect its school computer network to the Internet.

On the other hand, the district really isn't that small—comparatively. More than 500 students (nearly the town's total population) attend the elementary, middle, and high schools on the upper end of Main Street. Most of the children live outside of town in the Black Hills National Forest, which makes up 87 percent of the district, or in the nearby communities of Keystone, Silver City, and Rochford. Students call themselves "Rangers," and Hill City is the only district in the country that can claim Smokey Bear as its mascot. The honor was bestowed by the USDA Forest Service after several schoolchildren helped fend off a forest fire threatening the town in 1939.

Rapid City Area School District
300 Sixth Street, Rapid City
(605) 394-4037 (elementary)
(605) 394-5147 (secondary)
www.rcas.org
Approximately 13,000 students attend classes in South Dakota's second-largest school district, which includes 16 elementary schools (including one for children with disabilities), five middle schools, two high schools, three alternative academies that allow at-risk students to work at their own pace (in some cases, over the Internet) toward a diploma, and a technical school (see the Western Dakota Technical Institute listing below).

The district is committed to giving its youths a solid academic foundation from the very beginning of their educational career. The school board lowered student-teacher ratios in the earliest grades as a means of increasing literacy from the start. Outstanding primary programs such as this one have garnered honors for the district. Rapid Valley Elementary School won a national Blue Ribbon Award in 1997 from the U.S. Department of Education, one of 262 schools to be recognized for excellence. The school combines multiage classrooms, looping (where teachers remain longer with the same group of students), and traditional self-contained classes with progressive teaching techniques and a welcoming, "community of learners" atmosphere that makes children want to go to school—really! Some of its other progressive approaches to education include a money responsibility program, in which students can earn "Best Bills" play money they can use to pay fines for late homework or save to purchase items at the school store, and extended school days on Monday, Tuesday, Thursday, and Friday, which leaves Wednesday afternoon free for staff development and networking.

On the secondary level, Central and Stevens High Schools consistently excel in track, cross-country, and music (both band and orchestra). Stevens is usually noted for its wrestling, golf, and theater programs, which are consistently ranked as the best in the state, while Central takes top honors in volleyball and soccer and has a federally funded learning center for Native American students.

Overall, the district prides itself on doing a good job teaching basic skills and on the success of its science students in local and national competition. Noteworthy, too, is an active, successful exchange program with educators from Rapid City's Japanese sister city, Imaichi.

Southern Hills

Custer School District
147 North Fifth Street, Custer
(605) 673-3154
www.csd.k12.sd.us

Technology programs and boys' basketball have made Custer a standout school district. Presently, it is one of three districts in the Black Hills to operate on a four-day week. When the schedule changed in 1995, closing school on Friday and adding almost an hour a day Monday through Thursday was supposed to save the district money. In fact, savings were realized in transportation but little else, yet district voters overwhelmingly chose to continue the four-day week. According to the school superintendent, both rural and town residents like having their children home an extra day each week, and teachers like the longer class periods. In addition, cocurricular activities on Friday no longer interrupt instructional time.

Custer schools use computer technology across the curriculum at all levels, from kindergarten through 12th grade. A few students even use the Internet to take classes that earn them high school and college credit. Advanced placement classes are offered in calculus, with plans to add chemistry.

In the athletics arena, the names of Coach Larry Luitjens and the Custer High School boys' basketball team are practically synonymous with the title "state championship." Together, they've won five since 1990. Of course, like any sports team they've suffered setbacks, including the 1999 death of a star player and a bicycling accident in 2003 that seriously injured Coach Luitjens. Yet the team carries on with incredible support, not just from the community but from the entire state, as evidenced by a 2002 resolution passed by the South Dakota legislature congratulating Luitjens on garnering the most wins of any basketball coach in state history. Academic honors have included placing in the Odyssey of the Mind world finals and a Sallie Mae national teaching award for a

teacher at the rural school in Spring Creek.

The Custer district has three rural schools that teach kindergarten through eighth grade, including one in Fairburn. It's one of only a few two-room rural schoolhouses built in the last 50 years in South Dakota. In the city of Custer are one elementary, one middle, and one high school. A program for at-risk students is in place.

The school district embraces Custer State Park and Wind Cave National Park within its boundaries, and the superintendent points out that his district has 1,000 students, 1,100 square miles, and 1,500 bison.

Hot Springs School District
1609 University Avenue, Hot Springs
(605) 745-4145
www.hssd.k12.sd.us

Maybe it's the Southern Hills' gorgeous scenery and pleasant climate that produce top athletes at Hot Springs High School. The girls' track and cross-country teams consistently rank as the top in the state, and the volleyball team won the state championships in 2000 and 2001.

But students also focus on academics and technology skills. Hot Springs High School has an 11 to 1 student-teacher ratio and runs several special programs, including a business and marketing class that integrates computer technology and an annual trip to Washington, D.C., that affords students a close-up look at American government. The district, after observing the benefits in nearby Custer, went to a four-day school week in 2003.

Approximately 980 students attend elementary, middle, and high school in Hot Springs and a rural school in Oral that goes through grade eight. A program for at-risk students helps keep struggling scholars on track to graduation.

PRIVATE SCHOOLS

With the exception of Montessori schools, private schools in the Black Hills generally are religious institutions. Many of them are affiliated with a specific church and can be located through the churches. Check the Yellow Pages or inquire at the local school district for information. Here we've listed several private schools, including one that principally serves Native American students.

Central Hills

Rapid City Christian High School
1212 East Fairmont Boulevard, Rapid City
(605) 341-3377
Approximately 145 students in grades 7 through 12 attend this interdenominational Christian school, which opened in 1981. Accredited by the state and the Association of Christian Schools International, the school combines religious instruction with a traditional approach to basic learning. Students are required to enroll in a Bible class every semester and attend chapel once a week, and they must be committed to learning through a Christian world view. A full activities schedule also keeps them busy in football (the team competes in two conferences), basketball, volleyball, track, drama, and more.

The school occupies space in the Bible Fellowship Church building but is not affiliated with the church. The school bought the Hart Ranch Arena and 20 acres of land south of Rapid City and plans to convert it into a campus in time for the 2006 school year.

Sioux Chapel & Lakota Christian Academy
415 MacArthur Street, Rapid City
(605) 341-0652
www.wnam.org
Operated by Wesleyan Native American Ministries, Sioux Chapel & Lakota Christian Academy teaches nearly 50 students in grades kindergarten through 12. About 80 percent of the student body is Native American, but enrollment is open to all. And despite the school's affiliation with the Wesleyan church and its Christian emphasis, non-Christians are welcome. The unaccredited school uses the School of Tomorrow curriculum for an individualized approach to self-motivated learning. Classrooms are arranged by age, with more than one grade level per room. Student athletes compete in the Christian Athletic Conference in flag football, boys' basketball, and girls' volleyball.

St. Elizabeth Seton School
431 Oakland Street, Rapid City
(605) 348-1477

St. Thomas More High School
300 Fairmont Boulevard, Rapid City
(605) 343-8484
These two fast-growing, accredited Catholic schools comprise a single school system under the auspices of the Saint Elizabeth Seton Central Catholic School Corp. Recently, enrollment at St. Elizabeth Seton was 520 students in preschool through grade eight, with a waiting list in every grade. St. Thomas More had 257 scholars in grades 9 through 12. About 90 percent of the students came from Rapid City, and about one-fourth were non-Catholics.

Both schools strive to deepen understanding of the meaning and importance of the Catholic faith, and in addition to receiving religious instruction, students participate in regular prayer services and retreats. Eighth-graders take on a community service program, and seniors must complete a 30-hour Christian service project to graduate. Academic performance is boosted by strong discipline and a heavy homework load, backed by vigorous parental involvement and commitment to the schools' vision.

St. Elizabeth Seton School opened in 1961, replacing the Cathedral school that had been established in 1916. St. Thomas More High School began humbly, taking up temporary quarters at National American University in 1991 after the closure of St. Martin's Academy, a coed high school started by Benedictine nuns more than a century ago.

Commitment to St. Thomas More was such that enough money was donated to

Willard Water

It heals burns, grows gargantuan squash, helps you sleep, relieves pain, and keeps your pets healthy. Those are some of the claims made by folks who swear by Willard Water, a mysterious fluid discovered in the 1960s and patented by John Willard, a chemistry professor at South Dakota School of Mines and Technology in Rapid City.

Doc Willard, as he was called, developed "catalyst altered water" as a solvent but found it had health properties when he used it to soothe a burn on his arm. Once on the market it naturally attracted considerable curiosity, and in 1980 veteran TV reporter Harry Reasoner interviewed Doc Willard and a number of Willard Water devotees on *60 Minutes*. The testimonials claimed all sorts of benefits and no bad effects. Independent lab tests and a congressional investigation found it to be harmless. But no one could explain why Willard Water worked. As Doc himself said, "I see it but I still don't believe it."

One hypothesis holds that by altering the molecular structure of ordinary water, Willard Water boosts the assimilation of nutrients and hastens the elimination of toxins. It's also said to be a powerful antioxidant that helps the body rid itself of damaging free radicals. Users who drink it mixed with filtered water say they can't taste it, but they can tell a difference in the way they feel. And they say they feel better.

Doc Willard passed away in 1991, but Willard Water is still manufactured in Rapid City by his heirs and associates and distributed on a limited basis. There are imitations and diluted forms on the market, too, and representatives of Nutrition Coalition, a Moorhead, Minnesota, marketer, say the only way to know whether you're getting the real thing is . . . if you get results. If you're curious about Willard Water, call Nutrition Coalition at (800) 447-4793 for more information.

permit groundbreaking for a new building in 1994. The high school with a chapel in its center opened the next year.

St. Thomas More offers an accelerated college preparatory program with advanced placement courses, traditional college prep, and general studies for those who plan to go on to junior college or vocational school. For students needing extra help, tutoring is provided. In general, however, all students take the same level of course work. As a member of the South Dakota High School Activities Association, St. Thomas More competes with other local schools in football, basketball, wrestling, golf, debate, and many other activities.

Southern Hills

Bethesda Lutheran School
1537 Baltimore Avenue, Hot Springs
(605) 745–6676

Between 40 and 50 youngsters attend this grade school, which is a ministry of Bethesda Lutheran Church and is accredited through National Lutheran Schools. Located in the church complex, the school teaches a standard curriculum like that found in public schools, with the addition of a literature-based reading program and Lutheran doctrine. Pupils receive religious instruction four days a week and attend chapel one day a week. Kindergartners attend class for half a day, sharing a room with first-graders. Second and third grades are combined, as are fourth, fifth, and sixth. The school, which opened in 1980, is affiliated with the Missouri Synod and is open to all students.

MONTESSORI SCHOOLS

Maria Montessori was the first woman in Italy to receive a medical degree. Her work as a doctor led to her belief that children learn best at their own pace, a philosophy that has been the cornerstone of Montessori education since she opened her first school in 1907. The classroom materials she designed then are still in use today.

Children's House Montessori
3520 West Main Street, Rapid City
(605) 341–0824
www.chkids@rushmore.com

Bringing the outdoors in is one area of focus at this school for children from age three through grade five. Raising butterflies, tending a butterfly garden, growing pumpkins, and building a compost heap on the one-and-a-half-acre wooded campus are just a few of the activities that are integrated into the classroom. Studies include individual and group learning in a variety of subjects. Children also participate in a cultural exchange by visiting and writing to their peers in the Montessori school at Red Cloud Indian School on the Pine Ridge Indian Reservation. A multigenerational exchange takes place when parents and grandparents volunteer their time for reading, gardening assistance, and other activities.

Preschool and kindergarten are offered on a part-time basis, with limited extended care before school and at lunchtime. Teachers are required to obtain Montessori certification. But after a snowfall, even they can turn into kids again when everybody goes sledding.

Children's House is closed during the summer.

Life Tree Montessori School
2110 St. Martins Drive, Rapid City
(605) 343–1541

Life Tree Montessori School offers part-time and full-time programs for children from age 18 months through sixth grade. Tykes up to age 3 enroll in the toddler program; from 3 to 6 they're in preprimary, which includes kindergarten; and 6- to 12-year-old students receive elementary instruction. Extended care is available before and after school for students who attend Life Tree. All activities take place in open, sunny classrooms under the nurturing tutelage of Montessori-certified teachers. Parental involvement is evident, too, in the wooden play equipment that was built by a parent for the big outdoor playground.

HEAD START PROGRAMS

As the name implies, these publicly funded programs give preschoolers a solid foundation before they enter kindergarten. Call the programs for income

Most South Dakotans who take General Educational Development (GED) tests are between the ages of 20 and 24 and have completed 10th grade. The minimum age to take the tests is 16.

guidelines. For private preschool programs, check the Yellow Pages, and see the Child Care chapter for information about locating a day-care center.

Dakota Transitional Head Start
612 Crazy Horse Street, Rapid City
919 Main Street, Suite 201, Rapid City
57701 (mailing address)
(605) 341-3163

This center-based program serves 75 Native American children ages three to five and their families who move to the Rapid City area from an Indian reservation. Because the transition may involve several moves back and forth, enrollment is open at all times. Students learn typical preschool skills like math concepts and motor development, but they also learn about Lakota language and culture. Four classroom sessions are offered Monday through Thursday for the youngsters, and their parents can find assistance with their own educational and social needs, including obtaining a GED, planning for career development, and finding work and housing.

Dakota Transitional is under the auspices of Rural America Initiatives, 919 Main Street, Rapid City, (605) 341-3339, an organization that offers education-related services to Native American youth.

Youth and Family Services
1920 Plaza Boulevard, Rapid City
(605) 342-4195
www.youthandfamilyservices.org

This comprehensive agency offers a wide range of services (see the Child Care

---

If you know someone who needs help learning to read, have him or her call the South Dakota Literacy Council in Pierre at (800) 423-6665, or inquire at the local library. In Rapid City call (605) 394-4171; as soon as the recorded greeting starts, the caller should dial 255 and leave a message after the beep. Messages are retrieved daily.

---

chapter), including home-based and center-based Head Start programs for educational enrichment, starting at age four, with strong parental involvement. A center-based Early Head Start program promotes healthy relationships between parents and children from birth to age three. Youth and Family Services also administers home-based Head Start programs in Butte, Custer, Fall River, Lawrence, and Meade Counties.

COLLEGES AND TECHNICAL SCHOOLS

The Black Hills are a favorite location for students who love the area's recreational opportunities, but they also come here for a quality education. Many of them are non-traditional and international students who find the courses they need at our post-secondary schools. For information about attending intercollegiate sports events, turn to the Spectator Sports chapter.

Northern Hills

Black Hills State University
1200 University Station, Spearfish
(605) 642-6343, (800) 255-2478
www.bhsu.edu

This small public university is situated on a pristine 123-acre campus on the west side of Spearfish. Aside from its desirable setting and academic programs, it prides itself on an outstanding athletic facility, the Donald E. Young Sports and Fitness Center. The $10.5 million center opened in 1990, the result of a cooperative funding effort by the school, the city, the state, and private sources, including alumni. It serves the entire community with two swimming pools, a wide range of athletic facilities, and classroom and meeting space (see the Spectator Sports chapter for more information).

BHSU, one of six state-run colleges in South Dakota, was founded in 1883 as a teachers' training institution called

Spearfish Normal School. Many old-timers still call it that, even though for many years it was Black Hills State College before getting the university designation. Although primarily a school for aspiring teachers, it draws more business majors than any other South Dakota school.

Today BHSU has three colleges: Arts and Sciences, Business and Technology, and Education. The university is also home to the Center for Tourism Research, the Center for Indian Studies, and the Center for the Advancement of Mathematics and Science Education, which provide academic resources to students and private companies alike.

Major courses of study for a bachelor of arts or bachelor of science degree include, but are by no means limited to, such fields as accounting, American Indian studies, art, biology, business administration, chemistry, communication arts, mass communication, environmental physical science, history, human resource management, English, Spanish, outdoor education, political science, psychology, speech, theater, vocal music, tourism and hospitality management, human services, and education.

The school has two-year preprofessional programs in agriculture, dentistry, forestry, law, nursing, medicine, and other subjects. Associate degrees are offered in administrative assistance, drafting technology, general studies, tourism and hospitality management, and a number of computer and technology-related fields.

Master's programs are offered in education and tourism.

The school's athletes are known as the Yellow Jackets, and its colors are green and gold. Football, men's and women's basketball, and volleyball are high-profile competitive sports at BHSU. The football field, Lyle Hare Stadium, seats 3,200 and hosts high school as well as college football games.

Many of the university's 3,900 students live in residence halls, since state law requires unmarried undergraduates to live on campus for at least their first two years. Extension courses are offered over the Internet or in person at Ellsworth Air Force Base, Rapid City Regional Hospital, South Dakota School of Mines and Technology, and other locations.

Central Hills

South Dakota School of Mines and Technology
501 East St. Joseph Street, Rapid City
(605) 394-2400, (800) 544-8162
www.sdsmt.edu

Started as the Dakota School of Mines in 1885, Tech, as it's called today, has been known for its science and engineering programs for the last half century or more.

Four colleges—Materials Science and Engineering, Earth Systems, Interdisciplinary Studies, and Systems Engineering—provide courses of study toward 10 undergraduate degrees in engineering and 6 in science. There are master's programs in 12 disciplines and 3 doctoral programs in science and engineering.

The Institute of Atmospheric Sciences, established in 1959, is located on campus, and students are encouraged to take part in research there. The institute collaborates with the National Weather Service, which has a station nearby, through a student internship program and by helping develop models for more accurate weather prediction. A fiber-optic cable connected to weather service computers affords the institute instant access to data so scientists can watch storms as they develop; that information is then used in research and teaching.

The institute also works with the EROS (Earth Resources Observation Systems) Data Center in Sioux Falls, the world's largest storehouse of earth science information, to interpret and use data to delve into problems such as pollution, climate change, and weather phenomena. The institute has performed major weather-modification field research for several federal agencies and has developed studies for air quality and air pollution. Also, scien-

Billy Mills and Randy Lewis

Billy Mills and Randy Lewis didn't have to take up mining to find gold. They used their talents and worked hard to win gold medals in Olympic competition—20 years apart. So far, they're the only South Dakotans ever to do so.

Billy, an Oglala Lakota from the Pine Ridge Indian Reservation, became the only American in Olympic history to win the 10,000-meter running race. A virtual unknown, he stunned the crowd at the 1964 Tokyo games when, with a mighty burst of speed, he shot ahead of the front-runners and crossed the finish line in a record 28 minutes, 24.4 seconds, beating a world champion. The spectacular win caused such a sensation that it halted his victory lap. Winning the gold made Billy a national hero, but it didn't make him conceited. Instead, he became a role model for Native American youth.

Billy had been orphaned at age 12 and sent to an Indian school in Kansas. Later, at the University of Kansas, he'd competed in track and field, then joined the U.S. Marine Corps after graduating in 1962. In 1965, when he was already an Olympic champion, he won the U.S. national championship in the 6-mile run and set another world record. Billy retired from track and field due to injuries in 1968, but he was later inducted into the National Track and Field Hall of Fame and the U.S. Olympic Hall of Fame. A movie, *Running Brave,* was made about him.

All the while Billy never forgot his roots or the folks back home struggling with deprivation. After 23 years in the insurance business, he sold his company to become a full-time motivational and inspirational speaker. He formed the Billy Mills Speakers Bureau in Fair Oaks, California, and became national spokesperson for Running Strong for American Indian Youth. In the latter capacity he visited the Loneman School on the Pine Ridge reservation in 1997 to hand out awards in a student poster contest. Billy also wrote a book, *Wokini: A Lakota Journey to Happiness and Self-Understanding,* published in 1991.

While Billy was making history, Randy Lewis was a little boy growing up in

tists there use the world's only armor-plated, instrumented airplane capable of penetrating hailstorms in their studies of thunderstorm development. Currently, institute staffers are looking into the ways human activity affects Earth's atmosphere, a science called biogeochemistry.

The Museum of Geology on the Tech campus welcomes visitors who want to ogle dinosaur skeletons, meteorites, minerals, and other fascinating objects from the natural world. Read about the museum in the Attractions chapter.

About 2,400 students attend Tech, 500 of them housed in campus dorms. Under the watchful eye of their mascot, Grubby the miner, the blue-and-yellow Hardrockers compete in football, basketball, volleyball, track and field, and cross-country. O'Harra Stadium, with its playing field and all-weather running track, is surrounded on three sides by terraces where some 300 cars can park while their occupants watch college and high school sports.

Rapid City. He was still young, just 10 years old, when he started wrestling. He was a natural at it, and Olympic gold soon became his goal. He worked hard at his studies too, keeping up his grades at Stevens High School as he won three state wrestling championships. He even set a national record with 45 consecutive pins. The year he graduated, 1977, he won a junior world championship and two national championships. While studying business at the University of Iowa, Randy won two National Collegiate Athletic Association (NCAA) championships and others besides. In 1980 he qualified as the youngest member of the U.S. Olympic wrestling team, but his hopes were dashed when President Jimmy Carter decided the United States would boycott the games. Randy got his chance four years later in Los Angeles, though, and in 1984 he won the gold medal in the 136½-pound weight class.

In his wrestling career Randy was victorious over eight other world or Olympic champions and scored wins over dozens of other top wrestlers. For about eight years he was rated among the world's top

GREAT FACES

three wrestlers, and he won numerous championships. But possessing excellence didn't go to his head, and, like Billy, Randy wanted to pass on something of value to the next generation. Even before he became an Olympic star, he had developed a series of summer wrestling camps for elementary and high school athletes, and after graduating from college in 1982 he coached his alma mater's postgraduate Hawkeye Wrestling Team for 13 years. His days on the mat ended after that, and at this writing Randy was living in Arizona, running a business. He was inducted into the National Wrestling Hall of Fame in 1998.

South Dakota State University College of Nursing
1011 11th Street, Rapid City
(605) 394-5390, (888) 819-1725
www3.sdstate.edu
Nursing students need not attend the main South Dakota State University campus in Brookings to obtain a bachelor of science or master of science degree in nursing. This Rapid City department offers all the courses needed. Through a consortium agreement, students take support courses such as biology, anatomy, and

microbiology at South Dakota School of Mines and Technology in Rapid City. They may elect to take other classes through Black Hills State University, either on the Spearfish campus or at the Ellsworth Air Force Base branch. The remaining classes are offered at the nursing school's main building downtown. The R.N. Upward Mobility Program allows registered nurses with associate degrees to earn a four-year degree in three semesters.

With a bachelor's degree in nursing and a year of work experience, students may enter the graduate program to study for a master's degree in any of several tracks: family nurse practitioner, educator, administrator, or clinical nurse specialist.

Presently, 200 students are pursuing degrees here. All are on their own for housing and meals, since the school does not have student housing or a cafeteria.

South Dakota State University
West River Graduate Center
501 East St. Joseph Street, Rapid City
(605) 394-6823
www3.sdstate.edu

This SDSU extension offers master's programs in education administration, curriculum and instruction, and counseling. All classes are held in the evening on the South Dakota School of Mines and Technology campus; student housing and meals are not provided. Recent enrollment was approximately 130 students in all three programs; enrollment is limited for the counseling program, based on factors that vary from semester to semester.

The University of South Dakota
1011 11th Street, Rapid City
(605) 394-6720, (800) 233-7937
www.usd.edu

The state's largest public university operates two education-related programs in Rapid City through the Division of Technology for Training and Development. The first is a master of science program designed to help students use technological resources for teaching and learning; the second is a specialist program designed to build on the master's degree.

The USD graduate extension offers a master's program in business administration with a health-service option and master of science programs in administrative studies with three options: human resources, health services, and interdisci-

plinary studies. About 90 students take advantage of this program. All classes are offered at night. Students live and dine off campus.

The USD School of Medicine, which is located on the main campus in Vermillion, has a West River campus at 3625 Fifth Street, Suite 200, in Rapid City, (605) 394-5105, where third- and fourth-year medical students can complete a portion of their studies.

Western Dakota Technical Institute
800 Mickelson Drive, Rapid City
(605) 394-4034, (800) 544-8765
www.westerndakotatech.org

One of four state-created technical schools in South Dakota, Western Dakota Technical Institute provides training for jobs in the fields of medicine, engineering, science, law, agriculture, mechanics, and more. Students can choose from among 25 programs that lead to an associate of applied science degree or a diploma. Courses of study at the accredited school include accounting, agriculture, business management, automotive technology, business management and marketing, cabinetmaking, collision-repair technology, computer-aided drafting (architectural and mechanical), industrial electronics, law-enforcement technology, medical transcription, paralegal/legal assistance, pharmacy technician, phlebotomy/patient care technician, practical nursing, welding, and others. A ranch management program is offered on a 496-acre working ranch in Sturgis.

The approximately 4,000 students who go to school here have the use of on-site child care and a retail clothing store where they can get outfitted for a job interview or internship for a reasonable price. Students can buy meals on campus; however, they must find their own housing.

CHILD CARE

In a state where wages are relatively low, few families can afford to have a parent who doesn't work. In fact, recent statistics show that South Dakota has the highest percentage nationally of working mothers with preschoolers (well over 70 percent versus the national average of about 65 percent). Other numbers show that more than 80 percent of South Dakotan women with school-age children work, well above the national statistic of around 75 percent. As a result, child care is an important issue among South Dakotans in general, and Black Hills residents especially.

There's an enormous demand for quality child care, an issue that's an increasingly high priority for state officials and communities. The state even has a coordinator of child-care services to help us do a better job of watching over our kids. There's widespread agreement that more infant and toddler care is needed here, and the state is doing its best to create more slots with a new reimbursement rate structure and more accessible training for child-care providers.

In the Black Hills especially, both providers and parents have an outstanding number of training opportunities. In addition, numerous agencies provide services or referrals for special-needs children. You'll find some of both listed in the following information.

We're also innovative when it comes to looking after children when they're not in school. In Rapid City, for instance, the YMCA and the school district joined forces to create the Kidstop program that provides before- and after-school supervision and activities in many elementary schools. You can learn more about their approach by calling the YMCA at (605) 718-9622 or by visiting www.rcymca.org.

Although the Black Hills is a strongly traditional and conservative area, long based on standard eight-to-five jobs, a growing tourist industry and increasing population base mean that more and more workers are taking shifts on weekends and during the evenings. In response, more child-care providers have been experimenting with extended hours. And as day care becomes a more permanent fixture in our lives, we're seeing a growing array of public and private child-care options, from licensed day-care centers and home-based facilities to preschools and after-school programs. Some schools have day-care programs for students who are raising children.

With so many choices, be sure to shop around. Use the resources listed in this chapter to find the right place for your child.

LOCATING CHILD CARE

If you're new to the area or to the demands of finding child care, Rapid City-based Early Childhood Connections, (605) 342-6464 or (888) 999-7759, is a good place to begin your search. This nonprofit group can produce a customized list of child-care providers to anyone who calls. Just answer a few simple questions (such as the hours you'll need and the neighborhood and town in which you live) and staffers will supply you with a list of all the licensed providers that

---

Rockin Robin Fizz Kids, 120 Knollwood Drive in Rapid City, (605) 342-1818, has a Parents' Timeout program that provides two hours of supervised play for your child—and freedom for you—for a fee. For more information, see the Rockin Robin Fizz Kids listing in the Kidstuff chapter.

meet your criteria. Their list of providers, which they maintain with the help of the Department of Social Services, covers all of the Black Hills and much of western South Dakota. They also print a regular newsletter and offer some enrichment and training classes for day-care providers and new parents. All of these services are provided free of charge.

Classes, workshops, and published materials for parents are also available through the South Dakota Parent Resource Network, (605) 348-9276 or (800) 219-6247, in Sturgis. The network especially focuses on getting parents involved in their children's education, but it also covers topics like violence and community service. It doesn't keep a list of child-care providers, however; to obtain one, see the Early Childhood Connections description above or call the South Dakota Department of Social Services. The latter maintains the Office of Child Care Services, which has on hand lists of both licensed and unlicensed child-care providers across the state. There are several offices scattered throughout Black Hills towns. For their numbers, either contact a local chamber of commerce or consult the government pages of a Black Hills phone book.

WHAT TO ASK

One of the most important steps in choosing a caregiver is often overlooked: visiting the home or center you are considering before you enroll your youngster. While there, observe how staff members interact with children, look over the facility to ensure that it's clean and spacious enough for the number of children who stay there, and inspect the outdoor play area.

Questions you should ask include: How long has the provider been in business? What are her or his ideas about discipline and learning? What kinds of age-appropriate activities are offered? What kinds of meals and snacks are served? How many children attend each day, and what are their ages?

You'll also need to know whether there's a policy that requires you to have backup care if your regular provider gets sick or has an emergency, and whether the day care closes for staff vacation time.

It's a good idea to ask for parent references and to find out whether parents are welcome to drop in unannounced—if not, you might want to look elsewhere.

TRAINING AND OTHER SUPPORT

Whether or not you work outside the home, the time you spend with your child is precious. Here is a partial—and we do mean partial—list of services and training opportunities that can help enrich the hours you have together. These agencies serve the entire Black Hills. For information about Head Start programs and preschools, turn to the Education chapter.

Parents as Teachers
236 West Jackson Boulevard, Spearfish
(605) 642-9088

730 East Watertown Street, Rapid City
(605) 348-WARM, (800) 219-6247

215 North Third Street, Custer
(605) 673-2660
Program staffers make free home visits to families with children up through age five, providing information about growth and

ℹ️ *The Rapid City Area Chamber of Commerce and the city of Rapid City recognize registered family home day-care providers who show proof of 20 hours of training a year. They receive a certificate signed by the mayor and the chamber president and are placed on the Blue Ribbon Provider Recognition List. To request a copy of the list, call (605) 343-1744.*

development as well as age-appropriate activities for parents and children to do together. Other services include developmental screenings, group meetings for parents, referrals to other services, and toy-lending programs.

Single Points of Contact

Northern Hills Interagency Network
2885 Dickson Drive, Sturgis
(605) 347-6260, (800) 219-6247

Pennington County Interagency Network
1719 West Main Street, Rapid City
(605) 394-6089

Youth and Family Support Network
1039 Montgomery Street, Custer
(605) 673-5600, (888) 673-2660
These agencies provide screening for developmental delays, help set up evaluations, and assist parents in locating and coordinating medical, educational, social-services, and mental-health resources for special-needs children from birth to age three. They're also an information resource for families with children of any age.

Youth & Family Services
1920 Plaza Boulevard, Rapid City
(605) 342-4195
www.youthandfamilyservices.org
Youth & Family Services is a comprehensive agency whose services include the YFS Counseling Center, with a 24-hour crisis line, (605) 342-4303, for children and families. Free training in drug-abuse and violence prevention is available to school districts, individuals, and community groups through the Western Prevention Resource Center. Turn to the Health Care chapter for information about other mental-health and emergency resources.

REGULATION

The state of South Dakota keeps a vigilant eye on those who tend and nurture children by setting strict standards and making regular inspections to enforce them.

State law requires licensing for any day-care center that serves 21 or more children, as well as for group family day-care centers that serve 13 to 20 children. Providers who care for up to 12 children in their homes must register with the state if they or their clients receive public funds. In other cases, family home day-care registration is voluntary, but providers who don't register also don't get listed with the Office of Child Care Services or notified of certain training opportunities.

From a parent's point of view, registration may offer added reassurance since it extends systemwide screening for reports of child abuse and neglect to anyone age 10 or older who lives in the provider's home.

All licensed and registered providers must meet in-service training requirements that range from 6 to 20 hours a year, comply with nutrition standards, and keep up-to-date immunization records on the children in their care. Additionally, licensed day-care center directors are required to have a combination of education and experience in the early childhood field. Everyone who works in a regulated child-care facility has to maintain current certification in CPR and first aid.

There are limits to the number of children who can be supervised by one adult. For infants and toddlers, the limit is 5 children to 1 adult; for children ages 3 to 6, it's 10 to 1; and for school-age youngsters, it's 15 to 1.

State fire, health, and safety codes offer further protection for kids in day care, as do local city ordinances that may require criminal background checks, business permits, fenced yards, building code inspections, or other areas of compliance. Call city hall to find out what's required in your community.

HEALTH CARE (H)

Tourism and retail are easily the Black Hills' largest industries, especially in Rapid City. The growing number of giant retailers on the community's east and north sides and the construction of new office complexes downtown are evidence enough. However, a quick look at Rapid City's southern district will tell you that the medical industry runs a close second. Rapid City Regional Hospital, just one player among dozens of local clinics and medical centers, is the largest private-sector employer in the region, boasting a staff of about 2,000 (not including consultants, contractors, and employees of the other clinics the organization owns—see its listing for details). Other major medical facilities include the Rapid City Indian Hospital, the Black Hills Surgery Center (see their listings later in the chapter), as well as several clinics for spine injuries, orthopedics, and radiology, among others.

But Rapid City isn't the only place you can receive medical care in the region. Most major Black Hills towns have a hospital or clinic as well as independent doctors (some of whom still make house calls). Even tiny Deadwood, less than 15 miles from facilities in Sturgis and Spearfish, has its own hospital (which it shares with its sister city, Lead). Although there aren't many wellness or spa facilities in the Black Hills, this sector of the health-care community is also growing. More middle- and high-income residents coming to the area means there is a broader customer base for these sorts of facilities, and the commercial sector is beginning to respond.

With ranching still playing a major role in the economy, keeping animals healthy is also a big business in the Black Hills. You'll find a small number of veterinarians listed at the end of this chapter. Because of the nature of the region, many of them are just as experienced with dogs and ferrets as they are with horses and bison.

HOSPITALS

Northern Hills

Fort Meade VA Medical Center
113 Comanche Road, Fort Meade
(605) 347-2511, (800) 743-1070
www.va.gov
Fort Meade VA Center is part of the Department of Veterans Affairs (VA) Black Hills Health Care System that provides primary and secondary medical and surgical care along with domiciliary, extended nursing home, and tertiary psychiatric inpatient care services for veterans residing in South Dakota and portions of Nebraska, Wyoming, North Dakota, and Montana. Other specialty programs include addictive disorders, post-traumatic stress, and compensated work therapy. VA Black Hills features medical centers at Fort Meade and Hot Springs along with many community-based outpatient clinics, including Rapid City. It is ranked among the nation's top five VA health-care facilities for patient satisfaction.

Fort Meade VA Center, 2 miles east of Sturgis, has been a VA facility since the birth of the VA in the 1940s, but there has been a hospital at the 120-year-old fort since its founding. Today it features inpatient and outpatient care, an inpatient psychiatric unit, and a rehabilitation-focused nursing-home care unit.

Lead-Deadwood Regional Hospital
61 Charles Street, Deadwood
(605) 722-6101
www.rcrh.org
A $1.8 million project gave the hospital a

new lobby, an entrance and parking for the disabled, renovated rehabilitation facilities, and expanded services. The primary-care hospital has been in existence since 1878.

Services include an emergency room, cardiac care, obstetrics, cardiac and pulmonary rehabilitation, home health, respiratory and physical therapy, and medical equipment. The facility has 18 beds.

Spearfish Regional Hospital
1440 North Main Street, Spearfish
(605) 644-4000
www.rcrh.org
A primary-care facility with 40 beds, Spearfish Regional was named one of the top-100 hospitals in the nation and one of the top-38 rural care facilities. It has an adjacent family medical center, an emergency room, home health care (for in-home visits), rehabilitation services, a women's health-care center with eight birthing suites, and an award-winning cardiopulmonary rehabilitation program.

Spearfish Regional belongs to the Black Hills Regional System of Care.

Sturgis Regional Hospital
949 Harmon Street, Sturgis
(605) 347-2536
www.rcrh.org
This 25-bed primary-care facility has an adjacent family medical center, emergency room, a medical equipment component, a home-health program, and rehabilitation services for the elderly and the disabled. The hospital also has an 84-bed Medicare-certified nursing home and offers wellness and education programs.

Central Hills

Black Hills Surgery Center
216 Anamaria Drive, Rapid City
(605) 721-4700, (800) 818-1890
www.bhsc.com
Rapid City's smaller licensed hospital was built by doctors. It is a specialty hospital where many surgical procedures can be

Rapid City Regional Hospital has a benefit for patients' families: discount rates at the Best Western Town & Country Inn, 2505 Mount Rushmore Road, just 2 blocks from the hospital. Request a Hospital Visitor Card at the hospital's information desk and present the card at the motel to receive a discounted rate. The hospital also has "accommodation rooms," which are rented for a minimal charge. Inquire at the information desk.

performed, including neurosurgery and dental, pediatric, gynecological, and other operations. This 23-bed center does not accept heart attack victims or patients requiring intensive care, as it does not have an emergency room or intensive-care facilities. It specializes instead in most routine (and some advanced) surgical procedures, both inpatient and outpatient.

Rapid City Indian Hospital (Sioux San)
3200 Canyon Lake Drive, Rapid City
(605) 355-2500
www.ihs.gov
This Indian Health Service primary-care hospital is one of just three such facilities in the nation not located on a reservation. It was founded in the early 1950s as a tuberculosis sanitarium. Operated by the federal government, the 32-bed hospital treats only Native American patients.

Services and facilities include an emergency room, community health nursing (home care), specialty clinics such as dentistry and optometry, walk-in clinics, and the only mental health inpatient unit in the Indian Health Service. There are no facilities for surgery or obstetrics, which are handled at Rapid City Regional Hospital.

Rapid City Regional Hospital
353 Fairmont Boulevard, Rapid City
(605) 341-1000
www.rcrh.org
Rapid City Regional Hospital was created in 1973. It is a 417-bed regional medical center providing services in more than 40

There are plenty of specialist physicians in Rapid City, and many medical offices have sprung up near Rapid City Regional Hospital, creating a sort of "medical neighborhood." New offices have become concentrated in the area bordered by U.S. 16, Cathedral Drive, and South Fifth Street. Specialists are listed by their specialties in the Yellow Pages under "Physicians."

medical specialties. The hospital complex encompasses the Cancer Care Institute, Black Hills Rehabilitation Hospital, Regional West Behavioral Health Center, the Heart Care Center, Same-Day Surgery Center, and other components. Emergency services include a 24-hour emergency department and regional LifeFlight, a 24-hour emergency air- and ground-transport service.

Southern Hills

Custer Regional Hospital
1039 Montgomery Street, Custer
(605) 673-2229
www.rcrh.org
Custer's hospital is a 16-bed primary-care facility with a 24-hour emergency room and an adjacent urgent care and family practice facility. It also has a home-health program. It operates two smaller rural clinics in nearby towns: the Hill City Medical Clinic and the Edgemont Memorial Clinic.

Hot Springs VA Medical Center
500 North Fifth Street, Hot Springs
(605) 745-2000, (800) 764-5370
www.va.gov
The Hot Springs VA Medical Center—like the VA Medical Center in Fort Meade—is part of the Department of Veterans Affairs (VA) Black Hills Health Care System that provides primary and secondary medical and surgical care along with domiciliary, extended nursing home, and tertiary psy-

chiatric inpatient care services for veterans residing in South Dakota and portions of Nebraska, Wyoming, North Dakota, and Montana. The Hot Springs facility was founded in 1907 as the Battle Mountain Sanitarium. Today it features inpatient and outpatient medical care and residential-based programs.

INFORMATION AND SERVICES

Alzheimer's Association of Western South Dakota
701 St. Joseph Street, Rapid City
(605) 718-5766
The local Alzheimer's Association chapter has a wealth of information for caregivers of Alzheimer's patients. Telephone counseling can help guide the caregiver in new or difficult situations, and there's a library with informative videos, books, and audiotapes. Free brochures are available on numerous aspects of coping with Alzheimer's. The Alzheimer's and Related Dementia Care Group meets twice a month at the office, from 1:30 to 3:30 P.M. on the second Tuesday of the month and from 6:00 to 8:00 P.M. on the third Tuesday of the month.

American Cancer Society, South Dakota Division Inc.
2465 West Chicago Street, Rapid City
(605) 342-7740, (800) 227-2345
www.cancer.org
Above and beyond raising money for research, the local office of the American Cancer Society provides educational materials and programs to heighten cancer awareness, and it has a number of volunteer services for patients. In the Reach to Recovery program, for instance, volunteers who have survived breast cancer help current patients understand what to expect and how to care for themselves during treatment. Additional volunteer services include transportation to treatment centers and assistance with appearance, such as help with skin care from

Support Organizations
and Other Information Numbers

AIDS Hotline	(800) 592-1861
	(800) 342-2437
Al-Anon/Alateen	(605) 394-8250
Alcohol/Drug Helpline	(605) 394-6128
Alcoholics Anonymous	(605) 721-4552
Church Response	(605) 342-5360
Crisis Hotline	(605) 342-4303
Family Violence Hotline	(800) 430-7233
Gamblers Anonymous	(888) 781-4357
Gay and Lesbian Coalition	(605) 391-8080
Poison Control	(800) 222-1222
South Dakota Parent Resource Network	(605) 348-9276
Working Against Violence	(605) 341-4808
	(domestic violence crisis line)
	(605) 341-2046
	(sexual assault crisis line)

trained cosmetologists. Pamphlets that explain different cancers and treatments are available from the office, which is located in west Rapid City. The office serves the entire Black Hills area.

NONTRADITIONAL AND ALTERNATIVE TREATMENTS

A growing number of alternative health-care practitioners are relocating to the Black Hills. Some offer services such as acupuncture, reflexology, herbal remedies, yoga classes, and more.

In all cases, ask about the practitioner's certification. *NOTE:* Some alternative treatments are offered by spas and fitness centers, listed later in this chapter.

Acupuncture Clinic of the Black Hills
2720 West Main Street, Rapid City
(605) 342-4333
Gary Gamache, a certified acupuncturist, also operates the Westside Chiropractic Clinic at the same location. Patients come to be treated for chronic health problems and pain, among other ailments.

Body Systems
512 Main Street, Rapid City
(605) 484-6742
www.body-systems.net
What started as a homemade effort to create natural soaps and lotions that wouldn't trouble owner Teri Lang Peterson's sensitive skin has turned into a stylishly successful product line. Teri now manufactures and sells a variety of body care products from her home. Though she sells to individual customers around

Medical Centers and Day Clinics

Some of these clinics are open early and late for minor emergencies, sudden illnesses, routine physicals, or when your regular doctor isn't available. Many take walk-in patients; some require appointments. For major emergencies, go to a hospital emergency room instead.

Northern Hills
Belle Fourche Regional Medical Clinic
2200 13th Avenue, Belle Fourche
(605) 892-2701

Lead-Deadwood Regional Medical Clinic
71 Charles Street, Deadwood
(605) 578-2364

Spearfish Regional Medical Clinic
1445 North Avenue, Spearfish
(605) 644-4170

Massa Berry Regional Medical Clinic
890 Lazelle Street, Sturgis
(605) 347-3616

Queen City Medical Center
1420 North 10th Street, Spearfish
(605) 642-8414

Spearfish Health Center
550 Colorado Boulevard, Spearfish
(605) 642-2030

Sturgis Medical Center
1010 Ball Park Road, Sturgis
(605) 347-3684

Central Hills
Black Hills Pediatrics and Neonatology
2905 Fifth Street, Rapid City
(605) 341-7337

Family Practice Residency Center
502 East Monroe Street, Rapid City
(605) 719-4060

Foothills Family Clinic
8075 Stage Stop Road, Black Hawk
(605) 718-7625

the world via her Web site, her biggest clients are day spas and health stores located across the globe, including the Mandalay Bay Resort and Casino in Las Vegas and a few in East Asia. If you'd like to get some of her products while you're in the Black Hills, give her a call or stop by Spa 80 for Women in Rapid City (see the listing below).

Halina Hladysz
1320-B Mount Rushmore Road
Rapid City
(605) 342-7543
Halina Hladysz is an herbalist and certified iridologist who offers health and fitness

consultations and iris photography and analysis. In the field of iridology, the iris is a sort of mirror of the changes taking place in the body; it is analyzed to determine the cause of illness. She uses vitamins and minerals, homeopathic remedies, flower essences, essential oils, books, and herbs.

JSL Enterprises
2425 Mount Rushmore Road, Suite C
Rapid City
(605) 343-2322
www.shaklee.com
This small independent store distributes products of the Shaklee company, a national company that manufactures food

Hill City Medical Clinic
114 East Main Street, Hill City
(605) 574-4470

Medical Arts Clinic
717 St. Francis Street, Rapid City
(605) 388-4640

Medical Associates of the Black Hills
640 Flormann Street, Rapid City
(605) 718-3100

Piedmont Medical Center
8018 Stage Stop Road, Piedmont
(605) 787-6714

RapidCare Medical Center
408 Knollwood Drive, Rapid City
(605) 341-6600

Rapid City Community Health Center
504 East Monroe Street, Rapid City
(605) 394-6666

Rapid City Medical Center
2820 Mount Rushmore Road, Rapid City
(605) 342-3280
2201 Jackson Boulevard, Rapid City
(605) 348-4645
902 Columbus Street, Rapid City
(605) 348-2273
3810 Jackson Boulevard, Rapid City
(605) 343-4050

Rapid City VA Health Clinic
3625 Fifth Street, Rapid City
(605) 718-1095
(accepts veterans only)

Southern Hills
Custer Clinic
1041 Montgomery Street, Custer
(605) 673-4150

Edgemont Memorial Clinic
908 H Street, Edgemont
(605) 662-7250

products and household cleaners based primarily on herbs and plant material. You can purchase or order any Shaklee product from owner Jan Spicer, from pain medication and skin-firming lotion to glass cleaner and water filters.

SPAS AND FITNESS CENTERS

Some spas and fitness centers require memberships in order to use their facilities, but they also offer day or temporary passes for visitors. In addition, the charge is often lower if you are visiting the spa with a current member. If you are looking for therapeutic massage (check the Yellow Pages under "Massage"), ask about the types of massage therapy offered—such as Swedish, Esalen, sports, and deep tissue techniques.

Northern Hills

Frankly Hair
795 Main Street, Deadwood
(605) 578-2355
www.historicfranklinhotel.com
Frankly Hair is a small salon located on the main floor of the Historic Franklin

Hotel, one of the largest hotels on Dead-wood's Victorian Main Street (see its listing in the Accommodations chapter). Jill and Shanna cut and style hair, give pedicures and manicures, and apply makeup. Individual treatments and salon services vary but are generally less expensive than similar businesses in Rapid City.

Central Hills

Mystique Edge Salon and Spa
509 Seventh Street, Rapid City
(605) 737-0095
www.mystiqueedge.com
This spa's downtown location means that it attracts a lot of businesspeople; it even has specially designed massage packages for executives with only a few minutes to spare. However, the spa has extended therapies that last anywhere from an hour to all day. Salon services include haircuts, pedicures, manicures, facials, and waxes. It offers dozens of body wraps and treatments, a sauna, a hydrotherapy tub, and licensed masseurs. Packages range from $80 to $345. Massages run from $35 to $85, depending on length, and individual treatments start at $25. Owner Lori Eggersgluess and her staff are both friendly and professional, and they ensure that customers feel relaxed from the moment they walk in the door.

Spa 80 for Women and Pace Fitness
512 Main Street, Rapid City
(605) 342-8080
This fitness center is for women only. It offers aerobics, step aerobics, body toning, stair climbers, treadmills, weight machines and free weights, a circuit training program called Pace, a whirlpool, and a sauna. Tanning beds and a nursery are available, too, but there's an extra charge for those services. The spa has a certified personal trainer on staff. It offers nutrition classes and fun classes in stationary biking and spinning, which will really help you work up a sweat.

The Weight Room
601 12th Street, Rapid City
(605) 348-5070
www.theweightroom.net
This center specializes in the heavy stuff: weight lifting, free weights, Hammer-Strength equipment, and bodybuilding. Personal trainers are on staff and vitamins and protein supplements are for sale.

YMCA
815 Kansas City Street, Rapid City
(605) 342-8538
www.rcymca.org
The YMCA offers a new gym, drop-in child-care center, and the Randy Travis Wellness Center in honor of the singer who performed a benefit concert to raise money for the facilities. The wellness center has free weights, cardiovascular machines, Nautilus weight-lifting machines, and more, including an indoor track, racquetball courts, and three gyms. Fitness trainers are available for fitness testing, health appraisals, consultations, and exercise prescriptions (in collaboration with Rapid City Regional Hospital). Massage therapy is available by appointment.

Three indoor pools get a lot of use. One is a training pool (4-foot maximum depth) where water aerobics and other water workouts are held; the others are 25-meter pools for general use.

Many classes are offered at the YMCA, including aerobics and Jazzercise. Call to ask what's scheduled.

Southern Hills

Springs Bath House
146 North Garden Street, Hot Springs
(605) 745-4424, (888) 817-1972
www.springsbathhouse.com
This bathhouse has brought the day-spa concept back to Hot Springs, where such facilities were once common.

Springs Bath House offers therapeutic massage, juice and oxygen bars, reflexology, cleansing steam therapy, and many different kinds of healing baths, including aromatherapy, mud, milk, herbal, and mustard (good for when you have a cold).

The famous Hot Springs water has a high mineral content and is used in the handmade soaps, lotions, shampoos, conditioners, bubble baths, and face creams carried in the gift shop, where you can also purchase gift baskets.

WELLNESS CENTERS

Central Hills

Black Hills Health & Education Center
19 Battle Creek Road, Hermosa
(605) 255-4101
www.bhhec.org
A true wellness facility, the center uses education to improve the lives and health of its participants. It is open year-round, with the possible exception of December, and programs run from 5 to 20 days. Participants stay at the center and learn new ways of improving their health. They hike; work out; attend lectures on medicine, nutrition, cooking, and stress; and enjoy massages and hydrotherapy monitored by two staff physicians. Meals are vegan (no meat, eggs, or animal products), as the staff are members of the Seventh-day Adventist Church. The center, however, is nondenominational and nonprofit.

VETERINARIANS

Most area veterinarians work with small and large domesticated animals and livestock. Most can care for horses, either off-site or in their facilities, but we recommend you call ahead and ask.

Northern Hills

Belle Fourche Veterinary Clinic
406 Summit Street, Belle Fourche
(605) 892-2618

Johnson, Jones & Ireland Veterinary Clinic
713 Anna Street, Sturgis
(605) 347-3606

Metzger Animal Clinic
729 Seventh Street, Spearfish
(605) 642-3422

Spearfish Animal Hospital
710 East Colorado Boulevard, Spearfish
(605) 642-5771

Sturgis Veterinary Hospital
2421 Vanocker Canyon Road, Sturgis
(605) 347-4436

Tri-State Veterinary Clinic
Highway 212 West, Belle Fourche
(605) 892-2844

Central Hills

Animal Clinic
1655 East 27th Street (Valley Drive),
Rapid City
(605) 342-1368

Black Hills Animal Hospital
2909 U.S. Highway 79 South, Rapid City
(605) 343-6066

Canyon Lake Veterinary Hospital
4230 Canyon Lake Drive, Rapid City
(605) 348-6510

Dakota Hills Veterinary Clinic
1571 U.S. Highway 44 East, Rapid City
(605) 342-7498

Green Meadows Veterinary Clinic
3400 Elk Vale Road, Rapid City
(605) 348-3727
Meiners Animal Clinic
220 Krebs Drive, Rapid City
(605) 343-5089

Mountain View Animal Hospital
1112 Jackson Boulevard, Rapid City
(605) 343-8050

Noah's Ark Animal Hospital
1315 Mount Rushmore Road, Rapid City
(605) 343-3225

Southern Hills

Fall River Veterinary Clinic
Fall River Road, Hot Springs
(605) 745-3786

U.S. Highway 385 South, Custer
(605) 673-4018

RETIREMENT 🌴

For a certain number of Black Hills residents, retirement means winters on the sunny golf courses of Arizona. For others, it can mean moving to the Hills to live full-time in the family vacation cabin. Some build a dream home and settle down after years of moving around in the military or another line of work. Still others see retirement as a time to start a new career—it's not uncommon to see someone in her golden years taking a computer class, giving tours at a history attraction, or volunteering at an archaeological dig.

Whatever your lifestyle, retirement brings change. In this chapter we'll direct you to some of the opportunities and challenges reserved for retirees. We'll tell you about a couple of retirement communities where you can live in comfort and privacy with others who share your interests. And we'll provide information about some of the many services that are available to you.

For a comprehensive look at housing and medical care, turn to the Relocation and Health Care chapters.

INFORMATION AND SERVICES

Advocacy groups, financial and legal services, support groups, and other resources can be found throughout the Hills.

Hills-wide

Dakota Plains Legal Services
528 Kansas City Street, Suite 1, Rapid City
(605) 342-7171
(800) 742-8602 (SD residents)
Dakota Plains Legal Services provides free legal help to U.S. citizens age 60 or older regardless of income, as well as to income-qualified younger people. Areas of assistance include Social Security, Medicaid and Medicare, elder abuse, spousal abuse, powers of attorney and living wills, housing and homelessness issues, employment, and more. The agency covers the entire Black Hills and beyond. Call for an appointment.

MEALS Program
303 North Maple Avenue, Rapid City
(605) 394-6002
Seniors can enjoy a hot noon meal five days a week at sites throughout the Black Hills, and volunteers deliver meals to those who are homebound because of a mental or physical disability. Participants must be 60 or older, but their spouses younger than 60 are also welcome. Operating under the auspices of Western South Dakota Senior Services, the agency provides information about home health-care agencies in Rapid City and makes referrals to the state Department of Social Services. Payment is by donation; those younger than 60 pay a flat fee of $5.00. Call to reserve a place at the table, or sign up at one of the meal sites.

Several senior centers participate in the program, including Belle Fourche Senior Center, Custer Senior Citizens Center, Hill City Senior Citizens Center, Springs Senior Citizens Center, Keystone Senior Citizens Center, Canyon Lake Senior Citizens Center, and Minneluzahan Senior Citizens Center. See the Senior Centers section of this chapter for addresses and phone numbers.

In addition, some apartment buildings in Rapid City are in the program.

Call the main number above for other serving sites, brochures, menus, and service.

SHIINE Program
2628 West Main Street, Rapid City
(605) 342-3494, (800) 822-8804
SHIINE stands for Senior Health Information and Insurance Education. Trained vol-

unteers in almost every county in the state help seniors sort out the complexities of health insurance, including Medicare, private long-term or supplemental insurance, and other benefits. One-on-one meetings can be arranged when questions are too involved to be handled by phone. All services are free of charge.

Central Hills

American Association of Retired Persons
AARP Connections
2200 North Maple Street
(Rushmore Mall), Rapid City
(605) 394-7798
www.aarp.org

The American Association of Retired Persons is practically a one-stop shopping information outlet for people age 50 and older. Not only does the advocacy organization have its own education and assistance programs—for instance, a safe-driving course and help at tax time—but volunteers keep an astounding list of resource people and organizations that can answer your questions and direct you to service providers. So whether you want to find out if there's a local adult soccer team, get help with a legal or medical problem, obtain a list of nursing facilities, or get information on just about any topic, the AARP can tell you where to turn.

The office is open and staffed by volunteers from 10:00 A.M. to 3:00 P.M. Monday through Friday. Two chapters hold regular meetings, so ask about joining.

Financial Services Exchange
2040 West Main Street, Suite 310
Rapid City
(605) 348-4573

Using dedicated computer software, an independent financial consultant can help you decide how much money you'll need for retirement and how to invest for it. You'll get help analyzing your current savings situation and understanding different kinds of Individual Retirement Accounts and pension plans. Setting aside funds for

your children's college education, learning to manage your portfolio, and estate planning can be addressed as well. Charges for services vary.

Pennington County Council on Aging
Rapid City
(605) 348-0403, (605) 574-2273

The council advocates for seniors and puts them in touch with some of the services and benefits available to them in Pennington County, such as transportation. A board of directors oversees the council, which is funded through a county appropriation and membership dues of $5.00 a year. Membership is open to people of any age; meetings are at 1:30 P.M. the second Friday of the month at Minneluzahan Senior Citizens Center, 315 North Fourth Street, (605) 394-1887.

Widowed Persons Service
(605) 341-3255, (605) 394-7798

Volunteers who have experienced profound loss through widowhood themselves provide one-on-one support and understanding for the newly widowed. Meetings are arranged individually with an outreach volunteer who treats each situation with the strictest confidentiality. Literature also is available to help the bereaved cope with the changes faced after losing a spouse. Support groups for younger as well as senior survivors meet to help sustain members over the long term. They also sponsor a men's breakfast club, a lunch group, a monthly potluck, and other programs. Call for information about meeting times and places, as they vary. Begun in 1994, the organization is cosponsored by the AARP (see the listing above).

RETIREE HOUSING

When it's time to move into a smaller home, many seniors want to retain their independence while finding comfort, convenience, and companionship among their own age group in a retirement community. Regional Senior Care, a division of

Rapid City Regional Hospital, operates several assisted-living facilities around the Black Hills, including Fairmont Grand Manor and Fox Run in Rapid City, Wedgwood in Custer, and Golden Ridge in Lead. While these retirement communities offer a range of independent and assisted-living options, the majority of residents are older and generally need regular health monitoring. For more independent options, try some of the facilities listed below.

Northern Hills

Juniper Court
430 Oriole Drive, Spearfish
(605) 642-4744
Each of the 14 apartments here is at ground level and has a walk-out patio and a small plot for a flower garden. Seniors 62 and older can rent a one- or two-bedroom apartment but must bring their own clothes washer and dryer—a plus if you swear by your own appliances. There's a community room for socializing. Juniper Court is part of Evergreen Management Services, which operates a handful of other housing units in Belle Fourche, Sturgis, and Gillette, Wyoming.

Central Hills

Primrose
224 East Minnesota Street, Rapid City
(605) 342-6699
www.primroseretirement.com
Primrose has 48 one- and two-bedroom apartments for seniors 60 and older, 16 of which are for those who require residential care or assisted living. Each unit has a fully equipped kitchen and, depending on whether it's on the first or second floor, a patio or a balcony. In the common area are a library, cozy fireplace, exercise room, entertainment center, and multipurpose room. During the summer, residents can have a garden spot on the grounds.

Under South Dakota law, door-to-door salespeople must advise you of your right to cancel purchases of $25 or more made in your home and provide you with a cancellation form. You have three days in which to mail the form, preferably by certified mail, if you want to return the merchandise for a refund.

Westhills Village Retirement Community
255 Texas Street, Rapid City
(605) 342-0255
www.westhillsvillage.com
You don't have to be retired to move into one of the 202 lovely private apartments at Westhills Village, a life-care community that compares itself to a first-class hotel with five sizes and floor plans from which to choose (all with fully equipped kitchens). If you're 62 years old and capable of living on your own, you're eligible. Get your application in early; you can expect to be on the waiting list for at least a year, so plan ahead.

Established in 1984, the nonprofit and Christian-based Westhills Village offers a full spectrum of options for moderate-income seniors. In addition to the apartments already mentioned, 31 private suites at adjacent Westhills South offer assisted living with staffers on hand around the clock. For those needing the highest level of care and supervision, Westhills Village Health Care Facility is a state-licensed, Medicare-approved skilled-nursing facility with 44 beds in private and semiprivate rooms. Registered nurses are on staff 24 hours a day. The Home Health Agency of Westhills Village provides in-home care in Rapid City and the surrounding area.

The monthly service fees for Westhills Village apartments include a daily meal, utilities, and many services such as limited housekeeping and scheduled transportation. Woodworkers, gardeners, and crafters find ample space for their pastimes in the common area, and the beauti-

Comanche and Tipperary

Two of the most famous Black Hills retirees were horses. Comanche was a steady, faithful Seventh Cavalry steed. Tipperary, Comanche's temperamental opposite, was an outlaw bronc that was never tamed.

When troopers reached the battle-field at Little Bighorn—site of the "last stand" of Lt. Col. George A. Custer's Seventh Cavalry—two days after the 1876 battle, they found only one participant still alive: the seriously injured Comanche. He had been ridden into the battle by Capt. Myles Keogh, the commander of I Company.

The stoic horse eventually recovered and spent the rest of his life as the pet of the Seventh. By regimental order, he was retired, never to be ridden or worked again. He participated only in ceremonies, draped in mourning and led by a trooper. During the Seventh Cavalry's nine years at Fort Meade, Comanche lived a life of ease, had the run of the grounds, and reportedly developed a taste for treats and beer, panhandled from his fond fellow soldiers.

In 1888 the Seventh was sent to Fort Riley, Kansas, where Comanche died in 1891 at the age of 31 (or 28, depending on the source). His battle-scarred body was stuffed, mounted, and caparisoned, and it is still on display at the University of Kansas Natural History Museum in Lawrence.

Tipperary was born in 1905 near Camp Crook, north of the Black Hills. A range horse, he gave little indication of his ability to buck off the best until 1915, when Ed Marty tried to break him. The wild ride lasted only seconds. The cowboy gingerly picked himself up from the mud and broke into the popular refrain, "it's a long way to Tipperary," and the horse had his name.

The outlaw bronc loved cowboy busting and constantly learned new tricks to outwit them. He could rear straight up, twist, jump, sunfish, and buck, anything to get a rider off his back. Although he was mounted about 100 times, only eight men were not thrown from him.

Tipperary was retired in 1926. But he made his final appearance at the 1931 Black Hills Roundup in Belle Fourche (see the Annual Events chapter), where he had thrown so many riders. He stood there, head down, feeble, tired . . . until the band struck up "Tipperary." Then the old bronc raised his head and, keeping time to the music as he had done in his younger days, strutted proudly before the cheering crowd one last time.

Tipperary died during a 1932 blizzard on the rangeland of his birth. A monument to the great horse stands in Buffalo, South Dakota.

fully manicured grounds feature gardens and walking paths.

SENIOR CENTERS

Nearly every community in the Black Hills has a senior center where you can engage in fun activities, make friends, and find out about local services such as transportation. We've listed a number of senior centers here, but check phone book listings or contact the local chamber of commerce for others. There is no residency requirement for the centers listed below, so you can join any or all of them, regardless of where you live. Most of these sites serve meals, and you'll find information about that under the Information and Services section. Blood-pressure checks and other wellness clinics often are provided, too, as well as assistance with income tax preparation.

Northern Hills

Belle Fourche Senior Citizens Center
828 Kingsbury Street, Belle Fourche
(605) 892-6285
Members here take part in line dancing, cards and other games, pool, holiday dances, and a greeting card recycling program.

Members must be at least 45 years old (voting privileges come at age 55) and pay an annual fee of $7.00.

Meade County Senior Citizen Center
919 Second Street, Sturgis
(605) 347-5877
The center serves about 5,000 breakfasts during the annual Sturgis Rally & Races (see the Annual Events and Festivals chapter) each August. It also provides Meals on Wheels weekly to senior citizens and shut-ins. The rest of the year, members get together for card games, dances, choral performances, crafts, and sewing for the center's semiannual craft fairs. Special activities include potlucks and fund-raising meals, dances, exercise

classes, and a thrift shop. Annual dues are $10 for membership at age 55 or older.

Spearfish Senior Service Center
1306 10th Street, Spearfish
(605) 642-2827
Members here enjoy pool, card games, bingo, chorus and band, exercise classes, and dances. Other activities include monthly breakfasts, potluck luncheons, a bridge club, and fund-raisers (all on different days). Achieving age 50 and paying annual dues of $10 are the only membership requirements.

Twin City Senior Citizen Center
609 West Main Street, Lead
(605) 584-1261
Bingo, card games, and aerobics are available to members age 50 and older who pay their yearly $10 dues. Monthly potlucks and fund-raisers are on the agenda, and efforts are being directed at arranging regular Sunday social activities.

Central Hills

Canyon Lake Senior Citizens Center
2900 Canyon Lake Drive, Rapid City
(605) 721-8710
www.canyonlakecenter.com
Seniors age 60 and older find a wealth of activities and services here, including aerobics, bingo, cribbage, bridge, a discussion group, ceramics, dances, Ping-Pong, pool, shuffleboard, line dancing, exercise classes, and limited computer training. There's a rug loom for weavers, a library for book lovers, and a garden where you can rent space for summer flowers and veggies. Those with a flair for the performing arts

The Social Security Administration has an office at 605 Main Street, Suite 201, in Rapid City. Call (605) 342-1819 between 9:00 A.M. and 4:00 P.M. Monday through Friday, or call (800) 772-1213 for automated service.

will want to take part in community presentations by the Joyful Guys and Gals singing group and the center's drama group. Special activities include cross-country ski trips, golf lessons, hikes, and more. Yearly dues are $10, and there's a small fee for certain activities. The center claims more than 1,800 active members.

Hill City Senior Citizens Center
303 Walnut Avenue, Hill City
(605) 574-2988
Recent remodeling added new windows, an office, and an entryway for greater comfort at the center, where members participate in a greeting card recycling program, pool, the Merry Music Makers singing group, and birthday potlucks. New ideas are welcome, as are members of any age. Only those 60 and older can vote, though. Dues are $5.00.

Keystone Senior Citizens Center
517 First Street, Keystone
(605) 666-4808
The center is used mostly for community functions, but seniors congregate here to share meals (especially at holiday times), celebrate birthdays, and talk. Dues are $5.00 a year for members 55 and older.

Minneluzahan Senior Citizens Center
315 North Fourth Street, Rapid City
(605) 394-1887
There's no excuse for idleness when exercise classes, dances, bingo, cards, table tennis, crochet classes, pool, shuffleboard, volleyball, and so much else is available here. The musically inclined will find a place in the Rambling Larks singing group or the Merry Music Makers "kitchen band."

ℹ️ *In the Northern Hills, Prairie Hills Transit, 430 Oriole Drive, Spearfish, (605) 642-6613, operates a fleet of vans and buses that provides transportation to and from doctor appointments, stores, restaurants, and other destinations. Buses also go to Rapid City.*

Potlucks for members and suppers that are open to the public provide additional social opportunities, and a monthly bus trip to Deadwood provides a change of scenery. Members make good use of "retired" items through a greeting card recycling program and a thrift room where used clothing and household items are sold. Those 55 and older pay $5.00 a year to belong.

Southern Hills

Custer Senior Citizens Center
538 Mount Rushmore Road, Custer
(605) 673-2708
You don't need to be a senior citizen to enjoy the benefits of membership at this center. Associate members of any age pay $5.00 a year to belong; those 60 and older pay $12.00 and get voting privileges. Line dancing, exercise classes, bingo, greeting card recycling, ceramics, movies, a Stitches 'n' Sew group, pool, and card games are some of the activities found here. The center has a support group for widowed people, as well as programs for greeting new area residents and visiting or staying in touch by phone with those who are alone or isolated. The local ministerial association's food pantry is located in the center, and the Coalition on Aging holds its meetings here.

Springs Senior Citizens Center
206 South Chicago Avenue, Hot Springs
(605) 745-6123
Bridge, cribbage, and pinochle are some of the card games members enjoy playing here. Pool, exercise classes, and, occasionally, a dance offer additional opportunities for fun and well-being. Bingo players find their game of choice at the regularly scheduled potlucks, and fund-raisers, greeting card recycling, and a small rummage area for nonclothing items help support the center. Seniors 55 and older pay $7.50 a year or $50.00 for lifetime membership.

WORKING AND VOLUNTEERING

Looking for work and volunteer opportunities? Here are a few agencies that can help in the search for both. If you're interested in volunteering, also check with hospitals, libraries, schools, community sports programs, national organizations, and the USDA Forest Service. And don't forget about the valuable contribution to be made by serving on a civic committee or board.

Hills-wide

Retired & Senior Volunteer Program (RSVP)
333 Sixth Street, Rapid City
(605) 394-2507

236 West Jackson Boulevard, Spearfish
(605) 642-5198

919 Second Street, Sturgis
(605) 347-5048
www.seniorcorps.org
This national organization has put the skills of seniors age 55 and older to use on worthy community projects for a quarter of a century. Local chapters provide services to nonprofit agencies that ask for help with anything from collating bulk mailings to tutoring in schools to pushing the juice cart at the local hospital. The organization tries to match individual skills and training to specific tasks, be it helping other seniors fill out their tax returns, working in a literacy program, guiding children safely across the street as a crossing guard, or joining a chorus to entertain nursing home residents. In Spearfish, RSVP and other community volunteers gather each spring to replenish RSVP Memorial Garden on North Main Street with eye-catching colorful flowers.

Work Experience (Hills-wide)
2500 Minnekahta Avenue, Hot Springs
(605) 745-5101

(Northern Hills)
(605) 347-9362

111 New York Street, Rapid City
(605) 394-1745
It's been more than three decades since former first lady Lady Bird Johnson urged Americans to plant a tree, a bush, or a shrub to beautify our highways. But the Green Thumb program implemented by the Johnson administration in 1966 has branched out to include more people doing more jobs.

Seniors 55 and older who are eligible to work in the United States can get help finding employment through Work Experience, the nation's largest organization of its kind. You'll find Work Experience representatives serving the entire Black Hills; in the Northern Hills, however, there's no permanent office, and you'll need to call ahead.

An offshoot of Work Experience, Experience Works Staffing Service, 1719 West Main Street, Rapid City, (605) 394-5755, is a temp agency for mature workers of all ages and income levels. Skills assessment and testing are done here at no charge.

Central Hills

Community Development Department
300 Sixth Street, Rapid City
(605) 394-4181
www.rcgov.org
If serving on a city committee, task force, or commission is up your alley, contact the mayor's office at (605) 394-4110.

For an hourly rate of $8.00 to $12.00, Needful Things Errand Service Inc. in Rapid City will dispatch a driver to run your errands or to give you a ride. Drivers are available from 9:00 A.M. to 3:00 P.M. Monday, Tuesday, Thursday, and Friday. Call (605) 341-6308, or leave a message on the voice pager at (605) 394-1471.

MEDIA 📺

Visitors to the Black Hills will find plenty to listen to, watch, and read—on the radio and television and in print publications, that is. You'll find a diversity of music, a smattering of homegrown magazines, plenty of newspapers, and a wide variety of television programming.

Just for fun, we've included information about our film industry. After your visit here you may catch some big—or small—screen films or advertisements in which the landscapes look very familiar.

NEWSPAPERS

If you're interested in learning about daily life in Black Hills towns, local newspapers are your best source. The largest, the *Rapid City Journal*, offers state, national, and international coverage, as well as general coverage of smaller towns. However, many small papers provide thorough and personal coverage of their own hometowns, from community news and local government information to features and the quaint community and small-town neighbor news that defines the distinct personality of each area.

Northern Hills

DAILIES

Black Hills Pioneer
315 Seaton Circle, Spearfish
(605) 642-2761
www.bhpioneer.com
A daily tabloid (Monday through Saturday), the *Black Hills Pioneer* is distributed in the Northern Hills and focuses on the news and events in Lead, Lawrence County, and Spearfish. It's one of the larger papers, with a circulation of 3,500, and it includes an advertising supplement, the *Weekly Prospector*, on Tuesday.

WEEKLIES

Belle Fourche Bee/Post
1004 Fifth Avenue, Belle Fourche
(605) 892-2528
www.bfpost.com
The *Bee,* a weekly founded in 1891, comes out on Saturday. Its sister paper, the *Post,* comes out on Wednesday. Both serve the Northern Hills, with a focus on Belle Fourche and surrounding areas.

Together, their circulation totals 1,700, and both papers have won South Dakota Newspaper Association and state American Advertising Federation awards.

Black Hills Press/Meade County Times-Tribune
1238 Main Street, Sturgis
(605) 347-2503
www.meadecountytimes.com
The *Black Hills Press* is issued each Saturday and the *Times-Tribune* each Wednesday. Both have a circulation of 2,100 and serve the Northern Hills, focusing on the Sturgis and Meade County area.

Lawrence County Journal
376 Main Street, Deadwood
(605) 578-3305
This weekly comes out on Thursday and has a circulation of 800. It covers the Northern Hills and is distributed throughout the Spearfish, Deadwood, and Lead areas.

Tri-State Livestock News
1022 Main Street, Sturgis
(605) 347-2585
www.tsln.com
The *Tri-State Livestock News* is published weekly on Saturday. It has served the Midwest's agricultural industry for four decades, and if you're a farmer or rancher, you'll find its reports and news helpful. If you're not an agriculturist, it's a great way to learn what the real "cowboy life" is like.

Central Hills

DAILIES

Rapid City Journal
507 Main Street, Rapid City
(605) 394-8300, (800) 843-2300
www.rapidcityjournal.com

The *Journal* is the largest newspaper in the Hills, with a circulation of 35,000 and bureaus in Spearfish and Pierre. It focuses on the entire Hills area and also covers eastern Wyoming, northern Nebraska, and the rest of South Dakota. It provides national and international news and features. A daily morning paper founded in 1878 as the *Black Hills Journal*, the *Rapid City Journal* is sold in vending boxes and stores in all Hills towns.

Wednesday editions include advertising supplements (the majority of which are grocery store ads) and the *Rapid City Advertiser* (the *Northern Hills Advertiser* goes to towns north of Rapid City). Friday editions have weekend entertainment information, and Saturday editions offer religious articles and church service listings. Sunday editions include *Parade* magazine and the most extensive help-wanted ads of the week.

WEEKLIES

Hill City Prevailer News
114 Main Street, Hill City
(605) 574-2538
www.hillcitynews.com

The *Prevailer* is published on Wednesday; its 1,100 copies are distributed throughout both the Central and Southern Hills. The *Western Trader* is its weekly shopper supplement.

Lakota Journal
1321 Concourse Drive, Rapid City
(605) 399-1999
www.lakotajournal.com

Native news is what concerns this newspaper that is run by Tim Giago, the founder of the nationally known newspaper *Indian Country Today*; he sold that paper in 1998 and it is now based out of

It isn't easy to find the New York Times *in the Black Hills. It's easier to find the Sunday* Denver Post *or* USA Today. *You can find the Sunday* Times *in some convenience stores, bookstores, grocery stores, and hotels. You can read the daily* Times *at the Rapid City Library, which receives its copies by mail, three days late.*

New York. In 2000, Giago got back in the business by starting the *Lakota Journal*. This weekly paper comes out on Thursday and has a circulation of 8,000.

Pennington County Courant
212 Fourth Avenue, Wall
(605) 279-2565

The *Courant* circulates 1,000 copies throughout eastern Pennington County. It's an award-winning broadsheet that was founded in 1906 and is a window to the happenings in Wall, the Badlands, and surrounding area.

Southern Hills

WEEKLIES

Custer County Chronicle
522 Mount Rushmore Road, Custer
(605) 673-2217
www.custercountynews.com

The *Chronicle* calls itself "your hometown newspaper" and is one of the oldest newspapers in the Hills. In fact, it celebrated its 125th anniversary in 2004.

Distributed in the Southern Hills on Wednesday, the *Chronicle* has won South Dakota Newspaper Association awards for excellence and best feature story.

Hot Springs Star
107 North Chicago Avenue, Hot Springs
(605) 745-4170
www.hotspringsstar.com

The *Star* was founded in 1885, is published on Tuesday, and serves the Southern Hills.

It focuses on the people and events in and around Hot Springs and also publishes a shopper, the *Hot Springs Star Extra*.

MAGAZINES

An array of locally published magazines can be found in the Black Hills. Some are published "East River," far from the Hills, but they're popular and available here (some by subscription only, though). Each is a resource to learn more about an aspect of the Hills, from business and culture to hobbies and attractions.

Dakota Outdoors
333 West Dakota Street, Pierre
(605) 224-7301
This midwestern sportsperson's magazine offers information on outdoor recreation in the Dakotas, with a focus on hunting and fishing. In the Black Hills area it's available by subscription only for $10 per year. (It's on newsstands east of the Missouri River.) *Dakota Outdoors* is published monthly, and two stand-alone issues are included with subscriptions: the *Fishing Guide* in January and the *Hunting Guide* in August.

Deadwood Magazine
93 Sherman Street, Deadwood
(605) 722-7111
www.deadwoodmagazine.com
Deadwood Magazine has returned home to the town for which it was named. After being published in Rapid City for over a decade, Deadwood-based TDG Communications, a full-service advertising, marketing, and public relations firm, purchased the magazine in the summer of 2005 and is

now responsible for bringing the wild and woolly characters of Deadwood's past to life. As a result, *Deadwood Magazine* has gone through several changes under the new ownership. It is now a 24-page, full color, monthly publication with a circulation of 10,000 copies. *Deadwood Magazine* is distributed throughout the region and has subscribers from around the world.

Rapid City Home Journal/Black Hills Home Journal
507 Main Street, Rapid City
(605) 394-8300, (800) 843-2300
This is a two-in-one monthly real estate publication (produced by the *Rapid City Journal*) with listings arranged by real estate agency. One half contains Rapid City listings; flip it over to check out listings for the Black Hills.

South Dakota Conservation Digest
412 West Missouri, Pierre
(605) 773-3485
www.state.sd.us/gfp
This magazine started in 1934 as mimeographed sheets produced by the state's Department of Game, Fish & Parks. Today the bimonthly has a circulation of 16,000 and is still devoted to outdoor recreation, wildlife, and conservation. Its articles are about hunting, fishing, camping, wildlife, parks, and issues relating to all these. The November/December issue contains a calendar of events for the following year. You can't buy *South Dakota Conservation Digest* on newsstands, but you can subscribe for just $5.00 per year.

South Dakota Hall of Fame Magazine
1480 South Main Street, Chamberlain
(605) 734-4216, (800) 697-3130
This magazine provides a wealth of information about our South Dakota heritage. The nonprofit Hall of Fame began in 1974 to recognize those "who have contributed to the development and heritage of South Dakota." Since then, hundreds of noteworthy people, living and deceased, have become hall of famers commemorated in this quarterly magazine. The mag-

The daily **Rapid City Journal** *includes a list of the day's television programming. A separate television supplement, with program listings for the coming week, is published with the* Journal's *Saturday edition.*

azine is published once a year.

Fifteen people are inducted each year, in 15 categories, including agriculture, Indian heritage, religion, professional cowboy, and "unsung heroes and good hearts." The Hall of Fame sells books and displays a photo collection, and its magazine files are open to the public. The historically valuable archives are computerized, and a database is available for public use.

You won't find this magazine on newsstands, but it's available at most South Dakota libraries. Both subscriptions and single copies are available at the number above.

South Dakota Magazine
410 East Third Street, Yankton
(605) 665-6655, (800) 456-5117
South Dakota Magazine was founded in 1985 and has been highly successful, now reaching 100,000 readers with bimonthly issues.

It celebrates the heritage of South Dakota with a rich mix of articles about interesting characters, small towns, historical events, fascinating wildlife, and local lifestyles. It's a well-loved magazine, produced by people who obviously care deeply about the state. The extensive monthly collection of letters to the editors saying "thanks for the memories" and enthusing "I remember that!" attests to its popularity. South Dakota Magazine is available on newsstands around the state or by subscription.

RADIO

This being the Wild West, you'll find several country music stations (both contemporary and classic styles), but the airwaves also carry choices for fans of talk radio, rock, oldies, alternative, and Christian.

These radio stations are listed by format, not region, so you can easily find the type of music you prefer.

Many stations are powerful enough to span more than one of our usual geo-

graphical designations, but the Hills themselves may interfere occasionally with your reception of less-powerful stations, especially as you drive.

The talk, country, and Christian stations are probably the most popular local stations. However, the harder and classic rock stations have a substantial following in the Northern and Central Hills, due in part to some colorful radio personalities. South Dakota Public Radio is another favorite choice, as it can be received almost anywhere in the state, including the entire Interstate 90 corridor. The soothing, conservative NPR programming is on par with the values of many South Dakotans.

Alternative

KBHU The Buzz 89.1 FM

Christian

KLMP 97.9 FM (inspirational and talk)
KSLT 105.7/107.3 FM (adult contemporary Christian)

Country

KBHB 810 AM (traditional country)
KIMM 1150AM (classic country)
KIQK Kick 104.1 FM (contemporary country)
KOUT Kat Country 98.7 FM (contemporary country)
KZZI KZ Country 95.9 FM (mainstream country)

Oldies

KDSJ 98 AM (golden oldies)
KKLS Kool 92 AM (good-time oldies, '50s, '60s, '70s)

Public Radio

South Dakota Public Radio:
KBHE 89.3 FM, Rapid City
KPSD 97.1 FM, Northern Hills

Rock

KDDX X-Rock 101.1/103.1 FM (album-oriented rock)
KFXS The Fox 100.3 FM (classic rock)
KKMK Magic 93.9 FM (adult contemporary)
KQRQ 92.3 FM (classic hits)
KRCS Hot 93.1 FM (top 40 contemporary hits)
KSQY K-Sky 92.1/95.1 FM (adult-oriented rock)
KZLK 106.3 FM (adult contemporary/soft rock)

Talk

KOTA 1380 AM (news/talk)
KTOQ K-Talk 1340 AM (news/talk)

TELEVISION

Although cable or satellite service isn't necessary to receive network stations in most Black Hills locations (it does improve reception, however), many consumers here do subscribe.

There are several Black Hills companies to choose from, including Black Hills FiberCom, (605) 721-2000; Direct Satellite TV, (888) 441-7233, (605) 343-3806, or

Channel 100 is the local government access channel. You can view it if you subscribe to Prairie Wave Communications, (605) 721-2000. It's a good way to stay informed about Rapid City government, because Channel 100 broadcasts city council meetings, board of education meetings, and other informative public service programs.

(605) 343-0755; DirecTV, (605) 341-1323; and Midcontinent Communications, (800) 888-1300 or (605) 343-3402.

Local Television Stations and Affiliates

There are six local stations, listed below with their network affiliates and their local channel numbers. Channel numbers will be different if you're watching a television with cable or satellite service.

KBHE Channel 9, South Dakota Public Broadcasting (PBS)
(605) 394-2551, (605) 677-5861
(800) 456-0766 (administration)
(800) 568-6922 (network production)

KCLO Channel 15 (CBS)
(605) 341-1500, (800) 888-KCLO

KEVN/KIVV Channel 7 (Fox)
(605) 394-7777, (888) 394-7775

KKRA Channel 24 (PAX)
(605) 355-0024

KNBN Channel 27, Rapid City; Channel 31, Lead/Deadwood (NBC)
(605) 355-0024, (877) 4-KNBN-TV

KOTA Channel 3 (ABC)
(605) 342-2000

FILM

South Dakota Film Office
711 East Wells Avenue, Pierre
(605) 773-3301, (800) 952-3625
The beauty of the Black Hills and Badlands has enticed many a filmmaker to bring camera and crew to South Dakota. Thus, the state's Department of Tourism created a film office to promote South Dakota to the film- and video-producing industries and to assist and support filmmakers when they arrive.

South Dakota Public Television

South Dakota Public Television celebrated its official 39th anniversary in 2006. Although educational television station KUSD-TV first went on the air in 1961, the South Dakota State Legislature secured a federal grant (with matching funds from the state) in 1967 to increase the station's power, create more transmitters, and form a board of directors. The board was given the task of creating a network of stations across this huge state so that every single school could access instructional television programming for classroom use. Today, there are nine television/radio transmitters in place, with coverage areas that blanket the entire state.

Public television in South Dakota provides national programming and news from the Public Broadcasting System; South Dakota–oriented programs such as *Arts Advocate Report, Buffalo Nation Journal,* and legislative reports from the state capital; and programs for children and teens. In addition to instructional television programs broad-cast to schools, it offers adult continuing education telecourses, overnight educational programs that teachers or day-care providers can tape and use later, and live videoconferences for professionals via the Rural Development Telecommunications Network.

More than 20,000 people are Friends of South Dakota Public Broadcasting, supporting quality cultural and educational programming with both their financial contributions and their time and energy as volunteers. To become a Friend, call (800) 333-0789.

The popularity of Kevin Costner's *Dances with Wolves* brought the state's visual attributes to the attention of many. A state with open spaces and gorgeously varied vistas; herds of buffalo, horses, and cattle; eager extras; Old West–style towns and buildings; skilled horse riders; and Mount Rushmore is a real find in the film industry.

The Badlands have been especially popular among Hollywood directors since the 1950s, and they served as the backdrop for prominent westerns like *Chief Crazy Horse* and *How the West Was Won.* In recent years the Badlands have helped to tell stories of racism and poverty in the movies *Lakota Woman, Thunderheart,* and

Skins. They've also been tapped to serve as other planets (or an asteroid, as the case may be) for the films *Starship Troopers* and *Armageddon.* Directors have given nods to the timeless beauty of the Black Hills over the decades, using them for movies from Hitchcock's *North by Northwest* to the modern thriller *Mercury Rising.* You'll also find South Dakota scenery in the opening scenes of the movie *Twister.*

South Dakota, the Black Hills, and the Badlands are also popular with producers of commercials and still photographers seeking scenery for advertising, magazine, and fine art photographs.

WORSHIP AND SPIRITUALITY

Black Hills residents are firmly rooted in faith. In a place where many claim pioneers as their recent ancestors, it's not surprising that the faith of those forebears plays an essential role in modern life. Also, in a part of the world where so many depend on nature and weather for their livelihood (farmers, ranchers, and loggers come to mind), faith and religion keep people going when those two unpredictable elements sometimes disappoint.

The mix of religions in the Black Hills is typical of religious representation in America's heartland. That is, you won't find many alternative or New Age religions common in cities such as Boulder, Santa Fe, or San Francisco. What you will find is a healthy traditional religious foundation, a solid bedrock of spirituality that is rooted in everyday life.

Ancient forms of spirituality were permeating the lives of the Native people when the Black Hills were "discovered" by newcomers seeking gold. Other religions (also ancient, but new to this area) came along with the pioneers. Each of these developed, changed, and grew right along with the burgeoning Black Hills population.

The majority of religions here are traditional: mainstream and nonaffiliated Protestant, Catholic, and Jewish. Most have a solid base in the community and devoted members who are committed to their faiths. They also have interesting histories that reflect the immense changes that began here in 1876 with the gold rush.

PROTESTANTS AND CATHOLICS

The first Episcopal service conducted by an ordained priest was in 1878. It was held

in Rapid City, when the town was so new and tiny that it had only one street. A story tells that Reverend Edward Ashley was in town to attend court as a witness. The courtroom was above the saloon, so the enterprising priest asked if he could hold a church service in that room the following Sunday. He put up notices around town, but on Sunday morning Reverend Ashley and the saloon's janitor were the only worshippers present at the appointed time. After waiting 20 minutes, the good reverend was ready to give up when a large group of noisy folk came pounding up the stairs and into the courtroom, singing "Hold the Fort for I Am Coming," and the service began.

The first Episcopal service conducted by a resident, however, was the funeral of Preacher Henry Weston Smith in 1876. Deadwood Sheriff Seth Bullock borrowed a Book of Common Prayer to conduct the burial service for Smith, who was, interestingly enough, a Methodist clergyman. Preacher Smith had heard the call to minister to the people of Deadwood and had held services on an itinerant basis for just a few months before he was murdered by someone whose identity remains a mystery. The devout minister was the Hills' only clergyman at that time and its first religious martyr. Sheriff Bullock wrote that the funeral "was the most serious business that ever happened in the Hills, a lot of wicked, illiterate miners burying a minister, a man of God."

Both gold-rush and pioneer towns attracted clerics and missionaries who intended to save the souls of the residents and build up a bedrock faith. Many of the new pioneers had left more "civilized" eastern towns and discovered—some with glee, some with shock—that the recently sprung-up Black Hills towns

Lakota Creation Story

The Lakota people have a beautiful creation story. They believe they came from their First World into another life, the Second World or Root Nation. They then evolved into the Third World and lived at Wahutopa Oyate, the Four-Legged Nation, where their bodies and spirits were their beloved buffalo. The people came up to the earth's surface through the "breathing cave"—Wind Cave, in the southern Black Hills. They lived there with all their many relatives, those who lived in the water, walked on the land, and flew through the air, all part of Creation.

had a shortage of law enforcement, schools, churches, and civilized behavior.

The devout men of the cloth were respected and appreciated by most, but they still contended with the rough-and-tumble life of the frontier, with all its lawless, sometimes downright wacky, behavior. In 1882, for example, the *Black Hills Journal* carried this story: "Rev. Ira Wakefield, well known here, was surprised, while riding along the road near Custer recently, by the report of a pistol shot, followed by another and another, and hearing the bullets whistling, in what he imagined to be close proximity to his head, he pulled up, and was immediately joined by a man coming from the rear, who said he had merely wanted the reverend gentleman's company on the road, and took that method of bringing him to, until he could overtake him."

As men who had come to the Hills to look for gold began to send for their waiting families, as women and children began to move into the towns, and as merchants set up shops, more and more religious organizations formed. These had little

effect on the hard-drinking, rowdy types who made the gambling halls, saloons, and brothels so successful, especially in Deadwood. But perhaps those "unchurched" folks actually managed to encourage the growing number of congregations as counterpoints to the seamier side of life in these small towns.

Religious congregations often met in any space available until they could build their own house of worship, and the citizens of smaller, less-populated towns usually had to conduct their own services, or wait until a circuit-riding minister or priest made his rounds. As their num-

There are several religious bookstores in the Black Hills. In Rapid City, you'll find Bible & Book Store at 618 Main Street, (605) 343-3720, (800) 888-1639; Gospel Garden Book Store at 610 Seventh Street, (605) 348-6313, (800) 843-8080; and Mustard Seed Catholic Book Store at 708 St. Joseph Street, (605) 348-5228, (800) 456-1893.

Some local denominations have church camps or conference and retreat centers, a way to combine a pleasant vacation in the Black Hills with spiritual refreshment and personal enrichment. Inquire at the church of your choice to learn if such facilities are available.

bers grew and they raised funds, however, these groups built their own buildings.

The first religious organization in the Hills was Deadwood's First Congregational Church, founded in 1876. Its members met in two different hotels, then a carpenter's shop (a nice bit of symbolism), before building a structure in 1877.

The first Catholic priest in Deadwood, Father John Lonergan, arrived in 1877 and conducted the first Mass in another carpenter's shop. He and his parishioners built their church that year. Another priest preceded Father Lonergan to the Black Hills, however. Father Pierre DeSmet, a Jesuit pioneer missionary, visited the Native American tribes of the area in 1848.

Father B. Mackin established Catholic parishes in Lead and Central City in 1878 but also covered much of the Black Hills in his circuit-riding ministry. He brought the Holy Cross Sisters to Deadwood to establish a hospital in 1878. The first Mass in the Southern Hills was in 1887 at St. Anthony of Padua Catholic Church. The historic building no longer exists, but the parish still functions in Hot Springs. The first church in Rapid City was a Catholic church, constructed in 1882 at a cost of just $345. Although the building is gone, it boasted the first church bell in town.

Just two years after Preacher Smith's untimely death, another Methodist minister, Rev. James Williams, organized a congregation in Deadwood in 1878, but it was not until March of 1883 that the church was completed. A mere two months later the building was destroyed in a flood, and the Episcopal congregation generously offered the basement of its own church until the Methodists could complete a new structure in 1885.

That structure stood until 2002, when the city of Deadwood decided rehabilitating the crumbling building would be near impossible, no matter how many gaming-financed historic preservation dollars they could gather. Most of its artifacts—including stained-glass windows, a massive leather-bound Bible, and a baptismal font dating back to the original 1883 church—were saved and can be seen on display in the visitor center at Mount Moriah Cemetery (see the Attractions chapter).

THE JEWISH FAITH

Jewish people came to the Black Hills from other sections of the United States and from Europe, arriving during the gold rush to set up shops that provided goods and services to miners and pioneers. The impressive tombstones—beautifully inscribed in Hebrew—of some of those early Jewish merchants and their families can be seen at Deadwood's Mount Moriah Cemetery in the Hebrew Hill section.

Soon after Rapid City was founded in 1876, Jewish services began there. They were first held in local homes; it wasn't until the 1960s that they were moved to the chapel at Ellsworth Air Force Base. Worshippers built their own Rapid City building, the Synagogue of the Hills, in 1996. The synagogue's Torah is the original scroll used by Deadwood's early Jewish population. It came from Konigsberg, Germany, in 1888, along with Freda Lowensberg, who traveled here to join her sweetheart, settler Benjamin Blumenthal.

NATIVE AMERICAN SPIRITUALITY

Spirituality pervades the daily lives of many Native Americans and is not seen as separate from other aspects of life. Religious ceremonies such as sun dances and sweat lodges are not usually open to non-Indians, whose participation in such rites

An Indian Prayer

O Great Spirit, whose voice I hear
in the winds, and whose breath gives life
to all the world, hear me!

I am small and weak.
I need your strength and wisdom.

Let me walk in beauty, and make my eyes
ever behold the red and purple sunset.

Make my hands respect the
things you have made and my ears
sharp to hear your voice.

Make me wise so that I may understand
the things you have taught my people.

Let me learn the lessons you
have hidden in every leaf and rock.

I seek strength, not to be greater
than my brother, but to fight my
greatest enemy—myself.

Make me always ready to come to you
with clean hands and straight eyes.

So when life fades, as the fading
sunset, my spirit may come to
you without shame.

*Reprinted with the kind permission
of Red Cloud Indian School,
Pine Ridge, South Dakota*

often evokes controversy. A few area Christian churches have predominantly Native American congregations, but these are not listed as Native in the Yellow Pages. If you are interested, you will need to call the denomination of your choice and ask if such a church is in the area.

Visitors may not realize that powwows are also sacred ceremonies, ancient worship services celebrated with dancing (the Dakota, Lakota, and Nakota word for powwow means "dance"), singing, drumming, and much symbolism. Powwows, unlike some other ceremonies, are open to visitors, and there's one held nearly every weekend in the summer at reservations or in Black Hills towns. Call the South Dakota Department of Tourism, (605) 773-3301, for information on annual powwows. You'll find a write-up on the best-known event, the Black Hills Pow Wow, in the Annual Events and Festivals chapter.

Powwows are important in the spiritual lives of Native Americans. Organizers ask that visitors conduct themselves with respect, wear modest clothing, speak quietly, and always ask for permission before taking pictures. Photography may, in fact, be prohibited at powwows, and some elders may not want to be photographed.

HISTORIC HOUSES OF WORSHIP

Of the many houses of worship built in the Black Hills, many original buildings no longer exist, having been lost to time, weather, or "progress." One of the remaining, and the oldest continuously used, is St. John's Episcopal Church at 405 Williams Street in Deadwood. It was completed in 1881, and the congregation still uses its 554-pipe organ that was built in 1904.

Rapid City's Emmanuel Episcopal Church, 717 Quincy Street, still stands as well. It was completed in 1887 and is listed on the National Register of Historic Places. When its elegantly cut sandstone blocks were cleaned by sandblasting in 1976, it was discovered they had been cemented with good old Black Hills mud, a common technique in those days.

The modern era saw the construction in 1963 of the Cathedral of Our Lady of Perpetual Help, 520 Cathedral Drive, in Rapid City. It is a richly symbolic building and the largest church structure in the Hills. Anyone may view the architectural features and stained-glass work by requesting a tour at the rectory office.

RELIGION TODAY

Whatever religion or denomination you're looking for, a quick glance through the Yellow Pages will help you locate it. You'll have no trouble finding a Baptist, Methodist, Lutheran, or Catholic church. You will, however, have fewer choices if you're looking for an Assembly of God, Jehovah's Witnesses, Church of God, Reformed, Church of Christ, Episcopal, Mormon, or Presbyterian church.

Jewish, Unity, Salvation Army, Pentecostal, Christian Science, Nazarene, Quaker, Eckankar, Unitarian Universalist, Christian & Missionary Alliance, and Seventh-day Adventist faiths are represented by just one congregation each. There are several interdenominational, nondenominational, and community churches in the region as well.

Whatever religion or faith you claim, whether you're visiting for just a single worship service or looking for a new spiritual home, you'll most likely be welcomed wholeheartedly by any Black Hills congregation. These strong and devoted people know that their historically strong faith becomes even more unshakable when it's shared.

INDEX

ABOUT THE AUTHORS

T. D. GRIFFITH

Tom Griffith attended the University of London before he graduated from the University of Wisconsin–Eau Claire. He worked as a reporter, photographer, and managing editor of award-winning newspapers in Arizona, Montana, and South Dakota before serving as director of communications for the Mount Rushmore Preservation Fund, a nationwide campaign that raised $24 million to preserve and improve the mountain memorial. In addition to writing articles for dozens of newspapers and magazines, Tom is the author of five books, including *America's Shrine of Democracy* with a foreword by President Ronald Reagan; *South Dakota,* a comprehensive guide to the state; and *Greeno, A Winning Tradition of Teaching and Coaching* with a foreword by NBC's Tom Brokaw. He has co-authored more than 20 travel guides to date. Tom and his wife, Nyla, make their home in the Black Hills of South Dakota, where they operate an advertising, marketing, and public relations firm. In their spare time, they enjoy trout fishing, motorcycling, and travel.

DUSTIN D. FLOYD

A fifth-generation South Dakotan, Dustin D. Floyd was raised at the base of the Black Hills in Rapid City. He studied history at Oxford University before graduating magna cum laude from Coe College, a small liberal arts school in Cedar Rapids, Iowa, with a B.A. in English and public relations. He is currently a marketing manager with TDG Communications, a Deadwood-based marketing and public relations firm, where he has helped write and revise a number of articles and books on the Dakotas, Montana, and Wyoming. He also serves as executive editor of *Deadwood Magazine,* a monthly periodical that focuses on the history, culture, and people of the Black Hills and the American West.